Canadian Cities

in Transition

D0898437

EDITED BY

Trudi Bunting

and

Pierre Filion

Toronto/New York/Oxford
OXFORD UNIVERSITY PRESS

Oxford University Press, 70 Wynford Drive, Don Mills, Ontario M3C 1J9

Toronto   Oxford   New York
Delhi   Bombay   Calcutta   Madras   Karachi   Kuala Lumpur
Singapore   Hong Kong   Tokyo   Nairobi   Dar es Salaam
Cape Town   Melbourne   Auckland

and associated companies in
Berlin   Ibadan

Canadian Cataloguing in Publication Data
Main entry under title:

Canadian cities in transition

Includes bibliographical references and index.
ISBN 0-19-540794-6

1. Cities and towns – Canada. I. Bunting, Trudi E.,
1944–   . II. Filion, Pierre, 1952–   .

HT127.C35 1991   307.76′0971   C91-093347-2

Design by David Montle

Copyright © Oxford University Press Canada 1991
OXFORD is a trademark of Oxford University Press
2 3 4 – 94 93 92
Printed in Canada by Gagné Printing

Contents

INTRODUCTION

1

Introduction: Perspectives on the City

PIERRE FILION AND
TRUDI E. BUNTING

There are many reasons to pay attention to cities. As the living environment for the vast majority of Canadians and the site of most production, consumption, and administrative activities, cities play a crucial role in the country's economic and political life. Urban problems, such as traffic congestion and housing shortages, have a deleterious impact on economic performance, not to mention their effect on urban residents' living conditions. This book is about cities—how they work, their appearance, their evolution, and their problems.

The book singles out Canadian cities as a field of enquiry. This group of cities constitutes a distinct entity in that they can be seen as juxtaposed between European and US urban forms. For example, population densities and the use of public transportation in Canadian cities are higher than in the US but trail far behind those of European cities.

This introductory chapter first presents the purpose and structure of the book and describes briefly its different chapters. The introduction then moves on to suggest an interpretation of the city that stresses the importance of proximity, spatial relations, and the enduring nature of city buildings and infrastructures. It then charts the theoretical and methodological evolution of approaches to the city from the inter-war period until now. The focus is largely on urban geography and to a lesser extent on planning. The evolutionary perspective suggests a trend towards diversification—that is, the existence side by side of different approaches—which requires the acknowledgement of the relativity of various theoretical and methodological points of view.

PURPOSE AND ORGANIZATION OF THE BOOK

The book looks at the urban phenomenon through the lenses of different disciplines. While most chapters are written by urban geographers, three are written by planners (Chapters 6, 19, and 20), one (Chapter 16) is written partly by a planner, one by an engineer (Chapter 11), and another by a political scientist (Chapter 18). As such the book is primarily targeted at urban geographers. It is also aimed at urban planners in that it provides chapters that develop a distinct planning perspective and chapters that deal with the functioning of cities and that, therefore, offer essential background knowledge. This book is also useful for students approaching the city from the vantage point of other disciplines. This is because, since both geography and planning integrate a number of disciplines, the reader will find economic, sociological, and ecological treatments of the city. Moreover, the book's chapters written from a political science and engineering perspective are particularly useful to students belonging to these disciplines. The book is also a testimony to the diversity of approaches to the urban phenomenon. Contributors have organized their chapters and carried out the background research according to their preferred approach. This is why chapters run the full gamut from a heavy use of quantitative data to subjective, personal discussions. As well as attempting to consider different approaches to the city, the book endeavours to present a comprehensive treatment of the different aspects of Canadian cities. To achieve this end, it is organized in five parts, each looking at the Canadian city from a particular perspective.

Part 1 looks at the urban phenomenon at a national level, examining characteristics that concern urban Canada as a whole. Chapter 2 reviews the recent development of Canadian cities, and discusses the issues that are both currently affecting these cities and that are most likely to affect them in the future. Chapter 3 makes a case for Canadian cities as a distinct object of study. It highlights features that differentiate Canadian cities from their closest relatives, US cities. Chapter 4 follows the evolution of Canadian urban settlements from their seventeenth-century origin until the 1960s. It describes the emergence, over the last two centuries, of a demographic and economic heartland in southwestern Quebec and southern Ontario. As such, it provides a historical foundation for Chapters 5, 7, and 8, which focus on the Canadian urban system as a whole. Chapter 5 is the first of three chapters that allude to interactions between urban centres (the others are Chapters 7 and 8 in Part 2) rather than focusing on what happens within cities. These chapters consider the specialization of urban centres as well as the nature and extent of the exchanges that link these centres to each other. In Chapter 5, Simmons examines the uneven distribution of economic activities among Canadian cities, which is responsible for the existence of a Canadian urban hierarchy centring on Toronto. Chapter 6 ends this part of the book by reflecting on the likely impact of electronic communications and more generally, high technology, on urban form and urban life.

Part 2 focuses on regional perspectives defined both in terms of cities' zones of influence and the uneven distributions of population and economic activity across the country. In Chapter 7, Preston uses central place theory as a framework to define individual cities' zone of influence. These zones are measured according to migration flows, newspaper circulation, and airline journeys. Chapter 8 describes the evolution over the last decades of Canada's most urbanized region, the corridor that runs from Windsor to Quebec City, which is sometimes referred to as Canada's 'Main Street' (Yeates 1975; 1987). It identifies both the conditions behind this region's enduring demographic and economic domination within the country, and shifts occurring within the corridor. Finally, Chapter 9 explores changes occurring in rural belts encircling cities. These sectors experience the vagaries of agricultural markets and the encroachment of both urban residents settling into close-by rural areas and urbanites seeking occasional rural recreation.

While the previous part considered cities' external links, Part 3 is devoted to intra-urban perspectives—that is, to the form of, and social cleavages within, cities. It also looks at forces that shape urban areas. In Chapter 10, Olson demonstrates how the history of a city is reflected in its layout and buildings. In other words, she looks at the factors leading to the production of the urban built-environment through time. She also describes contemporary Canadian urban form, which she criticizes from an energy consumption and environmental point of view. The following chapter probes the interplay between transportation and land use by showing the historical correspondence between different modes of transportation and particular urban patterns. The chapter describes in some detail methods of transportation planning, and highlights their responsiveness to current and anticipated demand levels. Chapter 12 deals with social aspects of cities as places where people live. It considers models of population growth and social variations in inter- and intra-urban structure. And lastly, in Chapter 13 Ley looks at social change occurring within central neighbourhoods. He describes the ascending socio-economic trends experienced by many such neighbourhoods and discusses the tensions this generates.

Urban functions are the object of Part 4. This part groups chapters that look at the nature of activities taking place within cities, and at the locational and other characteristics of the facilities accommodating these activities. Chapter 14 focuses on housing. It emphasizes and explains differences between Canadian cities' housing stock and narrates the evolution of housing in Canada. It also discusses social issues arising from inequalities in housing conditions. In the next chapter, Jones offers a perspective on the recent evolution of retailing within Canadian cities. The attention is directed at the nature, size, and location of shopping facilities, as well as on their impact on the urban structure. The object of Chapter 16 is industrial location within cities. The chapter narrates both an overall declining trend in manufacturing relative to other sectors of employment and the redistribution of manufacturing employment, from the centre to the periphery of metropolitan regions. Chapter 17 focuses on offices, where much of contemporary employment growth takes place. It addresses the recent distribution of office types in different sectors within metropolitan regions.

Part 5 deals with social issues and the role of the public sector in a Canadian urban context. In Chapter 18, Sancton considers urban policy-making. He concentrates on changing styles of local politics, alternative forms of metropolitan government, and the distribution of urban policy-making responsibilities between senior and local governments. Chapter 19 considers urban planning. It traces the evolution of Canadian urban planning models and practice, and identifies contemporary planning issues affecting Canadian cities. Finally, in Chapter 20, Moore Milroy explores the difficulties individuals belonging to disadvantaged groups face in their attempts to make use of urban opportunities. It also demonstrates how these difficulties limit the education, employment and other options that are open to such individuals and, as such, contribute to confining them to a life of poverty.

The book also includes five appendices. The first presents Statistics Canada's definitions of census metropolitan areas, census agglomerations, and related terms. The second consists of a list of Canadian cities with 10,000 population and over. Appendix 3 assembles a number of critical demographic and socio-economic features pertaining to Canada's twenty-five census metropolitan areas. Appendix 4 introduces and describes sources of data on housing. And finally, Appendix 5 identifies special-need groups, the agencies catering to their housing needs, and the forms of housing available to these groups.

TOWARDS AN INTERPRETATION OF THE CITY

The urban literature offers multiple interpretations of the city, focusing variously on its social, political, cultural, physical, and economic attributes.[1] It is important to begin this book by describing the urban phenomenon in a way that provides an understanding of how cities work and a sense of the wide range of issues that can be labelled urban. This is why we propose an interpretation that is both broad and inclusive, and that aspires to capture in particular the geographic essence of the city.

Individuals and organizations locate in cities primarily to reduce inter-action costs and thereby facilitate the carrying out of exchanges on a frequently repeated basis with other persons or organizations. Exchanges are defined here as interactions that involve the *movement* of persons and goods; these exchanges entail merchandise, services, and inter-personal, face-to-face communication. Decisions to locate in cities are explained by a desire to achieve proximity in order to reduce the transportation and communication costs inherent in pursuing these recurrent exchanges. Cities are places where different markets of frequently repeated exchanges converge, with the daily labour market playing a dominant structuring role by setting the extent of metropolitan regions. Daily labour markets are defined by the range of commuting journeys (Harvey 1989, 19 and 128). In fact, Statistics Canada uses the proportion of residents of areas surrounding an urbanized core who commute to this core and of residents of the core who commute to these outlying areas as a measure to set the boundaries of CAs (census agglomerations) and CMAs (census metropoli-tan areas) as detailed in Appendix 1. The importance of labour markets as a factor of urban growth is expressed by the dominance of work availability as a reason for people to either stay in, or migrate to, cities. In this respect, Chapters 4, 5, 7, and 8 link demographic with economic vitality to explain the population rise of various urban centres.

The case is often made that accessibility constraints on labour markets are currently relaxed by advances in electronic communication such as computer networks, facsimile transmission, and fibre optics. In this view, the electronic transmission of information, insofar as it replaces the need for the physical movement of persons and goods, reduces the need for agglomeration and, as a result, the attraction of urban locations. Much has been written over the last decade on the imminence of diffused forms where individuals are able to pursue their work at home away from major centres, being connected to these centres by cheap and instantaneous electronic channels (Brotchie *et al.* 1985; Gappert and Knight 1982). Chap-ters 6 and 9 discuss the social and spatial implications of electronic com-munication. Face-to-face contacts remain, however, important in the sharing of non-standardized information, as well as in discussions that are an essential component of most significant decision-making processes. In any event, the urbanization wave of the 1980s, which was particularly felt in large agglomerations such as Toronto, Vancouver, and Ottawa-Hull (see Appendix 3 for 1981–1986 CMA growth rates), demonstrates that de-urbanization resulting from innovations in electronic communication has yet to materialize.

In spite of its undeniable importance, the daily urban market is by no means the only market of frequently repeated exchanges to which cities owe their existence. One example of a non-labour market are firms seeking proximity to each other in order to maintain intense patterns of linkages that involve frequent deliveries. Along with access to a plentiful labour force, this constitutes the principal reason for firms to opt for urban locations.

There are many other examples of non-labour markets operating within cities. One can think here of interactions between consumers and services such as retail facilities, and cultural and recreation activities.[2] Herein lies another important lure to cities—the archetypical 'bright lights'. Moreover, for many categories of individuals, such as the poor and the sick, it is vital to maintain easy accessibility to health and welfare services. It is therefore not surprising that, as noted in Chapter 20, poorer residents tend to locate in neighbourhoods that offer a wide range of welfare services. At a more personal level, exchanges may also consist of regular visits to family members or friends. The elderly, for example, will often move close to their children in order to enjoy family support. It is important to recognize that, in all these cases, ease of accessibility allowing for, or facilitating, frequently repeated exchanges is the main motive to locate in cities.

Given this concern over accessibility, it is hardly surprising that proximity is at the core of the urban space economy. A widespread aspiration to partake in the markets that compose the city drives competition for urban space. This aspiration explains the considerable premium placed on urban land by comparison to rural land. Urban land values account for the absence from cities of activities such as farming that yield a modest return relative to their surface. In these circumstances, urban households are forced to compromise between optimal locations in terms of accessibility, the sums they are willing or able to pay for such locations, and their need to consume urban space in order to carry out domestic activities (eating, sleeping, the rearing of children, etc.). The overlapping of income differences and uneven distributions of accessibility advantages and amenities within cities translate into residential segregation. Chapter 12 describes the relationship between urban land economics and social segregation within cities.

The particularity of exchanges defining cities is highlighted when intra-urban markets are compared to exchange patterns that link self-standing cities or metropolitan regions to their hinterland and to other agglomerations. These latter types of exchanges are typically not as frequent and are, in any event, more expensive to carry out and more time consuming, which tends to rule out many forms of exchanges taking place on a frequent basis within cities. Daily commuting is the most obvious example of an exchange that cannot practically take place beyond a certain distance. It is important to note that inter-urban exchanges support the existence of systems of cities, which consist of relatively stable exchange patterns between cities, and in this fashion, allow the economic and political specialization of cities. For example, Ottawa pools financial resources across the country through taxation; in return, it produces political decisions and public sector services for the country as a whole. But Ottawa also imports most of the goods it consumes, either from other Canadian cities or from abroad. Were it not for inter-urban systems there would be little variation in the size of cities, and all would offer similar activities. Chapters 5, 7, and 8 provide a fuller discussion of inter-urban systems. Chapter 5 does so by focusing on the economic specialization of the different Canadian cities, Chapter 7 by examining specific links that tie Canadian cities to each other, and Chapter 8 by emphasizing the disparity between Canadian regions, and the changing importance of different urban centres within the Windsor-Quebec City corridor.

The present interpretation incorporates another feature of the city: the cost and permanence of its built environment, which includes roads, subways, sewers, parks, all types of buildings, etc. Because it is expensive to produce, the built environment does not lend itself easily to radical transformations, as evidenced by the high cost of the public-sector urban renewal operations of the 1950s and 1960s. In this sense the existing built environment limits future urban possibilities. This explains a frequent lack of correspondence between changing accessibility potentials and land-use patterns. For example, it takes time for the density and nature of activities within a residential area to adapt to an increase in accessibility brought about by a new subway line. Zoning regulations, by specifying the size and role of future buildings, are also responsible for such an absence of adaptation. At the moment, the rebuilding of existing sectors, which is limited to central business districts and old industrial areas, is pretty much the preserve of governments and large development firms (Lorimer 1978).

The considerable sums invested in the built environment also explain the vested interest of landlords and owner-occupiers in protecting the value of their property. Attempts by owner-occupiers to prevent the location of unwanted facilities because of the threat they represent to house values—the 'Not In My Back Yard' (NIMBY) syndrome—now represent a mainstay of local politics as documented in Chapter 18. Associated with financial attachment are sentimental ties to a home or a neighbourhood.

Another influence of the built environment that stems from both its fixity and permanence is its pervasive impact on urbanites' lives. The urban built environment channels our movements and as such defines what we can do in the city (Harvey 1989, 83). Because of its lasting nature, the urban built environment assures the persistence of life-styles that are not necessarily consistent with contemporary social values and demands. In this respect, feminists have criticized suburbs on the ground that they are no longer adapted to women's new role in the work place and the family (Hayden 1984; Wekerle 1984; see also Chapter 14). According to this argument, the domestic tasks generated by the suburban single-family home, and the distance between the home and essential services and activities in a suburban environment, aggravate already severe time constraints placed on the working woman. In a similar vein, in its discussion of the urban form's symbolic dimension, Chapter 10 makes the point that older buildings project economic and political relations as well as values of the past into the contemporary urban landscape.

The combination of these two aspects of the urban phenomenon—the need for proximity and the lasting nature of the built environment—provides both a spatial and a temporal dimension to our interpretation. The proximity principle, which derives from the need to carry out frequent exchanges, explains the existence of cities and the distribution of people and activities within cities. Meanwhile, the permanence of the built environment and the attendant mobilization of resources and interests around its existence account for the relative inflexibility of urban space.[3] The permanence of the built environment also explains the myriad of urban issues that are triggered by physical and functional changes occurring within cities. In this respect, Chapter 18 gives to property-related interventions a core position among municipal government functions.

The above discussion provides a perspective on the essence of the urban phenomenon. But this discussion is not as effective in accounting for the substance of particular cities—that is, their definite form and features. It needs to be stressed that the general urban principles developed here are in reality specified by the societal contexts in which cities exist. Cities reflect the economic and technological development of a society. For example, Chapter 4 demonstrates how urbanization in Canada was shaped by the evolution of the economic system, itself closely associated with technical—in particular transportation—innovations. Likewise, in Chapter 15 we see how the progression in the size of shopping centres follows the growth of property development corporations. Cities also bear the mark of a society's political priorities, as shown by the different emphasis given to either public or private transportation infrastructures in various cities (see Chapter 11). In this same vein, Chapter 12 demonstrates how cities reproduce social cleavages that exist at a national level.

The impact of society's class structure on the possibility to take advantage of urban opportunities is particularly apt to illustrate this specification. Urban advantages are generally produced and distributed according to market principles. As a result, wealthier people are best positioned to secure these advantages. A society's inequality is therefore reflected, and possibly exacerbated, by the city. For urban residents, the ideal compromise is to live in pleasant surroundings while maintaining a large reachable territory that maximizes the number of possible exchanges. More concretely, this high accessibility potential translates into a better choice of jobs, consumer goods, cultural activities, educational establishments, etc. (Brehemy 1978, 463). The development of the middle- and upper-class suburb, which coincided with major urban expressway expenditures in larger metropolitan regions, can be perceived as an attempt to combine high accessibility potentials with attractive housing and neighbourhood conditions that are generally defined in terms of modernity and generous land consumption. In this light, these suburbs provide an example of how urban advantages are produced. This form of suburban development comes at a high cost, however: private costs include the purchase and maintenance of a house and of one car or more; public costs include the construction of extensive infrastructures such as expressways, arterial roads, sewers, and water systems to cater for low-density development.

In an urban context, poorer residents are confined to built environments that are disregarded by wealthier households. This explains the unsatisfactory conditions these poorer residents endure in housing units and neighbourhoods that are often older and inadequately maintained. Furthermore, poorer individuals suffer from accessibility difficulties, which compress the range of activities they can reach (Falcocchio, Pignataro, and Cantilli 1972; Paaswell and Recker 1978). These difficulties are the result of problems in purchasing and maintaining a car, and of the frequent location of low-cost housing in remote suburban enclaves or in job-depleted inner-city sectors. (Chapter 16 documents the serious decline in manufacturing employment that has affected central areas within Canadian cities.) Poor residents are thus denied many of the advantages of living in a city. Also, the narrow range of jobs accessible to them constitutes a serious obstacle to their social and economic advancement (Clark and Whiteman 1983, 85–6; Hutchinson 1978).

This interpretation of the city, which is, incidentally, only one among many, has the merit of highlighting the multiplicity of issues that can be defined as urban. Of course, one can think here of issues that pertain to accessibility and transportation matters, the accessibility advantages and disadvantages of different urban locations, the production and consumption of the built environment, inequalities in the capacity to use the built environment, and mobilizations over issues pertaining to urban accessibility as well as to the built environment. But a number of other issues can also be appended to the list. These issues relate to the everyday needs of people living within the confines of urban areas. Accordingly, the production and consumption of services required by urbanites, such as education and health services, also qualify as urban issues. Tensions created by proximity can be another source of urban issues—for instance in cases of conflicts over the location of incompatible facilities such as land-fill sites, as well as intolerance between social classes or ethnic groups that are located close to each other. It is clear from this list that urban issues pertain to the economic, social, and political spheres of human activity. The environmental dimension of the urban phenomenon is also highly relevant because of its consequences on the health of residents as well as on the natural environment.

APPROACHES TO THE CITY

The multiplicity of issues identified above suggests a large number of possible approaches to the urban phenomenon. This number becomes virtually unlimited when we consider the wide range of possible permutations between: (1) the urban issues under investigation; (2) the discipline adopted (e.g. geography, planning, sociology, political science, physical ecology); (3) the theoretical framework selected within a given discipline (e.g. positivism, Marxism, behaviouralism); (4) the methodology employed (e.g. direct observation, survey, statistical analysis); and (5) the scale of the field of enquiry (e.g. systems of cities, metropolitan regions, neighbourhoods, households). It is important to realize, however, that urban approaches are neither spread evenly across all possibilities nor distributed in a purely random fashion. Rather, as we shall see, a consistency prevails within approaches between issues under investigation, theory, method, and scale. In addition, approaches either evolve gradually within established schools of thought or are the product of break-away schools. This is a function of how knowledge evolves, or more to the point, of how it is produced.[4]

The evolution of a discipline is driven by the scrutiny to which any study is subjected. This leads to an action-reaction development process whereby new studies often respond to perceived deficiencies of previous studies. This response can consist of minor theoretical and methodological adjustments or can lead to the development of entirely new theories and methods in opposition to existing ones.

The remaining portions of this chapter consider the evolution of approaches to cities since the inter-war period. This historical account encompasses urban studies in general, but does give a privileged status to urban geography and planning. Also, because Canadian scholars partake extensively in international intellectual movements, it is impossible to limit our consideration to Canadian studies alone. The discussion on the evolution of approaches embraces, along with Canadian works, major sources of influence on Canadian scholars such as the English-speaking world, the French-speaking world and, to a lesser extent, other parts of the Western world. Because of space limitations this account is limited to a brief discussion of these major approaches.[5]

Early Approaches

Inter-war and immediate post-World War II approaches to the city showed little concern over matters of methodology. These approaches were mostly descriptive, relying on a mixture of direct observation and intuition. Concern was over the particularity of specific areas and populations, regardless of whether they were cities, neighbourhoods, ethnic groups or social classes. Researchers gave scant importance to the duplication or generalization of observations and explanations.

The foremost example of this period's urban theory is provided by the Chicago School of urban ecology, which associated neighbourhood location and characteristics with the gradual assimilation of immigrant populations to mainstream US society. It drew a parallel between movements from the inner-city high-density neighbourhoods to wealthy sub-urbs, and the acquisition of 'American' values (Park, Burgess, and McKenzie 1925). The Chicago School borrowed its theoretical framework from the then-favoured social application of Darwin's 'survival of the fittest' ecological model. Its findings were derived from a direct observation of the evolution of Chicago's neighbourhoods (Smith 1984, 357). It is also worth noting that the relative absence of methodology hindered the replication of these findings in other urban settings.

Positivism

In the early 1960s, a reaction against earlier forms of urban studies began to take shape. In line with the tenets of positivism—which consists in the application of natural science methods to the study of social life—this reaction purported to model social science after natural science. By the late 1960s it had completely transformed urban geography. This led to a remodelling of urban geography approaches along 'hard science' principles such as objectivity on the part of the researcher (which implies a lack of personal judgement on the observed situation) and the reliance on methodologies that permit a replication of the procedure behind findings (Johnston 1983, 5). Also, unlike earlier approaches, which celebrated the particularity of a given object of inquiry, the emphasis turned to the identification of laws by generalizing empirical findings from one place to another (Garner 1967; Harvey 1969).

Positivism created a context that became particularly favourable to the use of quantitative data since this form of data fulfils replication and generalization requirements. Over the 1960s human geography was traversed by what was to become known as the 'quantitative revolution' (Burton 1963). Matters of causality were then largely addressed by using statistical inference.[6] It is no accident that this 'revolution' coincided with the spread of powerful computers. In these circumstances, economics became a major source of inspiration for urban geographers. Most positivist studies of the city share the neo-classical premise of economics that trends result from aggregates of decisions taken independently by 'economic persons'. These abstract persons are deemed to be both rational and aware of all options.

The positivist method and its reliance on quantified data played a major role in the definition of objects of inquiry. These objects were likely to be chosen according to the availability of relevant data. This explains the proliferation of socio-economic studies that depend at least in part on existing data bases such as censuses (for example, Ley 1985; Murdie 1969).

A final point of importance is positivism's self-avowed hegemonic position. According to its proponents, only knowledge that emanates from a positivist method can lay claims to a scientific status. But, from the late 1960s and with an added vigour in the 1970s and 1980s, positivism was challenged by a number of emerging approaches. We now consider three such approaches: behaviouralism, phenomenology and structuralism. The first is considered because it amends the positivist method while incorporating most of its tenets; the second because it emphasizes subjectivity and direct experience, thus rejecting the positivist call for detachment and objectivity; and the third because it offers both a radical critique and an alternative while reorienting the study of cities.

Behavioural Geography

Behavioural geography arises from a dissatisfaction with positivism's exclusive concern with the aggregate effect of individuals' actions and its reliance on the 'economic person' abstraction. This causes positivist methodologies to overlook the motivations and processes that underlie human behaviour. Behavioural methods attempt to identify the steps involved in decisions made by individuals (see for example, Brown and Moore [1970] for an urban migration decision-making model) and constraints wherein these decisions are made (see for a discussion of time and space constraints, Parkes and Thrift 1975). One of the constraints that has become a particularly well-researched object of study is one's incomplete awareness of available options. In this respect, the drawing of mental maps has been a widely used means to measure one's fragmentary knowledge of a city (Downs and Stea 1973).

The behavioural approach shares with positivism an objectivity and value-free assumption as well as a predilection for quantitative data. The main methodological difference between the two approaches is behaviouralism's wide use of questionnaires targeted at individuals to expose the decision-making process orienting their actions. (See Golledge and Stimpson [1987] for a general discussion of behaviouralism within geography.)

Phenomenology

Another reaction against positivism comes from phenomenology, which emphasizes subjectivity, individual experience, and intuition. Very succinctly, for phenomenologists there is no objective world that is independent of experience; all knowledge is subjective. In an urban context, this approach is therefore devoted to examining how individuals experience the city. Methodologies are often interactive in that they involve extensive dialogue between researcher and subject. Phenomenology also lends itself to investigators' narration of their own subjective experience. In this respect it shares with early approaches a reliance on direct observation. Rowles' study of the elderly offers a revealing example of how a phenomenological study can be carried out (1978). In this study, Rowles shared the lives of a limited number of ageing urban residents so that he could document the adaptation of their use of the city to declining capabilities. In reporting the results of the research, Rowles quotes extensively from comments made by the elderly themselves. (For further discussion of phenomenology within geography, see Relph 1970; 1981.)

Structuralism

Structuralism originated from linguistics and later spread to anthropology. This analytical framework posits the existence of systems of rules that are invisible and unconscious, and that determine perceptible events, including conscious behaviour. For this framework, explanations do not arise from observable facts in the positivist fashion, but rather from underlying structures—hence the structuralist label. Accordingly, in order to understand social reality, observable events are important insofar as they point to the existence and functioning of underlying structures. For example, Levi-Strauss' anthropological studies of primitive societies revealed complex and enduring systems of rules—such as numerous restrictions on the choice of a spouse—that guide most aspects of behaviour. It became clear that such rules are not perceived by these societies' populations as socially formulated restrictions but are rather seen as part of a natural order that is not subject to question (Levi-Strauss 1963). Structuralism is discussed here because of its ties with Marxism, which has generated a large number of urban studies. (The Marxist approach is sometimes referred to as the 'Marxian' approach in order to distinguish the social science school of thought from the political movement.)

The structuralist perspective can be seen as embracing Marxism because Marxist explanations of social phenomena rest on underlying historical laws that guide the evolution of the economic system and thus play a pivotal role in the progress of society as a whole. The invisible and unconscious manner in which they operate and their determination of observable events qualify these historical laws as structures. But unlike the linguistic and anthropological understanding of the concept, which stresses structures' immutability, Marxism's historical laws unfold over time. In the late 1960s and the 1970s, a group of French scholars, sometimes referred to as 'structuro-Marxists', expressly acknowledged and developed the association between Marxism and structuralism (Althusser 1969; Althusser and Balibar 1970).

When applied to the study of cities, Marxism represents the most radical critique of positivist urban studies. This is because the structuralist dimension of Marxism challenges positivism's explanations, which derive from an analysis of observable facts. For Marxist scholars these facts are relevant in that they reflect the unfolding of historical laws leading to an increasing concentration of economic power within capitalism and intensifying class struggle. Another Marxist challenge stems from its rejection of the value-free assumption that is central to positivism. According to Marxism, all approaches are tied, albeit usually in an unacknowledged fashion, to the interests of specific classes. Marxist scholars have described positivist urban studies as bourgeois-oriented because they see them as being at the service of business interests and governments that favour these interests (Castells 1969).

Marxism has ushered in a new set of preoccupations within urban studies: social justice (Harvey 1973; Lefebvre 1968); the state as a factor of inequality (Castells 1977); adverse consequences of capitalist laws of development (Smith 1979; 1982); and collusion between political and economic establishments in matters of urban development.[7] Essentially, Marxist studies critique reality and promote an alternative future.[8]

As expected, critiques aimed at Marxism are concerned with its overly theoretical nature and the endless discussions that stem from a lack of clear empirical validation for its positions. Another source of disagreement is the lack of attention given to the urban phenomenon *per se*, which in Marxist studies is seen essentially as an expression of wider societal tendencies (Castells 1983). Finally, the determinism inherent in the reliance on structural explanations has also been an object of criticism. This criticism was targeted at the absence of room that structural determinism leaves to human agency or, in other words, to the possibility for individuals to have an impact on society by exerting their own free will. In response to this objection, two approaches seek to redress the balance between structural determinism and human agency: the realist approach (Bhaskar 1975; Sayer 1984; 1985) and structuration theory (Giddens 1979).

Post-Modernism
We now turn to the contemporary state of urban studies and, more particularly, urban geography. The above discussion should not give the impression that 'reaction approaches' obliterate and replace existing approaches. It is rather the case that older approaches generally persist, which makes for an ever growing number of approaches. Moreover, recent years have witnessed a flurry of new urban research directions in the wake of the Marxist challenge to positivism's value-free assumption. These directions do not subscribe to constitutive characteristics of Marxism, such as economic determinism and a predominance of class struggle over all forms of social cleavages. Many of the new directions could be referred to as expressions of an 'urban advocacy geography' where researchers both espouse and promote the interests of the groups they investigate. This is the case, for example, of the underprivileged (Badcock 1984; Dear and Wolch 1987), ethnic and racial groups (Peters 1988), and especially women from a feminist perspective (Hayden 1984; Mackenzie 1989). (Feminism strives to make women's experience and values visible in a historical and contemporary context.) One may add to this list of advocates, researchers from other disciplines such as those who champion the environmental cause (Gordon 1990).

The post-modern label is affixed to the present period because the term generally refers to a diversity of perspectives and the loss of clearly articulated points of reference (Soja 1989, 60). In other words, an erstwhile search for absolute truth has been replaced during the current post-modern period by intellectual relativism (Palm 1983, 109).

Post-modernism may result from a cumulative wisdom fostering the realization that no single approach is apt on its own to capture the full complexity of the city. The present diversity may equally be attributable to a decline in intellectual proselytism following the realization over time that one can rarely convince researchers committed to one approach of the superiority of another approach. This is because there is no reason to bestow a privileged status on any given theoretical viewpoint (Dear 1988). Finally, the current variety also results from the multiple purposes of urban studies: government reports, private sector consultation, background information for activist groups, as well as pure academic research, etc.[9]

Planning Models

Much of planning theory consists of normative models. These models identify roles that planning should play in guiding urban development, and put forth a range of planning processes tailored to these roles. Interestingly, the trajectory of this body of planning theory closely resembles urban studies' tendency towards diversification.

The first model, which was developed in the 1950s and the 1960s, views planning as a technical activity carried out by experts. The model is labelled *rational-comprehensive*: rational, because it consists of steps that should make it possible to define and select the best solution to a problem; comprehensive, because it attempts to look at all aspects of the current situation and explore all possible solutions. As in the case of positivist urban geography, the rational-comprehensive model became quantitative in the 1960s (Branch 1975).

Three main critiques were levelled at this model: (1) It is essentially technocratic since it offers a top-down approach to planning practice, which is left in the hands of experts; (2) It assumes interest-free goals and processes that will permit the identification of the best solution to a problem; (3) It does not acknowledge the reality of organizations' operations, where cost and time considerations limit information gathering and consideration of options.

Alternatives to the rational-comprehensive model were formulated to address these critiques. According to the first alternative, *incremental planning*, changes do not result so much from extensive and structured planning exercise as from coalitions and compromises. These lead to a number of minor changes consisting more in adaptations than profound changes— hence the label incremental (Lindblom 1959). Another alternative is *transactive planning*, which views planning as a social learning exercise where the planner learns from the client as does the client from the planner. According to this perspective, it is from an expert-population dialogue that valid planning solutions emerge (Friedmann 1973; 1987). *Advocacy planning* holds that planners ought to defend the interests of the members of society who are least able to fend for themselves and as a result who suffer the most from current planning practice: the poor, minorities, the elderly, some women, etc. (Davidoff 1965). Finally, *radical planning* defines for planners and planning a catalytic role in bringing about a change of society (Goodman 1971).

As in the case of urban studies, it has proven difficult to establish the superiority of one planning model over the others. Years of practical experience and of theoretical debates have established the relativity of interests within society and the need for planning to acknowledge this diversity. Another lesson is that planning processes must adapt to the different circumstances in which planners operate and the different roles they play.

THE BOOK'S APPROACH TO THE CITY

Many of this book's chapters criticize the current conditions of cities and urban systems, and suggest solutions. In this sense they reflect changes that have transformed urban studies since the advent of the Marxist approach and the 1960s' unrest by attempting to increase these studies' social relevance. Chapter 2 sets the tone by pointing to a number of contemporary issues facing Canadian cities. Some chapters tackle uneven and unfair distribution of resources and power between cities and regions (Chapters 4, 5, 7, 8) and between social groups. In this latter case, Chapters 14 and 20 focus on the condition of women and disadvantaged groups and thus adopt somewhat of an advocacy stand. From an institutional framework perspective, Chapter 18 identifies problems in managing cities. Chapter 19 examines planning problems and Chapters 10 and 16 raise environmental issues.

The presence of a diversity of approaches side by side within the book sets it within the contemporary post-modern current. It also demonstrates that there are many ways of doing and reporting urban-related research. Interestingly, rather than adhering strictly to the assumptions and methodology of a single approach, individual chapters generally blend aspects of different approaches. This is to avoid gaps that would be left in the discussion of a predefined empirical dimension of the city by the adherence to one approach. In this fashion, composite approaches stem from the requirements of empirical investigation. Many chapters lean towards positivism in their methodology and the use of quantitative data. As seen, however, they usually combine these elements of positivism with a focus on social concerns. Others depart quite sharply from the positivist mode. This is particularly the case of Chapter 6, which relies on a qualitative scenario-building methodology, and Chapter 10, which is written largely from a personal, subjective point of view and which, therefore, broadly espouses the phenomenological approach.

All the chapters in this book share a concern over themes that highlight the geographical and planning dimensions of the urban phenomenon and that relate to the interpretation of the city introduced earlier in the introduction. These themes are the use of space, movement within and between cities, the built environment, and the management of cities. The themes are discussed in the light of contemporary issues confronting the Canadian city: uneven growth distribution within individual cities and the Canadian urban system as a whole; resulting infrastructure congestion and housing affordability problems in certain centres or sectors, and the consequences of urban decline in other centres or sectors; growing urban poverty; the increasing role NIMBY plays in municipal politics; and air, water, and soil pollution generated by cities within or outside their perimeter.

NOTES

1. See Mumford (1938) for a cultural definition, Weber (1958) for a political and administrative definition, and Castells (1977) for a definition that emphasizes public sector services and infrastructures.

2. On the interaction within cities between households, the employment market, and consumption facilities, see Broadbent (1977).

3. It is interesting to note the resemblance between the implications of this interpretation of the city and the agenda Wirth (1964, 68) set for urban sociologists in 1938: 'The central problem of the sociologist of the city is to discover forms of social action and organization that typically emerge in relatively permanent, compact settlements of large numbers of heterogeneous individuals'.

4. See Kuhn (1962) and Popper (1959) for conflicting views on the evolution of science.

5. For alternative views on the evolution of urban geography see the annual progress reports in *Progress in Human Geography* and Palm (1981, 3–12). Readers may also want to consult Bird (1989), Holt-Jensen (1988), and Johnston (1983) for recent perspectives on the evolution of human geography, and Alexander (1986) and Friedmann (1987) for an account of changes within planning practice and theory.

6. For a similar evolution within urban sociology in the 1960s and 1970s, from ethnographic studies to a greater reliance on factorial ecology, see O'Brien and Roach (1984).

7. This latter theme was the object of the most elaborate Marxist investigation of a Canadian city—Quebec City. This study was carried out by the Etude des zones prioritaires (EZOP-Québec) group (EZOP-Québec 1981 [1972]).

8. Any impression that Marxist studies monopolize the critical scene should be dispelled, however. Canada witnessed over the last two and a half decades a flurry of studies of different persuasions questioning cities' political and social organization. Some of these studies narrate the actions of movements challenging this organization. One thinks here of books such as *Up Against City Hall* (Sewell 1972) and *The Milton-Park Affair: Canada's Largest Citizen-Developer*

Confrontation (Helman 1987) as well as many articles published in *City Magazine* and *Our Generation*.

9. It is interesting to note that post-modernism within urban geography coincides with a post-modern architectural movement. This movement has replaced the formerly dominant international style—responsible for the rectangular steel and glass towers of the 1950s, 1960s, and early 1970s—by more diversified stylistic experiences. Likewise we may also perceive a post-modern urban form in recently developed urban sectors. These sectors are indeed often characterized by an amorphous landscape, devoid of a clearly identifiable hierarchy of centres and thus of major points of reference.

REFERENCES

ALEXANDER, E.R. 1986 *Approaches to Planning: Introducing Current Planning Theories, Concepts, and Issues* (New York: Gordon and Breach Science Publishers)

ALTHUSSER, L. 1969 *For Marx* (London: Allen Lane)

—— and BALIBAR, E. 1970 *Reading Capital* (New York: Pantheon Books)

BADCOCK, B. 1984 *Unfairly Structured Cities* (Oxford: Basil Blackwell)

BHASKAR, R. 1975 *A Realist Theory of Science* (Brighton: Harvester Press)

BIRD, J. 1989 *The Changing Worlds of Geography: a Critical Guide to Concepts and Methods* (Oxford: Clarendon Press)

BRANCH, M.C. ed. 1975 *Urban Planning Theory* (Stroudsburg, Penn.: Dowden, Hutchinson and Ross)

BREHEMY, M.J. 1978 'The Measurement of Spatial Opportunity in Strategic Planning', *Regional Studies* 12, 463–79

BROADBENT, T.A. 1977 *Planning and Profit in the Urban Economy* (London: Methuen)

BROTCHIE, J., NEWTON, P., HALL, P. and NIJKAMP, P. 1985 *The Future of Urban Form* (London: Croom Helm)

BROWN, L.A. and MOORE, E.G. 1970 'The Intra-urban Migration Process: a Perspective', *Geografiska Annaler* 53B, 1–13

BURTON, I. 1963 'The Quantitative Revolution and Theoretical Geography', *The Canadian Geographer* 7, 151–62

CASTELLS, M. 1969 'Théorie et idéologie en sociologie urbaine', *Sociologie et sociétés* 1, 171–92

—— 1977 *The Urban Question: a Marxist Approach* (London: Edward Arnold)

—— 1983 *The City and the Grassroots: a Cross-cultural Theory of Urban Social Movements* (Berkeley: University of California Press)

CLARK, G.L. and WHITEMAN, L. 1983 'Why Poor People Do Not Move: Job Search Behaviour and Disequilibrium Amongst Local Labour Markets', *Environment and Planning A* 15, 85–104

DAVIDOFF, P. 1965 'Advocacy and Pluralism in Planning', *Journal of the American Planning Association* 31, 331–8

DEAR, M.J. 1988 'The Postmodern Challenge: Reconstructing Human Geography', *Transactions of the Institute of British Geographers* 13, 262–74

―――― and WOLCH, J. 1987 *Landscapes of Despair: From Deindustrialization to Homelessness* (Princeton, N.J.: Princeton University Press)

DOWNS, R.M. and STEA, D. 1973 *Image and the Environment; Cognitive Mapping and Spatial Behavior* (Chicago: Aldine Publishing Co)

EZOP-QUEBEC 1981 *Une ville à vendre* (Laval, Que.: Editions coopératives Saint-Martin) (1st edition, 1972)

FALCOCCHIO, J.C., PIGNATARO, L.J. and CANTILLI, E.J. 1972 'Modal Choices and Travel Attributes of Inner-city Poor', *Highway Research Record* 403, 6–17

FRIEDMANN, J. 1973 *Retracking America* (New York: Anchor-Doubleday)

―――― 1987 *Planning in the Public Domain: From Knowledge to Action* (Princeton, N.J.: Princeton University Press)

GAPPERT, G. and KNIGHT, R. eds 1982 *Cities in the 21st Century* (Beverly Hills: Sage Publications)

GARNER, B.J. 1967 'Models of Urban Geography and Settlement Location' in R.J. Chorley and P. Haggett eds *Models in Geography* (London: Methuen)

GIDDENS, A. 1979 *Central Problems in Social Theory* (London: Macmillan)

GOLLEDGE, R. and STIMPSON, R. 1987 *Analytical Behavioral Geography* (London: Croom Helm)

GOODMAN, R. 1971 *After the Planners* (New York: Simon and Shuster)

GORDON, D. ed. 1990 *Green Cities: Ecologically Sound Approaches to Urban Space* (Montreal: Black Rose Books)

HARVEY, D. 1969 *Explanations in Geography* (London: Edward Arnold)

―――― 1973 *Social Justice and the City* (Baltimore, Maryland: Johns Hopkins University Press)

―――― 1989 *The Urban Experience* (Oxford: Blackwell)

HAYDEN, D. 1984 *Redesigning the American Dream: the Future of Housing, Work and Family Life* (New York: W.W. Norton)

HELMAN, C. 1987 *The Milton-Park Affair: Canada's Largest Citizen-Developer Confrontation* (Montreal: Véhicule Press)

HOLT-JENSEN, A. 1988 *Geography: History and Concepts, a Student's Guide* (London: Paul Chapman)

HUTCHINSON, P.M. 1978 'Transportation, Segregation, and Labour Force Participation of the Urban Poor', *Growth and Change* 9, 31–7

JOHNSTON, R.J. 1983 *Philosophy and Human Geography; an Introduction to Contemporary Approaches* (London: Edward Arnold)

KUHN, T.S. 1962 *The Structure of Scientific Revolutions* (Chicago: University of Chicago Press)

LEFEBVRE, H. 1968 *Le droit à la ville* (Paris: Anthropos)

LEVI-STRAUSS, C. 1963 *Structural Anthropology* (New York: Basic Books)

LEY, D. 1985 *Gentrification in Canadian Inner Cities: Patterns, Analysis, Impacts and Policy* (Ottawa: Canada Mortgage and Housing Corporation)

LINDBLOM, C.E. 1959 'The Science of Muddling Through', *Public Administration Review* 19, 59–88

LORIMER, J. 1978 *The Developers* (Toronto: James Lorimer)

MACKENZIE, S. 1989 *Visible Histories: Women and Environment in a Post-war British City* (Montreal: McGill-Queen's University Press)

MUMFORD, L. 1938 *The Culture of Cities* (New York: Harcourt Brace)

MURDIE, R. 1969 *Factorial Ecology of Metropolitan Toronto, 1951–1961: An Essay on the Social Ecology of the City* (Chicago: University of Chicago, Department of Geography, Research Paper No. 116)

O'BRIEN, D.J. and ROACH, M.J. 1984 'Recent Developments in Urban Sociology', *Journal of Urban History* 10 2, 145–70

PAASWELL, R.E. and RECKER, W.W. 1978 *Problems of the Carless* (New York: Praeger)

PALM, R. 1981 *The Geography of American Cities* (New York: Oxford University Press)

——— 1983 'Progress Report: Urban Geography, City Structures', *Progress in Human Geography* 7 1, 109–15

PARK, R.E., BURGESS, E.W. and MCKENZIE, R.D. 1925 *The City* (Chicago: University of Chicago Press)

PARKES, D.N. and THRIFT, N. 1975 'Timing Space and Spacing Time', *Environment and Planning A* 7, 651–70

PETERS, E. 1988 'World [Third?] Within a World [First]: Canadian Indian People' in J. Norwine and A. Gonzales eds *The Third World: States of Mind and Being* (London: Unwin Hyman)

POPPER, K.R. 1959 *The Logic of Scientific Discovery* (London: Hutchinson)

RELPH, E.C. 1970 'An Inquiry Into the Relations Between Phenomenology and Geography', *The Canadian Geographer* 14, 193–201

——— 1981 'Phenomenology' in M.E. Harvey and B.P. Holly eds *Themes in Geographic Thought* (London: Croom Helm)

ROWLES, G.D. 1978 *The Prisoners of Space?; Exploring the Geographical Experience of Older People* (Boulder, Colorado: Westview Press)

SAYER, A. 1984 *Method in Social Science: a Realist Approach* (London: Hutchinson)

——— 1985 'Realism and Geography' in R.J. Johnston ed. *The Future of Geography* (London: Methuen)

SEWELL, J. 1972 *Up Against City Hall* (Toronto: J. Lewis and Samuel)

SMITH, N. 1979 'Towards a Theory of Gentrification: a Back to the City Movement by Capital not People', *Journal of the American Planning Association* 45, 538–48

——— 1982 'Gentrification and Uneven Development', *Economic Geography* 58, 139–55

SMITH, S.J. 1984 'Practicing Humanistic Geography', *Annals, Association of American Geographers* 74, 353–74

SOJA, E.W. 1989 *Postmodern Geographies; the Reassertion of Space in Critical Theory* (London: Verso)

WEBER, M. 1958 *The City* (New York: Collier Books)

WEKERLE, G.R. 1984 'A Woman's Place is in the City', *Antipode* 16 (3), 11–19

WIRTH, L. 1964 'Urbanism as a Way of Life' in *Louis Wirth on Cities and Social Life* A.J. Reiss ed. (Chicago: The University of Chicago Press)

YEATES, M. 1975 *Main Street: Windsor to Quebec City* (Toronto: Macmillan)

——— 1987 'The Extent of Urban Development in the Windsor-Quebec City Axis', *The Canadian Geographer* 31, 64–69

PART ONE

NATIONAL PERSPECTIVES

2

Addressing the Canadian City: Contemporary Perspectives, Trends, and Issues

LARRY S. BOURNE

Canada became an urban country, at least statistically, around 1924. At that time, more than 50 per cent of the nation's population resided in urban settlements of 1,000 or more.[1] It became, again in strictly numerical terms, a predominantly metropolitan country in 1965, when more than 50 per cent of Canadians lived in urban centres of over 100,000,[2] and an overwhelmingly suburban nation in about 1972. By that time, over 50 per cent of all urban residents lived outside the administrative boundaries of the central cities (that is, the municipality encompassing the original settlement of the metropolitan region; this municipality is usually at the centre of the metropolitan region).[3] These dates, although clearly arbitrary as reference points, do signal that the timespan of a predominantly urbanized society in Canada is relatively short, which means that its inherited urban fabric is of less extent than that of most other western nations (Stone 1967; Gertler and Crowley 1977; Artibise and Stelter 1979; Stelter and Artibise 1986; Bourne 1991).

This does not mean, however, that we can ignore the historical evolution of urbanization and settlement and the inheritance of the city-building process. In fact, precisely the opposite is true. The location of most of Canada's cities, and thus the basic geography of the Canadian urban system, was determined in the first centuries of European settlement, through the needs of the fur trade, military imperatives, the exploitation of resources, and the extension of the agricultural frontier westward. The internal form and structure of our cities also still mirror the land surveys and road systems laid down in the seventeenth, eighteenth, or nineteenth centuries. The message here is that while we may emphasize the rapidity of recent change in urban Canada in the post-war period, we should not lose sight of the historically-given pattern of settlement and the imprint of city development and planning decisions made years ago (see Chapter 4 for a more detailed history of Canadian urban development).

This chapter provides an overview of the transformation of urban Canada, and identifies some of the issues that flow from that transformation. The emphasis is on the last two decades, although attention will be paid to the historical context and to the possible emergence of new trends and issues.

ADDRESSING THE CITY

The term 'addressing' in the title of this paper is used to stress two important but often overlooked preconditions for the study of cities and the urban process more generally.[4] First is the obvious need to place each individual city in its appropriate geographical context: that is, to recognize its location within the larger system of cities of which it is a part, and to acknowledge the relationships that follow from that situation. With the increasing integration of the economies of cities, at national and international scales, these relationships become even more crucial. Cities clearly do not exist in isolation from each other or, perhaps even more obviously, from the structural and socio-political relations of that society.

Second, the term is used in its conventional sense of speaking to, or directing one's interest to, a specific audience or object. In this case, the urban process is the object of analysis. How we approach that object substantially shapes and colours our impressions, influences our selection of the facts that seem most relevant, and delimits the conclusions that we draw. This implies that we cannot study cities as independent artifacts, and must clearly indicate our assumptions, frameworks, and points of departure.

Consider two contrasting points of departure in the study of cities, each involving very different geographical scales of analysis yet illustrating in simple terms the importance of 'address' in its precise geographical sense. We can start with the specific question, 'Where do you live?' The answer or answers to this question are revealing, and depend not only on where you are but who you are talking to. To a person familiar with the area, you might give an address such as 276 George Street, 12A Water Street, or 1246 West 49th Avenue. To a visitor from out of town you might instead name a locale such as Ste. Foy, the Beaches, or Kitsilano; to a foreigner you may name a city such as Halifax, Montreal, or Kelowna.

Each 'address'—the home, the neighbourhood, the city or the region—
tells us something about the person giving the answer: his or her living
environments, perhaps their language and social status, and possibly their
life styles and attitudes.

Whether you start with a macro-scale study of the entire urban system
and move to a micro-scale study (the place of residence) or work in the
reverse direction, is not all that important. What is important is that one
sees the interrelationships among the different scales or 'addresses' in
which we live, from local to national or international scales. It is also
important to adapt these scales to the audiences that we are attempting to
'address'. At any given time, we approach the study of cities, and analyses
of urban growth and change and the varied experiences (positive and
negative) of urban living, with our own particular language, prejudices,
and standards of comparison. We also bring our own intellectual baggage.
This baggage has been described in some detail by the editors in the
preface to this volume and in an extensive literature on the philosophy of
geography and social-science research (Johnston 1987).

THE URBAN TRANSFORMATION

Within this general framework, we can examine the transformation of
Canada from a rural to an urban country. Both the scale and rapidity of
that transformation have been impressive (Table 2.1). In 1921, for example,
just over 4.2 million or 48 per cent of Canadians resided in urban areas of
all sizes. At that time, there were only six urban centres with populations

Table 2.1
The Urban Transformation of Canada: Population by Place of Residence and
Urban Size Category 1921–1986[d]

	1921[a] (000)	Per-centage	1941[b] (000)	Per-centage	1961 (000)	Per-centage	1981[c] (000)	Per-centage	1986[c] (000)	Per-centage
Rural: Total	4,531	51.6	5,254	45.7	5,266	28.9	5,907	24.3	5,957	23.5
Farm	na	na	3,117	27.1	2,238	12.3	1,435	5.9	890	3.5
Non-farm	na	na	2,137	18.6	3,028	16.6	4,472	18.4	5,067	20.0
Urban: Total[b]	4,257	48.4	6,252	54.3	12,972	71.1	18,436	75.7	19,397	76.5
<100,000	1,907	21.7	2,765	24.0	5,048	27.7	4,561	18.7	4,224	16.6
100,000–1 M	2,350	26.7	2,337	20.3	3,926	21.5	6,792	27.9	7,440	29.4
> 1 M	0	0	1,150	9.9	3,998	21.9	7,083	29.1	7,733	30.5
Canada	8,788	100	11,506	100	18,238	100	24,343	100	25,354	100

Sources: Census of Canada, various years; Stone 1967; Simmons and Bourne 1989.

Notes: na = not available.
  a = Farm/Non-farm distinction not available until the 1931 Census.
  b = Based on census definitions of 'urban' at each date. The 1941 figures use Stone's (1967)
  concept of the 'major urban complex'.
  c = Based on 1986 definitions of census metropolitan areas (CMAs) and census agglomerations
  (CAs).
  d = Definitional changes, particularly with respect to the geographical boundaries of CMAs and
  CAs, make comparisons of population change over time very difficult. The expanding
  boundaries of the CMAs and CAs account for a significant part of the decline in population
  of smaller settlements since 1961.

of over 100,000 population and no Canadians lived in settings that were truly metropolitan (with populations over 1 million population). By the beginning of the post World War II era, after nearly two decades of slow growth in both population and the economy because of the Depression and World War II, the proportion of the population classified as urban had increased to 54 per cent (6.4 million out of 12 million). With the incentives of post-war reconstruction and promises of rapid economic and population expansion, however, the stage was set for the explosion of urban growth in the post–1945 years (see Chapter 4).

From 1941 to 1961, the population of urban Canada nearly doubled to 13 million, and the proportion classified as urban increased from 54 per cent to over 71 per cent. The number of people living in rural areas also grew, but the proportion living on farms declined in absolute and in relative terms (from 27 per cent to just over 12 per cent). At the same time, the distribution and size of Canadian cities, as well as the local environments in which Canadians lived, also changed dramatically. The most rapidly growing size-category of urban places was the metropolitan category. By 1961, nearly 8 million people or 43 per cent lived in eighteen urban places with over 100,000 population; two of these places (Montreal and Toronto) had over 1,000,000 people. The contemporary Canadian settlement fabric was by this time firmly in place.

Over the next two decades, from 1961 to 1981, the urbanization process continued but at a somewhat reduced rate as the rural pool of migrants shrunk. The geography of change also seemed to differ widely from one five-year period to another (Simmons and Bourne 1985). By 1986, over 76 per cent of the nation's population or 19.4 million persons were classi-fied as urban residents, of which 15.2 million or almost 60 per cent resided in twenty-five census metropolitan areas. Over 30 per cent now lived in the three national metropolises. Thus, in the short space of forty-five years, the total urban population has trebled, the number of large urban centres has grown over three-fold, and the metropolitan population has increased by almost five times.[5]

One result of this massive expansion of the nation's settlement system has been a sharply differentiated hierarchy of urban places (Appendix 2). The twenty-five largest urban centres vary widely, not only in their size but in terms of their socio-economic attributes, in their inherited building fabrics, and in their social landscapes, living environments, and sense of place. Metropolitan areas in Canada differ in size by a factor of 30 (from Toronto to Saint John), and exhibit similarities and contrasts that reflect this size differential. They also differ according to their region (contrast Atlantic cities with those in British Columbia or the Prairies), their age (Quebec City and Calgary), local economies (contrast government and service centres, such as Ottawa or Victoria, with older industrial cities such as Winnipeg or Hamilton) and their social and demographic composition (contrast the homogeneity of cities in the Atlantic region and Quebec with the diversity of cities in southern Ontario and the Prairies).[6] These similarities and differences are both explicitly and implicitly addressed throughout the chapters to follow and more particularly so in Chapters 5, 7, and 8 which deal with the Canadian urban system.

THE POST-WAR PERIOD: AN OVERVIEW

It is possible to identify phases or different directions of urban growth and change in Canada over this extended period—phases that capture a significant part of the very complex set of processes involved. Table 2.2 offers a summary of the principal directions of change in Canadian settlement over the post-war period. Three phases are identified; the growth trends and characteristics of each phase are expressed at different spatial scales.[7]

Allowing for some over-generalization, the first phase (1945–64) may be characterized as the period of rapid growth in population and urban areas. Population in almost all cities and regions of the country increased, floating on a combined wave of high fertility (the baby-boom and marriage boom) and high immigration. The level of urbanization increased sharply and metropolitan growth accelerated, adding to the long-standing process of a concentration of population, economic wealth, and political power in the upper levels of the urban hierarchy. The hierarchy itself was redefined, as Toronto enhanced its national primacy and Calgary surpassed Winnipeg on the Prairies.

In the second phase, the late 1960s and the 1970s, the overall growth rate slowed, as fertility rates and immigration dropped. Regional differentials in growth increased because of variations in resource endowments (and resource prices) and industrialization. In the latter part of the 1970s in particular, the decline in manufacturing and the increase in oil prices shifted urban growth and migration flows away from the industrial heartland of southern Ontario and Quebec towards resource areas, and especially to cities in the West. This also meant that medium-sized and smaller centres, again most noticeably those in the west (e.g. Edmonton, Calgary) grew more rapidly than the larger centres of the industrial heartland. Urban decline became especially widespread in the East and the North. The overall result was a significant deconcentration of population at the national level and a redistribution of urban growth downward within the urban hierarchy—small centres growing faster than large centres. This period was as close as Canada has come to a period that others have described as one of counter-urbanization or deurbanization.[8]

This trend in urban and regional growth, however, was short-lived. It was brought to an abrupt end by the severe recession of the early 1980s. When the country subsequently came out of that recession, beginning in 1982–3, a new and somewhat surprising geography of change emerged (Simmons and Bourne 1989; Gad 1989). Growth returned with a vengeance

Table 2.2
Major Phases in Canadian Urban Development, 1945–1990

Geographical scale	Early post-war 1945–1964 *Urban boom*	Later post-war 1965–1980 *Deconcentration and decline*	Post-recession 1981– *Concentration and renewal*
National urban system	Rapid population growth; high fertility (*baby boom*) and high immigration; economy booming	Declining rate of growth; lower fertility and immigration; economic restructuring and manufacturing decline	Slow population growth; stable natural increase; ageing population; service economy dominates growth
Level of urbanization and urban/rural balance	Rapid increase in percentage of urban population; rural farm population decline	Stabilizing level (%); rural farm population decline; rapid non-farm growth	Stable level (76%) in urban population; slower non-farm rural growth
Regional variations	Rapid growth in industrial heartland and selected resource locations; some growth almost everywhere	Slower growth in heartland; rapid growth in West; widespread decline in East and North	Renewed growth in heartland; slower growth in West and resource periphery; retirement/leisure centres boom across the country
Urban size hierarchy	Massive concentration in metropolitan areas; relative decline of small towns	Slower metropolitan growth; middle-size cities growing rapidly; absolute decline of towns common (deurbanization)	Modest metropolitan revival; city-size influences growth; small towns decline except in metropolitan commuting fields and leisure areas
Intra-urban form and development	Highest growth in suburban areas; inner cities declining; slow growth on rural-urban fringe	Rapid decentralization; outer suburbs and exurbs growing rapidly; jobs spreading to suburbs; core jobs increase, but population declines (despite revitalization)	Continued rapid decentralization; outer suburbs and rural-urban fringe booming; downtown growth accelerates; central-area population stable or growing

to the industrial heartland, and especially to urban centres in south-central Ontario and to the greater Toronto area in particular. Only a few selected locations in other parts of the country, notably in Vancouver and south-western British Columbia participated fully in this recovery.

This development produced a result rather different from that of the previous period: a process of geographical concentration in economic and population growth was clearly in evidence, and the largest metropolitan centres (excluding Montreal) literally boomed. Resource-based communities and the national periphery suffered badly as most resource prices remained depressed. Regional variations again increased, but for different reasons, and, with the exception of the lastingly beleaguered Atlantic region, in other areas. By 1988, however, the boom was off. The fourth phase of urban growth, still to be defined, had begun.

CONTEMPORARY TRENDS IN URBAN FORM AND STRUCTURE

Within this evolving settlement system, the character and spatial structure of individual urban areas in Canada have been transformed substantially, and in some instances almost beyond recognition. The principal dimension of change has been the vast increase in the size of urban areas—in population, jobs, capital investment, infrastructure, and most of all in the extent of urban land development and the scale of the rural areas over which the metropolis casts its shadow. The dominant contributor to this scale increase, as well as the principal outcome of post-war urban growth, has been the suburbanization process.

The effects of this process have been wildly uneven from decade to decade. Our urban areas are in fact layered, with each ring of suburban growth added to and modifying that of previous periods, in a complex sequence of development. Most Canadian cities display a distinct break between their pre–1929 landscape and the post–1945 suburban landscape. The older fabric consists of high densities with mixed uses, heavily dependent on railways for goods transportation and on public transit. The more recent landscape is built at much lower densities, with a variety of building and house forms, regional shopping centres, and massive new clusters of work places, spatially organized largely around the widespread ownership and use of automobiles and trucks (for a more detailed discussion of the interaction between urban-land patterns and transportation, see Chapter 11).

The densities of urban development have declined everywhere. Newly constructed suburban neighbourhoods have also become massive in scale, and, until recently, more homogeneous in social composition and housing. Development firms of increasing size have created entire suburbs as a single unit—a process referred to as the emergence of the 'corporate' suburb (Lorimer and Ross 1976; Bourne and Bunting 1991). Jobs have become more diverse, in skills and remuneration, and much further removed from places of residence, in part because of forms of planning dominated by zoning practices; these practices have for most of the post-war period discouraged the mixing of residential and commercial and industrial activity (see Chapter 19).

This physical separation and homogeneity of use in turn has necessitated the construction of massive road and expressway systems to bring a labour force that is more and more dispersed to work places that are themselves more widely distributed (Bourne 1989). These road systems and associated parking, transfer, and storage facilities for cars and trucks also require immense amounts of space, adding further to the geographical dispersion of urban land uses.

Lower densities have also vastly increased the cost of providing local infrastructure (water and sewers most obviously) and public services such as schools, community and recreational facilities, as well as essential health and welfare services. Moreover, in those urban areas in which there are several independent political jurisdictions—the classic case of the fragmented metropolis—these services may be difficult to finance, and thus may be very unevenly distributed across the urban landscape.

The older downtown commercial cores of Canadian cities have been extensively demolished and redeveloped. Although redevelopment has been a part of the urban development process throughout the history of our cities, the pace of change in the decades after 1965 has been unprecedented. With the exception of a few listed historical buildings and a limited number of heritage districts, the occasional leisure place, and a few forgotten areas of derelict industrial buildings, most of the pre-war building fabric in the downtown of the larger metropolitan areas is now gone. High-rise mega-structures, new in-town shopping centres, and large comprehensive redevelopment schemes, all interspersed with parking lots, now dot the central urban landscape. In some instances, the same corporate developers and designers have been behind these schemes, producing a degree of uniformity and homogeneity from city to city that not only obliterates the historical record but often makes it difficult to tell where you are.

Between the downtown core and the suburban margin, the urban landscape has also changed, physically and socially, but in a much more discontinuous, multiform pattern. This pattern has evolved through localized redevelopment, principally around transit stations, along main arterial intersections, and adjacent to unusually rich amenity areas (e.g. parks, lakeshores), and through in-fill developments and widespread rehabilitation. Here the tension between the desire to maintain an older building fabric and preserve familiar living environments and the pressures for reusing or replacing that fabric have been most pronounced and most visible. Neighbourhoods have borne the brunt of this conflict, as planners, local community organizations, and politicians strive to find an appropriate balance between the desire for stability, the preservation of the old, and the need for change and renewal. These conflicts may indeed be the essence of the post-war political debates concerning questions of land development and the management of urban growth (see Chapter 19).

The structure and ambience of Canadian cities have changed in many other but rather more subtle ways, and often these changes initiate similar kinds of conflict and debate. Our cities have become much more complex in functional terms, through the expansion and restructuring of local economies and the reorganization of the linkages between productive sectors of those economies. Traditional land-use patterns have given way, although not entirely, to new forms combining multi-use buildings and specialized commercial and industrial districts. Nowhere is this more evident than in the emergence of massive suburban office parks and arterial highway ribbons, and in concentrations of new high-technology industry and employment (Gad 1989).

The character of the nation's social geography has also changed, perhaps even more dramatically. The well-known demographic transition of the post-baby-boom era, leading to smaller families and much more diverse types of non-family households, has altered the social composition of neighbourhoods and the use of the housing stock that is required for that population (Miron 1988). Earlier, the baby-boom (1948–64) generated a massive demand for schools, day-care and youth services, as well as for family-oriented housing. The inevitable result—extensive suburban development—helped to accelerate the already long-established tendency for production facilities and employment to migrate to the suburbs. Both trends were supported (at least initially) by a public sector willing to provide the necessary infrastructure.

This boom was followed by the baby-bust, beginning in the late 1960s, and deepening in the 1970s. Rapidly declining fertility levels, and associated life-style changes, produced a much smaller cohort of children and an increase in the number of childless couples. The result was another shift in the choice of living arrangements and thus in the demand for housing and in the locations at which that demand has been expressed (Bourne and Bunting 1991). Established neighbourhoods, even without a change in the number of dwelling units, witnessed a drop in their populations of over 25 per cent through 'demographic thinning'. The per-capita consumption of housing and urban land increased accordingly.

At the same time, many households with few (or no) children and two earners chose not to move to the suburbs, but to occupy older neighbourhoods near the city centre, where many held white-collar professional jobs. This process, widely known as revitalization, or gentrification, transformed numerous inner-city neighbourhoods in most of the larger metropolitan areas in the 1960s and 1970s. This movement displaced many of the previous residents, especially low-income tenants (Wilson 1965; Bunting and Filion 1988; Ley 1991). Moreover, demographic change and increasing affluence, supported by life-style and preference shifts, contributed to the redesign of other inner-city landscapes by encouraging the construction of luxury condominiums. In most of the larger Canadian centres, condominiums have been responsible for widespread social upgrading of older neighbourhoods, either through the conversion of existing rental housing to ownership status, or more dramatically through new construction. The latter, most often expressed in the form of high-rise buildings, have transformed old and derelict industrial and port districts (e.g. Harbourfront in Toronto and False Creek in Vancouver) and

Figure 2.1
Population Change: Toronto CMA, 1981-1986

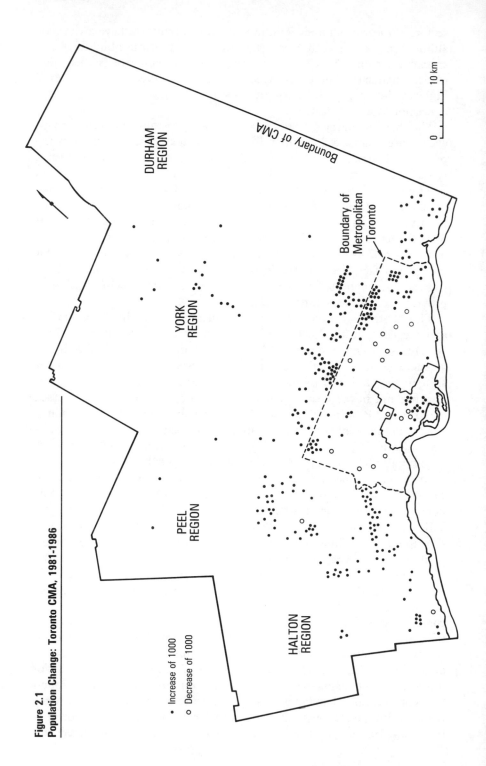

added new residential uses at other locations throughout the older urban landscape (Chapter 13 offers a more detailed discussion of the social trends affecting the inner-city). Less well known perhaps, new condominium construction has altered the physical landscape of the suburbs at least as much as that of the central core.

Patterns of Growth and Decline

The combined impacts of these trends on the distribution of urban population growth are clearly evident in the pattern of change for the Toronto CMA in the 1981–6 period (Figure 2.1). The areas of most rapid growth, as expected, are those on the suburban fringe. Interestingly, the overwhelming majority of this growth took place on the immediate margins of the built-up area, in the corporate suburbs described above, rather than in the outer reaches of the CMA. At the same time, however, population growth has returned to the central core, after four decades of continuous decline.[9] This growth, primarily attributable to new condominium or rental building, and to a lesser extent social housing construction, calls into question textbook accounts of density gradients where core densities necessarily decline as outer suburbs develop.

Finally, the areas of population decline have moved further out from the city centre. These areas form a more or less continuous ring embracing suburban areas built in the 1950s and 1960s. Most of these suburbs are going through a process of population ageing or 'maturing' as neighbourhoods, and thus show demographic thinning as described above. The next census will show this area of decline to have shifted even further from the city centre, into the newer suburban areas of the 1970s and 1980s. This decline in population, it should be added, is not necessarily a problem, although it does carry consequences for some public facilities (e.g. schools) and for some retail and business services, nor is it necessarily permanent.

The New Social Mosaic

One further consequence of this new urban demography, again accentuated by associated changes in life style, occupations and jobs, household incomes, and in housing stock composition, has been the emergence of a more polarized social landscape (Murdie 1990; Ley 1991). Up-scale elite neighbourhoods, some with the pretence of 'designer-label' status, now co-exist with down-scale neighbourhoods and deteriorating public housing projects in a complex geographic mosaic. Our old image of a visibly depressing, impoverished, and crime-ridden inner city surrounded by an increasingly homogeneous and affluent suburban belt, an image fostered by generations of American urban textbooks, is now out-dated. In its place we require a new image, one that conveys a sense of the much more complex and varied social landscape of Canadian cities, a landscape in which variations in social status are sharper, more distinctive, and less easily mapped. Both inner city and suburb have become less homogeneous, and richer and poorer, at the same time.

The visible face that our social geography presents has also changed, with new sources of immigrants and revised government policies on immigration. Between the 1950s and the 1980s the principal areas supplying immigrants to Canada shifted away from traditional sources in Europe and North America to Asia, the Caribbean, and the Third World (Balakrishnan 1988). This has added immeasurably to the ethnic diversity, neighbourhood vitality, and life-styles of our cities, as well as to the characteristics and skill levels of the labour force and entrepreneurial classes. With the changing ethnicity of immigrants has come a different urban social mix, including new racial and ethnocultural attributes. This in turn has led to a richer social environment, as well as to an enhanced awareness of the uncertain position and problems of visible minorities in Canadian life, including our Native peoples. The potential for social progress and improved social relations is there; so too unfortunately is the potential for misunderstanding and unrest. Whatever the outcome, the social composition of urban Canada will continue to be redefined by the descendants of these migrants, and by the continued flow of new and distinctive migrants, over the long term.

The geographical impact of these immigrants has also been uneven. The immigrant flows tend to be telescoped on particular urban areas, especially the larger urban centres (and particularly those in southern Ontario and British Columbia). This is because immigrants tend to be attracted to areas with high levels of employment (and investment possibilities), and follow the networks established by previous migrants. Within the large centres the focus of the immigrant flows has been redirected away from the traditional 'reception' areas in the inner cities to the expanding outer suburbs where housing and jobs (particularly blue-collar jobs) are more readily available. This shift has changed the ethnocultural and social profile of much of suburban Canada, again calling for a revision of our traditional images and public policies.

The Role of the Public Sector

The public sector—that is, government and its attenuated agencies and actors—is implicated in all of the changes described briefly above. The public sector at the local level dispenses essential services, both hard and soft, to its residents and their employers, within its territorial jurisdiction. Some of these services are innocuous (e.g. sewers, water); others are not (e.g. waste disposal). Some services convey obvious benefits on nearby households (e.g. parks, community centres); others involve negative impacts (e.g. a road widening which induces heavier traffic levels). Still others are perceived to offer benefits (e.g. road closing) or costs (e.g. group homes), whatever the evidence may be. Since most of these examples impact on residents over only a limited geographical area, their external effects are also by definition socially uneven (Pinch 1985). Clearly geography matters. How the local state distributes these 'goods and bads' certainly influences the quality of neighbourhood life, and more concretely, the value of housing and land, and thus ultimately the distribution of real income and well-being among urban residents.

Governments, of course, also act as regulators of private sector land development, and serve as mediators between competing interests in the use and reuse of urban land. In Canada, these responsibilities are shared between local and provincial governments (on the distribution of urban-related responsibilities between levels of government, see Chapter 18). As regulators, governments establish subdivision and building standards, set zoning by-laws regulating the use, density, and physical form of the built environment, and produce official plans to guide future urban growth in desired directions. Land that has development permission and infrastructure in place, or redevelopment permission in the case of older built-up areas, has more value than land that does not. Thus, the exercise of government regulatory powers acts to redistribute values within the urban landscape—in theory, in directions that serve a wider community purpose. This redistribution, by definition, not only shifts land value increments (or surpluses) from area to area, but from one set of landowners to another. Needless to say, this produces an endless series of conflicts and appeals, thereby transforming the local political process into an arena for resolving interest-group conflict in land and property development.

The structure and quality of our communities are shaped by the actions of governments, including those of the federal government; these actions often have little or nothing to do in their initial design with urban land or development. In fact, however, many of these actions become quickly embedded in the local markets for land and housing, and specifically into the relationships between local capital and labour, builders and residents, and between residential spaces and work places. Examples include the full range of social and welfare policies, at least those that influence a household's choice of living arrangements, household's position in the labour market, and access to housing. The way governments treat the taxation of capital investments, for example, or their practices for insuring residential mortgages and/or subsidizing declining industries, quickly find their way into the daily lives of households and into urban neighbourhoods and work places. More removed perhaps, government decisions on airport location, road construction and transit financing, and on the location of government facilities and employment, further augment the contribution of the public sector in determining the fortunes and misfortunes of cities and neighbourhoods. Clearly, urban development in Canada is a public process as well as a market process. Our cities, and our policy agenda, reflect the complex interactions of these two powerful sets of forces.

ISSUES IN URBAN POLICY AND RESEARCH

The preceding overview of urban growth and change in post-war Canada raises a number of key issues, both explicitly and more often implicitly, that will confront policy-makers, researchers, and students well into the next century. As a conclusion to this chapter, and as an incentive to readers to think about these questions as they progress through the chapters in this volume, this section outlines some of these issues in a succinct—and intentionally provocative—fashion. The discussion frequently takes the liberty of going beyond the context established above and often well beyond that for which we have sufficient and concrete evidence in hand.

Managing Growth: Equity or Efficiency?

The first issue has to be that of managing urban growth, an issue that emerges at several geographical scales: the national (urban system); regional (metropolitan area); and local (community or neighbourhood). As we know, economic growth is clearly not evenly distributed across the country, or even within regions. This unevenness invariably leads to inflation (in living costs and thus in wage demands), social tension, congestion, and pollution in growing areas. At the same time, as a consequence, levels of poverty, unemployment, physical deterioration, and social alienation increase in stagnating areas.

The post-recession period after 1982 seems to have accentuated these regional differentials. How do we reconcile these persistent regional inequalities in economic opportunities? What role does urbanization or, more specifically, the emergence of large cities, play in stimulating lagging regions? Our major urban centres are now fully part of a 'global urban system'; how then do we develop a national urban policy? Can we remain competitive in international markets by improving the economic efficiency of our urban system, while at the same time redistributing growth through public action so as to even out the social opportunities and costs that growth provides? Will the political climate after the rejection of the Meech Lake accord make political action at the national urban system level even more difficult?

At the metropolitan and local level the issue of managing urban growth is perhaps more familiar and immediate. To what extent is it possible to plan the development—the size and the spatial structure—of an entire urban region? How should urban governments be organized to facilitate the management of growth? How does the planner bring together the immense variety of legitimate but often competing interests in the development process—the landowners, developers, governments, investors, and households—to establish long-term goals for the region? To many people, managing growth instead means slowing or stopping the process through the imposition of growth limits, controls, or freezes (the lifeboat principle). But who then represents the next generation of residents and workers?

Public Service Provision: Who Benefits and Who Pays?

A related issue looks at the provision of particular public 'goods and bads' and asks the related question of who benefits and who pays. Within cities, as has been widely demonstrated here and elsewhere in the literature, the external impacts generated by decisions on what kinds of services to provide to whom, where, and at what cost, hold significant implications for the quality of urban living (Pinch 1985). Where should services such as waste disposal, group homes, police stations, and hospitals be located? Should those who suffer as a result, if they do in fact suffer, be compensated accordingly? How should such questions be decided? Who should decide what trade-offs are possible and necessary? What level of government should provide which services? Who can resolve the invariable political conflicts? What role, if any, should the private sector have in providing traditional public services? Would privatization lead to reduced or increased conflicts and costs?

Moving Around: Transportation, Densities and Urban Structure
One of the major sectors of public involvement is in urban transportation. Recent decentralization trends in urban development have undoubtedly accelerated the basic demand for transportation, even with the growth of communications technology, often because travel is seen by consumers as a relatively low cost good. The increasing separation of offices and factories, and thus of housing and jobs, and their widespread geographical dispersion throughout the metropolitan area, pose a daunting challenge to planners and politicians. Who will pay for transportation facilities? How should they be financed? Where should they be built? What balance of transportation modes (roads vs. transit) is appropriate, and/or most efficient? Will computer networks replace travel? Would it be preferable to restructure urban land uses, allowing for more mixed uses and higher densities, rather than build new transportation facilities? Will the latter not, in turn, lead to an even more dispersed pattern of land uses and travel behaviour? (These considerations are further discussed in Chapters 6 and 7).

Redesigning or Preserving Neighbourhoods
Whatever route we decide to adopt for new transportation infrastructures other issues then leap off the page. Providing new transportation facilities, for instance, may eat up valuable agricultural land on the fringe and disrupt older neighbourhoods in the inner city and suburbs. Higher densities of development, on the other hand, may reduce rates of rural land consumption, but within existing built-up areas they typically generate strong neighbourhood protests and outright resistance (NIMBY—the Not In My BackYard syndrome). The protection of existing neighbourhoods, against unwanted traffic, new roads, high-density redevelopment, or social housing is, in fact, the *raison d'être* of most community organizations. New suburban neighbourhoods quickly become organized to prevent these kinds of development.

But how do we achieve change, aware as we are of the necessity of responding to the increased demands for travel and living space generated by a growing population and increasing affluence? How do we accommodate those less fortunate households in our society without modifying existing or new neighbourhood compositions? What, more generally, is the appropriate balance between the legitimate aspirations of local residents for stability and security, and the collective needs and goals of the wider community, not to mention future generations, in accommodating growth?

Housing: What Price? What Place?

The issues of urban transportation and neighbourhood stability are invariably tied to concerns over housing, and vice versa. At what cost and in what places should old housing be preserved? Where and at what prices should new housing be provided? In most of the larger Canadian cities, rapid growth in the 1980s has made it increasingly difficult for many households to obtain housing at prices that are affordable and in environments that are suitable and supportive.

Undoubtedly, the overall standards of housing available to the average urban Canadian have improved significantly over the post-war period, but not in the same degree for all groups or in all places (Miron 1988). In growing cities, housing is often in short supply and expensive, largely because of demand pressures. Speculation in urban land, unreasonably high servicing standards, and efforts to protect neighbourhoods from the intrusion of new housing have also been contributing factors. The provision of new transportation facilities in outer suburban areas, as noted earlier, would release more rural land for residential development and likely reduce price escalation. But those facilities, as noted above, raise other thorny political difficulties. An alternative is to build housing at higher densities within established neighbourhoods, either as in-fill or redevelopment (the 'intensification' process); yet this solution, too, is fraught with complications. How do we resolve these issues, and who should be responsible for these decisions?

In one sense there appears to be a 'conspiracy of silence' on urban housing issues. Municipalities, for instance, pay lip service to the provision of more affordable housing while at the same time imposing higher development levies (fees for services) on new housing and often refusing to zone for higher densities (lot sizes) and smaller houses. Senior levels of government, meanwhile, have resisted pressures to augment their financial allocations to local governments, non-profit groups or the housing industry to meet the increasingly high costs of new residential development. Most of the signposts in housing policies now point in the wrong direction.

Coping with Social Diversity

All Canadian cities now accommodate a much more diverse set of populations than in the past, and this diversity is likely to increase in the future. A series of waves of demographic and life-style changes have rolled over the post-war urban landscape, reordering the demand for jobs, housing, and for all kinds of public and private services. An ageing population, for example, has quite different needs and attitudes than the earlier baby-boom generation. As the 'boomers' themselves age, the urban policy agenda must shift accordingly.

Can the form and structure of the city, the means by which we provide public services and housing, and the governing bodies and regulatory agencies of urban Canada, respond to these changes? In one sense, the task may seem straightforward—for example, vacant schools can be converted to retirement, bingo, and leisure centres. In a broader and certainly more realistic sense the task is much more challenging. When one considers the social and ethnic pluralism produced by new sources of immigration, in particular the new dimension provided by visible and linguistic minorities, the challenge of coping with diversity is obviously extended and complicated. So, too, are the opportunities for social progress in a multicultural society.

Poles Apart: Segregation and Polarization
Another outcome of the increased size of cities, the increased cost of housing, and the greater degree of social diversity is that the neighbourhoods become more visibly differentiated, by income, by stage in the life cycle (young adulthood, middle age, retirement) and by ethnocultural background. Residential segregation tends to increase, either through choice or through the constraints imposed on choice by the available housing stock. To some observers this geographical separation, if voluntary, is on balance a positive feature. It allows for mutual social support, better access to services, institutional completeness, and the nurturing of shared values in culture and life style.

To others the effects of geographical separation are largely negative. Geographical separation is restricting in terms of residential choice, and it may encourage misunderstanding if not outright discrimination in access to housing and public services. Indeed, some argue for explicit policies to encourage greater social mix within both old and new neighbourhoods through the provision of a wider range of housing types (including social housing). But, for whom is this residential clustering a problem? Why? Conversely, what are the benefits of greater social mix? Will levels of urban social differentiation decrease in the future as new immigrants assimilate, or will it increase if, as expected, incomes become more unevenly distributed?

Those Left Behind
Part of the challenge posed by social diversity and differentiation is to recognize and then respond to the urgent needs of those left behind by the growth process and the economic progress that has clearly benefited the vast majority of urban residents. While there has always been a poor

and disadvantaged population in Canadian cities, there is a widespread feeling that new and distinctive disadvantaged groups have appeared. Economic restructuring, occupational deskilling, technological change, and employment uncertainty have combined with new social situations to disadvantage particular individuals in certain settings.

Among the more obvious disadvantaged groups are the street people, transient youth, and certainly the homeless. But there are others—those on fixed incomes, those with low-paying jobs and marginal incomes, women with divided family responsibilities, and households faced with severe housing constraints (e.g. those living in suburban, crime-invested, high-rise social housing or decaying inner-city apartments or rooming houses)—for whom the situation has very likely worsened during the 1980s. These are individuals and groups who have obviously not been beneficiaries of economic change and urban growth. Indeed, their problems may have worsened precisely because of the rapidity, selectivity, and concentration of urban growth. How can these and other vulnerable groups be protected from the pressures of urban development and the social costs invariably associated with that process? Can the effects of urban growth on city dwellers be made more equitable?

Soiling the Urban Place

Most readers would readily agree that one serious issue faced by urban policy-makers is environmental degradation. The evidence is abundantly clear: closed beaches, foul air, toxic soil, piles of garbage and litter, and visual pollution—garish signs, telephone poles, dead spaces, and ugly buildings—testify to our continued misuse of the urban physical environment in Canada. And we have done it to ourselves; we are both the problem and the potential solution. What price for a clean environment?

Urban growth and form also play a secondary but still important part in pollution. Notably, as our cities are laid out primarily to serve the use of automobiles and trucks, exhaust emissions from vehicles are a principal cause of air pollution; indifference and a lack of investment in appropriate environmental technology accounts for most of the rest. The rate of growth itself becomes a contributing factor when that rate is either too fast or too slow (meaning decline). If it is too fast, the demands imposed by the growing population, vehicles, and new industries overwhelm the existing infrastructure (e.g. roads and sewage) and the capacity of the urban environment to absorb the output of waste products and pollutants. If, on the other hand, growth is slow or negative, there is much less incentive and even fewer resources available (e.g. public and private capital) to repair environmental damage.

The challenge then is to find a rate of urban growth and change that meets our expectations for improved living standards, is equitable and at the same time sustainable in terms of the quality of our urban environments. The next generation will not forgive us if we fail to meet this challenge.

NOTES

1. The definition of urban includes only incorporated settlements as defined by the Census of Canada at that time. Regional variations in the historical growth of urbanization are considerable: Ontario and British Columbia reached the 50 per cent level in 1911; the Prairies reached this level in 1961.

2. Defined as census metropolitan areas (CMAs) at the time of the 1961 Census.

3. This figure is open to question since the boundaries of central cities are not fixed over time. The expansion of central cities through the annexation of outlying areas would of course reduce the suburban population as defined here.

4. The urban process may be defined as incorporating the macro-scale process of urbanization and the more micro-scale processes involving the growth and development of individual urban areas and regions.

5. By 1986, Canada had 25 CMAs and three other places (census agglomerations) of over 100,000 (Kingston, Moncton, and Sydney). The more rapid growth of the larger metropolitan areas, and the decline in the number of middle-size and smaller places, is in part attributable to two statistical adjustments: 1) the growth of smaller places into the metropolitan size category (from the census agglomeration to the census metropolitan area category, see Appendix 1 for definitions); 2) the expansion of the boundaries of the CMAs by Statistics Canada, often resulting in the incorporation of formerly free-standing smaller urban areas into the larger metropolises. Statistically at least the smaller places then disappear.

6. See Bourne (1989), Simmons and Bourne (1989), and Forward (1990) for recent and comparative analyses.

7. An earlier version of this table appeared in Bourne (1991).

8. The counter-urbanization process, defined as a situation in which non-metropolitan areas grow faster than metropolitan areas and net migration flows shift towards the former, is described in an extensive literature. See Berry (1976) and Champion (1989).

9. Gentrification has not been a major direct factor here simply because neighbourhoods that are gentrified generally show reduced total populations, at least initially.

REFERENCES

ARTIBISE, A. and STELTER, G. eds 1979 *The Usable Urban Past* (Toronto: Macmillan)

BALAKRISHNAN, T.T. 1988 'Immigration and the Changing Ethnic Mosaic of Canadian Cities' (Ottawa: Health and Welfare Canada)

BERRY, B.J.L. ed. 1976 *Urbanization and Counter-Urbanization* (Beverly Hills: Sage Publications)

BOURNE, L.S. 1989 *On the Spatial Structure of Metropolitan Areas in Canada* (Toronto: Centre for Urban and Community Studies, University of Toronto) Research Paper No. 172

―――― 1991 'The Changing Settlement Environment of Housing' in J. Miron ed. (forthcoming) *Housing Progress in Canada* (Ottawa: CMHC)

―――― and BUNTING, T. 1991 'Housing Provision, Residential Development and Neighbourhood Dynamics' in L.S. Bourne and D.F. Ley eds (forthcoming) *The Changing Social Geography of the Canadian City* (Montreal: McGill-Queen's University Press)

BUNTING, T. and FILION, P. eds 1988 *The Changing Canadian Inner City* (Waterloo: Department of Geography, University of Waterloo)

CHAMPION, A.G. 1989 *Counterurbanization* (London: Edward Arnold)

FORWARD, C. 1990 'Variations in Employment and Non-Employment Income in Canadian Cities as Indicators of Economic Base Differences', *The Canadian Geographer* 34, 120–32

GAD, G. 1989 'The Metropolitan Areas of Canada in the 1980s' in R. Vogelsang ed. *Canada in the 1980s* (Bochum: Universitatsverlag Dr. N. Brockmeyer)

GERTLER, L. and CROWLEY, R. 1977 *Changing Canadian Cities* (Toronto: McClelland and Stewart)

JOHNSTON, R.J. 1987 *Philosophy and Human Geography* (London: Edward Arnold)

LEY, D. 1991 'Past Elites and Present Gentry: Landscapes of Privilege in Canadian Cities' in L.S. Bourne and D.F. Ley eds (forthcoming) *The Changing Social Geography of Canadian Cities* (Montreal: McGill-Queen's University Press)

LORIMER, J. and ROSS, E. eds 1976 *The City Book* (Toronto: James Lorimer)

MIRON, J.R. 1988 *Housing in Post-War Canada: Demographic Change, Household Formation and Housing Demand* (Montreal: McGill-Queen's University Press)

MURDIE, R. 1990 'Economic Restructuring, Changes in Central City Housing and Social Polarization: A Toronto Case Study' mimeo, Department of Geography, York University

PINCH, S. 1985 *Cities and Services* (London: Pion)

SIMMONS, J.W. and BOURNE, L.S. 1985 *Recent Trends and Patterns in Canadian Settlement, 1976–81* Major Report No. 23 (Toronto: Centre for Urban and Community Studies, University of Toronto)

―――― 1989 *Urban Growth Trends in Canada, 1981–86: A New Geography of Change* Major Report No. 25 (Toronto: Centre for Urban and Community Studies, University of Toronto)

STELTER, G. and ARTIBISE, A. eds 1986 *Power and Place* (Vancouver: University of British Columbia Press)

STONE, L. 1967 *Urban Development in Canada* (Ottawa: Dominion Bureau of Statistics)

WILSON, G.W. et al. 1965 *Canada: An Appraisal of Its Needs and Resources* (Toronto: University of Toronto Press)

3

The Canadian City in Continental Context: Global and Continental Perspectives on Canadian Urban Development

JOHN MERCER

There is little doubt that from a global perspective Canadian and American cities are seen as being more similar to each other than either group is to West European cities or to cities in the 'developing world'. For Europeans, for example, there is validity in the notion of a North American city (see Clout *et al.* 1985; Paterson 1989). The general characteristics of this urban form are well known. There is at the centre the principal retail and office business core; adjacent high-rise apartment areas; outlying commercial centres and strips, including the regional shopping centres; various industrial zones; and the different classes of residential areas, all with particular spatial relationships and all connected by streets, arterials, and freeways in the typical grid-radial pattern. The location factors for an oil refinery in the Montreal or Philadelphia metropolitan areas are not likely to be substantially different. Regional shopping centres in suburban Calgary and suburban Denver are essentially similar in location, market orientation, and internal spatial layout. In both Canadian and American cities there are highly diversified neighbourhoods, with some inner-city older areas now experiencing gentrification (although more so, perhaps, in Canada than in the US). Many Canadian and American neighbourhoods also have a visible and vital ethnic identity serving as the home for recent immigrants, who have now replaced earlier immigrants in these same core neighbourhoods. The outer suburbs are seen as essentially similar by many; Bunge and Bordessa (1975, 316) for example describe the 'most American' part of Toronto as being the rich side of town, the affluent suburbs.

Despite these broad similarities, the concept of a North American model of urban form masks or excludes significant differences in housing; in transportation systems and usage; in social geographies, and in institutional structures. These will be explored more fully in this chapter. Subsequent chapters provide further details regarding specific features of the Canadian city.

URBAN CANADA

In the late twentieth century, about three-quarters of Canada's population reside in its urban settlements. On a world scale, this is quite a high proportion, akin to highly urbanized countries in Western Europe and similar to that in the United States. Canada's unmistakably urban face is largely a product of the last hundred years or so. For instance, in the mid-nineteenth century the urban proportion of the total population was a little over one-tenth and by 1881 it was only one quarter. The absolute numbers of urban dwellers have also increased dramatically. As the twentieth century began, there were just over 1 million people resident in the principal metropolitan regions whereas by the 1990s there are between 16 and 17 million people living in Canada's 25 Census Metropolitan Areas (see Appendix 1 for a definition of Census Metropolitan Areas).

These high rates of urbanization and urban growth are broadly similar to those occurring in other industrially-based Western market societies, including the US (see Figure 3.1). The concentration of this explosive growth in the major metropolitan areas has concerned Canadians. A theme that pervaded policy debate in the 1960s and 1970s, for example, was coping with what was viewed as the excessive growth expected in the Toronto, Montreal, and Vancouver metropolitan regions (see, for example, such influential studies as Lithwick 1970 and Gertler and Crowley 1977).

Within the dominant metropolitan areas and the more moderately sized but still rapidly growing cities recent growth has occurred primarily in suburban settings. In media terms, this led to the 'exploding metropolis', developing rapidly beyond the bounds of the political limits of the central city (that is, the municipality which encompasses the original settlement of a metropolitan region and which is generally at the centre of the metropolitan region). Even this view underestimated the degree and nature of suburbanization for earlier suburbs had been annexed as central city limits were adjusted. Rapid suburbanization is often portrayed as a post-World War II phenomenon; this view points to a period characterized by a very vigorous urban building cycle and, in demographic terms, a remarkable event epitomized in the concept of the post-war 'baby boom'.

Figure 3.1
Per cent of Population Living in Urban Areas, Canada and the US, 1890-1980

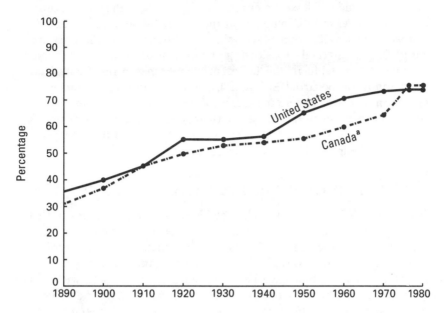

SOURCE: *Historical Statistics of Canada* [2nd ed., 1983], A67-74; Census of Canada, 1981, Cat. No. 92-901; *Historical Abstract of the U.S.; Colonial Times to 1970*, p. 11; Statistical Abstract of the U.S., 1984, p. xvii.

[a]For Canada, census information is gathered in the first year of a decade (i.e., 1891, 1901, etc.).

The initial spread of Canadian suburbs occurred in the expansionary decades of the 1950s and 1960s, as others have shown (Carver 1962; Gertler 1976; Gertler and Crowley 1977). This is a common experience among other market societies. For some urban theorists, such as Harvey (1975) and Walker (1981), the production of the suburban landscapes across North America and in Western Europe is a necessary corollary of the structure of late capitalism with capital flowing into finance and real estate markets, and less into industrial development and the expansion of the factory landscape. Others argue that the suburbs provided an impetus for the consumption of durable goods and as such were important in contributing to the economic expansion that took place in the decades following World War II.

Censuses taken in the early 1980s revealed that the rapid metropolitan growth of previous decades had considerably slowed down over the 1970s both in Europe and the US (Berry 1981; Hall 1984; 1985). Non-metropolitan regions that had for decades been areas of population loss or stagnation were experiencing growth, and the inner city (which refers to older central-city neighbourhoods surrounding the central business district—see Chapter 13 for a fuller definition) sank deeper into an already established declining trend. In fact, the inner city was widely recognized as a public problem requiring policy intervention. This latter feature was particularly felt in the US and to a lesser extent the UK. (As a result the term 'counter-urbanization', i.e. growth in non-metropolitan areas, became fashionable).

Canadian urban development certainly exhibited some of these features. The 1970s were marked by a slowing of annual urban growth rate, which was especially notable in the larger metropolitan centres. Central city population losses occurred, although by no means in every instance, and population increased in certain peripheral (i.e. non-metropolitan) regions. But, as the next section will show, there were some important cross-national differences between Canada and the US. These differences pose a potential challenge to the concept of a common North American outcome.

THE MYTH OF THE NORTH AMERICAN CITY[1]

This section challenges empirically the idea of the North American City. It does so not out of a sense of a narrowly based nationalism or innate superiority about the quality of urban life in Canada but from a position that when general processes of urban development interact with particular historical structures that have been created in a society and within its regions, a distinctive urban experience can result. Thus, the cities of Canada can only be fully understood by a joining of the general and the particular, the global and the local, set within the context of an emerging national state over the last 150 years.

Population and Household Change
One of the variables used almost diagnostically by urban geographers and other analysts is the rate of population change in metropolitan areas and their components, especially the central city. Population decline is taken

Table 3.1
Change in Metropolitan and Non-metropolitan Populations by Regions and Provinces, Canada, 1981–1986

	Metropolitan Population (%)	Non-Metropolitan Population (%)
Atlantic	4.4	1.2
Newfoundland	3.8	−1.1
Nova Scotia	6.6	1.3
New Brunswick	0.2	2.2
Quebec	2.3	0.5
Ontario	7.1	1.9
Prairies	7.0	2.5
Manitoba	5.6	0.8
Saskatchewan	11.2	0.4
Alberta	6.6	4.6
British Columbia	9.0	5.1

SOURCE: Census of Canada, 1986.

to be symptomatic of a general urban malaise, whereas growth is taken to be positive. Though simplistic, this accords with media and political perceptions. On this dimension, it is evident that Canadian cities, as a whole, appear to be converging with the American metropolitan experience; at the same time, notable differences persist.

During the 1960s and 1970s, Canada's CMAs grew faster than US Standard Metropolitan Statistical Areas (SMSAs). In the meantime, the Canadian central city fared better that its US counterpart, although in both countries population losses were felt in central cities within the largest metropolitan regions. In the latter part of the 1970s more (22) central cities gained than lost population in Canada, and in absolute terms, a net increase of just over 100,000 people took place between 1976 and 1981. While there were central cities in the US that were 'gainers' too, these were swamped nationwide by the massive haemorrhaging from America's leading urban centres. While there was some convergence in the two nations' aggregate metropolitan experience, important differences persisted. The Canadian experience was typified by less extreme growth and decline and by 'healthier' central cities in terms of population gain or stability.

Did these trends and cross-national differences persist in the 1980s? Only a partial answer can be given until the data from the 1990 and 1991 censuses are available. It is clear that, from 1981 to 1986, population growth in metropolitan areas in all parts of Canada, save for New Brunswick, exceeded that of non-metropolitan areas of the country (Table 3.1). This challenges the counter-urbanization thesis whereby growth would now mostly take place in non-urban areas. Meanwhile, on average, US metropolitan areas and central cities grew faster in the early 1980s (Table 3.2). There is clearly more variability in the US distribution as shown by the standard deviations. A distributional measure, the median, indicates higher metropolitan growth in Canada but lesser population growth in

Table 3.2
Population Change in American and Canadian Metropolitan Areas

| | CANADA (1981–86) | | USA (1980–84) | |
	Metropolitan Areas[a]	Central City	Metropolitan Areas[b]	Central City
Mean	4.8	2.4	5.3	3.1
Std. Dev.	4.0	4.3	6.7	7.2
Median	5.2	0.5	3.9	1.4
(n)	(25)	(25)	(258)	(240)
ANNUAL RATE				
Mean	0.96	0.48	1.33	0.78
Std. Dev.	0.80	0.86	1.68	1.80
Median	1.04	0.10	0.78	0.35

Source: Census of Canada, 1986; State and Metropolitan Area Data Book, 1986.

Notes: [a]Census Metropolitan Areas
[b]Standard Metropolitan Statistical Areas

Figure 3.2
Population Gains and Losses Among Canadian Census Metropolitan Areas and Central Cities

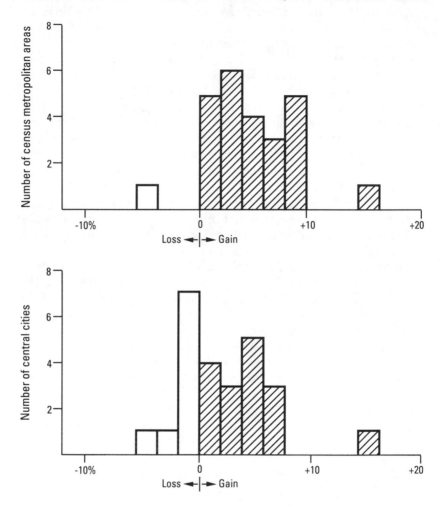

the central city. The actual distributions of population change in Canada's metropolitan areas are revealing (Figure 3.2). Only one metropolitan area grew in excess of 10 percent, whereas 21 American ones did so (in proportional terms this is 4.0% of all cases against 8.2%). Equally, only one suffered a loss, whereas 49 American areas did so (again, proportionally this is 4.0% against 19.0%). However, no US loss exceeded 5 percent and so the American mean is raised by the rapid growth of a small subset of metropolitan areas. This distributional difference is not as pronounced in the case of central cities. Overall, almost the same proportion of all central cities were gainers and losers in both countries; just under two-thirds were gainers (64% in Canada, 62% in the US) and over one-third lost population

(36% in Canada, 38% in the US). These data tend to support the idea of convergence. The sole notable difference is in the positive range. Only in one instance (or 4% of all cases) did a Canadian central city grow by more than 10 per cent but 30 US central cities did so (or 12.5% of all cases). These distributional differences for both metropolitan areas and central cities are captured in the higher US standard deviations.

The preliminary conclusion would be cross-national similarities with respect both to summary measures and to a lesser extent distributional characteristics. Clearly there is still considerable variability in both urban systems, especially in the American case. A positive relationship between economic growth and metropolitan population change is suggested in these data. America's economy recovered more quickly than did Canada's from depression in the early 1980s and this probably underpins a more buoyant population growth. What may surprise is the relatively strong population gains achieved in the early 1980s in many American central cities. This reminds us that it is erroneous to read substantial population losses evident in the largest central cities onto the entire system and misleading to talk generally about 'the' central city experience. The population losses for the Canadian central cities are also suggestive of a relationship between population change and regional economy. Of the nine Canadian central cities showing absolute loss in the 1981–86 period, all are located in Atlantic Canada, Quebec or the resource-based region of Northern Ontario.

Although rate of population change is an important and useful variable in urban analysis, it has received disproportionate attention, especially in comparison to numerical change in, and the composition of, urban households. Aggregate household change is important because households generate demand for housing, and for many other goods and services. For a city or district to experience a net loss in the number of households is to suffer a weakening in demand with attendant adverse consequences for the urban economy. For example, the loss of effective demand, even from lower income households, is a key in understanding housing abandonment in the US inner city.

The evidence indicates that population losses notwithstanding, Canadian central cities did not experience a net reduction of households in recent years whereas for a minority of US central cities this has been both a reality and a policy dilemma. This situation is most acute in the largest metropolitan areas. In the 1970s, for example, eight of the twenty largest US metropolitan areas suffered a household loss in their central cities, while another six 'stagnated' (where stagnation is defined as a growth rate of less than 0.5 per cent per annum). Of all Canadian metropolitan areas, only Montreal fell into this latter category. Language policies were possibly acting in Montreal as an impediment to in-migration. Also, apprehension over separatism and economic decline accelerated the out-migration of both employment and English-speaking households.

Urban Form

A useful parameter of urban form is the urban population density gradient, which measures differences in the density of metropolitan concentric zones from the core to the periphery (for a more detailed discussion of this statistical model see Cadwallader 1985). The comparison of density gradients for US and Canadian metropolitan areas provides a readily grasped measure of population concentration and dispersion. There are three simple points to be made concerning US-Canadian similarities and differences on this measure. Firstly, there is no notable cross-national difference with respect to decentralization within urban areas. In both cases, central densities fell on average by 50% from 1950–51 to 1975–76. Again, for both sets of metropolitan areas, the density gradients also fell on average during this interval. The decline was more pronounced in Canada than in the US, the density gradient values going from 0.93 to 0.42 (a 55 per cent change) in the former, and from 0.76 to 0.45 (a 41 per cent change) in the latter. Secondly, there persists a striking difference in central densities; Canadian central densities averaged twice the US figure, even though there were broadly similar declines in central density values over time in both countries. Thirdly, a consistent pattern is revealed with respect to the distribution of gradients by size of metropolitan popula-tion—Canadian density gradients were either similar to those in the US (for the both smallest and largest places in 1976/86) or considerably steeper (for places between 500,000 and 1,000,000 population). These results indi-cate overall a markedly more compact urban form in the urban areas of Canada compared with those in the US. There are many factors that help to explain this difference. Among the more important are variations in the rates of car ownership and the size of expressway networks and public transit use between the two countries. The extensive development of mass transit and expressway systems has played a key enabling role in the rapid growth of the outer city (Muller 1981). By using a standardized measure of capacity—the number of expressway lane miles per capita—it has been shown that there were just over four times as many lane miles of urban expressway per 100,000 metropolitan resident in the US as in Canada. US metropolitan areas are much more oriented to the automobile. On the other hand, Canadian mass transit systems had nearly 2.5 times the number of revenue miles per capita as their US counterparts. Given that there was no appreciable difference in the proportion of the metropolitan area population served by public transit, Canadian transit systems are much denser and serve their respective areas more intensively than equivalent US systems. In short, Canadian cities rely more on a dense public transit system, whereas American urban areas rely much more upon extensive freeway networks. An extensive reliance on cars and expressways is condu-cive to urban sprawl while high public transit use fosters more focused forms of development.

Another facet of urban form, which too reflects transportation-induced density differences, is revealed by examining the proportion of the housing stock comprised of single detached units which predominate in the low-density suburbs. There was a distinct US-Canadian difference in urban housing stock composition for 1970–1 within both central cities and suburban rings. In both sectors, the mean proportion of single detached units was significantly higher in the US cities, indicating overall lower densities. By 1980, the proportion of single unit structures in the metropolitan stock of all US metropolitan areas had declined, but at 62.5 per cent, it was still greater than an equivalent Canadian measure, which in 1986 was 54.1 per cent. A substantial difference still exists between the metropolitan areas on this revealing variable, but the magnitude has narrowed. What this suggests is a certain long-term stability in the stock in Canada's metropolitan areas whereas, overall, the American stock is experiencing greater change and tending towards the Canadian norm.

Social Patterns
The social diversity of and complex social order within metropolitan areas are vast topics in themselves as shown in Chapter 12 of this text. They encompass fundamental matters pertaining to such factors as class, racial and ethnic groups, and life cycle as well as these factors' geographical distribution. There are distinct differences in the social geographies of Canadian and US cities. These are demonstrated by a few selected variables although it is acknowledged that these measures cannot do full justice to the complex socio-geographic structures which constitute everyday social life in the metropolis (see for example, Ley 1983).

As Ley points out in Chapter 13, the research literature on the US city is replete with images of affluent suburbanites withdrawing behind exclusionary barriers, leaving behind a poverty-stricken central city, particularly in its inner parts. With respect to geographic disparities in socio-economic status, there is a clear difference in Canadian cities. The key indicator utilized here is the ratio of central city to metropolitan household income; a ratio of less than 100 indicates a central city that is poorer than the metropolitan area as a whole, whereas a ratio of over 100 expresses the converse. The US-Canadian difference has been marked: the ratio for both mean and median income was closer to 100 for the Canadian cases and the overall US-Canada difference was about 5 to 6 points lower. The distributions were also significantly different, as the Canadian cities shared almost equal ratios, tightly clustered around the value of 98. Spatial disparities in affluence are more sharply defined in metropolitan USA. For example, 30 per cent of US cities have ratios of less than 90 for mean household income, rising to 48 per cent for median household income; in Canada, the equivalents are 10 and 14 per cent.[2] Thus, the relative poverty of the US central city is clear and has not been found to the same extent in Canadian urban areas. In 1980, the US average central city per capita income represented 93.1 per cent of that of the metropolitan areas, whereas in Canada (1981) the central city average represented 99.7 per cent. This partly confirms previous 1970/71 findings. More recent work on Canadian CMAs further confirms these trends (Filion and Bunting 1990). Even if one turns from aggregate data taken over the entire metropolitan system to particular and controlled comparisons between selected US and Canadian pairs of metropolitan areas, the general conclusion holds (Goldberg and Mercer 1986, 158). In sum, there is a greater geographic disparity in socio-economic status (as measured by income) between the central city and the suburbs in metropolitan USA.

Various stages in the life cycle have been identified by social scientists as being important in terms of urban analysis. Despite the explosive growth of non-family households (common to both Canada and the US) the family household remains a key social unit. Its significance is captured in the concept of familism, where the family is seen as the highly valued centre of social life. Previous empirical analysis show a stronger association between Canada's central cities and family households than occurs in the US. The widely documented 'white flight' from the US central city to the suburbs, in search of affordable housing, jobs, and segregated school systems, has taken its toll. By 1971, on average only 40 per cent of all households in the central city were families with children at home; many of these would be non-white and female-headed. A capacity to retain families is suggested by the Canadian equivalent of 57 per cent. Canadian central city neighbourhoods are still seen as eminently suitable locales for family life, supported by fiscally sound school systems and a prevailing sense of public order, evidenced in the substantially lower urban crime rates of Canadian central cities, particularly those for violent crimes. However, the Canadian data precede the rapid increases in many central city house prices which have caused families of more modest means to look to the suburbs for affordable housing. Increasingly, only the more affluent families, often with two incomes, can settle in prestigious centrally located neighbourhoods.

To the external observer, such as a European, the US is historically marked as a racially divided society (it was for Myrdal [1944] 'The American Dilemma'). This deep-seated and often bitterly contested duality has set the US and Canada apart within North America, although Canada is changing in nature as a result of different immigrant streams (Mercer 1989). Not surprisingly, this distinction is clearly exhibited in the cities, where the proportion of non-whites in US urban areas has been of an order of magnitude of six or greater than the corresponding level in urban Canada.

Urban differences related to immigration are possibly less readily acknowledged. Americans are often quick to assert and celebrate their immigrant heritage. But Canada is equally an immigrant society and the impact on Canadian cities in recent years has been remarkable. The distribution of foreign-born people within the metropolitan population is yet another basis for social distinctions within urban North America. The average proportion in Canadian cities and metropolitan areas has been about four to five times greater than in the US equivalents. The average foreign-born proportion in the population was just under 15 per cent in Canada's metropolitan areas in 1986, almost the same as in 1971. As in earlier periods, the urban areas of Atlantic Canada and Quebec, except for Montreal at the median value of 16.3%, attract few foreign-born immigrants. The attractive destinations are still in southern Ontario, especially Toronto, where over one-third of the entire population is foreign born, and western Canada, other than Saskatchewan's cities which are well below the mean (see Appendix 3).

The Urban Geography of Economic Activities
The decentralization of people within urban areas in both countries has been paralleled by a decentralization of economic activities. This is a difficult topic on which to make careful comparisons. Others have shown the relative decline of the CBD in many US centres; in some sectors, the declines have been absolute. It has been more difficult with lags in data availability to analyze trends in Canadian CBDs, although a clearer picture has emerged from the valuable work of Jones and Simmons (1987). Some of this work is described in Chapter 15. A few summary points can be made concerning the Canadian business core. As in the US, the CBD share of metropolitan area sales has declined in the face of widespread retail developments in the outer city. But core growth can and does still occur within the context of this relative shift, as is illustrated by the case of downtown Toronto. Stores increased there by more than 50 per cent in the 1971–76 period after almost no change in the previous twenty years. The retail core of most Canadian cities has been transformed over the last two decades through the joint redevelopment efforts of private developers and supportive city administrations. As recently observed, retail sectors of Canadian downtowns have done better overall than those in the US (Jones and Simmons 1987, 387). This is related to the maintenance of household income in inner districts and to the strong service and retail base of many Canadian cities.

What has been shown for an earlier period is that economic activity was relatively more concentrated within the central cities in Canada. Relative to the metropolitan area, the central cities retained a higher proportion of various classes of economic activity such as retailing, business services, and to a lesser extent, wholesaling and manufacturing. More specifically, it was concluded that for manufacturing in the US a substantial amount of activity had relocated across regions and beyond boundaries of metropolitan areas. There was considerable central-city growth, especially in smaller cities in regions favoured by new investment and this needs to be borne in mind against significant losses. In Canada, manufacturing remains a predominantly metropolitan activity, with decentralization occurring to suburban locations. There can be no denying that warehousing activities once located by the waterfront or central railroad terminals have been reproduced on an even larger scale in the expressway-rich suburbs in both countries. But, whether one assesses the location of wholesaling establishments, retail sales, or the distribution of employment, Canadian central cities contained a significantly higher proportion of each than did US central cities in the early 1970s. It probably remains so now. This cross-national difference was particularly notable in those metropolitan areas with populations over 1 million, more so for services such as business, personal, recreational, and cultural, than for retailing. Such a finding is quite consistent with a vital, growing and hence attractive inner city in Canada and a concentration of personal services in the CBD.

A Multivariate Perspective

To this point, the evidence reviewed and presented on the myth of the North American City has largely consisted of single variables or measures considered separately. Yet many of these measures are interrelated and deserve simultaneous treatment. Three forms of multivariate analysis, namely factor analysis, cluster analysis, and discriminant analysis have been used to assess just how distinctive and recognizable are Canadian cities as a group within the larger continental metropolitan system.[3]

Factor analysis reduced a selected set of 20 variables to four. In the project reported on here, the four factors accounted for 86 per cent of the total variance. Each factor was interpreted in terms of the variables which clustered together, thereby constituting the factor. The four factors were, in ascending order of importance: suburban demographic change; central city/suburban fiscal contrast; minority population/disadvantage; central city share of economic activity. When factor scores were computed, clear US-Canadian differences became apparent. On average, the US scores were lower than the Canadian ones by an amount of seven or nine to one. Also, for each of the four factors, the mean scores had different signs for the two sets of urban areas. This analysis, suggestive of important differences, did not, however, directly answer the question of the existence of a distinctive coherent group of Canadian cities. But a series of cluster analyses did yield the general conclusion that the Canadian cities are places that have more in common with each other than they do with US cities. The variables chosen differentiate Canadian cities effectively from US ones; thus the distinctiveness thesis has been strongly supported in this type of analysis.

Another multivariate analysis permitted the identification of precisely which variables were the most important in setting apart Canadian from US cities. These were shown to be the proportion of central-city households which were families with children still at home, and the proportion of the population that was foreign born.

In general, US and Canadian metropolitan centres were clearly separated as the selected variables formed a function that discriminated very effectively between the groups. The most important discriminatory variables were indicators of the relative viability and hence, by inference livability and attractiveness of the central parts of Canadian metropolitan areas compared to the more disadvantaged and less livable inner sections of US metropolitan areas.

Integrating the Perspective

In the above discussion, a clear picture emerges that challenges the continentalist conceptualization of a North American City. Canadian cities are generally more compact in urban form with a greater reliance on public transportation to serve the agglomeration. They have had a different experience with respect to basic population changes but cross-national differences are now less evident in the early 1980s. Of equal importance, however, has been the absence of net household loss in the Canadian central city and an apparent ability to retain a higher proportion of family households. Also, the economic strength of central business cores and more generally, the central city *vis-à-vis* the whole metropolitan area is greater in Canada. In terms of social patterns, Canadian urban areas have less of a socio-economic disparity between the central city and the suburban ring, exhibit a much greater share of immigrants in their populations, especially in the central city, and are as ethnically, though much less racially, diverse and less racially segregated than their US counterparts.

The above distinctions are strongly supported by survey evidence (see Goldberg and Mercer 1986, 58–59). This latter evidence is quite compelling in terms of its portrayal of the inner and outer parts of US cities compared with those in Canada. Canadians did not abhor cities, liked living in them, and, even in certain instances, rated parts of cities as better places to live than the suburbs. In contrast, while the residents of US central cities also expressed satisfaction with living in the city, many expected to move out and were less enamoured of their community as a place to raise children. This supports the view that it will be more difficult for the large US central cities to retain their population, specifically family-oriented households, than for the Canadian central cities. Moreover, US central cities' attraction to residents living outside their boundaries is limited since suburbanites and residents of non-metropolitan areas hold an extremely negative view of the city. These central city differences in perceived livability are of major significance for they point to different structures and mechanisms at work in Canada's cities as well as to Canadians' different perception of the central city.

A second major distinction are differences in the type of public sector involvement. In Canada there has been more intervention from senior levels of government in achieving local fiscal balance and setting up metropolitan and regional planning areas. In other words, there has been less demand for 'local rule' in Canada as compared to the US. This has been difficult to show empirically without intensive careful comparisons.

Extensive cross-national comparisons as reviewed in this section cannot show this directly, though there are several clear suggestions that governments play a key role in sustaining the livability of Canada's central cities in, for example, the importance given to public transportation systems and public schools, and to the maintenance of a sense of public safety and order. A recent major account of urban and regional planning issues in Canada concludes that

> ... Canadian urban and regional planning [has] a more wide-ranging and acceptable role than is the case in the United States. It stops short, however, of fully accepting the degree of discretionary controls which characterize the British planning system. (Cullingworth 1987, 462)

Understanding Urban Development in Canada and the US
This section aims to provide a partial understanding of the differences reviewed above. The emphasis is principally on a series of contexts within which urban development occurs. This means particular attention needs to be directed towards distinctive political histories, the evolution of particular institutional arrangements, and the character of the societies that have developed on the continent. Certain belief systems or ideologies, themselves historically fashioned, anchor these arrangements and continue to support current ways of doing things.

Both Canada and the US are of course federal nations but at their inception, urban affairs were not prominent in terms of the fundamental division of powers. Local governments such as cities exist as legal entities within the domain of the states and provinces. What then is the federal role *vis-à-vis* cities and metropolitan areas? The role has emerged quite differently in the two countries and has changed over time, reflecting in part the more general evolution of federal powers and responsibilities. In the US, the federal government was conceived initially as a weaker unit *vis-à-vis* strong states but this changed dramatically over two centuries as a result of judicial decisions and the changing national economy. As the federal role expanded especially in the trauma of the 1930s, the roots of US federal intervention in the urban arena were planted (Gelfand 1975). In Canada, the initial conception was for a strong central government and weaker provinces—in fact the comparison having been made, the American model was one to be avoided. Paradoxically, as Gibbins (1982) has shown, there has been in Canada a general tendency towards stronger provinces, their strength arising from revenues obtained through expanding resource-rent-driven provincial economies. Thus, some provinces, such as the Atlantic provinces, have remained weak and are fiscally dependent on federal transfers. Others, most notably Ontario and British Columbia, have consistently been powerful and are well positioned to challenge the federal government.

When the Canadian federal government, in response to interest-group pressures, a misplaced perception of an urban crisis, and a desire to expand its scope, sought to enlarge its role in urban affairs in the 1960s and early 1970s, it found itself being opposed most vigorously by provinces like Ontario and Quebec, who saw this as an encroachment on their jurisdictions. With the federal role limited, Canadian provinces and cities have had to fend for themselves in terms of urban development and local transportation. But it would be erroneous to depict Canada's federal government as bereft of authority in urban affairs. The Central (later Canada) Mortgage and Housing Corporation (CMHC) through its post–1954 mortgage policies has promoted the spread of suburbs by initially putting price ceilings on houses eligible for insurance, an impact very similar to that of the US Department of Housing and Urban Development (HUD) in the post-World War II era. To a lesser extent CMHC policies for urban infrastructure have also promoted suburbanization. Similarly, Canadian federal port and airport policies have potential impact on urban form. This point is elaborated on in Chapter 19.

There is a vast literature that documents and interprets the US federal government's impact on cities and metropolitan areas (for an excellent assessment, see Glickman [1980] and for an historical interpretation, see again Gelfand [1975]). What is particularly striking in comparison to Canada is the strong direct linkage that has been developed between the central cities and the federal authorities, reflecting partisan Democratic connections, aggressive innovative programs—such as Urban Renewal, Model Cities and more recently the UDAG program (Urban Development Action Grants), and the general lack of political will on the part of state governments to become involved in urban affairs. One could further cite the critical and substantial federal role in various housing programs and the funding of local public housing authorities (although this has been sharply curtailed) and fiscal support for mass transit improvements (also curtailed under the Reagan administration). Of major importance to the growth and form of US cities have been the massive underwriting of the federal interstate highway system, which has had a tremendous impact in enhancing accessibility in the outer city. For those increasing numbers of households living in outer suburban zones, this changing pattern of accessibility leads to an increasing physical and psychological detachment from the metropolitan core. The destabilization of inner-city housing markets and the stimulation of the production of low density, auto-oriented suburbs can also be in part attributed to this federal action, which has had therefore profound consequences for urban form. At a more regional level, it is necessary to recognize, for example, the vitally important federal actions in water distribution, irrigation, and power projects. These have been a necessary prerequisite to large scale urban development and growth in much of the arid West and Southwest (the case of Phoenix, Arizona, is a fine example). Yet again and in a different context, the federal revenue-sharing program (see US ACIR, 1980; 1981) which benefited the fiscally hard-pressed central cities (although it was not limited to them) is another example of federal-local linkages. This program was however terminated during the Reagan presidency. Most Americans have lived through an era in which the federal government in its various bureaucratic forms and under a bewildering array of programs spanning, for example, housing, transportation, fiscal assistance, infrastructure, education, and environmental protection, has been intimately involved in 'urban fortunes' (Logan and Molotch 1987). Although there has been, in the Reagan presidency, a politically inspired effort to roll back this involvement and shift more responsibility and the fiscal burden on to state and local governments, one can foresee new demands on the federal government. People and media opinion leaders expect the federal government to do 'something' about the homeless, for example.

A second crucial context for understanding urban development is the social composition of the two societies and its geographical expression. This is a topic of great magnitude and of necessity the treatment here is much abbreviated. This discussion focuses on certain fundamental dualisms that capture essential social characteristics.

The first dualism, of profound importance in understanding the geography of US cities, is one expressed in racial terms (black-white). Until quite recently (consider Toronto), the presence of racial subgroups has only been important in the social geographies of a few Canadian cities—Halifax, Vancouver, Victoria come readily to mind. A principal hallmark of US cities has been the remarkable persistence of a high level of residential segregation by race. This is expressed in a most territorial notion, the (black) ghetto. This persistence, and the reasons for it, have been much studied and are well understood (for an excellent recent appraisal, see Tobin 1987). At root, there is a strong antipathy on the part of white Americans against sharing their residential areas with blacks who, on the other hand, express a strong preference for racially integrated areas (at least demographically speaking, since co-residence does not necessarily result in social interaction). To prevent co-residence, white Americans and the institutions they control have resorted to a number of stratagems, too numerous to detail here. Even though individually based discrimination in housing markets is illegal and even though the racially restrictive residential covenant that permitted and maintained all white areas was ruled unconstitutional over forty years ago, there is still a cumulative legacy of the effects of historic and continuing discrimination. This discrimination is of such a scale that scholars talk of dual housing markets: one white; one black. The history of low-rent public housing in US cities is also fundamentally structured on a racial basis. Finally, one can note that in many other contexts, the metropolitan area has become literally the arena for group struggles in which it is enormously difficult to disentangle the complex concepts of race and class. The politics and geography of urban education and the development of split labour markets are but two powerful examples of these other contexts.

This US experience is almost totally foreign to the Canadian urban experience. What both countries have in common is an urban geography of residential differentiation or separation that is structured by a mainly private housing market, and is therefore based on class capacities, exercised by individuals who 'choose' housing and locations in these metropolitan markets. Those most able to pay are able to buy the choicest sites and geographic locales. Social differentiation is also structured by ethnic identity and a desire to live with fellow ethnic group members, even when the economic capacity to live elsewhere in more ethnically diverse settings exists. Thus, as the major descriptive work of Bourne et al. (1986) shows clearly, there is a considerable amount of metropolitan area residential segregation for many of Canada's diverse ethnic groups, though the index values do not attain those for black-white segregation in the US. No doubt such ethnically structured separation also exists in US cities (see the Atlas by Allen and Turner 1988). Unfortunately, the Bourne et al. study is not able to tell us how residential segregation between ethnic groups might vary by socio-economic status or class. Extensive sociological and geographical research tells us that ethnicity and class are related in Canada; for instance, factorial ecologies of western Canadian cities (Davies and Barrow 1973) depict the lower social standing of Ukrainian origin peoples vis-à-vis more socially dominant groups. Therefore, some of the ethnic separations are likely a product of class-based segregation working through housing market mechanisms.

Historically, and still today, one of Canada's definitive dualities is the French-English dialectic. Interestingly, the context it provides for urban development differs from the black-white duality of the US in one important respect—scale. Whereas significant numbers of black and white Americans live, work, and reside in the same metropolitan areas, the French-English separation is more at the regional scale. Of the metropolitan centres, only Montreal and Ottawa-Hull are places where there are really significant numbers of both socio-linguistic groups. The concentration of francophones in Quebec means that on this dimension alone, Quebec's principal urban areas are distinctive and set apart from the rest of Canada. Moreover, these cities have been governed by a series of provincial administrations that are historically different from those in other provinces.

Quebec cities are somewhat distinctive, too, in terms of their housing stock and urban form, certainly in relation to centres in Ontario and the West, but less so in relation to those in Atlantic Canada. Figure 3.3 shows these differences in graphic terms. The siting of Quebec's urban centres within the Canadian context is a topic needing much more systematic research than it has received to date. For instance, other than Montreal, Quebec cities have had an immigration experience largely different from the rest of Canada; of the lowest five positions in a rank ordering of Canada's CMAs by the proportion of foreign born in the population (1986

Figure 3.3
Differences in Census Metropolitan Areas' Forms of Housing

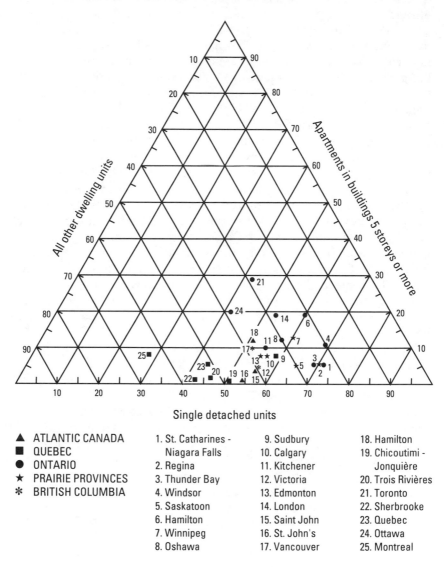

Single detached units

▲ ATLANTIC CANADA	1. St. Catharines -	9. Sudbury	18. Hamilton
■ QUEBEC	Niagara Falls	10. Calgary	19. Chicoutimi -
● ONTARIO	2. Regina	11. Kitchener	Jonquière
★ PRAIRIE PROVINCES	3. Thunder Bay	12. Victoria	20. Trois Rivières
✳ BRITISH COLUMBIA	4. Windsor	13. Edmonton	21. Toronto
	5. Saskatoon	14. London	22. Sherbrooke
	6. Hamilton	15. Saint John	23. Quebec
	7. Winnipeg	16. St. John's	24. Ottawa
	8. Oshawa	17. Vancouver	25. Montreal

data), four are occupied by Quebec CMAs (see Appendix 3). Even Ottawa-Hull (ranked 15th) reveals an interesting situation when prised apart provincially. The proportion in the Quebec part of the Ottawa-Hull CMA places it in the bottom five, whereas the Ontario proportion is ranked above the median.

One consequence of this particular duality is that one of Canada's great cities, Montreal, is a unique place within Canada and North America. The great majority of Quebec's anglophones dwell in this area and remain largely residentially separate from the French-speaking population. This duality is affected by the various immigrant groups, themselves multilingual. Thus, the pattern of residential segregation is both ethnic and linguistic, since the new immigrants have clustered, at least initially, in a geographic and cultural niche between the two principal populations. Although most of the immigrants adopted English, they were socially and economically separate from the anglophone élites who have until recently controlled the entrepreneurial and financial empires based in Montreal.

The last duality briefly noted is the US-Canada relationship itself. The creation and maintenance of Canada in opposition to the American revolutionary state was not unimportant for the siting and functions of settlements, some of which became metropolitan centres (e.g., London, York [later Toronto], Kingston). The revolutionary war also strongly influenced the tenor of US-Canada relations for over a century. The dependent nature of the Canadian economy has more and more come to mean a dependence on the United States in particular. The amount, form, and geographic direction of 'American' capital as investment has had a great impact on the geographic distribution of employment, on urban growth, and perhaps even on urban form (in the nature of the suburbanization of office employment, for example). To the extent that certain areas, like southern Ontario, have embedded in them and in their larger economic content a branch-plant economy, the provocative notion of the Canadian city arising from an economic colonial context merits some examination (Semple and Smith 1981). Finally, Canadian communities have often borrowed extensively from the US in terms of ideas (e.g. the city-manager system, first introduced in Westmount, a Montreal suburb, in 1913) and practices (street cars and street railway systems). More recently, there is a vigorous debate about the 'Manhattanization' of Toronto's core and central waterfront. In many respects, the Canadian reference point is the United States and in both direct and indirect ways this transfers down to or into the urban level.

CONCLUSION

This chapter ends with a provocative discussion of the distinctiveness of the Canadian City. It serves both to summarize and capture the shades and degrees of difference expressed in this brief comparative assessment of national contexts (for another comparative perspective on continental differences see Michalos 1980a; 1980b; 1982). The assertion is that Canadian cities are more public in their nature and US ones more private. Rather than these being sharply drawn polarities, the notions should be thought of as having both a range and overlap on a public-private continuum (see Figure 3.4).

Figure 3.4
The Public-Private Continuum

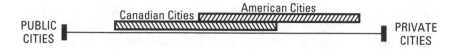

The conception of the American city as 'private' is not entirely original, owing something to Warner (1968). It attempts to express a strong commitment to individualism and individual freedoms; to the protection of private property rights under the Constitution; to the reliance on private mechanisms and individual user fees in the provision of infrastructures and goods and services; to homeownership, especially of the single detached residence; and to the concept of autonomy in local government, the profusion of special purpose districts and small municipalities being seen as virtual private extensions of relatively homogeneous social groups. In a privatized society, problems are solved in a highly personalized fashion. In America, conditions of life in many central cities and certain large metropolises have led to withdrawal to the safer ground of suburban jurisdictions. The above listing is not inclusive but conveys something of the complexity and essence of the notion of the privatized city.

The public city is more attuned to Canadian values, ideologies, and to current practices. It expresses a strong commitment to a greater emphasis on variously defined collectivities; to the maintenance of social goals and order rather than individual freedoms; to a greater trust and belief in the competence of government and its bureaucracies; and to the idea of active intervention in the form of urban planning by city, suburban and various more innovative forms of metropolitan government. The public city is also a place where there is a higher quality of urban development consistent with high servicing standards set by local authorities, a well developed and high quality public transportation system, an extensive system of community and recreation centres with quality parks and open spaces, all publicly provided, a public school system that is not seen as having virtually collapsed in central cities and where central city-suburban disparities are not acute in fiscal or educational terms. Again these themes could be pursued further in terms of the multi-faceted presence in Canadian cities of a more extensive welfare state, of health care and hospital services, of policing, of the presence of a wide array of Crown corporations and so on.

The distinction between the private US and the public Canadian city is not so much a reflection of different levels of government intervention as it is a result of the nature of this intervention. Governments in the US have been particularly active in their support of private consumption. This is best illustrated by considerable urban expressway expenditures which encourage the use of the private car. By contrast governments in Canada have adopted a more balanced approach to urban transportation. Along with expressway investments, they have supported public transit through both capital and operation grants. Another source of divergence between the two countries that is responsible for Canadian cities' stronger public dimension is the willingness of provincial governments to reorganize the administration of metropolitan regions. Many of the large metropolitan regions are now at least partly administered by metropolitan governments. Such governments assure a more even distribution of municipal services and a more integrated planning process. In the US, state governments have tended to be more sensitive to the 'home rule' arguments voiced by municipalities that are opposed to metropolitan governments. As a result sharp variations persist in service standards and property tax levels across US metropolitan regions.

Several years ago, the question was put: 'Is there a distinctive Canadian city?' (Kerr 1977). The answer can now be given more confidently than before and it is definitely 'Yes, but . . .' There is an important qualifier. It must be acknowledged that cities in Canada, like Canadians themselves, are North American in nature and experience an openness to continental interaction and influences.

NOTES

1. This chapter makes considerable use of empirical analyses reported in Gold-berg and Mercer's *The Myth of the North American City*. Rather than make repeated reference to this book, it should be noted that the details summarized here can be found there in full, especially in Chapters 7 through 9. Occasionally, where a specific point needs substantiation, I refer to the appropriate location in the book.

2. The mean is skewed upwards by the presence of many exceptionally wealthy households. Accordingly, many argue that the median is the more appropriate figure.

3. Briefly, factor analysis is a technique (or rather a generic for a series of generally similar techniques which, depending on the problem at hand, use different statistical methods to manipulate multivariate space) that uses a correlation matrix to identify interrelationships between original input variables describing where each empirical unit, i.e. in this case the city, sits with respect to a particular variable—household occupational status for example. It produces sets, or factors, on the basis of correlates with each of the original input variables. A factor matrix shows how much each variable contributes to each factor and how much each factor accounts for the original variance—e.g. Factor 1, 35 per cent Factor 2, 20 per cent etc. In this way, if the factors are strong, one can use a few factors (in this case, four) to replace a larger set of original variables (in this case 20). Factor scores show where each original observation unit (city) is positioned on each factor. Chapter 12 gives further examples of the application of factor analysis to geographic problems.

Cluster analysis is a multivariate technique that uses input variables, or factor scores in the data set, using one of a set of possible statistical grouping procedures. The analysis attempts to achieve an optimal grouping of the original observation units based on similarities in their relative positioning on input variables.

Discriminant analysis is a technique which begins with *a priori* groupings—the groupings derived from the cluster analysis—along with the variables that describe each observation (city) in each cluster. By comparing scores for each cluster in multivariate space, this technique is capable of showing which are the most important variables differentiating or discriminating between each of the input clusters or groupings.

FURTHER READING

AGNEW, J., MERCER, J. and SOPHER, D. eds 1984 *The City in Cultural Context* (Boston: Allen and Unwin)

ARMOUR, L. 1981 *The Idea of Canada and the Crisis of Community* (Ottawa: Steel Rail)

BUNGE, W. and BORDESSA, R. 1975 *The Canadian Alternative: Survival, Expeditions and Urban Change* York Geographical Monographs, No. 2 (Toronto: York University)

COLCORD, F.C. Jr 1987 'Saving the Central City' in E.J. Feldman and M.A. Goldberg eds *Land Rites and Wrongs: The Management, Regulation and Use of Land in Canada and the United States* (Boston: Oelgeshlager, Gunn and Hain)

GOLDBERG, M.A. and GAU, G. eds 1983 *North American Housing Markets into the Twenty-First Century* (Cambridge, Mass: Ballinger)

——— and MERCER, J. 1986 *The Myth of the North American City* (Vancouver: University of British Columbia Press)

HARLOE, M. 1981 'Notes on Comparative Urban Research' in M. Dear and A. J. Scott eds *Urbanization and Urban Planning in Capitalist Society* (New York: Methuen)

KETCHAM, R.L. 1987 *Individualism and Public Life: A Modern Dilemma* (Oxford: Blackwell)

LIPSET, S.M. 1990 *Continental Divide* (New York: Routledge)

MERCER, J. 1979 'On Continentalism, Distinctiveness and Comparative Urban Geography' *The Canadian Geographer* 23, 119–39

SANCTON, A. 1983 'Conclusion: Canadian City Politics in Comparative Perspective' in W. Magnusson and A. Sancton eds *City Politics in Canada* (Toronto: University of Toronto Press)

STELTER, G. and ARTIBISE, A. eds 1986 *Power and Place: Canadian Urban Development in a North American Context* (Vancouver: University of British Columbia Press)

VANCE, J.E. Jr 1987 'Revolution in American Space Since 1945 and a Canadian Contrast' in R.D. Mitchell and P.A. Groves eds *North America: The Historical Geography of a Changing Continent* (Totowa, New Jersey: Rowman and Littlefield)

WALTON, J. 1981 'Comparative Urban Studies' *International Journal of Comparative Sociology* 22, 22–39

REFERENCES

ALLEN, J.P. and TURNER, E.J. 1988 *We the People: An Atlas of America's Ethnic Diversity* (New York: Macmillan)

BERRY, B.J.L. 1981 *Comparative Urbanization: Divergent Paths in the Twentieth Century* (New York: St. Martin's Press)

BOURNE, L.S. et al. 1986 'Canada's Ethnic Mosaic: Characteristics and Patterns of Ethnic Origin Groups in Urban Areas' Major Report No. 24 (Toronto: Centre for Urban and Community Studies, University of Toronto)

BUNGE, W. and BORDESSA, R. 1975 *The Canadian Alternative: Survival Expeditions and Urban Change* Geographical Monographs No. 2 (Toronto: York University, Department of Geography)

CADWALLADER, M. 1985 *Analytical Urban Geography* (Englewood Cliffs, New Jersey: Prentice-Hall)

CARVER, H. 1962 *Cities in the Suburbs* (Toronto: University of Toronto Press)

CLOUT, H. et al. 1985 *Western Europe: Geographical Perspectives* (New York: Longman) especially chapter 4, 'Urban Development'

CULLINGWORTH, J.B. 1987 *Urban and Regional Planning in Canada* (New Brunswick, New Jersey: Transaction Books)

DAVIES, W.K.D. and BARROW, G.T. 1973 'A Comparative Factorial Ecology of Three Canadian Prairie Cities' *The Canadian Geographer* 17, 327–53

FILION, P. and BUNTING, T.E. 1990 'Socioeconomic Change Within the Older Housing Stock of Canadian CMA's: Social and Policy Implications' *Housing Studies* 2, 75–91

GELFAND, M.I. 1975 *Nation of Cities: The Federal Government and Urban America, 1933–1965* (New York: Oxford University Press)

GERTLER, L.O. 1976 *Urban Issues* (Toronto: Van Nostrand Reinhold)

—— and CROWLEY R. 1977 *Changing Canadian Cities: The Next 25 Years* (Toronto: McClelland and Stewart)

GLICKMAN, N. 1980 *The Urban Impact of Federal Policies* (Baltimore: Johns Hopkins University Press)

GIBBINS, R. 1982 *Regionalism: Territorial Politics in Canada and the United States* (Toronto: Butterworths)

GOLDBERG, M. and MERCER, J. 1986 *The Myth of the North American City* (Vancouver: University of British Columbia Press)

HALL, P. 1984 'The Urban Culture and the Suburban Culture' in J. Agnew, J. Mercer and D. E. Sopher eds *The City in Cultural Context* (Boston: Allen and Unwin)

—— 1985 'Dutch Urban Planning within the Perspective of European Development' in A. Dutt and F.J. Costa eds *Public Planning in the Netherlands* (New York: Oxford University Press)

HARVEY, D. 1975 'The Political Economy of Urbanization in Advanced Capitalist Societies—The Case of the United States' in G. Gappert and H. Rose eds *The Social Economy of Cities* (Beverly Hills: Sage Publications)

JONES, K. and SIMMONS, J. 1987 *Location, Location, Location* (Toronto: Methuen)

KERR, D. 1977 'Review of George A. Nader, Cities of Canada, Vols. I and II' *Annals, Association of American Geographers* 61, 163–65

LEY, D.F. 1983 *A Social Geography of the City* (New York: Harper and Row)

LITHWICK, N.H. 1970 *Urban Canada: Problems and Prospects* (Ottawa: Canada Mortgage and Housing Corporation)

LOGAN, J.R. and MOLOTCH, H.L. 1987 *Urban Fortunes: The Political Economy of Place* (Berkeley: University of California Press)

MERCER, J. 1989 'Asian Migrants and Residential Location in Canada' *New Community* 15, 185–202

MICHALOS, A.C. 1980a 'Foundations, Population and Health' *North American Social Report: Volume 1* (Boston: D. Reidel)

—— 1980b 'Crime, Justice and Politics,' *North American Social Report: Volume 2* (Boston: D. Reidel)

—— 1982 'Economics, Religion and Morality' *North American Social Report: Volume 5* (Boston: D. Reidel)

MULLER, P.O. 1981 *Contemporary Suburban America* (Englewood Cliffs, New Jersey: Prentice Hall)

MYRDAL, G. 1944 *An American Dilemma: The Negro Problem and Modern Democracy* (New York: Harper and Row)

PATERSON, J.H. 1989 *North America* 8th ed. (New York: Oxford University Press)

SEMPLE, R.K. and SMITH, W.R. 1981 'Metropolitan Dominance and Foreign Ownership in the Canadian Urban System' *The Canadian Geographer* 25, 4–26

TOBIN, G.A. 1987 'Divided Neighborhoods: Changing Patterns of Residential Segregation' *Urban Affairs Annual Reviews Vol. 32* (Beverly Hills: Sage Publications)

US ADVISORY COMMISSION ON INTERGOVERNMENTAL RELATIONS 1980 AND 1981 *The Federal Role in the Federal System: The Dynamics of Growth* (Washington, D.C.: United States Government Printing Office)

WALKER, R.A. 1981 'A Theory of Suburbanization: Capitalism and the Construction of Urban Space in the United States' in M. Dear and A.J. Scott eds *Urbanization and Urban Planning in Capitalist Society* (New York: Methuen)

WARNER, S.B. 1968 *The Private City* (Philadelphia: University of Pennsylvania Press)

4

Canada Becomes Urban: Cities and Urbanization in Historical Perspective

LARRY D. MCCANN AND PETER J. SMITH

Canada became an urban country only recently. At Confederation, fewer than one in five Canadians lived in towns and cities of 1,000 or more population. A slight majority claimed urban status at the close of the 1920s, but the two-thirds mark was not met until 1961; and maturity or a levelling-off in the urbanization process took place just in the 1980s. The demographic trend of urbanization has been matched by an increasing number of cities anchoring the Canadian space economy. Over 750 communities—ranging in size from small resource towns, through regional service centres and large manufacturing cities, to the metropolis Toronto—now make up Canada's urban system. There is no doubt that Canada has become urban, nor that the changing character of the Canadian city has played an all-important role in recasting society and economy across the country.

This chapter examines the urbanization of Canada over almost four hundred years, as we trace the process from initial town settlement, through the rise of mercantile towns and commercial cities, across the critical threshold of urban-industrial development, and onwards to maturity in a post-industrial world. As a theoretical concept, urbanization has three components: *demographic*—the increase in the urban proportion of a country's population; *structural*—the redistribution of population and economic functions among towns and cities in a changing urban system; and *behavioural*—the effects that urbanization has on the behaviour of people (Stelter 1990). Our analysis focuses upon the first two components and their effects in the period before the 1960s, particularly during the Great Transformation (1880s–1920s), when the urban pattern of Canada was fixed firmly in space. By emphasizing the conditions that led to a discrepancy between the heartland (where major cities, industries, and decision-making are concentrated) and the hinterland (which is by comparison sparsely populated and dependent on natural resources) this chapter provides a historical background to Chapters 5 and 8.

CONTEXT: DIMENSIONS OF SPACE AND TIME

The French historian Fernand Braudel has written that 'geographical space as a source of explanation affects all historical realities, all spatially-defined phenomena' including cities and settlement systems (Braudel 1984, 21). He also argues, like sociologist Immanuel Wallerstein and economist Harold Innis, that the fundamental dimension and explanatory power of space is the division between core and periphery, metropolis and hinterland, or centre and margin (Wallerstein 1974; Innis 1930; 1946).

Geographers also share the opinion that centres and peripheries are of critical importance in shaping the urban character of a country (McCann 1987a; Ray 1974). Core areas usually possess favourable physical qualities and they are always accessible to markets. They display a diversified profile of secondary, tertiary, and quaternary industries as well as a full division of labour; they are well-advanced along the development path and possess the capacity for innovative change; they are characterized by a highly urbanized and concentrated population forming a well-integrated urban system; and they are able to influence and usually control—through the metropolis—economic, social, and political decisions of national importance. Peripheral areas are distinguished by the opposite qualities: an emphasis on primary resource production; a scattered population; limited innovative capacity; restricted political power; and narrowly based urban economies and weakly integrated urban systems (McCann 1987b, 4). These spatial attributes critically affect the urban process. Who can deny the favoured economic position of southern Ontario cities in the Canadian space economy? What Maritimer, facing the choices of career and residence, fails to notice the limited opportunities offered by regional cities?

Our interpretation of urbanizing Canada emphasizes the growth of cities and types of settlement systems that have evolved to characterize the core and peripheral regions. But we must also create meaningful divisions of time to analyze and to explain urban change. The existence of towns and cities rests fundamentally on their economic activities, and these change over time in response to the unfolding, or stage development, of capitalism (Heilbroner 1985; Johnston 1982). Capitalism is an elusive, slippery concept, but it basically refers to the process by which essential factors of production (labour, entrepreneurship, technology, and especially capital) interact to generate wealth. As David Harvey argues, the structure of capitalism is a basic determinant of the urbanization process (Harvey 1985). In Canada this relationship between urban change and capitalist development begins with the mercantile era of trade and commerce (from the early seventeenth to the mid-nineteenth centuries). The links then develop more firmly under industrial capitalism (early nineteenth to mid-twentieth centuries), when new machine and managerial technologies, financial systems, and divisions of labour shaped the modern industrial city, and integrated metropolis and hinterland. Finally, there is the maturing of the urbanization process after the mid-twentieth century under late capitalism, when corporate and state agencies came more strongly to the fore.

These dimensions of space and time support a concept that is central to an interpretation of Canada's urban development—metropolitanism. In many respects—economically, socially, politically, even culturally—Canadian urban development is based on the staging of the metropolis-hinterland relationship. As defined by Maurice Careless, 'metropolitanism is at root a socio-economic concept . . . [implying] the emergence of a city of outstanding size to dominate not only its surrounding countryside but [also] other cities and their countrysides, the whole area being organized by the metropolis, through control of communication, trade, finance, into one economic and social unit that is focused on the metropolitan "centre of dominance" and through it trades with the world' (Careless 1954, 17; 1979). The metropolis, located at the economic core, operates from a position of strength achieved through successive phases of capitalist development. Given its superior trading, manufacturing, transportation, and financial roles, the metropolis takes a leading role in defining—even dominating —the urban character of a country. Canada has been and still is under the influence of world metropolises. Such an external role has been associated with the outreach of London, New York, and more recently Tokyo. Internally, all of Canada feels the influence of Montreal and Toronto. For all Canadian towns and cities, the 'sting' of the metropolis can be deeply felt.

GENESIS: OUTPOSTS OF EMPIRE

Canada's inclusion within the capitalist world economy took place very gradually after the early exploratory voyages of Cabot, Cartier, and others in the late fifteenth and sixteenth centuries. Subsequently, the cod fishery attracted mainly seasonal migrants to Newfoundland's Grand Banks and Acadia's shores. Further inland, the fur staple created some settlement along the St. Lawrence River and beyond. But the European peopling of Canada prior to the eighteenth century constituted a marginal, peripheral society at the outer edge of a European metropolitan core—'the radial margin kept firm, coherent, and operative by spokes connecting it to an inner hub' (Bailyn 1984, 328).

There were very few places on this outer edge that could claim urban status before 1700. In New France, Quebec City's administrative, military, and religious roles were supplemented by overseas trade; Montreal was the outfitting centre for western fur-trading ventures; and Trois Rivières was a small trading centre. All three were almost exclusively French in social make-up, and their respective populations in 1698 totalled 1,988, 1,185, and 250—or about 20 per cent of the colony's population of European origin. France's mercantilist policies of limited colonization restricted their further expansion. No comparable towns existed in Britain's domain. Annapolis Royal's 450 turn-of-the-century inhabitants, by then under British rule, were linked through trade and migration to neighbouring New England. St. John's wintering-over population of Irish, English, and some Scots in 1696 was only about 350, a reflection of England's anti-settlement laws (Nader 1975).

In time, the political and economic interests of both France and England towards Canada changed, and 'towns . . . became vanguards of . . . imperial expansion' (Stelter 1983, 171). The most significant expressions of the new political economy were the founding of Louisbourg (1713) and later of Halifax (1749). The former was selected as France's naval fortress in North America, but it also attracted merchants, artisans, labourers, and fishermen in pursuit of profit from the local fishery. Similarly, while Halifax was created as the military counterpoint to Louisbourg, it was also the 'metropolis' for Nova Scotia's anticipated commercial development. Like other newly-settled outposts, Halifax's success through its formative period was tenuous at best. A high turnover of people and business was the most characteristic pattern throughout the eighteenth century.

TRADE: MERCANTILE TOWNS AND THE SETTLEMENT SYSTEM

By the opening of the nineteenth century, Canada was an established and expanding staple hinterland for metropolitan interests in Europe, especially in Great Britain. The cod fishery was now attracting permanent settlers throughout the Atlantic realm, and the fur trade had pushed west to the Pacific coast. Increasingly, as the Baltic timber trade went into decline, the rich pine forests of Nova Scotia, New Brunswick, and Lower Canada were exploited for their naval masts, house timbers, and shipbuilding materials. Political revolution in the United States had forced Loyalist immigrants north, opening the agricultural lands adjacent to Lake Ontario and Lake Erie shores.

But it would be wrong to label these newly-settled regions as frontiers, for they were not regions of self-determination. Rather, they were peripheries, areas that remained attached, spoke-like, to a metropolitan hub. There were about 340,000 people living in British North America in 1800. All were ultimately governed from London. The urbanization level, which would dip lower when scores of British immigrants later took up farming, still stood at 20 per cent. The economic prospects of towns and cities were also linked abroad, since there was relatively little inter-regional trade among the British North American colonies. The prosperity of urban places relied instead on metropolitan government policies, foreign trading relationships, and a town's ability to tap a local hinterland. Halifax waxed and waned through war and peace and the ups and downs of the West Indies fish and sugar trade. Quebec City's fortunes rose and fell with the British demand for squared timber. In these and other towns, the radial arm of mercantilist policies prohibited diversified manufacturing. Canada was not a frontier of advancing goals but a dependent periphery.

The settled periphery fixed the rim of Europe's metropolitan wheel. In 1800, there was a fairly continuous belt of population distributed adjacent to the St. Lawrence River, but thin and isolated fragments elsewhere. Quebec City (8,000 people), Trois Rivières (1,500), and Montreal (6,000) maintained an urban presence in Lower Canada. Nova Scotia focused on Halifax (8,000), with notable outliers at Lunenburg (500), in the Annapolis Valley, and around Pictou. The Saint John River valley in New Brunswick was headed at tidewater by mercantile Saint John (2,500) and inland by Fredericton, the government seat (1,000). Prince Edward Island and much of Newfoundland were ringed by small, isolated outports. St. John's with 3,000 people was the urban exception. On the western margin, in Upper Canada, Kingston (500) was the only so-called urban place; a decade of Loyalist settlement was still rural-oriented and bound by mainly subsistence agriculture (Nader 1975). As Cole Harris has written, 'people lived in patches of isolated settlement and no one town, unless it were London, dominated the entire area' (Harris 1987, plate 68).

Yet, despite fragmentation and isolation, settlement systems of inter-connected places were taking root in the various regions. Coastal and river valley areas featured a major port like Halifax, St. John, Quebec City, or Montreal that was attached through maritime links with its foreland in Europe. These links were the principal route of connection in a so-called network system, along which investment capital, manufactured products, and immigrant labour flowed inward, or staple commodities in demand at foreign markets moved outward (Hohenberg and Lees 1985, 59–60; Johnston 1982, 56–63). Secondary lines of communication, of much less importance, ran out laterally along a coastline or inland through a river valley. Here were situated the smaller places for gathering staples or distributing trade imports—the size, spacing, and number of such places determined, foremost, by the actual production of the staple. James Vance labels the ports entrepôts, and the gathering/distributing places staple depots (Vance 1970, 148–67). Vance further argues that a central place system did not exist in the initial settlement phase. This is defensible, because New World settlement growth was at first externally-led. Later, as the density of population in the periphery increased and local production and exchange occurred, propositions of central place theory are entirely reasonable. The gathering/distributing places began to service tributary areas, taking on particular functions in relation to improved accessibility and increased market thresholds. A hierarchy of settlements then emerged to meet the diverse needs of the peripheral area's population. In this way, the network system and the central place system began to complement each other. (For an explanation of central place theory, see Chapter 7.)

Throughout British North America there is ample evidence of this evolutionary sequence—whether it be from coastal Newfoundland or the Maritimes; inland New Brunswick or the St. Lawrence Valley region; or the emerging Great Lakes system. An area that combines coastal and inland territory to illustrate the general case is the Bay of Fundy region, specifically the Saint John River valley and the southern coast of New Brunswick. The great staple giving initial shape to the network was timber, but in time land was cleared for agriculture, facilities for transportation and communications were set in place, and a capitalist market system prevailed—all leading to a scattered rural population and a hierarchy of central places that met the diverse needs of the growing settler population (Wynn 1987a; 1987b).

TRANSITION: FROM STAPLE ENTREPÔTS TO COMMERCIAL CITIES

During the first half of the nineteenth century, foreign trade remained at the forefront of the expanding colonial economy. Fish, timber, minerals (chiefly coal), and agricultural products were traded abroad for a variety of manufactured goods. This was the pattern established and enforced by imperial policies, perpetuating the global core/periphery relationships of mercantile capitalism. Holding the spokes to the metropolitan-controlled rim remained the responsibility of the long-established entrepôts, such as Halifax and Montreal.

Complementing the imperial network system was the quite considerable settlement of agricultural lands across British North America, particularly in Upper Canada (later Canada West). Here, thousands of Irish, English, and Scottish immigrants pushed the settled periphery north towards the Canadian Shield. As the process gained momentum, a mix of small towns (Guelph, Goderich, Owen Sound) and larger places (Toronto, Hamilton, London) gained increased prominence over the rural countryside (Spelt 1972). The urbanization level at mid-century stood below 15 per cent, but a substantial domestic market economy, based on commercialism and fuelled by rising incomes, was clearly in the making. In the face of this new reality, and challenged by a wide range of changing technologies, imperial policies could no longer constrain local manufacturing. The repeal of the English corn laws and other trade restrictions in the 1840s was the death blow against this form of metropolitan control. Numerous mercantile towns responded by moving to diversify their economies, thus adding new functions to the structure of the settlement system.

This growing commercialism was played out most fully in the largest cities. Because of initial advantages construed by location, size, or imperial preference, they were best able to take advantage of new trends in transportation and communication. The largest places were the first to woo the steamship companies and to offer bonuses to railways. Telegraph systems served them ahead of smaller rivals. The results were cumulative. They were able to offer a wider range of financial, wholesale, retail, and other business services. To serve these enterprises further, domestic manufacturing expanded in such areas as printing, machine repair, and agricultural implement production. This was not a full embrace of industrialization— that would follow after Confederation—but was a selective use of new industrial processes to meet domestic needs.

Montreal, the emerging commercial metropolis of pre-Confederation Canada, epitomizes the rise of the so-called commercial city. From its splendid gateway location on the St. Lawrence River, it controlled the import-export trade of a vast trading empire that stretched west, north, and even east across the country. The 'river barons' of Montreal promoted canal building, new railroad ventures, a telegraph system, resource enterprises, and a variety of manufacturing sectors, all in the name of progress and the desire to build a centre of dominating importance (Tulchinsky 1977). They were indeed successful. From a population of 22,000 in 1825, Montreal nearly tripled to 58,000 in 1851. Business depressions buffeted this upward growth, and the attachment to London and New York financial services remained in place. But as the country moved towards Confederation, no Canadian city was in a position to challenge Montreal's commercial prominence.

The rise of commercialism and a growing national market; the accelerating pace of changes in communication and transportation technologies; and the tentative beginning of large-scale manufacturing enterprise—all had an effect on the urbanization process. Demographically, the movement of foreign immigrants to both town and countryside was generally balanced, holding the rural-urban ratio at about six to one in 1851. Differences in birth rates favoured the countryside, but this was offset by some rural-urban migration. Structurally, the most notable developments focused on the entrenchment of core-periphery settlement patterns within each of the British North American colonies. The most articulated system at mid-century existed in Canada West, where all the spatial characteristics of a core region were strongly in evidence (Whebell 1969). Nevertheless, as Peter Goheen has recently argued, an autonomous Canadian system of

Table 4.1
The Changing Urbanization of Canada and its Regions, 1851–1961

	1851	1861	1871	1881	1891	1901	1911	1921	1931	1941	1951	1961
Canada (excl. Newfoundland)	13.1	15.8	18.3	23.3	29.8	34.9	41.8	47.4	52.5	55.7	62.9	70.2
Canada (incl. Newfoundland)	—	—	—	—	—	—	—	—	—	—	62.4	69.7
Newfoundland	—	—	—	—	—	—	—	—	—	—	43.3	50.7
Prince Edward Island	—	9.3	9.4	10.5	13.1	14.5	16.0	18.8	19.5	22.1	25.1	32.4
Nova Scotia	7.5	7.6	8.3	14.7	19.4	27.7	36.7	44.8	46.6	52.0	54.5	54.3
New Brunswick	14.0	13.1	17.6	17.6	19.9	23.1	26.7	35.2	35.4	38.7	42.8	46.5
Quebec	14.9	16.6	19.9	23.8	28.6	36.1	44.5	51.8	59.5	61.2	66.8	74.3
Ontario	14.0	18.5	20.6	27.1	35.0	40.3	49.5	58.8	63.1	67.5	72.5	77.3
Manitoba	—	—	—	14.9	23.3	24.9	39.3	41.5	45.2	45.7	56.0	63.9
Saskatchewan	—	—	—	—	—	6.1	16.1	16.8	20.3	21.3	30.4	43.0
Alberta	—	—	—	—	—	16.2	29.4	30.7	31.8	31.9	47.6	63.3
British Columbia	—	—	9.0	18.3	42.6	46.4	50.9	50.9	62.3	64.0	68.6	72.6

SOURCE: D. Michael Ray, ed., *Canadian Urban Trends*, Vol. I (Ottawa: 1976) Ministry of Supply and Services Canada, 1976.

core-periphery relationships had yet to develop (Goheen 1986). Urban relationships between the colonies existed, to be sure, but fragmentation—not integration—remained the more characteristic pattern. Integration awaited the unifying force of Confederation and the era of the new industrialism.

INDUSTRIALIZATION:
FORGING AN URBAN-INDUSTRIAL NATION

After mid-century, and particularly following Confederation, Canada became a 'nation transformed' (Brown and Cook 1974). Political union was, of course, a principal factor of change. It certainly provided an environment that facilitated the growth of industrial and financial capitalism. But labour, entrepreneurship, technology, capital, and rich resources of land and sea were also mixed together in different ways to cause an urban-industrial revolution. These factors of production became the building blocks of a more complex society and economy. The integrating force of the new industrialism of steam and rail in the era of the Great Transformation from the 1880s to the 1920s was substantial (Heron 1989; Kerr and Holdsworth 1990). Industrialization created new focal points of settlement and growth across the country, and so set the now-familiar pattern of heartland and hinterland, or core and periphery.

The broad progression of the urbanization process to 1961 is recorded clearly in Table 4.1. Canada as a whole increased its urban proportion by five to seven percentage points every decade between 1881 and 1921, finally tipping the 50 per cent level by 1931. The biggest surges—in the 1880s and 1900s—were linked to immigration. There were strong regional differences as well. The core regions of Ontario and Quebec crossed the urban threshold years before peripheral areas in the Maritimes and western Canada. For example, Saskatchewan waited a half-century longer than Ontario to achieve the 50 per cent mark. Over time, rural-urban migration was a long-lasting agent of urbanization in peripheral regions like the Prairie provinces. By contrast, a new round of urban-oriented immigration, complemented by inter-city migration within Canada, triggered the substantial urban population growth of post-war Ontario (Stone 1967).

Industrialization in Canada, as in Britain and the United States, began in the countryside, but its most significant impact on economic and population growth was felt in towns and cities. The older forms of staple production—sawmilling, grist milling, fish processing, shipbuilding, coal mining—had a strong rural focus. But the new industrialism—iron and steel production, textiles, appliance and automobile manufacture—generally required the agglomerative advantages of an urban location. Concentration near a labour supply or near linked industrial and consumer markets, for example, was essential. The result was a binding relationship between industrialization and urbanization. This is illustrated by Table

Table 4.2
The Urbanization and Industrialization of Canada During the Great Transformation, c.1890–1931[a]

	1890, 1891	1910, 1911	1929, 1931
Total population[1]	4,833,239	7,206,643	10,376,786
Percentage of population urban[1]	29.8	41.8	52.5
Number of urban places[1] (1,000+ population)	274	396	503
Gross value of production[2]			
Primary industries ($000s)	585,625	1,177,735	2,061,585
Manufacturing ($000s)	623,205	1,383,760	1,802,960
Changing labour force (%)[3]			
Primary	50.0	39.6	34.0
Secondary	25.3	26.9	25.3
Tertiary	24.7	33.5	40.7
Miles of railroad operated[4]	17,657	24,730	41,380
Pig iron produced (long tons)[5,4]	23,891	917,635	1,080,160
Steel ingots and steel castings produced (short tons)[5,4]	13,000	882,396	1,543,427

[a]Population and labour force data are for 1891, 1911, and 1931. All other data are for 1890, 1910, and 1929.

Sources: [1]Canada, *Census of Canada* for 1891, 1911, and 1931 (Ottawa).
    [2]Alexander, D. (1978) 'Economic growth in the Atlantic Region' *Acadiensis* 8, 60.
    [3]Green, A. G. (1971) *Regional Aspects of Canadian Economic Growth* (Toronto: University of Toronto Press) Appendix C.
    [4]Urquhart, M. C., ed. (1965) *Historical Statistics of Canada* (Toronto: Macmillan) 532.
    [5]Donald, W.J.A. (1915) *The Canadian Iron and Steel Industry* (New York: Houghton Mifflin) and Urquhart, 484.

4.2, which reveals the quite considerable restructuring of labour force activity; the ways in which different trends of industrial development (manufacturing output, railroad construction) correlate positively with urban development; and the increasing level of urbanization. Canada today ranks in the top ten of world industrial nations, and it is well to remember that the drive to this position began in earnest with the National Policy of industrial incentives shortly after Confederation (Williams 1983).

A Model of Urban-Industrial Growth

How do cities grow? And why have certain cities in Canada grown larger than others? To interpret the rise of the Canadian city in the era of the new industrialism, we need to examine the growth possibilities that exist in a core-periphery or heartland-hinterland space economy. After all, this was the settlement system that took shape during the Great Transformation (McCann 1987a).

From a heartland-hinterland perspective, the economic character of cities stems from their handling of the factors of production, as these are channelled between core and periphery. Cities function as intermediaries, interacting with one another and integrating regional network systems. Interaction therefore creates cities whose livelihoods depend on some combination of transportation, wholesale-trading, manufacturing, and financial and business activities. One or more of these sectors, but espe-

Figure 4.1
The Process of Urban Growth in a Heartland-Hinterland Space Economy

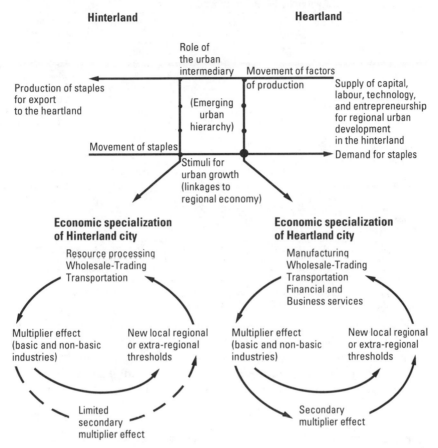

cially industrial activity, triggers a circular and cumulative growth process that is sustained by the strength of the multiplier effect and by the size of critical market thresholds (refer to Figure 4.1).

Heartland and hinterland cities differ in their responses to the industrialization process. The degree of specialization and the composition of economic sectors will vary in each situation. Thus it is unlikely that a hinterland city's economy will be fully diversified, because depending upon the type and distribution of natural resources, towns and cities within the periphery will function chiefly as resource towns, central places, break-in-bulk or trans-shipment points; or where location or circumstance favours diversification, as multi-functional centres. In most heartland cities, on the other hand, manufacturing plays a key role because the core area's accessibility to national markets creates certain economic advantages (e.g. external economies), making possible the manufacturing of a wide

Table 4.3
The Changing Economy of Three Canadian Cities, 1881–1931
(Distribution of Labour Force by Industrial Groups)

Industrial Group[1]	Quebec City 1881	1911	1931	London 1881	1911	1931	Edmonton 1911	1931
Primary	1.3	.8	.8	1.1	1.0	1.9	5.6	9.0
Manufacturing	18.2	34.6	16.6	24.4	43.0	19.1	19.5	9.7
Construction	9.5	11.5	7.4	8.6	7.5	7.3	16.1	6.4
Transportation	9.2	5.4	7.7	4.8	8.2	7.1	7.5	7.5
Communications	—	.7	1.9	.6	1.0	2.1	.6	1.7
Utilities	—	—	.7	—	—	.8	—	1.0
Trade	7.7	20.2	13.3	9.7	17.0	15.7	14.8	14.0
Finance	.2	1.2	.3	.7	1.5	.4	1.8	.3
Insurance and real estate	.3	.9	1.0	1.4	1.3	1.3	3.6	1.3
Community, business, and personal services	27.0	16.5	35.8	26.5	15.4	31.4	22.3	34.7
Public administration	2.0	8.3	3.8	1.8	3.4	3.3	7.4	3.1
Others	—		11.1	3.8	.8	9.5	.8	11.0
Unspecified	2.7			3.8		.1		.1
Commercial clerks	7.5			7.3				
Labourers	14.4			8.4				
Total labour force	23,442	25,656	49,266	6,712	19,851	29,004	12,535	33,317
Population	62,446	78,710	130,594	19,746	46,300	71,148	24,900	79,197

SOURCES: Compiled from data in Canada, *Census of Canada* for 1881, 1911, 1931.

[1]To ensure comparability over time, the labour force data for each year were reclassified according to Canada, DBS, *Standard Industrial Classification Manual* (Ottawa, Queens Printer, 1960).

range of primary, producer, and consumer goods. Hinterland cities, by contrast, generally lack these opportunities and advantages. Manufacturing in all cities is supplemented during the development process by service sector activity, and in core cities by highly specialized financial and management activities—all spin-offs from the major industrial stimulus.

The Model Applied

The changing labour force characteristics of representative heartland and hinterland cities over the course of the Great Transformation demonstrate the utility of the general model (Table 4.3). Quebec City, London, and Edmonton grew appreciably between 1881 and 1931. All experienced a burst of manufacturing activity at the turn of the century, followed by diversification and expansion in the service sector. Wood products, textiles, and shoe manufacturing spurred Quebec City; food processing and agricultural implements fuelled London; and milling and meat packing led Edmonton. Later, government services and attention to community and personal needs supplemented the initial industrial stimulus, and manufacturing fell back. This was the common path followed by most Canadian cities. Manufacturing, however, remained most pronounced and diversified in core-area cities like Hamilton, Kitchener-Waterloo, and Brampton, where external economies favoured industrial concentration. Specialization in a few manufacturing lines characterized staple production in Vancouver (wood products), Sydney (steel), and other peripheral places.

Besides stimulating urban population growth, industrialization reinforced the developing heartland-hinterland structure of the Canadian
space economy. In 1700 and 1800, as previously discussed, the urban
system was weakly articulated and linked primarily abroad. By the mid-
nineteenth century, however, the settlement pattern of central Canada
possessed core-like features, forming the nucleus of a national system of
urban places, which, in 1900, was differentiated quite strongly by core and
periphery (Figures 4.2 and 4.3). Yet, by world standards, the pattern was
a modest one. About one in three Canadians lived in some twenty-five
urban places with populations greater than 10,000, whereas Britain at this
time was nearly three-quarters urbanized, and the United States about
50 per cent. There were several hundred large urban places in both countries; and London and New York still held sway over critical industrial
and financial sectors of Canada's economy.

The axis of the internal metropolitan wheel stretched between Windsor
and Quebec City, with the main hub of the system centred on Montreal. In
1901, Montreal outdistanced Toronto, its nearest rival, in both population
(267,000 to 208,000) and manufacturing output ($71 million to $58 million). The spokes integrating the system ran mainly throughout southern
Ontario and Quebec; and although a railroad network now stretched across
the country, facilitating integration, peripheral nodes of interaction were
few and far between. Well over 70 per cent of Canada's urban-based
economic activity and urban population were concentrated within the
Industrial Heartland. Places here interacted in numerous ways. For example, capital moved from headquarter banks in Montreal and Toronto to
hundreds of regional branches. Successive bank acts, beginning in 1871,
encouraged this centralized banking system. Further, steel was shipped
by rail from Hamilton to linked industries in Brampton, London, Oshawa,
and elsewhere. Government bounties in support of United States' (but not
Nova Scotian) coal provided a considerable inducement to the growth
of Ontario industries and their urban places. In short, the cumulative
advantages of a core area location weighed heavily in shaping Canada's
turn-of-the-century pattern of urban-industrial activity. They help to
account for the large number and considerable size of central Canadian
cities relative to the periphery.

DOMINANCE: METROPOLITANISM AND THE EVOLVING URBAN SYSTEM

As Canada became more urban and less rural, several cities played leading—even dominating—roles. Montreal, Toronto, Winnipeg, Calgary,
Edmonton, and Vancouver are the principal metropolitan centres that
have shaped the heartland-hinterland system. The largest and most
important of these—the metropolis—functions from a position of acquired
power. Rising through successive tiers of economic strength, the metrop-

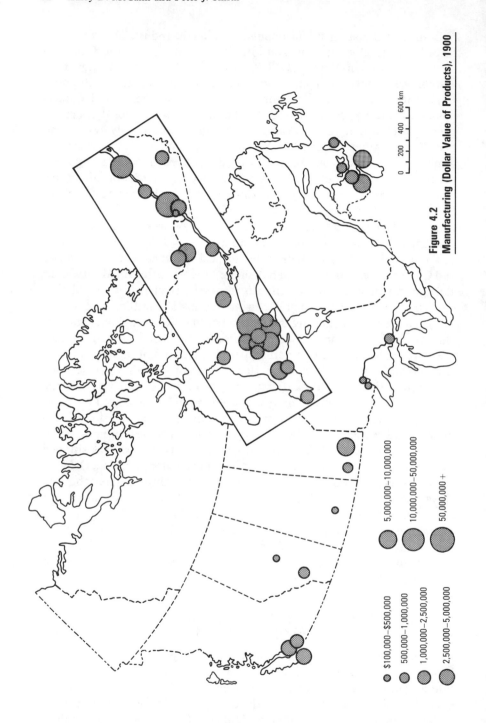

Figure 4.2
Manufacturing (Dollar Value of Products), 1900

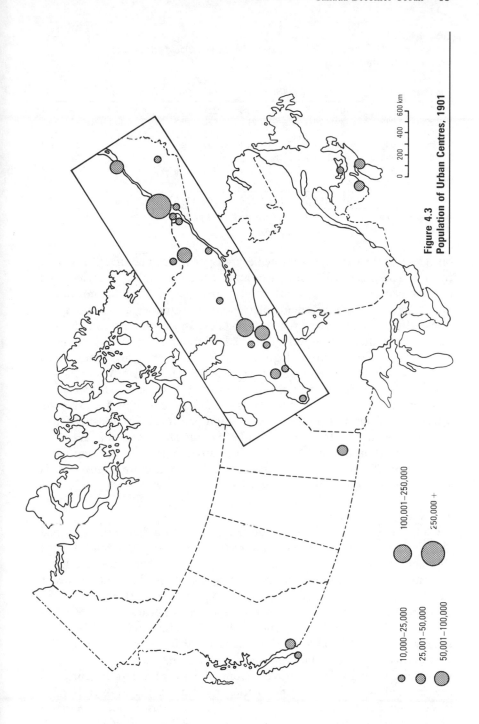

Figure 4.3
Population of Urban Centres, 1901

0 200 400 600 km

10,000–25,000

25,001–50,000

50,001–100,000

100,001–250,000

250,000 +

Table 4.4
The Changing Size Distribution of Canadian Towns and Cities, 1871–1951
(by population size classes)

Population Size Classes	1871 (No.)	1871 (%)	1891 (No.)	1891 (%)	1911 (No.)	1911 (%)	1931 (No.)	1931 (%)	1951 (No.)	1951 (%)
1,000– 2,499	103	64.5	166	60.5	238	60.1	289	57.4	408	57.1
2,500– 4,999	32	20.0	59	21.5	76	19.2	101	20.1	141	19.7
5,000– 9,999	16	10.0	28	10.2	38	9.6	51	10.1	73	10.2
10,000– 24,999	2	1.2	12	4.4	27	6.8	34	6.8	48	6.7
25,000– 99,999	6	3.7	7	2.6	12	3.0	20	4.0	32	4.5
100,000–249,999	1	.6	1	.4	3	.8	4	.8	6	.8
250,000 and over			1	.4	2	.5	4	.8	7	1.0
Total	160	100.0	274	100.0	396	100.0	503	100.0	715	100.0

SOURCE: Compiled from data in Canada, *Census of Canada* for 1871, 1891, 1911, 1931, and 1951.

olis gains prominence in commerce, transportation, manufacturing, and finance. The metropolis influences greatly the economy and society of a country because of its concentration of people, wealth, and innovating power. In fact, it is only when a metropolitan centre becomes innovative, transmitting social values, political potency, and economic control well beyond its traditional hinterland into a larger arena, that it wins status as a metropolis. Once achieved, its power of dominance overshadows all other towns and cities, rendering them of lesser importance. Montreal and Toronto long ago demonstrated their ability to control vast hinterlands, and some would argue that this status is shared today with, for example, Vancouver, Calgary, Edmonton, and Winnipeg (McCann 1981a). Thus, metropolitanism is the historical and geographical process that accounts for the growth of a city that enables it to attain a position of dominance in national life, and so creates the geographical structure of metropolis and hinterland found in all capitalist societies.

The Rise of the Metropolis
We turn now to a discussion of the competition between Montreal and Toronto for metropolitan dominance in Canada, but first we need to examine two features of structural urbanization that place this long-standing rivalry in context and in clearer perspective. The first feature is the changing number of cities by population size classes; the second is the changing urban hierarchy of the leading Canadian cities.

In 1871 there were 160 so-called urban places in Canada; in 1951 the total was 715 (Table 4.4). This is a substantial increase, but what is its significance for understanding metropolitanism? Canada was slowly urbanizing throughout this period (from 18 per cent to 63 per cent), and the proportion of the urban population residing in places over 100,000 gained considerable ground. At the same time, the vast majority of urban places remained small; in 1951, 87 per cent (622) had fewer than 10,000 people. As a country of towns and small cities, Canada was fertile ground

Table 4.5
Changing Population of Canada's Largest Urban Places, 1871–1986
(Ranked by dominant Census Metropolitan Area in 1986)

Metropolitan Centre	1871	1901	1931	1961	1986
Toronto	59,000	208,040	631,207	1,824,481	3,427,168
Montreal	115,000	267,730	818,577	2,109,509	2,921,357
Vancouver		26,183	246,593	790,165	1,380,729
Ottawa	24,141	59,928	126,872	429,750	819,263
Edmonton		4,176	79,197	337,568	785,465
Calgary		4,392	83,761	249,641	676,321
Winnipeg	241	42,340	218,785	265,429	625,304
Quebec City	59,699	68,840	130,594	357,568	603,267
Hamilton	26,850	52,634	155,547	395,189	557,029
St. Catharines	7,864	9,946	24,753	84,472	343,258
London	18,000	37,981	71,148	181,283	342,302
Kitchener	2,743	9,747	30,793	154,864	311,195
Halifax	29,582	40,832	59,275	92,511	295,990
Victoria	3,270	20,919	39,082	154,152	255,547
Windsor	4,253	12,153	63,108	193,365	253,988
Oshawa	3,185	4,394	23,439	62,419	203,543
Saskatoon		113	43,291	95,526	177,641
Regina		2,249	53,209	112,141	186,521
St. John's				90,838	161,901
Chicoutimi	1,393	3,826	11,877	31,657	158,468
Sudbury		2,027	18,518	110,694	148,877
Sherbrooke		11,765	28,933	66,554	129,960
Trois Rivières	7,570	9,981	35,450	53,477	128,888
Saint John	41,325	40,711	47,514	63,633	121,265

SOURCE: Compiled from data in Canada, *Census of Canada* for 1871, 1901, 1931, 1961, and 1986.

for the seeds of metropolitan dominance as practised by Montreal and Toronto. The many small places lacked the economic and political organization to compete against the few large cities. Moreover, the changing order of the twenty or so largest urban places indicates a high degree of stability at the top of the hierarchy, suggesting that the initial advantage of size was easily sustained (Table 4.5). This points to the cumulative advantages that accrued to the largest Canadian cities, and particularly to Montreal and Toronto. The major shifts in position coincided with the opening of new territory (e.g. Winnipeg and Vancouver during the settlement of the West), the decline of older regions (e.g. Saint John in the Maritimes), and the intensification of urban development in central Canada. These are trends that we will return to later.

What is the place of Montreal and Toronto within urbanizing Canada? It has become commonplace to equate the metropolitan outreach of the Canadian heartland in the late nineteenth and early twentieth centuries with the nation's largest urban centre—Montreal (Careless 1989; Kerr 1968; and Semple and Smith 1981). This assumption is based in part on Montreal's larger population size (outdistancing Toronto by about 230,000 over their respective metropolitan areas in 1931), but also on its well-known prominence as an industrial, transportation, and financial centre.

Montreal had always led Toronto in manufacturing output (although only slightly since World War I); its import-export and transportation functions were more dominant, for here were located the headquarters of the Canadian Pacific Railway and various national shipping companies; and although Toronto's banks competed almost evenly across Canada with their rivals from Montreal, in the sphere of international banking and stock exchange activity, Montreal remained the clear leader through the 1930s and early 1940s (Higgins 1986).

These facts are well known, but did Montreal hold sway over all the Canadian regions and in all business sectors during the Great Transformation? It is relatively straightforward to recognize the economic strength of the metropolis, but rather more difficult to measure the nature of metropolitan dominance, and hence to answer the question. Such economic criteria as a metropolitan centre's share of national manufacturing employment and production, bank clearings and stock transactions, or corporate assets and revenues easily identify concentration in an urban system, but they tell us little about the integration of metropolis and hinterland. On the other hand, analyses of trade in commodities, flows of bank capital, and movements of people provide measurements of relationships in the space economy, but individually they lack comprehensiveness. To try to overcome that difficulty we here consider control over branch businesses as a key indicator of metropolitan influence. Metropolitanism implies the extension, into the hinterland, of economic activities headquartered in the metropolis, so branch businesses may be regarded as emissaries of the metropolis, advancing its business interests and consolidating its empire throughout the hinterland. Amongst other activities, branch businesses engage in manufacturing; they facilitate the distribution of goods; they channel capital flows; and they sell and service the products of the metropolis.

In this section we present the major findings of an analysis of some 15,000 branch businesses and their metropolitan linkages in 1891, 1911, and 1931 (McCann 1983; 1989). To return to the question of whether Montreal dominated in all business sectors and all Canadian regions during the 1891 to 1931 period, the analysis indicates that Montreal (21.1 per cent) had lost its edge in headquartering branch business activity to Toronto (23.8 per cent) by World War I (Table 4.6). Other Canadian cities offered little competition. We should thus ascribe to Toronto more prominence in Canadian business affairs than previously recognized, although this does not necessarily mean that Toronto was more important than Montreal as a national metropolis. It could be, for example, that Toronto's branch business network was focused largely in Ontario. Nor does Table 4.6 allow us to assert that these two metropolitan centres actually dominated business activity across the country.

Our data shed light on this puzzle in two ways. First, the regional focus of metropolitan branch business investment points to the nation-wide

Table 4.6
Metropolitan Headquarters of Urban-Based Branch Businesses, 1891–1931
(Ranked by dominant centre in 1931)

Metropolitan Centre	1891 No.	1891 Percentage of total branch businesses	1911 No.	1911 Percentage of total branch businesses	1931 No.	1931 Percentage of total branch businesses
Toronto	221	16.9	1,051	23.8	2,590	28.9
Montreal	261	19.9	926	21.1	2,347	26.2
Winnipeg	31	2.4	224	5.1	482	5.4
Vancouver	11	.8	73	1.6	255	2.8
Calgary			60	1.4	244	2.7
Hamilton	44	3.4	161	3.6	172	1.9
London, England	20	1.5	65	1.5	149	1.7
New York	28	2.1	86	2.0	102	1.1
Quebec	27	2.1	176	4.0	101	1.1
Ottawa	21	1.6	96	2.2	86	1.0
Regina	1		11	.2	75	.8
Saint John	8	.6	49	1.1	61	.7
Edmonton			7	.2	50	.6
Victoria	8	.6	23	.5	47	.5
Chicago	1		42	1.0	45	.5
Saskatoon			3	.1	36	.4
London, Ont.	1		12	.3	32	.4
Detroit	21	1.6	25	.6	29	.3
Other places	611	46.5	1,307	29.7	2,061	23.0
Total branch businesses	1,315	100.0	4,397	100.0	8,964	100.0

SOURCE: Data compiled from the *Mercantile Agency Reference Books* of Dun, Wiman and Company and R.G. Dun Company.

investment practices of heartland cities, especially by 1931; and, conversely, to the limited regional outreach, with the exception of Winnipeg and Calgary, of cities in the hinterland. In 1891, Montreal had the most pronounced national outreach, dividing its activity between Quebec and Ontario about equally and reaching as well into the Maritimes and the West. No other city then matched this spatial range. By 1931, however, Toronto shared this national business outlook, tapping opportunities in all regions in a quite significant fashion. Second, when we turn to an examination of metropolitan control of regional branch businesses, we can safely assert that Toronto accounted for the single largest share of branch business activity across most Canadian regions, even challenging Montreal in its own backyard of Quebec. What is most striking, in fact, is the extent to which Toronto had already surpassed Montreal and the lesser regional centres in the control that it exercised.

Does the increasing ascendancy of Toronto over Montreal, and its achievement of leading status, mean that Montreal's business community failed to participate in the managerial revolution of the late nineteenth and early twentieth centuries? Comparison of the changing structure or make-up of branch businesses headquartered in Montreal and Toronto suggests that this was not the case (Table 4.7). The two metropolitan centres controlled similar ranges of branch businesses, led strongly by finance, then followed at some distance by manufacturing, which was a short step ahead of wholesale and retail trade. The difference in their

Table 4.7
Metropolitan Domination of Regional Branch Businesses, by Major Business Sector, 1891–1931

	1891 Control of regional branch businesses				1911 Control of regional branch businesses				1931 Control of regional branch businesses			
Region and major business sectors	Montreal (No.)	(%)	Toronto (No.)	(%)	Montreal (No.)	(%)	Toronto (No.)	(%)	Montreal (No.)	(%)	Toronto (No.)	(%)
CORE												
Quebec												
Manufacturing	25	37.3	8	11.9	53	16.8	78	24.4	122	23.5	149	28.7
Wholesale trade	7	20.0	6	17.1	5	5.7	22	25.0	45	16.4	83	30.2
Retail trade	10	41.7	2	8.3	11	18.6	12	20.3	79	26.6	63	21.2
Finance, insurance and real estate	51	60.0	4	4.7	152	31.0	55	9.9	485	82.9	100	17.2
Ontario												
Manufacturing	20	13.7	20	13.7	15	12.5	29	24.2	169	19.1	194	21.9
Wholesale trade	15	14.4	8	7.7	3	8.8	3	8.8	116	21.8	152	28.6
Retail trade	12	8.2	9	6.2	3	4.8	8	12.7	89	11.3	283	35.9
Finance, insurance and real estate	72	21.1	138	40.5	146	29.8	348	62.5	347	37.6	564	61.0
PERIPHERY												
Maritimes												
Manufacturing	8	32.0	—	—	20	27.0	11	14.9	38	20.8	54	29.5
Wholesale trade	—	—	—	—	6	11.8	5	9.8	21	25.0	12	14.3
Retail trade	—	—	—	—	3	3.8	2	4.3	17	8.8	39	20.2
Finance, insurance and real estate	7	8.6	—	—	66	13.5	16	2.9	89	55.6	68	42.5
Western Interior												
Manufacturing	2	22.2	2	22.2	42	19.8	52	24.5	84	15.9	137	26.0
Wholesale trade	3	11.1	4	14.8	22	11.1	35	17.6	64	10.9	91	15.5
Retail trade	—	—	1	6.7	8	18.2	15	18.5	41	9.1	105	23.4
Finance, insurance and real estate	7	31.8	5	22.7	77	15.7	96	17.2	164	50.0	161	49.1
British Columbia												
Manufacturing	4	33.3	1	8.3	30	20.4	18	12.2	55	16.9	66	20.2
Wholesale trade	—	—	—	—	11	15.3	8	11.1	33	15.1	34	15.5
Retail trade	—	—	1	11.1	8	22.2	4	11.1	10	5.7	30	17.0
Finance, insurance and real estate	5	41.7	—	—	49	10.0	42	7.5	94	57.7	69	42.3
CANADA												
Manufacturing	59	22.8	31	12.0	107	19.3	110	19.9	468	19.2	600	24.6
Wholesale trade	25	13.7	18	9.8	42	11.8	51	14.3	279	16.4	372	21.9
Retail trade	22	10.3	13	6.1	22	8.5	29	11.2	236	12.4	520	27.3
Finance, insurance and real estate	142	26.4	147	27.3	490	33.2	557	37.8	1178	54.5	962	44.5

SOURCE: Data compiled from the *Mercantile Agency Reference Books* of Dun, Wiman and Company and R.G. Dun Company.

status rested rather in the numbers of branch businesses controlled by each centre and in Toronto's greater diversification. It was from a broad, numerically strong base that Toronto overtook Montreal and achieved dominance in most Canadian regions, as well as in most sectors of the regional branch business economy. Montreal retained a slight superiority in financial services in the peripheral regions in 1931, but elsewhere, except for wholesaling and retailing activity in the western interior, where Winnipeg and Calgary stood ahead by a slight amount, and in British Columbia, where the same sectors were controlled marginally by Vancouver, Toronto dominated manufacturing distribution, wholesale functions, and retail trade. In fact, its leadership had been won by 1911, to be accentuated over the next two decades.

Clearly, there are different ways of assessing the question of metropolitan dominance in Canada. The above discussion cautions us that measures of urban concentration are not sufficient by themselves. The interplay between cities and their hinterlands reveals essential elements of dominance. From this perspective, Toronto functioned as a national metropolis much earlier in the twentieth century than is commonly appreciated.

Consolidating the Urban-Industrial Core
Montreal and Toronto had the strongest impact of all places on the evolving Canadian space economy, but they were not alone in integrating the nation's core and periphery system. Southern Ontario and southern Quebec possessed all the essential characteristics of a core area that facilitated control: a diversified labour force; the capacity for innovation; and a highly urbanized and concentrated population, linked by rail, road, and other communication networks into a well-integrated urban system. The 'Golden Horseshoe', ringing the western end of Lake Ontario, and the Montreal-centred region were the focal points of the system. In fact, by 1961 there were over eighty places of 10,000 or more population comprising the industrial heartland. The rest of the country had barely three-quarters of this total. (The recent evolution of the Canadian heartland and hinterland is contrasted in Chapter 8.)

Most of these heartland places had been fuelled by the industrialization process. They distributed their products across Canada, beating out hinterland competition along the way. Steel from Hamilton; automobiles from Windsor, Oshawa, and Oakville; rubber from Kitchener; plastics from Sarnia; textiles from Sherbrooke—the list of such common products, as well as more specialized ones, could be extensive. Urban growth and development was aided and abetted by many economic and geographic factors: agglomeration economies that encouraged linked activities; a skilled labour force; access to regional markets that reduced production costs and in turn made long-distance shipping across Canada more bearable; nearness to the United States manufacturing belt; availability of raw materials; cheap hydroelectric power and later natural gas; and others.

Social and political actions further propelled the cumulative growth of cities: immigration and internal migration (the demographic basis of urbanization); government tariff policies; regional development incentives—all these played a role. In short, by the close of World War II, the consolidation of urban-industrial strength in Canada's industrial heartland was an unmistakable and established fact (Kerr 1987; Semple and Smith 1981).

Uneven Development: Expanding and Contracting Peripheries
Canada's peripheral regions have become urban in quite different ways. De-industrialization and underdevelopment plague the Maritimes and Newfoundland, retarding urbanization. The Canadian Shield is characterized by single-enterprise resource towns tied closely to metropolitan enterprise. Across the western interior, agriculture and oil production have shaped pattern and process in unique ways. In British Columbia, which crossed the urban threshold before even Ontario, the urban system is dominated by the concentrating effects of Vancouver. Despite these broad differences, however, the urbanization of all the peripheral regions since the late nineteenth century has been played out on the metropolis-hinterland stage, offering a perspective from which to examine some of the salient features of regional urban development (Preston 1980).

The Maritimes is Canada's least urbanized region. Yet, it showed strong promise of urban development in the 1880s, when the various National Policy incentives stirred industrial activity and fostered considerable town growth (Acheson 1972; McCann 1979). Canada's steel industry was established in Nova Scotia in 1882, and since mid-century coal from Cape Breton and Pictou County had fuelled the St. Lawrence region. Small towns—New Glasgow, Amherst, Moncton, Marysville—made the transition from mercantile to industrial capitalism. For a brief span, their steel mills, railroad car plants, and textile factories were prominent on the national stage. But the urban system was fragmented, little integrated, and weakly-led by its regional centres. Halifax and Saint John battled most strenuously with each other, not as major industrial or financial centres, but as national ports competing for the products of distant markets.

The region's urban-industrial revolution collapsed with devastating effects in the 1920s. The cumulative disadvantages of earlier business takeovers by Montreal corporations, the new Toronto outreach, a peripheral location and marginal resource base, regressive government policies (e.g. severe cuts in rail and industrial subsidies) and hesitant investors, among other factors, caused industries to close and many towns to lose population (Forbes 1977; McCann 1981b). Rather than move into towns and cities, many Maritimers chose to retain a small farm and work a seasonal round of rural (and sometimes urban) activities to earn a livelihood. Such pluralistic patterns of work and residence help to explain the limited urbanization of the region even today (McCann 1988). Against this trend, Halifax, Saint

John, and a few other cities attracted the region's young and footloose, but few foreigners. No urban centre functioned alone to control the Maritimes. Only in the 1970s and 1980s did Halifax emerge as a place of singular importance. In Newfoundland, St. John's—a government, import-export, and service centre—long held a degree of control over the many isolated and weakly-linked coastal settlements. But it too suffers from the tyranny of a marginal location within Canada, and is now of secondary importance to Halifax in the Atlantic provinces.

Resource towns are a distinguishing feature of Canadian urbanization, particularly in areas of mining and forestry activity across the Canadian Shield (Robinson 1962). These communities have created, in fact, one of the anomalies of urban Canada. On a proportional basis, most people living in northern resource areas are urban—or, at least, town—dwellers, not rural residents. Yet these small resource towns, usually with less than 5,000 people, are often isolated by hundreds of miles from one another; their links are strongest with the metropolitan south. Mining towns, for instance, have been most strongly tied to Toronto, where the promotion, capitalization, and organization of resource activity on the stock exchange has traditionally been greater than in Montreal. Pulp-and-paper towns, on the other hand, have shared connections with both Montreal and Toronto. Often, too, international links with parent companies in places like New York are of paramount importance.

Besides capital, other metropolitan production factors—labour, technology, entrepreneurship—shaped the ever-moving, outward rim of the resource periphery. Resource town development was extended, spoke-like, along routes of access in response to increased demands by industrial nations for pulp and paper, nickel, copper, gold, and other valuable resource commodities. The first burst of concentrated mining town development was focused on the nickel belt in northwestern Ontario. Sudbury was established there in 1883—more by chance than by design—when the Canadian Pacific Railway (CPR) opened up the district. It became the central place of a cluster of smaller communities that included Copper Cliff, Conniston, and Levack (Stelter 1974). Silver mining at Cobalt and nearby places like Timmins and Kirkland Lake in the early 1900s followed the construction northwards of the Temiskaming and Northern Ontario Railway. Later, in the 1920s, an outlier at Rouyn-Noranda pushed the periphery into Quebec. Pulp-and-paper towns, by contrast, have followed rivers into the periphery, seeking sites for water, power, and log transport. By World War I, they formed a crescent-shaped pattern along the southern flank of the Canadian Shield. During the inter-war period, the need for larger pulpwood sources forced some companies to move northward, advancing further into the headwaters of rivers emanating in the Shield. In this way, Espanola, Dolbeau, and Baie-Comeau were added to Canada's growing resource town inventory. The few new towns of the post-World War II era (e.g. Marathon and Terrace Bay) were responses to technological advances in the industry that intensified the peripheral distribution pattern (McCann 1980). The consequences of metropolitan control over resource town development have been all-pervasive. Not only did large metropolitan corporations, both domestic and foreign, determine such matters as the location, scale, and timing of development, but they frequently built and controlled the towns that supported the resource operations. Company towns no longer contribute to the urbanization process, but their legacy is ever-present in the physical form of the resource community (Robson 1986).

In the western interior, in contrast to the fragmentation and lack of integration that characterize the Maritimes, there is a certain symmetry to the urban pattern, derived from the interweaving of network and central place systems of urban settlement. From the late nineteenth century through much of the twentieth century, Winnipeg functioned as a 'gateway' city (Burghardt 1971). Investment capital, manufactured goods, immigrant labour, and business expertise from eastern Canada and abroad flowed inward through it; and agricultural staples (e.g. wheat and meat products) in demand elsewhere, but especially in industrializing Britain, moved outwards. In this way, the commercial and transportation sectors held prominence in Winnipeg's economy. Across the West and spaced fairly evenly along the many thousands of miles of railroad tracks, were hundreds of staple depots. The grain elevators and general stores of these typically small places were the means of connection with external markets and suppliers. In larger places banks, immigration halls, and wholesalers added depth to the network. But as the West was settled, attracting nearly 1.5 million people by World War I, the staple depots took on additional functions to service tributary areas, creating an overlying central place system.

Alan Artibise and Paul Voisey have demonstrated that much more than geography and economic rationale were involved in shaping the West's urban pattern (Artibise 1981; Voisey 1975). Order and symmetry aside, metropolitan interests and boosterism played decidedly-important roles. It might appear, for example, that Winnipeg was a natural choice on locational grounds alone for the region's gateway city, but only City Council bonuses to the CPR—incentives that competitors like Emerson and Selkirk could not match—ensured its success. Then, once the railway was in operation across the West, the shipping and freight rail policies of the Montreal-based CPR favoured Winnipeg's dominance as a transshipment centre. Although ruled as unfair practice shortly after the turn of the century, such policies gave Winnipeg an initial advantage over its competitors that lasted for many years (Smith 1972; 1984a).

Coincidental with the achievement of provincial status (1905) and the fleshing out of the central place system, Alberta and Saskatchewan developed their own distinctive settlement systems. In the case of Alberta, in particular, there were key spatial transformations that accompanied

Figure 4.4
Diagrammatic representation of the evolution of the Alberta settlement system by stages in the modernization of the space economy

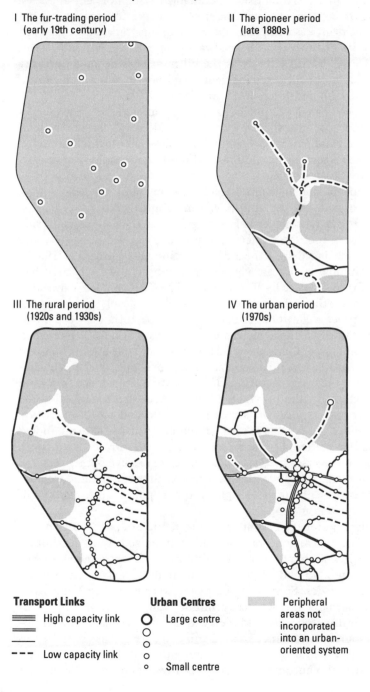

I The fur-trading period
  (early 19th century)

II The pioneer period
  (late 1880s)

III The rural period
  (1920s and 1930s)

IV The urban period
  (1970s)

Transport Links

≡≡≡ High capacity link

——— Low capacity link

Urban Centres

O Large centre

o Small centre

Peripheral areas not incorporated into an urban-oriented system economic modernization (Figure 4.4). Following the fur trade era and the initial period of farming and cattle ranching, Alberta went beyond a mere network pattern to establish a hierarchical system of central places. Moreover, as the settlement system matured, Calgary and Edmonton functioned to some degree as complementary places, illustrating the dispersed city hypothesis. The two cities have always competed against each other, but they do so now with Calgary as the oil industry's headquarters city and Edmonton as the oil-servicing centre and provincial capital (Smith 1984b; 1987; Smith and Johnson 1978; Zieber 1973).

Prior to 1961, urban development in the West suffered the consequences of a hinterland economy shaped by long distances to markets, a small regional market, and federal government policies—all of which hindered fully-diversified economic development. Cities lacked a solid manufacturing base partly because transportation costs were high, and tariff policies favoured concentration in central Canada. Even flour processing took place largely outside the region, the victim—some would say—of a discriminatory freight rate. Nevertheless, largely because of the region's rich resource base, cities of the western interior have enjoyed prosperity and expansion far beyond that of the Atlantic region (Barr and Lehr 1987).

British Columbia is also an expanding periphery, but its basic urban pattern was firmly in place by World War I. The CPR reached Vancouver in 1886, and soon thereafter a core-periphery system took shape that the urbanization process continues to reaffirm. Once Victoria was beaten out, Vancouver attained regional metropolis status by 1914, at a time when British Columbia's population was just over 50 per cent urban (McCann 1978; McDonald 1981). With a population then of about 100,000, Vancouver dominated the manufacturing, import-export, transportation, and financial functions of the province. Its hinterland stretched east to the Prairie provinces; its foreland across the Pacific and to Europe. As a sawmilling centre it was Canada's leader, but other manufacturing industries were rather limited. So was its own financial sector, for it relied on eastern banks and overseas investment for much of its development capital. In short, Vancouver was, and still is, a paradox: although it could implant its own spokes throughout the periphery, other spokes ran to the hub of the distant Canadian metropolis.

The resource periphery beyond Vancouver, Victoria, and other places in the Georgia Strait region, was also highly urbanized. With agriculture rather limited in scale but forestry and mining activities strong in possibility, most immigrants and migrants lived in dispersed, often isolated resource communities. Some of these places were linked to Vancouver, but others, especially the Kootenay mining towns, dealt mainly with Spokane in Washington state, and even with far away Calgary and Winnipeg. This resource base of incredible depth and variety has continued to support an ever-expanding regional economy that has become more and more controlled by Vancouver. Government investment in rail, road, and power networks has facilitated this situation, creating the cumulative advantages for large-scale metropolitan development. British Columbia is the 'company province', and most of its population prior to 1961 were industrial migrants from Britain who had come from an established urban background to shape another urban community. The recency of this urban experience and the dominating role of Vancouver distinguish British Columbia from other peripheral regions.

CONCLUSION

Our examination of urbanization in Canada has identified the economic and political factors that have led first to early urban settlements and then to economic regions characterized by distinct urbanization patterns. The chapter has demonstrated that nineteenth century economic conditions have favoured the emergence of a heartland containing most large cities, manufacturing enterprises, head offices, and political agencies and decision-making centres. The Great Transformation period (that ran from the 1880s to the 1920s) has further entrenched the economic and political domination of the heartland over the hinterland. The enduring nature of the heartland/hinterland dichotomy from the nineteenth century to the present is remarkable. Numerous and costly government programs that have attempted to decentralize economic development over the last thirty years have largely failed in their attempts to reduce this disparity. This persisting imbalance points to the heartland's wide range of economic advantages acquired for the most part over the nineteenth and twentieth century. These include: accessibility to a large labour pool and consumer market, extensive industrial and service linkage potentials, and good transportation links with the remainder of the country as well as with other nations.

By describing the circumstances that have led to the formation of the Canadian urban system and of its dominant heartland/hinterland feature, this chapter provides a historical background to later chapters that explore this systems' recent evolution and contemporary characteristics (Chapters 5, 7, and 8). Furthermore, its discussion of Toronto's gradual accession to the role of nation's corporate centre over the inter-war period sets the stage for these chapters' analysis of recent changes at the summit of the Canadian urban hierarchy.

FURTHER READING

CARELESS, M. 1979 'Metropolis and Region: The Interplay Between City and Region in Canadian History Before 1914' *Urban History Review* 3, 99–118

MCCANN, L.D. ed. 1987 *Heartland and Hinterland: A Geography of Canada* (Scarborough: Prentice-Hall)

NADER, G.A. 1975 *Cities of Canada: Theoretical, Historical and Planning Perspectives* (Toronto: Macmillan)

PRESTON, R.E. 1980 'Notes on the Development of the Canadian Urban Pattern' in R.E. Preston and L.H. Russwurm eds *Essays on Canadian Urban Process and Form II* Publication Series No. 15, Department of Geography, University of Waterloo

STELTER, G.A. 1990 'Introduction' in G.A. Stelter ed. *Cities and Urbanization: Canadian Historical Perspectives* (Toronto: Copp Clark Pitman)

WYNN, G. 1987 'A Region of Scattered Settlements and Bounded Possibilities: Northeastern America 1775–1800' *The Canadian Geographer* 31, 319–38

REFERENCES

ACHESON, T.W. 1972 'The National Policy and Industrialization of the Maritimes, 1880–1910', *Acadiensis* 1, 2–34

ARTIBISE, A.F.J. 1981 *Prairie Urban Development, 1870–1930* Historical Booklet No. 34, Ottawa: Canadian Historical Association

BAILYN, B. 1984 'New England and a Wider World: Notes on Some Central Themes of Modern Historiography' in D. Hall and D.G. Allen eds *Seventeenth Century New England* (Charlottesville: University of Tennessee Press)

BARR, B.M. and LEHR, J. 1987 'The Western Interior: The Transformation of a Hinterland Region' in L.D. McCann ed. *Heartland and Hinterland: A Geography of Canada* (Scarborough: Prentice-Hall)

BROWN, R.B. and COOK, R. 1974 *Canada 1896–1921: A Nation Transformed* (Toronto: McClelland and Stewart)

BRAUDEL, F. 1984 *The Perspective of the World* translated by Sian Reynolds in vol. 3 of *Civilization and Capitalism 15th–18th Century* (New York: Harper and Row)

BURGHARDT, A.F. 1971 'A Hypothesis About Gateway Cities', *Annals, Association of American Geographers* 61, 269–85

CARELESS, M. 1954 'Frontierism, Metropolitanism, and Canadian History', *The Canadian Historical Review* 35, 1–21

—— 1989 *Frontier and Metropolis: Regions, Cities, and Identities in Canada before 1914* (Toronto: University of Toronto Press)

FORBES, E. 1977 'Misguided Symmetry: The Destruction of a Regional Transportation Policy for the Maritimes' in D. Bercuson ed. *Canada and the Burden of Unity* (Toronto: Macmillan)

GOHEEN, P.G. 1986 'Communications and Urban Systems in Mid-Nineteenth Century Canada' *Urban History Review* 14, 235–45

HARRIS, R.C. 1987 'Eastern Canada in 1800' in R.C. Harris ed. *Historical Atlas of Canada* (Toronto: University of Toronto Press)

HARVEY, D. 1985 *The Urbanization of Capital* (Oxford: Basil Blackwell)

HEILBRONER, R. 1985 *The Nature and Logic of Capitalism* (New York: Norton)

HERON, C. 1989 'The Second Industrial Revolution in Canada, 1890–1930' in

D.R. Hopkin and G.S. Kealey eds *Class, Community and the Labour Movement: Wales and Canada 1850–1930* (St. John's: Canadian Committee for Labour History)

HIGGINS, B. 1986 *The Rise and Fall? of Montréal* (Moncton: Canadian Institute for Research on Regional Development)

HOHENBERG, P.M. and LEES, L.H. 1985 *The Making of Urban Europe, 1000–1950* (Cambridge, Mass.: Harvard University Press)

INNIS, Harold 1930 *The Fur Trade in Canada* (New Haven: Yale University Press)

—— 1946 *The Cod Fisheries* (New Haven: Yale University Press)

JOHNSTON, R.J. 1982 *The American Urban System* (New York: St Martin's)

KERR, D.P. 1968 'Metropolitan Dominance in Canada' in J. Warkentin ed. *Canada: A Geographical Interpretation* (Toronto: Methuen)

—— 1987 'The Emergence of the Industrial Heartland c. 1750–1850' in L.D. McCann ed. *Heartland and Hinterland: A Geography of Canada* (Scarborough: Prentice-Hall)

—— and HOLDSWORTH, D. eds 1990 *Historical Atlas of Canada* (Toronto: University of Toronto Press)

MCCANN, L.D. 1978 'Urban Growth in a Staple Economy: The Emergence of Vancouver As a Regional Metropolis, 1886–1914' in L.J. Evenden ed. *Vancouver: Western Metropolis* Western Geographical Series Volume 16 (Victoria: Department of Geography, University of Victoria)

—— 1979 'Staples and the New Industrialism in the Growth of Post-Confederation Halifax', *Acadiensis* 8, 17–79

—— 1980 'Canadian Resource Towns: A Heartland-Hinterland Perspective' in R.E. Preston and L. Russwurm eds *Essays on Canadian Urban Process and Form II* Geography Publication Series No. 15 (Waterloo: Department of Geography, University of Waterloo)

—— 1981a 'The Myth of the Metropolis: The Role of the City in Canadian Regionalism', *Urban History Review* 9, 52–8

—— 1981b 'The Mercantile-Industrial Transition in the Metals Towns of Pictou County, 1857–1931', *Acadiensis* 10, 29–64

—— 1983 'Metropolitanism and Branch Businesses in the Maritimes, 1881–1931', *Acadiensis* 12, 111–25

—— ed. 1987a *Heartland and Hinterland: A Geography of Canada* (Scarborough: Prentice-Hall)

—— 1987b 'Heartland and Hinterland: A Framework for Regional Analysis' in L.D. McCann ed. *Heartland and Hinterland: A Geography of Canada* (Scarborough: Prentice-Hall)

—— 1988 'Living a Double Life: Town and Country in the Industrialization of the Maritimes' in D. Day ed. *Geographical Perspectives on the Maritime Provinces* (Halifax: St Mary's University)

—— 1989 'Metropolitan Dominance in the Emerging Canadian Urban System, 1867–1931' Unpublished paper, Centre for Canadian Studies, Mount Allison University, Sackville, New Brunswick

MCDONALD, R.A.J. 1981 'Victoria, Vancouver and the Evolution of British Columbia's Economic System, 1886–1914' in A.F.J. Artibise ed. *Town and City: Aspects of Western Canadian Urban Development* (Regina: Canadian Plains Resource Centre)

NADER, G.A. 1975 *Cities of Canada: Theoretical, Historical and Planning Perspectives* (Toronto: Macmillan)

PRESTON, R.E. 1980 'Notes on the Development of the Canadian Urban Pattern' in R.E. Preston and L.H. Russwurm eds *Essays on Canadian Urban Process and Form II* Publication Series No. 15, Department of Geography, University of Waterloo

RAY, D.M. 1974 *The Urban Challenge of Growth and Change* (Ottawa: Ministry of State for Urban Affairs)

ROBINSON, I. 1962 *New Industrial Towns on Canada's Resource Frontier* Research Paper No. 73 (Chicago: Department of Geography, University of Chicago)

ROBSON, R. 1986 *Canadian Single Industry Communities: A Literature Review and Annotated Bibliography* Rural and Small Town Research and Studies Programme, Mount Allison University, Sackville, New Brunswick

SEMPLE, R.K. and SMITH, W.R. 1981 'Metropolitan Dominance and Foreign Ownership in the Canadian Urban System', *The Canadian Geographer* 25, 4–26

SMITH, P.J. 1972 'Changing Forms and Patterns in the Cities' in P.J. Smith ed. *The Prairie Provinces* (Toronto: University of Toronto Press)

────── 1984a 'Urban Development Trends in the Prairie Provinces' in A.W. Rasporich ed. *The Making of the Modern West: Western Canada Since 1945* (Calgary: University of Calgary Press)

────── 1984b 'The Changing Structure of the Settlement System' in B.M. Barr and P.J. Smith eds *Environment and Economy: Essays on the Human Geography of Alberta* (Edmonton: Pica Pica Press)

────── and JOHNSON, D.B. 1978 *The Edmonton-Calgary Corridor* (Edmonton: University of Alberta)

SPELT, J. 1972 *Urban Development in South-Central Ontario* (Toronto: McClelland and Stewart)

STELTER, G.A. 1974 'Community Development in Toronto's Commercial Empire: The Industrial Towns of the Nickel Belt, 1883–1931', *Laurentian University Review* 6, 3–54

────── 1983 'The Political Economy of the City-Building Process: Early Canadian Urban Development' in T. Sutcliff ed. *The Pursuit of Urban History* (London: Edward Arnold)

────── 1990 'Introduction' in G.A. Stelter ed. *Cities and Urbanization: Canadian Historical Perspectives* (Toronto: Copp Clark Pitman)

STONE, L. 1967 *Urban Development in Canada* (Ottawa: Dominion Bureau of Statistics)

TULCHINSKY, G. 1977 *The River Barons: Montreal Businessmen and the Growth of Industry and Transportation, 1837–53* (Montreal: McGill-Queen's University Press)

VANCE, J. 1970 *The Merchant's World: The Geography of Wholesaling* (New York: Prentice-Hall)

VOISEY, P. 1975 'The Urbanization of the Canadian Prairies 1871–1916', *Histoire sociale/Social History* 15, 77–101

WALLERSTEIN, I. 1974 *The Modern World System* (New York: Academic Press)

WHEBELL, C.F.J. 1969 'Corridors: A Theory of Urban Systems', *Annals, Association of American Geographers* 59, 1–26

WILLIAMS, G. 1983 *Not for Export: Towards a Political Economy of Canada's Arrested Industrialization* (Toronto: McLelland and Stewart)

WYNN, G. 1987a 'Maritime Canada, Late 18th Century' in R.C. Harris ed. *Historical Atlas of Canada* Plate 32 (Toronto: University of Toronto Press)

―――― 1987b 'A Region of Scattered Settlements and Bounded Possibilities: Northeastern America 1775–1800', *The Canadian Geographer* 31, 319–38

ZIEBER, G.H. 1973 'The Dispersed City Hypothesis with Reference to Calgary and Edmonton', *The Albertan Geographer* 9, 4–13

5

The Urban System

JIM SIMMONS

Urban places are something more than places to live, work, and shop. They provide a home for institutions and activities that, when linked together into an urban system, integrate and co-ordinate the development of different regions of the country. Thus, in addition to the economic and demographic concentrations that we call cities, the urban system includes the flows of information, goods, capital, and migrants that tie these places together, as well as the processes by which an event in one location is transformed into growth or decline at another place. This chapter describes the main features of the Canadian urban system, beginning with a description of the economic and social variations among the cities themselves, and the major linkages that integrate the system. The latter portions of the chapter turn to the processes of change, in order to understand how the Canadian urban system evolves over time. A particular problem for this turbulent space economy is the maintenance of stable growth within a 'boom and bust' environment.

THE URBAN SYSTEM IN CANADA

The Importance of the Urban System
No matter how we define the urban system, it dominates the Canadian economy and society. For the purpose of this chapter the urban system

consists of the 140 or so urban places with more than 10,000 people. These places are mapped in Figure 5.1, and are listed in Appendix 2. Table 5.1 shows the relative importance of cities in different size ranges and Table 5.2 shows the regional distribution of cities within these ranges. Urban nodes collectively occupy only 3 per cent of the Canadian land mass, but include 76 per cent of the population and 80 per cent of the economic

Table 5.1
Cities by Population, Size, and Income, 1986

	Population	(%)	Area (km²)	(%)	Income ($ m)	(%)	Income per capita
Largest 25 cities	15,155,000	(59.9)	71,104	(0.8)	204,990	(66.5)	13,500
Next 25 cities	1,872,000	(7.3)	24,753	(0.3)	19,318	(6.3)	10,300
Next 50 cities	1,658,000	(6.6)	197,153	(2.1)	18,148	(5.9)	10,900
Largest 100 cities	18,685,000	(73.8)	293,010	(3.2)	242,456	(78.7)	13,000
Rest of Canada	6,624,000	(26.2)	8,927,965	(96.8)	65,609	(21.3)	9,900
Canada	25,309,000	(100)	9,220,974	(100)	308,065	(100)	12,200

SOURCE: Statistics Canada, *Census of Canada, 1986.* Catalogue 94–127, 94–128.

Table 5.2
Hierarchical and Regional Variations in Urban Characteristics

Number of Urban Places

Size category	Region or province					
	British Columbia and Territories	Prairies	Ontario	Quebec	Atlantic	Total
Over 1 million	1	0	1	1	0	3
300,000—1 million	0	3	5	1	0	9
100,000—299,999	1	2	5	3	5	16
30,000— 99,999	10	7	14	14	6	51
10,000— 29,999	13	10	17	13	7	60
Total	25	22	42	32	18	139

Urban Population (000)

Size category	Region or province					
Over 1 million	1,381	—	3,427	2,921	—	7,729
300,000—1 million	—	2,081	2,375	603	—	5,059
100,000—299,999	256	388	851	417	800	2,712
30,000— 99,999	571	329	892	626	270	2,688
10,000— 29,999	239	157	277	236	117	1,026
Total	2,447	2,955	7,822	4,803	1,187	19,214

Average income per capita ($ 1985)

Size category	Region or province					
Over 1 million	13,900	—	15,100	12,600	—	14,200
300,000—1 million	—	13,700	13,600	12,000	—	13,101
100,000—299,999	13,100	12,800	12,800	10,600	11,000	12,000
30,000— 99,999	11,100	12,200	12,100	10,400	10,200	11,300
10,000— 29,999	11,800	11,800	11,800	10,000	9,200	11,100
Total	13,000	13,300	13,900	11,900	10,700	13,000

SOURCE: Statistics Canada, *Census of Canada, 1986.*

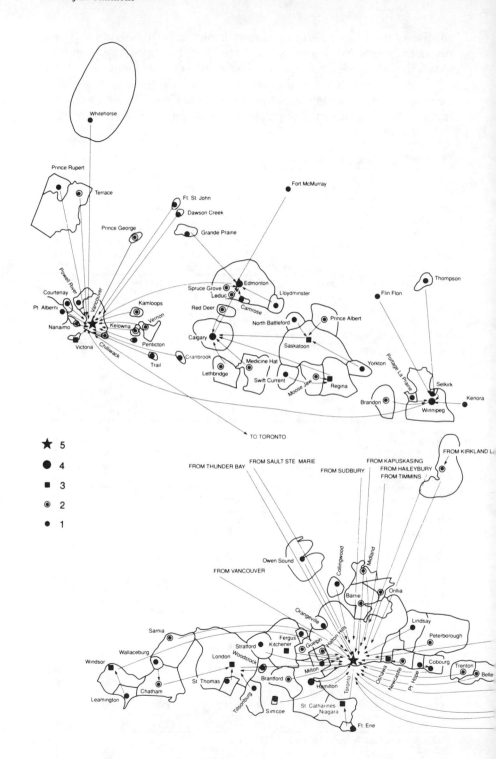

**Figure 5.1
Distribution of Canadian Cities by Size, 1986**

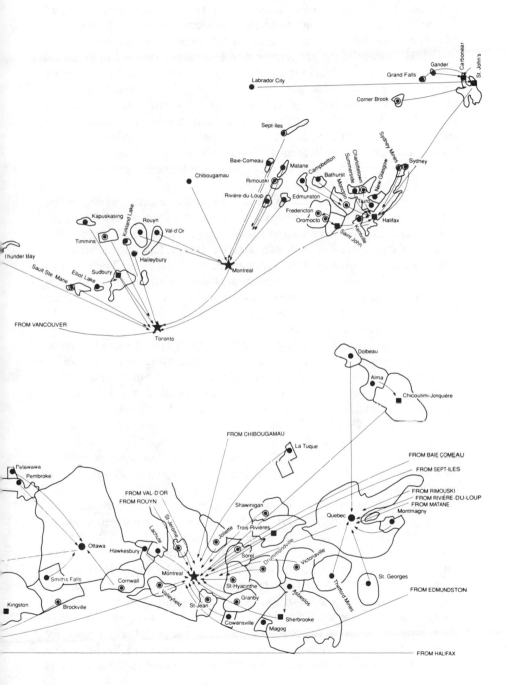

activity (here defined as income). For most practical purposes the urban system *is* Canada. The relationships among cities define the major geographical regions of the country.

In Canada, the concept of an urban place is a statistical artifact developed by Statistics Canada. In most provinces, municipal units are a hodgepodge of archaic boundaries and political convenience that woefully underbound our usual concept of the geographic city. In order to provide more useful and consistent measures of urban activity, Statistics Canada has developed the concept of the census agglomeration (CA): an urbanized core of at least 10,000 persons, together with adjacent urban and rural areas which have a high degree of economic and social integration with that core. If the urbanized core includes over 100,000 persons, the agglomeration is called a census metropolitan area (CMA). The procedures currently used by Statistics Canada to define various levels of settlement types are summarized in Appendix 1.

No matter how the definitions are laid down, the results are roughly the same: the same set of urban nodes that include 65 per cent to 80 per cent of the population and economic activity emerge. This stability reflects the enormous concentration of urban activity into a few large centres—a fundamental property of urban systems in every country. Toronto and Montreal include one-quarter of the population of Canada; the ten largest cities include almost half. In measures of social or economic activity, what happens around the edges of these places or at the lower end of the urban hierarchy matters rather little.

Even the non-urban parts of the country are strongly affected by activities in the urban nodes. Figure 5.1 shows that most of the Canadian ecumene (that is, the settled portions of the country) can be allocated to the service area, or hinterland, of one urban node or another. In this example the hinterlands of urban areas are defined by the isoline of 20 per cent migration. Within this boundary line, more than 20 per cent of all out-migrants from each census subdivision relocate into the census agglomeration at some time in their lives, often in their later years. One would find similar urban-hinterland delineations based on shopping trips or mail flows.

Unlike some other countries, where settlement occurs more regularly in space, Canadian urban activity occurs at three different geographical scales. First, beyond the limits of the ecumene (which excludes 85 per cent of Canada's land area) there is virtually no urbanization. The urban settlements in that part of the country are marginal by any definition. The ecumene itself can be divided into two subregions with different settlement densities. In the core region in southern Ontario and Quebec (the Windsor-Quebec Corridor of Chapter 8) there are 52 cities, one for every 3,400 km². In the rest of the ecumene, known as the periphery, the density of cities drops to one-quarter, with one city for every 13,200 km². The service areas of urban places in the periphery are larger in area, with less competition among nodes. As we will see later in this chapter, the core and periphery differ fundamentally in economic function and growth processes.

The other important feature shown on Figure 5.1 is the network that links together the cities of the urban system. These lines can be derived from a variety of other sources, for example, telephone calls, airline trips, or freight flows. They represent the routes by which money, information, people, or growth impulses move easily through the system. But in an urban system where there are such enormous differences in size of node and distance between nodes, the pattern of linkages is roughly hierarchical. Typically, the strongest link from each city goes to the nearest largest place: Sydney to Halifax, Halifax to Toronto, and so forth. This network traces the linkages of the distribution system: goods flow from Toronto to Halifax to Sydney, tying together the service areas of individual urban nodes into a series of larger and larger trade areas. Ultimately, Toronto serves all of Ontario and much of the rest of the country as well as its immediate hinterland. The growth of this high-order centre will depend on the growth of all the places that it serves.

The Emergence of the Urban System

Although Canadian myths stress the frontier, the North, or agricultural settlement, the urban system has always played a central role in the settlement and development of the country, as shown in the previous chapter. Canada was settled late and largely bypassed the development stage of subsistence agriculture, although the economy of natives and smaller early European settlements was of a subsistence nature. From the time of European settlement, rural areas produced staple products—cod, beaver, wheat, lumber, minerals—and the production was organized and marketed through the networks of the urban system. The nation began at the urban nodes—St. John's, Quebec, Montreal, Halifax, Victoria—and then settled the surrounding hinterlands. Only in the final stage of development were hierarchical regional systems linked together into a national urban system.

A map of the Canadian urban system of a century ago based on railway flows (*Historical Atlas of Canada*, Vol. III, Plate 10) describes a much more fragmented urban system than the one we know today. Much of the West is simply blank. Newfoundland is independent. The Maritime Provinces are tenuously linked to central Canada by one railway line, the Intercolonial. Only southern Ontario and southern Quebec display any degree of interaction among urban places as measured in terms of rail traffic. Even so, many towns and villages are still essentially unconnected from the rest of the nation. The great urban concentrations that now polarize the rest of the nation were then quite weak: Montreal had 250,000 people; Toronto 180,000; Vancouver did not exist. As production nodes or markets, these current metropolitan giants affected only a few nearby centres.

By 1921, a national urban system had emerged. An enormous investment in railways and roads linked each community into the national market. National banks, wholesalers, and retail chains distributed goods and money throughout the country. And the main urban centres had begun to take their places within the urban hierarchy: Montreal (700,000); Toronto (600,000) and Vancouver (200,000). But, in many ways, the country was still a set of separate economies and life-styles. While tariffs on imported consumer goods forced people in all parts of the country to buy the goods manufactured in central Canada, the peripheral regions still produced primary products for export. Because communities in Nova Scotia or British Columbia produced only one or two commodities, with price that varied dramatically over time, these economies suffered dramatic booms and busts. Thus, although central Canada was integrated with markets in the rest of the country, the rest of the country was still not integrated with central Canada.

Since the 1960s, the degree of integration has progressed considerably, as will be shown in later sections of this paper. Massive inter-regional flows of funds from various programs help to even out the level of consumption across the country, as for example when the wealth of Alberta and Ontario flows eastward to Newfoundland (mediated, of course, by the federal government). The dependence of peripheral communities on world markets is offset by the compensating links to the national or provincial capital. National institutions have further expanded—in finance, transportation, communications, distribution systems, cultural agencies, unions, and corporations of all kinds. The tension between regional and national institutions is now giving way to the competition between national and international institutions.

While the concentration of population and economic activity in urban nodes is readily visible, it is more difficult to demonstrate the flows of information, money, and goods that support the concentrations and shape the structure of spatial systems around regional, national, or international centres. That is the challenge in the rest of the paper: to fill out the structure and meaning of the linkages sketched out here.

STRUCTURE AND ORGANIZATION

Geographers are interested in the way that the spatial pattern of urban characteristics reflects and is reflected in the way the urban system operates, thus in the day-to-day processes (such as economic transactions and political decisions) that support, reproduce and modify the Canadian way of life. This section examines three aspects of the urban system in cross-section, beginning with the *space-economy* (that is, the spatial dimension of the Canadian economy). We have observed that the Canadian economy is relatively open. Our rate of growth is determined by events in markets outside our boundaries. Most Canadian cities are highly specialized in the production of one or two commodities. As a result, urban growth tends to follow the traditional economic or export-base model.[1] A signal from the world economy affects a subset of Canadian urban economies, which then transmit these growth impulses to nearby centres. The demography of cities responds appropriately, generating or attracting migrants to match the economic change, but always lagging behind because of the inherent conservatism of demographic processes. In Canada, the political system fills the gap between the economic impulses and the demographic responses by transferring income among locations. This transference takes place within the constraints imposed by the spatial structure of political units and the constitutional responsibilities assigned to different levels in the political hierarchy. Unemployment benefits, health care, education, pensions, and family allowances are part of this income-transferring process.

Finally, this section will explore the pattern of linkages among cities, and what these linkages mean for the urban system. The most intense linkages in the production system are not the same as those of the demographic system. The fact that growth-signals from the economy trace different routes than demographic responses has significant implications for policy decisions.

Economic Specialization

The economic base of most Canadian cities is intensely specialized in two or three commodities, and often these cities' options in terms of alternative economic activities are limited. Vancouver depends on forest products; Calgary on oil and gas; Winnipeg on prairie grain. Figure 5.2 shows the pattern of economic specialization in 1981.[2] The most striking feature of Figure 5.2 is the concentration of manufacturing activity in the Windsor-Quebec corridor. The heartland-periphery pattern this produces is now considered to be a primary feature of Canadian geography (see for example, McCann 1987, and Chapter 8 in this text). Despite the efforts of policy-makers for generations, the pattern of spatial economic specialization has intensified: the rest of the country harvests and processes primary products, usually for export. With the exception of automobile production (sold largely to the US), most Canadian manufacturing output is consumed in Canada. As soon as the tariff boundary was drawn over a century ago to define the Canadian market, the location advantages of central Canada became overwhelming. And as manufacturing activity stimulated the growth of cities in the corridor, the national market itself became more and more centred in this area.

For the most part, smaller cities in the rest of the country produce one or two primary products—from mineral and wood products in the North to farm products, oil, and gas in the West. There are no substitutes, so that when the resource runs out or the price drops below the cost of production, the community dies. The periphery is full of ghost towns or

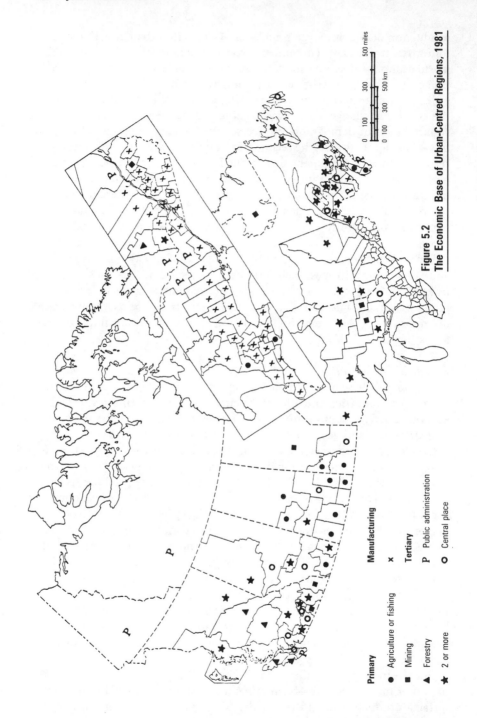

Figure 5.2
The Economic Base of Urban-Centred Regions, 1981

Primary

● Agriculture or fishing

■ Mining

▲ Forestry

★ 2 or more

Manufacturing

✗

Tertiary

P Public administration

O Central place

potential ghost towns from the Klondike area to Elliot Lake or Labrador City. Larger cities in the periphery—the regional centres like Winnipeg or St. John's—survive and grow because they serve the economies of several different urban regions with varying economic bases. They grow as the whole province grows.

In both the corridor, with its manufacturing towns, and the periphery, with its resource centres, the smaller places are linked together by the hierarchical network of service and administrative centres that provide trade and service activities as well as public administration and transportation (see Chapter 7). Many places that specialize in services have prospered because of the steady expansion of these labour-intensive activities at the expense of industries that produce goods, but the advantage is partly offset by the shift of many service activities down the urban hierarchy. Thus, instead of importing wholesale or medical services from Toronto or Regina, smaller places now provide these themselves. The increasing use of telecommunications facilitates this type of decentralization, as is shown in the following chapter.

The dramatic differences in the economies of different regions and cities result in equally dramatic differences in the per-capita-income levels of different places (Table 5.2 and Appendix 3, column 11). The patterns are not necessarily predictable; cities in the periphery share both the highest (Fort McMurray) and the lowest (Carbonear) income levels across the country. It depends in what primary sector, hence in what region— given regions' specialization in specific sectors—the boom (which makes cities rich) or bust (which makes them poor) is taking place. These income levels are only partly the result of the local economy. They also include the various public-sector income sources that reduce place-to-place and region-to-region variations. The most regular pattern is the consistently higher income earned by residents of large cities, a reflection of scale economies: that is, the savings in production costs achieved at these locations by large-scale operations.

Demographic Processes
The basic demographic facts of age and sex show little variation from one urban region to another (Simmons 1980). Much more interesting are the city-to-city differences in population growth, and especially in the sources of population growth. Urban population grows in three ways in Canada: by natural increase, or births minus deaths; by net internal migration from other places in Canada, or in-migrants minus out-migrants; and by net international migration. Each process displays a different spatial pattern, and these spatial patterns shift over time. From 1976 to 1981 there was an extraordinary concentration of growth in Alberta. In the next five years, the growth shifted back to central Canada.

Natural increase is largely dependent on the age structure of the parent population. As such, it is relatively regular in space and quite stable over time (at least since the end of the baby boom in the late 1960s). Three kinds of spatial variation are visible, however: first, differences in rural and urban life-styles show up as higher rates of natural increase in smaller places. Second, natural increase is also higher in places that have high rates of net in-migration, because the latter process shifts the age structure towards fertile age groups. Finally, there is a low rate of natural increase in Victoria, Canada's leading retirement centre.

Net internal migration is responsible for most of the inter-regional variance in population growth, and for most of the temporal variation as well. Some places—for instance, Alberta and British Columbia in the late 1970s—gain; while others—the Atlantic Provinces and Quebec—lose. Much of this variation can be associated with the growth rate of the local economy, particularly the rate of job creation. Over the last two decades, the direction of net migration—in- or out-—has reversed at least once for every province. Persistent in- or out-migration alters the demographic structure, and in turns affects natural increase, as we saw above. With respect to city size, net internal migration is neutral because cities of all sizes are found in both slow-growth and high-growth regions.

The overall level of net international migration depends on the federal government's immigration policy, but the spatial distribution is linked to the pattern of economic growth, with the added constraint that certain regions with strong ethnic-group institutions have an advantage. This benefits large cities like Vancouver and Toronto. Francophone Quebec and the Maritime Provinces have little recent history of immigration, hence few prospects for rapid growth in population in the future. In general, an increased contribution of immigration to Canada's growth means that larger cities grow more rapidly.

It should be emphasized that there is a powerful interdependence between the patterns of economic change and the levels of internal and international migration. Much of Canada still grows in booms and busts, with rapid increases and decreases in the amount of labour required in different regions, so we need the capacity to move workers quickly from one location to another. In the past, this requirement has often overtaxed the migration system: about 400,000 Canadians move from one province to another each year, with a net interprovincial migration of 50,000 to 90,000. If the space-economy changes more rapidly than this, so that the net interprovincial shift of jobs requires more movement, traditionally we have looked outside the country—importing workers from abroad for the growing regions, while losing workers to the US from the declining regions. Now both of these external linkages have been restricted. The United States government has made entry to the US more difficult, and Canada has restrictive immigration policies. This means we must either slow down the rate of spatial restructuring of the economy, or we must accelerate the level of internal migration.

Linguistic differences complicate the problem. Francophones are largely concentrated in the Province of Quebec and adjoining parts of Ontario and New Brunswick. Francophones and anglophones tend to move within their language group; relatively few cross the boundary. This suggests a need to keep each labour market—anglophone and franco-phone—separately in balance. Surplus workers in Quebec City are unlikely to respond to a job surplus in Edmonton, and vice versa.

The Public Sector

Governments in Canada have come to play an important intermediate role between the rapidly changing economic geography conditions and the much-slower-to-respond demography. But not all governments: in the issues that we discuss here, municipal governments are largely irrelevant. A metropolitan region will have several municipal governments, often pulling in different directions; and, even if these governments were united, there is no evidence that they could influence the level or direction of economic or demographic development. Urban growth responds to signals from the urban system outside the urban region, and the urban system is managed by higher levels of government namely the provincial and federal agencies.[3]

The provinces control many aspects of the hierarchical relationship between the metropolitan regions and smaller centres. They build roads and other infrastructure that shape accessibility and favour one city rather than another. Provincial governments locate court-houses, hospitals, and universities, all of which bring large numbers of jobs. In addition, they redistribute large sums of public funds down the urban hierarchy from the big cities to small towns and rural areas. The money comes from taxes paid by urban workers, or perhaps from the federal government, and is spent on roads, schools and hospitals throughout the province. These public services flow to all citizens, in all locations—rich or poor, growing or declining.

So sizable have these expenditures become, and so diverse the levels and nature of expenditures among provinces, that provincial boundaries have become the most significant geographical features in the country (Simmons 1984). When you cross a provincial boundary you may find that tax structures, spending priorities, language, and liquor laws have changed. The enormous revenues that came from oil and gas production in the West accentuated these variations. For a while, in the 1970s, it was worth several thousands of dollars a year to live in Alberta rather than across the border in Saskatchewan. The effect of provincial financing on municipal economies shows up in two ways. Although income taxes are largely determined by income level, provincial governments contribute to regional variations. Quebec, for instance, has a much larger public sector than Ontario; this shows up both in higher taxes and higher public employment. Alberta's oil and gas revenues permit the province to impose taxes that are low relative to the income level.

It is the task of the federal government to carry out the redistribution of funds among the regional subsystems of the urban hierarchy, for example, between urban regions centred on Calgary and places served by Halifax. It does so in four ways. First, on the taxation side, it collects personal and corporate taxes at a higher rate in rich and growing communities: the higher the income, the higher the tax bracket. Second, it redistributes money among the provinces as equalization payments according to a complex formula designed to make the per-capita-tax base of each province the same. This affects the income available to government employees, and the number of employees each province can have. Third, it redistributes large sums of money in transfer payments to individuals on the basis of their unemployment (the inverse of local economic activity) and demographic status (e.g. pensions and family allowances). This is the major source of income redistribution between regions. High unemployment regions with an ageing population or with above-average proportions of children in the population benefit the most from transfer payments. Finally, the government spends money, collected elsewhere, on government employment to provide a variety of human services and administer its own operations. The effect of these expenditures is most notable in the national and provincial capitals, but in other locations tends to reflect the demand for services, again a reflection of the local demography.

The net effect of all this government activity is to cause the income map to match the population map; it results in a significant alleviation of the place-to-place, region-to-region variation in earned income. Whereas private-sector-earned income ranges from plus or minus 50 per cent of the national average, income adjusted by government activity and transfers varies much less widely—less than half of that. In some small communities in the periphery, when the local economy is having a bad year, the level of government expenditures, especially unemployment benefits, replaces the economic base, maintaining the level of services in both private and public sectors.

Interdependence

It is possible to produce an atlas of maps that differentiate the cities of the urban system. To the basic elements of economy, demography, and public sector-activity we could add maps of life-style, illness, education, or religion. An infinite set of maps could be drawn to represent the ways Canadian cities are linked together: mail flows, money flows, movements of goods by road or rail, etc. Figure 5.1 showed the most important linkage for each city in the urban system—the place to which it is most closely tied. The volume of flows throughout the system as a whole could also be mapped. Such a map would show that the volume of movement among urban nodes is concentrated in a small number of routes.

A small number of nodes account for the bulk of Canadian urban activity. The interaction between locations has been shown again and again to be related to the size of the nodes at either end of the route, and inversely to the distance between the nodes. Not surprisingly then, the greatest flows occur between Toronto and Montreal, the largest nodes, which are, by Canadian standards, relatively close together. A map of the largest flows would show the 'Main Street' effect that links the largest regional centres across the country: Halifax, Toronto, Montreal, Ottawa, Winnipeg, Calgary, Edmonton, and Vancouver. These flows tie the various regions of the country into a national urban system; they are consistently stronger than the connections southward to cities in the United States. And maps of economic links show that Ontario and Quebec as the two major concentrations of manufacturing and financial activity in the country, are strongly linked economically.

THE DYNAMICS

Embedded in the structure of the urban system is a logic that describes how the system must evolve over time. In this open spatial system, in which most cities depend on the fortunes of one or two economic sectors, the location of urban growth is determined outside Canada by world commodity markets and by the relative effectiveness of resource producers that compete with Canada. Economic change, often encompassing violent shocks in commodity prices and in the level of economic activity in a community, is felt most directly in the small cities of the periphery. Agricultural income, for example, may change as much as 30 per cent in one year.

These shocks are gradually moderated as the impulses of growth or decline are transmitted through the network of linkages. These transmit commodities to market, act as the distribution system for consumer products, or provide public services. In a variety of ways the urban system seeks stability resisting and modifying the external pressures for change in the system. Nonetheless, ultimately the system must respond, as certain cities and certain regions grow faster than others, leading in turn to a reorganization of the spatial system by the creation of new spatial linkages. If the Alberta economy grows faster than the Manitoba economy, Calgary begins to take over Winnipeg's service role; first by expanding its own trade area into Saskatchewan, and ultimately stealing all of Winnipeg's high-order service activities.

Indeed, as Figure 5.3 suggests, the urban system has changed dramatically over the last fifteen years. For Canada as a whole, the population growth is 17.3 per cent, but for particular urban regions, growth is as high as 78 per cent (Kelowna) and as low as minus 13 per cent (Kirkland Lake) which means a 13 per cent decline in population. The cumulative pattern over this time period shifts the national economy westward to Alberta and

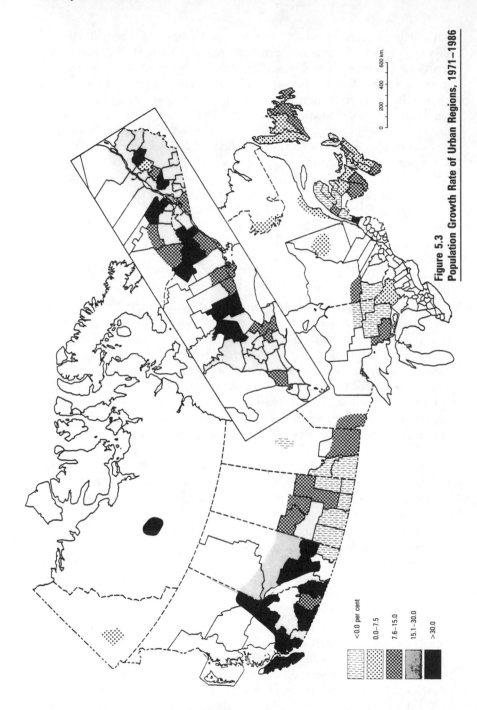

Figure 5.3
Population Growth Rate of Urban Regions, 1971–1986

<0.0 per cent

0.0–7.5

7.6–15.0

15.1–30.0

>30.0

0   200   400   600 km.

British Columbia, and away from the Atlantic Provinces and Quebec. Ontario resists the change, by virtue of its control of the national market. In manufacturing, distribution, and public activity Ontario serves the urban system as a whole, growing as the system grows, or slightly faster.

The Variability of Urban Growth

The fundamental problem in Canadian regional policy is not the disparity in incomes (as shown in Table 5.2), nor the associated pattern of urban growth (Figure 5.3), but the differences in the degree of variability in urban growth rates, shown in Table 5.3. The most volatile local economies are those that lie in the front line of the growth process. They are the smallest centres in the primary producing regions—grain-growing centres like Brandon, or mining towns like Timmins or Fort McMurray. Even if, like agricultural communities, these centres are able to retain employment and population in the presence of drought or steep declines in farm prices, they often suffer striking changes in the standard of living, as shown in Figure 5.4. From one year to the next, such places may have to deal with a growth or decline of up to 20 per cent in real income.

The problem is less severe in central Canada, which largely produces goods for the Canadian market rather than for export (the major exception is the automobile industry). The demand for these products depends on the aggregate growth of the Canadian market (up to 4 per cent per year), a growth that is managed, so far as is possible, by the actions of the federal government. The growth of the largest cities in the urban system is much more regular than the growth of smaller places. Big cities serve extensive trade areas, which average out the fortunes of several different economic

Table 5.3
Hierarchical and Regional Variations in Urban Growth

Average Urban Growth Rate for CMAs and CAs (1981–1986)

Size category	British Columbia and Territories	Prairies	Ontario	Quebec	Atlantic	Total
Over 300,000	8.9	6.3	5.9	1.0	—	5.4
100,000—299,999	5.8	11.2	2.5	2.3	2.5	3.8
30,000— 99,999	3.8	8.0	2.6	0.9	1.7	3.0
10,000— 29,999	−3.7	3.8	0.1	−1.4	−3.6	−0.9

Standard Deviation of Urban Growth Rates

Size category		Region or province				
Over 300,000	—	0.9	4.0	3.3	—	3.7
100,000—299,999	—	4.9	5.4	1.9	3.7	4.8
30,000— 99,999	5.8	5.2	3.6	0.9	3.4	4.4
10,000— 29,999	5.2	6.0	3.3	6.0	9.0	6.0

SOURCE: Statistics Canada, *Census of Canada, 1986.*

Figure 5.4
Income Variability in Canadian Cities (1961-1986)

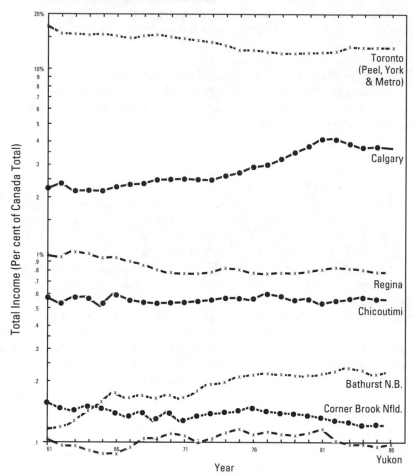

sectors. So, as we see in Figure 5.4, relative to Canada as a whole, Toronto's income curve remains stable. Corner Brook's income is erratic—even after the corrective actions of government programs. Most cities in the periphery are subject to sudden drops or surges in growth.

Openness
The overall growth rate of a spatial system and the variability of growth in time and space are the result of the openness of the system boundaries. Just as banks weigh the risk of extending a loan against the rate of return, so countries must balance policies favouring economic sectors that promote growth against such sectors' instability or vulnerability. Closed spatial systems cannot grow more rapidly than the rate of reproduction of

the labour force, or the rate of savings and investment within the society. Both of these growth processes are spatially conservative, tending to create growth in the same spatial pattern as the existing urban system. In an open system, in contrast, natural increase can be augmented by net immigration or undermined by emigration; and these latter processes, as we have seen, show much greater variability in space and time. First, spatial systems that are open to international trade and investment are more likely to demonstrate spatial specialization. What would farmers grow on the Prairies if grain could not be exported? Second, such systems have the potential for much greater swings between periods of growth and decline, reflecting the exaggerated fluctuations of world commodity prices and competition. In combination, these two conditions generate great uncertainty in the growth of many Canadian cities.

The openness of the Canadian economic system is displayed in Figure 5.5. In spite of wide annual variations in growth rates, the overall level of Canadian exports has remained relatively constant, ranging from 13 per cent to over 20 per cent of the gross national product (GNP) since 1951. Since that year, the composition of exports has varied dramatically, however. First agricultural products led the way; these were followed by mining products and energy, and more recently automobiles and forest products. Changes in each export sector affected certain regions of the country disproportionately. Specialization in these export activities imparts an extraordinary amount of economic variation into the Canadian urban system. The Economic Council of Canada, for example, has calculated that two-thirds of Saskatchewan's income variation can be traced to the uncertainty of farm incomes (Jobin 1984). For Canada as a whole, the temporal variation in farm income—mostly from prairie grain-growing— is responsible for one-third to one-half of the year-to-year fluctuations in income.

The demographic numbers are just as sensitive to the openness of the urban system. While the level of natural increase has remained relatively constant since 1970, the rate of net immigration has varied with the growth of the economy. And just like the effect of exports, levels of immigration and the uneven distribution of immigrants within the urban system will affect the spatial structure of population growth.

The map of economic growth changes quickly from year to year, and significantly over a five-year period. A small city can gain or lose 10 per cent of its work-force in a few months. Early in 1990, Canso, Nova Scotia, was estimated to have lost considerably more of its workforce as a result of the closure of the local fish-packing plant. Population growth processes are much slower: it is difficult to gain or lose more than 3 per cent or 4 per cent of population in a year. The map of population growth in any census period is strongly correlated with the pattern from the previous period. And, as we have seen in earlier sections, the spatial processes that generate economic and demographic change are only loosely related. How

Figure 5.5
Openness of the Canadian Urban System

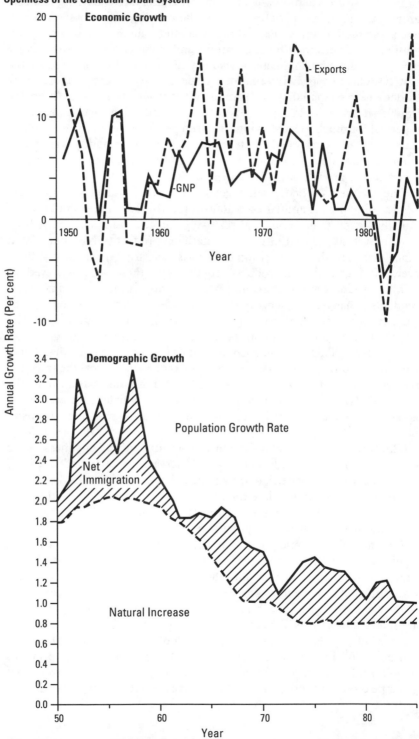

then, do we keep the number of workers and population roughly in proportion to the number of jobs in all these different locations? Historically, a variety of mechanisms have operated. In pre-history, tribal starvation or invasion was common; in the period of European settlement, immigrants flowed easily in and out of the country, filling jobs in 'boom' locations, and abandoning 'bust' locations to go to the United States. In Canada's first century, 5 million people arrived, and almost as many left (Leacy 1983). More recently, government policy has intervened, trying to weaken the close relationship between economic growth and income by transferring funds and creating jobs where there are surpluses in the labour force, in the expectation that sooner or later the resource economy will rejuvenate the regional economy.

Stabilization
The Canadian economy depends on exports. The export economy requires spatial specialization in production. Canada's investments in transportation and communications, and our long-standing barriers to the import of manufactured goods, have encouraged this pattern. This spatial economic specialization leads to substantial variability in urban growth rates across the country. Variations in urban growth, in turn, lead to social problems such as unemployment, inadequate local support for health care, education and other public services, and out-migration. It is not the fault of a miner in Glace Bay that his job disappears; and if he is over forty years of age there is not much point in moving him to some other employment location. But if the economy as a whole is to succeed—that is, to benefit from the productivity of economic specialization—then it must pay the inevitable costs. As a result, the Canadian urban system has developed an elaborate set of mechanisms that spatially redistribute income and public services to mitigate the impact of economic uncertainty.

The importance of these mechanisms depends on the size of the public economy. The three levels of government in Canada collectively spent $221 billion in 1986, equal to 43 per cent of the GNP. Most of that expenditure stabilized the space economy in some fashion, either by simply slowing down the rate of spatial change in the economy, or by actively redistributing funds from one location to another to resist the direction of change in the private sector. The variety of mechanisms, calculated for 1976, is shown in Table 5.4. The index of redistribution shows how much the map of income across the country changed as a result of each program. The correlation coefficient (r) indicates whether the program alleviates (r positive) or exacerbates (r negative) the problem of regional disparity in income per capita.

In terms of magnitude of impact, the income paid to government employees, especially federal and provincial, is most important (the capital-city effect), but with relatively little effect on income per capita. The latter is most sensitive to federal income tax and transfer payments, espe-

Table 5.4
The Mechanisms of Income Stabilization, 1976

		Index of redistribution		Correlation (r) with income per capita	
Indices of Spatial Redistribution	Value of program (millions of	Income base			
Program	dollars)	(millions of dollars)	Population base	Income base	Population base
Federal income tax	14,541	510	1,636	0.779	0.972
Provincial income tax	5,852	489	594	−0.225	0.688
Total income tax	20,393	629	2,073	0.526	0.957
Family allowances	1,758	193	88	−0.854	−0.057
Net unemployment benefits	2,009	728	616	−0.692	−0.595
Old-age pensions	1,978	306	387	−0.050	0.261
Net CPP/QPP	−229	85	88	0.083	−0.096
Total transfers	5,516	977	623	−0.782	−0.509
Federal employment	4,542	1,541	1,466	0.042	0.213
Provincial employment	6,159	1,513	1,363	−0.214	0.129
Municipal employment	5,659	455	648	0.055	0.574
Total employment	13,360	2,367	2,421	−0.095	0.365
Net benefits	1,483	3,517	3,426	−0.543	−0.370

$$\text{Index } j = \frac{1}{2} \sum_{i=1}^{124} \left| \left(\frac{\sum_i I_{ij}}{Y_i} \cdot Y_i \right) - I_{ij} \right|$$
where Y_i is the income of place i, and I_{ij} is the value of program j at place i

cially family allowances and UIC benefits. The provincial income tax has a regressive effect, increasing income differences because the poorer provinces are forced to tax more heavily to support a similar level of services. By increasing the role of the provinces relative to the federal government, we increase regional disparity. By increasing the role of the local government, we increase the differences between rural and urban places.

Figure 5.6 illustrates the stabilization process, using the example of Saskatchewan. The values above the line refer to the private sector; below the line they refer to the public sector. Note the extraordinary year-to-year variation in farm income, which drives the rest of the private economy even though tertiary activities take up part of the slack and moderate the variability. Government also moderates the private economy by collecting income tax at higher rates when times are good and income per capita is greater. Below the line are two kinds of government expenditures. Transfers to individuals are modestly counter-cyclical; these transfers include unemployment benefits and the demographic programs of pensions and family allowances. Government expenditures on schools, hospitals, and roads stabilize the economy because they change very gradually over time, since governments are able to borrow in bad years and save in good times.

Looking to the Future
How is the Canadian urban system likely to evolve in the future?
1. Regardless of the impact of free trade with the US, there is likely to

Figure 5.6
Income Stabilization in Saskatchewan

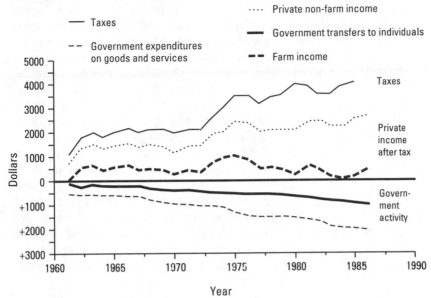

be an increase in the ratio of exports to the GNP, and hence an increase in the quantity of uncertainty imported into the economy. As the economy becomes more open, the federal government will lose its ability to manage the overall level of demand in Canada, and we will depend more, not less, on other countries and international institutions. Free trade means that cities in the periphery will gain access to US markets and pay lower costs for consumer goods. Manufacturers and services in central Canada will face greater uncertainty as they lose their captive markets in the rest of the country. Over time, we can expect the gradual erosion of east-west channels of transportation and communication and the strengthening of north-south ties.

2. If, at the same time we (and the Americans) restrict the flow of international migrants, we may well find that the space economy changes more rapidly than the level of internal migration. The resultant bottlenecks in labour supply can initiate or diffuse inflationary pressures, and/or leave permanent pockets of unemployment in some locations.

3. Given the stabilizing effects of the public sector, it seems unlikely that the role of government will be permitted to decline in the urban system of the future. On the contrary, an ageing population will generate increased expenditures on pensions and medical care, further separating the geography of demography from the geography of production.

4. National and international institutions will grow in importance at the expense of the local and regional institutions. The sequence of recent economic events in Alberta illustrates the problem. Despite a decade of spectacular growth, the province was unable to generate substantial alternatives to its primary economic base. The vulnerability to energy policies and prices led to the collapse of local financial institutions as the regional economy declined sharply. Only national or international economic institutions can survive the uncertainty of regional markets.

5. Quebec, less closely linked demographically to the rest of the country than other provinces, may lead the way towards integration with United States' institutions. Ontario, with strong cultural ties to almost every country in Europe, may maintain contacts with the European Economic Community, although the integrated automobile industry ties the province to the US market. Western Canada, especially British Columbia, may strengthen trading ties with Asia. After a long period of building national institutions at the expense of provincial ones, we may find that the growing importance of international markets and institutions pulls different regions of the country in opposite directions. While this suggests a need for national policies to compensate for these differences, a national solution is not inevitable.

6. Stronger national institutions accelerate the growth of cities that serve the nation as a whole, for example, Toronto, relative to cities that serve particular sectors or regions, for example, Calgary. Stronger international ties weaken this national role, and could reverse the recent polarization of urban growth. At any rate, we can expect a gradual increase in the variance of urban growth rates across the country as regional specialization intensifies.

CONCLUSIONS

Canada operates as a spatial system in which each urban node is intricately linked with other nodes and with the rest of the world. To manage the system, we need to know something about the processes that drive and control this system, spread growth from one region to another, and keep the economy and demography in balance. This system is managed, in more ways than we realize, by a variety of economic, political, and social mechanisms. Social processes diffuse new techniques, new attitudes, and new consumer needs across the landscape; the economy sends signals, by way of prices, that lead to investment, production decisions, and trade. The political system has built up program after program to mitigate the uncertainties that are inherent in the economic system. It is a complex system, but it is fascinating as well; and even the people who ostensibly manage it don't fully understand it.

NOTES

1. The export base model is a model of urban economic growth that assumes that the trigger effect for growth comes from the sale of a specialized material, good, or service (basic products) to outside markets. A second sector in the local economy—the service, non-basic, or residentiary sector—develops to serve the needs of people and establishments (e.g. consumer goods, business products, education, health care) in the export sector. The relationship of non-basic to basic employment is termed the multiplier effect. Given that forecasters can estimate growth in export activity, the multiplier coefficient facilitates the forecasting of total economic growth. Most standard texts in urban and economic geography provide summaries of export base modelling. (See Lloyd and Dicken [1977].) The staple theory of Canadian economic development (as discussed in Chapter 4) is related to the export base model.

2. Note that this map required three modifications to the conventional census data. First, the urban centres were combined with their surrounding counties or census divisions so that the economic base of the hinterland could be included. Yorkton, Saskatchewan, for example, depends on the production of farmers in the surrounding area. Second, the map combines primary production and processing by reassigning certain manufacturing activities to appropriate primary categories. Thus, pulp-and-paper workers are placed in the forest product industry. Third, the map ignores those tertiary activities that serve the local population, and focuses on the economic base.

3. This does not, however, discourage municipalities from attempting to create local economic growth. This trend, which has grown in recent years, is discussed further in Chapter 18.

FURTHER READING

BORCHERT, J.R. 1967 'American Metropolitan Evolution', *Geographical Review* 57, 301–32

—— 1983 'Instability in American Metropolitan Growth', *Geographical Review* 73, 127–49

BOURNE, L.S. and SIMMONS, J.W. eds 1978 *Systems of Cities: Readings in Structure, Growth and Policy* (New York: Oxford University Press)

COFFEY, W.J. and POLESE, M. eds 1986 *Still Living Together: Recent Trends and Future Directions in Canadian Regional Development* (Halifax: Institute for Research in Public Policy)

SIMMONS, J.W. 1986a 'The Impact of the Public Sector on the Canadian Urban System' in A.A. Artibise and G. Stelter eds *Power and Place: Canadian Urban Development in the North American Context* (Vancouver: University of British Columbia Press)

—— 1986b 'Concepts of Urban Systems' in J.R. Borchert et al. eds *Urban Systems in Transition* (Utrecht: Netherlands Geographical Series No. 16)

YEATES, M. 1985 *Land in Canada's Urban Heartland* (Ottawa: Environment Canada)

REFERENCES

Historical Atlas of Canada Vol. III 1990 (Toronto: University of Toronto Press)

JOBIN, J. 1984 *Farm Income Instability on the Prairies* Discussion Paper No. 273 (Ottawa: Economic Council of Canada)

LEACY, F.H., ed. 1983 *Historical Statistics of Canada* 2nd ed. (Ottawa: Statistics Canada)

LLOYD, P.E. and DICKEN, P. 177 *Location in Space* 2nd ed. (London: Harper and Row)

McCANN, L.D. 1987 'Heartland and Hinterland: A Framework for Regional Analysis' in L. D. McCann ed. *Heartland and Hinterland: A Geography of Canada* (Toronto: Prentice-Hall)

RICHARDSON, H.W. 1973 *Regional Growth Theory* (London: Macmillan)

SIMMONS, J.W. 1980 'Changing Migration Patterns in Canada', *Journal of Regional Science* 3, 139–62

—————— 1984 'Government and the Canadian Urban System: Income Tax', *The Canadian Geographer* 28, 18–45

6

High Technology, Societal Change, and the Canadian City

LEN GERTLER

This chapter starts with an outline of its theme: the relationship of information technology, as a form of high technology, and the development of cities. This view is shown to be important in the evolution of cities as focal points of communications. A strong emerging tendency is for such focal points to become nodes in computer-communication networks. The chapter explains how state-of-the-art information technology enables effective networks at three levels: local, metropolitan, and wider, which may be national or international. Each has the potential to affect the location and relationship of human activities and land uses; and in that way to reverberate on the parts or functions of cities, on individual cities, and indeed on the entire Canadian urban system. There is mounting evidence that the spread of these networks is an important part of a process that is moving Canadian society, at least in terms of occupational structure, from its resource industry and manufacturing base towards information-related activities. This transformation is sometimes characterized as an evolution to a post-industrial society.

In considering the implications of information technology for the Canadian city, the case is made for a scenario approach to 'discovering' the future. Such scenarios, systematic forecasts of a developing or future state, should be both qualitative and quantitative. They must be societal, considering the city in context, because technology does not operate in isolation, and the city as product very much reflects the influence of broad economic, political, and social factors. Information technology, in this light, represents a relatively new set of powerful tools that can help us towards Paradise Gained, or if we fail, hasten us towards Paradise Lost. The kind of choices we make have consequences. This is illustrated in three optional scenarios developed by a research team on Technological Change and Human Settlement which was sponsored by the Canada Mortgage and Housing Corporation.[1] These scenarios were termed 'business-as-usual', 'high tension', and 'development', which reflect different sets of assumptions about technology, economic policies, our political values, and society generally. At the very least, we must understand the city/information-technology relationship if we would act upon it benignly.

The concept of 'high' technology is time-bound. The high technology of yesterday is either a museum piece or commonplace today. In this, there is a technological lineage from the birch-bark canoe that provided access to the interior in the seventeenth century to the sophisticated jet aircraft in the late twentieth century. If technology is 'the organization of knowledge for the achievement of practical purposes' (Mesthene 1970), then high technology is a relatively new embodiment of knowledge. Because of the presumption that knowledge is cumulative and progressive, high technology represents the most advanced application available—the compact disk compared to the stereo record or tape.

In this chapter the particular form of high technology that will be considered is information technology. This term refers to 'electronic systems for communication, computing, and control concerned with collecting, storing, retrieving, processing, distributing and applying information' (Laver 1982). In brief, information technology is the combination of computers and telecommunications. The introductory chapter in this text stressed that cities are fundamentally communications systems; their geographic layout maximizes spatial interaction. Thus information technology reverberates on the model city by creating networks, and thereby influencing the location of and linkage among human activities; for example, where we live and work.

PERSPECTIVES ON THE CITY

In treating the relationship of information technology and the city, this chapter will keep in view two perspectives: the city as product and the city as process (Stelter and Artibise 1986, 3–6). The first, which is deeply grounded in Canadian urban studies and ably treated in this volume (see Chapters 3, 4, 5, and 7) is the view that no city exists in splendid isolation. It is both a subsystem in a system of cities, and a reflection of broader societal forces. The second is the understanding that, within such constraints, there is an urban process that enables the individual city to influence its own destiny, and which then reverberates back on the urban system and on society at large.

In this chapter, only a broad appreciation of this duality is important as part of the context for looking at the relationship between city, technology, and society. There is, however, a specific observation on each aspect of this duality that also informs the approach to the subject. From a product perspective, it is important to note, first, that hierarchy and dominance of a few big centres, the major metropolitan areas, is a persisting feature of the Canadian urban system; and second, that the information-based measure of centrality, 'exported daily newspapers', became the critical factor in the 1970s and early 1980s in determining the central-place order of the larger places. While the spheres of influence of the main regional centres, from Vancouver to Halifax, did not expand, Toronto emerged as 'the metropolitan centre of Canada'. Preston (1986, 19–22) attributes this pattern on the one hand, to the limitations of the regional cities as information centres, and on the other, to the pre-eminence of Toronto as the fountain-head of business information for the entire country (see Chapter 7).

From a process perspective, it is important to appreciate the city as a creative force in society. This is not only because it is the place where the sources of power tend to be concentrated (Galbraith 1983), but because of its human dimension. As Reissman (1964, 13) in his seminal work *The Urban Process* observed: 'Cities are communities only because they command allegiance, social consensus and belief, and even at times, a civic spirit'. This creative aspect is the underpinning of the social and political ferment that can be observed in the evolution of Canadian cities, and which indeed is the very basis of community mobilization, planning, and action. This legacy may be observed in terms of emerging ideas (e.g. 'healthy cities'); tangible policy and program achievements (e.g. in social housing); and in institutions, both formal and informal (e.g. city and regional planning offices and a plethora of voluntary groups) (Board of Health, City of Toronto 1988; Hodge 1986, 75–107).

Gerald Hodge (1986), in his overview of Canadian community planning experience, throws light on the role of the planner and of planning as an active force in the life of the city and therefore on the city as process. In two critical periods of Canada's history, the planner joined forces with broader movements and assumed a public role as educator and social reformer. In these circumstances, planners influenced public opinion and generated the political support deemed necessary to address some urgent issues. Early in this century, during the time of the Commission on Conservation, these issues were public health, housing, civic government, and conservation; and, much later, the issues of massive urban growth and automobile-led suburbanization after World War II, were signalled by the formation of the Community Planning Association of Canada in 1946 (see Chapter 19 for further detail on the evolution of Canadian planning). The first effort laid the foundation for modern community planning in Canada;

and the second was instrumental in establishing planning as a function of local and regional government throughout the country. Changes of this type represent a creative legacy that must be constantly renewed to avoid the setting in of bureaucratic arteriosclerosis.

Our two perspectives on the city also help to explain the historic role of communications in the development of cities. Richard L. Meier, who has formulated *A Communications Theory of Urban Growth* has explained the nature of his subject: 'Communications represents a cooperative attempt on the part of a sender and a receiver to expand the realm of ideas, impressions, and experiences they hold in common'. (Meier 1962, 8.) Information technology is a major modern means of communication. The evolution of cities in a market society like Canada may be thought of in terms of the emergence and then the strengthening, stage by stage, of a number of communication focal points. This is illustrated in Figure 6.1.

Figure 6.1 illustrates a 'cumulative communications cycle', made up of

Figure 6.1
The City in History: A Cumulative Communications Cycle

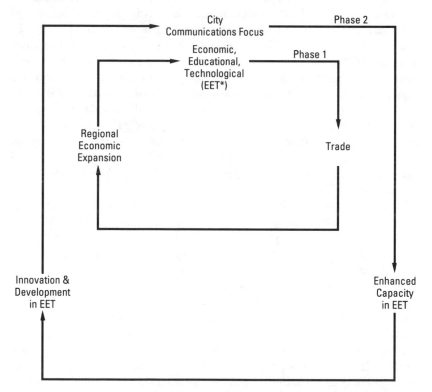

Economic: Production and trade; *Educational:* Research and learning;
Technological: Developments such as information hardware and software

three kinds of communication—economic, educational, and technological—which is focused on a city. In the first phase of the cycle, trade or communication between urban sellers and rural buyers provides an economic base for a town. Town and region, bound by a multitude of transactions, are interdependent and mutually reinforcing. They contract or expand in unison.

The City of Calgary in its original relationship to the ranching economy of southern Alberta provides an example of the first phase cycle. Both 'product' and 'process' forces were at work, but product predominated. The city's growth as a major urban centre of well over 80,000 people by the late 1920s was to a great extent due to its strategic transportation position at the confluence of the Bow and Elbow rivers (attracting in the 1860s and the 1870s the 'whisky traders' and then a post of the North-West Mounted Police); and as an important railway centre on the CPR main line, which reached Calgary in 1883 (*The Canadian Encyclopedia* 1985, 255–7).

The second phase of the communications cycle builds on the first. In the case of Calgary, additional regional stimulus is provided by the discovery of major oil reserves. As the financial and management centre for the industry, Calgary becomes a critical node in an international communications network linking New York, Dallas, and Oklahoma City—head office locales of the big multinationals—to oilfield exploration and exploitation at Leduc, Pembina, and Redwater (*Communications Focus—Economic*). The rising economic stature and wealth of Calgary leads to the development of its cultural facilities, such as the Southern Alberta Institute of Technology, the University of Calgary, and the Calgary Centre for the Performing Arts (*Communications Focus—Educational*). A whole new set of communication linkages are set in motion. The growth of the city takes off. By 1981, it is the sixth largest metropolis in the country.

Calgary's enhanced capacity for *innovation and development* indicates that 'process' forces have become increasingly important. We see the emergence (not without risk) of aggressive, Calgary-based, Canadian firms, such as Nova and Dome, in the petroleum industry. A community-wide initiative brings the 1988 Winter Olympics, which, in turn, links Calgary to an international marketing and information network. A recent development illustrates the interplay of product and process forces. Calgary's regional role as an 'information city' led in 1980 to its selection as a production and distribution centre for Alberta by Canada's national daily newspaper, the *Globe and Mail*. The early morning edition of the *Globe* is transmitted, using a satellite communications network, for printing, after conversion by laser scanners, on offset presses in Calgary. Ironically, this highly successful operation, which reflects the communications clout of the city (*Communications Focus—Technological*), serves to demonstrate the position of Calgary as 'product' in the central-place hierarchy of Canada (Hepworth 1985, 414–17). Indeed, in the case of the *Globe and Mail* example, the decision to raise Calgary to the status of provincial communications centre was taken in Toronto, not in Calgary.

The model presented here illustrates the relationship between product and process forces in urban development. There is a strong presumption that external factors weigh heavily in the pioneer phase of a city's development. As a place reaches a certain threshold in communications capability in its economic, educational, and technological dimensions, process forces, based on the innate qualities of the people and the region, take hold. As this chapter unfolds, these two aspects of the contemporary city—the determined (product) and the proactive (process)—will be kept in sharp focus. This synoptic view is essential for placing high technology in a proper context: a powerful societal force, as constraint or opportunity, that is, nevertheless, amenable to public policy.

INFORMATION TECHNOLOGY AND THE CITY: EMERGING TENDENCIES

To consider the relationship of information technology and the city is to be concerned with the spatial implications of this technology. It is essential in turn to grasp the implications of networks. 'Networks' in this case refers to a characteristic topology that includes: computers and terminals; telecommunications for data transmission (e.g. telephone, cable, satellite); and communication processing equipment (e.g. concentrators, laser scanners) (Hepworth 1985, 414). The combination of these components provides the basis for two primary network capabilities: first, to act as a medium for the rapid and continuous distribution of information, both locally and over long distances; and second, to provide 'material inputs into production', in the form of software or facsimiles that may have the effect of transferring gains in productivity from one place to another (Hepworth 1985, 408 and 416–20). From these technical capabilities other generic capacities follow: the power to inform or obscure, to centralize or decentralize, and to concentrate or distribute decision-making and control (Coates 1982).

With the current state-of-the-art technology, networks can be created at three critical scales of human activity: at a specific site, in the form of a local area network (LAN); for a region, for example a metropolitan area network (MAN); and between regions, a wide area network (WAN). At the largest scale, the network using satellites may be global (Hepworth 1987, 256–9). At each of these levels computer networks may have repercussions on the city, on the urban system as a whole, or on both. Information technology will be an important factor, perhaps critical in some cases, in affecting the mix of 'product' and 'process' forces in city development.

The LAN provides the backbone for the concentration of the most advanced information services within a single building or in a multifunctional complex. Maranouchi Intelligent City, a 32-building complex in central Tokyo, probably provides the clearest contemporary prototype (Nobuyuki 1986). This kind of facility is becoming the stock-in-trade of sophisticated office construction as practised by the leading developers around the world, such as the Canadian firms, Olympia and York (World Financial Center, New York) and Marathon Realty (Railway Lands Project, downtown Toronto). In this form, LANs have the potential for intensifying both functional and physical concentration within major business centres. LANs become nodes within nodes which reverberate, through ripple effects on land values, rents, ancillary activities, and traffic, on the entire urban fabric (Hepworth 1987, 259; Nobuyuki 1986, 157–8).

At the level of the metropolitan area, the powers of MANs have stimulated speculation about the 'tele' phenomenon in a multitude of forms: telecommuting; telemarketing; telebanking; telelearning; teleworshiping; even teledoctoring (Dorney *et al.* 1984, 23–37). These represent possibilities, viewed with varying degrees of scepticism, that are still unfolding. The forte of computer networks, the real time (or spontaneous) distribution of information and technique, leads to the expectation that the historic tie between home and work will be severed. A corollary is the freedom to choose residence on the basis of preferred environments and life-styles (Shortreed, Dust, and May 1984). That potential could translate into a society composed of a myriad of communities reflecting the whole range of human preference and diversity: 'in the mature information society of the future, nature communities, non-smoking communities, energy conservation communities and many other types of voluntary communities will prosper side-by-side' (Masuda 1985, 629).

Experience to date prompts a more pragmatic view. There is indeed the possibility to carry further a tendency documented authoritatively for the first time in the *Regional Survey of New York and its Environs*, Vol. I (Haig and McCrea 1974 [original, 1927]). Reference here is to the splitting-off of functions (e.g. head-office administration, sales and manufacturing) within the metropolis. Thus the front office of a corporate headquarters adheres to the face-to-face, decision-making ambience of the downtown core; while the routine back-office relocates perhaps as far as 60 kilometres from the core, taking advantage of lower locational costs and the 'second income' labour market of middle-class housewives (Nelson 1986). This kind of centrifugal thrust, however, is limited by some very practical interests. These are to maintain access for many services to the external economies of the metropolis, especially mass transit, and to have the opportunity for convenient periodic personal contact between back-office and headquarter personnel.

There are also some noteworthy spatial effects of metropolitan area networks when they are used in industry. In flexible manufacturing systems, computer networks facilitate the physical separation yet functional integration of the phases of the production process: design; materials or parts supply; manufacturing distribution. The presumed advantage of this separation is the just-in-time delivery system, which is supposed to result in lower inventory costs and flexibility in responding to the vagaries of the market. The economic effectiveness of this arrangement, however, is based on the assumption of a rapid response of supplier/contractor to producer/assembler, and this requires these two groups to be physically close. The search for capital and market flexibility using computer communications may lead to spatial clustering of the phases and components of the production process (Gertler, M. 1988, 422–3). One of the best examples of this in Canada is the General Motors Autoplex in Oshawa. This 'largest manufacturing complex in North America' features, in addition to its manufacturing facilities, a sub-complex producing automotive components. This includes some in-house capacities, and a cluster of independent suppliers in nearby plants delivering components to GM on a just-in-time basis.

Overall, the critical literature on computer networks suggests very clearly that the impact of that technology is strongly shaped by economic forces and by human and social factors (Bereiter 1983; Black and Bengston 1977; Calhoun 1984; Forester 1985; Mandeville 1983; Menzies 1984). For example, the romance of the new 'cottage industry' is somewhat deflated by pressure on the domestic scene, and by the possible loss for those working at home of job benefits and security. Moreover, informal information exchanges that take place around the coffee machine and at lunchtime have proved to be invaluable in helping employees understand how their organization operates, achieve promotions, and satisfy desires for gossip. And the video or digital classroom cannot replace the personal relationship, critical for many subjects, in the learning process (Nelson 1986, 4).

'The new source of power', writes John Naisbitt, 'is not money in the hands of a few but information in the hands of many' (Naisbitt 1984, 35). This is the perspective that has led some social commentators to stress the potential of local and regional cable TV to foster a stronger sense of community identity; and of computer-communication networks to broaden the base of political participation and give neighbourhoods better access to city hall. But another view is not so rosy. It is that the affluent, the well-educated, the powerful will take command of 'high-tech' communication, and use it to perpetuate exclusive privilege and environments (Goldmark 1972; Castells 1985, 19).

Wide area networks (WANs) conjure up the image of 'a vast electronic highway or utility accessible to anyone anywhere in the world' (Menzies 1984, 20). The key point about WANs is that they greatly enhance the technical capacity to establish and sustain large-scale systems, operating on either a centralized or decentralized basis. In the Canadian context, however, in which the urban system has marked hierarchical features, and in which the corporate structure is notoriously concentrated (and becoming more so, it seems) the tendency is for WANs to be used as instruments for strengthening centralized directions (Francis 1987; Hepworth 1985 and 1987). The largest metropolitan areas in Canada (the nine above 500,000 in population, 1981) are the locations of the head offices of Canada's dominant corporations (Gertler 1985, 59–61). These same head offices are the locus of the great bulk of Canada's computing capacity and that capacity is being utilized to expand market reach and tighten organizational control (see Chapter 7, and Hepworth 1985, 413; 1987, 258; Menzies 1984, 20; Conklin and St-Hilaire 1988, 88).

It is not the purpose here to demonstrate empirically that WANs are instruments for intensifying spatial centralization and urban hierarchy in Canada. Instead, it is to make a more modest and relatively unassailable assertion: that the information factor supports the dominance of a relatively few metropolitan areas which are also the major communication nodes. To all of the 'classical' agglomeration economies (the benefits of 'public goods', the hedges against uncertainty, and congenial decision-making environments) are added the formidable powers of computer networks (Gertler and Crowley 1977, 148–9).

The cumulative impact of the three levels of networks on the Canadian economy is far-reaching. It should not be surprising that close to 49 per cent of Canada's labour force (1981) was made up of 'information' workers, who were employed as producers, distributors and processors, or in infrastructure. These jobs cut across the conventional boundaries of the economic structure; primary, secondary, tertiary sectors and upwards. This percentage was up from 44 per cent in 1971 (Hepworth 1985, 409–11). A recent study on Canadian high-technology observes: 'The importance of high technology for productivity improvements throughout the entire economy cannot be overemphasized' (Conklin and St-Hilaire 1988, 87). This phenomenon has broad societal implications. It is said to mark the transition from an energy-based society to a knowledge-based society, sometimes called 'post-industrial', with correspondingly cosmic changes in prevailing value systems and in the very basis of societal power (Brotchie et al. 1985, 7).

What seems clear from this overview of the computer-communications networks at the three scales, from the highly local to the global, is that they represent a powerful technology, which may, depending on the context, be used to reinforce either the product forces or process forces in city development. The pre-existing centralized Canadian space economy predisposes the use of WANs to intensify the concentration of decision-making, and to decentralize economic activities. As nodes in a network, cities may be initiators strengthening their own positions, or products of initiatives or directives taken elsewhere, say Calgary vis-à-vis Toronto.

Similarly, metropolitan area networks (MANs) may be used to intensify the dominance of a single downtown core, or to foster a poly-centred association of communities. And local area networks have potential for either building up the communication power of a subregional centre, say

Dartmouth versus Halifax, or for augmenting the metropolitan, national, and international dominance of an existing financial centre. In fact, the pendulum may swing back and forth between product, externally determining, and process, internally inspired, forces.

PROSPECTS FOR THE CITY: A SCENARIO APPROACH

It is now legitimate to ask what implications this subject has for the evolving Canadian city. In addressing this question, a number of clues to a response have already been inferred. It is advisable to consider the influence of technology in association with other societal forces. Technological determinism is out. Each generation of high technology opens up both unprecedented opportunities and constraints. The city responds to and reflects the societal dimensions—technological, socio-economic, institutional—but it is not a mere passive product. It is the medium for an urban process that is itself a creative force within the city and which reverberates on its region, the system of cities as a whole, and society in general.

In assuming a proactive or planning approach to urban development, it is well to be aware of some of the Canadian realities: the persistence of hierarchy and dominance in the Canadian urban system; the importance of communication power as a touchstone of centrality; and the background of struggle for more liveable environments in Canadian cities.

Similarly, planning should be informed of the powers and limitations of information technology, particularly of the ubiquitous computer networks. At each level—site specific, metropolitan, and national/international—there may be repercussions on the spatial structure of the city and on the urban hierarchy. Overall, the planner must be attuned to the presumed economic and social repercussions of an emerging 'information society'.

In considering the prospects of the Canadian city, an approach or methodology is required that incorporates some of these 'clues'. Synoptically, the approach will possess two main features: first, it will be societal—the city and the urban growth forces, including technology, will be considered in context; and second, it will be normative—the prospects that are explored will frankly represent images of how the forces we have to work with may be shaped in different ways by different prevailing value systems and public policies.

The Canada Mortgage and Housing Corporation-sponsored research team referred to at the opening of this chapter found that the method that most appropriately encompassed the two main features was a form of social forecasting called scenario-building (Hirschorn 1980; Jantsch 1967). It has been aptly described as 'the formation of a synoptic (and dynamic) view of as many developments as can be grasped and as may appear relevant to an experimental simulation of a possible reality' (Jantsch 1967, 180–1).

The scenarios that were formulated and are outlined below were built around seven societal dimensions: technology; institutions; economy; values and life-styles; population; resources; and human settlements. The research approach was eclectic, combining scenario-building and computer-based modelling, qualitative and quantitative, judgemental, and statistical elements. Within the structure of these dimensions, causal processes were explored and some policy levers identified. The scenarios were used as devices for releasing the creative imagination, recognizing that their formulation is as much a matter of 'art' as 'science'. In the scenario-building process, the researchers were able to combine some of the advantages of the Delphi approach—drawing upon the opinions of an interdisciplinary expert group—and the brainstorming approach—an exchange and dialogue of a considerable variety of 'world views'. In essence, the scenario approach has been used to reduce the 'uncertainty space' by defining and delineating three scenarios, each representing different potential futures (Embree 1986, 32–7). Finally, the qualitative scenarios were made more useful as policy tools by the generation of numerical simulation models, using an analytical framework known as SERF, the Socio-Economic Resource Framework.[2]

The construction of the scenarios by the research team proceeded in several steps:

1. Probes were done on major trends in the above-mentioned seven societal dimensions—for example, under the heading, Institutions: What are the expected repercussions of increasing corporate concentration in the business world?
2. The results were presented and critically discussed by the research team, with particular attention to the impact of information technology and the implications for human settlements.
3. Simultaneously, historical data sets (available in SERF) were examined, as well as the extrapolation of historical trends and alternative simulations (for example, high, moderate and low rates of future population growth).
4. With the foregoing as background, the research team met in a series of exploratory, scenario-building sessions. The scenarios were to be qualitative, at the national level, long-range and societal in scope. Within the general environmental rubric, the team had diverse backgrounds: architecture, ecology, regional planning, social psychology, sociology, and spatial systems planning. In this role, the group acted as a panel of experts in an asymmetrical probe—that is, as a variety of experts addressing a multi-faceted problem (Helmer 1983, 59–63).
5. At each of the scenario-building sessions, each participant had a 'time at bat' to present his/her synoptic view of the emerging future. These views were discussed and ideas traded. A summary record of the discussion was kept for collective meditation until the next session.

6. After three or four sessions, the co-ordinator of the study, drawing on the scenario-building sessions, prepared three alternative draft scenarios. After review and comments by members of the team, the scenarios were revised for publication (Gertler and Newkirk 1988).
7. The qualitative scenarios became the basis for the selection and adaptation of three scenarios in the SERF modelling repertoire. These projections were the closest quantitative expression, the closest fit, to three, decidedly different, world views.

THREE SCENARIOS: SOCIETY AND THE CITY

The themes of the three, national-level societal scenarios that were formulated are termed Business-As-Usual, the High Tension Society, and the Developmental Society (see for a more detailed presentation, Gertler and Newkirk 1988). These are presented in relation to major societal dimensions in Table 6.1. With regard to information technology, the first scenario reflects the somewhat uneven, fitful, and, in global terms, precarious pattern of the *status quo*. The second scenario assumes that the technologi-

Table 6.1
Scenarios: Societal National

	Business-As-Usual (BAU)	High Tension Society (HT)	Developmental Society (DVT)
Technology	Turbulent R&D: Weak, uneven	High-Tech R&D: Strong, uneven	Strategic R&D: Strong, balanced
Institutions	Non-intervention Privatization Economic concentration	Elites on top Continental, corporatist	Development strategy Greater public sector intervention
Economy	Instability Rising disparity Rising unemployment	High growth High levels of disparity Rising unemployment	Steady Towards equity Declining unemployment
Values	Market ethic Preservation & exploitation	Technocratic and consumerist Polarized, paternalist	Development and equity Environmental quality
Population	Low growth Regional imbalance	High growth Extreme regional imbalance	Moderate growth Regional balance
Resources	Uncertain markets Energy sources erratic	Corporate control and high demand for energy	Management Mixed energy sources
Human Settlements	Growth in large centres causing social and economic tensions and decline in many other regions	Big Metros sprawl Environmental degradation	Strong core & regional centres Regional City: Urban/ Rural conservation

cal imperative is taken to its limit. And the third represents a well-balanced development in which the application of information technology is tempered by human, social, and environmental considerations. In following the features of these scenarios, it will be helpful to note the mix of product- and process-forces shaping the urban and regional environments. A clue to these distinctions is the role of public policy, not only for cities, but with respect to Canada as a whole. Do we bring together the disparate conditions and forces of this country into a coherent strategy, or do we follow a policy of drift and expediency? Hence the choice of three terse titles—almost slogans—to capture the spirit of each scenario. A synoptic interpretation of each of the scenarios follows.

Business-As-Usual
This scenario represents a Canada in which the present, historically-influenced tendencies have full sway. Not animated by major consensual purposes, destinies will be shaped by the influence and sometimes the encounter of major forces. Information technology in its computer and telecommunications aspects will continue to expand, but with a decreasing Canadian industrial component. A non-interventionist and privatizing federal government espousing competitive market philosophy will ironically give full scope to corporate consolidation and concentration.

An industrial structure featuring a high degree of centralization of ownership and control will use the power of computer networks and all forms of communications to consolidate and extend head-office domination (both national and expatriate). Concentration of economic power may be accompanied by spatial decentralization—internationally, nationally, and regionally. Head offices concentrated in Toronto and a few lesser corporate centres could take advantage of these new forms of communication to relocate administration and production operations to more distant lower-cost regions in Canada, or abroad in developing countries.

The conspicuous absence of planned development strategies, together with a waning research and development effort, and subservience to US and Japanese techniques, will prove to be a recipe for economic uncertainty and instability. In this atmosphere, population fertility rates will probably remain low, and immigration policy cautious and defensive. Unemployment, chronic and cyclical, will create rising social stress.

The quality of renewable resources of agricultural soils, forests, fisheries, and water will be in peril because of inadequate management practises and unsafe levels of pollution (e.g. in streams and lakes). Downward pressure on commodity prices internationally will destabilize mineral, energy, and agricultural industries, and jeopardize availability of capital and human resources for insuring efficiency, productivity, and control of pollution.

Human settlement patterns will reflect the foregoing societal dimensions. Nationally, centralization and decentralization factors will offset each other, resulting in the centre-periphery imbalance characteristic of the mid–1980s described in detail in Chapter 5. There may even be some selective increase in regional disparities. Weak resource-based industries will be reflected in stressed agricultural communities and northern resource towns, which will increasingly become non-viable, socially and economically. Surplus labour will stream to the larger urban areas. Downsizing of fishing fleets and processing industries brought about by diminishing supplies will cause economic stress on both coasts.

Regionally, the relatively high growth rate of metropolitan centres in a climate of commercial boosterism will produce an expansive and volatile urban-rural fringe. Stress points will be housing and the environment. The quality of residential communities and the countryside will be in jeopardy, in the midst of rising public agitation. In the forefront of a critical public response will be an emerging non-governmental Third Sector, an increasingly well-informed coalition of voluntary groups aggressively asserting an environmental ethic.

The High Tension Society
In this perspective, some of the major tendencies of 'business-as-usual' are carried to the ultimate limit. This is an unrestrained, corporate, continentalized Canada, growing and developing as a component of the American system. 'High-tech' is in the saddle. Information technology through the use of computer networks and teleconferencing, becomes a tool for the integration of the economy, nationally and internationally.

Canada, increasingly presided over by a corporate and professional élite, becomes a high-growth, high-income and, at the same time, substantially (and tragically) polarized society. The inequity takes several forms: in income structure, in bias within research and academic establishments (towards technology rather than towards natural science, social science, or the humanities), and in resource-use patterns. International markets (e.g. the London Metal Exchange, the Chicago Board of Trade), by maintaining the downward pressure on commodity prices, virtually 'whip-saw' producers. The family farm is finally replaced by corporate and franchise farming. Canadian mining, petroleum, forestry, and fishery enterprises are bought up by and consolidated with large, strongly capitalized, national and international corporations. Even the Bay Street investment community will be increasingly dominated by a few big internationally-oriented financial 'superhouses'. These will operate in deregulated global markets made effective by the fast flow of information through computers and automated systems.

The ultimate expression of the foregoing trends will be the rise of the 'virtual corporation'. This is the contemporary multinational, expanded and dominant—a corporate empire, controlled from metropolitan centres by a small coterie of high-level management through self-contained, transitory units, lacking local and regional interests, established for component production, research and development, service and marketing. These units will be distributed and relocated around the world in search of cheap labour, capital, material, and favourable taxation rates; and to gain access to markets and minimize political risk. The virtual corporation will exploit to the full the technology of the communications satellite, fibre optics, and miniaturization in electronic equipment (even production facilities will be transportable) to effectively link together for management purposes its spatially dispersed organization.

The monumental scale and highly abstract monetary character of the prevailing business organization will preclude regional and personal loyalties. Managers need not know or care where things happen in real socio-economic space. Pride of place and civic responsibility will not be in the lexicon of the twenty-first century executive. A Canadian society, dominated by the virtual corporation will give low priority to environmental values—rhetoric usually replaces action; resource management will be an area of neglect; and the highly centralized corporate structure with headquarters in a few major communication nodes will be reflected in a highly centralized Canadian settlement pattern. The big metropolitan centres of over 500,000 people will increase their demographic dominance as regional centres decline. In this neo-industrial scenario, there will be even fewer constraints than in the 'business-as-usual' future to urban sprawl and a degraded countryside.

Not surprisingly, the economic, social, and regional disparities of this scenario will generate a great deal of social discontent and distress. This is a society that is not only 'high-tech', but high tension. Government will intervene to maintain social peace by paternalistic redistributive policies such as 'guaranteed annual income' and social housing. But the general tenor of society will be one of precarious polarization. Similarly, concern and alarm about global environmental issues will produce some concessions on that front.

The Developmental Society

The distinguishing feature of this third scenario will be the emergence of national strategies that address the major issues of Canadian development. Science and technology will be an area of deliberate public-policy concern. All of the instruments of government—expenditures, taxation, regulation, public corporations, education, and persuasion will be bent towards various national goals. Typically, these will be concerned with promoting innovation in high-tech industries, such as micro-electronics and communications; and in cultivating a strong Canadian-led research and development effort, involving both industries and universities. A strenuous effort will be made to avoid the disrupting effects of new technology, and instead to reap the benefits—economical, social, and intellectual—that it can bring. Canada will become a learning society.

This kind of positive direction will not be attainable by government fiat. It will depend upon a groundswell of change in human values in directions already inherent in the 'business-as-usual' society. Some of the more important of these values are: conservation; participation; voluntarism; lifetime learning; the urge to excellence; physical fitness; personal fulfilment; and global responsibility. Cumulatively-reinforcing processes of transformation will result from the interaction of public policy, education, both higher and popular culture, science and technology, industrial development, and public attitudes. The precipitating motive may be no more than enlightened self-interest—the requirements of surviving in a highly competitive world. But the inevitable political expression of the new values will invoke, reshape, and modernize the tradition of developmental democracy (e.g. John Stuart Mill's concept of the good society) as one that fosters the development, enjoyment, and fulfilment of individual capacities for all of its citizens.

Based on this kind of 'equal opportunity' ethic, Canada's development strategy would move in the direction of reducing inequalities between social classes, attaining greater balance in regional development, and opening our doors to a reasonable flow of immigrants. The Developmental Society would also give high priority to scholarship, to meaningful work, and to sustainable development. Economic expansion will not attain the heights of the High Tension Society, but it will be marked by greater equality and stability.

The rationalization of the supply and demand of renewable and non-renewable resources—a classical Canadian issue—will be confronted directly. Agriculture, forestry, and mining will be encouraged in the most productive regions. Policies of regional adjustment will be pursued. Canada's comparative advantage in hydroelectric power will be fostered by increased production for export both interprovincially and to the US, in Quebec and Manitoba. Long-term capital will be made available for investment in forestry and fisheries, especially for reforestation and aquaculture.

Declining or low commodity prices, tragic for the resource sector in other scenarios, are turned to an advantage in a national development strategy. The accompanying decline in rural land prices is seized upon as an opportunity to redesign the 'unfinished landscape'. The diverse regional landscapes of Canada, particularly the areas of interface between town and country, undergo comprehensive reconstruction. The process of degradation is halted, and positive measures are taken to protect and preserve good soils, clean up streams and save aquifers, rehabilitate excavated areas and restore them to productive use, and combine in a positive way unique natural and cultural features (e.g. eskers and escarpments, woods and ravines, mill sites and country schools, formal parks and vacant lots) into multi-purpose open-space systems that extend from the countryside to the heart of the city. Urban agriculture will be in vogue. The reconciliation of environmental and economic values will be found in the concept of 'sustainable development'.

The human settlement system of the Developmental Society will not be able to transcend entirely the constraints of the 'business-as-usual' Canada. But the biases will be clear: less dominance by metropolitan areas, more growth in the moderate-sized centres of 10,000 to 99,999 people; less regional disparity in economic development and population growth. Computer networks will be used as instruments of policy to promote the linkages, within and between regions, that will modify the traditionally acute centre-periphery biases of the Canadian space economy. Computers and telecommunications will provide the infrastructure for the 'regional city', which enjoys at the same time the benefits of high-level services and a low-key residential environment. Growth in these largely self-contained centres throughout the country will reduce the sprawling expansion of the larger metropolises.

In the ambience of developmental democracy, the Third Sector will become a force in national development. Since many of the voluntary groups that make up that sector are active at the local level—concerned with issues of pollution, environment, land use, employment, housing, etc.—the municipal realm will assume greater importance. This movement will be reinforced by the need, in a society undergoing drastic change in its industrial structure, for organized, self-help, and innovative activities based upon local and regional potentials. There is a prospect for a kind of libertarian municipalism—a veritable subculture that will exert an increasing influence on public policy. This will have the support of a broad electorate, which will include paradoxically both the new information constituency and 'the technologically displaced strata which can no longer be integrated into a cybernetic and highly mechanized society' (Bookchin 1987, 32). On this basis, the Third Sector will emerge as a counterpoint in the power structure to Big Government and Big Business. Thus, its influence in important policy areas, such as housing and public goods, will generally be contra-polarization in the direction of greater mix and the forms of organization and tenure that favour popular control and decision-making power. One of the possible, interesting prospects is the emergence of a coherent aesthetic expressed in architecture and urban design that affirms humanistic values, in contrast to the cold, corporate monumentalism of the 'High Tension Society', and the cacophonous commercialism of 'Business-As-Usual'.

The exposition of the three scenarios should serve to show that a developmental city, one in which creative process forces are released, depends on a developmental society. This will be a society in which technology is used deliberately as an instrument for building a certain kind of Canada: less centralized in its economic structure than at present; regionally balanced; more participatory in decision-making; and more sustainable in development.

CONCLUSIONS

The scenario approach illuminates the policy challenge in several ways. It demonstrates that the pattern of city development is not capricious and reflects both 'product' and 'process' orientations—for example, the impact of the corporate structure, on the one hand, and of the struggle for the 'good city', on the other. It draws attention to the consistencies of development within the assumptions and parameters of each scenario. At the same time, by conveying some of the complexity of the context, it provides a caution against single-factor and overly-simplistic solutions.

With regard to 'high-tech', in particular information technology, the scenarios illustrate the possible repercussions of a new set of technical capabilities. The problems and the opportunities that follow in the wake of computer networks are different more in degree than in kind from those of the preceding period. This is largely because of the way in which information technology is inextricably bound up with and conditioned by the structural features of Canadian development: centre-periphery; urban hierarchy; the topology of the multi-locational enterprise; the subcontinental scale of the country. This is reflected in the way computer networks at various scales can be used to both centralize control and decentralize activities; in the High Tension Society that bow is stretched to its ultimate limits.

In one respect, however, the inner logic of computer-telecommunications networks, as well as the short but dramatic history of their use, demonstrates the potentials of the power to communicate in real time. What it means is that, if we wish to pursue a city form that is genuinely decentralized, we now have at our disposal an appropriate infrastructure. The potentials exist in several realms: in private corporate organization and decision-making, in local government (bring 'city hall' to the people), and in the cultural life of the region. While the technical capabilities are available, the three scenarios should provide a sobering indication of the forces of inertia that would have to be overcome, for example in moving from 'Business-As-Usual' to 'The Developmental Society'. At the very least, as prospective policy advisers and possibly policy-makers, we know that we have to work on several fronts: the institutional, with regard to both public and private decision-making; technological, in terms of facilitating an appropriate infrastructure; and educational in three forms. These are: the development of knowledge to generate creative responses to societal change; training for skills to manage the technology; and broad communication and debate on the public issues provoked by the spread of information technology.

The importance of the city (as incubator, receiver, and disseminator) in the development of information technology raises a conjecture about the role of informatics—the study of information, its use, management, and repercussions in city planning. On this, Hepworth has put forward a provocative agenda. It has four main thrusts: (1) *development of a comprehensive information base* on economic and technical trends, including the impacts of networks on urban and regional land-use patterns; (2) *local government initiatives*, including technology centres, multi-interest group networks, public data bases, training programs, and an information hardware/software public utility; (3) *public policy advocacy* beamed at the appropriate levels of action on such matters as the locational, investment, and purchasing strategies of multi-locational organizations, the regulation of telecommunications, and the distribution and pattern of infrastructure; and (4) *a program of public information and education* on the information economy and its repercussions, benign or otherwise, on individuals, social groups, and communities (Hepworth 1987, 259–62). This is an excellent contribution to the debate, but to this, one should add a 'fifth business'; that is an active program of scenario-building as part of the struggle to keep a handle on the complexity of the Technology/City/Society relationship, and as insurance against technocratic myopia.

NOTES

1. The author wishes to acknowledge the value of his association with the other members of the research team on Technological Change and Human Settlements (University of Waterloo), namely R. Dorney, C. Knapper, S. Lerner, R. Newkirk and L. Richards; and to express appreciation for research support to the Canada Mortgage and Housing Corporation.

2. SERF was developed by the Structural Analysis Division of Statistics Canada. The data within SERF are expressed in terms of 'real' rather than monetary units, and encompass a myriad of time series in four major blocks: demography, consumption, production, and material resources (Hoffman 1986). It is programmed to make projections, on an annual basis, to the year 2031, and to do so while maintaining internal consistency with respect to accounting identities, say the relationship between population, housing preferences, and the supply of housing stock by dwelling type. SERF also embodies the design approach to modelling, explicitly providing for the interaction of scenario-builder and policy-explorer with the physical transformation processes, which are expressed in the statistical output. While the projections provide an enlightening demonstration of consequences in Canadian society, it is the qualitative scenarios that are the foundation of the entire exercise.

FURTHER READING

BOOKCHIN, M. 1987 *The Rise of Urbanization and the Decline of Citizenship* (San Francisco: Sierra Club Books)

BROTCHIE, J., NEWTON, P., HALL, P., and NIJKAMP, P. 1985 *The Future of Urban Form* (London: Croom Helm)

CASTELLS, M. 1985 'High Technology, Economic Restructuring and the Urban-regional Process in the United States' in M. Castells ed. *High Technology, Space and Society* (Beverly Hills: Sage Publications)

DAKIN, J. 1979 *Feedback From Tomorrow* (London: Pion Limited)

FORESTER, T. 1985 *The Information Technology Revolution* (Cambridge, Mass.: M.I.T. Press)

GAPPERT, G. and KNIGHT, R. eds 1982 *Cities in the 21st Century* (Beverly Hills: Sage Publications)

HODGE, G. 1986 *Planning Canadian Communities* (New York: Methuen)

MARIEN, M. ed. 1987 *Future Survey Annual* (Bethesda, Maryland: World Future Society)

MENZIES, H. 1984 *Women and the Chip* (Montreal: The Institute for Research on Public Policy)

WORDS ASSOCIATES and NEWTON, K. *Workable Futures: Notes on Emerging Technologies* (Ottawa: Supply and Services Canada)

REFERENCES

BEREITER, S. 1983 'The Personal Computer Invades Higher Education' *IEEE Spectrum* 20 (6), 59–61

BLACK, K. and BENGSTON, V. 1977 'Implications of Telecommunications Technology for Old People, Families and Bureaucracies' in E. Shanas and M. Sussman eds *Family, Bureaucracy and the Elderly* (Durham, N.C.: Duke University Press)

BOARD OF HEALTH, CITY OF TORONTO 1988 *Healthy Toronto 2000, A Strategy for a Healthy City* Report of Healthy Toronto 2000 Sub-Committee (Toronto: City of Toronto)

BOOKCHIN, M. 1986 *The Limits of The City* (Montreal-Buffalo: Black Rose Books)

———— 1987 *The Rise of Urbanization and the Decline of Citizenship* (San Francisco: Sierra Club Books)

BROTCHIE, J., NEWTON, P., HALL, P. and NIJKAMP, P. 1985 *The Future of Urban Form* (London: Croom Helm)

CALHOUN, C. 1984 'Tomorrow's Global Village Fragments Community Life' *IEEE Spectrum* 21 (6)

CASTELLS, M. 1985 'High Technology, Economic Restructuring and the Urban-regional Process in the United States' in M. Castells ed. *High Technology, Space and Society* (Beverly Hills: Sage Publications)

COATES, J.F. 1982 *The Future of the Built Environment: Factors and Forces* Draft Report for the Advisory Board of the Built Environment (Washington: National Academy of Sciences)

CONKLIN, D.W. and ST-HILAIRE, F. 1988 *Canadian High-Tech in A New World Economy: A Case Study of Information Technology* (Halifax: The Institute For Research on Public Policy)

DORNEY, R., GERTLER, L., KNAPPER, C., LERNER, S., NEWKIRK, R., and RICHARDS, L. 1984 *Technological Futures and Human Settlements* (Waterloo, Ont.: Faculty of Environmental Studies, University of Waterloo)

EMBREE, C. 1986 *Planning and Scenario Development: The Case of Telecommunications and Urban Form* Senior Honours Essay for B.E.S., Urban and Regional Planning, University of Waterloo (Waterloo, Ont.: University of Waterloo)

FORESTER, T. 1985 *The Information Technology Revolution* (Cambridge, Mass: M.I.T. Press)

FRANCIS, D. 1987 *Controlling Interest: Who Owns Canada?* (Toronto: Seal Books, McClelland-Bantam, Inc.)

GALBRAITH, J.K. 1983 *The Anatomy of Power* (Boston: Houghton Mifflin Company)

GERTLER, L.O. 1985 'The Changing Metropolis and the Blumenfeld Blues' in J.R. Hitchcock and A. McMaster eds *The Metropolis* (Toronto: Department of Geography and Centre for Urban and Community Studies, University of Toronto)

—— and CROWLEY, R.W. 1977 *Changing Canadian Cities: The Next 25 Years* (Toronto: McClelland and Stewart)

—— and NEWKIRK, R.T. 1988 *Technological Futures and Human Settlements: Three Possible Views of a National Context* (Waterloo, Ont.: Faculty of Environmental Studies, University of Waterloo)

GERTLER, M.S. 1988 'The Limits to Flexibility: Comments on the Post-Fordist Vision of Production and its Geography' *Transactions of the Institute of British Geographers, N.S.* 13, 419–32

GOLDMARK, P.C. 1972 'Communication and the Community', *Scientific American* 227, 142–48

HAIG, R.M. and MCCREA, R.C. 1974 *Regional Plan of New York and Its Environs* (New York: Arno Press) (originally published in 1928)

HELMER, O. 1983 *Looking Forward, A Guide to Futures Research* (Beverly Hills: Sage Publications)

HEPWORTH, M. 1985 'The Geography of Technological Change in the Information Economy', *Regional Studies* 20, 407–24

—— 1987 'The Information City', *Cities* August, 253–62

HIRSCHORN, L. 1980 'Scenario Writing: A Developmental Approach', *Journal of the American Planning Association* 46 (2), 172

HODGE, G. 1986 *Planning Canadian Communities* (Toronto: Methuen)

HOFFMAN, R. 1986 *Overview of the Socio-Economic Resource Framework* (Ottawa: Statistics Canada)

JANTSCH, E. 1967 *Technological Forecasting in Perspective* (Paris: Organization for Economic Cooperation and Development)

LAVER, M. 1982 'Microelectronics and Tomorrow's Communities', *Town and Country Planning* 51, 211–13

MANDEVILLE, T. 1983 *The Trouble with Technology: Explorations in the Process of Technological Change* (London: Pinter)

MASUDA, Y. 1985 'Computopia' in T. Forester ed. *The Information Technology Revolution* (Cambridge, Mass.: M.I.T. Press)

MEIER, R.L. 1962 *A Communications Theory of Urban Growth* (Cambridge, Mass.: M.I.T. Press)

MENZIES, H. 1984 *Women and the Chip* (Montreal: The Institute for Research on Public Policy)

MESTHENE, E.G. 1970 *Technological Change* (New York: Mentor)

NAISBITT, J. 1984 *Megatrends* (New York: Warner Books)

NELSON, K. 1986 'Automation, Skill and Back Office Location', presented to Association of American Geographers Annual Meeting, Minneapolis, May 3–7

NOBUYUKI, K. 1986 'Intelligent Buildings Rise in Tokyo', *Japan Quarterly* 33, 154–58

PRESTON, R.E. 1986 'Stability and Change in the Canadian Central Place System Between 1971 and the Early 1980s', *Mitteilungen der Geographischen Gesellschaft* 76, 3–31

REISSMAN, L. 1964 *The Urban Process: Cities in Industrial Societies* (New York: The Free Press)

SHORTREED, J., DUST, E., and MAY, P. 1984 *The Effect of Future Trends on Trip Patterns, Urban Commercial Structure and Land Use* Transportation Research Board, Ontario (Waterloo, Ont.: Transportation Research Group, Civil Engineering, University of Waterloo)

STELTER, G.A. and ARTIBISE, F.J. 1986 *Power and Place* (Vancouver: University of British Columbia Press)

THE CANADIAN ENCYCLOPEDIA, Volume 1 1985

WORDS ASSOCIATES and NEWTON, K. *Workable Futures: Notes on Emerging Technologies* (Ottawa: Supply and Services Canada)

PART TWO

REGIONAL PERSPECTIVES

7

Central Place Theory and the Canadian Urban System

RICHARD E. PRESTON

This chapter examines the role of cities as central places (regional service centres) in the recent development of the Canadian urban system. It contributes to the urban systems section of this book by emphasizing central place theory as a framework for studying urban systems and by following a flow-based approach to the interpretation of such systems.

The chapter covers six topics: (1) Christaller's central place theory; (2) the Canadian central place system in the late 1980s; (3) stability and change in that system between 1961 and 1988; (4) the increasing importance of Toronto as the nation's chief central place; (5) an example of change in a central place system in a region experiencing population decline and located outside the national heartland; and (6) generalizations about the structure and formation of the Canadian central place system.

CENTRAL PLACE THEORY AND ITS APPLICATION

This interpretation of the Canadian central place system follows Christaller's (1966 [1933]) original statement and rules for application of his central place theory. Christaller offered a partial theory of the space economy, one that attempted to describe and explain, at the inter-city scale, the location and development of retail and service trades, transportation and communication activities, wholesaling, public and cultural institutions, some financial activities, and certain types of market-oriented industries.

Christaller's theory focuses on the *region-serving importance* (i.e. the central place function) of towns, or what he called their *'Centrality'*. The concept of centrality was intended to represent the outflow of *'Surplus'* central goods and services from a central place to consumers and activities that are not located in that place but are located within the larger system of which it is a part. In Christaller's interpretation, settlements 'became' central places, usually through competition with other places over time. At any point in time, therefore, specific settlements can be *central places* (those providing surplus goods and services to dependent centres and consumers), *deficit places* (those providing insufficient central goods and services to meet the needs of their residents and are thus dependent on central places for such goods), or *auxiliary places* (neither clearly central or deficit). No other approach to the study of central place patterns uses this three-part classification of settlements.

Christaller (1966, 164) defined *'Central Place Systems'* as a number of central places grouped around a system-forming central place according to certain rules. He identified the system elements as: the system-forming central places; the central places grouped around them; the distances (interpreted as subjective economic distance) between the central places; the location of smaller places in relation to both system-forming and other central places in the system; and the complementary region of the system-forming central place.

The importance of any place in the system at any point in time is identified by the magnitude of its centrality. Christaller saw the spatial organization of central places as dynamic; that is, as elements in a constantly evolving constellation of hierarchies, each of which is organized by changing flows of region-serving or surplus central-place activity (e.g. retail and service, administrative, cultural, health related, wholesale, and transportation and communication activities).

Christaller explains stability and change in both the importance of central places and in the organization of hierarchies in terms of: (1) ongoing competition among the bundles of forces driving each of his three pure principles of central place organization (*marketing, transportation*, and *administration*); (2) by a group of general factors (including distribution, density, and structure of the population; type, price, and production cost of central goods; transportation technology; region of natural resources; and the range of central goods); and (3) by the influence of numerous exogenous and endogenous forces including business cycles, long-distance trade, industrial development, urban population growth, metropolitan expansion, and unique local events (Christaller 1966, 27–132). The results of such competition are the thousands of combined or mixed central place hierarchies that constitute settlement patterns in the real world (Preston and Mitchell 1987; Preston 1989).

Regarding the study of urban systems in general, it important that classical central place theory's emphasis on centrality (or surplus central activities) places it under the broader approach to the study of space economies offered by both *economic base* and *input-output* theories (Mulligan 1984; Hewings 1985; Preston and Mitchell 1987). In its simplest form, the economic base approach states that the reason for both the existence and the growth of a city or region lies in the goods that it produces and sells beyond its borders. Such efforts are called 'basic', while all local serving or non-exports are called non-basic. The greater the value of the exports, the greater the local return, local investment, and local stability and growth. The *input-output* approach focuses attention on relationships (flows of commodities and money) between activities both within and between regions. The links between central-place and economic-base and input-output theories are clear; namely, that part of a town's total production of central goods and services accounted for by centrality can be considered basic, while that part accounted for by local consumption can be considered non-basic. In this context, all linkages and multipliers are amenable to description and explanation in an input-output format.

Since the appearance of Christaller's basic work in 1933, numerous theories of central places have been proposed and applied (e.g. Losch 1954; Berry and Garrison 1958; Beckmann 1958; Smith 1965; Berry 1967; White 1974; Beavon 1977; Allen and Sanglier 1979; and Berry *et al.* 1988). A key theoretical and practical difference among these theories lies in their claimed explanatory power, which ranges from Christaller's specifically defined region-serving or surplus importance (centrality) to aggregate overall importance (nodality) or city size.

Contemporary research on central place theory that goes beyond the description and testing of the original contributions can be summarized in terms of both two broad research themes and specific areas of research. According to Berry *et al.* (1988, 79–118), key themes are the elaboration and extension of traditional Christaller and Losch models (e.g. by focusing on their logical structure and geometrical properties) and the development of alternatives to them, usually by either increasing their theoretical generality or by making them more realistic. Within these broad themes, several specific research foci stand out (King 1984, 76–90): (1) consumer behaviour and central places; (2) central place theory and the location of production; (3) the dynamics of central place systems; (4) formal restatements of central place theory; and (5) alternative approaches to settlement theory.

Measuring Central Place Importance and Dominance
In this study, Canada's most important central place systems were identified for 1987–8. Next, they were organized first into regional systems and then into a national system. Then, patterns of territorial stability and change in those systems were described for the time periods 1961–71, 1971–81, and 1981–8.[1] Examined for at least two time periods were: (1)

distribution of central place importance, (2) composition of the central place hierarchy, (3) territorial patterns of daily newspaper dominance, and (4) territorial patterns of regional and national dominance based on intermetropolitan migration and air passenger flows. Attention was then given to the changing role of Toronto in the national central place system and to change in Saskatchewan's central place system.

The central place importance of each system-forming place was established by applying Christaller's (1966, 16–18) conceptual centrality model: $C = N - L$, where C is surplus importance or centrality; N is the sum of the importance of a place as a consuming unit plus its surplus importance, its absolute importance or nodality; and L is the importance of a place as a unit consuming central goods and services, or local consumption. Total daily newspaper circulation served as a measure of nodality, the number of newspapers consumed locally as a measure of local consumption, and the difference between nodality and local consumption as a measure of centrality.

THE CANADIAN CENTRAL PLACE SYSTEM
IN THE LATE 1980S

Figure 7.1 shows the territorial arrangement of central places in Canada that offered a daily newspaper in 1987–8. Central place importance, or centrality, is shown by circles and is described further by patterns showing the ratio of centrality to nodality. The higher the centrality percentage, the greater the likely contribution of the central place function to an overall urban economy, and by contrast, the lower that percentage, the greater the likely contribution of local consumption or non-central place activities.

Figure 7.2 and Figure 7.3 show the national central place hierarchy for 1971–88 in a centrality-based rank-size arrangement and in terms of daily newspaper dominance. The individual central place systems were defined initially and combined with daily commuting flows for the early 1970s (Preston 1984b). The daily newspaper component was updated for 1981 (Preston 1986a), and again for 1987–8. These central place systems were organized into regional systems on the basis of intermetropolitan migration flows (Figure 7.4) and into a national system according to airline passenger flows (Figure 7.3 and Figure 7.5).

Toronto is Canada's dominant central place. Montreal and Vancouver form a well-defined second order. Quebec City, Halifax, Edmonton, Ottawa-Hull, Winnipeg, and London comprise the third order. The remainder of the important regional system-forming central places fall in the fourth order: Saint John; Calgary; Trois-Rivières; Hamilton; Kitchener-Waterloo; Regina; Sherbrooke; Chicoutimi; Victoria; Windsor; Saskatoon; Moncton; Kingston; and St. John's.

Figure 7.1
The Pattern of Central Place Importance in 1988

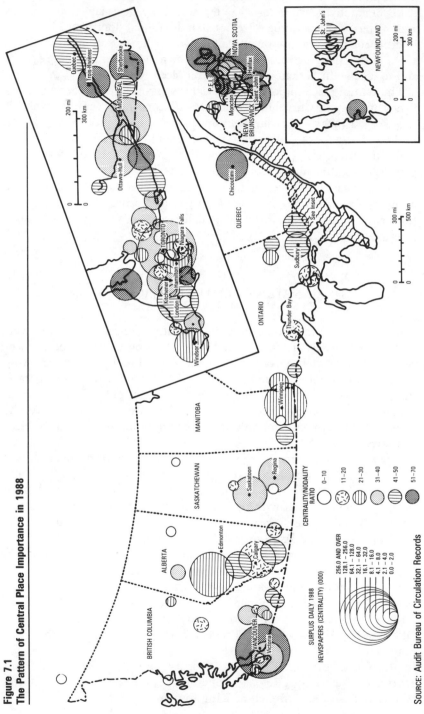

SOURCE: Audit Bureau of Circulation Records

Figure 7.2
The Canadian Central Place Hierarchy: 1971, 1981, and 1988

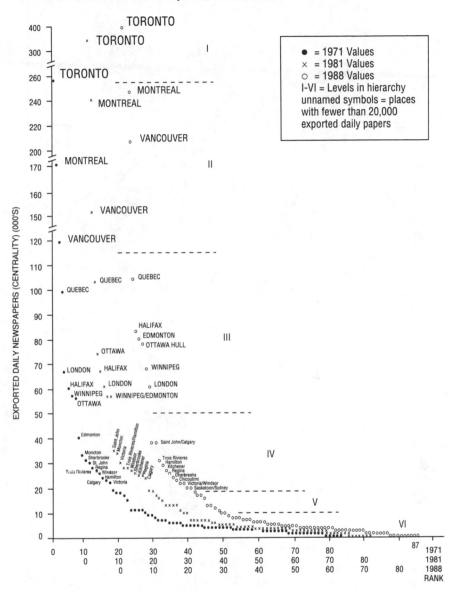

Figures 7.1 and 7.3 show that the main concentration of central places with relatively large centrality values is in the Windsor to Quebec City corridor. This situation highlights the country's two largest and most complex urban systems focusing on Toronto and Montreal and underscores the significance of the central place function in the economies of numerous cities in the nation's urban-industrial heartland.

Figure 7.3
The Canadian Central Place System: 1987 and 1988

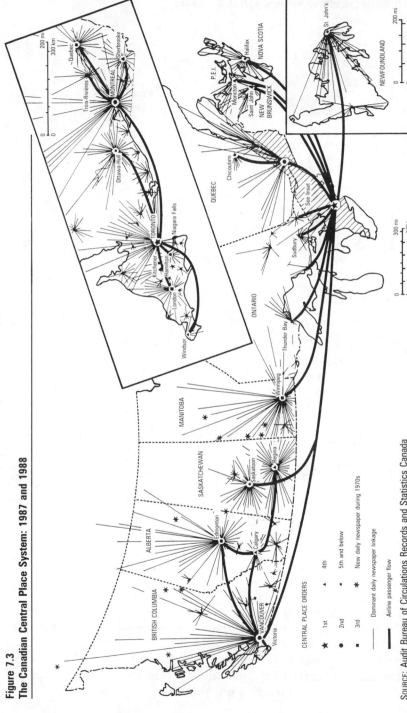

CENTRAL PLACE ORDERS

★	1st	
●	2nd	
●	3rd	
▲	4th	
•	5th and below	
✳	New daily newspaper during 1970s	

— — — Dominant daily newspaper linkage

——— Airline passenger flow

SOURCE: Audit Bureau of Circulations Records and Statistics Canada
Air Passenger Origin and Destination Reports, Domestic Reports

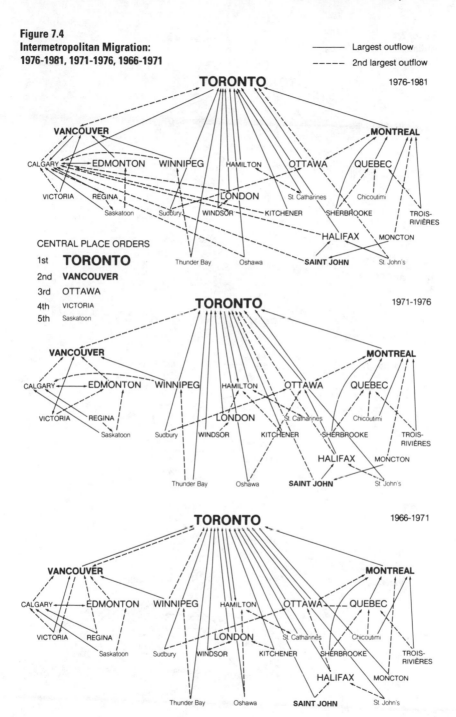

Figure 7.4
Intermetropolitan Migration:
1976-1981, 1971-1976, 1966-1971

——— Largest outflow
– – – 2nd largest outflow

1976-1981

CENTRAL PLACE ORDERS

1st **TORONTO**
2nd **VANCOUVER**
3rd OTTAWA
4th VICTORIA
5th Saskatoon

1971-1976

1966-1971

Source: Statistics Canada

Figure 7.5
Airline Passenger Flows:
1987, 1981 and 1971

——— Largest outflow

- - - - 2nd largest outflow

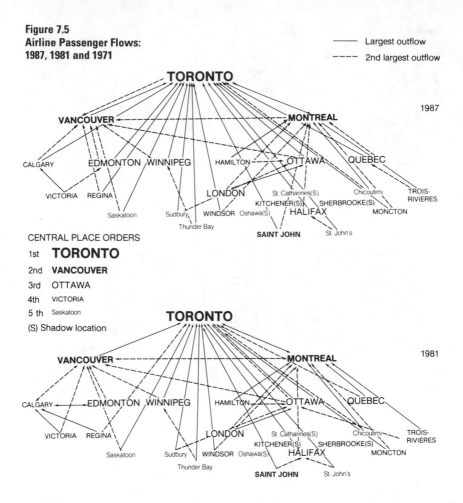

CENTRAL PLACE ORDERS

1st **TORONTO**

2nd **VANCOUVER**

3rd OTTAWA

4th VICTORIA

5 th Saskatoon

(S) Shadow location

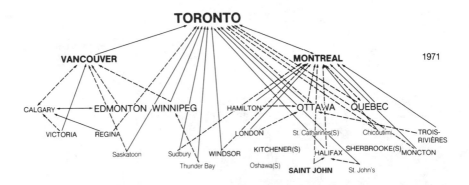

SOURCE: Statistics Canada, Air Passenger Origin and Destination Reports 1971, 1981, 1987.

Toronto's regional urban system comprises a much larger critical mass and is far more complex than Montreal's. It includes the central place subsystems of third-order Ottawa and London, fourth-order Hamilton, Windsor, Kitchener, and Kingston, and fifth-order Owen Sound, Sudbury, St. Catharines, Brantford, and North Bay. By contrast, the only significant subsystems in Montreal's system are those of third-order Quebec City and fourth-order Trois-Rivières, Sherbrooke, and Chicoutimi.

Also emphasized by their centrality magnitudes are the key regional system-forming central places outside the national heartland: Vancouver, Edmonton, Calgary, and Winnipeg in the West, and Halifax in Atlantic Canada. Other hinterland cities with relatively large centralities are St. John's, Saint John, Moncton, Charlottetown, and Sydney in Atlantic Canada, and Victoria, Regina, and Saskatoon in the West. Still smaller places whose centralities stand out on Figure 7.1 are Lethbridge and Red Deer in Calgary's system, and Sudbury in northern Ontario.

Without exception, and by contrast with the systems focusing on Toronto and Montreal, the urban systems located outside the national heartland are characterized by poorly developed rank-size distribution: that is, there are few centres between the main system-forming central places and a cluster of much smaller places.

There is little relation between central place importance (centrality) and size of centrality/nodality ratio beyond the expected tendency for larger and economically more diversified cities to have smaller values. Low ratios also marked many peripherally-located resource towns in the West and manufacturing-based cities in southern Ontario. This emphasizes that places, especially smaller ones, specializing in primary and secondary economic activities tend to have weak central place functions.

Patterns of dominance by the regional system-forming central places are well-defined, and, outside of southern Ontario, are simple in structure (Figure 7.3). Vancouver dominates British Columbia (except for the south-eastern corner) and the Yukon Territory. Edmonton dominates central and northern Alberta and the western section of the Northwest Territories. Calgary's sphere of influence includes Alberta from Red Deer south and south-eastern British Columbia. Saskatchewan's settlement pattern is divided into two tiers of influence, focusing on Saskatoon in the north and on Regina in the south. Winnipeg dominates all of Manitoba and parts of north-western Ontario.

Toronto dominates all of Ontario except for the far north-west (Preston 1979). In the north, spatially separate systems centre on Thunder Bay, Sudbury, Sault Ste. Marie, and the mining towns of the north-east. In the south, well-defined central place systems are nested within Toronto's system, and include those focusing on Windsor, London, Kitchener-Waterloo, Hamilton, St. Catharines, and Ottawa-Hull.

Montreal dominates Quebec, with well-developed subsystems focusing on Trois-Rivières, Quebec City, and Sherbrooke. Central place systems in the Atlantic Provinces are fragmented. Halifax dominates Nova Scotia. St. John's dominates Newfoundland except for the south-west coast where Corner Brook is becoming an important regional centre. New Brunswick is divided along linguistic lines into spheres focusing on Saint John and Moncton, with an area of overlap in the northern part of the province, especially in the north-east. Prince Edward Island is divided into small systems centering on Charlottetown and Summerside.

When the central place systems in Figure 7.3 were organized into larger regional systems on the basis of intermetropolitan migration flows for the period 1976–81, four well-defined regional systems appeared. They focused on Vancouver, Toronto, Montreal, and Halifax (Figure 7.4). All of these regional systems were, in turn, tied by their largest extra-regional migration outflow to Toronto. However, the second largest outflows of virtually all of the country's larger central place systems, with the exception of Montreal, were oriented to British Columbia and Alberta. It is important to emphasize, however, that in the 1980s the situation just described changed. Interprovincial migration estimates show that during the early and middle 1980s the pull of the West weakened while that of central Canada gained strength. By the late 1980s, however, British Columbia joined Ontario as an important intraprovincial migration destination and Alberta was also beginning to show positive net migration. Whatever the overall spatial orientation of flows, intermetropolitan migration patterns emphasize the importance of the key regional centres in the organization of the Canadian urban system.

As noted, the central place systems comprising each of the regional migration systems form clear spatial structures. In the West, the central place systems focusing on Edmonton, Calgary, Regina, Saskatoon, and Winnipeg form a migration system centering on Vancouver. Central place systems in central Canada are linked to either Toronto or Montreal, and form two separate regional migration systems. Toronto dominates all subsystems in Ontario. In this regard, it is significant that Toronto's link with Ottawa was twice the size of that between the national capital and Montreal. Montreal is the migration focus for Quebec and northern (Acadian) New Brunswick. In Atlantic Canada, migration flows link the central place systems focusing on St. John's and Saint John to Halifax, which, in turn, is linked to Toronto.

Not surprisingly, Toronto and Montreal are linked by the nation's largest single intermetropolitan migration stream. The flow from Montreal to Toronto, however, was seven times greater than that from Toronto to Montreal, and while Montreal's single most important migration destination was Toronto, Toronto's main outflows were to Calgary, Vancouver, Hamilton, and Edmonton, in that order.

Toronto's domination of the nation's intermetropolitan migration pattern between 1976 and 1981 was striking, and it is emphasized further by Toronto's appearance in six of the ten largest intermetropolitan migration links. Its closest rivals, Montreal and Calgary, by contrast, appear in only three of the top ten linkages. Equally striking was the westward orientation of intermetropolitan migration systems during the 1970s, a situation revealed by the westward focus of the second largest outflows in general and by the fact that Toronto's largest outflow was to Calgary.

When the nation's central place systems were organized into a national system on the basis of domestic airline passenger flows for 1987, the patterns in Figures 7.3 and 7.5 appeared. When the airline passenger pattern was compared with that for intermetropolitan migration, there were similarities and differences in both the interregional flows and in the role of some of the system-forming central places. Similarities were: (1) Toronto's national dominance as the attractor of largest outflows; (2) the absolute dominance of the Toronto-Montreal link (1,224,290 passengers in 1987); (3) the westward orientation of second largest outflows; (4) domination by Toronto, Montreal, Vancouver in their respective regions; (5) consistency in the overall rank order of the largest centres in the three major regional subsystems outside of Atlantic Canada; and (6) the firm inclusion of Ottawa's central place system within Toronto's regional system.

Toronto's domination of the national air passenger system deserves comment. Table 7.1 shows that in 1987 Toronto appeared in the four largest air passenger links, with Montreal, Vancouver, Ottawa, and Calgary, in that order. Toronto also appears in seven of the top ten links and in thirteen of the top twenty five. No other city appeared in more than eight links (Vancouver). Toronto's increasing dominance is also shown by the fact that it accounted for three (St. John's, Quebec City, and Regina) of the four new links among the top twenty five for 1987.

Differences between the air passenger and migration flows reflected the overwhelming dominance of interaction between Toronto and Montreal in the national air passenger system, competition between Toronto and Vancouver for air passengers from central place systems in Manitoba and Saskatchewan, and competition among Toronto, Montreal, and Halifax for air passengers from central place systems in the Atlantic region. Vancouver's pattern of air passenger dominance was territorially smaller than its intermetropolitan migration system. Calgary, Edmonton, and Vancouver were part of Vancouver's regional system on both measures, but, while Saskatoon and Winnipeg were part of Vancouver's migration system, they were linked to Toronto by their largest air passenger flow. Toronto's attraction was also reflected in the fact that while Vancouver's main migration link was with Calgary, its main air passenger link was with Toronto. Toronto's attraction appeared again in Atlantic Canada, where central place systems focusing on Halifax, Saint John, Moncton, St. John's, and Charlottetown, have direct air passenger links to Toronto, instead of linking with Toronto through Halifax as they did through intermetropolitan migration.

Table 7.1
Twenty-five Largest Airline Passenger Links: 1987 (Pairs Ranked by Total Inbound and Outbound Passenger Volumes)

Link Rank 1971	1981	1987	City Pair	Magnitude 1987 (thousands of passengers)	Per cent of Total	Cumulative percentage
1	1	1	Montreal-Toronto	1224.3	10.47	10.47
4	4	2	Toronto-Vancouver	686.4	5.87	16.34
2	3	3	Ottawa-Toronto	671.4	5.74	22.08
11	6	4	Calgary-Toronto	482.2	4.12	26.20
5	5	5	Calgary-Vancouver	396.4	3.39	29.59
6	9	6	Toronto-Winnipeg	353.5	3.02	32.61
3	2	7	Calgary-Edmonton	328.4	2.81	35.42
16	8	8	Edmonton-Toronto	323.5	2.77	38.19
7	7	9	Edmonton-Vancouver	322.5	2.76	40.95
8	10	10	Halifax-Toronto	307.1	2.63	43.58
9	11	11	Thunder Bay-Toronto	187.2	1.60	45.18
14	12	12	Vancouver-Winnipeg	159.9	1.37	46.55
15	15	13	Montreal-Vancouver	156.2	1.34	47.89
18	19	14	Halifax-Montreal	126.9	1.09	48.98
xx	xx	15	St. John's(Nd)-Toronto	124.9	1.07	50.05
25	13	16	Kelowna-Vancouver	121.5	1.04	51.09
23	16	17	Calgary-Winnipeg	117.7	1.01	52.10
xx	23	18	Ottawa-Vancouver	111.8	.96	53.06
12	25	19	Toronto-Windsor	107.1	.92	53.98
xx	xx	20	Halifax-Ottawa	104.3	.89	54.87
xx	xx	21	Quebec-Toronto	101.7	.87	55.74
20	20	22	Sault Ste Marie-Toronto	100.8	.86	56.60
18	14	23	Prince George-Vancouver	98.1	.84	57.44
xx	18	24	Calgary-Montreal	97.7	.84	58.28
xx	xx	25	Regina-Toronto	88.9	.76	59.04

xx = Not present in the top 25 linkages in a particular study year

SOURCE: Statistics Canada, *Air Passenger Origin and Destination: Domestic Flight, 1971, 1981, 1987.* Ottawa: Minister of Supply and Services Canada.

CENTRAL PLACE STABILITY AND CHANGE: 1961–1988

The number of central places competing for the national daily newspaper market (the total number of newspaper readers in the country) increased by about 10 per cent between 1971 and 1986 from 87 to 101. All but three of these new central places were in western resource-based towns located at considerable distance from the main regional centres (Figure 7.3): Whitehorse in the Yukon Territory; Terrace, Dawson Creek, and Fort St. John in northern British Columbia; Fort McMurray in north-eastern Alberta; Lloydminster, on the provincial boundary between Saskatoon and Edmonton; and Dauphin, Flin Flon, Roblin, Swan River, and Thompson, forming an arc through the resource extraction region of Manitoba. The three exceptions were Cobourg, Ontario, and Sackville and Caraquet in New Brunswick. Newspapers in at least three towns also declined from daily to weekly status between 1971 and 1988: Brampton and Oakville in Toronto's metropolitan area, and Fort Frances in north-western Ontario.

Table 7.2
Stability and Change in the Canadian Central Place System: 1961–1988

Period	1961–71		1971–81		1981–88	
Change	(No.)	(%)	(No.)	(%)	(No.)	(%)
Growth	73	82	42	51	24	28
Stable	13	15	24	29	41	48
Decline	3	3	16	20	21	24
Total	89	100	82	100	86	100

SOURCE: Preston (1984) and Audit Bureau of Circulations.

Comparison of central place hierarchies for 1971, 1981, and 1988 revealed reasonably clear and comparable breaks in the distribution for the first four orders for both study years, overall stability among the larger places, and considerable movement among the middle-sized and smaller places (Figure 7.2). Toronto occupied the first rank and increased its lead over Montreal. Montreal and Vancouver formed the second rank. The third order included Quebec City, Ottawa, Halifax, London, and Winnipeg in all three years, and added Edmonton in 1981. Within that group, Ottawa and Halifax improved their positions while London and Winnipeg declined. Within the fourth order, between 1971 and 1981, Kitchener was the new entry, Victoria showed the greatest upward shift, and Sherbrooke and Regina the greatest decline.

Differences in the national pattern of centrality values between the 1960s, 1970s, and 1980s were substantial (Figure 7.6 and Figure 7.7 show the patterns for 1961–71 and 1981–8 respectively). During the 1960s, virtually every central place in the country that offered a daily newspaper increased its central place importance (Preston 1984b). The pattern for the 1970s, by contrast, was mixed, with numerous smaller central places in the heartland and in the West, as well as larger central places in the West and Quebec, showing either stability or decline. The trends of the 1970s continued into the 1980s with stability being a consistent trait in the national heartland, decline characterizing numerous smaller central places in the West, and a mixed pattern in Atlantic Canada.

A summary of stability and change in central place importance between 1961 and 1988 is given in Table 7.2. The proportion of central places in the growth category declined from 82 per cent to 28 per cent, the stable class increased from 15 to 48 per cent, and the decline group increased from 3 to 24 per cent.

The pattern of stability and change between 1961 and 1988 by hierarchical level shows that increasing central place importance characterized the larger central places (orders 1 and 2) in all three decades (Tables 7.2 and 7.3). Among the smaller centres (orders 3 and 4), by contrast, stability has increasingly replaced growth since 1971. Among fifth order central places, there has been a complete turn around from the growth-dominated situa-

Figure 7.6
Change in Central Place Importance 1961–1971

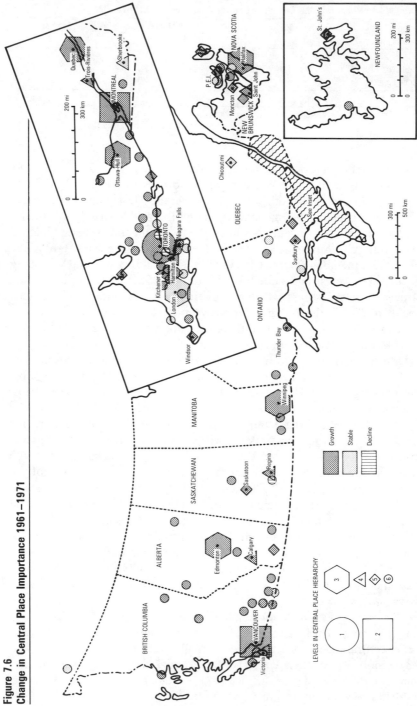

Figure 7.7
Change in Centrality 1981–1988

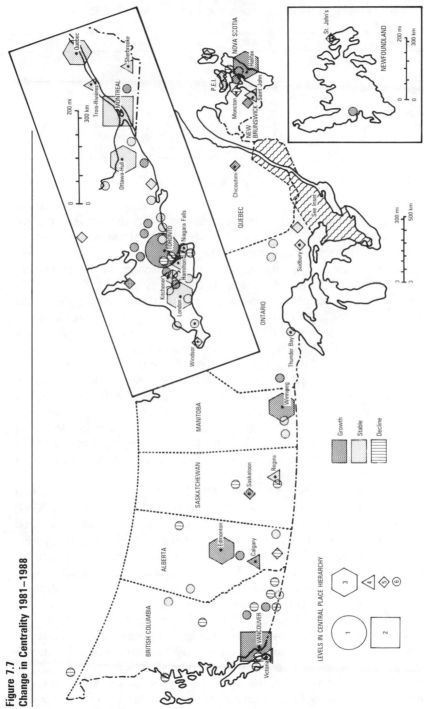

Table 7.3
Stability and Change in the Canadian Central Place System by Hierarchical Order:
1961–1988

Period	1961–71			1971–81			1981–88		
Type of Change	G	S	D	G	S	D	G	S	D
Order									
Order 1	1	—	—	1	—	—	1	—	—
Order 2	2	—	—	2	—	—	1	1	—
Order 3	5	1	—	4	2	—	3	3	—
Order 4	7	1	—	3	3	2	1	8	—
Order 5	13	1	—	8	5	1	4	6	4
Order 6	42	10	2	25	14	13	14	24	17

(G = Growth, S = Stable, D = Decline)

SOURCE: Preston (1984) and Audit Bureau of Circulations.

tion in the 1960s. A roughly equal division of growth, stability, and decline prevailed during the 1970s, while stability was the dominant state in the 1980s. Among sixth order central places, the situation was one of growth during the 1960s, an upsurge of stability and decline in the 1970s, and dominance by stable and declining central places in the 1980s.

Stability and change in central place importance in the 1970s and 1980s as revealed by our analysis of surplus daily newspaper distribution exhibited some clear differences. In the 1970s, the most outstanding growth situation was the rapid increase in the central place importance of Toronto. Substantial relative growth elsewhere in the national system was shown by: (1) Montreal, Ottawa, Kitchener, and Kingston in the heartland; (2) Vancouver and Victoria in the Georgia Strait urban region; (3) Edmonton, Lethbridge, and Red Deer in the Alberta development corridor; (4) Winnipeg, Portage La Prairie, and Brandon in Manitoba; and (5) Halifax, Saint John, St. John's, Charlottetown, and Fredericton in Atlantic Canada. Most of the growing central places were thus the nation's main regional system-forming centres.

In the 1970s, stable central places included many of the important system-forming centres: Calgary, Saskatoon, and Regina in the West; London, Windsor, Trois-Rivières, and Quebec City in the heartland; and Moncton and Sydney in the Atlantic hinterland. In addition, there were noticeable concentrations in the western and northern parts of the national hinterland, especially in interior British Columbia. Declining places were for the most part either, or both, smaller places or places dependent on traditional manufacturing or resource industries. Their greatest concentration was in southern Ontario, where the decline in the central place role of older manufacturing towns was evident. Prominent central places in the heartland that declined markedly were Sherbrooke, in Montreal's system, and the mining centre of Sudbury in north-eastern Ontario.

In the 1980s, by contrast, there were only a few growth situations, and they were mainly the largest central places. There were no regions where growth was widespread. Among the major system-forming central places, only Toronto, Vancouver, Edmonton, Calgary, Winnipeg, Saskatoon, and Halifax showed strong growth. The national heartland and Atlantic Canada were dominated by stability, with key central places like Montreal, Quebec, Trois-Rivières, Sherbrooke, Ottawa-Hull, and London falling into this group. Moreover, declining central place functions were exhibited in the heartland by Windsor and several other centres west of Toronto. Moncton and St. John's showed decline in the Atlantic Region. Decline was also frequent among smaller places outside of Vancouver and Victoria in British Columbia.

When the above observations on stability and change were combined with the fact that none of the main system-forming places experienced decline between 1961 and 1988, it suggests that the larger regional centres withstood Canada's economic difficulties during the 1970s and 1980s far better than the smaller ones.

A perspective on the extent to which the central place systems outlined in Figure 7.3 were reorganized territorially during the 1970s and 1980s can be gained by a comparison of patterns of dominance for 1971 with those for various dates in the 1980s. The result of this comparison is that, with the exception of the embryonic complementary regions associated with the new newspaper towns, the patterns of territorial dominance exhibited by individual newspaper towns have remained virtually unchanged since the early 1970s.

A comparison of intermetropolitan migration flows for 1966–71, 1971–6, and 1976–81 (Figure 7.4) and of interprovincial flows for 1981–6 revealed: (1) the persistence and growth of Toronto as the chief migration destination for all regional systems; (2) an overall stability in the relative size, composition, and organization of the regional systems focusing on Toronto, Vancouver, Montreal, and to a lesser extent, on Halifax; (3) a substantial reorientation of the national system towards the West (to Calgary and Vancouver) between 1976–81; (4) an increase in importance of Calgary as a destination not only for the West but for the East; (5) a reorientation of Toronto's main outflow from central Canada to Calgary in the 1970s; (6) the relative decline of Montreal's system as a migration destination; (7) the strong orientation of Ottawa to Toronto; and (8) the orientation of all Atlantic systems to Toronto.

It is important to remember, however, that migration data for the early- and middle–1980s show a reorientation of the national intermetropolitan migration system away from the West and back to central Canada, especially to southern Ontario. During that period, therefore, the attractiveness of Alberta and British Columbia as migration destinations for opportunity seekers from elsewhere in Canada, and especially from Ontario, diminished. At the same time, the fortunes of Ontario as a destination for immigrants from other parts of Canada, and especially the West, was once again on the upswing. This shift in interprovincial migration patterns became clear in 1982–3, and was related to an improvement in the heartland's economy, on the one hand, and to a deterioration in British Columbia's and Alberta's, especially Calgary's, on the other (Statistics Canada, various years). By the end of the decade, however, British Columbia, especially Vancouver, was once again an important migration destination and Alberta, especially Calgary, was also attracting migrants.

A comparison of how airline passenger flows organized the nation's central place systems into larger regional systems and into a national system in 1971, 1981, and 1987 revealed: (1) an overall stability in the territorial organization of largest air passenger outflows; (2) a persistent and increasing national dominance by Toronto; (3) an overall reorientation from the east to west especially to Vancouver and in terms of secondary links; (4) an increasing orientation of Atlantic central place systems to Toronto, shown by direct links from Halifax, Saint John, St. John's, and Moncton to Toronto (bypassing Halifax and Montreal); (5) Moncton's reorientation from Montreal to Toronto, a situation that appears to indicate a continued reduction in the size of Montreal's area of influence and an intrusion by Toronto into an area that is partly French speaking; (6) a stable boundary zone between Toronto and Vancouver air passenger systems; and (7) increasingly strong ties between Ottawa and Toronto (Figures 7.3, 7.5 and Table 7.1).

The Increasing Importance of Toronto

Strong themes in this chapter are stability in the rank order and territorial extent of the areas of dominance of the country's main regional capitals and the increasing importance of Toronto as the nation's chief central place. Toronto's increasingly dominant role in the nation's central place system has already been demonstrated on several measures. However, as Matthew (1989) and Semple and Green (1983) have shown, Toronto's importance as the control centre of the national economy is best shown by the city's ability to attract corporate head offices. Table 7.4 ranks by population the nation's nine census metropolitan areas with over 500,000 inhabitants, and shows for various measures the number of head offices that each city hosted in 1988. The data source was *The Financial Post 500* (1988), and distributions are shown for 'The Top 100 Industries', 'The Top 100 Financial Institutions', 'The Top 100 Private Companies', and the 'Top 500 Industries'. Toronto's dominance in every category, especially in comparison with Montreal and Vancouver, is both striking and apparently increasing.

When Toronto's increasing national dominance is combined with the fact that during the 1970s and 1980s the main regional system-forming central places have either increased or maintained their central place importance, it is clear that there has been a concentration of nation- and region-serving central place functions in Toronto and the regional capitals (Figures 7.6 and 7.7, and Tables 7.2, 7.3, and 7.4). It is suggested, moreover,

Table 7.4
Corporate Control Points in the Canadian Urban System

Central Place	Population (millions)	Top 100 Industries	Top 100 Financial Institutions	Top 100 Private Companies	Top 500 Industries
Toronto	3.43	44	50	49	201
Montreal	2.92	19	17	22	125
Vancouver	1.38	9	7	2	42
Ottawa	.82	1	4	2	14
Edmonton	.79	1	3	2	10
Calgary	.67	12	3	1	42
Winnipeg	.63	6	1	3	17
Quebec City	.60	—	4	—	2
Hamilton	.56	1	1	3	11

SOURCE: *The Financial Post 500*, Summer, 1988.

that this concentration has been at the expense of smaller and more specialized urban centres.

Given the strength of the nation's regional capitals since 1971, it appeared reasonable that at least some of them should have expanded their spheres of influence over the 1970s and 1980s, for example, Toronto, Montreal, Vancouver, Edmonton, Calgary, Winnipeg, Halifax, Ottawa, and Quebec City. However, when extra-provincial daily newspaper circulations (both first and second most important links) for 1971 were compared with those for 1983, it was clear that except for Toronto, which expanded its influence dramatically, and for Montreal, which experienced a contraction in its area of influence, the expected pattern of expanded regional spheres of influence and of direct competition among regional capitals beyond their home provinces did not take place. Rather, the patterns present in the early 1970s persisted (Figure 7.3); for example, Vancouver's dominance in the Yukon Territory, Edmonton's influence in the western Northwest Territories and in north-eastern British Columbia, Calgary's influence in south-eastern British Columbia, Winnipeg's influence in the central Northwest Territories and that city's declining influence in north-western Ontario; Ottawa's dominance in adjacent Quebec; Montreal's declining influence in eastern Ontario; and Halifax's influence in Prince Edward Island.

The most significant change in the national pattern of daily newspaper dominance has been the increase in both volume and areal coverage of Toronto newspapers. This situation suggests that the increasing importance of Toronto, the decline of Montreal, and stability in the pattern of dominance of the main regional centres are all associated with Toronto's rapid development as the nation's key business centre, and thus its most important central place.

Moreover, it is suggested that the failure of regional centres to prevail as suppliers of the latest specialized information to expanding regions, or even to their traditional regions, also reflects Toronto's increasing ability to provide this type of information for most of the nation. The nationwide increase in Toronto newspapers appears to be related directly to the city's expanding central place function as the national centre for business information conveyed by the daily, weekly, and monthly business press.

At the outset of the 1970s Canada did not have a national daily business press (Preston 1986a). The task of spreading business information by newspaper fell to the region-serving daily papers in each province and to nationally-distributed weekly and monthly business publications. This situation changed dramatically between 1971 and 1981, and that change was linked directly to a rapid increase in national coverage by the Toronto *Globe and Mail* (Figure 7.8). Facilitated by satellite transmission and same-day publication in four locations outside of Toronto (Vancouver, Calgary, Ottawa, and Moncton), by the early 1980s the *Globe and Mail* had won a strong presence in every major central place system in the country. This situation suggests that 'the nation's business had become Toronto's business and vice versa'.

The key element in the nationwide appeal of the *Globe and Mail* has been demand for its 'Report on Business'. This is a daily survey of national and international business and financial matters plus special reports on subjects of interest to business people. The performance level of the Report on Business has surpassed and replaced attempts by metropolitan and regional newspapers elsewhere in the country to develop or maintain a regionally dominant daily national business section.

The Toronto *Globe and Mail* experience during the 1970s was only part of the story of recent events highlighting the increasing importance of Toronto in the territorial reorganization of Canada's business press. The city was also making significant strides toward becoming the national centre for weekly and monthly business publications.

The weekly business press has been dominated by two newspapers, the *Financial Post* and the *Financial Times* (which added a daily edition in 1989). The French language entry in this arena is *Les Affaires*, but its circulation is and has been largely restricted to Quebec. In 1966, the *Financial Times* was published in Toronto and the *Financial Post* and *Les Affaires* in Montreal. In 1975, however, the Montreal-based *Financial Post* moved its editorial offices and point of publication to Toronto. Thus, by 1976 Toronto offered a combined weekly business press circulation of 213,746, of which 137,000 served locations outside Ontario, while Montreal's contribution to the national weekly business press after 1976 did not rise above the 40,000 copies of *Les Affaires*, almost all of which were consumed in Quebec, and which were matched in volume of circulation in Quebec by the Toronto-based English language weekly business press. In the weekly business press at the national scale, therefore, Toronto's dominance has become overwhelming.

In 1966, the leading monthly English-language business magazine in Canada was *Canadian Business* published in Montreal. The leading French-

Figure 7.8
The Distribution of the Toronto Globe and Mail Outside of Ontario: 1971 and 1981

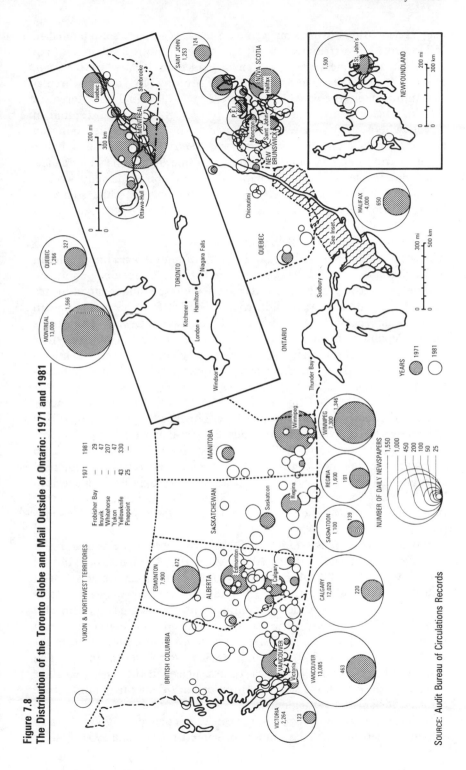

SOURCE: Audit Bureau of Circulations Records

language monthly business magazine was *Revue Commerce*, also published in Montreal but distributed mainly in Quebec. Montreal's dominance of the monthly business press in Canada ended in 1979 when *Canadian Business* moved its base of operation from Montreal to Toronto. Circulation immediately increased by 70 per cent to 83,421 in 1981. Moreover, this increase was distributed over all provinces with the exception of Quebec where circulation was stable. Based on the record for these monthly business publications between 1966 and 1986, Toronto's position has changed from one of a non-contributor to one of national dominance. Therefore, because of Toronto's national domination of the daily, weekly, and monthly business press, the city has become the chief source of business information for the nation.

A Peripheral Central Place System in the 1960s

This section focuses on stability and change in central place importance in Saskatchewan (Preston 1984a), a province that is experiencing population decline and out-migration and is located beyond the immediate influence of both the national urban-industrial heartland and the nation's main metropolitan regions (Ray and Brewis 1976). Saskatchewan's economy is largely dependent on staple resources; since World War II, the province has experienced substantial out-migration. The provincial settlement pattern is dominated by numerous small centres and by a large rural non-farm population.

Saskatchewan's population is small, 926,242 in 1986—and is concentrated in the southern half of the province. The space economy is organized around two metropolitan areas of modest size and of roughly equal importance: Regina (population 139,470) and Saskatoon (126,450). There is no dominant metropolitan centre and little overlap between the commercial areas of dominance of the two cities. Both urban systems are characterized by poorly-developed central place hierarchies in the sense that together they contain no places with over 35,000 inhabitants and only five with populations of over 10,000.

Saskatoon's system is comprised of three distinct subsystems in addition to its own. They focus on Prince Albert (28,465), North Battleford (14,500) and Lloydminster (8,690). By contrast, the small urban systems east of Saskatoon and those lying near the boundary of the Saskatoon and Regina systems do not contain clearly dominant places. Regina's system also includes four territorially distinct subsystems in addition to its own, which includes Moose Jaw (31,855). These subsystems centre on Swift Current (15,415), Yorkton (13,340), Weyburn (8,815) and Estevan (9,150). The majority of these towns are typical central places in the sense that their chief function is that of a service centre for both their surrounding trade area and for smaller settlements.

Both the pattern of change and the causes of change in Saskatchewan's settlement pattern has been known for some time (Hodge 1965; Stabler

1987). The reorganization of the provincial settlement pattern since World War II has influenced the number of centres, the distribution of various types of centres, the density and spacing of centres, and the performance of trade centres in particular spatial situations. The key shaping forces have been depopulation resulting from increased farm size and new agricultural technology, increasing consumer mobility as a result of widespread car ownership and highway improvements, and increased incomes. The results of these forces have been elevated thresholds for central place functions and more multiple-purpose shopping trips. The impact of these changes on the settlement pattern have been those suggested by Christaller (1966, 88–90, 117–9, 165), namely:

1. The weaker (smaller) central places die away first.
2. The decrease in the number of nodes in a particular system is accompanied by a transformation of the system in which, first, the most favourably situated places are sought out by investors and thus tend to maintain themselves, and, second, the most unfavourably situated central places are neglected by investors and tend to lose their central place status.
3. The demand for central goods tends to migrate to either the more favourably situated central places in a distressed region or to central places in neighbouring regions with stable or expanding populations.
4. The trade areas of the larger stable or growing central places expand at the expense of smaller declining places.

In summary, Christaller suggested that in urban systems in decline, the original systems are transformed into ones comprised of fewer places, and in which the survivors tend to be the larger and economically more diversified centres with relatively healthy central place functions. Moreover, smaller places suffer first and often stagnate, decline (frequently losing their central place function), and become either dependent noncentral places (Christaller called them auxiliary and deficit places) or disappear.

Empirical studies have shown that change in Saskatchewan's settlement pattern have followed Christaller's interpretation (Hodge 1965; Stabler 1987): (1) the very small trade centres (hamlets) have been for some time declining faster than the larger ones; (2) the trade-centre needs of rural and small town consumers are increasingly being served by larger trade centres; (3) decline in small trade centres is especially pronounced close to large cities; and (4) small trade centres are farther apart today than in the pre-World War II situation.

Figure 7.9 shows stability and change in the central place importance of settlements with over 1,000 inhabitants in Saskatchewan between 1961 and 1971. Seen in the light of the changes in the provincial settlement pattern just listed, and especially in relation to the well-documented widespread decline of small centres with less than 1,000 inhabitants, the map

Figure 7.9
Centrality Differences for Incorporated Centres, 1961–1971, Saskatchewan

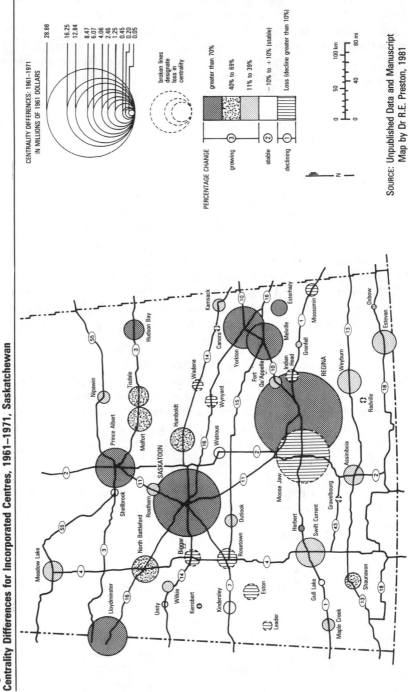

CENTRALITY DIFFERENCES: 1961–1971
IN MILLIONS OF 1961 DOLLARS

28.88
16.25
12.84
8.47
6.07
4.06
2.46
1.25
0.45
0.20
0.05

broken lines
designate
loss in
centrality

PERCENTAGE CHANGE

greater than 70%
40% to 69%
11% to 39%
–10% to +10% (stable)
Loss (decline greater than 10%)

growing ③
stable ②
declining ①

SOURCE: Unpublished Data and Manuscript
Map by Dr R.E. Preston, 1981

emphasizes both the viability of the larger central places and the weaknesses of many of the smaller ones.

Several central places showed centrality increases of greater than 70 per cent between 1961 and 1971. Conforming to Christaller's interpretation, they were the larger places, for example, Regina and Saskatoon, and the key places in the main central place subsystems: Melville, Yorkton, Prince Albert, and Lloydminster. Smaller places showing vitality were Esterhazy, Hudson Bay, and Herbert. Complementing this group were those showing increases between 40 and 69 per cent, viz. Shaunavon, Humboldt, Tisdale, North Battleford, Grenfell, and Melfort. Virtually all of the growing smaller places were located between strong central places on important highways serving Regina or Saskatoon.

Among the larger and rapidly growing central places, Yorkton, Lloydminster, North Battleford, and Prince Albert demonstrate the viability of the principal foci of the important central place subsystems in Saskatchewan. It is also significant that the remaining critically located central places, such as Swift Current, Nipawan, Meadow Lake, Assiniboia, Weyburn, and Estevan, experienced at least modest growth in their central place function.

The main points here are that between 1961 and 1971: (1) virtually all of the larger and more important central places fell into a centrality growth group; (2) central places of all sizes that occupied focal points in the provincial central place system showed expanding centralities; (3) no significant component of the provincial settlement system was without at least one expanding and relatively large central place that was accessible to virtually all settlements in the system of which it was a part; (4) with the exception of Moose Jaw, all declining or stable central places had small populations; and (5) the proximity of many stable or declining places to locations with expanding centralities suggests that some functions formerly offered by the stable and declining centres are increasingly being offered by growing central places located nearby.

Overall, and in the context of Saskatchewan's continuing state of rural and small-town population decline, it would appear that the provincial central place system is undergoing a transformation towards a new situation in which it will be composed of 'fewer but stronger central places'.

CONCLUSIONS

This interpretation of recent patterns of stability and change in the Canadian central place pattern was based on Christaller's (1966 [1933]) original theoretical statement. Accordingly, the explanatory power of his key concept of central place importance, centrality, was emphasized. This approach revealed the following general conclusions and possible trends regarding the Canadian central place system. The performance of the Canadian central place system during the 1960s was dominated by growth.

By contrast, central place performance during the 1970s and 1980s was mixed, and demonstrated few well-defined territorial patterns. Stability in rank order and in overall territorial organization, of slow growth by over half of the places, and of decline among an increasing number of smaller places were the most common states.

Over the thirty year study period a number of situations emerged, at least some of which may indicate trends:

1. The most spectacular change was the increased importance of Toronto as both a region and nation-serving centre, especially when compared with the performance of Montreal. This confirms Semple and Green's (1983) conclusion that Toronto has become 'the metropolitan centre' of Canada in the sense that the concentration in Toronto of national and branch corporate headquarters offices and financial institutions is continuing, and that the city is increasing its business and financial domination of the national urban system.

2. Confirmed was Montreal's decline in status in the national urban system from the position as the dominant centre, first to one rivalled by Toronto, then to one dominated by Toronto, and now to its present role as chief regional centre for French Canada.

3. The sheer concentration of strong and growing larger central places between Windsor and Quebec City confirms the continued strength of the Toronto and Montreal urban systems in the organization of the national system.

4. Vancouver showed strong growth in the context of the West, a region where only a few centres showed an increased region-serving importance during the 1970s. The source of Vancouver's strength poses an interesting question, at least part of the answer to which may lie in the city's increasing role as a centre for Canada's involvement with the nations of the Pacific Rim.

5. In general, regional capitals and larger central places exhibited stronger growth during the 1970s and 1980s than did smaller places, and, overall, there was an improvement in the position of western versus heartland and eastern metropolitan areas.

6. At one level, there was a continued orientation of the nation's regional systems towards Toronto, and, at another level, towards the West, especially towards Vancouver, Calgary, and Edmonton. Associated with these regional shifts was a decline in regional orientation towards Montreal by parts of its traditional urban system, and by the cities of the Atlantic region.

7. By 1981, Ottawa's urban system had become firmly integrated into Toronto's larger regional system. The question, which was still open during the early 1970s, of whether Ottawa would fall to either Montreal or to Toronto, or whether it would remain tied equally to both appears to have been answered.

8. A continuing decrease in the size and complexity of Montreal's area of influence is indicated by increasing Toronto-dominance in eastern Ontario, the integration of Ottawa's urban system into Toronto's regional system, an increasing presence of Toronto's newspapers in Quebec, and the partial reorientation of Moncton's system from Montreal to Toronto.

9. The smaller central places that fared worst over the 1970s and 1980s were dependent on natural resources or traditional manufacturing.

10. In regions of population decline, for example, the Prairies, central place systems are undergoing a pattern of reorganization that is resulting in systems comprised of fewer but stronger central places.

ACKNOWLEDGEMENTS

I would like to thank the Social Sciences and Humanities Research Council of Canada for supporting the research underlying both this chapter and the larger project of which it is a part.

NOTES

1. The central place importance for the period 1961–71 was based on surplus retail and service sales for each place, while that for the two later periods was based on surplus daily newspaper circulations. These measures are highly correlated (Preston 1971).

FURTHER READING

ALLEN, P.M. and SANGLIER, M. 1979 'A Dynamic Model of Growth in a Central Place System', *Geographical Analysis* 11, 256–72

BEAVON, K.S.O. 1977 *Central Place Theory: A Reinterpretation* (London: Longman)

BERRY, B.J.L., PARR, J.B., EPSTEIN, B.J., GHOSH, A., and SMITH, R.H.T. 1988 *Market Centers and Retail Location: Theory and Applications* (Englewood Cliffs, N.J.: Prentice-Hall)

KING, L.J. 1984 *Central Place Theory* (Beverly Hills: Sage Publications)

MULLIGAN, G.F. 1984 'Agglomeration and Central Place Theory: A Review of the Literature', *International Regional Science Review* 9, 1–42

PRESTON, R.E. 1983 'The Dynamic Component of Christaller's Central Place Theory and the Theme of Change in His Research', *The Canadian Geographer* 23, 201–21

WHITE, R.W. 1974 'Sketches of a Dynamic Central Place Theory', *Economic Geography* 50, 219–27

REFERENCES

ALLEN, P.M. and SANGLIER, M. 1979 'A Dynamic Model of Growth in a Central Place System', *Geographical Analysis* 11, 256–72

Audit Bureau of Circulations (Toronto, Chicago), Annual Audit Reports for Daily Newspapers, Annual FAS, FAX, and Annual Fact Book, various dates since 1971

BEAVON, K.S.O. 1977 *Central Place Theory: A Reinterpretation* (London: Longman)

BECKMANN, M. 1958 'City Hierarchies and the Distribution of City Size', *Economic Development and Cultural Change* 6, 243–48

BERRY, B.J.L. and GARRISON, W.L. 1958 'Recent Developments of Central Place Theory', *Papers and Proceedings of the Regional Science Association* 4, 107–20

——— 1967 *Geography of Market Centers and Retail Distribution* (Englewood Cliffs, N.J.: Prentice-Hall)

——— and PARR, J.B., EPSTEIN, B.J., GHOSH, A., and SMITH, R.H.T. 1988 *Market Centers and Retail Location: Theory and Applications* (Englewood Cliffs, N.J.: Prentice-Hall)

CHRISTALLER, W. 1966 *Central Places in Southern Germany* translated by C.W. Baskin (Englewood Cliffs, N.J.: Prentice-Hall) This book contains about 80 per cent of W. Christaller 1933 *Die zentralen Orte in Süddeutschland* (Jena: Gustav Fischer Verlag)

HEWINGS, G.D. 1985 *Regional Input-Output Analysis* (Beverly Hills: Sage Publications)

HODGE, G. 1965 'The Prediction of Trade Center Viability in the Great Plains', *Regional Science Association* 15, 87-115

KING, L.J. 1984 *Central Place Theory* (Beverly Hills: Sage Publications)

LOSCH, A. 1954 *The Economics of Location* (New Haven: Yale University Press)

MATTHEW, M.R. 1989 *Toronto Offices: Suburban Patterns and Processes* Unpublished Ph.D. Thesis, Department of Geography, University of Waterloo

MULLIGAN, G.F. 1984 'Agglomeration and Central Place Theory: A Review of the Literature', *International Regional Science Review* 9, 1–42

PRESTON, R.E. 1971 'Toward Verification of a 'Classical' Centrality Model', *Tijdschrift Voor Economische en Sociale Geografie* 62, 301–7

——— 1979 'The Recent Evolution of the Ontario Central Place System in the Light of Christaller's Concept of Centrality', *The Canadian Geographer* 23, 201–21

——— 1983 'The Dynamic Component of Christaller's Central Place Theory and the Theme of Change in His Research', *The Canadian Geographer* 23, 201–21

——— 1984a 'Relationships Between Classical Central Place Theory and Growth Center Based Regional Development Strategies' in C.R. Bryant ed. *Waterloo Lectures in Geography, Volume 1* Department of Geography Publication Series, No. 23 (Waterloo: University of Waterloo)

—— 1984b 'The Canadian Central Place System' in F. Helleiner ed. *Proceedings of the 1983 Symposium of German and Canadian Geographers: The Cultural Dimension of Canadian Geography* (Peterborough: Trent University Occasional Papers in Geography, No. 10)

—— 1986a 'A Business Press Perspective on the Emergence of Toronto as Canada's Dominant City' in J.G. Borchert, L.S. Bourne, and R. Sinclair eds *Urban Systems in Transition: Netherlands Geographical Studies* 16, 70–84

—— 1986b 'Stability and Change in the Canadian Central Place System Between 1971 and the Early 1980s' in F.N. Nagle ed. *Beitrage zur Stadtgeographie II: Stadtentwicklung in Ubersee* (Hamburg: Mitteilungen der geographischen Gesellschaft in Hamburg) 77, 3–31

—— and MITCHELL, C.J.A. 1987 'Possible Contributions of a Combined Economic Base-Central Place Theory to the Study of Urban Systems' in L. Guelke and R. Preston eds *Abstract Thoughts and Concrete Solutions: Essays in Honour of Peter Nash* Department of Geography Publication Series No. 29 (Waterloo: University of Waterloo)

—— 1989 'Christaller's Contribution to Development of the Mixed Hierarchy Concept' Paper read at the First General Meeting of the IGU Commission on Urban Systems and Urban Development, Paris, France

RAY, D.M. and BREWIS, T. 1976 'The Geography of Income and Its Correlates', *The Canadian Geographer* 20, 41–71

SEMPLE, R.K. and GREEN, M.B. 1983 'Interurban Corporate Headquarters Relocation in Canada', *Cahiers de Géographie du Québec* 27, 389–406

SMITH, J. 1965 'The Growth of Central Places as a Function of Regional Economy and Population', *Swedish Journal of Economics* 67, 279–307

STABLER, J.C. 1987 'Trade Center Evolution in the Great Plains', *Journal of Regional Science* 15, 87–115

STATISTICS CANADA, various dates *Quarterly Estimates of Population for Canada and the Provinces* (Ottawa: Minister of Supply and Services) Catalogue 91–001

WHITE, R.W. 1974 'Sketches of a Dynamic Central Place Theory', *Economic Geography* 50, 219–27

8

The Windsor-Quebec Corridor

MAURICE YEATES

The Windsor-Quebec City corridor lies within parts of the southern areas of the provinces of Quebec and Ontario, extending some 1000 kilometres from Windsor to Quebec City. The area demarcated in Figure 8.1 has been defined on the basis of major spheres of urban influence, relatively high population densities, and physical features (Yeates 1975). At the outset, the most important concept to recognize with respect to the corridor is that it serves as the core, or 'heartland' in the geography of the Canadian economy (McCann 1987). As a consequence, urban development in the area is a direct outcome of the 'core' function, and the differing rates of urban growth that occur are related in part to the changing role of the corridor in the economy. Throughout this chapter the terms corridor and core are used interchangeably.

THE IMPACT OF THE CORE FUNCTION ON URBAN DEVELOPMENT IN THE WINDSOR-QUEBEC CITY CORRIDOR

The core/periphery model introduced earlier in Chapter 4 and Chapter 5 argues that in any country (or region) there is usually a core that is the focus of innovation and entrepreneurship, interaction, manufacturing, and the controlling levers of society (banking, financial investments, political

Figure 8.1
Concentration of Population in Metropolitan Areas, 1986

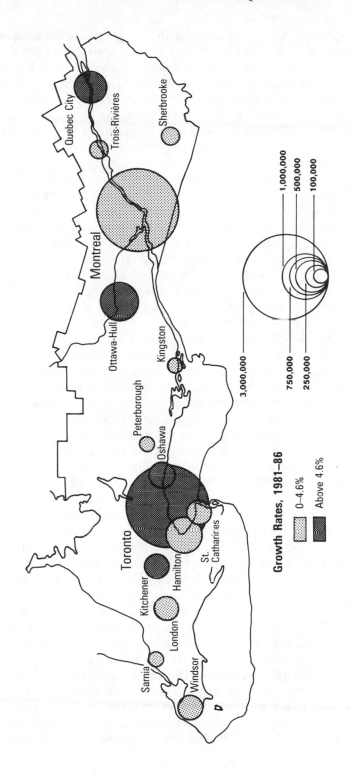

Quebec City

Trois-Rivières

Sherbrooke

Montreal

Ottawa-Hull

Kingston

Peterborough

Oshawa

Toronto

St. Catharines

Kitchener

Hamilton

London

Sarnia

Windsor

1,000,000
500,000
100,000

3,000,000

750,000
250,000

Growth Rates, 1981–86

0–4.6%

Above 4.6%

influence). Around this core is the periphery, which tends not to have many of the levers of financial or political control. The periphery consists of many distinct parts that are linked to each other primarily through the core. It depends on the core for innovation, and is mostly raw-material producing. It is often argued that the core accrues some of the economic surplus produced in the periphery because of the ways in which the economic activities are organized. On the other hand, the core may also be thought of as the engine upon which much of the economic health of the nation depends (Yeates 1985a).

The role of the corridor as the core of the Canadian economy can be illustrated in two ways. First, particular indicators comparing the corridor with the rest of Canada are developed, and then used to demonstrate recent changes in the economic importance of the area. Second, measures concerning interaction are presented to show the ways in which the different parts of the country are organized internally with respect to the core, and externally with respect to the rest of the world. The first group of indicators are static descriptors of the core and the periphery, while the second set relates to flows pertaining to both components.

Recent Changes in the Importance of the Corridor
While there have been some fluctuations in the indicators listed in Table 8.1 since 1971, the information emphasizes the continuing vital role of the corridor in Canada. Over 54 per cent of the population of the country is located in the corridor, which constitutes an estimated 14 per cent of the 'occupied' area. This high concentration of population in a core region is similar in magnitude to that experienced in some other countries—in Japan, 54 per cent of the population is located in the Tokaido region, and in the United States 41 per cent of the population of the country is in the Lower Great Lakes/eastern seaboard area. In 1971, the core population was, on average, 10 per cent wealthier than in the periphery, but by 1981 the average income level was about the same (Yeates 1985b).

These recent changes in the distribution of wealth between the core and the periphery are reflected in the changing proportion of the population found in the two parts. Employment opportunities and good income attract people to move. Thus, changes in the proportion of the total population found in the core since 1921 reflect the fluctuating fortunes of the core relative to the periphery. The period between 1921 and World War II was one in which neither component grew at the expense of the other. Between 1951 and 1971, the core grew much faster than the periphery, but between 1971 and 1981 the periphery (in general) increased in population at a greater rate. This has again reversed during the 1980s.

A major distinguishing feature of the corridor is clearly its dominance in manufacturing. Seven out of every ten manufacturing jobs are located within the area, and this concentration has not fluctuated much in recent years. Regardless of attempts to generate manufacturing employment in

Table 8.1
Some Indicators of the Changing Role of the Windsor–Quebec City Corridor in Canada, 1971–1986

Indicators	Corridor	Rest of Canada	Per cent in Corridor
Area (000 km^2)			
Total area	175	9,799	1.8
Occupied area	175	1,099	14.0
Population			
1971 (000)	11,920	9,648	55.3
1981	13,194	11,154	54.2
1986	13,804	11,550	54.4
Total National Income			
1970 ($ millions)	30,946	19,873	60.9
1981	125,967	108,027	53.8
Manufacturing Employment			
1971 ($ millions)	1,173	464	71.7
1980	1,355	495	73.2
Value Added			
1971 ($ millions)	16,132	5,286	75.6
1980	50,486	19,409	72.2
Farm Cash Receipts			
1971 ($ millions)	1,747	2,766	38.7
1981	6,356	12,325	34.0
Hectares in Farmland			
1971 (000)	8,950	59,714	13.0
1981	8,075	57,815	12.0
Tertiary Employment			
1971 (000)	2,821	2,159	56.6
1981	4,393	3,407	56.3

various parts of the hinterland, the core remains the focus of industrial activity. In contrast, the corridor appears to play no special role in service employment which, as might be expected, is distributed roughly in accordance with the population share. These figures are, however, slightly misleading because service employment is not only large (63 per cent of the national labour force), but also covers a wide variety of different types of activities. The core area does have a concentration of employment in finance and insurance activities, which accounts for the 2 percentage point difference between the population and service employment shares in 1981.

Farm cash receipts and hectares in farmland provide indicators of the relative importance of staples in the economy of the periphery compared with that of the core. Only 12 per cent of the nation's area in farmland is located in the core, and both the total area and the proportion have been declining in recent years. However, this relatively limited amount of farm land produces over one-third of the total cash receipts received by the nation's farmers. Agricultural activities within the corridor are generally intensive in nature, involving high-revenue activities per hectare (Bryant

Table 8.2
Leading Domestic Airline Journeys: Ranked in Order of Traffic Volumes in 1986
(inbound and outbound) 1968–1986

City Pairs	Passengers (in Thousands)			Change (%)	
	1986	1978	1968	1978/86	1968/78
Toronto-Montreal	1221	949	547	29	73
Toronto-Vancouver	784	347	117	126	197
Toronto-Ottawa	635	513	227	24	125
Vancouver-Calgary	493	320	111	54	188
Toronto-Calgary	427	241	65	77	272
Edmonton-Vancouver	401	278	102	44	172
Edmonton-Calgary	311	551	173	− 43	218
Toronto-Edmonton	307	196	52	57	275
Toronto-Halifax	282	165	63	71	150
Toronto-Thunder Bay	206	165	63	25	162

SOURCE: Statistics Canada (1968; 1978; 1986) Airline Passenger Origins and Destinations: Domestic Report, Ottawa: Minister of Supply and Services 1968, 1978, 1986.

and Russwurm 1981). Smaller farms and intensive agricultural production mean that farm employment in the corridor is high compared with the rest of the country. In fact, about 45 per cent of the proportion of the country's labour force that is employed in primary activities (agriculture, fishing, forestry, and mining) resides within the corridor.

Interaction

Measures of interaction, involving goods, people, or messages, provide an excellent means for illustrating the ways in which the different parts of the country, and hence the urban areas, are interconnected and growing (or declining) relative to each other. As was pointed out in Chapter 5, interaction is a reflection of the economy, and flows are important because they are a dynamic representation of that economy. Furthermore, fluctuations in flows through time illustrate how the economic interrelationships between places are changing (Yeates 1982).

Internal Interaction

One of the simplest ways of representing the interrelationship between places, and the change in this interrelationship through time, is with airline passenger flows. These data are presented in Table 8.2 for the ten pairs of metropolises with the largest number of passenger flows for three years. The information shows, for example, that the Toronto-Montreal city pair had the highest volume of traffic (both ways) for the three years, but that the rate of increase for 1978 to 1986 was a great deal less than that for 1968 to 1978 (even taking into account the fewer number of years).

The airline traffic data demonstrate that the business of the country is organized primarily around Toronto. Seven of the top ten city pairs include that particular metropolis, and involve interconnections with the west, east, and the Shield. Of course, a lot of the traffic originating from, or destined for, Montreal with respect to western cities passes through

Figure 8.2
Canadian Urban System Structure
According to Airline Passenger Flows, 1986

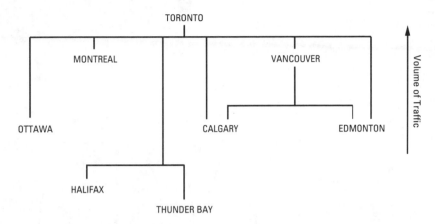

Toronto, so the Montreal connection may be under-represented. Also, it is interesting to note the growth in importance of Vancouver, as the conduit to the Pacific rim. The Toronto-Vancouver link is now even more voluminous than the Toronto-Ottawa link despite the much greater distance. The final point to notice is that the volume of traffic in the Calgary-Edmonton link is evidently influenced a great deal by the vibrancy of the oil industry, for this pair had the second-largest volume of traffic in 1978, but dropped to the seventh-largest in 1986.

The airline traffic information in fact provides a very interesting set of indicators relating to the changing structure of the Canadian economy, and, therefore, to differential urban growth. The structure of the Canadian urban system that appears to have emerged by 1986 is indicated in Figure 8.2, which illustrates the almost unitary direction of the economy with respect to the corridor in general, and Toronto in particular. This is reflected in the pattern of differential urban growth within the axis (Figure 8.1), for the Oshawa/Toronto/Kitchener-Waterloo area has been growing in recent years at a rate above the corridor average.

External Interaction
Much of the economic development, and hence urban growth, in the Windsor-Quebec City axis is derived from international trade. The greater the volume of trade (exports and imports), the greater the level of economic activity in the country, and hence the greater the rate of urban development. The types of products imported and exported, and the geographic origins and destinations of the imports and exports, influences urban development to an extraordinary degree. In general, the exports from the core area tend to be manufactured products, and the exports from the

Figure 8.3
Cartogram of Exports and Imports, 1982 (Exports/Imports by per cent)

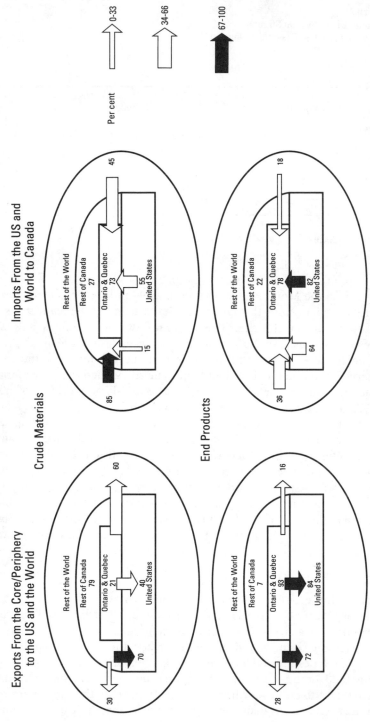

SOURCES: Statistics Canada, *Summary of External Trade, Dec. 1982,* (Feb. 1983), and Ontario Ministry of Industry and Trade, *Ontario Exports and Imports, 1982,* (Nov. 1983).

periphery tend to be more raw material oriented; 93 per cent of Canada's exports of manufactured goods come from Ontario and Quebec, whereas only 21 per cent of the value of raw materials that are exported come from this core area. On the other hand, 79 per cent of the raw materials exported from Canada are derived from the peripheral provinces (Yeates 1987a).

The contrast between the areas of export and import of raw materials and that of fully manufactured products demonstrates a clear geographic pattern (Figure 8.3). Seventy per cent of the raw materials exported from the periphery go to the United States, and 84 per cent of the exported end products from the core are also destined for the United States. On the import side, 82 per cent of the end products coming to the core are from the United States, and a large share of raw materials entering Canada also comes from the US. It should be noted that on the import side, the periphery is slightly less US-oriented than the core. Nevertheless, the salient feature is that, with respect to both exports and imports of raw materials and end products, Canada and the US are highly interdependent. Clearly, the Canada-United States General Trade Agreement will translate into an intensification of this interdependence.

DIFFERENTIAL URBAN GROWTH

Explaining variations in the rates of urban growth—differential urban growth—is difficult because not all places within the core region, and not all those in the peripheral areas, are affected by the same forces. Table 8.3 lists the populations and growth rates for 1981 to 1986 of all urban areas that had a population of 100,000 or more. These twenty-eight cities included more than 60 per cent of the population of the country; the country's population was somewhat more concentrated in these cities in 1986 than it was in 1981. In general, therefore, the population of the country has become more 'big-city' located during the 1980s than it was in the 1970s.

It is, however, evident that there are wide variations in growth rates among and within the major regions. At the national level, the greatest concentrations of growth are in central Canada and in cities in the western part of the country. The average growth rates of the cities with populations of 100,000 and more is significantly greater than the national population-growth-rate. On the other hand, there was in general a small relative dispersal of population away from the cities in the Maritime Provinces, and either stagnation or a decrease in the larger mining communities on the Shield.

Within most of the regions, there are particular sub-areas where cities or groups of cities have experienced greater or lesser growth relative to the average urban-growth-rate for its region. Within central Canada, it is quite evident that the Oshawa-Toronto-Kitchener/Waterloo area, along with Ottawa/Hull, is growing the fastest, and Montreal-Trois Rivières-

Table 8.3
Population in Major Census Metropolitan Areas and Census Agglomerations
(Population Greater than 100,000), 1981/1986

Metropolis, CMA/CA	Population (in 000s) 1981	1986	Per cent Change
Central Canada			
Toronto	3,130	3,427	9.5
Montreal	2,862	2,921	2.1
Ottawa/Hull	744	819	10.1
Quebec City	584	603	3.3
Hamilton	542	557	2.8
St. Catharines/Niagara	343	343	0.2
London	327	342	4.7
Kitchener/Waterloo	288	311	8.1
Windsor	251	254	1.2
Oshawa	186	204	9.2
Sherbrooke	125	130	3.8
Trois Rivières	125	129	2.8
Kingston	115	122	6.4
Total	9,622	10,162	5.6
The Shield			
Chicoutimi/Jonquière	158	159	0.2
Sudbury	158	149	−4.6
Thunder Bay	122	122	0.2
Total	438	430	−0.2
The West			
Vancouver	1,268	1,381	8.9
Edmonton	741	781	6.0
Calgary	626	671	7.2
Winnipeg	592	625	5.6
Victoria	241	256	5.8
Saskatoon	175	201	14.6
Regina	173	187	7.7
Total	3,816	4,102	7.6
The East			
Halifax	278	296	6.6
St. John's	155	162	4.6
Saint John	121	121	0.2
Sydney	123	119	−2.7
Moncton	98	102	3.8
Total	775	800	3.2
Canada	24,343	25,354	4.2

SOURCE: Statistics Canada (1987) 'National Package'.

Quebec City have experienced low growth rates. Nearly all the major metropolises in the West experienced significant growth during the first half of the 1980s, while in the Maritimes only Halifax exhibited growth significantly above the national average.

Factors Influencing Differential Urban Growth
The basic patterns of national concentration, regional concentration, and local deconcentration that have been identified above, are listed in Table 8.4. Within each of these national, regional, and local patterns are particu-

Table 8.4

Major Processes Affecting National, Regional, and Local Patterns of Differential Urban Growth, 1976/81, 1981/86

1976–1981		1981–1986	
PROCESSES	PATTERNS	PROCESSES	PATTERNS
SOCIAL/CULTURAL	NATIONAL	SOCIAL/CULTURAL	NATIONAL
Declining birth	Deconcentration	Declining birth	Deconcentration
rates	Core decline	rates	Core decline
French language	Western growth	Aging population	Western growth
Female	•	Female	•
participation	•	participation	•
Immigration	•	Immigration	•
•		•	
•		•	
•		•	
ECONOMIC	REGIONAL	ECONOMIC	REGIONAL
Energy prices	Concentration	Energy prices	Concentration
Manufacturing	Southern Ontario	Manufacturing	Toronto region
change	Vancouver-Victoria	concentration	Vancouver-Victoria
Financial	Calgary-Edmonton	Financial	Calgary-Edmonton
concentration	•	concentration	•
•	•	Producer services	•
•	•	Value of dollar	•
•		•	
		•	
GOVERNMENTAL	LOCAL	GOVERNMENTAL	LOCAL
Equalization	Deconcentration	Equalization	Deconcentration
payments	Inner-city decline	payments	Inner-city decline
Quebec separation	Gentrification	US/Canada	Suburbanization
US/Canada	Exurbanization	auto pact	Redevelopment
auto pact	•	•	Exurbanization
National Energy	•	•	•
Policy	•	•	•
•			•
•			
•			

lar areas of concentration and deconcentration. The question concerning individuals involved in planning and development is, what are the processes that influence these patterns? The first observation is that, just as the patterns change over time, so do the processes that influence them. The second point is that each of the patterns of change are influenced by a variety of interlinked processes (Bourne 1984).

These two points—change over time, and the interlinked nature of the process—can be discussed in the context of a comparison between the basic patterns of change in the period from 1976 to 1981 compared with 1981 to 1986. In order to simplify matters, three categories of processes are considered in Table 8.4: socio-cultural; economic; and governmental. The types of socio-cultural processes that appear to have had an influence on differential growth are declining birth rates; the ageing population; immigration; the increase in participation of females (particularly those in the 25–40-year-old group) in the labour force; and the affirmation of French-language primacy in Quebec (considered a strong force in 1976 to 1981, but less influential in the 1981–1986 period).

One of the consequences of declining birth rates is that migration has become a much more important determinant of differential urban growth (or decline) than it was 20 to 30 years ago. The affirmation of French-language rights in Quebec in the 1970s is considered to have resulted in a far greater than normal out-migration of anglophones and recent immigrants from that province. Coupled with the great decline in birth rate, this movement has contributed to very low rates of urban growth in the province. This out migration has contributed towards the growth of urban places in southern Ontario, an area that has been particularly stimulated in the 1980s by the resurgence of the automobile industry under the Automotive Trades Agreement (the Auto Pact) with the United States (which was signed in 1965), and the lower value of the Canadian dollar.

Likewise, rising energy prices caused a boom in the petroleum industry in the West in the late 1970s, and led to enormous migration to Calgary and Edmonton. On the other hand, falling energy prices in the 1980s are having the opposite effect—dampening growth somewhat in the West, but fostering manufacturing employment in central Canada through lower energy and raw-material costs. On the governmental side, equalization payments of various kinds have had the effect of decreasing the amount of out-migration from the Maritime Provinces.

Economic processes have, in general, a powerful effect on differential urban growth, as has been emphasized in general terms in the discussion of the core/periphery nature of the Canadian economy. An aspect of economic processes that is rather more subtle relates to the effect of changes in economic structure on the location of population within cities. For example, one feature of the 1980s has been the growing influence of Toronto in the financial community as the link between Canada and the global financial markets. At the same time, there has been an increasing concentration of employment in financial activities in the downtown area, and the growing importance of the producer-services industries. (Producer services are all those activities that support production—finance, insurance, marketing, computer service operations, law firms servicing the corporate sector, and so forth.) These activities concentrate in the downtown areas of such metropolises as Toronto, Vancouver, and Montreal; and some individuals working in these offices are now choosing to locate close to their place of work in the inner cities. Thus, the continuous underlying trend for deconcentration at the local level is being offset by downtown redevelopments that cater to this return to the inner city.

It should, therefore, be clear that the possible array of processes affecting differential growth at the national, regional, and local levels is extremely large. Many of the processes work in complicated ways that might be reinforcing in some cases, and offsetting in others. Furthermore, the processes that appear to be extremely powerful in one period may have a small or negative effect in the next. The patterns of differential urban growth are thus in a continual state of flux, for it does not take that much to influence local, regional, and national migration patterns. It is also important to recognize that public policy, which influences many of the processes referred to in this section, have either a direct or an indirect effect on differential urban growth at every geographic scale.

The Spread of Urban Development in Central Canada
The key dates for tracking the spread of urban development in the Windsor-Quebec City corridor are perhaps 1921, 1951, 1971, and 1981. These represent major turning-points in the relationship between the core and the periphery, and the consequent movement of population (Yeates 1984). The geographic units that are used to examine urban development are census subdivisions, and for the sake of simplicity, 684 of these have been defined for each time period for the entire area. An 'urban' census subdivision is defined as one that has a population density in excess of 60 persons per square kilometre; a 'semi-urban' census subdivision has a population density between 25 and 60 persons per square kilometre (Yeates 1987b).

On the basis of these definitions, the spread of urban areas across the axis since 1921 has been fairly consistent through the decades. The map for 1921 (Figure 8.4) shows that the basic skeleton of the urban system was in place by that time, though settlements had not spread out too much. (It should be noted that on Figures 8.4, 8.5, 8.6, 8.7, and 8.8 the density of 60 persons per square kilometre and the range of 25–60 persons per square kilometre are averages relating to entire census subdivisions; these numbers do not imply that the total area of each census subdivision is populated at these densities. The implication is, however, that an entire census subdivision placed in the 'urban' category is under the direct or indirect influence of urban development.)

The growth in extent of urban development on the basis of this classification is itself instructive. In 1921, about 50 per cent of the population in the Windsor-Quebec City corridor was located in census subdivisions defined as urban. These census units made up just over 4 per cent of the areas defined as being part of the corridor. By 1981, however, the census subdivisions defined as urban involved 15 per cent of the area of the corridor, and contained more than 80 per cent of its population (see Figure 8.7). Furthermore, the census units defined as urban and semi-urban had converged by 1981 to form an almost continuous macro-urban strip between Windsor and Quebec City, though the infertile Shield forms a physical wedge between south-western Ontario and Ottawa-southern Quebec.

Figure 8.4
Areas Defined as Urban, Semi-urban, and Rural/Sparsely Populated in the Windsor-Quebec Axis, 1921

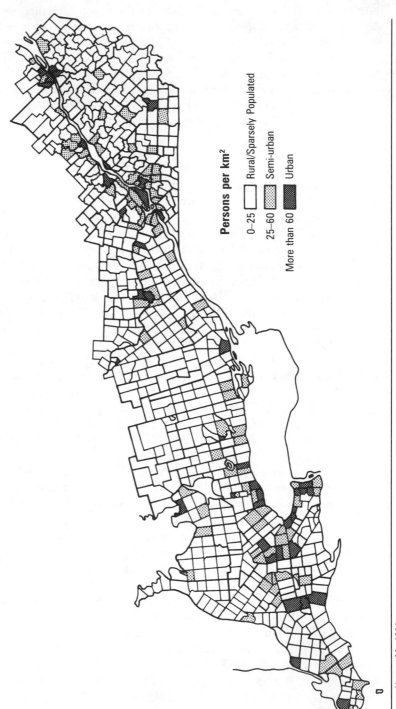

Persons per km²

☐ 0–25   Rural/Sparsely Populated

▨ 25–60   Semi-urban

■ More than 60   Urban

Source: Yeates, M., 1984.

This physical control points to two general characteristics of the maps. First, the area defined as 'sparsely populated' appears to be fairly consistent throughout the period represented, with the Shield area and the Appalachian intrusion being inimical to permanent settlement for most people. Second, urban expansion has occurred in an east-west corridor fashion, with very little urban expansion to the north except from Toronto and Montreal.

Urban Growth in the Period of Consolidation, 1921–51
The urban response to comparative prosperity in the 1920s, economic depression in the 1930s, and the exigencies of war in the 1940s, was slow but steady population growth in most settlements, with the larger places growing fastest. The major population movement in the country, and particularly within the corridor, was rural to urban. While the population located in urban census subdivisions more than doubled between 1921 and 1951, the population in areas defined as rural declined. This general consolidation of growth within and around census units classified as urban in 1921 is apparent in Figure 8.5, which exhibits little spatial change, other than an increase in urban intensity, over Figure 8.4.

The tendency for the greatest population growth to occur in the largest places is illustrated in Table 8.5, which contains information (and the definitions used) for the four largest metropolitan regions in the corridor. In order to have comparable information for the entire set of years under study, the urban areas of Ottawa-Hull and Quebec City are defined by a 25-kilometre radius, which is the distance around these cities that embraces census subdivisions defined as urban in Figure 8.7. The urban regions pertaining to Montreal and Toronto are defined as within a radius of 65 kilometres from the centre of each, since it is from within these areas that most of the commuting to the two major municipalities occurs. Between 1921 and 1951, the population in these four urban areas increased by 82 per cent, compared with a 58 per cent increase in the corridor as a whole.

Urban Growth in the Period of Concentration, 1951–71
Apart from a brief recession in the mid–1950s, the period from 1951 to 1971 was one of almost continuous economic growth, matched by unprecedented urban development within the corridor. Most areas experienced an increase in population (except on the more marginal lands some distance from the larger metropolises), but much of the growth occurred in the census subdivisions defined as urban (see Figures 8.5 and 8.6). The urban-located population within the corridor almost doubled to 9.5 million by 1971, whereas the population of the country as a whole increased by little more than 50 per cent in two decades. On the other hand, rural depopulation continued, particularly with large-scale farm abandonment on the marginal lands in the sparsely populated part of the axis.

Figure 8.5
Areas Defined as Urban, Semi-urban, and Rural/Sparsely Populated in the Windsor-Quebec Axis, 1951

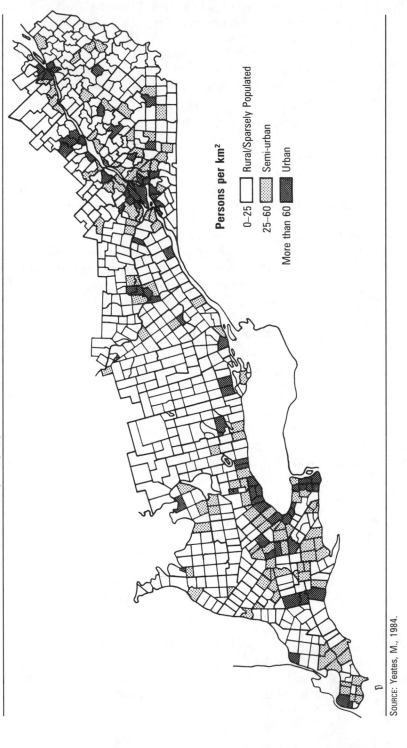

Persons per km²

0–25   Rural/Sparsely Populated

25–60   Semi-urban

More than 60   Urban

SOURCE: Yeates, M., 1984.

Table 8.5
The Population Concentration (1,000s) within Four Major Urban Areas in the Windsor-Quebec City Corridor 1921–1981, and projection to 2001

Metropolitan Region	1921		1951		1971		1981		2001	
	Pop	% of corridor	Pop	%	Pop	%	Pop	%	Pop	%
Montreal (within 65 km)	1,103	22.0	1,840	25.3	3,174	26.6	3,350	25.4	3,567	23.8
Toronto (within 65 km)	929	20.2	1,696	23.3	3,413	28.6	3,935	29.8	5,216	34.8
Ottawa-Hull (within 25 km)	177	3.9	305	4.2	586	4.9	680	5.2	793	5.3
Québec City (within 25 km)	157	3.4	321	4.4	507	4.3	580	4.4	554	3.7
Total	**2,266**	**49.5**	**4,162**	**57.2**	**7,680**	**64.4**	**8,545**	**64.8**	**10,130**	**67.6**

Figure 8.6
Areas Defined as Urban, Semi-urban, and Rural/Sparsely Populated in the Windsor-Quebec Axis, 1971

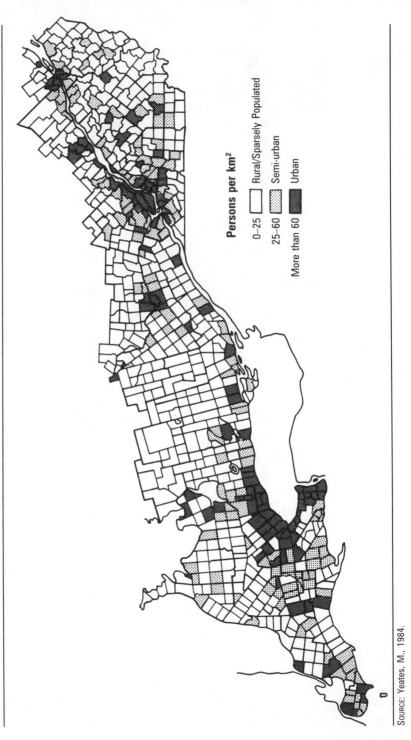

Persons per km²

0–25 Rural/Sparsely Populated

25–60 Semi-urban

More than 60 Urban

SOURCE: Yeates, M., 1984.

Figure 8.7
Areas Defined as Urban, Semi-urban, and Rural/Sparsely Populated in the Windsor-Quebec Axis, 1981

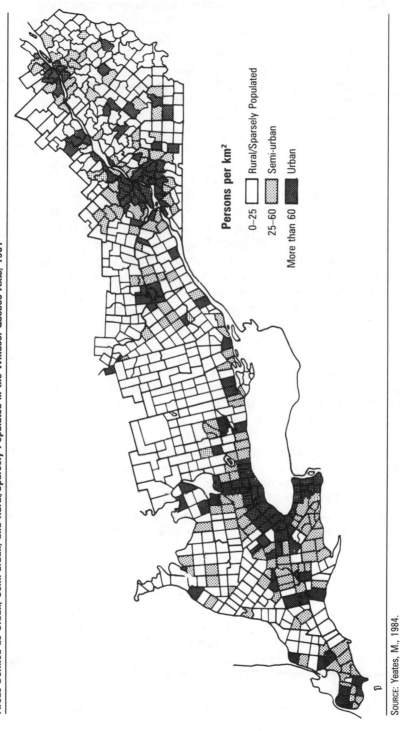

Persons per km²

0–25 ☐ Rural/Sparsely Populated

25–60 ▨ Semi-urban

More than 60 ■ Urban

Source: Yeates, M., 1984.

This was a period of extraordinarily high natural-population increase, high immigration, and considerable gains in employment in manufacturing and service industries. The net result was a spectacular surge in metropolitan growth and expansion. The population became even more concentrated in the larger urban areas, so that by 1971 the share of the corridor population located within the four major metropolitan regions had increased to more than 64 per cent. In particular, by 1971 the metropolitan region around Toronto exhibited a larger population than the area around Montreal. This concentration of metropolitan expansion around Toronto and into south-western Ontario is related to the growth of industry, the focusing of new immigrants to the region, and the gradual shift of financial activities from Montreal to Toronto.

At the same time, there was also a deconcentration, or suburbanization, of population and economic activities within these regions. High rates of population increase occurred in the census subdivisions surrounding the major metropolitan areas; around some of the smaller urban agglomerations such as Sherbrooke and Kingston (related primarily to growth in post-secondary education employment); and around Sarnia (due primarily to an expansion of refining and petrochemical facilities using recently developed western oil supplies). The counterpoint to this shift to the suburbs was the much lower growth rates in the densely populated inner cities of Toronto and Montreal.

The outcome of this massive urban development was the emergence of a fairly contiguous macro-urban region extending from Windsor to Quebec City. The smaller urban areas around Montreal and Toronto coalesced with the major city; the whole area between these two cities became one long, highly-integrated corridor in terms of the flow of goods, people, and information. Urban areas physically merged in some places; and the establishment of a limited-access highway system across the two provinces extended commuting fields, and permitted the decentralization of a number of different types of economic activities. Although the general east-west spread of the corridor along the traditional line of transport arteries is the dominant feature, significant extensions to Barrie and Orillia north of Toronto, and to a lesser extent into the Laurentians north of Montreal, also emerged (Figure 8.6).

Urban Growth in the Period of Contraction, 1971–
The processes affecting urban growth in the current era are quite different from those occurring in the 1951–71 period. The two greatest differences lie in the realms of demography and socio-economic influences. Whereas the 1951–71 era was characterized by a very high rate of natural increase, and large volumes of immigration, the current era is characterized by low rates of natural increase (below the replacement level for the baby-boom generation) and low volumes of immigration. The consequence of this is that internal migration, and the factors that influence internal migration

(such as employment opportunities and amenity locations), are now the most important determinants of urban growth.

The second great difference has occurred with respect to the economy. The 1951–71 period was one of almost continuous economic expansion, particularly with respect to employment in manufacturing and service industries within a framework of known and fairly well-understood technologies. The current era involves a rapid restructuring of manufacturing, the growth of employment in particular kinds of producer-service activities, and enormous increases in the number of women in the paid labour force, all occurring within a framework of new, rapidly changing, and little understood technologies. The net result is greater spatial competition for job-providing economic activities—hence the incorporation of functions related to development in many municipal planning offices during the 1980s (discussed further in Chapter 19).

During the past twenty years there have been two types of general population and economic change (concentration/deconcentration) at three different geographic levels. At the core/periphery level, there was some deconcentration of population and economic activities during the decade 1971 to 1981, in particular towards cities in western Canada. Since that time this trend has been reversed, and the core is once again growing faster than the rest of the country. It is instructive to note that this core/periphery flow of people involved a net loss from the core of 27,000 persons per year in the 1971–81 period, and a net gain to the core of about 12,000 per year during the 1981–86 period. This rate of annual net gain does, however, appear to be much larger (perhaps about 25,000 per year) during the 1986–91 period.

Within the corridor, there has been a significant concentration of population and economic activities towards Toronto and south-western Ontario in general. This is exemplified in Figure 8.7 and Table 8.5. Whereas Montreal experienced a decrease in its share of the corridor population between 1971 and 1981, Toronto increased its share, and in 1986 more than 4 million people resided within 65 kilometres of the downtown area. The spatial competition for economic activities that has been referred to previously is, therefore, reflected in a contraction within the core. For the first time in more than fifty years, the concentration of growth that occurred in all four metropolitan nodes across the corridor has been broken, and it is apparent that one area is beginning to dominate in terms of size.

The low rate of population growth, or decline, in the centre of some cities has been matched by continuing suburban growth, expansion of the urban fringe, and the repopulation of some rural areas that had been growing slowly, or even declining, in recent decades. The extensive areas of population growth are related to suburbanization and also to exurbanization. (Suburbanization involves out-migration and urban development that is relatively contiguous to existing urban areas; exurbanization refers to the out-migration of households from urban areas to rural areas, small towns, and cities that are some distance from existing metropolises. These households remain, however, economically dependent upon the metropolises.)

THE CORRIDOR IN THE YEAR 2001

Although population forecasting is a hazardous business, and particularly so at the small-area level, nevertheless it is useful to translate the general trends outlined above into numbers that indicate what might happen if the present situation continues. The forecasts have been made on the basis of trends in the rate of net natural increase and net migration for each county in the corridor; these county forecasts are then factored on the basis of recent patterns of population change to the census-subdivision-level (Yeates 1985b). The forecasts have been prepared in five-year intervals on the basis of presumed continued decreases in fertility rates over the 1981–2001 period, and declining levels of foreign immigration. One of the fundamental assumptions in the forecasting model is that the existing pattern of net migration by county will also continue during the twenty-year period. All of these assumptions are, of course, open to serious question.

The forecast to the year 2001 suggests the following:

1. The population of the corridor will increase, but at a rate somewhat less than that experienced in preceding decades.

2. The growth rates of population in the corridor will be greater than that for the rest of the nation because of continuing migration to the area, particularly from the Prairie Provinces and eastern Canada.

3. The population within the corridor will continue to concentrate around the major metropolises (Table 8.5 and Figure 8.8), but the focus of the concentration will be on Toronto and south-western Ontario.

4. There will be an increase in the extent of urban development along the entire corridor. In particular, urban growth between Kitchener-Waterloo and Toronto, and along Lake Ontario as far east as Port Hope will be quite dramatic. Urban development northwards to Barrie and Orillia will yield an extensive area of suburban and 'countrified' exurban developments.

5. There will also be an increase in the number of census subdivisions defined as urban around Montreal and Ottawa-Hull. There is no doubt that the concentration of more than five million people around Toronto will create special needs, as well as providing considerable economies of scale for industry and service activities.

Figure 8.8
Areas Defined as Urban, Semi-urban, and Rural/Sparsely Populated in the Windsor-Quebec Axis, 2001

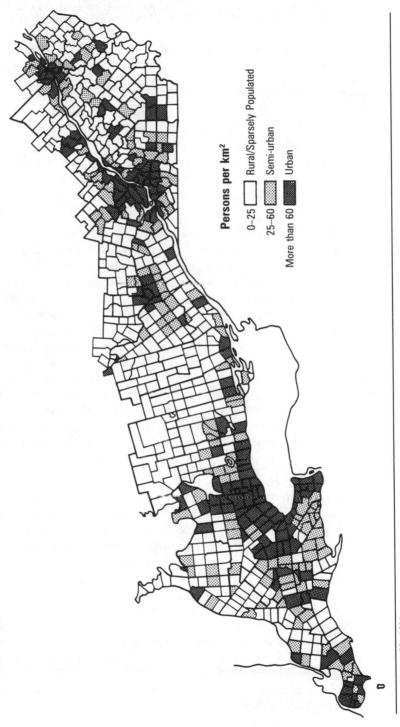

Persons per km²

0–25 ☐ Rural/Sparsely Populated

25–60 ▨ Semi-urban

More than 60 ■ Urban

SOURCE: Yeates, M., 1984.

PUBLIC POLICY AND PLANNING ISSUES RELATED TO URBAN DEVELOPMENT WITHIN THE CORRIDOR

With the increase in the overall rate of population growth in the corridor, there has been a concomitant increase in interest by provincial and local governments in problems arising from urban growth. This increase in interest has, unfortunately, come at a time when continuing budget deficits at the federal and provincial levels make it difficult for public funds to be diverted to address pressing urban problems. The issues being faced within the corridor can, perhaps, be discussed in terms of two types of growth scenarios (rapid growth and slow growth) in two sizes of cities (large and small). These scenarios should also be considered in conjunction with the technological parameters discussed in Chapter 6.

Issues Facing Faster-Growing Urban Places

Faster-growing urban places are defined as those that have a growth rate in excess of the increase in Canada (4.2 per cent) between 1981 and 1986 (Table 8.3). Table 8.6 lists some examples of the range of issues facing high-growth-rate urban areas, the kinds of planning objectives that arise as a result of these issues, and some of the policies and programs developed to deal with such problems. A distinction is made between the larger and smaller urban areas because population size affects the ability of urban areas to respond to growth issues. The absence of a planning office in many smaller places, for example, creates difficulties over and above those experienced in larger, high-growth places. Of the issues facing the faster-growing places, probably the three that will receive the most attention are the high price of housing and land; urban encroachment on rural land; and traffic congestion and the maintenance of transport infrastructure.

The High Price of Housing

As pointed out in Chapter 14 and extensively publicized by the media, one of the chief issues facing the faster-growing urban areas has to do with the high price of housing. The price of housing is, in general, determined at the fringe of the city by the price of new housing. Even though new housing adds only a minute proportion to the existing housing stock in an urban area, it does provide a considerable proportion of the housing that is in the market. Thus, new housing influences the general level of house prices for an entire urban area. The price of new housing is, therefore, of special concern, and the factors that may cause rapidly escalating prices are of particular importance in a political system that tries to ensure that all households can participate in the housing market, either as renters or as home-owners. In the Toronto region between 1985 and 1989, the dearth of serviced land was seen as a primary cause of an escalation of new housing prices, and therefore of higher overall housing costs.

Table 8.6
Problems, Planning Objectives, and Possible Ameliorative Policies Relating to Different Growth

Growth Situation	Problems/Needs	Planning Objective	Ameliorative Policies/Programs
Rapid Growth particularly in urban areas and metropolises of greater than 40,000 population	• urban encroachment on prime land • financing basic services and amenities • high price of housing and land • traffic congestion • difficulty absorbing newcomers	• to protect prime farmland • meet postponed infrastructure and service needs • control price of housing and land • develop balanced transport system • develop suitable inner-core family housing • control in migrants	• land preservation • infrastructure and service assistance • land assembly and land banking • multi-nodal metropolis • housing assistance • immigration policy • examine role of rent control
Rapid Growth particularly in small places	• same as above • uneven, cyclical growth • comparatively large infrastructure costs • conflict between new and old inhabitants • lack of forward planning	• same as above • even-out cycle of development • infrastructure and service needs • harmonize relationships • provide a development plan	• same as above • diversity in economic base • special assistance • social engineering • shared-cost planning assistance
Slow Growth in metropolises and urban places of greater than 40,000 population	• expenditure in excess of revenues • vacancies, deterioration of some areas • lack of opportunities for young • increase in dependent population • decline in quality of services, etc.	• maintain financial visibility • revitalize deteriorating neighbourhoods • link educational opportunities to employment • maintain service facilities for dependent population • maintain quality of services • improve economic base	• controlled budget cuts • neighbourhood improvement • co-operative apprenticeships • health and welfare programs • transfer payments • industrial- and tertiary-activity incentives
Slow Growth in small places	• same as above but aggravated because of small size	• improve local economy • plan decline of some places • protect service environment	• industrial incentives • subsidize relocation costs • transfer service costs

SOURCE: Modified from Ira Robinson, *Canadian Urban Growth Trends* (Vancouver: University of British Columbia Press, 1980), Figures 3 and 4.

The types of public policy that may be pursued to address the high price issue depend on the various causes of the problems that are considered to be important.

1. *The demand-pull hypothesis* states that prices go up because of excessive demand arising from changes in the demographic structure of the population, and increases in the level of real household income. The public policy consequences of accepting this argument are invariably to allow market forces to respond to price increases by raising the level of housing starts.

2. *The conspiracy school* claims that, as the ownership of land becomes concentrated in the hands of a few companies, and the building industry is dominated by a few major developers and construction firms, these groups take advantage of the pressure for housing by forcing up prices. Also, as these groups do not like government interference in the housing market (through such means as rent control), they cease to build rental accommodation. Acceptance of this view leads to a demand for greater public involvement in the housing market through such measures as the construction of public-housing units, the release of government-held land, and high taxes on speculative gains.

3. *The cost-push hypothesis* argues that rising costs of production are the real problem. These rising costs occur as a result of inflation of prices in building materials, labour, and land; and because of increased housing standards required by continually expanding local-planning and -building codes. Policy recommendations involve the introduction of methods to increase productivity (output per person hour), maintain low rates of inflation, and restrict the proliferation of building codes.

4. *The multiple-bottleneck* argument is similar in some elements to the cost-push hypothesis in that it emphasizes the effect of governmental control on construction. In nearly all jurisdictions, construction and renovations usually require some combination of approvals with respect to environmental impact, water availability, adequate sewage disposal, planning assessment, access to roads, types of building materials used, and lot coverage. All these necessary approvals create bottlenecks. The argument does not suggest that approvals should be eliminated, but that their administration could be streamlined.

5. *The radical view* argues that private and governmental institutions are so structured as to allocate housing differently to the various classes in society. Public policy proposals for those accepting this view favour greater public ownership of land and housing; requirements for the construction of affordable housing for certain disadvantaged groups in the population (the elderly, single parents, the handicapped, and so forth); and national management of differential urban growth.

These various perspectives are all, to a degree, reasonably persuasive. All the positions tend to be ideologically-based in a political sense, and they all contain some messages that need to be addressed. Government bureaucracies do entwine the building industry sector in red tape, and procedures must be streamlined. Private and governmental institutions have fostered the allocation of resources on a class basis, and procedures are required for the reversal of this situation. Demand is high because of the concentration of economic growth in one part of the Windsor-Quebec City corridor. The ameliorative policies listed in Table 8.6, therefore, require serious considerations. Another way of dealing with these growth pressures would be to pursue economic decentralization policies actively. Such policies could diffuse growth and reduce development pressures on the Toronto region. Thirty years of federal-government regional economic involvement indicate, however, that firms are generally oblivious to government decentralization incentives (Savoie 1986).

Urban Encroachment on Rural Land
Population growth has created strong demands for new urban land at the periphery of most urban areas, whatever their size. Nevertheless, although there has been a considerable decrease in the total amount of land used for farming in the Windsor-Quebec City corridor, urban growth was responsible for the direct consumption of only a small amount of the land withdrawn from agricultural use. In fact, much of the land lost to agriculture was unimproved farmland, and where improved land was lost it was usually compensated for by the cultivation of formerly unimproved areas. However, the more important issue here relates not to the absolute loss of land, but rather to the loss of prime land, that is, the most productive land in the most favourable climate for agricultural production. About one-half of the prime land in Canada is located in southern Ontario, and is in the path of urban expansion—over 60 per cent of the land lost to urban expansion has been prime land.

The Niagara Fruit Belt provides an example of a particularly important area of prime land being subject to considerable urban encroachment (Krueger 1982). The amount of land in Canada with soil and climatic conditions suitable for the production of tender fruit crops is limited to the lower Fraser Valley and the southern Okanagan Valley in British Columbia, and a small part of the Niagara peninsula. As the Niagara peninsula is in the most highly urbanized part of the Windsor-Quebec City corridor, the region is particularly important because it is highly accessible to the bulk of the market. Historically, the area of tender fruit production increased until 1951, and since that time urban expansion has resulted in the loss of about one-quarter of this maximum area.

The response to this issue in Ontario has been the enunciation of a set of foodlands guidelines, which are to be considered and implemented by local municipalities. As local governments are invariably more responsive to developments that increase their tax base, the guidelines are rarely implemented. In Quebec, the government introduced Bill 90, an act to protect agricultural land in 1978, which seeks to stop the conversion of agricultural land to non-agricultural uses and return vacant land to agricultural use in protected zones. This legislation has had some limited success, but its effect depends upon the political support given to the Commission for Agricultural Land Protection, which has the responsibility for implementing the principles.

Traffic Congestion and the Maintenance of Infrastructure
Many of the larger metropolises in central Canada are now facing a crisis in the provision and maintenance of facilities for transportation. This crisis has two components: the facilities for private transportation, and those for public transportation. Both components involve the expenditure of public funds, either through provincial and local government organizations, or through special bodies such as transit commissions.

The main transport facility that ties the Windsor-Quebec City corridor is the 'main street' involving Highway 401 and Route 20 (Yeates 1975). This facility is now severely overloaded immediately west and east of Toronto, and west of Montreal. Furthermore, there has been little maintenance of many sections of the highway and bridges since they were originally built in the 1960s. Similarly, many limited-access highways within the metropolises are overloaded or in a poorly maintained state or both. The 'Autoroute Métropolitaine' through Montreal has been so poorly maintained that the surface is now a danger to most motor vehicles. The Gardiner expressway in Toronto is almost as dangerous, and the Don Valley expressway is congested for most of the day.

The great growth in public transit, particularly rapid transit, occurred in Toronto during the 1950s and 1960s. By contrast, Montreal went ahead with important extensions throughout the 1970s and 1980s. Nevertheless, both the Toronto and Montreal rapid-transit systems are now grossly overloaded, particularly at the intersection of the Yonge and Bloor lines in Toronto and on the Berri-UQAM/Henri-Bourassa segment of the Montreal Line 2. These transit systems require new equipment, improvement, and extension if they are to cater for future demands.

One way of ameliorating overload on intra-urban expressways and highways is through the improvement of regional transport systems, particularly those connecting the suburbs and local communities with the downtown office areas of the major metropolises. The extension of the Toronto GO Transit train network to surrounding cities such as Oshawa, Brantford, Guelph, and Newmarket might alleviate some of the rush-hour traffic on the freeways. There are, however, few public-transit opportunities for improving the cross-town commuting problem in Toronto.

Issues Facing Slower Growing Places
Just as growth creates certain sets of issues that have to be faced by communities, so slow growth and decline create other sets of urban issues that need to be addressed. The major issues arising from slow growth

(Table 8.6) relate to a lack of employment opportunities; a declining tax base; and a limited ability among governments at all levels to maintain existing sets of services and physical infrastructure. These difficulties arise in two types of geographic locations: inner cities, and slow-growth or declining regions within the corridor.

Slow Growth or Decline in Inner Cities
Most inner cities within the corridor are experiencing relatively slow growth or declining population. One consequence of this slow growth or decline in population, and the much more rapid growth of suburban areas, is a continuous decentralization of, in particular, commercial activities. The newer department stores and shopping centres exist in suburban areas, leaving many parts of inner cities inadequately served by the larger commercial enterprises. The effect of this is felt particularly in smaller towns, such as Trois Rivières and Sarnia, where the old central commercial areas are particularly deserted.

There have been efforts in many communities to revive the central commercial cores with planned developments, financed jointly by the public and private sectors (see Holdsworth 1985). The Farmer's Market in Kitchener is an attempt towards this type of development. In many cities the downtown core has, however, become a collection of specialty stores catering for the local, and occasionally for the tourist, market. In Kingston, for example, the downtown area appears reasonably healthy; its activity is based on the needs of tourists, university students, and families who have chosen to reside in the older houses bordering the downtown, or in new condominiums and apartments along the waterfront. Accordingly, the potential for downtown revitalization hinges to a large degree on the nature of a city's economic base. This potential is low for industrial cities, particularly for declining industrial cities. Meanwhile, downtown redevelopment shows considerably more promise in service-oriented cities.

Regional Stagnation or Decline
There are four areas of general slow growth or decline within the Windsor-Quebec City corridor. The two areas of greatest decline are in the Appalachian area of southern Quebec to the US border (area A in Figure 8.9), and on the Shield north of Trois Rivières (area B on Figure 8.9). Area A has a number of mining centres (Asbestos, Thetford Mines) that are victims of restrictions on asbestos use, and otherwise consists of generally infertile upland. In a similar way, the pulp-, paper-, and wood-processing industries in area B are gradually losing their resource base.

The Shield areas of eastern Ontario through to the Gatineau (area C) are mostly in population decline as farms are abandoned or become weekend retreats for urban dwellers. This is an area of extremely poor soils, and it is amazing that farming became established in the pockets of better land

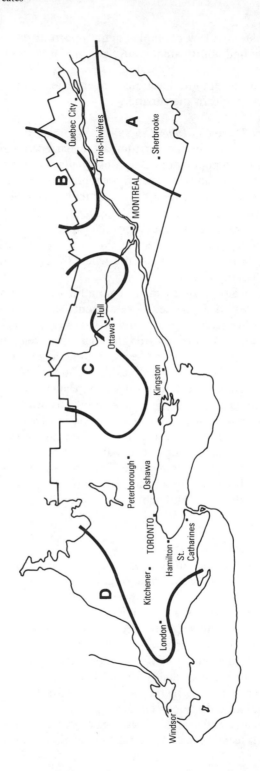

Figure 8.9
Regions of Slow Growth or Decline in the Windsor-Quebec Axis

SOURCE: Yeates, M., 1984.

in the first place. As a consequence, ever since the 1930s, there has been continuous out-migration from this region. The lands bordering Lake Erie, the St. Clair River, and Lake Huron (area D) are not declining in population, but they are growing very slowly. The industrial centres of Windsor and Sarnia have not exhibited vibrant economies in the 1980s, and the smaller industrial towns such as Goderich and Owen Sound have lost much of their traditional manufacturing base. This, along with a continual decline in farm population, which has been only partially offset by an increase in the non-farm population, has resulted in a generally slow-growth situation.

The various policies that may be introduced to ameliorate conditions of this type are listed in Table 8.6. The most important debate arises with respect to the need for sustaining economic opportunities in such areas. One school of thought argues that people have moved and should move to where the jobs are located, even though that means depopulation in the area of out-migration. Under such circumstances, public policy would focus on maintaining essential elements of the social (such as, education) and physical infrastructure in the areas of out-migration. An alternative approach is to argue that jobs should be taken to the people so as to ensure community survival and a more balanced array of local opportunities. Under these circumstances, public policy focuses on local job creation using incentives for new firms, and the transference of governmental operations from faster-growth areas.

CONCLUSION

The Windsor-Quebec City corridor is the most heavily urbanized area in Canada. More than 80 per cent of the 13.8 million people living in the area reside in census subdivisions defined as urban, and the trend towards the concentration of people in these areas, and the outward spread of urban development, continues. The basis for urban growth has always been manufacturing, services, financial, and government activities. These activities are concentrated in the Montreal area and particularly in Toronto and south-western Ontario. The result is quite wide disparities in growth performance within the corridor, with some areas experiencing accelerated development, and others growing extremely slowly or declining. The concentration of the growth in employment opportunities in a few places is not likely to diminish, and will only serve to accentuate disparities in growth performance within the corridor in the future.

FURTHER READING

MCCANN, L.D. ed. 1987 *Heartland and Hinterland: A Geography of Canada* (Toronto: Prentice-Hall)

SAVOIE, D.J. 1986 *Regional Economic Development: Canada's Search for Solutions* (Toronto: University of Toronto Press)

YEATES, M. 1975 *Main Street: Windsor to Quebec City* (Toronto: Macmillan)

────── 1985 *Land in Canada's Urban Heartland* (Ottawa: Environment Canada, Lands Directorate, Land Use in Canada Series No. 27)

REFERENCES

BOURNE, L.S. 1984 'Urbanization in Canada: Recent Trends and Research Questions' in L. Gentlecore ed. *China in Canada: A Dialogue on Resources and Development* (Hamilton: Department of Geography, McMaster University)

BRYANT, C.R. and RUSSWURM, L.H. 1981 'Agriculture in the Urban Field: Canada, 1941–1971' in K.B. Beesley and L.H. Russwurm eds *The Rural-Urban Fringe: Canadian Perspectives* (Toronto: York University Press, Geographical Monographs No. 10)

HOLDSWORTH, D. ed. 1985 *Reviving Main Street* (Toronto: University of Toronto Press)

KRUEGER, R.R. 1982 'The Struggle to Preserve Specialty Crop Land in the Rural–Urban Fringe of the Niagara Peninsula of Ontario', *Environments* 14, 1–10

MCCANN, L.D. ed. 1987 *Heartland and Hinterland: A Geography of Canada* (Toronto: Prentice-Hall)

SAVOIE, D.J. 1976 *Regional Economic Development: Canada's Search for Solutions* (Toronto: University of Toronto Press)

YEATES, M. 1975 *Main Street: Windsor to Quebec City* (Toronto: Macmillan)

────── 1982 'Urbanization, Economic Growth, and Transport Development in Canada' in H. Becker ed. *Kulturegeographische Prozesforschung in Kanada* (Bamberg, FRG: Bamberger Geographische Shriften)

────── 1984 'Urbanization in the Windsor–Quebec City Axis, 1921–1981', *Urban Geography* 5, 2–24

────── 1985a 'The Core/Periphery Model and Urban Development in Central Canada', *Urban Geography* 6, 101–21

────── 1985b *Land in Canada's Urban Heartland* (Ottawa: Environment Canada, Lands Directorate, Land Use in Canada Series No. 27)

────── 1987a 'The Industrial Heartland: Its Changing Role and Internal Structure' in L.D. McCann ed. *Heartland and Hinterland: A Geography of Canada* (Toronto: Prentice-Hall)

────── 1987b 'The Extent of Urban Development in the Windsor–Quebec City Axis', *The Canadian Geographer*, 31, 64–9

9

The City's Countryside

CHRISTOPHER R. BRYANT AND PHILIP M. COPPACK

The countryside that surrounds today's city can rightly be called the city's countryside, for it provides the stage on which several acts of city life are played out. The collection of environments comprising the city's countryside (Bryant *et al.* 1982) provides the support base for a variety of activities and functions, including recreational activities, the production of commodities, and residential development, that are tied into the city. The city's countryside is therefore a complex environment with multiple dimensions.

The changing relationships between city and countryside reflect a complex set of processes operating at the regional scale and within the broader fabric of society. In particular they reflect the shift from an industrial to a post-industrial society that has been increasingly evident since the 1950s. The nature of the relationship between Canadian cities and their countrysides shares much with that of the United States, but the specific geographic forms that have resulted differ because of differences in the political and cultural environments. The differences in form between the Canada and Western Europe situation are even greater because of economic, political, and cultural differences. An example of the difference is the greater role played by public transportation in the major metropolitan regions of Western Europe. Furthermore, the settlement structure of European countries is considerably older and more densely populated than that of North America.

The changing relationship between the city and countryside in Canada and the resulting changing form of the settlement pattern is manifest in changing life-styles, land use and demographics. Any system that undergoes change experiences a certain degree of stress, and this is as true of the city's countryside as of any other environment. These stresses are manifest in conflicts between different uses of the land, and between the various groups (e.g. recreationists, residents [both new and long-time], farmers, and industrialists) using the surroundings of the city. When those stresses involve significant divergences between individual and collective values associated with, say, the land resource, then public intervention in the form of management and planning may be necessary.

In this chapter we explore the evolution, form, and processes underlying the structure of the city's countryside. First, we consider two generic frameworks that deal with the formative processes and the settlement structure of the city's countryside in Canada in the context of post-industrial society. Second, we introduce a framework that allows us to address the issue of regional and subregional specificity in the city's countryside by focusing on the multiplicity of environments in this complex geographic zone. Finally, we consider the implications of the changing relationships and settlement form for planning and management, and how the public sector has responded to the challenges that these present.

CITY-COUNTRYSIDE RELATIONSHIPS

Forces and Processes of Change in Post-industrial Society
Settlement structure in its broadest sense incorporates the built environment; the various land uses resulting from human activity (e.g. residential, industrial, commercial, agricultural, recreational); the various functions supported by both the biophysical and the built environment (e.g. work, play, living); and the interactions that tie the different elements together into some sort of functioning system. Settlement structures evolve as the result of a multitude of decisions taken by individuals, households, firms, agencies, and governments at all levels. These decisions reflect sets of values, and changes in these values, that are influenced by forces operating and interacting at a number of levels. While factors influencing decisions at, say, the individual household or firm level are significant, the total set of decisions being made cannot be understood without first understanding the broader context in which they occur.

The broader context of change that has to be addressed is the transition from an industrial to a post-industrial society that was recognized during the mid-twentieth century (Bell 1973). Much has been written about the attributes of this transition, but generally it has been characterized by the growth and development of a variety of service sectors, the growing importance of knowledge as capital, the increasing openness in the economic system, huge advances in communications technology, and the growth of a whole host of new consumer 'needs' (Bryant 1988; Bryant and Johnston forthcoming).

How have these broad changes been reflected in the evolving settlement system in the city's countryside? Human activities can be thought of as functioning within 'systems of exchange' involving, for example, the transfer of ideas, commodities, and information. These systems operate at and across a variety of different geographic scale levels. The changes have worked their way through the various systems of exchange and have modified their boundaries. Some of the results have been the development of an extended urban life-space around cities and the development of the city's countryside.

A whole range of geographic scales exists from the macro (international and national), through the meso (e.g. urban field, regional city) to the micro (e.g. firm, individual). Socio-economic systems function through various forms of interaction or various systems of exchange. Interaction occurs between units that reside at the same geographic scale (e.g. between households or between firms within the same broad region) and between 'units' at different scales of geographic analysis. Thus, an individual firm can be tied into both a national system and an international system of production and consumption. Some systems of exchange can be very localized, such as the production of farm produce for sale in pick-your-own outlets around Toronto, where the market is predominantly from the local urban and exurban population. Other systems of exchange are more regional, such as the commuting flows that tie residence in the city's countryside to work environment in the urban core. Still others are tied into national and international systems of exchange (e.g. wheat production around Regina and Saskatoon in Saskatchewan).

The exchanges or interactions that link decision-making units within or between different geographic scales of analysis include flows of people (e.g. commuting patterns), goods (e.g. farm produce), information, money, capital, and ideas. These exchanges can be influenced by changing values, technologies, and institutions. Although the broad changes can be seen as 'megatrends' (Naisbitt 1982), or very general trends in society, it is important to realize that their influence is transmitted both upward and downward through the various systems of exchange to produce the changing settlement structure that we observe in the city's countryside.

The broad trends associated with the evolution of post-industrial society have been summarized elsewhere in terms of: (1) the development of 'new needs' in society; (2) the changing nature of communications technology; and (3) the changing nature of production technology (Bryant 1988; Bryant and Johnston forthcoming). All of these trends can be linked to various changes that have occurred, and continue to occur, in the settlement structure of the city's countryside.

'New needs' are related to increasing levels of disposable household income; changing values regarding life-styles (e.g. an increased value attached to natural environments and outdoor recreational experiences, and changing values associated with accumulating tourist experiences); changing personal-health-care values; greater values placed upon education; and, more generally, a greater emphasis on 'quality of life', however elusive that may be as a concept. Not all people have adopted or developed these values to the same extent, of course, and we have to recognize the variety of combinations of values and needs held by different individuals and groups in society (Walker 1987).

In the city's countryside, we can easily observe the effects of the values noted above. For example, people seeking country living can be observed in exurban residential development, both in its scattered form and in smaller settlement nodes. The development of outdoor recreational opportunities has grown remarkably over the past few years. Parks, go-kart tracks, horse-riding establishments, ski-trails, ski-slopes, and other recreational opportunities such as theme parks (e.g. Canada's Wonderland, north of Toronto) are now commonplace in the city's countryside. Furthermore, frequent trips to the countryside for the 'rural' experience of shopping in a small town are embedded in the commuting field of a major city (Bunce 1981; Coppack 1988b). The development of pick-your-own farm produce outlets that are common around Metropolitan Toronto (Johnston and Bryant 1987) also reflect the search for new experiences by city-based consumers.

Changes in communications technology have been fundamental to the development of the settlement system in the city's countryside. The development of truck transportation and the supporting public investment in highway infrastructure in Canada has been critical to the dispersal of industrial and commercial activities to suburban locations and smaller towns and cities found in the city's countryside of the larger metropolitan centres (on retail dispersion, see Chapter 15, and on industrial dispersion, Chapter 16). But it was the development and rapid diffusion of the private automobile that really characterized the scattered residential development prevalent in the city's countryside in the 1950s and 1960s. This settlement form differs considerably from that found around many West European cities, where public transportation played a much more significant role in the early stages of the spread of urban influences into the countryside. The private automobile continues to play a role in the development of the city's countryside in Canada, but public transportation has also become a factor in some metropolitan regions (e.g. the GO Transit system centred on Toronto, and the metropolitan subway system in Montreal that has facilitated the growth of such suburban centres as Longueuil, St-Bruno, and Mont-St-Hilaire because of their highway links to the South Shore terminal).

Improvements in goods transportation systems have significantly altered the boundaries of the systems of exchange in which many of the economic activities in the city's countryside function. For example, agricultural activities in the city's countryside can be influenced as much by competition from producing regions on the other side of the world, as by pressures from a nearby expanding urban centre.

These transportation technologies have their roots in technologies that developed in industrial society. Other communications technologies, namely telecommunications, FAX, the use of computer networks for transferring information—in fact, all the artifacts of our 'information society'— have been more closely associated with the development of post-industrial society. These new and rapidly evolving forms of communication have radically altered the life-styles and relationships between residence and work place for some people. It is not uncommon for some executives whose work place is in downtown Toronto to spend two days each week working at home, some 100 kilometres from the office, another one or two days in the office, and the rest of the week travelling. However, this type of work pattern has not yet been adapted in sufficient proportions to make a noticeable dent in rush-hour traffic congestion for people working in Vancouver, Toronto, or Montreal—people who use twentieth-century technology for travel, but remain prisoners of nineteenth-century attitudes regarding employee-employer-work place relationships. (Chapter 6 discusses further the impact of new communications technologies on urban residents).

Finally, although many of the changes in production technology also have their roots in the technological changes of industrial society, there has been an increasing emphasis placed upon knowledge as capital in these developments. In particular, research and development plays an increasingly important role. At one end of the spectrum, some technological changes simply continue patterns of substitution of capital for labour (e.g. farm mechanization). These patterns go back to the nineteenth century, and can still be seen operating in many agricultural areas in the city's countryside in Canada. Other industrial technologies, such as assembly-line production, helped fuel the development of industrial production in the peripheries of urban centres because they needed large areas of land at relatively cheap rates. At the other end of the spectrum, the advanced technology of the microchip and microprocessor have placed more and more emphasis upon the need for a professional and specialized work force with all the associated values that a highly-educated work force demands. Now, the industrial park is giving way to the 'prestige business park'. Small towns in the city's countryside can extoll the virtues of a high 'quality of life' for the professional personnel of the newer industries, while offering all the advantages of proximity to the facilities and amenities of a major urban centre. (Note that some of these factors are discussed in

Chapter 13 and noted as contributing to residential revitalization in the inner city.)

Settlement Organization in the City's Countryside
Since at least the 1920s, the concept of extended fields of urban influence over rural areas has been a central focus in urban and rural-urban fringe research. Several concepts have been developed to describe and explain these extended fields of interaction. Each concept reflects the central idea of a *nodal city region* and a rural periphery, woven into a 'city-region' tapestry (Dickinson 1947), or what has been called a *meso-scale* urban form (Preston 1977) (Figure 9.1).

Meso-scale urban forms centred on one dominant urban node are appropriately referred to as regional cities; however, urban meso-forms can take on different spatial configurations all of which involve the idea of the nodal region. These meso-scale urban structures, with their central cities and surrounding countrysides, together form one layer in a series of nested nodal regions that operate at different geographic scales (Figure 9.1). The hierarchy of nodal regions starts inside the city with activity nodes connected by flows (e.g. the Central Business District and its connections with suburban areas through commuting flows), and ranges up through the regional city scale comprised of one city core and its countryside to the urban field as a collection of regional cities. Finally, the whole national space economy can be seen as a collection of urban fields which may or may not (as in Canada's case) blanket the space economy.

In general, most concepts of the city's countryside are built upon the idea of the functional region, the area over which a given city core influences its immediate environs. For example, the labour- or commuter-shed (the area from which a city draws its labour pool) spreads far beyond the political boundary of Metropolitan Toronto (Ricour-Singh 1979; Coppack and Robins 1987). In areas such as Ontario's 'Golden Horseshoe' at the western end of Lake Ontario, the density of cities is such that a series of overlapping functional regions exists. This is leading to what has been termed 'megalopolitan' development (Gottmann 1961).[1]

In the decades following World War II, two phenomena have contributed to the development of the city's countryside. First, up to the mid–1960s, the process of metropolitanism accelerated, with suburban development spreading rapidly in the US and at a somewhat slower pace in Canada. Second, from the mid–1960s to the present, rural areas have seen an influx of city dwellers, either as permanent residents and cottagers, or as visitors to small communities within approximately two-hours travel-time of the respective urban centres. This 'extra-metropolitan' development has generated several conceptual models, among them that of the dispersed city (Burton 1959; Dahms 1984; Hart 1975), the regional city (Gertler 1972; Russwurm 1976) and the urban field (Coppack *et al.* 1988; Friedmann 1973; Friedmann and Miller 1965; Hodge 1967; 1972). The

Figure 9.1
Hierarchy of Nodal Regions

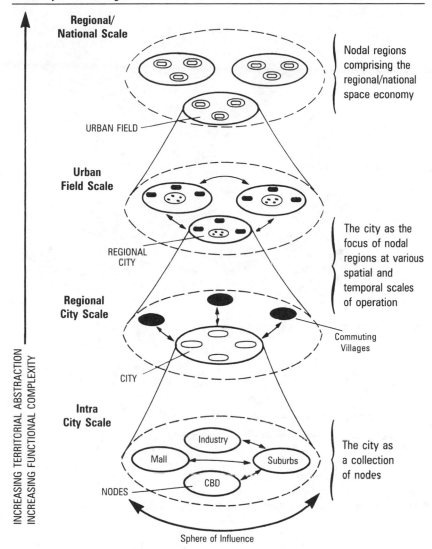

Regional/
National Scale

Nodal regions
comprising the
regional/national
space economy

URBAN FIELD

Urban
Field Scale

The city as the
focus of nodal
regions at various
spatial and
temporal scales
of operation

REGIONAL
CITY

Regional
City Scale

Commuting
Villages

CITY

Intra
City Scale

Industry

The city as
a collection
of nodes

Mall

Suburbs

CBD

NODES

Sphere of Influence

INCREASING TERRITORIAL ABSTRACTION
INCREASING FUNCTIONAL COMPLEXITY

idea of the city-centred functional region based upon shopping-and-work
interaction was also the basis of the Government of Ontario's planning
and development frameworks of the late 1960s and early 1970s (e.g. the
Design for Development strategy and the Toronto-Centred Region concept (Ontario, Government of 1966; 1970; 1974)).

The evolution of the city's countryside is the result of powerful technological, social, economic, and demographic forces, especially those related
to population redistribution into rural areas. The results of these forces

Figure 9.2
Stages of Growth of the Regional City

Centre A   Centre B

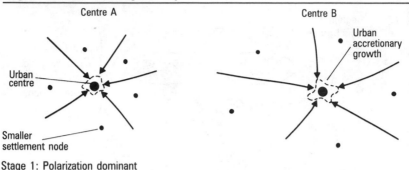

Urban centre

Urban accretionary growth

Smaller settlement node

Stage 1: Polarization dominant

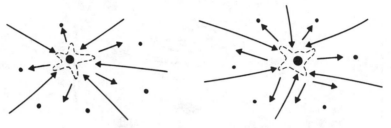

Stage 2: Residential dispersal with urban growth and transportation developments

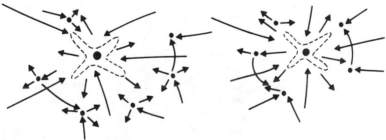

Stage 3: Dispersal of economic activities — nodal, axial, suburban

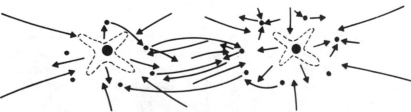

Stage 4: Integrated megalopolitan structure

SOURCE: Bryant et al., 1982.

can be conceptualized into a four-stage historical model which, while concentrating on population redistribution, has at its heart all of the factors mentioned above (Bryant *et al.* 1982; Coppack and Preston 1988). This historical and descriptive model (Figure 9.2) shows how population and economic activities were first polarized and then decentralized as technological, economic, cultural, and demographic forces changed in step with the evolution of post-industrial society.

In the first stage (1), a process of polarization proceeds apace with both population and economic activity focusing on larger urban nodes. This is the result of a complex set of forces that revolved around the mechanization of agriculture and the associated displacement of agricultural labour from rural areas; and to the willing search for the 'bright lights' of the city by rural people looking to better their lives by leaving low-paying farm jobs for higher-paying industrial and urban jobs. This movement was accentuated by the development of industrial agglomeration economies in the cities. The development of a transportation and, eventually, communications network capable of moving people and goods easily and freely within city and country alike reinforced this polarization pattern, and allowed wider use of the city by adjacent rural populations.

The influx of people to the city, somewhat paradoxically, set the stage for the eventual development of the city's countryside. As people moved into the city, suburban development occurred, leading to residential enclaves and commercial and industrial nodes around the city periphery. These, in turn, acted as stepping-stones to development further afield (for example, workers who live an hour's drive into the countryside, and are employed in industrial or office developments in the Metropolitan-Toronto fringe or in adjacent municipalities). While the physical or formal edge of the city may have been well defined, usually by the built-up area and political boundary, the actual influence of the city spread much further afield. The commercial activities of the suburbs provided employment and retailing opportunities to an increasingly mobile rural population close to the city. The resulting patterns of commuting and shopping tied the rural surroundings ever closer to the city cores. This situation is typified by the second stage (2) of the model and represents the early stages of regional city development.

Eventually, as the settlement form matures in the third stage (3), industrial and residential nodes develop further out into the countryside proper and, where urban areas of influence overlap, the development of an integrated megalopolitan structure occurs (the fourth stage on Figure 9.2). Ontario's 'Golden Horseshoe' area was clearly in the 1980s in the transitional phase between stages three and four. Here, clear structural distinctions between one urban area and another, or between urban and rural areas, are increasingly difficult to discern. While political boundaries might proclaim spatial divisions, patterns of economic, social, and population interaction tell a much different story. However, there are still powerful centralizing forces at work, illustrated by the continued dominance of the built-up area centred on Toronto shown by employment pull and the heavy volumes of road traffic on such key arteries as Highways 401, 400, and 403. Such continued centralizing pressures are fuelled by the development industry and local planning policies, and by the continued substantial public investment in highways and the public transportation system. Together, these factors slow down the achievement of a truly decentralized multi-nodal urban system.[2]

It is not surprising that stages 3 and 4 have not developed to their fullest extent around isolated or relatively small urban centres such as Regina, Saskatoon, or Saint John's. The most complex and highly developed cities' countrysides are found in those regions that have experienced continuing trends of meso-scale polarization in the space economy. These result in the maintenance and further development of economic and demographic concentration within the broad functional regions centred on Toronto, Montreal, and Vancouver.

The forces underlying this model and its concomitant settlement form are complex; furthermore, they may also be historically specific to a large extent. For example, the centralizing and decentralizing patterns depended on the technological innovations of the automobile and its supporting infrastructure. Concentration of industry likewise had to wait for an improved accessibility to sources of energy, as well as changes in transportation and production technologies.

In recent years, the relationship between the concentrated built-up urban areas and their rural peripheries has become more intimate. Changing demographic and economic circumstances have given us an older, more affluent population. Rapid advances in communications and transportation technology (see Chapter 6) have led to increased levels of accessibility, while new needs and demands have prompted the pursuit of new and different life-styles oriented towards the consumption and use of rural resources (Cloke 1983; Moss 1978). Residential enclaves have sprung up on the peripheries of Canada's cities—commuter refuge from the stress of earning a living in the city. Old mills turn into 'Olde Mills' as grist mills turn to gift shops catering to well-heeled city dwellers seeking to purchase nostalgia and experience rural ambience for a day.

The process of economic reorientation in small towns and rural areas in the city's countryside has both positive and negative ramifications. Traditional values are eroded, but often replaced with new and equally valuable ones (Gilg 1985; Mathieson and Wall 1983; Westhues and Sinclair 1974). Economic activities change as country stores give way to specialized tourist retailing, and, while we may mourn their passing, their transformation has given a new lease on life to many small towns (Dahms 1984; 1985; 1988). Ironically, it is the search for historical character and rural atmosphere by newcomers that has guaranteed the continued existence and preservation of many towns in the city's countryside.

FORM OF THE CITY'S COUNTRYSIDE

Two of the most useful constructs for visualizing the form of the city's countryside are the regional city and the urban field. The urban field can be seen as a wider-reaching and more complex behavioural space comprised of three basic dimensions (Figure 9.3). First, the settlement form itself is comprised of a multi-centric arrangement of high-density urban clusters of all sizes, centred on a core city and surrounded by open space. Second, there exists a twofold set of relationships between the nodes based on: (1) physical flows of goods, services, and people—such as shopping, recreation, work trips; and (2) non-physical flows, such as electronic money transfers and ideas (which may also be seen as commodities, but transfer mores, values, and attitudes between urban and rural environments). Third, there are the periodicities over which the interactions occur. These revolve around the daily system (such as goods delivery and commuting), the weekend/weekly system (such as recreational day trips, overnight travel, and cottaging), and the seasonal system of flows that permeate the other two periodicities and define the outer limits of the field (Coppack 1988a).

The regional city includes the concentrated built-up core and commuting zone of the urban field. There is some use in considering the rural-urban fringe portion of the regional city as a series of land-use zones with specific characteristics (the inner fringe, outer fringe, urban shadow, and rural hinterland). However, it should be noted that not all regional cities exhibit all zones, and not all zones are characterized by all attributes, nor are zones always easy to discern.

The first two zones, the inner and outer fringes, comprise the rural-urban or simply urban fringe, and represent those areas close to the city (in terms of travel time and accessibility) in the most direct state of transition. These areas are exemplified by land uses such as idled farmland that will become residential or industrial subdivisions, cemeteries, scrapyards, and some 'nuisance' activities such as abattoirs and stockyards that are incompatible with most urban land uses (Russwurm 1977). All these land uses are also attracted by the relatively cheaper land costs and availability of space. Yet, while there are clearly discernable land uses—uses for example that would be easily seen on an air photograph—there are also more subtle and less discernable characteristics to the urban fringe. Ownership of land is frequently in the hands of farmers. Some are waiting for their land to fetch urban prices before selling; others continue to farm, resisting, coping with, or adapting to the pressures in the urban fringe.

Further out, in the urban shadow, urban influence is much more subtle and less visible, but nonetheless real. Typical of this shadow area are scattered country residential enclaves—single homes or country estates adjacent to small towns. These residents may commute an hour or more to the central urban node for employment, recreation, medical services, and the like. Beyond this shadow zone is the rural hinterland, where,

Figure 9.3
The Form of the Urban Field and Regional City

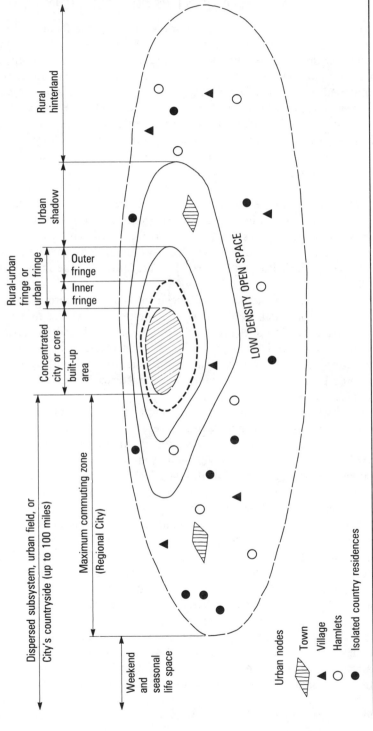

SOURCE: Adapted from Bryant et al., 1982.

again, urban influence is present but subtle, and the regional city proper merges into the urban field. Here small rural communities play host to thousands of urban visitors seeking rural ambience on summer weekends. These communities may even find themselves host to large manufacturing establishments that traditionally were bound to large urban centres. The recent decisions by Honda, Suzuki, and Stelco to locate in small Ontario communities (Alliston, Ingersoll, and Nanticoke respectively) are examples. These plants are removed from, but easily accessible to, the inputs and markets of the larger urban centres.

Beyond and overlapping the rural hinterland of the regional city lies a zone of seasonal use. Here the metropolitan influence is seen in cottage communities, ski resorts, and other recreational environments. Many of these cottage areas are fast turning into retirement enclaves as people choose to move from city to periphery.

THE ENVIRONMENTS OF THE CITY'S COUNTRYSIDE

The model of the city's countryside presented below deals with how it functions and its observable features. The conceptual model of the environments in the city's countryside is comprised of nine environments (Figure 9.4); these can be organized into three distinct dimensions that are 'wired' together by systems of exchange. The first major dimension, the physical dimension, contains two environments—the non-built environment (which includes 'natural' open space and managed open space), and the built environment. This dimension represents the *form* of the city's countryside. Many of the demands of the evolving regional city and urban field are directed at the land base in this physical environment. This is where most of the concerns about the impacts and stress created by the evolving settlement system have been expressed.

The second major dimension, the structural system, is comprised of three human environments—the living, working, and play environments. These are superimposed on the physical dimension. Together, the environments of the structural dimension give rise to the *functions* in the city's countryside. The living environment involves a range of actors including temporary, overnight inn-guests, cottagers, and permanent long-term or new residents. They live in spatially diverse places ranging from scattered country homes, cottages, and guest-houses to homes in the urban core itself. The play environment describes the leisure needs and demands of the residents, tourists, and recreationists, who seek rural places as one element in their recreational and leisure behaviour-space. The work environment is structured by the traditional agriculture/extraction, manufacturing, and services/retail sectors, each influenced by a heterogeneous set of considerations that give rise to a complex, integrated pattern of economic activity and exchanges.

Figure 9.4
A Multidimensional Framework for the City's Countryside

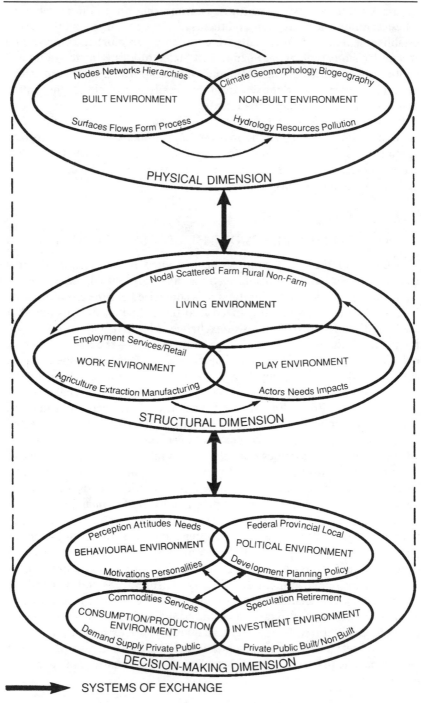

PHYSICAL DIMENSION

Nodes Networks Hierarchies

BUILT ENVIRONMENT

Surfaces Flows Form Process

Climate Geomorphology Biogeography

NON-BUILT ENVIRONMENT

Hydrology Resources Pollution

STRUCTURAL DIMENSION

Nodal Scattered Farm Rural Non-Farm

LIVING ENVIRONMENT

Employment Services/Retail

WORK ENVIRONMENT

Agriculture Extraction Manufacturing

PLAY ENVIRONMENT

Actors Needs Impacts

DECISION-MAKING DIMENSION

Perception Attitudes Needs

BEHAVIOURAL ENVIRONMENT

Motivations Personalities

Federal Provincial Local

POLITICAL ENVIRONMENT

Development Planning Policy

Commodities Services

CONSUMPTION/PRODUCTION ENVIRONMENT

Demand Supply Private Public

Speculation Retirement

INVESTMENT ENVIRONMENT

Private Public Built/Non Built

SYSTEMS OF EXCHANGE

The third major dimension is the decision-making dimension, which is comprised of four environments—consumption/production, investment, political, and behavioural. The investment environment is one of the corner-stones of the work environment because it involves allocation of the factors of production—land, labour, and capital. In the city's countryside, particular attention is paid to the land base—the demand for land and the various functions it supports is the principal manifestation of the changing values that underlie the evolving form of the regional city. The political and behavioural environments comprise the control subsystem which guide and constrain function and hence form. The political environment is most easily thought of as the formal control system, and includes federal, provincial, and municipal authorities. All actions and behaviour in the city's countryside can be thought of as passing through the filter of planning and development policy in the formal control environment, although only a subset of all possible actions are effectively open to scrutiny. The behavioural environment represents what might be called informal control. How people live reflects their perceptions of their environments, demands, needs, and means, as well as their motivations, personalities, demographic, social, and cultural attributes and those of the social system in which they function. The behavioural environment is truly a creation of its resident groups and individuals. Thus, in short, the decision-making environments, made up of countless decisions taken at various scales and levels, provide the *process* that drives the city's countryside.

At one level, all of these environments are superimposed on each other and overlap, and so give rise to a complex mosaic of land uses, functions, and values. But at another level, they are bound together by flows of ideas, commodities, and people at different scales in time and space to form a dynamic, integrated, functioning whole. Using some of the concepts outlined above, we shall now explore some selected attributes of the city's countryside in Canada, with particular emphasis on the Toronto, Montreal, and Saskatoon regional-city complexes. We shall concentrate on some of the more important attributes: population structure and change, employment structure and change, and central place structure.

EMPIRICAL ATTRIBUTES OF THE CITY'S COUNTRYSIDE

Population Structure and Change

The most evident manifestation of the evolution of the city's countryside is seen in population structure and change. The population of the city's countryside can be categorized into several components to represent the main elements of the regional city (Table 9.1 and Table 9.2). The *concentrated population* refers to the main concentration of the built-up area; the *dispersed population* (or permanent countryside population) refers to the city's countryside. This dispersed or countryside population can be further divided into farm and non-farm; the non-farm group can again be divided

Table 9.1
Regional City Populations and Percentage of Total Population, 1941, 1961, and 1981

		Atlantic[a]	Quebec	Ontario	Prairies	B.C.	Canada[a]
Regional City Population ('000)	1941	514	2,436	3,112	803	604	7,469
(% of total population)		(45.5)	(73.1)	(82.2)	(33.2)	(73.8)	(65.5)
	1961	751	4,134	5,344	1,529	1,234	12,992
		(50.7)	(78.6)	(85.7)	(48.1)	(75.8)	(73.0)
	1981	986	5,128	7,668	2,473	2,069	18,324
		(44.1)	(79.6)	(88.9)	(58.4)	(75.4)	(75.5)
Regional city population by component (%)							
1. Concentrated	1941	61.3	75.5	71.4	76.5	79.8	73.2
	1961	66.2	81.9	77.2	87.1	81.1	79.6
	1981	61.0	80.2	78.6	85.9	80.9	79.5
2. Dispersed population							
2.1 Dispersed non-farm nodal	1941	17.1	9.0	9.3	4.4	5.1	8.8
	1961	20.9	8.3	9.3	4.5	5.1	8.6
	1981	31.3	9.5	10.5	7.4	6.6	10.4
2.2 Rural non-farm scattered	1941	2.5	1.9	4.7	1.9	6.6	3.5
	1961	5.2	3.3	6.8	1.9	12.2	5.5
	1981	6.0	8.2	8.3	4.9	13.2	7.8
2.3 Farm	1941	19.0	13.5	14.7	17.2	8.4	14.3
	1961	7.7	6.5	6.7	6.5	3.9	6.4
	1981	1.6	2.1	2.6	2.5	1.7	2.3

[a]Newfoundland population excluded in 1941 and 1961. Newfoundland joined Canada in 1949; its 1961 population was 415,074

Source: Adapted from Russwurm et al., 1988, Table 7.3, p. 112.

into *dispersed or rural non-farm scattered* and *dispersed non-farm nodal* settlements (dispersed nodal settlements are settlements with populations from 50 to 10,000). With this in mind, population data are discussed below for Canada's regional cities by province, for rural non-farm population change and for two case studies of the urbanization landscape around metropolitan Toronto and Saskatoon.

The absolute numbers, relative shares, and proportional change components for 52 regional cities across Canada are summarized in Table 9.1 and Table 9.2 (Russwurm et al. 1988).[3] The 52 regional cities in Canada have accounted for an increasing proportion of the nation's population since 1941 (Table 9.1); the ratio of their 1981 to 1941 population was 2.46 compared to the national population ratio for 1981 to 1941 of 2.11. Other interesting trends occur within the regional cities where: (1) the concentrated urban populations have levelled off at about 80 per cent of total regional city population since 1961 (Table 9.1); (2) the rural non-farm scattered population component of the dispersed part of the regional cities has increased absolutely by over five times (a population increase of 163.7 per cent between 1941 and 1961, and of 107.1 per cent between 1961 and 1981 (Table 9.2)), while farm-population has declined to two fifths of its 1941 value (Table 9.2); and (3) the dispersed non-farm nodal popu-

Table 9.2
Population Change Rates (per cent), Canada and Provinces, 1941–81

		Atlantic[a]	Quebec	Ontario	Prairies	B.C.	Canada[a]
Region							
	1941–61	31.2	57.9	64.6	31.3	99.1	54.8
	1961–81	17.8	22.4	38.3	33.1	68.4	33.7
Regional Cities (Total)							
	1941–61	46.1	69.7	71.7	90.4	104.3	76.0
	1961–81	8.8	24.0	43.5	61.7	67.7	39.8
1. Concentrated							
	1941–61	57.8	84.1	85.6	116.9	107.7	90.1
	1961–81	6.9	21.6	46.1	59.5	67.4	40.4
2. Dispersed population							
	1941–61	27.6	25.4	37.0	4.2	91.0	32.8
	1961–81	51.2	35.1	34.6	77.2	69.1	42.1
2.1 Dispersed non-farm nodal							
	1941–61	78.4	55.7	72.0	97.1	103.2	77.4
	1961–81	50.7	41.9	62.0	165.2	117.5	63.0
2.2 Rural non-farm scattered							
	1941–61	300.0	189.4	151.7	81.3	205.0	163.7
	1961–81	51.3	207.4	74.8	262.0	81.1	107.1
2.3 Farm (decline)							
	1941–61	40.8	18.2	21.4	28.3	5.9	45.2
	1961–81	72.4	60.4	44.3	38.4	25.0	49.6

[a]Newfoundland and St John's were excluded for 1941 to 1961 calculations; Newfoundland joined Canada in 1949.

Source: Russwurm et al., 1988, Table 7.2, p. 111.

lation growth-rate, while slowing since 1961 (Table 9.2), has nonetheless maintained a steady increase in its share of total regional-city-population (Table 9.1). By 1981, the city's countryside had about eight exurbanite (or rural non-farm scattered) people for every two farm people. In the aggregate for the 52 regional cities in 1981, out of every 100 people, 80 lived in the concentrated category, 10 in dispersed towns and villages, 8 in scattered non-farm locations, and 2 on farms (Table 9.1). But there are also pronounced provincial differences; these reflect the degree to which post-industrial and urbanization forces have affected regional economies, and the different densities of settlement.

Another population perspective is offered through a more detailed case-study of the countryside surrounding two CMAs, Toronto and Saskatoon, since 1941. These two CMAs represent extremes in the Canadian urban system: Toronto, located in the industrial heartland in Ontario, is the largest city in Canada, and Saskatoon, located in the agricultural hinterland of the country, is the twentieth city in the nation by size. Saskatoon is also one of the most rapidly growing cities in Canada. Despite the differences in urban rank of these places, we shall see that the patterns of population structure are very similar, though at different scales and intensity.

Table 9.3
Farm and Rural Non-Farm Populations (Toronto Area), 1941–81

(A)	Farm Population					
Year	Farm Population by Ring*			Change by Ring (%)		
	25–50 km	50–75 km	75–100 km	25–50 km	50–75 km	75–100 km
1941	33,388	37,745	51,921	− 28.4	− 15.1	− 17.1
1961	23,904	32,048	42,997	− 40.9	− 31.1	− 34.4
1981	14,108	22,099	28,210			
Change						
1941–81	− 19,280	− 15,646	− 23,711	− 57.7	− 41.5	− 45.7

SOURCE: Statistics Canada, Census of Agriculture, 1941 to 1981, and Russwurm *et al.*, 1988, Table 7.4, p. 118

*The 25-km ring is virtually synonymous with Metropolitan Toronto so there are no township census subdivisions (CSDs) for this ring. Farm population totals have been calculated by the addition of the CSDs falling into each ring.

(B)	Rural Non-Farm Population					
Year	Rural Non-Farm Population by Ring*			Change by Ring (%)		
	25–50 km	50–75 km	75–100 km	25–50 km	50–75 km	75–100 km
1941	24,641	18,490	31,451	221.3	221.9	85.5
1961	79,175	59,520	58,329	60.8	90.9	90.0
1981	127,352	113,634	110,812			
Change						
1941–81	102,711	95,144	79,361	416.8	514.6	252.3

SOURCE: Statistics Canada, Census of Population, 1941 to 1981, and Russwurm *et al.*, 1988, Table 7.5, p. 119

*The rural non-farm category is derived by subtracting farm population from each CSD total, and is thus affected by changing definitions of census farms. Rural non-farm totals have been calculated by addition of the CSDs falling into each ring.

Studies of the areas within 100 kilometres of Metropolitan Toronto and Saskatoon show dynamics for the population components that are similar to those in the nation and provinces—that is declining farm populations and increasing rural non-farm population (Table 9.3 and Table 9.4). Yet another perspective is offered by Figure 9.5, which classifies each census subdivision in the Toronto and Saskatoon countryside according to the ratio of rural non-farm to farm population (Russwurm 1976; Russwurm *et al.* 1988). As we move through the rural to urban spectrum of this classification, it is reasonable to expect that decisions typifying urban rather than rural issues would become progressively more important in the management of both municipalities' and individuals' affairs. For example, close to the city, in the inner fringe, land conversion to residential or industrial purposes, frequently associated with idling of farmland prior to actual development, may occur. Further into the city's countryside, exurbanites may try to slow down development of their new-found rural communities as they seek to preserve their own particular vision of rural sentiment (Graber 1974; Pahl 1965; Westhues and Sinclair 1974). It is clear from Figure 9.5 that an obvious trend towards urbanization of Toronto's countryside has occurred since 1941; by 1981, it was difficult, if not

Table 9.4
Farm and Rural Non-Farm Populations (Saskatoon Area), 1961, 1971, and 1981, and Change 1971–1981, Ranked by Rural Non-Farm Change

Census Subdivision	Farm Population 1961	Farm Population 1971	Farm Population 1981	Change 1971–81 (%)	Rural Non-Farm Population 1961	Rural Non-Farm Population 1971	Rural Non-Farm Population 1981	Change 1971–81 (%)
Great Bend	948	764	517	−32.3	63	24	106	341.7
Vanscoy	872	833	717	−13.9	142	311	1,242	299.4
Laird	1,294	1,155	933	−19.2	5	63	231	266.7
Colonsay	526	492	350	−28.9	61	20	64	220.0
Harris	632	461	329	−28.6	4	21	63	200.0
Blucher	983	745	549	−26.3	176	286	738	158.0
Corman Park	4,837	3,401	3,396	−0.1	2,978	1,270	2,961	133.1
Perdue	701	469	418	−10.9	58	40	84	110.0
Aberdeen	1,212	726	553	−23.8	64	61	128	109.8
Rudy	768	552	439	−20.5	28	39	77	97.4
Hoodoo	1,495	1,158	750	−35.2	175	56	106	89.3
Dundurn	459	391	334	−14.6	197	149	234	57.0
Montrose	652	492	431	−12.4	161	159	237	49.1
Fish Creek	1,017	658	447	−32.1	74	45	63	40.0
Viscount	1,029	813	520	−36.0	117	121	160	32.2
Grant	1,008	606	522	−13.9	55	105	99	−5.7
Eagle Creek	865	687	484	−29.5	242	151	139	−7.9
Lost River	573	488	339	−30.5	7	47	43	−8.5
Rosthern	1,919	1,697	933	−45.0	149	426	231	−45.8
Rosedale	760	565	510	−9.7	38	42	18	−57.1
Bayne	1,268	1,011	750	−25.8	377	647	106	−83.6

SOURCE: Statistics Canada, Census of Canada, 1961, 1971, and 1981.

impossible, to find areas that were truly rural within 100 kilometres of Metropolitan Toronto. In the case of Saskatoon (Figure 9.5), a similar picture is painted, though here, because of the area's overall rural nature, the small size of the concentrated city, and land banking policies that have been in effect since the 1930s, the pattern of urban influence is much more concentrated, mainly within a 40-kilometre radius.

Two basic structural population changes have occurred since 1941 in the countryside surrounding Toronto, and since 1961 around Saskatoon. First, farm populations have steadily declined to a fraction of their previous size, both proportionately and absolutely. Second, the rural non-farm population has increased with equal speed, reflecting the second and third stages of the model previously presented (see Figure 9.2). This demonstrates how extended fields of urban influence have become a reality for many of Canada's cities (Hodge and Qadeer 1983; Lépine and Brunet 1984; Momsen 1984; Parenteau 1981). The countryside, at least in a population sense, is most definitely the city's countryside.

Characteristics of Urbanites in the City's Countryside
While population change tells much about the dynamics that drive

Figure 9.5
Urbanizing Landscapes, Toronto Urban Field and Saskatoon Area

Toronto

1941

Rural Non-Farm to Farm Population Ratios

Rural ≤0.29

Semi-rural 0.3-1.0

Semi-urban 1.1-5.0

Urban ≥5.0

Urban Areas

Lake Ontario

Lake Erie

Saskatoon

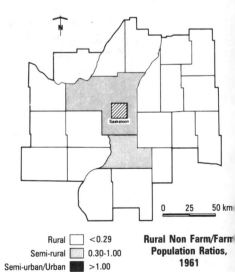

Rural		<0.29
Semi-rural		0.30-1.00
Semi-urban/Urban		>1.00

Rural Non Farm/Farm Population Ratios, 1961

SOURCE: Coppack, 1986, Russwurm et al., 1989

1961

1981

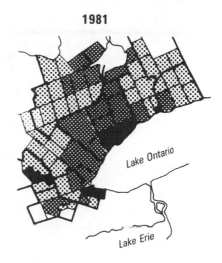

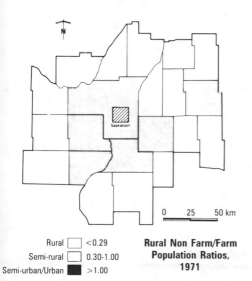

Rural	☐	<0.29
Semi-rural	☐	0.30-1.00
Semi-urban/Urban	■	>1.00

Rural Non Farm/Farm Population Ratios, 1971

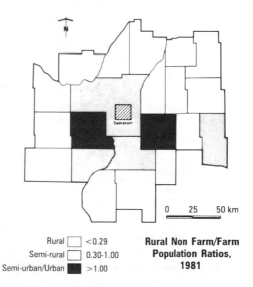

Rural	☐	<0.29
Semi-rural	☐	0.30-1.00
Semi-urban/Urban	■	>1.00

Rural Non Farm/Farm Population Ratios, 1981

Table 9.5
Characteristics of Urbanites in the City's Countryside: Selected Attributes

Spatial Criteria and Subgroups	Characteristics
REGIONAL CITY	
Guelph Regional City	• higher education • newer, higher-value homes • urban background • perceive community as changing, unsafe, and with noisy roads • satisfied with local medical services and facilities • rate Guelph moderately high as place to live • journey to cities to shop and visit
Kitchener CMA Regional City	• perceive local community as attractive, safe, with quiet roads and privacy • satisfied with local fire protection • optimistic about the future of their local community • journey to cities to work, shop, and visit
Stratford Regional City	• married • employed • older homes • perceive local community as unattractive, unchanging and not private • rate Stratford and Metropolitan Toronto relatively high as place to live • satisfied with local taxes
DISTANCE	
Near (< 20 km)	• upper household-income group • single-detached, custom-built, larger homes, large lot and home, and property in upper value category • urban background • strong community attachment • perceive local community as happy, well-kept, attractive, natural, a very good place to live with a lot of privacy, rich and very satisfactory • satisfied with local community as a place to live, the local goods and services, and police protection services • evaluate the local community now, past, and future, and the Kitchener CMA urban area good as a place to live • journey to cities to work, shop, and visit
Intermediate (20–40 km)	• newer homes • satisfied with local taxes and the services received for local taxes • evaluate local community now and past moderately high
Far (>40 km)	• older home • perceive local community relatively negatively (cf. the near-subgroup above) • satisfied with local welfare, garbage disposal, and recreation services • rate Guelph and Kitchener moderately high
SETTLEMENT TYPE	
Scattered (compared to Nodal)	• young and employed upper personal- and/or household-income group • newer, custom-built, single-detached homes, on larger lots, in upper value category • recent urban background • perceive local community as rural, young, well-kept, attractive, natural, private, agricultural, wealthy, and very satisfactory but far from conveniences and with heavy traffic on main roads • generally less satisfied with local government and services • rate local community of the past and Metropolitan Toronto relatively high • journey to cities to work, shop, and visit

---

RURAL URBAN DICHOTOMY

Urban (compared to Rural)	• higher education
	• upper personal- and/or household-income group
	• newer homes, larger lots, upper value category
	• recent urban background
	• improved quality of life
	• perceive local community as happy, attractive, a very good place to live, wealthy, and very satisfactory
	• not particularly satisfied with local fire protection, garbage disposal, or road maintenance
	• rate local community and Guelph high
	• journey to cities to work, shop, and visit

SOURCE: Beesley, 1988, Table 8.1, pp. 138–9.

---

regional city development, it is also interesting to investigate the attributes of the people involved in this settlement evolution. In a recent study of the Guelph, Stratford, and Kitchener-Waterloo regional cities in Ontario, Beesley (1988) analyzed attributes of exurbanites using four major criteria: the specific regional city to which they belonged; their distance from those regional cities; the settlement type in which they resided; and whether the respondents were of urban or rural origin. A summary of key results is given in the form of attribute profiles in Table 9.5. These reinforce the notion of a complex population structure within the city's countryside.

For visitors to the city's countryside, the tendency is to seek characteristics associated with what Bunce (1981) has called rural sentiment. Two recent surveys of visitors and tourists to small communities within the Toronto area have demonstrated that an important motivation for patronizing these small towns was to experience the 'atmosphere' of the 'rural' environment offered there. For example, in separate surveys of Elora and Stratford, Ontario, visitors tended to rank scenery, country atmosphere, historical character, and shops and restaurants as strong attractants for their visit (Mitchell 1988; Coppack 1988b). Furthermore, the growing number of visitors to picturesque and historic towns has provided a large part of the necessary market thresholds for the re-establishment of former retail functions. These functions had been in difficulty since the decline of the agricultural population (Coppack 1985). The search for rural sentiment, and the associated resurgence of retail functions, is related to many of the ideas contained within the conceptual models presented earlier in the chapter (Figure 9.4)—for example, the existence of complex interactions involving people, money, goods, and ideas within the regional city and urban field; the multiple roles that small communities play in the city's countryside; and the existence of residential, play, and production environments operating on a physical resource base that incorporates both the natural and built environments.

Employment Change

In an analysis of the Metropolitan Toronto area's employment structure between 1971 and 1981, Bryant (1988) demonstrated that there has been significant employment growth in the peripheral regional municipalities around Toronto (Table 9.6). This growth is especially marked when compared to the relatively slow overall growth occurring in the inner-urban core areas of Toronto, and especially to the absolute declines of manufacturing and commercial activity. The inner core still dominates in terms of the typical post-industrial activities of finance, insurance, and real estate, and socio-cultural, commercial, and personal services, and recreation activities. As well, Metropolitan Toronto still accounted for some 70 per cent of the employed labour force of the area in 1981. But the increasing importance of the peripheral areas is evident.

Reasons for these changes are complex, and while decline of the inner-core's industries is related to lack of space, obsolescence, zoning conflicts,

Table 9.6
Employment by Sector for the Toronto Region, 1971–81

Population		Metropolitan Toronto Inner Core (Toronto, York, East York)		Outer Core (Etobicoke, Scarborough, North York)		Adjacent Regional Municipalities (Durham, York, Peel, Halton)		Regional Total
		Number of people	%	Number of people	%	Number of people	%	Number of people (100%)
	1971	964,871	33	1,124,858	39	833,215	29	2,922,944
	1981	835,808	25	1,301,587	38	1,280,306	38	3,417,701
Employed labour force[a]								
Manufacturing								
	1971	139,100	39	113,195	32	104,631	29	356,926
	1981	110,750	24	180,520	39	167,430	37	458,700
Commerce								
	1971	100,465	45	76,405	34	47,207	21	224,077
	1981	93,860	28	103,800	39	110,345	33	308,005
Finances, insurance, real estate								
	1971	63,470	72	15,455	18	8,683	10	87,608
	1981	94,160	62	35,140	23	22,355	15	151,655
Socio-cultural, commercial, and personal services								
	1971	171,330	54	82,775	26	63,421	20	317,526
	1981	234,705	44	158,485	30	137,255	26	530,445
All activities								
	1971	614,590	49	351,650	28	289,815	23	1,256,055
	1981	678,810	37	602,400	33	556,115	30	1,837,325

[a]By place of work. 1971 data are based on 1976 municipal boundaries.

SOURCE: Census of Canada, 1971 and 1981 and Bryant, 1988, Table 5.1, p. 72.

poor accessibility, and a host of other inner-city problems, it is also related to the larger-scale changes associated with the restructuring of Western industry as a whole, and global economic change in general (Dicken 1986). As post-industrial society proceeds apace, older, less competitive industries suffer decline while new post-industrial activities, such as those related to finance, recreation, and information, thrive in the core and elsewhere. As well, commercial and retail activity is thriving. In the core, downtown retail and office developments have succeeded in rescuing many CBDs from the dereliction that has afflicted many downtowns in US cities. In the city's countryside, similar retail growth has occurred as population numbers (both residents and visitors) provide the necessary markets—or, in central-place theory terms, the necessary thresholds—for the development of many and different retail functions.

FUTURE OF THE CITY'S COUNTRYSIDE

It is appropriate in closing to consider planning and development in the city's countryside. This is an area where change is the only constant. Too often, it is an area that is seen in simplistic terms because of the relative lack of the built-infrastructure we associate with the city core. It should be clear that comprehensive planning and development of the city's countryside can only take place within a policy framework that recognizes the multi-dimensional nature of that particular part of the urban system. And, although we have not considered the structure and stresses created within the rural resource base, and especially the agricultural sector, any planning and development for the settlement structure has to deal with these concerns (see, for example, Bryant and Russwurm 1982; Johnston and Bryant 1987). The familiar refrain of 'environment as a resource', rather than the more simplistic idea of land as a commodity, must be echoed once again. At the same time, dealing with resource issues from a largely sectoral perspective, as has been the case generally (for example, the development of agricultural land-conservation policies, or aggregate mineral policies) ignores the interrelatedness at a regional level between the concentrated urban areas and the city's countryside.

Four key points must be noted if responsible planning and development policy of the city's countryside is to be a reality (Coppack and Russwurm 1988). First, while the city's countryside may be in large part a product of the city, it does not follow that city planning and policy can prevail in the countryside. The differences in roles, uses, and nature are too pronounced for such an approach. The city's countryside has much less built-infrastructure spread over a far greater areal extent and impinging on a much larger number of 'natural' environments. Thus physical planning for land uses takes on a much different complexion, requiring consideration of the multiple roles played by places and resources in rural areas. In the concentrated urban area, given the complexity of its built environment, the roles of particular areas are relatively clear-cut—for example, industrial, retail, and residential areas, despite transitional zones and recent mixing of uses. In rural areas, small communities support residential, recreation, commercial, tourism, and heritage functions, as well as providing a home for rare species and other uses, often at the same time and in the same place. Until the recent influx of exurbanites, the social structure of the countryside was more homogeneous within communities and areas, although sometimes quite different between communities and areas. Furthermore, rural communities have usually been established for long periods of time and often have extended family and social networks (Walker 1987). This stands in contrast to the city, where much of the growth has occurred since the mid-twentieth century and migration activity has usually been very pronounced.

Second, economic development of the city's countryside requires a more innovative and enlightened approach than that practised to date. Frequently, the conventional approach has viewed rural areas as either chronically backward and terminally ill, or as 'urban-areas-in-waiting'. Inadequate attention has been paid to the other, more positive, roles that the city's countryside plays in the urban life-space. This is particularly the case for city-core governments, whose tendency to see the countryside and its resources (especially its space) as bride-to-be and dowry (e.g., through successive annexations) has caused endless friction with politicians and polity alike in the countryside. The so-called 'top down' approach to development undoubtedly still has its role, but encouragement of a local-development or 'bottom-up' approach that relies more on self-reliance and the devolution of decision-making is required. It is perhaps time that we recognized that different non-traditional development options, such as tourism, exurban residential enclaves, and retirement communities, exist. These can substitute for more traditional activities such as agriculture and manufacturing, which are experiencing declines as employment generators in the face of global economic changes and the evolution of post-industrial society.

Third, the prevalent tendency to control by crisis management must change to one of proactive management in which the options are spelled out as scenarios to be explored rather than as problems to be resolved. This can only occur when complementary, conflicting, and compatible activities are identified within the multi-dimensional and multi-use nature of the city's countryside. Also, it must be recognized that city core and country are one entity, with no dominant partner, even though in political and economic terms the city core wields considerable influence. However, as society changes and new attitudes towards rural areas prevail, the strength and bargaining position of the countryside will increase concomitantly.

Fourth, as urban systems grow more complex, especially in terms of spatial size, they are usually accompanied by an emphasis on *aspatial* solutions and policy. These reflect the difficulties of handling the functional complexities of large urban systems. Despite these inherent difficulties, there is a growing and pervasive need for more integrated planning policy at a regional level. Yet, there appears to be no political inclination to develop such policy, largely because of the political difficulties of inculcating non-partisan attitudes in the partisan political structure of municipal systems. Use of the city's countryside will increase with the passing of time; whether or not the passing of responsible policy follows or leads remains to be seen.

NOTES

1. The mismatch of 'formal' and 'functional' urban region gives rise to fundamental management and political problems. Further discussion of these problems is found in Chapter 18.

2. Notable here are the differences in the form of post-World War II cities in the US as opposed to the form of Canadian cities. See Chapter 3 which is devoted to this theme.

3. These were defined for all cities that in 1976 had a concentrated population of 40,000 or more (as well as Charlottetown, Granby and Chilliwack in order to represent important areas otherwise not included) by including all census subdivisions (i.e., municipalities and Indian reservations) within a 50 km radius (60 km for Toronto, Vancouver and Montreal); areas of overlap were assigned on the basis of 1971 commuting flows.

FURTHER READING

BRYANT, C.R., RUSSWURM, L.H., and MCLELLAN, A. 1982 *The City's Countryside* (Toronto: Longman)

COPPACK, P.M., RUSSWURM, L.H., and BRYANT, C.R. 1988 *Essays in Canadian Urban Process and Form III: The Urban Field* (Waterloo: University of Waterloo, Department of Geography Publication #30)

DAHMS, F.A. 1988 *The Heart of the Country: From the Great Lakes to the Atlantic Coast—Rediscovering the Towns and Countryside of Canada* (Toronto: Deneau)

HODGE, G.D. and QADEER, M.A. 1983 *Towns and Villages in Canada* (Toronto: Butterworths)

RUSSWURM, L.H. 1977 *The Surroundings of Our Cities* (Toronto: Holt, Rinehart and Winston)

WALKER, G.E. 1987 *The Invaded Countryside: Structures of Life in the Invaded Fringe* (Toronto: York University, Atkinson College, Geographical Monograph #14)

REFERENCES

BEESLEY, K.B. 1988 'Living in the urban field' in P.M. Coppack, L.H. Russwurm, and C.R. Bryant eds *Essays in Canadian Urban Process and Form III: The Urban Field* (Waterloo: University of Waterloo, Department of Geography Publication Series No.30)

BELL, D. 1973 *The Coming of Post-Industrial Society: A Venture in Social Planning* (New York: Basic Books)

BRYANT, C.R. 1988 'Economic activities in the urban field' in P.M. Coppack, L.H. Russwurm, and C.R. Bryant eds *Essays in Canadian Urban Process and Form III: The Urban Field* (Waterloo: University of Waterloo, Department of Geography Publication Series No.30)

―――― and JOHNSTON, T.R.R. forthcoming *Agriculture in the City's Countryside* (London: Pinter Publishers)

―――― and RUSSWURM, L.H. 1982 'North American farmland protection strategies in retrospect', *GeoJournal* 6, 501–11

―――― RUSSWURM, L.H., and MCLELLAN, A. 1982 *The City's Countryside* (Toronto: Longman)

BUNCE, M. 1981 'Rural sentiment and the ambiguity of the urban fringe' in K. B. Beesley and L. H. Russwurm eds *The Rural-Urban Fringe: Canadian Perspectives* (Toronto: York University, Atkinson College, Geographical Monograph No.10)

BURTON, I. 1959 'Retail trade in a dispersed city', *Transactions of the Illinois State Academy of Science* 52, 145–50

CLOKE, P.J. 1983 *An Introduction to Rural Settlement Planning* (London: Methuen)

COPPACK, P.M. 1985 'A stage model of central place dynamics in Toronto's urban field', *East Lakes Geographer* 20, 1–13

―――― 1988a 'The evolution and modelling of the urban field' in P.M. Coppack, L.H. Russwurm, and C.R. Bryant eds *Essays in Canadian Urban Process and Form III: The Urban Field* (Waterloo: University of Waterloo, Department of Geography Publication No.30)

―――― 1988b 'The role of amenity in the evolution of the urban field', *Geografiska Annaler* 70B, 353–61

―――― and PRESTON, R.E. 1988 'Central place structure of the urban field' in P.M. Coppack, L.H. Russwurm, and C.R. Bryant eds *Essays in Canadian Urban Process and Form III: The Urban Field* (Waterloo: University of Waterloo, Department of Geography Publication No.30)

―――― and ROBINS, D. 1987 'Commuting patterns in the Toronto area, 1971, 1981', *Ontario Geography* 29, 63–78

―――― and RUSSWURM, L.H. 1988 'The future of the urban field' in P.M. Coppack, L.H. Russwurm, and C.R. Bryant eds *Essays in Canadian Urban Process and Form III: The Urban Field* (Waterloo: University of Waterloo, Department of Geography Publication No.30)

―――― RUSSWURM, L.H., and BRYANT, C.R. 1988 *Essays in Canadian Urban Process and Form III: The Urban Field* (Waterloo: University of Waterloo, Department of Geography Publication No.30)

DAHMS, F. 1984 ' "Demetropolitanization" or the "urbanisation" of the countryside; the changing functions of small rural settlements in Ontario', *Ontario Geography* 24, 35–62

—— 1985 'Ontario's rural communities—changing, not dying' in A.M. Fuller ed. *Farming and the Rural Community in Ontario: An Introduction* (Toronto: Foundation for Rural Living)

—— 1988 *The Heart of the Country: From the Great Lakes to the Atlantic Coast— Rediscovering the Towns and Countryside of Canada* (Toronto: Deneau)

DICKEN, P. 1986 *Global Shift: Industrial Change in a Turbulent World* (London: Harper and Row)

DICKINSON, R.E. 1947 *City, Region, and Regionalism: A Geographical Contribution to Human Ecology* (London: Kegan Paul Trench Truber)

FRIEDMANN, J. 1973 'The urban field as a human habitat' in S.P. Snow ed. *The Place of Planning* (Auburn, Alabama: Auburn University Press). Reprinted in L.S. Bourne and J.W. Simmons eds 1978 *Systems of Cities* (Toronto: Oxford University Press, 1978)

—— and MILLER, J. 1965 'The urban field', *Journal of the American Institute of Planners* 31, 312–20

GERTLER, L. 1972 *Regional Planning in Canada: A Planner's Testament* (Toronto: Harvest House)

GILG, A. 1985 *An Introduction to Rural Geography* (London: Edward Arnold)

GOTTMAN, J. 1961 *Megalopolis* (New York: The 20th Century Fund)

GRABER, E.E. 1974 'Newcomers and oldtimers: growth and change in a mountain town', *Rural Sociology* 39, 504–39

HART, J.F. 1975 *The Look of the Land* (Englewood Cliffs, N.J.: Prentice-Hall)

HODGE, G. 1967 'Emerging bounds of urbanism', *Community Planning Review* 18, 4–9

—— 1972 'The emergence of the urban field' in L.S. Bourne and R.D. MacKinnon eds *Urban Systems Development in Central Canada* (Toronto: University of Toronto Press)

—— and QADEER, M.A. 1983 *Towns and Villages in Canada* (Toronto: Butterworths)

JOHNSTON, T.T. and BRYANT, C.R. 1987 'Agricultural adaptation; the prospects for sustaining agriculture near cities' in W. Lockeretz ed. *Sustaining Agriculture Near Cities* (Ankeny, Iowa: Soil and Water Conservation Society)

LEPINE, Y. and BRUNET, Y. 1984 'Les variations spatiales de la présence exurbaine en milieu rural québécois' in M.F. Bunce and M.J. Troughton eds *The Pressures of Change in Rural Canada* (Toronto: York University, Atkinson College, Department of Geography, Monograph No.14)

MATHIESON, A. and WALL, G. 1983 *Tourism: Economic, Physical and Social Impacts* (London: Longman)

MITCHELL, C.J.A. 1988 'Recreation and culture in the urban field' in P.M. Coppack, L.H. Russwurm, and C.R. Bryant eds *Essays in Canadian Urban Process and Form III: The Urban Field* (Waterloo: University of Waterloo, Department of Geography Publication No.30)

MOMSEN, J. 1984 'Urbanization of the countryside in Alberta' in M.F. Bunce and M.J. Troughton eds *The Pressures of Change in Rural Canada* (Toronto: York University, Atkinson College, Department of Geography Monograph No.14)

MOSS, G. 1978 'Rural settlements', *Architects Journal* 18 January, 100–39

NAISBITT, J. 1982 *Megatrends* (New York: Warner Books)

ONTARIO, GOVERNMENT OF 1966 *Design for Development: Statement by the Prime Minister of the Province of Ontario on Regional Development Policy* (Toronto: Government of Ontario)

———— 1970 *Design for Development: The Toronto Centred Region* (Toronto: Government of Ontario, Ministry of Treasury, Economics and Intergovernmental Affairs)

———— 1974 *Central Ontario Lakeshore Urban Complex* (Toronto: Queen's Printer)

PAHL, R.E. 1965 *Urbs in Rure: The Metropolitan Fringe of Herefordshire* (London: London School of Economics, Geographical Paper No.2)

PARENTEAU, R. 1981 'Is Canada going back to the land?' in K.B. Beesley and L.H. Russwurm eds *The Rural-Urban Fringe: Canadian Perspectives* (Toronto: York University, Atkinson College, Department of Geography, Geographical Monograph No.10)

PRESTON, R.E. 1977 'A perspective on alternate settlement forms' in L.H. Russwurm, R.E. Preston, and L.R.G. Martin eds *Essays on Canadian Urban Process and Form* (Waterloo: University of Waterloo, Department of Geography Publication No.10)

RICOUR-SINGH, F. 1979 *Poles and Zones of Attraction* (Ottawa: Ministry of Supply and Services, Statistics Canada Census Analytical Study, No. 99–754)

RUSSWURM, L.H. 1977 *The Surroundings of Our Cities* (Toronto: Holt, Rinehart and Winston)

———— 1976 'Country residential development and the regional city form in Canada', *Ontario Geographer* 10, 79–96

———— COPPACK, P.M., and BRYANT, C.R. 1988 'Population in the urban field' in P.M. Coppack, L.H. Russwurm, and C.R. Bryant eds *Essays in Canadian Urban Process and Form III: The Urban Field* (Waterloo: University of Waterloo, Department of Geography Publication No.30)

WALKER, G.E. 1987 *The Invaded Countryside: Structures of Life in the Invaded Fringe* (Toronto: York University, Atkinson College, Geographical Monograph No.14)

WESTHUES, K., and SINCLAIR, P.R. 1974 *Village in Crisis* (Toronto: Holt, Rinehart and Winston)

PART THREE

INTRA-URBAN PERSPECTIVES

10

The Evolution of Metropolitan Form

SHERRI OLSON

The form of an object can be understood as a product of forces, for instance, the energies applied to clay by the potter, or by wind and water to a sand beach. The form of a city, or urban *morphology*, is an expression of forces exerted on it during the years of its existence. As D'Arcy Thompson expressed it with reference to shells and skeletons, 'The form of an object is a diagram of forces', and 'from it [the form] we can judge of or deduce the forces that are acting or have acted upon it . . .' (Thompson 1961 [1917], 11). In this essay, after some thoughts about the meaning of form as it applies to urban identity, we consider first the physical landscape on which the metropolis develops, then look at the structures we have built, examine the whole 'built landscape' as a product of flows of investment, and finally turn to the problems generated by massive flows of energy through our urban landscape. We shall see that the form of a city sets limits on our life-styles and creates problems which may mean life or death for urban residents.

IDENTITY AND FORM

Canadian cities share some formal properties because they were all shaped by the history of the nation, but each city also has features of its own.

Images of St-Hyacinthe (Quebec) and Winnipeg (Manitoba) about 1880 and Saint John (New Brunswick) in 1944 (Figures 10.1 to 10.3) present urban forms characteristic of particular places and moments in history. St-Hyacinthe grew from a village and was already well established by 1880, while Winnipeg was laid out in a gridiron pattern, new, expansive, and brash. The artists who drafted the two 'bird's eye views' shared certain ideas of the 1880s: an admiration for the riverfront site, an appreciation of the surrounding 'breadbasket' and a perception of smokestacks as an expression of the city's ambitions of industrial power. The 1944 artist erased the smoke instead of exaggerating it, and the improvements conceived for Saint John are present in other North American plans of the 1940s: a viaduct, a school set in a park, curving streets for single-family developments, and slab walk-ups rented by low-income families.

A generation later, when Expo '67 turned the spotlight on Montreal, local architectural critics pointed to the powerful verticals of the 'new city centre'. Slabs and point-blocks rising to forty-seven storeys expressed corporate ambitions. Melvin Charney referred to 'a mound fixation' and the pioneering underground city, while Norbert Schoenauer criticized the insular character of the buildings, and the failure to take full advantage of the topography and the surrounding urban fabric (Schoenauer 1967). Similar criticisms were made of Toronto and Vancouver.

To generalize about the common properties of our cities, or to enjoy their individuality, we observe volumes and spaces, colours and reflections. We examine a city from a distance, from close-up, and from inside. We take clues from its sensory, even sensual, properties: visual, tactile, and kinesic—rough or smooth, hard or soft, challenging the muscles for walking uphill or downhill.

Because the form of a city expresses our various ambitions and aspirations, observing the landscape we have created around us informs us about our society. It provides cues as to how, from generation to generation, our social relations have changed. Urban form offers a better appraisal of the balance of social forces at work than any other analysis. As an example, in Montreal restored vestiges of the Grey Nuns' eighteenth-century hospital adjoin rows of handsome warehouses which replaced the hospital—an urban renewal project of the 1870s. (A second round of renewal in the 1970s transformed the warehouses into condominium dwellings and offices). Dating from the same era as the warehouses are ornate banks at the centre, bulky tobacco factories and breweries flanking the city on the east and west, and superb stone mansions of the tobacco manufacturers and brewers overlooking miles of working-class rowhouses. Steeples of the same vintage are still focal points of dozens of neighbourhoods. In Point St Charles, two stone churches, cheek by jowl, St Charles and St Pierre, still shelter Irish and French Canadian neighbours at worship. Those remnants of earlier forms continue to provoke questions about our values and identities, past and present.

Figure 10.1

ST. HYACINTHE, P.Q.
1881.
VUE A VOL D'OISEAU DE

1. PALAIS DE JUSTICE.
2. CATHEDRALE.
3. TOUR.
4. ÉGLISE DE PAROISSE.
5. PRESBYTÈRE ANGL.
6. PRESBYTÈRE ANGL.
7. SÉMINAIRE.
8. MANUFACTURE DE LAINE.

9. MANUFACTURE DE L. CÔTÉ.
10. JAMBET ET LAFERLE.
11. FONTAINE, BERTRAND.
12. MANCHE.
13. MARCHÉ.
14. AULDIÈRE GÉNÉRARD.
15. TANNERIE DUCLAS & PAYAN.
16. STATION DU GRAND TRUNC.
17. MANUFACTURE DE PORTES, CHASSIS &
BOISERIE ETC.

Bird's-eye view of Saint-Hyacinthe, Quebec, in 1981. The artist sought to make every commercial building identifiable, used curling smoke and rippling water to make the industrial base more prominent, and at the same time gave detail and stature to monumental buildings, curving paths, and planned green spaces. Reproduced from a copy in the National Archives of Canada (NMC 8876), original at the Séminaire de Saint-Hyacinthe.

Landscape patterns reveal relationships. A landscape is an assemblage of objects in a space much larger than the individual human being, large enough for social interaction: a stage set. If we blow up a microphotograph of an intestinal wall or a computer chip, we perceive it as a landscape the moment we recognize that we can (in imagination) move in and out of it, bump into it, or inhabit it. Our conception of landscape therefore provides a scale and a perspective. We shift back and forth between the standpoint of observer and participant, distancing ourselves or becoming involved.

Walking down a hill in the country, we would see changes of slope and an adapted catena or chain of soils and plants. As we walk down Mountain Street in Montreal, or Wentworth Street in Hamilton, we observe a similar chain of house-types and household types. The sizes and heights of houses indicate a social chain of command, from which we can infer the meaning of social class. For larger regions, Humboldt (the grandfather of modern geography) used the heights of vegetation—grassland, scrub, or forest—as indicators of climate and relief.

Landscape has integrating power because people have the capacity to handle fabulous amounts of information in visual form. In the city we infer hierarchical relationships from the overlay of patterns at several scales. Urban forms fit together into a whole. The Aldred Building, built in 1928 on Place d'Armes, belongs to the Montreal skyline, and situates us in a 'central business district', a feature we expect to find in any big city.

Just as we are situated within the city's spatial frame, we are also situated inside its time-frame. Churches, war memorials, and shade trees have longer lives than our own, and the city testifies to a long sequence of human choices, to the exercise of power, and a succession of creative and destructive impulses. Even a small city like St-Hyacinthe (Figure 10.1) has the capacity to outlast us, overwhelm us, and still belong to us.

Modern geographical theories have failed to develop the full significance of urban morphology. Despite talk of 'space' and 'place' as defining concepts in geography, there has been little theorizing about scale in human geography.[1] Too little attention has been paid to form and classification of forms.[2] Urban spatial analyses of the 1960s were generally simplified to a two-dimensional geometry, and models were static rather than dynamic, snapshots rather than moving pictures.[3]

To develop more dynamic models, we are now beginning to employ tools such as film media, dynamic geometry, computer-assisted modelling and satellite imagery, and to look at urban forms as evidence of social processes. Even landscapes of repose, like those pictured in Figures 10.1 to 10.3, are a product of dynamic circulations. The city's boxes of wood, brick, and glass represent the accumulation of masses of capital, and the moving traffic and flashing signals inform us about flows of energy in the system, which are the basis of accumulation, reproduction and depreciation of that capital.

> Morphology is not only a study of material things and of the forms of material things, but has its dynamical aspect, under which we deal with the interpretation, in terms of force, of the operations of Energy (Thompson 1961 [1917], 14).

THE LAY OF THE LAND

The individuality of our cities is founded on the lay of the land, peculiar to each place. Urban morphology therefore begins with geomorphology: the study of land-forms. A surprising number of Canadian cities have as much as 100-metre variations in their relief, and therefore offer spectacular views. Their topography shapes the circulation of air, water, and energy, and the topography is itself re-shaped by the work of wind and water, as well as by bulldozers and piledrivers.

In classic descriptions of Canadian cities, the physical underpinnings have been discussed chiefly as economic assets or as initial reasons for the choice of a site. All writers attest to the historic importance of deep harbours at Halifax and Vancouver, the defensive promontory of Quebec 100 metres above the St Lawrence River, Montreal's origin at the head of navigation, and Ottawa's access to the water power available at the falls in the Ottawa River. Disadvantages are occasionally admitted, and even the most attractive sites have inconveniences such as the risk of floods in Winnipeg and Fredericton, the need for dredging the approaches to Saint John, poor drainage in Regina, earthquake risk in Chicoutimi, and a high water-table in Calgary.

The lay of the land influences the layout of our cities, sometimes constraining their design, sometimes provoking engineering ingenuity, sometimes creating problems for generations to come. Most cities, because of cost advantages for hauling, were founded at sea level and have tended to grow uphill, over rougher terrain and greater gaps. Nader (1976) notes the high cost of developing land around Halifax and Saint John because of bogs and outcroppings of rock. The cities of the Maritimes therefore developed narrow ribbons of settlement in the valleys, causing bottlenecks to traffic. At St John's, Newfoundland, rows of houses climb a 100-metre ridge, and some of the older streets are simply flights of stairs. In Calgary, the decision to thread a railroad along the Bow river determined where industry would locate. The technological challenge of bridging the St Lawrence River delayed suburban expansion of Quebec, Trois Rivières, and Montreal, and the costs of overcoming strong relief features long postponed residential expansion of Toronto across the Don Valley, and of Hamilton onto the escarpment 100 metres above Lake Ontario.

As rivers were roofed, swamps filled, and hills leveled, some landforms disappeared under the buildings. Riverfront, lakefront, and oceanfront have become the least 'natural' features of our cities—the ease of filling and dredging made it possible to crochet a more elaborate edging at the commercial interface between land and water. The 1986 Expo site in Vancouver was created on fill, and Hamilton has been greatly extended this way, as have the Toronto 'islands'. The Ontario Place development in Toronto was laid out on 2.5 million cubic metres of rubble from the excavation of subway tunnels and foundations for the new high-rise Toronto. With a new generation of tall buildings, Halifax is obliterating the harbour view from Citadel Hill, while Toronto and Calgary have put up artificial observation towers. A few major topographic features remain as landmarks—magical identifiers such as Mount Royal, the Niagara escarpment, or the "reversing falls" at Saint John, where tides eight or nine metres in height reverse the flow in the gorge. Because the ravines of Toronto and Edmonton and the gorges and falls near Hamilton were costly to build upon, their character was preserved, and they gradually became valued parts of stream valley park systems.

Climatic conditions, too, affect the shapes of cities. As a result of their northerly situation, most Canadian cities face long, very cold winters when artificial heat is needed, and heavy snowfalls that favour sales of snowplows and ski-doos. Each city is distinguished by its regional climate and vegetation: the wind in the Prairie cities, Calgary's milder winter, Victoria's gardens, Vancouver's combination of ski slopes and beaches, the brilliant fall colours of the Maritime cities. In some places, oceans or lakes modify the impact of each season, and a sharp break in relief, like the Niagara escarpment, can be noticed in local pockets of frost and fog. McCann (1987) gives a fine example of the way the contrast of lake and land in Hamilton generates breezes in the course of the day and the round of seasons. The influence of Lake Ontario produces comparable variations of micro-climate in St Catharine's and Toronto (Kerr and Spelt 1965) and unforgettable sunrises in Kingston.

As more land is paved and roofed for urban activities, the impermeable surfaces prevent infiltration, and storms produce more rapid run-off and flash floods. Materials like asphalt tend to store heat, and concrete canyons trap solar radiation and create a rough surface modifying the winds, so that a 'heat dome' is centred on the downtown (Oke 1987). Hamilton, under certain conditions, shows the curious variant of two warm cells, one centred over the downtown area and the other over the steel-making district. Local topography fosters situations in spring and fall when cold air (at lake level) is overlain by warmer air (at the level of the escarpment); under this stable situation of temperature inversion pollutants build up, trapped in the urban area (Rouse and Burghardt 1987).

Because local topography has that power of shaping the details of local climates, it indirectly affects the selection of sites for residential development, particularly the high-status areas occupied by people who can afford to choose. Every metropolis displays an example: Rosedale in the Toronto area, or the Mount Royal neighborhood of Calgary, laid out in the 1920s to follow the contours of the land. We see comparable 'contour plowing' in Shaughnessy Heights and Point Grey (Vancouver). Most of these areas used socially restrictive zoning covenants in their deeds, and even now provide great contrast with older working-class habitats such as low-lying 'Cork Town', 'Little Ireland', 'Cabbagetown', or 'The Ward' (Lemon 1985; Harris 1988). Quebec City had its 'Upper Town' and 'Lower Town', Montreal its 'City Below the Hill' (Ames 1972 [1902]), subject to flood, damp, and accumulation of pollutants. If asymmetry is an indicator of power relationships (Raffestin 1980), the topographic situation of those neighborhoods illustrates the power of social class.

A SUCCESSION OF BUILT FORMS

What we have built upon the land conveys a social interpretation of order and disorder. What we choose to conserve expresses the old order, or a certain conception of it, and what is proposed (as in Figure 10.3) is a conception of a new social order. In Ottawa, for instance, the elaborate rules for heights of buildings, public and private, formulate ambitions of national unity and deference for central institutions.

The morphology of everyday housing has everywhere been limited to a small range of basic building blocks. Early decisions about street grids, the sizes and shapes of building lots, and housing models created a cultural legacy of restraint on what could be done in the next generation. Regularity of layout and a symbolic centre recall notions of cosmic and social order (Wheatley 1971), but the choice of a plat (a model for laying out streets and lots) was often a crude speculative option. The gridiron of Winnipeg, evident in Figure 10.2, was a quick solution for surveying the town and offered developers as much buildable area as possible, at the expense of less public space. Ease of application and profitability for developers explains that the gridiron pattern became the norm in North America. With a two-dimensional parcelling of lots in place, the range was narrowed for planning three-dimensional shapes.

A powerful determinant of townscapes was the density of settlement, a product of economic forces. Eighteenth-century cities were built up with one- and two-storey dwellings, built one at a time, with gables, shingles, and chimneys. Narrow streets were laid with cobbles, and lanes were of dirt. Halifax blocks, for example, were small (120 feet by 320 feet), with streets 55 feet wide. At St John's, where colonial authorities sought to discourage residence and exercised no building regulations, frame shacks persisted. In small towns of western and northern Canada, a low-density 'western-style' pattern has continued into the twentieth century, with a grid plan, streets as wide as the surveyor's chain (66 feet), and low buildings of wood. The features shown for Winnipeg in 1880 (Figure 10.2) can still be seen at Rouyn-Noranda. St John's retains a frame architecture, and the Prairie cities, as well as suburbs of all Canadian cities, have retained wood as a material. Quebec small towns and suburbs still skimp on sidewalks,

Figure 10.2

Bird's-eye view of Winnipeg, Manitoba, in 1880. The artist, T.M. Fowler, displayed the ambitions of the city by projecting population from 6,000 to 10,000, exaggerating steamboat smoke, extending the geometry of streets and rendering a railway bridge that was completed a year later. Source: National Archives of Canada (NMC 15026).

and Vancouver houses exhibit not simply a 'west coast style', associated with a milder climate, but a 'twentieth-century style' (Holdsworth 1966).

As urban populations grew and cities spread out from their centres, competition grew more intense for space within walking distance of these centres. Until the 1890s most people walked to work, and, since they worked long hours, tried to live close to their work places. The pressure to stack homes and businesses higher is therefore best seen in cities that had grown large by the turn of the century.[4] Under the constraint of the journey to work, the larger cities, over the second half of the nineteenth century, increased their residential densities to a spectacular degree. Urban growth was accommodated by filling and squeezing and piling higher. For example, Montreal's rapid population growth between 1847 and 1901 (it doubled between 1847 and 1861, tripled in the next twenty years, and doubled again between 1881 and 1901), was accommodated largely by changes in urban form. Back lanes were built in already crowded areas, and dwellings were opened in rear lots. In the 1860s and 1870s builders shifted from two-storey to three-storey designs, and from gabled to mansard roofs, providing more interior space on the top floor. In the booms of the 1880s and the early 1900s they adopted larger lots and larger blocks, and new construction took the form of the triple-decker—three flats on three and a half floors, with an L-shape which let light into more rooms (Legault 1990). Tens of thousands of such triplex dwellings built between 1900 and 1940 have contributed to the urban identity of Montreal. Their neighbourly balconies and their twisting outside stairways, which squeeze more usable space out of the building lot are as distinctive a trademark as the Mount Royal.

A TRAJECTORY OF CAPITAL

David Harvey (1972 and 1978) has taught us to think of cities as *built capital*, including the streets, rail tracks, and sewers as well as houses and factories. This conception, derived from Marx's logic, reminds us that all these works were created from human labour, frozen into place for a century or more. The forms of the city reflect, therefore, the decisions of people who controlled property and deployed the labour of other people, with the object of raising the values of their private property. At every street corner or construction site we are led to wonder, Whose capital is invested? How has energy been deployed? at whose design? to whose benefit? at what human cost?

A powerful feature of built capital is its cyclical rhythm of accumulation.[5] Every twenty years or so, another boom produces another ring of suburban construction and another reconstruction of the centre. In each generation the buildings, like the ships and engines, are larger, taller, deeper, reflecting a new engineering, architecture, and taste. For all Canadian cities the waves of city-building are synchronized, but some cities have been more successful in a particular wave. As capital has moved westward, successive financial hubs were generated: at Halifax, Montreal, Toronto, and Calgary. Economic booms and city-building are synchronized with immigration. Immigrants followed economic activity and concentrated in cities, and waves of social change rippled outward from their centres. In Montreal the chunky lofts of garment factories marched north along the Main, parallel with the homes and shops and places of worship of successive populations of immigrant workers, the produce markets, and cheap entertainments. New populations succeeded one another in the old structures like new wine in old casks.

In each building boom, larger building blocks were employed. Gad and Holdsworth (1988) have described the office blocks of King Street, Toronto, as expressions of the increasing resources capitalists could amass. The streetscape reflected their ambitions, but as the human walking-scale was exceeded, the streetscape lost its diversity and vitality. Like the office blocks, the sizes and shapes of Canadian factories trace out a North American sequence of technological opportunities. In Montreal in the 1850s, Dow's brewery, Redpath's sugar mill, and Molson's bank were little larger than the mansions of their owners, but by 1900 you could put a dozen such mansions inside one of the top ten enterprises. Among the largest spaces were railway stations, department stores, gasholders, and cold-storage warehouses. Large firms like Sun Life and Bell Canada created the cement wedding-cakes of Montreal in the 1920s, and in the 1980s the glass ice-cubes of Toronto.

Nation-wide corporate institutions placed their signatures on Canadian cities. Central post offices designated downtown itself. Eaton's stores were scaled to the size of each central place, and the fashions in their windows were adapted to different living standards and mores, distinguishing the big city from the small town. The Canadian Pacific Railway fitted its stations to the pecking order of towns, but each was unmistakably 'CP', and its turreted hotels became landmarks in every metropolis. One of the dramas of the 1970s was the sudden failure of this city-defining role on the part of chain enterprises. The post office, VIA Rail, oil companies, and fast food restaurants abandoned their identification with a central site or a 'main street'. Since the 1970s, the strategy of each is to blare a little louder than the others, and television dramatizes their placeless symbols and colours coast to coast.[6]

Virtually all cities have an identifiable centre in which taller, more closely packed buildings reflect higher land values and a greater competition of users. Alonso (1964), more firmly than anyone else, established the importance of the land-value gradient to the centred pattern of land uses and the central business district (CBD) which is its kernel (this is discussed more fully in Chapter 12). Specialized and impressive buildings, such as railway stations and office towers, were erected in high-priced central sites. Even non-profit functions, like cathedrals and city halls, conscious of the competition of symbols, captured central sites. As we move away from the centre, we generally observe that the bulk and density of built forms diminishes.[7] Thus the basic gradient of land values forms the basis for building types and functions, and determines the evolution of urban form as discussed in Chapter 11.

As cities expanded, the process of land value differentiation snowballed. Higher land values stimulated investment in underground transit and made yet higher buildings profitable. Growth of the city as a whole produces an ever more powerful centrality and an ever greater differentiation of parts. For instance, in the central and oldest part of Montreal, residential population dwindled to nothing by 1860, but taxable commercial space continued to increase, tenfold in twenty years. The Banque du Peuple, built three storeys high in 1872, had six more storeys added in 1892. The Sun Life building reached six storeys in 1914, ten in 1924, and twenty-six in 1934. Place Ville-Marie, headquarters for ALCAN and the Royal Bank in 1959, reached forty-two storeys and dug its roots six storeys below street level. Establishment of underground mass transit in 1966 was associated with investment in tall buildings above many CBD stations, so that today the underground network can be inferred from the urban profile.

Public works, more particularly transportation facilities, are another important form of built capital. Continental decisions about canals, railroads, and pipelines have had exceptional importance for Canadian cities. As powerful speculative operations, they created a sense of opportunity and an indecent haste in the promotion of city sites (Nader 1976). Decisions about highways fostered strip development in building booms of the 1920s, 1940s, and 1960s. Stretches of the Trans-Canada highway in the 1960s bypassed city centres and undermined the economic vitality of the older strips and 'Main Streets' of small and large towns, drawing enterprises to a rim (Holdsworth 1985). Comparable readjustments occurred in port facilities, as larger ships required larger docks and back-up spaces. Their need for specialized facilities, 24-hour access, and tight security brought shipping into conflict with other city land uses and produced radical changes in waterfront management (McCalla 1988).

The great corridors of public works also give character to the landscape by creating paths through which we experience the city: rail lines along the waterfront, the expressway trench, the sodium glare of a highway, the lift of a bridge at Trois Rivières. They provide visual 'edges' for neighbourhoods and reinforce social separations (Lynch 1960). In the 1880s, the CP embankment separated Montreal's areas of rich and poor, Westmount and Saint-Henri; in the 1970s that gulf was reinforced by construction of a parallel highway. At that time, Félix Leclerc was singing about the telephone poles of Montreal as signs of domination of foreign capital; in the 1990s, the cartoonists' symbols of subservience are the pylons of high-tension lines bringing electric power from James Bay to New York as well as to Montreal.

THE CITY SPREADS OUT

The swift growth of the nineteenth-century metropolis produced monstrous problems. As we shall see, the concentration of built capital, and the haste to accumulate more, generated threats to health on an unprecedented scale. Concern about these threats led to new ideas, and by the turn of the century reformers had blueprints ready for a revolution in urban form. They saw congestion as the problem, and envisioned cheaper, faster transportation as the solution. Greater mobility would permit a more generous use of space, so that city-dwellers could 'breathe' again. It took nearly a century to achieve those objectives, and, as we shall see, to discover the drawbacks of the new spread-out city.

The great nineteenth-century threats in urban centres were fire and contagious disease. The high densities and cheap materials of Canadian cities permitted these threats to expand into massive conflagrations and epidemics. As the costs of these disasters became intolerable, cities were re-engineered to bring both threats under control through changes in shape and layout.[8] Under pressure of fire insurance costs, public water supplies were developed. While burned out districts were usually rebuilt in haste, each episode spurred fire-conscious regulations which contributed to shifts of local building styles: brick cladding for the frame houses of Montreal, fire escapes for theatres, dikes around fuel storage tanks, the choice of reinforced concrete for the skyscrapers of the 1920s.

As a response to the scourge of tuberculosis, more attention was paid to air quality and the provision of open space. Playgrounds and parks were conceived as 'lungs' for the city, porch-front dwellings became popular, zoning laws were written to separate homes from factories, and legislation required setbacks for skyscrapers, and ventilation for factories.

Also of epidemic proportions were the intestinal diseases (cholera, typhoid fever, and infant diarrhoea) transmitted by the contamination of drinking water by human wastes. Pumps from shallow wells and outhouses that drained to septic beds were imports from rural landscapes, and at urban densities they failed. Intestinal diseases, deadliest in summer, were brought under some control by public water management. By 1900 water towers were town landmarks, and large cities had public baths and drinking fountains. With the gradual acceptance of germ theory, water was piped from more distant sources (for example, water was sent into Winnipeg from ninety-five miles away), and human wastes were drained to points outside the city, downstream, or into the lake or ocean. The strategy proved effective, but it meant that the city was depending upon *externalities*, that is, on benefits captured from an environment outside its own territory.

About 1891, when cable-cars and electric tramways were introduced, cities began to spread rapidly. The higher speed and lower cost of mass transit made it possible for employees to live farther from work, and the central business district came to serve an area of larger radius. For example,

Figure 10.3

Bird's-eye sketch of central Saint John, New Brunswick, showing Master Plan proposals of 1944. Smoke and traffic are minimized; trees are reduced to a symbolic minimum. Clean lines and curves are reinforced, and all types of urban activity are packed in neat boxes. Source: Saint John Town Planning Commission (1946, p. 83).

Vancouver in the 1890s occupied two square miles (the peninsula between Burrard Inlet and False Creek); by 1912, it was spread over thirty square miles (MacDonald 1966). A hundred miles of street railway were built, the long ribbon of Kingsway was developed, and the downtown of three- or four-storey buildings was replaced by office blocks, hotels, and banks, eight to fourteen storeys high.

Introduction of automobiles reinforced the tendency of cities to spread. Parkways and viaducts were built. Suburbs were laid out on a large scale to make generous use of cheaper land. Schools, as well as factories and warehouses, adopted one-storey layouts. To slow automobile traffic in the new suburban areas yet accelerate its flow through the metropolis as a whole, city planners experimented with curves and a 'street hierarchy'. North American theories of city planning crystallized around a conception of generous low-density life-styles, with homes segregated from industry and business, and further segregated by levels of 'affordability' (see Chapter 19).

By the 1940s, 'master plans' like the one for Saint John (Figure 10.3) expressed these principles and identified 'blighted' areas where these standards had not yet been achieved. The average densities of cities were substantially reduced, and planners were beginning to congratulate themselves on having eradicated typhus, tuberculosis, and conflagration. Incinerator stacks and the trickling filters of sewage-works and water treatment plants had become major urban features visible from the air. They represented a new strategy of taking advantage of natural processes like gravity flow and microbial digestion. They also forced cities to *internalize* some of the costs of their metabolism. Those costs, as we shall now see, are very high.

THE COSTS OF THE LOW-DENSITY METROPOLIS

Metabolism is the rate at which a system uses energy. Extension of the city at lower densities implies changes in its metabolism because continuous inputs of energy are required to cover the greater distances. Calgary is a good example, a success story of prosperity and effective urban planning, characterized by a golden triangle of oil-company skyscrapers, high levels of car ownership, superb expressways, a preponderance of single-family detached housing, elaborately segregated residential neighbourhoods, and a green belt five miles wide. But these features mean that Calgary draws more kilowatts, guzzles more gasoline, and spews out more nitrogen oxides than in the past. Hamilton is an ecosystem with a still higher metabolism since its industries are exceptionally energy-intensive. The steel industry accounts for half the city's exports, but consumes three-quarters of its energy inputs (Lonergan 1987, 111).

Like Calgary, all cities now encounter threats to people's health due to air pollution and new costs arising from their high rates of metabolism.

Cities' energy consumption is not only related to daily heating, transportation and transformation requirements. In Dansereau's classification of landscapes (1985), urban land is the most radically transformed, since brick, glass, and concrete have baked into them large quantities of fossil energies. Hough (1984, 16–18) reports energy flow through a city as 100 times that through a natural ecosystem: 'Thus cities place enormous stresses on natural systems, depending on them for resource inputs and for the disposal of unwanted products', such as waste heat, cooling water, sewage, solid wastes (two to three cubic metres per person per year) and methane from their decomposition.

Canada has the highest per capita use of energy in the world. The heavy demand for fuels is attributable not so much to the cold climate as to the form of Canadian cities—the way they spread over the landscape. Half the energy consumed by the average urban household is used for driving cars. Sweden, with a comparable living standard, uses only three-fifths as much energy per person (Sanderson and Wolfe 1978).

High fossil fuel consumption made people feel independent of place and season: 'Bulldozers made all sites equivalent, and oversized heating and cooling systems made every house a blob of paradise' (City of Hamilton 1982, 21). The high metabolism also made city-dwellers vulnerable to changes in the energy supply system, evident in the years since 1973 as the world price of petroleum increased sixfold.

Associated with the higher demand for energy was a higher throughput of other materials and a higher excretion of waste substances, many of them uncommon in nature. Voracious cities forced massive environmental changes upon the entire Canadian landscape. Ontario cities depend for half their electricity on nuclear plants that continuously add to a stockpile of dangerous wastes—wastes that will have to be safeguarded for many generations, although after thirty years of design we still do not know how or where to do this. In Alberta, the exploitation of the tar sands remains 'an expensive and environmentally suspect technology' (Sanderson and Wolfe 1978, 7). In the North, power-related proposals such as further extension of pipelines (NWT) and hydroelectric developments in Quebec could cause oil spills, the melting of permafrost, and disruption of the ways of life of hunting peoples.

Waste products from central Canada, including lead, PCBs and hydrocarbons, are carried by prevailing winds and end up in groundwater, wetland environments, or the marine food web. The oxides of nitrogen from automobile emissions nearly tripled in the 1970s. Construction of tall stacks in the 1960s seemed to clean up towns like Sudbury, but instead exported sulphur and nitrogen components of 'acid rain' to a larger area. For instance, the 387m superstack at the Inco plant in Sudbury emits a cloud of pollutants that may arrive in Toronto, 400 km away, eighteen hours later, or, depending on wind direction, reach as far as the sensitive ecosystems in the Maritimes.[9] A decade ago it still seemed progressive to clean up the St Charles River at Quebec City by piping sewage and industrial wastes directly into the St Lawrence River and building a 10-metre dam to prevent their backing up into the St Charles at high tide (Nader 1976). We now recognize that such diversions, like the taller stacks, merely export the problem a little farther from its source.

In Saint John, as pictured in Figure 10.3, seventy-five outfalls were dumping raw sewage into the harbour. In Montreal, where the mountain functions as a natural 'reservoir', the St Lawrence River, in particular the wider, more tranquil reach of Lac Saint-Pierre, has become the sump of heavy metals. Industrial pollutants have accumulated over years in urban soils, in groundwater, and at the bottoms of the rivers. Virtually every city is discovering dangerous dumps, and the spoils from dredging harbours are highly contaminated. As a result of steel industry pollution in the Hamilton area, genetic deformities are reported for one-tenth of the worms at the base of the food chain. Divers have identified in the St Clair River near Windsor a 'blob' of the most contaminated material ever found in the Great Lakes (Sanderson 1988). Downstream, at Quebec City, the numbers of species of fish in the St Lawrence River have diminished (from forty-eight to thirty since 1940), and the beluga whales at its mouth are threatened with extinction.

Cities have become more hospitable to a few species, notably rats, squirrels, starlings, pigeons, and roaches, and less hospitable to great diversity of songbirds, butterflies, and small mammals. The effects of pollutants on human health are becoming apparent. One example is the gradual concentration of lead in urban environments: in the paint on old buildings, in dusts and residues from gasoline, in battery-disposal and recycling plants. Lead poisoning now affects the health of renovation workers, tunnel guards, and children of entire neighbourhoods (Olson 1979). Allergies and physiological responses to chemical residues and 'building disease' are complicated by smoking habits. City-dwellers are subject to progressive deafness from noise, and to the violence of spills, explosions, and collisions, which result from the magnification of human error in the handling of powerful, energy-driven machines.

THE REVOLUTION REQUIRED

Problems associated with energy use, waste disposal, and environmental hazards will be solved by joint efforts of all members of society or not at all. To bring urban metabolism under control calls for a re-concentration of urban activities, that is, another revolution in urban form. Trends can already be observed towards higher densities and a greater integration of activities, but the built landscape is so long-lived that its adaptation will take more than a generation. It will require a double process: control of new development and the retrofitting of existing habitats.

Some techniques for retrofitting have already been identified. A small example of the way individual households adapt a landscape for energy conservation is the clothes-line. These lines festooned the slums of the 1890s, but with the advent of washing-machines and laundromats they were left to rural settings; élite subdivisions outlawed them as unsightly. California cities are now re-writing the rules to require that new developments include a clothes-drying pole for every dwelling. At a more substantial level, a Saskatchewan study showed that energy-conscious site development and landscaping, combined with energy-efficient construction techniques, could reduce fuel consumption for space heating by 85 per cent compared with conventional suburban forms of development. Hamilton planners go a step farther: they assert that by the end of the century houses with zero fuel bills will be developed in southern Ontario (Hamilton, City of 1982, 32). Such dwellings, known as *passive solar*, will be built of conventional materials but designed to capture winter sunshine and provide shade in summer. Home heating bills can be reduced by planting deciduous trees or vines on the south side of a house and coniferous trees for shelter on the north side. Other techniques are effective when they are applied at the scale of an entire community. Shading parking lots, for example, reduce the urban heat load and the rate of precipitation run-off.

Energy-conscious plans favour cottage industries, narrower streets, bicycle paths and walkways, and greater social diversity of neighbourhoods. In the early 1970s, the design of Fermont, a mining town in subarctic Quebec, offered pointers towards energy conservation: its tallest buildings are situated to shelter the community from wind, and energy for steam heat is recovered from sewage and garbage. In 1979 Brampton, Ontario, was one of the first Canadian towns to establish a policy of securing 'access to sun' for all new buildings, by favouring the east-west orientation of streets and the north-south orientation of houses, controlling heights and setbacks to avoid winter shadows, and permitting ingenuity of layout.[10]

Cities spend energy as well as money trying to maintain the ecosystem in an unchanging and unnatural state. Harbours and channels are continually dredged. Reservoirs fill with silt from the erosion of soil from suburban construction sites. It costs $2 million a year to keep grass trimmed on the boulevards of Winnipeg (Hough 1984, 21) and $30 million to clear 'each last snowflake' from the streets of Montreal (Sanderson and Wolfe 1978). Instead, by taking advantage of natural processes, a city can be made more comfortable and more manageable. Winnipeg, faced with the projected high cost of extending storm sewers on low-lying land to detain rainfall, instead created lakes and ponds. The University of Alberta, to accommodate twice as many students, increased the built-up area of its Edmonton campus (from 15 per cent to 34 per cent) and at the same time made the campus more hospitable by disposing buildings so as to cut the wind and capture winter sunshine (Hough 1984, 98). The same tactics were applied to Ontario Place, on the Toronto lakefront: winter recreation areas are encircled by buildings and conifers.

The concept of retrofitting extends to cleaning up damaged urban habitats. Economies of energy have already produced marked improvements in the air quality in Montreal, as well as savings to industry from the recycling of chemicals.

Renovation of older inner-city neighbourhoods is occurring in every Canadian metropolis. While that trend suggests a return to high-density life-styles, it is accompanied by a proliferation of 'second homes' and by recreational and commercial expansion into a yet larger 'exurban' area (detailed in Chapter 9). The net impact is still to reinforce our dispersal, mobility, and dependence on high energy metabolism. The costs are not shared equally. Retrofitting of older areas is associated with 'gentrification', and low-income families, excluded from these neighbourhoods, tend to live in the suburbs of the 1960s and 1970s, where they bear the brunt of rising energy costs. Lower-income households are already spending one-quarter of the family budget on energy (Sanderson and Wolfe 1978).

Metropolitan areas are just beginning to face the real costs of their metabolism. The public debt of municipalities, or even the combined debt of all levels of government, is small relative to the environmental debt that has been contracted. As citizens become reluctant to accept or re-process wastes of other regions in their 'back yards', each metropolis is forced to internalize the costs of its metabolism and search for controls it can impose at source, and for changes it can make in life-styles (see Bunting 1987). The City of Montreal, after outlawing open burning and acquiring a huge quarry in which it could bury its garbage, is now preparing to shut down the dump in 1992 and re-landscape the site. It will have to monitor and re-process all storm drainage and recover methane from decomposition on this site for at least thirty years. And after 1992 what will the city do with its solid wastes?

The present-day wasteful and isolating habitats typical of the modern suburb will, a century from now, evoke the horror we feel when we look back at the teeming, contagious fire-trap cities of the Victorian era: 'The style and manner in which land has been developed for residential use in the past can hardly be justified in a time of escalating costs and a diminishing supply of non-renewable sources of energy. The challenge lies in modifying the urban form.' (City of Hamilton 1982, 2).

Retrofitting of cities implies that all elements of built capital must become more a part of their natural landscape. As there is little hint of a change in the capitalist process itself, retrofitting will be obstructed by powerful forces and undermined by opportunities for profit. The need to re-form cities will challenge the acquired 'rights' of high-income people to protect their privileged life-styles, and separate themselves from the habitats of others. 'Re-form' of the physical city will once again require social reform.

CONCLUSION

In this chapter we have seen that the form of the metropolis displays the effects of political, social, and economic forces. Canadian cities were laid out, each in its own topographic setting, and developed as a succession of 'built forms', changing their shapes with every surge of investment. Each new design provided protection and enjoyment for those who could afford the new, although urban dwellers incurred unexpected costs and spill-over effects.

Over generations, the development process has stimulated massive flows of energy through the urban landscape. In the course of the nineteenth century, cities were built to ever higher densities, creating risk of fire and contagion. In response to those problems, cities have, in the course of the twentieth century, been re-engineered into new patterns at much lower densities.

But today's sprawling metropolis, wasteful of energy, is vulnerable to the accumulation of its own waste products. Once again, in response to rising costs and risks, we are beginning to conceive of a revolution of metropolitan form. The future Canadian metropolis is likely to be more compact, more self-contained, more aware of its metabolism, and more conscious of the costs. At each excavation and construction site, we are challenged to ask, How is energy being deployed? How is capital being deployed? to whose benefit? at what human cost?

NOTES

*I am grateful for the help of colleagues Jeanne Wolfe (McGill School of Urban Planning) and Gunther Gad (University of Toronto Erindale College).

1. The remarkable exception is the extensive work of Hans Blumenfeld (1967).

2. The exceptions here are the fine work of German and Austrian geographers, and, in Britain, of Michael Conzen (1988) and Whitehand (1981).

3. Even the best texts, such as Cadwallader (1985) or Yeates and Garner (1980) have no discussion of built forms or three-dimensional shapes.

4. West of Montreal, cities did not reach that critical size until after the introduction of tramways, so that the predominant housing type remained the free-standing frame dwelling, and even the poor, confined to small, poorly insulated spaces, lived in houses rather than flats, or built shacks outside the city limits.

5. On the Kuznets cycle of urban construction—swings in economic growth rates with a duration of 15 years or more—see Gottlieb (1976) and, for further references to its geographical properties, Olson (1982).

6. An absurd example, at 359 St James Street, Montreal, is the blue and yellow plastic logo of the Royal Bank, mounted inside the elegant and well-preserved banking hall, all red and gold, of Italian Renaissance design.

7. Bid-rent curves are discussed in all texts in urban geography. Classic accounts of the density function are reviewed by Newling (1969), and applied to

Toronto by Latham and Yeates (1970). A novel model, still two-dimensional, is proposed by Batty *et al.* (1989).

8. Fire destroyed an entire downtown or a large share of the housing stock in Quebec City in 1845 and 1866, St John's in 1846 and 1892, Toronto in 1849 and 1904, Montreal in 1852, Halifax in 1859, Saint John in 1784, 1837, and 1877, and Ottawa-Hull in 1900. Norris (1987) argues that small towns were more vulnerable, less able to fight fires, less well insured, and consequently less able to compete with large cities. Frost and Jones (1989) confirm the improved durability of the urban built environment through time.

9. Maritime provinces are sensitive as a result of regional bedrock type, which has little alkalinity. Lakes and rivers have low buffering capacity. Salmon and phytoplanktons are subjected to a spring shock of nitrates, and acidic water mobilizes or dissolves metals such as aluminum from soils and sediments. These problems are well described in the essay of Ricketts in Day (1988).

10. Zoning conventions had to be rewritten to permit the slanting and staggering of lots along streets oriented in another direction, and keyed or chevron layouts. The clustering of houses permits densities of 50 to 75 dwellings per ha and reduced areas for road, sewer, water, and electrical networks. Leaders in implementing these methods have been the California State Energy Code of 1976, the Solar Rights Act and Solar Shade Control Act of 1978, the cities of Davis and Burbank, California, and Denver, Colorado. Especially valuable for Canadian cities are reports from Hamilton (Hamilton, City of 1982), Saskatoon (Saskatchewan Department of Mineral Resources n.d.), Province of Prince Edward Island (ca. 1981), and the work of Hough (1984).

FURTHER READING

BLUMENFELD, H. 1967 *The Modern Metropolis* (Cambridge, Mass.: M.I.T. Press)

CALVINO, I. 1972 *Invisible Cities* (New York: Harcourt Brace Jovanovich)

HARVEY, D. 1973 *Social Justice and the City* (Baltimore: Johns Hopkins University Press)

HOUGH, M. 1984 *City Form and Natural Process* (New York City: Van Nostrand Reinhold)

RAFFESTIN, C. 1980 *Pour une géographie du pouvoir* (Paris: LITEC)

ROBINSON, G.D. and SPIEKER, A.M. eds 1978 'Nature to be Commanded ...' Earth science maps applied to land and water management, U.S. Geological Survey Professional Paper no. 950

REFERENCES

ALONSO, W. 1964 'The Historical and Structural Theories of Urban Form', *Land Economics* 40, 227–31

AMES, H.B. 1972 [1902] *The City Below the Hill* (Toronto: University of Toronto Press)

BATTY, M., LONGLEY, P., and FOTHERINGHAM, S. 1989 'Urban Growth and Form: Scaling, Fractal Geometry and Diffusion-Limited Aggregation', *Environment and Planning A* 21, 1447–72

BLUMENFELD, H. 1967 *The Modern Metropolis* (Cambridge, Mass.: M.I.T. Press)

BUNTING, B.T. 1987 'Soils of the Hamilton Region: Profiles, Properties and Problems' in M.J. Dear, J.J. Drake, and L.G. Reeds eds *Steel City, Hamilton and Region* (Toronto: University of Toronto Press)

CADWALLADER, M. 1985 *Analytical Urban Geography* (Englewood Cliffs, N.J.: Prentice-Hall)

CITY OF HAMILTON 1982 *Design Criteria for Energy Efficient Neighbourhood Planning* (Hamilton: City of Hamilton, prepared by the Planning and Development Department of the Regional Municipality of Hamilton-Wentworth)

CONZEN, M.R.G. 1988 'Morphogenesis, Morphological Regions and Secular Human Agency in the Historic Townscape as exemplified by Ludlow' in D. Denecke and G. Shaw, eds *Urban Historical Geography, Recent Progress in Britain and Germany* (Cambridge: Cambridge University Press)

DANSEREAU, P. 1985 'Essai de classification et de cartographie écologique des espaces', *Etudes Ecologiques* 10

DAY, D. ed. 1988 *Geographical perspectives on the Maritime Provinces* (Halifax: St. Mary's University)

FROST, L.E. and JONES, E.L. 1989 'The Fire Gap and the Greater Durability of Nineteenth-Century Cities', *Planning Perspectives* 4, 333–47

GAD, G. and HOLDSWORTH, D.W. 1988 'Streetscape and Society: The Changing Built Environment of King Street, Toronto' in R. Hall, et al. eds *Patterns of the Past, Interpreting Ontario's History* (Toronto: Dundurn Press)

GOTTLIEB, M. 1976 *Long Swings in Urban Development* (New York: Columbia University Press)

HARRIS, R. 1988 *Democracy in Kingston: A Social Movement in Urban Politics, 1965–1970* (Kingston/Montreal: McGill-Queen's University Press)

HARVEY, D. 1972 *Society, the City and the Space-Economy of Urbanism* (Commission on College Geography, Resource Paper 18)

———— 1978 'The Urban Process Under Capitalism: A Framework for Analysis', *International Journal of Urban and Regional Research* 2, 101–31

HOLDSWORTH, D. 1985 *Reviving Main Street* (Toronto: University of Toronto Press)

———— 1966 'House and Home in Vancouver: Images of West Coast Urbanism, 1886–1929' in G.F. Stelter and A.F.J. Artibise eds *The Canadian City, Essays in Urban History* (Ottawa: Carleton Library no. 109, Macmillan reprint 1979)

HOUGH, M. 1984 *City Form and Natural Process* (New York City: Van Nostrand Reinhold)

KERR, D. and SPELT, J. 1965 *The Changing Face of Toronto—A Study in Urban Geography* (Canada, Department of Energy Mines and Resources, Geographical Branch, Memoir 11)

LATHAM, R.F. and YEATES, M. 1970 'Population Density Growth in Metropolitan Toronto', *Geographical Analysis* 2, 177–85

LEGAULT, R. 1991 'Architecture et forme urbaine: L'exemple du triplex à Montréal 1870–1914', *Urban History Review* (forthcoming)

LEMON, J. 1985 *Toronto Since 1918: An Illustrated History* (Toronto: James Lorimer)

LONERGAN, S.C. 1987 'Energy Flows and the City of Hamilton' in M.J. Dear, J.J. Drake, and L.G. Reeds eds *Steel City, Hamilton and Region* (Toronto: University of Toronto Press)

LYNCH K. 1960 *Image of the City* (Cambridge, Mass.: M.I.T. Press)

MACDONALD, N. 1966 'A Critical Growth Cycle for Vancouver, 1900–1914' in G.F. Stelter and A.F.J. Artibise eds *The Canadian City, Essays in Urban History* (Ottawa: Carleton Library no. 109, Macmillan reprint 1979).

MCCALLA, R.J. 1988 'Land Use Development in Cityport Waterfronts: A Model' in D. Day ed. *Geographical Perspectives on the Maritime Provinces* (Halifax: St. Mary's University)

MCCANN, S.B. 1987 'Physical Landscape of the Hamilton Region' in M.J. Dear, J.J. Drake, and L.G. Reeds eds *Steel City, Hamilton and Region* (Toronto: University of Toronto Press)

NADER, G.A. 1976 *Cities of Canada, Profiles of Fifteen Metropolitan Centres* (Toronto: Macmillan)

NEWLING, B.E. 1969 'The Spatial Variation of Urban Population Densities', *Geographical Review* 59, 242–50

NORRIS, D.A. 1987 'Flightless Phoenix: Fire Risk and Fire Insurance in Urban Canada, 1882–1886', *Urban History Review* 16, 62–8

OKE, T.R. 1987 *Boundary Layer Climatology* (London: Methuen)

OLSON, Sherri 1979 'An Ecology of Workplace Hazards', *Economic Geography* 55, 287–308

―――― 1982 'Urban Metabolism and Morphogenesis', *Urban Geography* 3, 87–109

PROVINCE OF PRINCE EDWARD ISLAND c. 1981 *Municipal Energy Management in Prince Edward Island* Report of a Study sponsored jointly by the Province of Prince Edward Island and the Government of Canada

RAFFESTIN, C. 1980 *Pour une géographie du pouvoir* (Paris: LITEC)

RICKETTS, P.J. 1988 'Shoreline Changes and Associated Coastal Management Issues in the Maritime Provinces' in D. Day ed. *Geographical Perspectives on the Maritime Provinces* (Halifax: Geography Department, Saint Mary's University)

ROUSE, W.R. and BURGHARDT, A.F. 1987 'Climate, Weather and Society' in M.J. Dear, J.J. Drake, and L.G. Reeds eds *Steel City, Hamilton and Region* (Toronto: University of Toronto Press)

SANDERSON, C. and WOLFE, J.M. 1978 *The Energy Crisis and Urban Planning, A Canadian Perspective* paper presented at Canadian Institute of Planners Annual Meeting, July 30th to August 3rd 1978, McGill University School of Urban Planning

SANDERSON, M. 1988 'The Blob', *Canadian Geographer* 30, 315

SASKATCHEWAN DEPARTMENT OF MINERAL RESOURCES, OFFICE OF ENERGY CONSERVATION (n.d.) *Energy Conscious Landscape & Urban Site Design* (Saskatoon, Saskatchewan)

SCHOENAUER, N. 1967 'The New City Centre', *Architectural Design* 37, 311–24

THOMPSON, D.W. 1961 [1917] *On Growth and Form* (Cambridge: Cambridge University Press)

WHEATLEY, P. 1971 *The Pivot of the Four Quarters* (Chicago: Aldine)

WHITEHAND, J.W.R. ed. 1981 *The Urban Landscape: Historical Development and Management, Papers by M.R.G. Conzen* Institute of British Geographers special publication. no. 13 (London: Academic Press)

YEATES, M. and GARNER, B. 1980 *The North American City* (New York: Harper and Row)

11

Metropolitan Transportation: Patterns and Planning

BRUCE G. HUTCHINSON

This chapter is primarily concerned with the interactive relationship that ties transportation to land use. The relationship is first considered through an overview of urban development patterns and then through a discussion of transportation planning as practised in Canadian cities. It begins with an introductory section that deals with the role that transportation, and more broadly speaking communication, plays in structuring urban growth and form. At this stage the attention is more specifically on the effect of transportation on land-use patterns. Subsequent sections deal with urban transportation demands, time horizons in transportation planning, transportation systems analysis, and the evolution of urban transportation policy and planning. In a manner that is consistent with predominant transportation planning practice, emphasis is given to the adjustment of transportation to demand levels that proceed from different types of land-use patterns and from other factors such as household size, car-ownership rates, and life-styles.

LAND USE AND TRANSPORTATION IN CITIES

Perhaps the most fundamental principle of city structure is that of the inextricable link between urban growth, land use, and transportation. In the early 1960s, Richard Meier (1962) detailed these fundamental inter-relationships in *A Communications Theory of Urban Growth*. In this work he demonstrates that throughout history major changes in urban growth rates, city size, and structure can be directly attributed to transportation and communication innovations. For example, steam transportation was a major factor underlying the revolutionary rates of urban growth that coincided with the Industrial Revolution. Thus, the patterns of urban development in Western Canada directly reflect the layout of nineteenth- and early twentieth-century rail transit routes.

Modes of transit were historically the main force shaping the internal form and structure of cities; they now share this role with planning policies. In the past when space friction costs (in other words, movement costs in terms of money and time) were high and when urban movement was primarily by foot the spatial extent of built-up urban areas could be reasonably traversed by pedestrians. Roughly circular or semi-circular geographic layouts were predominant as these were the most efficient geometric shapes for maximizing time-distance relationships. Also, densities of population were generally high. The inner cores of our Maritime cities exhibit characteristics of what has been referred to as the 'horse-cart-pedestrian city' (Yeates and Garner 1980). The old town in Quebec City is also a classic example of this form.

In the latter half of the nineteenth century and into the early parts of the twentieth century new modes of transit—the horse-drawn streetcar, railways, and, later, electric streetcars and various forms of rapid transit— had dramatic effects on time-distance relationships. These relationships were no longer relatively homogeneous across urban space. Time-distance was significantly reduced along transit routes. New heavy industry gravitated to rail lines to ease shipping and receiving of products and raw materials. Inevitably, poorer worker housing abutted these industrial sectors. The reasons for this concentration of housing were twofold. First, poorer households relied primarily on walking as a means of commuting. Second, the better-off households would not tolerate the noxious environmental conditions that were a direct by-product of heavy industrial processing. In contrast, in areas where travel time was reduced by new forms of infrastructure, such as streetcars and commuter trains, middle- and upper middle-classes inevitably took advantage of the reduced travel costs by moving to larger lots and less congested neighbourhoods at increasing distances from the Central Business District (CBD). Warner (1962) has used the term 'streetcar suburb' in reference to this phenomenon. The juxtaposition of high-income neighbourhoods along Yonge Street in Toronto or along the Lakeshore and the Two Mountain commuter train lines in the Montreal region are good examples of rail transportation's role in generating sectoral alignment of urban social structure. This sectoral pattern was also captured in one of the early 'land use' models developed by Homer Hoyt (1939) and discussed more fully in Chapter 12 of this volume.

The automobile city introduces further variation in the urban form. In the years following World War II, widespread automobile ownership brought great increases in personal mobility for the majority of urban households. As the cost of moving about in the city decreased, residential densities dropped dramatically. Compact, ring-like, and sectoral patterns persisted in the core areas of metropolitan regions, but the outer zones became characterized by low-density housing tracts that often sprawled for miles into the rural-urban fringe (Bryant *et al.* 1982). In the immediate post-war decades, unplanned strip development occurred along major traffic arteries such as Calgary's Ventura Boulevard (Boal and Johnson 1965). One noted theorist uses the term 'nonplace city' to describe this type of urban form (Webber 1964). In the United States, Los Angeles is an archetypical example; in Canada many unplanned suburban areas built up in the 1960s and 1970s took on characteristics of the 'nonplace city'.

With the advent of widespread ownership of automobiles, land-use segregation tended to increase. Specialized areas that are consistent with the Harris and Ullman (1945) multiple nuclei model began to appear. These areas took the form of industrial parks, regional shopping centres, and large residential sectors differentiated according to the type and cost of their housing. This type of land-use segregation led directly to increased distances between place of work and place of residence. Commuting increased in terms of distance. Also, growing labour force participation translated in larger numbers of commuters. As a result new and/or expanded freeway systems were needed to accommodate growing rates of trip generation especially as these occur at 'peak times' in morning and evening rush hours. The costs of this urban form were high, not just in terms of energy consumption and transportation infrastructure investments, but also in terms of noxious spin-offs such as high accident rates and air pollution that have come to characterize life in the post-World War II automobile city. (See Chapter 10 for an environmental critique of the contemporary urban form.)

In response to problems associated with the form of city that emerged with widespread automobile ownership, we are now witnessing a variety of attempts on the part of planners to 're-spatialize' the city—that is, to reduce the necessity for massive transportation investment merely by placing things closer together geographically and achieving overall higher urban densities. The aim is to produce an urban form with characteristics of the pre-World War II city. This will mean moving away from large-scale land-use segregation, for example from extensive tracts devoted solely to residential use, to a more balanced and integrated land-use pattern. One step in this direction is the City of Toronto's proposal to allow medium-density housing (of four or five storeys) over shops located along its major arteries. By bringing homes, schools, work, and shopping facilities closer together, overall transportation costs are reduced. This is especially important where place of work and place of residence are concerned, since urban transportation routes are designed to handle peak load, rush-hour traffic volumes.

The main points of discussion in this chapter are divided into three sections: the first deals with empirical aspects of transportation patterns in Canadian cities; the second examines transportation planning methods; and the third briefly outlines the evolution of urban transportation policy.

URBAN TRANSPORTATION PATTERNS

The relation between transportation and land use is bidirectional: transportation affects land use through variations in accessibility potentials which translate into land values differences, and land use patterns influence the demand for transportation infrastructures and services. We will now consider the impact of land use on transportation. This will be achieved by describing the types and levels of transportation demand generated by different forms of land use. A discussion of transportation planning processes will also shed light on how transportation infrastructures and services are made to cater to various demand levels, and on how these levels are partly a function of different types of land use. We will see that transportation planning involves also the consideration of many other factors that influence demand. These factors include variations in trips made per household, modes chosen, distribution of journeys throughout the day, and so on. We will also touch on land use interventions meant to shape transportation demand.

Other chapters have discussed the spatial structure of Canadian urban areas. They have shown that different spatial arrangements of homes, jobs, and other activities have evolved in response to different physical environments, different economic bases, and different social conditions. Differences in spatial structure lead to differences in travel demands, which in turn produce different opportunities for satisfying these travel demands. For example, the Toronto and Ottawa urban regions have relatively strong concentrations of jobs in their central areas that provide opportunities for public transportation to capture a significant share of the commuting market. In contrast, the suburbs of these urban areas contain dispersed job opportunities, producing diffuse patterns of travel demands that are difficult and very expensive to service by public transportation.

The essential goal of urban transportation planning is twofold: (1) to forecast the travel demands that are likely to be created by expected development patterns; and (2) to provide transportation facilities and services that are able to handle these transportation demands at appropriate levels of service to trip makers while creating acceptable environmental

Figure 11.1
Start Time Distribution for Total Person Trips Greater Toronto Area, 1986

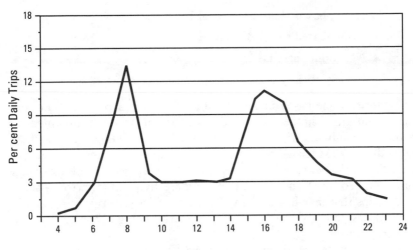

Trip Start Times in One Hour Intervals

SOURCE: Ministry of Transportation Ontario, 1988.

impacts. Transportation planning is not simply a reactive process of providing transportation facilities in order to serve demands. It also attempts to shape travel demands through land-use planning intervention (see also Chapters 10 and 19), traffic restraint, pricing, and other management policies.

Urban transportation problems are often perceived in terms of traffic congestion, where this congestion results largely from the peaking of travel demands during rush hours. Figure 11.1 shows the percentage of daily trips within the Greater Toronto Area (municipalities of Hamilton-Wentworth, Halton, Peel, Metropolitan Toronto, York, and Durham) that begin in each one-hour period. The diagram shows that the peak trip departure time occurs between 07:00 and 08:00. The afternoon peak trip departure time is spread over the hours between 15:00 and 17:00. It should be recognized that this graph illustrates only the trip departure times and does not show the duration of peak traffic flows on the transportation network, which is a much longer period. It should also be recognized that if the level of urban travel demands could be reduced at peak demand periods, significant improvements in the level of traffic and transit service would occur.

The urban travel market may be subdivided into a number of market segments, or travel by trip purposes. The following percentages of travel by trip purpose were observed in the Greater Toronto Area in 1986:

Home-based work	38.4%
Home-based school	10.8%
Home-based shop & personal business	18.8%
Home-based social & recreational	16.1%
Non-home-based	15.9%

(SOURCE: Ministry of Transportation Ontario, 1988)

The term home-based means that one end of a trip is at home. For example, morning home-to-work trips and afternoon work-to-home trips are both home-based trips. Non-home-based trips are those trips without one end being associated with a home. Examples are trips between two places of work, between work and shop, between work and a day-care centre, and so on. Non-home-based trips are frequently part of a set of linked trips that may begin or end with a home-based trip. For example, home to day-care, day-care to work; or, work to shop, shop to day-care, day-care to home.

Trips with different trip purposes have different departure time profiles; Figure 11.2 shows the departure profiles for home-based work and home-based shop and personal business trips. The diagram illustrates very clearly that work trips are the principal component of the morning peak demand. On the other hand, data on departure profiles would show that work trips and non-home-based trips are the principal contributors to the afternoon peak demand. Many of the non-home-based trips that occur in the morning and afternoon peak periods are also work-associated since they are part of a sequence of linked trips with one end of the trip sequence at work.

An important input to planning is the spatial structure of travel. In the case of the Toronto region, for example, commuting is dominated by travel to the Toronto CBD and the areas of job concentrations in Mississauga, Scarborough, and along the Yonge Street transit corridor.

Future travel in an urban area will not simply be an expansion of the existing travel structure since housing and job opportunities in the subregions of an urban area grow at different rates. Data relating to changes in work-to-home travel between 1971 and 1981 observed in the Toronto region show that the increases in travel demands were concentrated in Peel Region and in north-eastern Metropolitan Toronto. These are the subregions that grew rapidly as both residential and employment areas during the 1971–81 period.

Many Canadian urban areas have attempted to improve the quality of urban transportation by improving the efficiency of public transportation, and through this, attract trip makers away from private cars. Travel-to-work surveys conducted by Statistics Canada (1982a) revealed the proportions of commuting by transit for the eight largest metropolitan areas in Canada. The results of these surveys are illustrated in Figure 11.3. The

Figure 11.2
Trip Departure Profiles for Home-Based Work and Home-Based Shop and Personal Business Trips, Greater Toronto Area, 1986

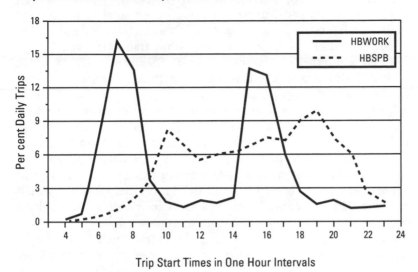

Trip Start Times in One Hour Intervals

HBWORK : home-based work
HBSPB : home-based shop and personal business

SOURCE: Ministry of Transportation Ontario, 1988.

Figure 11.3
Percentage of Commuters in Major Metropolitan Areas Using Public Transport

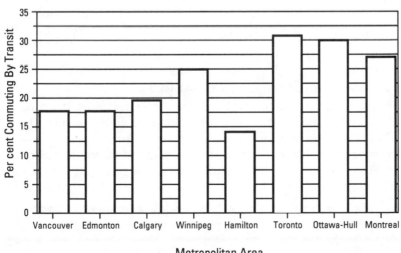

Metropolitan Area

SOURCE: Statistics Canada, 1982a.

diagram shows that the proportion of commuters using public transportation varies substantially across the major cities of Canada from a high of 31 per cent in the Toronto census metropolitan area (Metropolitan Toronto, Peel, York, and Durham) to a low of less than 15 per cent in Hamilton. An interesting case is that of the Ottawa-Hull CMA, which has about 30 per cent of its commuters using public transportation.

There are a number of reasons for these differences, most of which are related to differences in urban spatial structure. Toronto, Montreal, Ottawa-Hull, and Winnipeg have the strongest concentrations of jobs in their central areas. This type of geographic arrangement means that efficient public transportation services may be provided to the central areas of these cities, which helps to attract trip makers away from their cars. Hamilton, Calgary, Edmonton, and Vancouver have smaller proportions of their jobs in their central areas, which means that a smaller fraction of the commuter market may be served by the centrally-focused transit services. Similarly, there are strong variations in transit use throughout different areas of a metropolitan region. For example, in the Toronto area in 1986 approximately 26 per cent of trips in Metropolitan Toronto were made by public transit. This contrasts with a low of approximately 8 per cent in the Haldimand Region, which is located sixty kilometres south west of Metropolitan Toronto. (On the relationship between public transportation ridership and land-use patterns, see Pushkarev and Zupan 1977; and Thomson 1978.)

Increasing travel demands in Canadian urban areas are due to increases in the number of residents and in the average rate at which Canadian urban residents make trips. The following average trip rates were observed in the Greater Toronto Area in two surveys conducted twenty-two years apart:

	1964	1986	% increase
Average trips per day per person	1.3	2.1	38.1
Average trips per day per household	4.9	5.4	10.2

(SOURCE: Ministry of Transportation Ontario, 1988)

The average number of trips per day per person increased by 38 per cent, and the average number of trips per household increased by only 10 per cent. The smaller increase in trips per household reflects the rapid growth in the numbers of smaller households (one- and two-person households) in the Toronto area. The differential rates of growth of population and households are summarized below:

	1964	1986	% increase
Population	2,464,700	4,156,600	68.6
Households	652,400	1,470,300	125.4

(SOURCE: Statistics Canada, 1982b; 1987)

The growth in per capita travel is due to a number of factors. These include the rapid growth in female labour force participation, the increasing percentage of adults in the total population, and the sharp increase in car ownership per household, which stimulates larger numbers of non-work trips. The implications of these higher trip rates for travel demand in the Toronto region are summarized below :

	1.3 trips per capita	2.1 trips per capita
Total daily trips in 1964	3,204,000	
Total daily trips in 1986	5,400,000	8,730,000

(SOURCE: Ministry of Transportation Ontario, 1988)

These figures show that the total number of trips would have increased by about 2,200,000 if the trip-making rate of 1964 had remained unchanged. Instead there was the approximately 5,500,000 increase observed in the 1986 survey.

Another changing characteristic of urban travel that has contributed to greater peak-period congestion is increasing average trip length, particularly for commuting trips. For example, the increase in average trip length in the Toronto CMA was from 9.7 km in 1971 to 12 km in 1981. These increases reflect the fact that much of the commuting growth between 1971 and 1981 was from commuters drawn from the outer suburbs to jobs in the Toronto central area and other parts of Metropolitan Toronto.

This growth has had large impacts on the total amount of travel that has had to be handled by the regional road and transit systems. For example, given a total employment of about 1,900,000 in the Toronto CMA this increase in trip length means that the total daily work-trip travel load would increase from 18,400,000 kms per day to about 22,800,000 kms. This trend towards more and longer journeys has affected other Canadian metropolitan areas. In most cases, however, the impact was less dramatic than in the Toronto CMA because it was not accompanied by such a rapid rate of population increase.

TRANSPORTATION PLANNING

Our attention now shifts to the actual process of transportation planning as it has been practised in the latter decades of the twentieth century. This emphasis on the planning process *per se* is warranted on a number of counts. Two of the most important are: (1) the inextricable link between land use and transportation, which provides a basis for urban transportation planning; and (2) the extreme severity of transportation problems in most large Canadian cities and, concomitantly, the extreme importance of developing appropriate techniques for the solving of such problems.

Transportation planning occurs with respect to different time scales. Shaping travel demands through *interventions in the land development process* may only be achieved over 10- to 15-year time horizons, while traffic restraint and pricing schemes may be implemented over 2- to 3-year time horizons. *Urban strategic planning studies* have planning horizons of 20–30 years, and are concerned with the broad patterns of development and the demands placed on various infrastructure systems such as transportation, water supply, and sewage disposal. Strategic studies are usually conducted in association with the development of official municipal plans, and are frequently updated at about ten-year intervals. Transportation analyses at this level of planning are normally conducted with respect to a very broad transportation network, where the main concerns are traffic flows in major travel corridors and across critical screenlines delineating major sectors within metropolitan regions such as, for example, the central business district.

In contrast, *transportation systems studies* usually have time horizons of 10 to 20 years, and are directed towards a more detailed planning of the transportation network. Their purpose is to establish transportation system characteristics to the point where they may be used as a basis for functional planning and design. Transportation systems proposals are subjected to more detailed transportation systems analyses than proposals at the strategic planning level. Transportation flows are estimated in sufficient detail to allow the capacities required in major road and transit corridors to be calculated. Out of this work come *transportation systems management* studies, which have time horizons of 5 to 10 years and are concerned mainly with optimizing the use of existing transportation facilities. They are concerned with traffic engineering measures such as reserved lanes for high-occupancy vehicles and traffic signal co-ordination, traffic restraint schemes, the pricing of transit and parking facilities, and so on. Finally there is *development proposal analysis*. The analysis of development proposals is the most frequent type of transportation study. Developers seeking project approval from municipal governments must show that existing road facilities (and other infrastructure as well) will not be overloaded by the traffic generated by a particular development. If systems are expected to be overloaded, developers may have to transfer land to a municipality for road expansion, or pay for new road facilities.

A key component in any of the above types of transportation planning is the development of a thorough knowledge of existing and future travel demands in urban areas. In some studies a knowledge of travel in the entire urban area may be required, while in other studies the concern may be with only one part of an urban area.

As has been stressed, the amount and direction of urban journeys is influenced by the spatial organization of development in terms of residential, employment, and shopping/recreational areas and the densities of this development. Urban travel demands are normally calculated by a four-

Figure 11.4
Urban Travel Demand Estimation Process

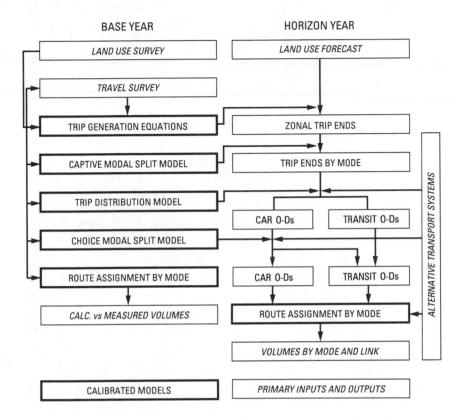

BASE YEAR   HORIZON YEAR

LAND USE SURVEY — *LAND USE FORECAST*

TRAVEL SURVEY

TRIP GENERATION EQUATIONS — ZONAL TRIP ENDS

CAPTIVE MODAL SPLIT MODEL — TRIP ENDS BY MODE

TRIP DISTRIBUTION MODEL — CAR O-Ds — TRANSIT O-Ds

CHOICE MODAL SPLIT MODEL — CAR O-Ds — TRANSIT O-Ds

ROUTE ASSIGNMENT BY MODE

CALC. vs MEASURED VOLUMES — ROUTE ASSIGNMENT BY MODE — *ALTERNATIVE TRANSPORT SYSTEMS*

VOLUMES BY MODE AND LINK

CALIBRATED MODELS   *PRIMARY INPUTS AND OUTPUTS*

stage procedure which involves trip generation, trip distribution, modal split, and traffic assignment. The four-stage analysis process is applied by dividing urban areas into a number of traffic analysis zones. In strategic planning studies of a large urban area some fifty to sixty traffic analysis zones may be used, while in the more detailed transportation systems and transportation systems management studies as many as 600 to 700 traffic analysis zones might be used.

The Travel Demand Estimation Process
The sequence of activities involved in urban travel demand estimation is illustrated in Figure 11.4. The basic aim of this process is to estimate the number of trips on each link of the road network and public transportation network of an urban area given a knowledge of the expected future land-development patterns and the future transportation system characteristics. The impacts of different transportation networks on traffic flow may be analysed, as well as the effects of different land-use patterns. Figure 11.4

illustrates that a number of component models are used to analyse land use and transportation system alternatives. These models are first calibrated to some base year condition; the calibrated models are then used to estimate the travel demands for a horizon year. Four component models are identified in Figure 11.4. These are:

1. Trip Generation Equations.

2. Modal Split Model (Captive and Choice).

3. Trip Distribution Model.

4. Route Assignment by Mode Model.

This sequence of models attempts to estimate, respectively, the number of trips by urban residents from and to each traffic analysis zone, the origin-to-destination patterns of these trips, the mode of travel used for these trips, and the road and transit network paths used by trip makers. The characteristics of each of these four phases of travel demand estimation are discussed in subsequent subsections.

1. TRIP GENERATION EQUATIONS The purpose of the trip generation analysis phase is to develop equations that allow the trip destinations for a particular trip purpose to be estimated from a knowledge of land-use properties. The broad proportions of trips performed for various trip purposes in urban areas have been identified in earlier discussion. It has been pointed out that the bulk of the trips are performed for purposes of work, with educational and shopping trips being the next most important trip purposes. It is important to introduce a few definitions at this time that relate to trip generation analysis:

Trip production This term is used to denote trips generated by households where these trips might be from households or to households. Examples of trip productions are home-based trips to work, home-based trips to shop, and so on.

Trip attraction This term is used to describe trips generated by the non-home end of home-based trips. In other words, it refers to the trips that are made to reach destinations such as employment, shops, and so on.

Trip purpose This refers to the principal activity engaged in at the end of a trip such as work, shopping, and so on. Urban travel market segments are defined according to trip purpose, for example, as work trips, educational trips, shopping trips, social-recreational trips, and so on. It has been pointed out that where several destinations are visited, say, between work and home, the trips are classified as linked trips.

Trip generation equations are developed that relate the rate at which trips of different purposes are created by various types of human activities. For example, a typical trip production equation for work trips is:

[1] Daily Work Trips Produced = 0.33 × Population of Zone

Clearly this coefficient of population 0.33 simply reflects the proportion of the population working, workers on vacation, and people not at work for various reasons. Similar equations may be developed for shopping trips, for example:

[2] Daily Shopping Trips Produced = 0.12 × Population of Zone

Trip attraction equations for various trip purposes relate to the activities at the destination end of the trip. A typical work-trip attraction equation is:

[3] Daily Work Trips Attracted = 0.84 × Employment of Zone

Trip generation equations are frequently developed using regression equation techniques to estimate the parameter magnitudes of equations of the following general form:

$$[4] \quad TG_i = a + b_1 {\cdot} X_{i1} + b_2 {\cdot} X_{i2} + ... + b_N {\cdot} X_{iN}$$

where TG_i = the number of trips generated by a zone i. The components $X_{i1}, ..., X_{iN}$ = the magnitudes of variables which describe the amount of human activity of various types in a zone; $b_1, ..., b_N$ = the partial regression coefficients estimated by regression analysis which reflect the rate at which each of the independent variables contribute to trip generation; a = a constant term estimated by regression analysis.

An example of a multiple regression equation for estimating work trip productions which attempts to capture in more detail the residential structure of zones is:

[5] WTP = 95 + 1.655 (No. Detached Dwelling Units) + 1.117 (Apartments)
+ 1.441 (No. Other Dwelling Units Types)

where WTP_i = the daily number of work trips produced by a zone i.

This equation recognizes that work trips are generated at different rates by different dwelling-unit types. This is because the different dwelling-unit types tend to accommodate households of different sizes. Single-family dwelling units tend to be occupied by the larger households and apartments by the smaller.

2. CAPTIVE MODAL SPLIT ANALYSIS Figures 11.5 and 11.6 demonstrate that modal split analysis is conducted in two phases; one before and one after the trip distribution phase. Modal split analyses are conducted to estimate the split of trip makers between the public transportation system and the road system. Studies of travel in urban areas have demonstrated quite clearly that there are essentially two separate submarkets for public

Figure 11.5
Sequence of Activities Involved in Horizon Year Travel Demand Estimation

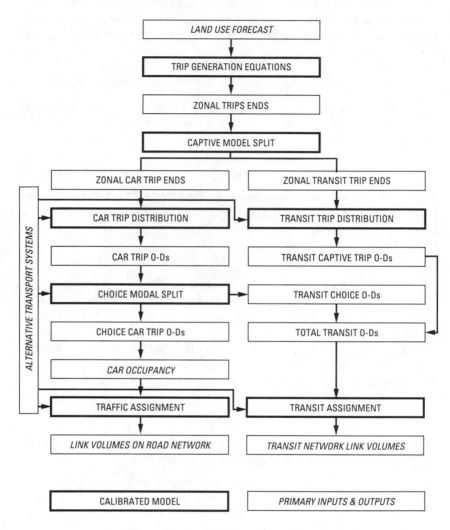

transportation services which might be labelled as captive riders and choice riders. Captive trip makers may be defined as those persons without access to a car for a particular trip. Choice riders are those people who have a car available but who use public transportation for a variety of reasons. In most small Canadian urban areas there are very few choice transit riders as there are few constraints (parking fees, congestion) on the use of private cars and the levels of transit are generally poor.

The purpose of the captive modal split analysis phase is to develop relationships that allow the production and attraction trip ends estimated

Figure 11.6
Simple Gravity Model Calculations

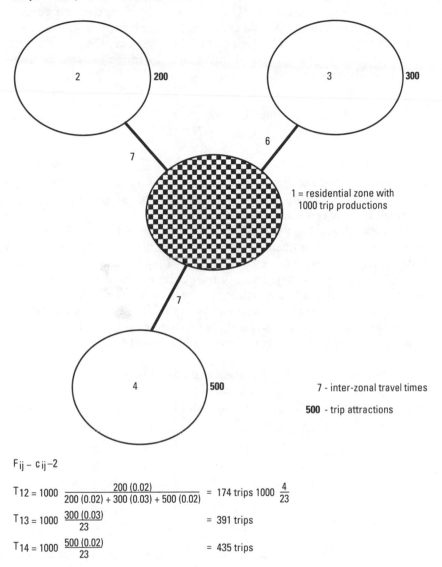

$F_{ij} - c_{ij} {-2}$

$$T_{12} = 1000 \ \frac{200\ (0.02)}{200\ (0.02) + 300\ (0.03) + 500\ (0.02)} = 174 \text{ trips } 1000 \ \frac{4}{23}$$

$$T_{13} = 1000 \ \frac{300\ (0.03)}{23} \qquad\qquad\qquad = 391 \text{ trips}$$

$$T_{14} = 1000 \ \frac{500\ (0.02)}{23} \qquad\qquad\qquad = 435 \text{ trips}$$

in the trip generation phase to be partitioned into two groups of trip ends known as transit captive riders and choice riders. Captive trip makers are usually identified through car ownership, which in turn is defined by socio-economic variables such as age and income. The role of the captive modal split relationships in horizon year travel demand estimation is illustrated in Figure 11.5 where zonal trip productions and trip attractions are split into two sets of trip ends.

3. TRIP DISTRIBUTION ANALYSIS The purpose of the trip distribution analysis phase is to calculate the trip linkages, or trip interchanges, between each pair of origin-destination (O-D) zones for both captive and choice riders. The technique used most commonly to synthesize these trip linkages is the gravity model. This type of model is widely used by geographers to describe many types of spatial interaction. In traffic forecasting it is often formulated as:

$$[6] \quad T_{ij} = O_i \frac{D_j F_{ij}}{\sum\limits_{j=1}^{N} D_j F_{ij}}$$

where T_{ij} = the number of trips between origins in zone i and destinations in zone j; O_i = the number of trips produced in zone i; D_j = the number of trips attracted to zone j; F_{ij} = some function of the generalized costs of travelling between zones i and j.

The term 'generalized costs' requires some explanation. A variety of factors are known to influence location and trip decisions. These include travel time, trip costs such as fares and out-of-pocket operating costs for cars, and the general convenience of travel. Each of these components of generalized cost is combined to produce one measure: the generalized cost of travel between two points. Travel time is the largest component of the generalized cost, and time is usually valued as some function of the average wage rate. The generalized cost concept is discussed in more detail later in this chapter.

The function F_{ij} in the above equation is usually referred to as the deterrence function, or the space friction factor, and it represents a trip maker's perception of the generalized costs of travel. Typical forms of this function which have been used are:

$$[7] \quad F_{ij} = c_{ij}^{-n}$$

$$[8] \quad F_{ij} = e^{-bc_{ij}}$$

$$[9] \quad F_{ij} = (c_{ij})^a e^{-bcij}$$

In the earlier versions of the gravity model, the F_{ij} function used was usually of the form specified in equation [7] with the exponent $n = 2$ and c_{ij} = the distance between two areas. It is this form of the spatial interaction model that gave rise to the name gravity model because of its resemblance to Newton's law of gravity. In most contemporary studies, the functions specified in equations [8] and [9] have been used and the parameters are estimated from survey data. The optimal parameter magnitudes are estimated by comparing the trip length characteristics calculated by the model with those observed in a survey, with the optimal magnitude being obtained when the model estimates and observed trip length frequency distributions are as close as possible.

A simple example of gravity model calculations is provided in Figure 11.6. It should be noted that the calculated trip interchange magnitudes in this example for the single zone of origin are less than the trip attraction magnitudes for zones 2 and 4 and greater than the trip attraction magnitudes for zone 3. Procedures for achieving balanced trip interchange magnitudes that are consistent with the production and attraction trip ends are used, but are beyond the scope of this chapter and are described, for example, in Black (1981).

4. CHOICE RIDER MODAL SPLIT ANALYSIS Figure 11.5 illustrates that a choice rider modal split analysis is conducted to split the choice trip interchange magnitudes into trips by public transportation and trips by car. Choice modal split models attempt to emulate the way in which choice trip makers travelling between an origin-destination pair will choose between the use of a car and public transportation for the trip.

Transportation studies have shown that choice trip makers consider a number of characteristics of both the trip by car and the trip by transit in making modal transportation choice decisions. These include: (1) the in-vehicle travel time; (2) the travel time spent outside of the line-haul vehicle, usually called 'excess travel time', which consists of walking and waiting times; (3) the out-of-pocket costs including the vehicle operating costs, parking charges, and transit fares; and (4) the reliability, comfort, and convenience of the transit modes. That is, modal choice decisions are influenced by the generalized costs of using the different modes. Generalized transportation costs are calculated for the trip by each of the modes of transportation and the difference in generalized cost is calculated and used to estimate modal split. A typical generalized cost function is:

$$[10] \quad Z^*_{ij} = a + u_m(b_{ij} - a_{ij}) + u_e(eb_{ij} - ea_{ij}) + u_i(tb_{ij} - ta_{ij})$$

where Z^*_{ij} = transit generalized cost minus car generalized cost (\$); a = a constant term whose significance is described below; u_m = the utility of the monetary costs of travel; b_{ij} = transit fare (\$); a_{ij} = out-of-pocket car costs including parking charges; u_e = the utility of excess, or out-of-vehicle travel time; eb_{ij}, ea_{ij} = the excess travel times by transit and car, respectively; u_i = the utility of in-vehicle travel time; and tb_{ij}, ta_{ij} = travel times by transit and car (minutes), respectively. A typical generalized cost function developed for modal choice decisions made by commuters to the CBD of Toronto is as follows:

$$[11] \quad Z^* = 0.0402 - 0.6933(b_{ij} - a_{ij}) + 0.0764(eb_{ij} - ea_{ij}) + 0.0328(tb_{ij} - ta_{ij})$$

The first point to be noted about the utility function is that positive values of Z^* represent a disadvantage to public transportation since the output is really the generalized cost difference of car minus transit. Negative values of Z^* represent an advantage to public transportation since car generalized costs are higher than transit generalized costs.

If equation [11] is applied to a zone for which transit has a $1.50 cost advantage (e.g., because of CBD parking charges), a 15-minute larger excess travel time than car travel, and a 15-minute larger travel time than car travel, then the estimated transit share may be calculated in the following way:

[12] $\quad Z^* = 0.0402 - 0.6933(1.50) - 0.0764(-15) - 0.0328(-15) = 0.6383$

and the magnitude of Z^* substituted into equation [11]:

$$[12a] \quad p(a) = \frac{1}{1 + e^{0.6383}} = 0.35$$

which means that the estimated transit share of travel between this residential zone and a CBD zone is 0.35. It should be noted that the coefficient of the excess travel time difference is about 2.3 times the coefficient of the in-vehicle travel time difference, showing that trip makers are more sensitive to the time involved in waiting, walking, and transferring. The coefficients of equation [12] may be used to estimate the value of travel time that commuters use in making modal transportation choice decisions:

$$[12b] \quad \frac{\text{utility of excess travel time (u/min)}}{\text{utility of money (u/\$)}} = \frac{0.0764}{0.6933} = \$0.11/\text{min} = \$6.60/\text{hour}$$

and the value of in-vehicle time would be:

$$[12c] \quad \frac{0.0328}{0.6933} = \$0.047/\text{min} = \$2.84/\text{hour}$$

If all the differences are set to 0, then $Z^* = 0.0402$ and $p(a) = 0.49$ which represents the prior or average probability of using public transportation. The transit share probabilities for individual zones will shift from this average depending on the relative costs and times of using the different modes.

5. ROUTE ASSIGNMENT ANALYSIS The purpose of route assignment analysis is to emulate the way in which the car and public transportation trips between each origin-destination pair distribute over the links of their respective transportation networks. In most urban areas the assignment to public transportation networks may be done by hand since the networks are not particularly complicated. However, the assignment of car trips to the road network requires a more formal procedure even in the smaller

urban areas. Traffic assignment procedures normally consist of three main components. These are:

1. a driver-route selection criterion;
2. a tree-building technique that identifies optimal vehicle routes through a network of streets, by sketching the shortest and fastest link between an origin and a destination; and
3. a method of allocating vehicle trip interchange magnitudes to the selected vehicle routes.

The travel time on alternative routes is usually used as the criterion of driver route choice. While this is an over-simplification since drivers also take into account the quality of the flow, it seems to explain the majority of route choice decisions.

Wardrop (1952) proposed a criterion of path choice: the trip times on all routes between an origin-destination pair that are actually used are equal to or less than those which would be experienced by a single vehicle diverted to any unused route. With the elementary traffic assignment methods, all vehicles are assumed to use the minimum travel time path between each origin-destination pair. This leads to the mapping of a minimum path tree by using the tree-building technique. A minimum path tree is simply the set of minimum paths between a particular zone of origin and all possible destination zones.

The third component of traffic assignment is a rationale for assigning trip interchange magnitudes between origin-destination pairs to the path or paths between each zone pair. With the so-called all-or-nothing assignment method the trip interchange magnitudes are assigned to the minimum time paths.

Clearly, as the traffic volumes are assigned to links within a network, the travel times will change and new paths through the network might represent the minimum paths. Sheffi (1985) discusses more advanced techniques that use capacity-restrained traffic assignment which recognize that link travel times change as the traffic volumes assigned to links change, thus accounting for the effect of congestion.

EVOLUTION OF URBAN TRANSPORTATION POLICY

Metropolitan transportation systems analysis has its origins in several large-scale urban transportation planning studies conducted during the late 1950s and early 1960s in a number of North American cities such as Detroit, Chicago, and Toronto. As has been pointed out in many other chapters in this volume, it was during these decades that urban areas were growing rapidly and car ownership was increasing. The aim of these earlier studies was to identify medium- and long-run capital investments in new transportation capacity. The planning and analysis processes developed in these original studies have been used in hundreds of urban areas over the

Table 11.1
Some Urban Transport Policy Instruments

Urban Strategic Planning

    Urban structure planning
    Phasing the development of residential and employment areas
    Zoning policies to increase residential and employment densities along transit corridors

Transport Systems Studies

    Investments in new public transport and road capacities
    Integration and co-ordination of regional transport services
    Major public transport and road pricing schemes
    Provision of special purpose transit systems for the handicapped and aged

Transport Systems Management Studies

    Flexitime and other work scheduling practices
    Optimization of traffic signal systems
    Pricing of travel services in specific areas
    Provision of high-occupancy-vehicle lanes
    Integration of public transport and private road transport through park-and-ride, etc.

Development Proposal Analysis

    Zoning by-laws
    Local area planning and transport management

past thirty years. These studies usually recommended heavy investments in freeway systems, particularly the studies conducted during the 1960s and early 1970s.

The mixed blessings of capital investments in freeways were recognized in the late 1960s and early 1970s as the large increases in freeway capacity tended to exacerbate the problems of traffic congestion and environmental degradation. The increased mobility of car owners provided by freeway systems stimulated the development of low-density urban areas with unstructured travel demands, resulting in substantial reductions in the per capita use of public transportation. Many transit properties were unable to provide adequate levels of service to newly developing residential and employment areas, thus compromising severely the mobility of those without access to a car.

During the 1970s and 1980s, urban transportation planners recognized that a much broader spectrum of policy instruments were available to address the many dimensions of urban transportation problems. Table 11.1 summarizes some of these instruments, classified according to the planning time horizons described earlier in this chapter.

SUMMARY AND CONCLUSION

This chapter has described the importance of transportation in shaping urban areas. It has shown the close association between modes of transportation and different forms of cities. With this in mind, the chapter has devoted most of its attention to recent transportation demand patterns and more particularly to transportation planning.

Four broad types of planning study have been introduced at the beginning of the chapter, and the four-stage-analysis procedure introduced above is adapted to the special needs of each of these planning study types. For example, at the strategic level the main concern is with the broad patterns of travel created by different arrangements of land use and the analysis emphasis is normally on trip generation and trip distribution with less emphasis being placed on modal split analysis and traffic assignment. Planners are usually interested in probable peak period flows along major travel corridors and the potential transportation facilities needs in these corridors. Information of this type provides an objective context for the more detailed transportation systems studies.

At the transportation systems analysis level the emphasis is usually on all four stages. The transportation engineer's concern is normally with reasonably detailed flows along major transit corridors and with traffic flows on freeways and arterials. This more detailed level of analysis allows the performance of alternative transportation supply options to be analysed in more depth.

At the transportation systems management level, the principal analytical concern is with very detailed traffic flows on links, with intersection movements, and with the scheduling of public transportation services. Their shorter time horizons allow the transportation planner to use existing trip-generation and trip-distribution patterns for these more detailed analyses.

The main focus in evaluating development proposals is usually on trip generation, say, by a proposed residential development, and the probable impacts of these trips on the adjacent street system. A major criterion is to establish if new developments are likely to generate travel demands that may exceed available transportation capacity.

It is worth ending by recalling the vast array of demand generating factors on which transportation planning relies for the forecasting of future flows: journey rates per household, distance travelled, types of trips, modal choice, and so on. Among these factors, anticipated land-use patterns play an important role in that they allow forecasts of population levels, as well as the nature and the distribution of activities within an area. Interestingly, transportation planning also has an impact on land use: within parameters set by planning regulations, urban development will tend to adapt to accessibility potentials provided by transportation systems.

FURTHER READING

ALTSHULER, A., WOMAK, J.P., and PUCHER, J.R. 1979 *The Urban Transportation System; Politics and Policy Innovation* (Cambridge, Mass: The M.I.T. Press)

BRUTON, M.J. 1985 *Introduction to Transportation Planning* (London: Hutchinson)

CERVERO, R. 1986 'Urban Transit in Canada; Integration and Innovation at Its Best', *Transportation Quarterly* 40, 293-316

COPPACK, P. and ROBINS, D. 1987 'Commuting Patterns in the Toronto Area: 1971-1981', *Ontario Geography* 29, 63-78

HANSON, S. ed. 1986 *The Geography of Urban Transportation* (New York: Guilford Press)

HUTCHINSON, B.G. 1974 *Principles of Urban Transportation Planning* (New York: McGraw-Hill)

—— 1986 'Structural Changes in Commuting in the Toronto Region 1971-1981', *Transportation Reviews* 6 (4), 311-29

MICHAELS, R.M. 1980 *Transportation Planning and Policy Decision Making; Behavioral Science Contribution* (New York: Praeger)

OWEN, W. 1972 *The Accessible City* (Washington, D.C.: Brookings Institution)

SHAEFFER, K.H. 1980 *Access for All: Transportation and Urban Growth* (New York: Columbia University Press)

STARKIE, D.N.M. 1976 *Transportation Planning, Policy and Analysis* (Oxford: Pergamon Press)

STOPHER, J.D. and MEYBURG, A.H. 1975 *Urban Transportation Modeling and Planning* (Lexington, Mass.: Lexington Books)

REFERENCES

BLACK, J. 1981 *Urban Transportation Planning* (London: Croom Helm)

BOAL, F.W and JOHNSON, D.B. 1965 'The Functions of Retail and Service Establishments on Commercial Ribbons', *The Canadian Geographer* 9, 154-69

BRYANT, C.R. et al. 1982 *The City's Countryside: Land and its Management in the Rural Urban Fringe* (London: Longman)

HARRIS, C.D. and ULLMAN, E.L. 1945 'The Nature of Cities', *Annals of the American Academy of Political and Social Science* 242, 7-17

HOYT, H. 1939 *The Structure and Growth of Residential Neighborhoods in American Cities* (Washington, D.C.: Federal Housing Administration)

MEIER, R. 1962 *A Communications Theory of Urban Growth* (Cambridge, Mass.: The M.I.T. Press)

MINISTRY OF TRANSPORTATION ONTARIO 1988 'An Overview of Travel Characteristics in the Greater Toronto Area' (Transportation Tomorrow Survey) (Downsview, Ontario: Ministry of Supply and Services)

PUSHKAREV, B.S. and ZUPAN, J.M. 1977 *Public Transportation and Land Use* (Bloomington, Ind.: Indiana University Press)

STATISTICS CANADA 1982a 'Culture Statistics: Travel to Work, 1975-1980', Cat. 87-503 (Ottawa: Minister of Supply and Services)

STATISTICS CANADA 1982b 'Occupied Private Dwellings: Types and Tenure', Cat. 92-903 (Ottawa: Minister of Supply and Services)

STATISTICS CANADA 1987 'Population and Dwelling Costs', Cat. 92-101 (Ottawa: Minister of Supply and Services)

SHEFFI, Y. 1985 *Urban Transportation Networks* (Englewood Cliffs, N.J.: Prentice-Hall)

THOMSON, J.M. 1978 *Great Cities and their Traffic* (Harmondsworth: Penguin)

WARDROP, J.G. 1952 'Some Theoretical Aspects of Road Traffic Research', *Proceedings, Institute of Civil Engineers*, London, Part II, 1.

WARNER, B. 1962 *Streetcar Suburbs: The Process of Growth in Boston* (Cambridge, Mass.: Harvard University Press)

WEBBER, M.M. 1964 'The Urban Place and the Nonplace Urban Form' in M.M. Webber et al. eds *Explorations into Urban Structure* (Philadelphia, Penn.: University of Pennsylvania Press)

YEATES, M. and GARNER, B. 1980 *The North American City* (3rd revised edition) (New York: Harper and Row)

12

Social Differentiation in Canadian Cities

TRUDI E. BUNTING

Throughout this volume Canadian cities are examined from a variety of perspectives. This chapter focuses on the social geography of our cities. As we have learnt, cities are places where specialized economic activity takes place. Among other things they have a relatively high-density built environment and distinctive infrastructure, but, above all else, cities are social settlements, places where *people* live and work. This chapter is concerned with social differentiations, which are particularly apparent in cities because cities tend to attract a diversity of social groups and because these groups are particularly visible in high-density environments. The chapter itself is divided into three major sections. First, it examines *demographic aspects of urban growth* which vary quite considerably from one urban area to another. A second section looks at *inter-urban variations* in the social composition of Canadian cities. The final portions of this chapter deal with *intra-urban variations* in economic and social structure, particularly with the spatial patterning of the distinct social areas that are found in all Canadian cities and with some of the more contemporary aspects of changing social patterns in cities, especially in suburban zones, which have not been singled out for special treatment elsewhere in this text.

DEMOGRAPHIC ASPECTS OF URBAN GROWTH

Knowledge of the basic demographic characteristics of urban populations is fundamental to understanding and managing cities. From the theoretical point of view, it is important to establish and explain interrelationships that exist between certain population characteristics, for example, growth rate and age-sex composition, industrial mix and income, size and labour force participation. From an applied or management point of view, one must have knowledge of the characteristics of the population that is to be served, and one must also be able to predict how the population is likely to change over time. It is also important to know how and why population characteristics vary from one area within a city to another. In this case, spatial variations in such demographic characteristics as number of households, growth rate, age distribution, occupation, and socio-economic status will be of interest to both the planner and the more theoretically-oriented urban researcher.

The obvious first question one wants to ask about urban social structure relates to how cities grow in population. In Chapter 5 we were introduced to the notion that cities grow as a result of two processes: natural increase (births minus deaths) and net migration (in-migration minus out-migration). Put simply, population growth at any particular time in the future (P_2) will be a function of the present population (P_1) plus natural increase and net migration. This process is depicted graphically in Figure 12.1. Rates of net migration are closely tied to growth in the local economy and also to government policy relating to foreign migration. As discussed in Chapter 5, the most common reason for household moves in Canada is to secure or improve on existing employment.[1] Natural increase is more a

Figure 12.1
A Simple Model of Population Growth

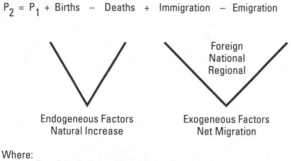

$$P_2 = P_1 + \text{Births} \ - \ \text{Deaths} \ + \ \text{Immigration} \ - \ \text{Emigration}$$

Endogenous Factors
Natural Increase

Foreign
National
Regional

Exogenous Factors
Net Migration

Where:
  P_1 = Population enumerated at time 1 (t_1)
  P_2 = Population enumerated at time 2 (t_2)

and

  births, deaths, immigration and emigration refer to the number of events occurring during the time interval $t_2 - t_1$

function of age-sex distribution within the urban population, though other factors such as cultural differences also affect rates of natural increase. Until the mid–1960s, rates of natural increase were, for example, considerably higher in Quebec cities and in francophone areas of the Maritimes than elsewhere in Canada. Since that time, values related to child rearing have changed quite dramatically in Quebec, especially so in the larger urban areas (see Mathews 1984). Montreal has one of the lowest rates of natural increase (21,226 live births in 1986 in the Montreal census division as contrasted with 30,793 in Toronto and 17,648 in Vancouver).[2] Natural increase and household formation are easier to forecast than net migration, at least in the short run where past trends are generally a good indicator of future rates of natural increase. However, it must be stressed that households born in a particular city are only marginally less likely to migrate to other cities than are households that have already migrated from some other place.

It must also be stressed that there are many complex and poorly understood factors affecting fertility rates—for example, economic growth, average age of marriage, proportion of women in the labour force and the like. With the rapidly inflating housing costs that have taken place in large, fast-growing cities over the last decade, some go so far as to argue that housing costs may have a deflating effect on household formation. Thus, for example, it is argued that grown children are less likely to leave their parental home when housing costs are high and/or vacancy rates excessively low (Miron 1988). Similarly, the elderly and other semi-dependent individuals such as the physically or mentally handicapped may be forced to live with their kin for economic reasons and not simply for health or socially-related ones. 'Homesharing' is a phenomenon that has begun to recur in the 1980s, just as it did in the less affluent pre-World War II years. On the other hand, as contrasted with the pre-World War II period there are factors that keep rates of household formation relatively high. Three are of particular importance. First, on the supply side, is the availability of small residential units, many of them in high-rise apartments, that facilitate the formation of small households simply by providing appropriate accommodation away from the original family home. Second is the trend for grown children to leave the family home at relatively early ages and set up their own households before marriage. As well, rates of marriage are down and rates of divorce are up. At the same time, people are living longer, and there are more widows and widowers among the population.

There are numerous methods of demographic forecasting. All tend to be based on past trends and on assumptions relating to factors that will affect future economic and demographic growth. This introduces a high degree of uncertainty into the forecasting exercise. As a result almost all city planners use 'high', 'medium', and 'low' estimates of growth, and monitor population change on an annual basis. Even then there is usually

Table 12.1
Real and Projected Population, Regional Municipality of Waterloo 1976–1986

	1976	1981	1986
Region			
Actual population	289,125	305,496	329,404
Projected population	297,810	351,500	412,100
Cambridge			
Actual population	72,383	77,183	79,920
Projected population	73,383	89,000	107,000
Kitchener			
Actual population	131,870	139,734	150,604
Projected population	135,000	155,000	179,500
Waterloo			
Actual population	46,623	49,428	58,718
Projected population	50,150	65,000	79,000

SOURCE: Regional Municipality of Waterloo, 1976.

a significant margin of error. Table 12.1, for example, shows the real and projected populations for the Regional Municipality of Waterloo over the period 1976 to 1986. In 1986, the error factor was 82,696, almost 25 per cent of the actual 1986 population (Regional Municipality of Waterloo 1976).

The most commonly-used population-forecasting technique is *cohort survival*, which begins with assumptions about natural increase, then uses life expectancy trends to 'age' the population over chronological periods, and then adds a net migration factor to each age cohort. It is not, however, within the scope of this chapter to provide a detailed discussion of population forecasting techniques. Useful treatment of the topic can be found in Jones (1981), McLoughlin (1969), and Woods (1975).

Figure 12.2 shows the population pyramids for Saint John, New Brunswick, a slow-growth city, and a fast-growing city, Calgary, for 1976 and 1986.[3] This figure shows how the cohorts can be 'aged' over time. In the case of Calgary, it also shows the dramatic impact of in-migration on a fast-growing city (most migrants fall in the 25 to 34 year age-range). Figure 12.3 shows net migration rates for Ontario cities with a population of 10,000 or greater over the period 1966–71, a time of rapid urbanization. The graph indicates that city size is of fundamental importance in attracting migrants. Yeates (1990, 3) gives evidence that this pattern is common across all regions of the country. He refers to Webster's (1985) work on Western Canada, Smith and Johnson (1978) on the Calgary-Edmonton corridor, Gibson (1976) on the Victoria-Vancouver urban region, and his own work (1984) on Southern Ontario. Not surprisingly, economic base is also important: Hamilton and Windsor, for example, have rates of migration that are much lower than their size would suggest because of the slow growth of their economies, which are dominated by traditional industries (respectively steel and car-making). Location is also significant.

Figure 12.2
Population Pyramids, Saint John and Calgary, 1976 and 1986

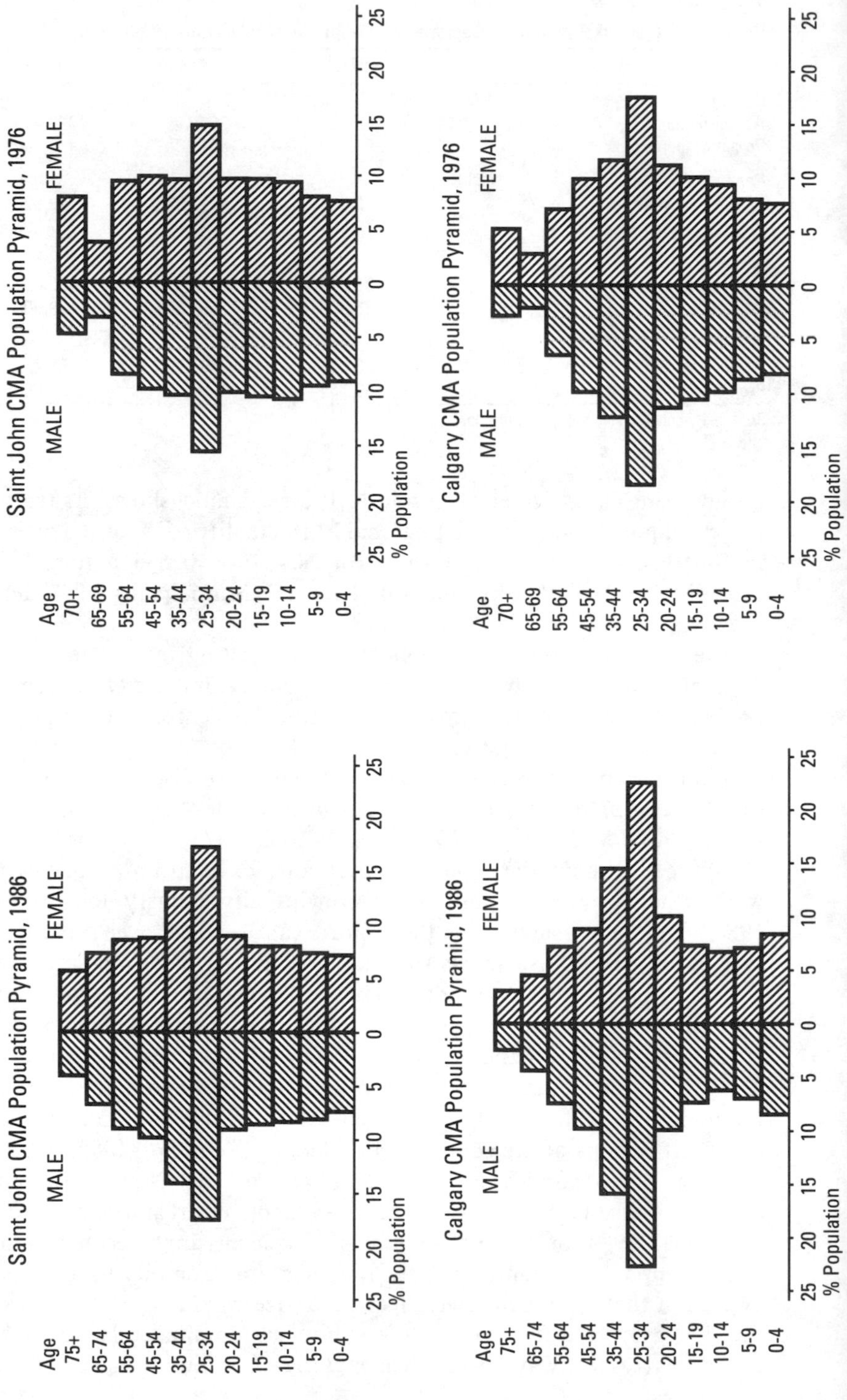

Saint John CMA Population Pyramid, 1986

Saint John CMA Population Pyramid, 1976

Calgary CMA Population Pyramid, 1986

Calgary CMA Population Pyramid, 1976

Figure 12.3
City Size and Growth, Ontario Cities over 10,000, 1966-1971

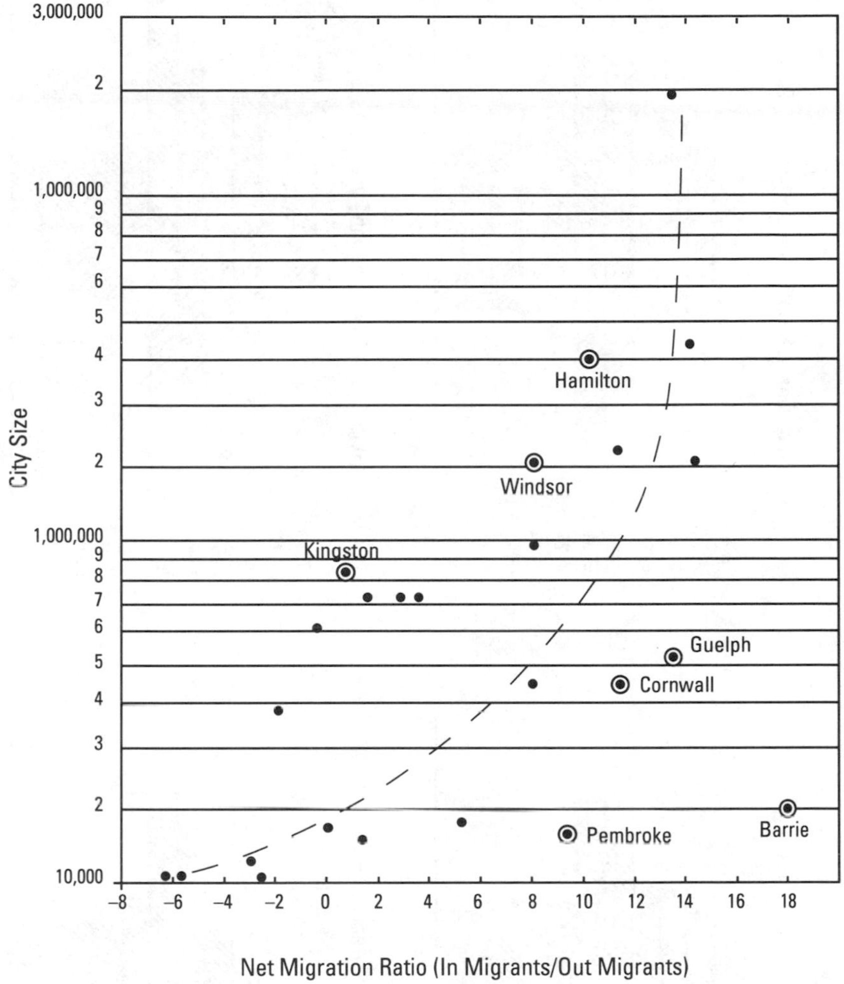

Net Migration Ratio (In Migrants/Out Migrants)

Smaller places that grow faster than expected are all within commuting distance of major metropolitan areas.

INTER-URBAN SOCIAL DIFFERENTIATION

As the subsequent section will show, differences in the social composition of CMAs across Canada are not as great as the differences found within any one metropolitan area. Nonetheless they are significant and deserve discussion here. The most obvious differences are size- and growth-related. These dimensions have been discussed at some length in most of the

Figure 12.4
Population Pyramids, Selected CMAs, 1986

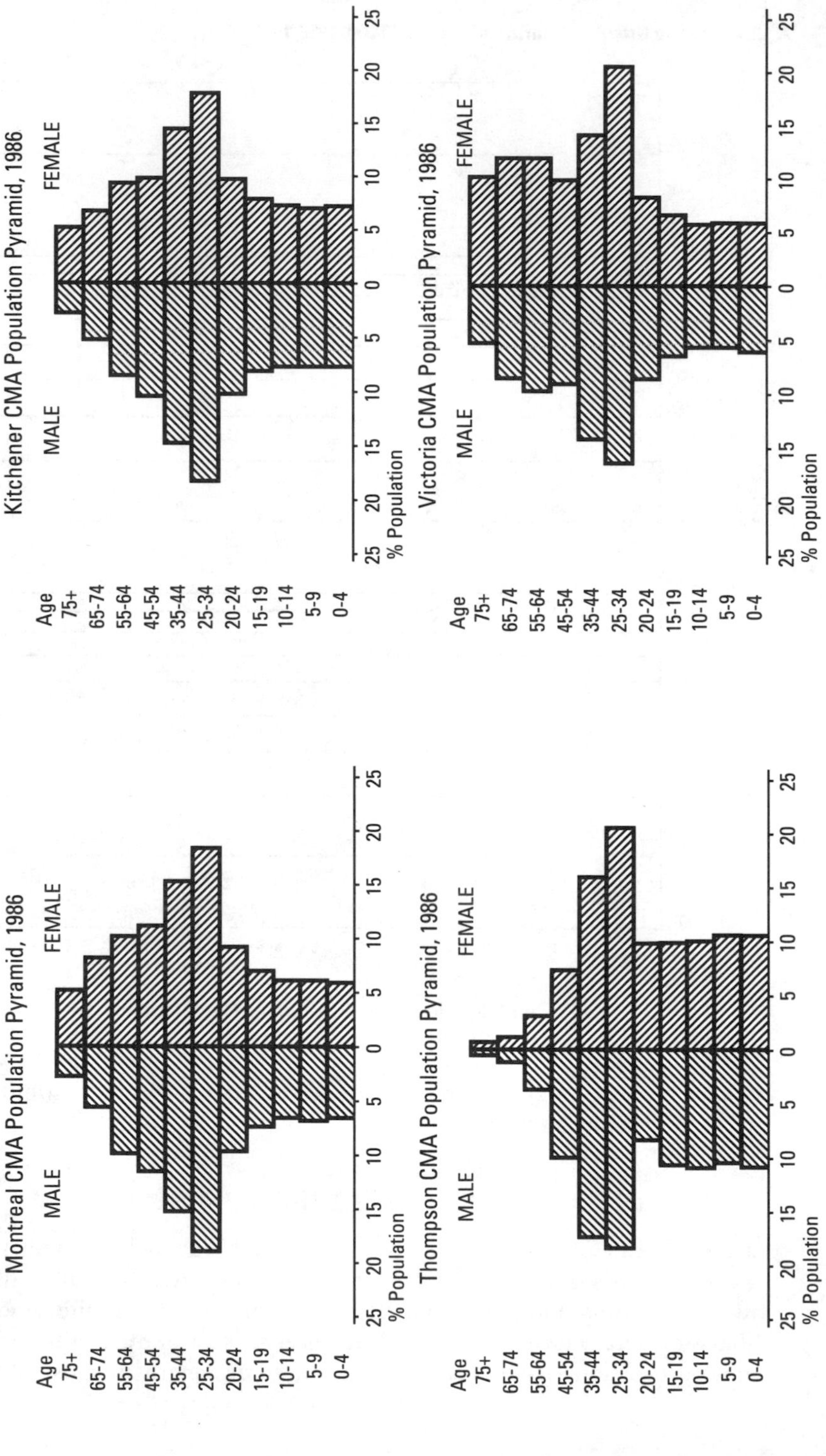

Montreal CMA Population Pyramid, 1986

Kitchener CMA Population Pyramid, 1986

Thompson CMA Population Pyramid, 1986

Victoria CMA Population Pyramid, 1986

chapters in this volume. Quite simply, social differences are greater in larger places because, among other things, there is more demand for an increased and often diversified labour force, foreign in-migrants also tend to be attracted to large cities, and large cities offer anonymity to people with alternative life-styles. There is also a tolerance of social differences that is widely rumoured not to exist in rural areas and smaller urban places. There are, of course, some extreme differences in urban social composition, especially among smaller urban places—for example, the growing number of planned and unplanned 'retirement' communities (see Kuntz 1989) as contrasted with our northern 'resource' communities, which are usually characterized by a youthful and often male-dominated population profile (Gill and Smith 1985). Even where the differences are more subtle, their implications are important. For example, the composition of a city's age/sex profile and its socio-economic mix will give rise to varying demands for public and private facilities; for instance, there is a demand for retirement homes, medical and para-medical facilities in Victoria (Canada's so-called 'retirement community') as opposed to a high demand for affordable low- to medium-density housing in Toronto's environs and, within Metropolitan Toronto itself, for megahousing.[4] Figure 12.4, which depicts the population profiles for four Canadian cities—two relatively 'typical' metropolitan areas, Montreal and Kitchener, and two rather 'atypical' places, the resource town of Thompson, Manitoba, and the city of Victoria—illustrates these differences quite dramatically.

One of the most fundamental differences between Canadian CMAs relates to their growth rate. A number of our urban indices shown in Appendix 3 relate to growth rate. The most obvious is shown in column 2, population change 1981–86. Here the high scorers are the large, fast-growing CMAs—Toronto, Vancouver, and Ottawa-Hull. Kitchener-Waterloo and Oshawa undoubtedly owe their relatively high growth-rates to their proximity to Metropolitan Toronto and, in comparison to Metropolitan Toronto, their relatively lower cost of living. The slow-growth places have declining economic bases, e.g. Windsor, Niagara-St Catharines, and Hamilton, or are generally peripheral resource towns. Wallace (1987) explains the slow growth of Canada's resource towns with reference to a number of factors: competition from new sources of supply in Third World countries; the decline in resource orientation throughout the global economy; and the weakened competitive position of the United States in heavy industrial sectors, particularly steel production. Many resource communities were also particularly hard hit by reduced demands from international markets that accompanied the world-wide recession of the early 1980s.

The percentage of immigration, column 3, Appendix 3, tends to follow overall growth rates with, not unexpectedly, Toronto and Vancouver being the leaders, followed by Calgary and Edmonton. Relatively low rates of foreign migrants choose Ottawa as a destination, indicating that the capital city grows primarily through internal migration (particularly of younger households with bilingual skills). Quebec cities are consistently low on foreign migration, suggesting that what little growth occurs in Quebec cities is a result of internal, probably primarily intra-provincial, migration flows.

When we turn to immigrant population as a percentage of the total 1986 population (column 4), Toronto and Vancouver are once again leaders as is Hamilton, which has a large southern European population, much of it 'spillover' from the growth that took place in Toronto in the 1950s and 1960s. Other cities with reasonably high rates of foreign immigration are located in Southern Ontario or British Columbia. Low rates of foreign-born within the population characterize many of the provincial capitals in the periphery and again, the resource towns. Labour-force participation rates as shown in column 7 reflect similar patterns. With the exception of Montreal, high rates are found in the fast-growing larger CMAs—Toronto, Ottawa-Hull, Edmonton, Calgary, and Kitchener-Waterloo—and lower rates in peripheral centres and resource-based towns. The two lowest rates of labour-force participation are found in resource-based cities in the province of Quebec—Trois Rivières and Chicoutimi-Jonquière. High unemployment ratios, as would be expected, also characterize cities with slow-growing economies, e.g. Saint John, Trois Rivières, Chicoutimi-Jonquière, and St John's. This pattern is shown clearly in column 8. In marked contrast, those places with relatively low unemployment are again the larger, faster-growing ones, viz. Toronto, Ottawa-Hull, London, Kitchener-Waterloo, and Oshawa.

The economic base of Canada's metropolitan areas varies widely. However, most would be classified either as manufacturing centres or regional service centres (see Chapters 5 and 7) with many of the provincial capitals in the periphery in the latter category. Appendix 3 shows high rates of manufacturing employment in Toronto and Montreal, and particularly high rates in urban areas within commuting distance of Metropolitan Toronto, for example, Hamilton, St Catharines-Niagara, Kitchener-Waterloo, and Oshawa. Windsor's manufacturing specialization is, of course, directly related to its proximity to the US automotive complex that is centred on Detroit. Again, the provincial and regional capitals and Ottawa tend to have low rates of participation in manufacturing activity and relatively high rates of participation in finance, insurance and real estate (FIRE), and government services as shown in columns 9 and 10 in Appendix 3. Toronto's relatively low rating, 9.6 per cent, on the latter category, belies the very large size and importance of its employment in this category. This in no way reflects a weakness in Toronto's financial sector. In fact, Toronto has the highest absolute number of persons employed in this sector in comparison to all other places in the country. However, its strength in other sectors—such as manufacturing—tends to mask Toronto's role as the major financial centre in the country.

Notwithstanding size and growth rates, probably the most obvious significant difference between CMAs across Canada lies in their socio-economic status. A good indicator of socio-economic status is income per capita, which is shown in Appendix 3, column 11, and ranges quite significantly from a high of $15,600 in Toronto to a low of $10,400 in Chicoutimi-Jonquière and Sudbury. This variable is most closely related, not surprisingly, to city size (Toronto and Ottawa rank top), because large cities tend to have more highly skilled workers, especially in the professional and managerial occupations, and because the cost of living is generally higher and wages tend to keep pace with living costs. Also important are recent growth rates (note the correlation here for the Montreal CMA between relatively high unemployment, low wages, and modest growth), economic base, and location (with the major exception of Calgary, cities in the periphery tend to have consistently lower per capita incomes).

Educational status tends to mirror patterns of income, with some notable exceptions. Halifax is approximately in the middle of the income scale. Yet Halifax boasts almost the highest education figure, with 14.3 per cent of its population having completed university degrees (column 6). This is probably explained by the large number of institutes of higher education that are located there (more than in any other urban area of the country), and by the fact that Halifax is a provincial capital and a regional public- and private-sector administrative centre for Atlantic Canada as a whole. It is notable in column 5 that Montreal, Quebec City, Sherbrooke, and Trois Rivières have the highest rates of population with less than grade 9 education, an indication of the low value given to education in Quebec before the 'Quiet Revolution' opened access to secondary and higher education.

INTRA-URBAN SOCIAL DIFFERENTIATION

Our concern now shifts to where different types of people live within the geographic boundaries of any one urban area; that is, with how households locate themselves in residential neighbourhoods or in distinctive social areas made up of people with similar incomes and/or social and ethnic backgrounds. Many complex and interrelated factors dictate who lives where in a city and why: societal values for different types of physical and social environments; disposable income and its relative distribution throughout a society; land values and the technology of building; the relative mobility of different households; changing land-use patterns, especially the suburbanization of employment centres; the operating practices of major financial institutions; household composition, especially as regards the changing role of women in society (discussed in some detail in Chapter 14); and the changing role of developers and planners, to name but a few. The task here is to relate these factors more specifically to the social configuration of geographic space within cities.

The following discussion deals first with the importance of households as the fundamental social unit within urban society, and then with the economics of urban real estate. Remaining portions deal chronologically with varying socio-residential patterns that have been put in place since the turn of the century. These varying patterns have led to successive modelling efforts by Burgess (1925), Hoyt (1939) and Harris and Ullman (1945). However, our observations also include more recent patterns of social segregation that have appeared in the last two decades.

The Household Unit

In preceding discussions we have looked at people in cities primarily from a population perspective. As we have seen, the number of people in a city can be of fundamental importance to researchers and practitioners alike. For example, if we are concerned about future trends in school enrolment, a simple head-count for children under the age of 16 years should suffice; we count transit riders to calculate the feasibility of various public transportation schemes, and governments use a head-count enumeration method to allocate public funds to urban areas. However, in many instances simple population counts are not enough. Most people do not live and carry out their activities in cities as individuals. This requires that we consider integral social units such as households or families. The obvious example is housing and hence residential location. Information about the total number of people in a city tells us little about overall housing demand, much less about demand by submarket, because people live in household or family units even if these are single-person households.

Statistics Canada (1987) identifies households as follows:

HOUSEHOLD TYPE
Refers to a person or group of persons (other than foreign residents) who occupy a dwelling and do not have a usual place of residence elsewhere in Canada. It usually consists of a family group with or without lodgers, employees, etc. However, it may consist of two or more families sharing a dwelling, a group of unrelated persons, or one person living alone. Household members who are temporarily absent on Census Day (e.g., temporary residents elsewhere) are considered as part of their usual household. For census purposes, every person is a member of one and only one household. Unless otherwise specified, all data in household reports are for private households only. Households are classified into 3 groups; Private Households, Collective Households and Households Outside Canada.

In subsequent discussion we will be dealing primarily with households because our fundamental interest is focused on the spatial pattern of their residential location.

The Economics of Urban Real Estate

Households' residential location is influenced by numerous factors. Many of these factors will be unique to individual households or specific household types. Probably the primary factors influencing, and in many cases determining, residential location are fundamentally economic in nature—who can afford what and where given the very real differential real-estate costs that characterize different neighbourhood locales and that are primarily transportation- and amenity-related. (This, of course, holds true for most other types of land use as well).

The primary factor influencing urban real-estate values tends to be distance from the Central Business District (CBD). As Figure 12.5A suggests, different uses compete for the scarce and highly accessible space in and around the CBD. This process is fundamental to the classic Von Thunen model of urban land use, though it is much less applicable today than it was in the pre-automobile city.[5] Today, land values tend to look more like a patchwork quilt with peaks at major subnodes (along public transit and expressway routes, and at points that have 'amenity' value, e.g. high-income status or scenic views, such as is found in the English Bay area of Vancouver).

In terms of residential land use, there are two main implications arising from urban land-value patterns. First, households are generally not able to compete with certain other types of land uses, e.g. commercial and office space, for the most accessible geographic locales. This is true not only for locations in and around the CBD.[6] As is shown in Figure 12.5B, similar patterns accrue at subnodes of access, such as the interchange of express-ways or major public transit routes. The second implication is that residen-tial values will lead to segregation in terms of both density and quality. The very highest valued land will generally be developed as either high-density housing, usually in the form of high-rise apartments (as, for exam-ple, at the interchange of the Don Valley Parkway and Highway 401 in Metropolitan Toronto or in the Longueuil Metro Station area on Mon-treal's South shore), or high-income single-family housing. Hoyt (1939) argued that higher income households generally seek out sites with scenic amenity and/or good transportation access, as in the case of the high-income residential neighbourhoods that parallel the Don Valley Parkway and the Yonge Street corridor in Toronto, and the mountain in West-mount in the Montreal area. In Kitchener-Waterloo, the high-income residential area has grown towards the University of Waterloo with its spacious grounds and social and symbolic 'prestige value'.

In large Canadian cities, the distinctly different geographic patterns of high-density units and single-family neighbourhoods was largely put in place in the 1960s during the apartment boom that accompanied the coming of age of the 'baby boom'. The patterns persist today and are simply expanding outward. However, the process has also been greatly influenced by planners, who tend to zone nodes of highest accessibility to high-density residential use—in part to capture the land value differential and in part to buffer lower density housing from major points of traffic noise and pollution.

Figure 12.5
Patterns of Urban Real Estate Values

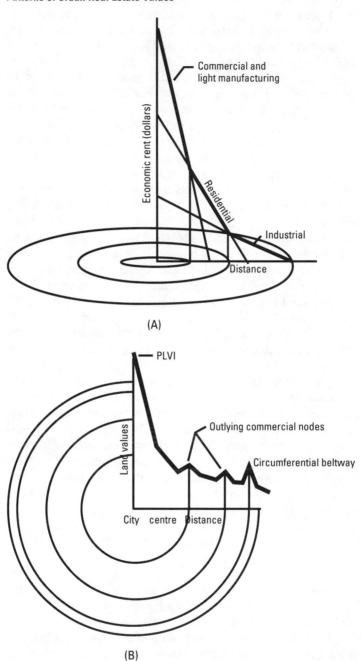

SOURCE: Hartshorn, 1980.

A final factor of note regarding urban real-estate values (see Figure 12.5B) is the steep 'drop off' that characterizes non-CBD inner-city land values. This rapid decrease in central-city real estate has been explained by the relative unattractiveness of older housing, taken against North American society's proclivity for newer, low-density suburban locales. The trend is accentuated by almost universal automobile ownership and the suburbanization of major employment nodes. The term 'filtering down' has been used to describe this process, whereby the better-off middle- and upper-middle-class households abandon the central city for the suburbs, leaving behind housing that is progressively passed on to lower income groups, which results in accelerated deterioration of an already ageing housing stock.

Another explanation for central-city decline comes from the neo-marxist or Marxian school of thought. This school uses the term 'land value valley' (see, for example, Smith, 1979; 1982) to describe extensive and purposeful disinvestment in central city properties by capitalistic investors and developers. An example would be 'redlining' on a large scale. Redlining refers to the fact that financial institutions have been known to draw solid geographic boundaries around central city areas that are not considered to have current investment potential, hence hastening their decline. It is argued that this and various other types of disinvestment occur in order that substantial gains may be achieved when the property is effectively devalued and ripe for reinvestment. Though the theoretical rhetoric behind such a conspiracy view of urban trends is strong, there has been little empirical evidence to support the case. One major exception comes from the work of Checkoway (1980), who has been able to show that the large-scale suburbanization that occurred in the United States in the 1950s and early 1960s was as much influenced by lobbying on the part of major development and automobile industries as it was by consumer demand.

In Canada, the downgrading process of central-city neighbourhoods has not occurred on as large a scale as it has in many US cities (see Chapters 3 and 13). There are many reasons for this. Among them are: the development of public housing in suburban neighbourhoods; the continued presence of high- and middle-income sectors within the inner city; the importance of public transit, especially in the larger cities; post-war foreign in-migration; and since the 1970s, protective zoning for many inner-city neighbourhoods. The question now arises as to how the urban real-estate market and other factors relate to the distinctive patterns of different social areas found in different locations throughout Canadian cities.

Social Area Analysis
In the pre-World War II years, a number of eminent scholars had examined patterns of social space in US cities. Three distinctive patterns emerged. These are shown schematically as Figure 12.6. The Park (1925) model or 'concentric zone theory' postulated a CBD, surrounded by a 'zone of

Figure 12.6
Schematic Illustration of Three Theories of City Structure

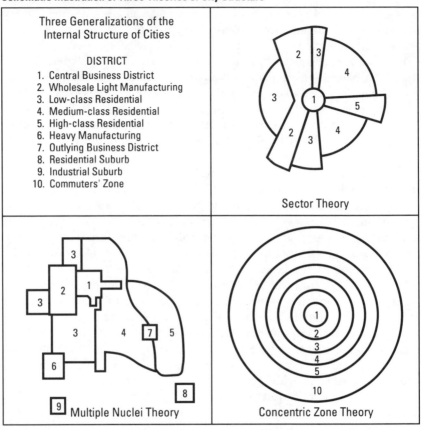

Three Generalizations of the
Internal Structure of Cities

DISTRICT
1. Central Business District
2. Wholesale Light Manufacturing
3. Low-class Residential
4. Medium-class Residential
5. High-class Residential
6. Heavy Manufacturing
7. Outlying Business District
8. Residential Suburb
9. Industrial Suburb
10. Commuters' Zone

Sector Theory

Multiple Nuclei Theory

Concentric Zone Theory

SOURCE: Harris and Ullman, 1945.

transition' largely characterized by deteriorated land use brought about through the process of speculation fuelled by anticipated CBD expansion. Outer zones were characterized primarily by residential use in a 'distance-decay' pattern whereby lower income households located in the less attractive, central-city locations close to their place of employment, and increasingly higher income households, who could afford some type of transportation facility, moved outwards in search of newer homes, larger lots, and, relatively speaking, 'amenity' landscapes. Though not classified as such by Park, the process he identified later came to be referred to as 'filtering down' (Lansing, *et al.* 1969; Smith 1964). As mentioned earlier, filtering down was viewed as a fundamental process of residential change. As housing aged, it deteriorated and became less valuable (socially and economically). Thus Park argued that as ageing housing was 'abandoned' by the middle- and upper-classes, it would be taken up by lower income groups, and eventually be subdivided by non-occupant owners and rented out to lower income tenants, dramatically speeding up the process of deterioration. This explains why some of the lowest income groups can be found on land with potentially high land-value in highly accessible central-city locations.

While 'filtering down' certainly took place in Canadian cities in the decades immediately following World War II, it did not occur on the scale observed in many US cities. There are numerous reasons for this: some of the main ones were the lack of racial discrimination in the inner zones of Canadian cities, the so-called middle-class exodus to the suburbs in the 1950s which was more pronounced in the US than in Canada, and high rates of foreign in-migration. (The new migrants tended to be attracted to the central city, and were also primarily interested in home purchase and 'do it yourself' styles of home improvement.) Another important factor was that rates of car ownership were much lower in Canada than in the United States.

The second model of social space shown in Figure 12.6, sector theory, was developed by Homer Hoyt (1939), who studied housing patterns in United States cities in the inter-war depression years. His model comprises a sectoral alignment of social space with higher-income residential neighbourhoods aligned along the better transportation routes and/or along scenic physical features such as ravines (e.g. Rosedale in Toronto) or shore fronts (e.g. the Northwest Arm in Halifax). On the other hand, heavy industry tended to abut major rail lines and, in turn, be abutted by worker housing. Examples would be the Weston Road area in Toronto and the St Henri district in Montreal.

The Harris and Ullman multiple nuclei model, the third model depicted in Figure 12.6, is in fact a land-use model and was not intended to deal with social space *per se*. It has, however, been shown that distinct nucleations of social groups do exist within cities, especially as regards ethnic groups. Africville in Halifax or the Chinatowns in Toronto and Vancouver are good examples. However, it should be noted that when these communities are large and there is little or no discrimination in the housing market, the neighbourhoods usually grow outwards in a sectoral fashion as in the case of the Italian community in Toronto. Nonetheless, the original 'port of entry' is usually maintained as a major focal point for commercial and cultural activity. In addition to the many ethnic neighbourhoods that characterize 'multicultural' Canada, other smaller pockets such as gay communities are also beginning to emerge as our society diversifies. Some are of increasing social concern, such as the rooming-house-based congregation of ex-psychiatric patients found in the Parkdale community of Toronto, which is located adjacent to Toronto's major mental hospital (Dear and Taylor 1982).

For some time in the mid-twentieth century scholars debated as to which of the three models of urban social space was most applicable.

Figure 12.7
Social Space in Metropolitan Toronto

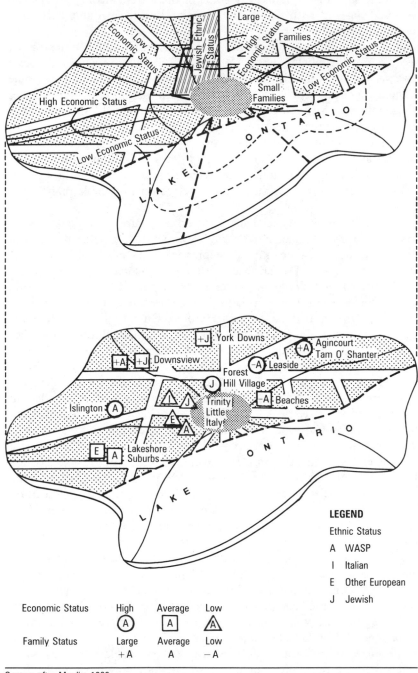

SOURCE: after Murdie, 1969.

Shevky and Bell (1955) argued quite definitively that all three fit in an overlapping and integratial fashion.[7] They developed empirical indices for each of the dimensions which, when applied to a variety of different cities, were all found to be major discriminants of urban social structure, each with its own distinctive spatial pattern as postulated by Burgess, Hoyt, and Harris and Ullman. The major criticism of social-area analysis as an empirical technique was that it selectively focused on specific variables that, it was argued, might or might not be the major discriminants of urban spatial structure.

The application of multivariate statistical techniques to geographic problems changed this critical viewpoint considerably. Murdie (1969) in his pioneering work applied a multivariate statistical technique—principal components analysis—to a wide array of socio-economic variables. The same three factors emerged as the most significant discriminants of residential structure in the Toronto Metropolitan area, i.e. socio-economic status, life cycle, and ethnicity as shown in Figure 12.7. Work since that

Figure 12.8
Dimensions of Social Space, Regina, 1961

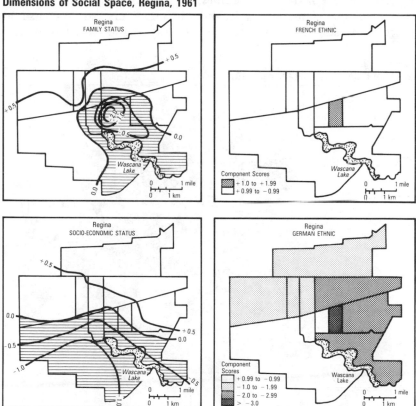

SOURCE: Davies and Barrow, 1973

time has confirmed the fundamental importance of these dimensions in spite of contemporary transformations affecting households and cities, for example, suburban diversification, changing patterns of household formation, and inner-city revitalization (Le Bourdais and Beaudry 1988; Davies 1984; Janson 1980; Schwirian and Maitre 1974). Figure 12.7 shows the original schematic model put forward by Murdie (1969). The similarity between the Murdie's original model and the 1961 pattern for the Regina CMA is remarkably close (see Figure 12.8). Similar associations are found on the socio-economic and ethnicity dimensions as revealed in cities across the country. Figure 12.9, which shows one index of life-cycle status for Montreal—one person as compared with middle-aged households—is a further example of the persistence of distinctive life-cycle patterning in a city with a very complex physical setting (the island, riverways, and mountain) and social setting (strong lines of ethnic and language segregation).

Despite the fact that social-area analysis and factorial-ecology statistical techniques (Davies 1978; Hunter 1972; Palm and Caruso 1972) have come under considerable criticism, there can be no doubt that at least to the present time the main dividing lines in Canadian urban society remain socio-economic status, life cycle, and ethnicity. This can, of course, be expected to change in the future, especially in association with government

Figure 12.9
Montreal CMA Household Changes, 1971–1981

< −1.00
One person households

> 1.00
Middle-age established families

0   20
    km

SOURCE: Le Bourdais and Beaudry, 1988.

policy on foreign immigration and trends in household formation. It will be interesting to see the extent to which changes appear when the 1991 census data are available for analysis.

SOME CONTEMPORARY ASPECTS OF SOCIAL CHANGE IN CITIES

Contemporary patterns of social segregation within urban space can be approached around the theme of social differentiation. Many issues arise from the current changing social composition of our cities. Many of them are not picked up by social-area analysis, which, being based on census tract data, gives a relatively aggregate picture of urban social change. Further, many of the changes are very current and are not easily seen in the analysis of data from the 1981 or 1986 census. These include: mixed-density housing in all but the most exclusive of neighbourhoods; less successful attempts at greater mix among households of different socio-economic status; gentrification; the feminization of poverty in the suburbs as well as in the central city (see Filion and Bunting 1990); incumbent upgrading, especially on the part of foreign in-migrants (see Bunting, 1987); increased problems of housing affordability, which has been felt particularly by the growing numbers of persons in the low-paid, slow-growth industrial sectors, the lower paid 'blue-' and 'pink-' collar workers, and the growing numbers of single-parent households. Overall, as regards housing and residential location, we seem to be seeing increased polarization between the 'haves' and the 'have-nots'.

Not all of the above issues can be dealt with in a chapter of this scope, although some of them are discussed by Moore Milroy in Chapter 20. The emphasis here is less on the 'problems' and more on contemporary patterns of social variation in Canadian cities. One area that has not received much attention is the changing nature of the social composition of our suburbs and of suburban development, unlike, for example, the inner city, which has been the focus of much attention and is treated in detail in Chapter 13. Nonetheless, the majority of Canadians live (and increasingly work) in suburban locales.

In the 1950s, 1960s and even 1970s, the central city and suburban components of cities were considered to be distinctly different. The suburbs were viewed as relatively homogeneous in social composition with family-oriented households and children living at home. In terms of social status, the householders were perceived to be middle class at one or the other end of the scale depending on location, and lot and house size. A prime example would be the extensive tracts of lower middle- to middle-income housing constructed in Scarborough in the 1950s and 1960s. Though less prevalent, higher-income suburban communities also grew up, usually in areas that had attractive physical settings and/or locations that offered good transportation access to the entire metropolitan area—

the Bayview area in Toronto and Beechwood in Kitchener-Waterloo are good examples of this more exclusive type of suburban residential development. These types of residential communities can be found throughout the outer zones of all Canadian metropolitan areas.[8] In fact, however, the suburban stereotype never really existed, and the differences between suburban neighbourhoods were probably as great as those found in the central city. Consider, for example, the differences between the Jane-Finch corridor in Toronto, the predominantly single-family lower middle class Rexdale, and the more substantially-housed neighbourhoods in the Bayview area of North Toronto. However, what most suburban neighbourhoods shared, relative to the central city, were relatively lower residential densities, a predominance of single-family housing, and strictly zoned land-use segregation with occasional nodes of high density at major transportation intersections.[9]

Current planning practices have changed, however, as the large-scale monolithic suburbs have created serious urban problems, most notably over-use of the automobile and attendant air pollution, and the consumption of prime farmland and other natural resources. A greater mix of employment centres with housing of varying density and socio-economic status is the current vogue among planning theorists. This type of community has the advantage of avoiding built-in obsolescence as, for example, in the school closures that have taken place in many of the suburbs built in the immediate post-World War II period. In a more balanced suburban community, the continued need to provide new facilities as the population ages can largely be avoided. In the Metropolitan Toronto Region, the planning of Scarborough Town Centre and Mississauga reflects something of this newer philosophy of city planning. Nonetheless, though the suburbs can be said to be urbanizing, becoming socially more diversified, and growing more like the central city, the differences between the two types of areas are still immense.

It has been argued that differences between the suburbs and the inner city are decreasing, and this certainly is the case in most Canadian metropolitan areas. And there is an abundance of evidence to support this case. However, where social differences are concerned, the central city has finer-grain differentials than the suburban zones, which tend to comprise larger-scale patchwork-like geographic zones. As has already been mentioned, suburbs also differ greatly among themselves. These differences are accentuated by relatively autonomous political jurisdictions whose goals for urban development can be found to be quite different. However, to date, social differentiation within suburban zones has not been closely examined in the research literature.

Many factors abound to produce an increasingly diversified suburban landscape. Life-cycle differences are an obvious example. In the outer suburbs, newer young households, most with children, predominate, whereas the inner suburbs are ageing and have a much more diversified population profile with a variety of residents at different stages of the life cycle. Ethnic differences also exist—witness the Asian population in Agincourt close to the edge of Metropolitan Toronto. Another example in the same city would be the suburbanization of the Italian population. Originally located in west-central Toronto neighbourhoods, this community has moved outwards in a sectoral pattern that now stretches beyond the outer suburbs to what were once independent cities outside the Toronto zone. In the case of the Italian community, its geographic bounds have extended into what was, a decade ago, predominantly agricultural land. This minority group has also encompassed small outlying communities like Woodbridge in the Toronto area.

As in the case of the inner city, one of the most prominent of the differences between suburban communities exists in their socio-economic differences. In Toronto, some of the poorest citizens reside in suburban areas. To a large extent, this has been the result of policies from various levels of government that have committed major public housing projects to suburban areas. On the part of the private sector, practices like the renting of basement apartments also serves to increase social diversity in suburban locales. Much of the subsidized housing for senior citizens has also been located in suburban zones. At the same time, processes like gentrification and commercial redevelopment have been major factors in reducing low-income residential units within the central city.

Patterns of socio-economic variation in the suburbs tend to follow those found in the central city. For example, in Toronto the more well-to-do residential housing is mostly found in the northern sector of the city following a pattern established in the late nineteenth and early twentieth century. Other pockets of high-income housing can be found in amenity locations, such as along the Don and Humber Rivers.

The above suggests that much of the US-inspired central city/suburban dichotomy did not develop on a large scale in Canadian metropolitan areas, and that over the last decade or so, the social differences are becoming even less marked. However, one must recognize that the suburbs were built on an entirely different scale than the central city. This facilitated the development of homogeneous communities on a scale not found in the central city. It also encourages strong interest groups—neighbourhood associations, for example—whose primary concern is the protection of property rights for single-family homeowners. Problems like NIMBY (Not In My Back Yard) can be traced directly to the attitudes of private-property home-owners wanting to protect their socially homogeneous neighbourhoods.

SUMMARY AND CONCLUSIONS

This chapter has focused on people in social groups in cities, and social differentiation within and between cities. It has dealt first with aspects of demographic growth, then with inter-urban differences in social organization, and finally with spatial variations in the internal social structure of our cities. It concludes with some brief and speculative comments as to what we might expect in the future. As we move towards the twenty-first century, social patterns in our cities may be expected to change quite dramatically, though we can probably expect that most people will continue to prefer living among people like themselves which will in turn perpetuate patterns of social differentiation. Thus, while geographic patterns may change, the presence of distinctive social areas is likely to persist. It is, of course, difficult to speculate about the exact nature of future social change. Recent and current trends suggest five important areas of change. The first is the impact of technological change, which is discussed in Chapter 6. The second trend is the slowing down of population growth. Current birth rates in our larger CMAs are below replacement level, with growth occurring mainly through internal and foreign in-migration. The implication of slow growth or no growth is that we can expect less new-housing development and more resale of existing properties. The implications for the development and renovation industries are profound. Related to this is a third trend towards smaller and less family-oriented households. If this trend continues, we can expect demands for different types of housing in different types of locations to increase. It is difficult to speculate on how the vast tracts of three-to-four bedroom single-family houses that now predominate in most Canadian suburbs might be altered to accommodate these smaller households. A fourth trend has already been mentioned. This is the apparent increasing polarization in the socio-economic structure of our society. Economic trends point to occupational growth in the service sector, with demands for large numbers of relatively unskilled and poorly paid service employees on the one hand and smaller numbers of high-order professional and managerial jobs on the other. This trend suggests that, all other things being equal, we can expect a significant increase in current problems of housing affordability, which will be accentuated by a fifth factor, the increasing number of single-parent, mother-led households (Bunting and Filion 1988). Finally, there is the issue of environmental quality. Here, on a more positive note, we can probably expect the quality of public life in our urban environments to improve, even if only marginally. Increased control of air-, noise-, and water-pollution and the 'regreening' of our urban environments will create more liveable public environments, though it is debatable as to what extent this might offset increasing constraints in the private housing market. Moreover, these constraints can probably be expected only to solidify and accentuate existing patterns of social diversification and residential segregation in Canadian cities.

NOTES

1. Some suggest that households' reasons for moving are becoming more complex with amenities and life-style factors being traded off for purely employment related benefits (see Coppack 1988). These trends can be expected to increase in the future with earlier retirements, shorter working weeks, the substitution of telecommunications for transportation, and the overall increase in 'home work'.

2. A census division refers to the general term applying to counties, regional districts, regional municipalities and five other types of geographic areas made up of groups of census subdivisions. In Newfoundland, Manitoba, Saskatchewan and Alberta, the term describes areas that have been created by Statistics Canada in co-operation with the provinces as an equivalent for counties (Statistics Canada 1987).

3. Note that in these population pyramids the number of years delineating cohorts varies from one age group to another.

4. Megahousing refers to the phenomenon whereby smaller, usually post-World War II houses (usually in good repair and located in the inner suburbs with good access to public transit and the expressway network) are 'knocked down' and replaced by large and usually luxurious new housing. To the average urban dweller the costs involved seem prohibitive. The process occurs because demand for high-quality housing with good access to all parts of the city, especially the CBD, is high and the supply cannot keep up with the demand.

5. The Von Thunen model is probably the most classic model of geographic land use segregation. It is based on the premise that establishments 'trade off' space for access—hence higher demand and higher densities and land values in locations of high accessibility, and lower values as one moves away from the most accessible places. For more detailed discussion of the Thunian model see Lloyd and Dicken (1977; 1990); Yeates (1990); Yeates and Garner (1980).

6. In the past, the main intersection in a city was generally the peak land value intersection (PLVI). This is less generally true today, as the relative importance of the CBD has declined.

7. Shevky and Bell (1955) also produce a very detailed theoretical explanation (Marxist in origin), as to why this type of social and residential segregation occurs in capitalistic society. It is not within the purview of this chapter to repeat these arguments. Useful summary discussions can be found in Ley (1983) and Yeates (1990).

8. The two somewhat aberrant cities in this respect are Vancouver and Montreal. In Vancouver, high-rise apartments with scenic views composed a much higher percentage of the housing stock than was the case in the average Canadian city. Montreal, too, was different, showing bias for higher density (though not high-rise) styles of housing, evidenced by larger tracts of duplexed suburban developments.

9. It should be noted that Canadian suburbs have always been more heterogeneous than their American counterparts. Reasons for this will not be repeated here. More detailed discussion is found in Chapter 3.

FURTHER READING

DEAR, M.J. and TAYLOR, S.M. 1982 *Not on Our Street: Community Attitudes to Mental Health Care* (London: Pion)

JANSON, C.G. 1980 'Factorial Social Ecology: An Attempt at Summary and Evaluation', *Annual Review of Sociology* 6, 433–56

LE BOURDAIS, C. and BEAUDRY, M. 1988 'The Changing Residential Structure of Montreal 1971–81', *The Canadian Geographer* 32, 98–113

LEY, D. 1983 *A Social Geography of the City* (New York: Harper and Row)

SCHWIRIAN, P. and MAITRE, M. 1974 'The Ecological Structure of Canadian Cities' in K.P. Schwirian ed. *Comparative Urban Structure* (Lexington, Ma.: Heath)

REFERENCES

BUNTING, T. 1987 'Home Purchase and Renovation Activity in the Inner Zones of a Medium-Sized Canadian City', *The Canadian Geographer* 30, 209–22

—— and FILION, P. 1988 'Introduction: The Movement Towards the Post-Industrial Society and the Changing Role of the Inner City' in T. Bunting and P. Filion eds *The Changing Canadian Inner City* (Waterloo: University of Waterloo, Department of Geography Publication Series No. 31)

BURGESS, E.W. 1925 'Growth of the City' in R.E. Park, E.W. Burgess, and R.D. McKenzie eds *The City* (Chicago: University of Chicago Press)

CHECKOWAY, B. 1980 'Large Builders, Federal Housing Programmes and Post War Suburbanization', *International Journal of Urban and Regional Research* 4, 21–44

COPPACK, P. 1988 'Reflections on the Role of Amenity in the Evolution of the Urban Field', *Geografiska Annaler* 70B, 353–61

DAVIES, W.K.D. 1984 *Factorial Ecology* (Hants: Gower)

—— 1978 'Alternative Factorial Solutions and Urban Social Structure', *Canadian Geographer* 22, 273–97

DEAR, M.J. and TAYLOR, S.M. 1982 *Not on Our Street: Community Attitudes to Mental Health Care* (London: Pion)

FILION, P. and BUNTING, T. 1990 *Housing Affordability in Canada* (Ottawa: Statistics Canada)

GIBSON, E. 1976 *The Urbanization of the Strait of Georgia Region* (Ottawa: Environment Canada, Geographical Paper No. 57)

GILL, A. and SMITH, G.C. 1985 'Residents Evaluative Structures of Northern Manitoba Mining Communities', *The Canadian Geographer* 29, 17–29

HARRIS, C.D. and ULLMAN, E.L. 1945 'The Nature of Cities', *The Annals of the Association of the American Academy of Political and Social Science* 242, 7–17

HOYT, H. 1939 *The Structure and Growth of Residential Neighbourhoods in American Cities* (Washington, D.C.: US Federal Housing Administration)

HUNTER, A.A. 1972 'Factorial Ecology: A Critique and Some Suggestions', *Demography* 9, 107–18

JANSON, C.G. 1980 'Factorial Social Ecology: An Attempt at Summary and Evaluation', *Annual Review of Sociology* 6, 433–56

JONES, H.W. 1981 *A Population Geography* (New York: Harper and Row)

KUNTZ, M. 1989 *Planned Retirement Communities in the Urban Field* (Waterloo: Department of Geography, unpublished M.A. Thesis)

LANSING, J.B. et al. 1969 *New Homes and Poor People* (Ann Arbor: Institute for Social Research)

LE BOURDAIS, C. and BEAUDRY, M. 1988 'The Changing Residential Structure of Montreal 1971–81', *The Canadian Geographer* 32, 98–113

LEY, D. 1983 *A Social Geography of the City* (New York: Harper and Row)

LLOYD, P. and DICKEN, P. 1977 *Location in Space: A Theoretical Approach to Economic Geography* (London: Harper and Row)

—— 1990 *Location in Space: Theoretical Perspectives in Economic Geography* (New York: Harper and Row)

McLOUGHLIN, J. 1969 *Urban and Regional Planning: A Systems Approach* (London: Faber and Faber)

MATHEWS, G. 1984 *Le choc démographique: Le déclin du Québec est-il inévitable?* (Montreal: Boréal Express)

MIRON, J. 1988 *Housing in Postwar Canada: Demographic Change, Household Formation and Housing Demand* (Montreal: McGill-Queen's University Press)

MURDIE, R.A. 1969 *Factorial Ecology of Metropolitan Toronto* (Chicago: University of Chicago, Department of Geography Research Paper No. 116)

PALM, R. and CARUSO, D. 1972 'Factor Labelling in Factorial Ecology', *Annals, Association of American Geographers* 62, 122–33

PARK, R.E., et al. eds *The City* (Chicago: University of Chicago Press)

Regional Municipality of Waterloo 1976 *Regional Official Policies Plan* (Waterloo, Ontario: Regional Municipality of Waterloo)

SCHWIRIAN, P. and MAITRE, M. 1974 'The Ecological Structure of Canadian Cities' in K.P. Schwirian ed. *Comparative Urban Structure* (Lexington, Ma.: Health)

SHEVKY, E. and BELL, W. 1955 *Social Area Analyses* (Stanford: Stanford University Press)

SMITH, N. 1979 'Towards a Theory of Gentrification: A Back to the City Movement by Capital Not People', *Journal of the American Planning Association* 45, 538–48

—— 1982 'Gentrification and Uneven Development', *Economic Geography* 58, 139–55

SMITH, P.J. and JOHNSON, D.B. 1978 *The Edmonton-Calgary Corridor* (Edmonton: Department of Geography, University of Alberta)

SMITH, W. 1964 *Filtering and Neighbourhood Change* (Berkeley: University of California Press)

STATISTICS CANADA 1987 *The Dictionary 1986* (Ottawa: Ministry of Supply and Services, Canada)

WALLACE, I. 1987 'The Canadian Shield: The Development of a Resource Frontier' in L. McCann ed. *Heartland and Hinterland: A Geography of Canada* (Scarborough: Prentice-Hall)

WEBSTER, D. 1985 'Canadian Regional Decentralization in the New Global Context: Myth or Reality', *The Canadian Journal of Regional Science* 8, 377–94

WOODS, R.I. 1975 *The Stochastic Analysis of Immigrant Distribution* (School of Geography, University of Oxford Research Paper No. 11)

YEATES, M. 1984 'Urbanization in the Windsor-Quebec City Axis, 1921–1981', *Urban Geography* 5, 2–24

―――― 1990 *The North American City* (New York: Random House)

―――― and GARNER, B. 1980 *The North American City* (New York: Harper and Row)

13

The Inner City

DAVID LEY

It has been said that all classifications are useful rather than true, and this statement applies particularly to the classification of geographical regions. A regional study must begin both by defining its region and by acknowledging that any such definition is arbitrary. While there are, undoubtedly, important themes shared by the ring of old neighbourhoods around the central business district (CBD) that we call the inner city, no single criterion, or even a combination of criteria, permits boundaries to be reliably drawn around urban districts.

In Canada, it has been the federal government that has most often undertaken the near impossible task of defining the inner city, in part to target and monitor its own programs and policies. This was the purpose of its first comprehensive definition, which used the common sense criteria of age and spatial proximity to downtown to define the inner cities of Canada (McLemore, Aass, and Keilhofer 1975). More specifically, an urban census tract was included within the inner city if the percentage of its housing stock built before 1946 was double the metropolitan average, and/or if the tract was surrounded by others that were so defined. In this manner isolated tracts with older housing were excluded while central tracts with newer housing (where redevelopment had occurred) were included. Based on the 1971 census, these criteria identified inner-city districts in ten large cities. These districts had populations ranging from 18,000 (St John's) to 644,000 (Montreal), and accounting for between 10 per cent and 24 per cent of the metropolitan total.

A second government document adopted a more flexible definition of the inner city (Brown and Burke 1979). The task of identifying inner-city districts in the twenty-three census metropolitan areas (CMAs) then in existence was delegated to local field officers, who were asked to employ the criterion of residential age but qualify it according to local considerations and perceptions. Overall, the inner city so defined comprised some 30 per cent of the metropolitan population in 1971 and 25 per cent in 1976. But with a less standardized classification, there were considerable departures from the mean and in 1976 the inner city, as defined in this second government document, ranged from only 7 per cent of the metropolitan population in Victoria to 40 per cent in Montreal, a somewhat disturbing range.

The third and most recent attempt by a federal department at inner-city definition in twelve cities revived an earlier and narrower classification that included the CBD, the surrounding areas of mixed land uses, and high density residential development (Ram et al. 1989). Trends in twelve CMAs were examined over the 1951–86 period, and the inner-city definition was fixed throughout to aid comparison. While understandable, this decision had the effect of freezing inner-city boundaries, even though inner-city processes (e.g. property ageing) were expanding beyond the area demarcated in 1951, and CBD expansion was removing housing from the core. The predictable outcome of this restrictive definition was that the inner-city's share of the metropolitan population in the twelve cities fell from 16 per cent in 1951 to 4 per cent in 1986, and by 37 per cent in absolute terms.

AN INITIAL PROFILE OF THE INNER CITY

What form of statistical profile of the inner city emerges from these attempts at region-building? In Figure 13.1, maps of family status, family income, and ethnic diversity are shown for metropolitan Winnipeg in 1971, with its inner city demarcated following the criterion of housing age. The visual evidence of the maps is reproduced in Table 13.1, which displays a set of variables comparing the inner city with the metropolitan area as a whole. With 17 per cent of the metropolitan population in 1971, Winnipeg's inner neighbourhoods contained, in general, smaller households with fewer children and a higher proportion of the elderly (Figure 13.1a). Household incomes were more than 20 per cent below the metropolitan average (Figure 13.1b) and unemployment rates at 10 per cent exceeded the mean by three percentage points. Educational attainment was lower in the inner city, with proportionately more blue-collar workers and fewer white-collar and professional workers—though these

**Figure 13.1
Selected Social Indices, Winnipeg CMA, 1971**

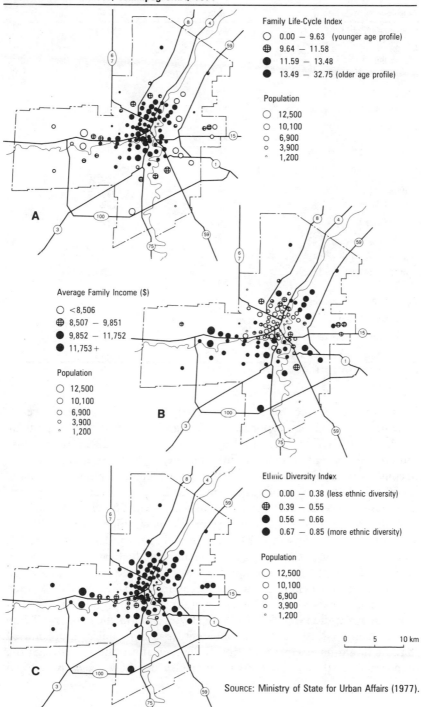

Family Life-Cycle Index

○ 0.00 — 9.63 (younger age profile)
⊕ 9.64 — 11.58
● 11.59 — 13.48
● 13.49 — 32.75 (older age profile)

Population

○ 12,500
○ 10,100
○ 6,900
○ 3,900
∘ 1,200

Average Family Income ($)

○ <8,506
⊕ 8,507 — 9,851
● 9,852 — 11,752
● 11,753 +

Population

○ 12,500
○ 10,100
○ 6,900
○ 3,900
∘ 1,200

Ethnic Diversity Index

○ 0.00 — 0.38 (less ethnic diversity)
⊕ 0.39 — 0.55
● 0.56 — 0.66
● 0.67 — 0.85 (more ethnic diversity)

Population

○ 12,500
○ 10,100
○ 6,900
○ 3,900
∘ 1,200

0   5   10 km

SOURCE: Ministry of State for Urban Affairs (1977).

Table 13.1
Data on the Inner City and Census Metropolitan Area of Winnipeg, 1971

Variable	Inner city	CMA
Population (% of CMA)	89,160 (17%)	540,240
Age groups:		
Less than 19	28%	34%
65 and over	15%	10%
Average household size	2.7	3.2
Average household income	$7,335	$9,380
Education:		
Less than grade 9	42%	31%
University graduates	5%	6%
Occupational groups:		
Blue collar	28%	25%
White collar	39%	44%
Professional	17%	19%
Unemployment	10%	7%
Born outside Canada	29%	20%
Type of dwelling:		
Single-detached	40%	63%
Apartment	53%	32%
Dwellings owner-occupied	37%	59%
Rooms per dwelling	4.8	5.2
Average annual gross rent	$921	$1,142
Overcrowding (over 1 person per room)	6%	6%

SOURCE: McLemore, Aass, Keilhofer (1975).

labour force differences were not particularly marked. There was, however, a significantly higher proportion of foreign-born residents than in the CMA as a whole. The map of ethnic diversity (Figure 13.1c) reveals that most inner-city census tracts fall into the category with the greatest degree of ethnic mixing. To accommodate this mainly tenant population, housing is more likely to consist of apartments, and have fewer rooms per person than the CMA as a whole, with annual rents some 20 per cent lower.

With few exceptions, the statistical profile of Winnipeg's inner city was shared by other CMAs in 1971 (McLemore, Aass, and Keilhofer 1975). The overall picture is confirmed by the more sophisticated methodology of factorial ecology (that is, the application of reordered matrices of correlation coefficients to demographic, socio-economic and housing data), which also uses census data to develop maps of broad social trends across Canadian cities (Murdie 1969; Davies 1975; Davies and Murdie in press). While the inner city-CMA contrast is apparent, it is nonetheless more muted than we might have expected across a number of variables. Although the demographic, ethnic, and housing variables do show a clearly defined gradient, the socio-economic differentials are slighter, and, in the case of occupational type, are of only a minor nature.

There are two further points we need to make here. First, it bears repeating that the stark image of polarization between inner cities and suburbs in the United States does not exist *at this scale* in Canada, though we shall see later that pockets of poverty are certainly a significant feature of the Canadian inner city. In many ways, the Canadian city continues to reflect the social area models put forward by members of the so-called 'Chicago' school of human ecologists, Burgess and Hoyt in particular.[1] In these models, demographic, housing, and life cycle variables are distributed concentrically, following Burgess, and thus highlight a distinctive inner-city profile, while socio-economic variables display a sectoral pattern, following Hoyt, thereby obscuring a distinctive status for the inner city.

Second, an important issue is the consideration of historic trends. What trends were discernible prior to 1971 and what have been discernible since? There is some evidence that in the twenty years up to 1971, differentials were becoming more marked in the case of income and family size. One demographic consequence was population decline but stability in the numbers of households. Across twenty three CMAs, inner-city population fell by 11 per cent between 1971 and 1976 but households increased by 2 per cent (Ley 1981), a trend that continued through the 1970s (Filion 1987). In the 1980s, at least within the narrow definition of inner-city districts employed by Statistics Canada, a significant shift has occurred: between 1981 and 1986, and for the first time in thirty five years, the inner-city population of twelve CMAs grew, by an average of 5 per cent (Ram *et al.* 1989). This increase is attributable in large measure to redevelopment, particularly of former industrial lands such as the St Lawrence and Harbourfront projects in Toronto, and False Creek in Vancouver. This trend can be expected to continue with ongoing projects in such districts as the Expo Site and Coal Harbour in Vancouver, The Forks in Winnipeg, the Lachine Canal in Montreal, and the Halifax Waterfront. In each instance waterfront industrial land is being recycled for mixed uses that include a substantial component of medium- or high-density housing units.

Meanwhile, the age profile of the inner city continues to highlight young adults in the age group of 20 to 35 years; by 1986, this cohort accounted for 37 per cent of residents (Ram *et al.* 1989). Associated with this trend has been significant growth of people living alone, who amounted to 56 per cent of inner-city households in 1986. Ethnic composition in the inner city and CMA as a whole has remained constant over the past twenty-five years: around 30 per cent of the inner-city population, and 22 per cent of the rest of the CMA population were foreign-born.

The tendency of inner-city residents to display higher attainment in advanced education has accelerated; in 1971, 25 per cent more of the inner-city residents of fifteen years and over had a university education than within the CMA as a whole, but by 1986 inner-city over-representation had reached 55 per cent (Ram *et al.* 1989). During the 1970s, the rate of expansion of degree holders in the inner city was double that of the CMA (Filion 1987). Other socio-economic measures are correlated with this, notably occupations: inner-city residents now show an over-representation of some 20 per cent in professional and managerial jobs. These two variables are indicators of the much discussed process of gentrification, known earlier in central Canada as 'white-painting', that is, the movement of middle-class professionals into lower cost inner-city districts, accompanied by the renovation or redevelopment of the housing stock. We shall have more to say about this process later, but for now it is necessary to add an important qualifier. Despite gentrification, there has not been an equally marked elevation of inner-city incomes relative to the CMA mean. In part, this is a product of the rapid growth of two-wage-earner families in the suburbs; in part, it is a function of the precise income definition used (the inner city performs more strongly on per capita income measures). Using Statistics Canada's narrower definition of the inner city, the measure of median family income indicates a *relative* earnings decline in the inner city across twelve CMAs between 1970 and 1985 (Table 13.2). In a second study, across Canada's nine largest cities, increases in median household income in the inner city during the 1970s attained 93 per cent of the increase achieved in the CMA; in Toronto, the rise in inner-city earnings exceeded that of the CMA (Filion 1987). Table 13.2 also shows the variation in earnings trends between metropolitan areas. The inner cities of three of Canada's four largest CMAs have improved their economic status both relatively and absolutely; the (unaccountable) exception

Table 13.2
Median Census Family Income (1985 dollars) of Selected Inner Cities and Census Metropolitan Areas, 1970 and 1985

City	1970			1985		
	Inner City	CMA	$\frac{\text{Inner City}}{\text{CMA}} \times 100$	Inner City	CMA	$\frac{\text{Inner City}}{\text{CMA}} \times 100$
Toronto	22,689	32,323	70	30,622	40,536	76
Montreal	18,715	27,684	68	24,445	33,498	73
Vancouver	21,620	29,569	73	23,197	36,645	63
Ottawa-Hull	23,977	33,166	72	31,282	41,776	75
Edmonton	23,170	29,803	78	27,367	37,568	73
Calgary	21,258	30,421	70	24,594	39,842	62
Winnipeg	18,552	27,804	67	16,026	34,794	46
Quebec	20,129	26,932	75	21,796	33,986	63
Total[a]	21,056	29,651	71	23,639	37,109	64

[a]Including figures for Regina, Saskatoon, Halifax, and Saint John, which are not shown separately because of small numbers of cases.

SOURCE: Statistics Canada (1988).

in these data is Vancouver (possibly the result of excluding medium-density gentrifying districts from the inner-city definition). The variation in performance between cities is marked. While Montreal and Winnipeg had virtually the same ratio of inner city-to-CMA median family incomes in 1970, during the ensuing years, the Montreal ratio rose five points while in Winnipeg it fell nineteen points.

This trend matches the result of other research (Ley 1985; Dansereau 1988) that has also indicated a growing polarization in terms of inner-city change between centres in the national urban system.

THE INNER CITY AS PERCEIVED: THE BIOGRAPHY OF A CONCEPT

As well as a seemingly objective profile, the inner city also has a subjective identity, projecting a topography of *meaning* in the minds of urban dwellers. Mainstream society in Western nations has commonly conferred a stigmatized meaning on parts of the inner city, and this perception has directed middle-class attitudes and actions.

As a general term, the inner city dates back to nineteenth century industrialization and the construction of high density and frequently shabbily-built housing for blue-collar workers around the new factories, warehouses, and construction sites, which offered semi-skilled and unskilled jobs for migrants to the city. The pace of growth, the limitations on mass transportation until the 1890s, and the paucity of municipal by-laws contributed to high residential densities, few public services, and little regulation of environmental quality. Members of the blue-collar labour force lived close to their place of work in often unhealthy conditions. The alienating environment of English inner cities was condemned in the mid-nineteenth century by observers with political commitments as varied as those held by Charles Dickens, Frederick Engels, and Benjamin Disraeli. Conditions no less horrendous were present in the United States. In New York City, infant mortality rates rose steadily through the nineteenth century from 135 deaths per thousand live births in 1810 to 240 in 1870. There was, of course, a geography to such conditions: in the first decade of the twentieth century, the Pittsburgh Survey recorded a four-fold differential in mortality rates between wards of that city, with the gravest rates occurring in the crowded immigrant districts located next to the iron-and-steel plants.

The deprivation and pathologies of the inner city led to middle-class avoidance, and rumour and stereotyping took the place of real knowledge. 'It is in the town and not in the country, that "terra incognita" needs to be written on our social maps' wrote Charles Booth, one of the earliest social-science explorers in London, England (Goheen 1970, 15), while his contemporary, William Booth, founder of the Salvation Army, asked as he confronted the British inner cities: 'As there is a darkest Africa is there not also a darkest England?'(Booth 1890). And from the high densities, the high crime, the desperation of the inner-city poor, emerged an anxious response from the middle class (Ward 1976). So we find a not untypical nineteenth-century view of the inner city expressed in England by Cooke Taylor: 'It is an aggregate of masses, our conception of which clothe themselves in terms which express something portentous and fearful' (Briggs 1965, 59). The substance, and often the rhetoric, of nineteenth-century images of the inner city have continued to the present, most notably in the United States in the polarized separations between racial minorities in the inner city and the middle class in the suburbs (Ley 1974). And behind the images survive realities of inequality. A celebrated map of infant mortality rates in Detroit indicates a four-fold variation between the inner city and the suburbs; inner-city rates are those of the Third World, while suburban rates reach the healthy standards of northern Europe (Bunge and Bordessa 1975).

To what extent do we find reflections of this tenacious image of the inner city as a spoiled identity in Canada? There are similar allusions in nineteenth- and early twentieth-century accounts of such inner-city districts as the immigrant North End of Winnipeg, Toronto's notorious Ward area, the poor working-class districts of Montreal, or the racial ghettos of Vancouver and Halifax. Inner-city conditions in Britain and the United States were well known in Canada—indeed, early in the twentieth century many immigrants were refugees from these hostile environments—and the writings of the Booths in London, and Riis (1971 [1890]) in New York, amongst others, were familiar to Canadian readers (Allen 1972). Tabloids in Canadian cities sensationalized conditions in the inner city and provided a regular reinforcement of an image of poverty and pathology. Rapid urban growth, particularly in the 1901–11 decade, and the arrival of immigrants from a plethora of sources seemed to be imitating earlier American experience. As Superintendent of All Peoples' Mission in Winnipeg, J.S. Woodsworth observed and reflected upon the impact of this rapid and largely unregulated growth, and found much he could recognize from Upton Sinclair's chronicle of the evils of the poor in Chicago in *The Jungle* (Woodsworth 1972 [1911], 70). His own Mission visitors were reporting similar conditions in Winnipeg:

> Shack—one room and a lean-to. Furniture—two beds, a bunk, stove, bench, two chairs, table, barrel of sauerkraut. Everything very dirty. Two families lived here. Women were dirty, unkempt, bare-footed, half-clothed. Children wore only print-slips ... The supper was on the table—a bowl of warmed-over potatoes for each person, part of a loaf of brown bread, a bottle of beer.

Montreal was the largest city in Canada with close to half a million inhabitants by 1911, and labour conflict, municipal corruption, and poverty conditions led a businessman, Herbert Ames, to embark on a social survey, and, like Woodsworth, launch a reform campaign (Ames 1972[1897]). Following its earlier history as a mercantile centre, exporting

Figure 13.2
Residential Location of Grand Trunk Railway Shop Machinists, Montreal, 1901

Places of Residence

▲   Anglophones
△   Francophones
○   Others

Mount Royal

Saint Lawrence River

Grand Trunk Railway Shops

Source: Hoskins, 1987.

staple products to Britain, Montreal emerged in the second half of the nineteenth century as a major water- and rail-based industrial centre. By 1881, 70 per cent of Montreal workers were employed in factories with work forces of over one hundred. Rapid industrialization was associated with rapid urbanization, and the city's population very nearly doubled in the 1850s and almost increased five-fold from 1852 to 1901 (Hanna 1986). Factory hands flooded the city from the francophone hinterland, from Britain, and from Ireland. Excess labour during much of the period kept wages down and generated social tension. Housing demand and marginal wages increased densities and decreased housing quality; the high level of working-class home-ownership existing in the 1840s was speedily reduced. Spatial sorting of residential districts occurred, of which the most striking was the social precipice in the city's west end (setting apart opulent Westmount and working-class St-Henri), strongly correlated with elevation above and below an escarpment.

As elsewhere, working-class districts were juxtaposed with local factories, and residential patterns overall were strongly influenced by the location of the place of work. Different districts had not only a distinctive class character, but also an ethnic and occupational emphasis. For example, one of the largest employers in the city was the repair and manufacturing shops of the Grand Trunk Railway in Point Saint Charles, with a work-force of between two thousand and three thousand during the first two decades of this century (Hoskins 1987). Some 90 per cent of this large work-force lived within a walking distance of less than two miles from the shops in 1902. The distribution of machinists, one of the better-paid trades, dominated by anglophones, showed a tight clustering around their work place (Figure 13.2), which created a significant bonding between home and work, and contributed towards a community resonating with the culture and landscape of what Ames called the real industrial class.

In 1900, the machinists were part of the labour aristocracy among the 38,000 people who comprised the city below the hill in the west end of Montreal. Their monthly average wage of $47.80 in 1902 compared favourably with $8.25, estimated by Ames to be the mean weekly income of local male wage-earners a few years earlier. Over 10 per cent of families fell below Ames' threshold of $5.00 a week, which to him defined the presence of poverty, and a further 25 per cent experienced unsteady work and irregular incomes. The indicators of disadvantage were enumerated: over 50 per cent of families had that 'insanitary abomination', an outdoor pit-privy, and with evident disfavour he reported the presence of one liquor store for every forty-five families. But the decisive statistic, which integrated all others, was the death rate. The figure for Montreal exceeded that even of New York and London; indeed, infant mortality at 293 per thousand births in 1859 was considerably in excess of the level in New York (Olson *et al*. 1987). Ames estimated that the overall death rate below the hill was 70 per cent higher than that of the middle-class district to the north.

One should not over-simplify the spatial differentiation that existed within the working-class. Not all of the inner city consisted of poorer households, nor were all poorer households inner-city residents—significant working-class suburbanization existed in Montreal (Lewis 1985) and Vancouver (Holdsworth 1979). But a combination of working-class households, environmental degradation, and poverty converged upon the inner city to create the popular stereotype of the slum behind the industrial waterfront and around the railyards of Canada's cities. Another variable, ethnic and racial status, compounded the difference between, and ignorance of, the inner city by the middle class; an ignorance assailed by Woodsworth and Ames, like the British and American reformers before them. Whether the outgroup was the Irish Catholics of Griffintown in Montreal, the Jews of Spadina in Toronto (Hiebert 1987), or the Chinese in Vancouver, the presence of this exotic population added to the strange and menacing image of the inner-city slum. Race and place were bound together in a value-laden perception. In the early twentieth century, the idea of Vancouver's Chinatown as a place of stigma perniciously led to a widely publicized harassment of the district by public officials, a practice that simply confirmed its unsavoury status, its otherness, for the population at large (Anderson 1987; 1988).

Popular stereotypes of the inner-city slums were compounded by the emergent social sciences. British and American reformers, as they seized upon the cultural and economic difference of the slums, aided the mental construction of a place apart, with its own and inherent culture of poverty (Ward 1984). Canadian reformers like Ames and Woodsworth drew heavily upon British and American authors and reached similar conclusions (Rutherford 1972). Their perceptions were immensely fortified by the inter-war social scientists of the Chicago School, for long the dominant tradition of urban sociology in North America. As the Chicago sociologists overlaid maps of social indicators in American cities, it seemed that whichever variable they selected, be it delinquency, crime, family breakdown, poverty, or mental illness, the maps all showed high levels of pathology in the inner city. The inner city seemed to them to be *inherently* pathological, characterized by social disorganization. Moreover, their analysis cast this mantle over broad areas; the slum appeared to be the natural condition of the whole inner city.

This image has proven extraordinarily tenacious, and provided a substantial motivation to the urban renewal and slum clearance programs in Canada and other Western nations in the post-war period. In city after city, the presence of old housing and high densities were sufficient condition to warrant the arrival of the federal bulldozer and the onset of the renewal process. But slowly a new perception of the inner city began to form. In the early 1960s, two important American social planners, Jane Jacobs (1961) and Herbert Gans (1962a), published ethnographic accounts of the inner city that severely challenged the dominant wisdom. Age and density, they showed, could be an asset rather than a disadvantage, sheltering a community where tight social networks and local institutions sustained a supportive social milieu not equalled in the frequently brutal landscapes of urban renewal. By the early 1970s, Jacobs had moved to Toronto and presented her optimism for the Canadian inner city in different media, including a film commissioned by the National Film Board (Jacobs 1971). Old buildings, social and land-use diversity, ethnic neighbourhoods, farmers' markets, pedestrian travel and public transportation, human-scale living environments, urban parks and waterfronts—Jacobs' broad vision celebrated exuberance, the cosmopolitan character of the inner city. It was opposed to the blandness of the freeway, the high-rise city of the renewal planner, or indeed the conformity of the distant suburban tract home.

The sometimes romantic vision of cosmopolitan vitality in the inner city has proven attractive to a significant minority of the professional middle class in metropolitan Canada since 1970. City living has regained the cachet it has not enjoyed since the eighteenth century, at least for the gentrifiers who have transformed the face of many older neighbourhoods

(Ley 1988). Consider the responses of new middle-class townhouse dwellers in the Vancouver inner-city district of Fairview Slopes (Mills 1989, 178):

> We both considered ourselves city people. I think that we like the amenities that cities have to offer, I think we like that sense of taking advantage of what we consider to be urban things . . . in being close to theatres and that kind of city life.

For these boosters of inner city living, it is now the suburb that generates a sense of desperation:

> I hope and pray that if I ever have to move on the basis of some really altered circumstances, I'll still be able to live in the city. I do not want to live in the suburbs, I don't think it would ever suit me . . .

INNER-CITY DIVERSITY

Both the progressive reformers of the early twentieth century and the Chicago sociologists who followed them erred in their perception of the inner city. Their portrayal of social disorganization was too one-sided, and it remained for a later generation to identify the social order that existed even in slum neighbourhoods (Suttles 1968). Moreover, a second error had been perpetrated in generalizing the conditions of the slum to the entire inner city. The truth is that central-city neighbourhoods display considerable diversity. One American account suggested five types of dwellers and districts in the inner city (Gans 1962b): areas of upper-class cosmopolitans, young singles, coherent ethnic communities, the deprived, and the trapped and downwardly mobile.

A thoughtful classification of inner-city districts in Canada recognizes this diversity (Table 13.3). Areas are categorized according to the dominant processes of change that are identifiable. As a result, neighbourhoods with different social characteristics may find themselves in the same category. While other classifications could be upheld, this process-driven typology provides a useful vehicle for discussing the broad spectrum of neighbourhoods that comprise the inner city. Four processes are identified: decline, stability, revitalization, and massive redevelopment.

Districts in Decline
In these districts, physical deterioration of the housing stock is associated with population loss, poverty, and social problems among the population. Property values increase slowly, and may even decline; residents are primarily tenants and turnover may be rapid. This set of traits characterizes areas that in the United States have reached the ultimate stage of deterioration—widespread housing abandonment (Dear 1976). This condition, which covers broad areas of such districts as the Bronx in New York and North Philadelphia, is unusual in Canadian cities. Where examples occur,

Table 13.3
Dimensions of the Four Inner-City Types

	Decline	Stability	Revitalization	Massive redevelopment
Population	Continuing loss of population	No significant losses or gains	Little change	Gain in population
Socio-economic status	Decreasing	Stable	Increasing	Increasing
Family status	Increasing proportion of non-family units & elderly	Maintenance of population mix	Maintenance of population mix	Loss of families, gain of singles
Ethnicity	Varies: can be influx of deprived ethnic group or breaking-down of traditional community	Sometimes strong ethnic community	Sometimes loss of ethnic groups	Seldom important
Community organizations	Poorly organized, unstable	Varies	Increasingly well organized	Usually unorganized
Physical conditions	Worsening	Stable	Improving	Improved housing, possible environment problems
Housing/land costs	Increasing much less than metro average	Increasing at same rate as metro average	Increasing more rapidly than metro average	Increasing more rapidly than metro average
Tenure	Increasing tenancy	Varies, but often high ownership	Little change	Tenancy
Non-residential functions	Loss of commercial-industrial functions with no replacement	Maintaining a mix of functions	Maintaining a mix of functions	Losing some commercial functions, but gaining others
Pressure for re-development	Low	Low	Strong, but controlled	High

Source: McLemore, Aass, Keilhofer (1975).

such as parts of the North Ends of Winnipeg and Halifax, Saint-Henri and Point Saint Charles in Montreal, or the Lower Ward of Toronto in the 1960s (Mann 1970), they are found in former working-class neighbourhoods where poor housing and the collapse of the local industrial economy has contributed to low levels of demand and property disinvestment. Often this is a transitional stage to a new round of development. For example, after decline in the 1970s Saint-Henri, especially zones adjacent to the Lachine Canal, experienced considerable apartment redevelopment and some warehouse conversion in the 1980s.

While there is certainly urban poverty in Canada, poverty areas are less concentrated and visible than in the United States. Elements of decline most commonly occur in scattered pockets coinciding with the location of particular poverty groups. A feature of most cities is skid row, an old district dominated by lodging houses and residential hotels and with an entourage of bars, soup kitchens, missions, and pawn shops serving a single-male population, including resident elderly and handicapped men and younger, more transient males. Skid row, commonly located near the bus and/or train station, is a district of discard and disinvestment.

In Vancouver, two railway stations and the bus station bound skid row on the south and west; in 1965, it included the city's major concentration of residential hotels, over 40 cheap cafés, 26 beer parlours, 2 liquor stores and 11 Christian missions. In the late 1980s, the district still contained 80 per cent of the city's premises with a full liquor licence. In Toronto, skid row is concentrated between Queen Street and Dundas Street, just east of the CBD. Its population consists of elderly men primarily from Atlantic Canada, low-income regions of Ontario and Quebec, and Indian reserves (Whitney 1970). Urban centres in the western provinces have substantial numbers of natives living around skid row, at least on a seasonal basis; in Winnipeg, surveys suggest a figure of up to 60 per cent (Rowley 1978). In the Winnipeg case unemployment is high, around 85 per cent, and may be associated with heavy drinking; over 70 per cent of men interviewed had received treatment at a detoxification centre.

Skid row is a district heavily supported by state-run social services and voluntary groups; almost forty social-service agencies operate in Vancouver's skid row, and proximity to these services offers a strong locational tie for residents. In Vancouver (unlike Winnipeg) the largest portion of the population consists of stable, elderly men without drinking problems, who have lived in rooms for some years. In addition, the district's coherence is strengthened by a strong neighbourhood association, which has challenged the permissiveness typical of skid row, improved social services, enforced building codes, controlled excesses at liquor outlets, and sponsored the construction of a number of non-profit housing projects (Ley 1990).

Other pockets of poverty and decline in the inner city are associated with a more dispersed rooming- and lodging-house population in the zone of housing conversions (where single-family homes have been subdivided into apartments or transformed into rooming houses). This population includes inhabitants of group homes for deinstitutionalised psychiatric patients and other community-based facilities. This is a group at considerable risk, who comprise perhaps a third of the nation's homeless population, estimated in 1986 to fall between 130,000 and 250,000 (Dear and Wolch in press). Due to the availability of suitable housing, proximity to necessary services, and the presence or absence of exclusionary zoning, group homes are frequently concentrated in specific inner-city districts. The Toronto district of South Parkdale contains no fewer that forty-nine group homes (more than a quarter of the City's total) which overwhelmingly serve psychiatric patients (Joseph and Hall 1985). Such a concentration of poor and handicapped residents in ageing lodging houses provides a local context for neighbourhood decline, as private reinvestment is unlikely to occur in a locale with a perceived stigma.

Poverty districts are associated with other marginalized populations, including such historically persistent communities as the racial and ethnic minorities of Vancouver's Chinatown or the North Ends of Winnipeg and Halifax. As we shall note later, poverty is also concentrated around the massive public housing projects of the 1950s and 1960s. It is linked as well to regional economies, for the structural unemployment of Atlantic Canada and parts of Quebec is manifested in a higher than average incidence of urban poverty. Montreal, Trois Rivières, Quebec City and, above all, Saint John, are all CMAs with twice as many census tracts as the national average showing extreme scores on an impoverishment factor (Davies and Murdie in press).

The visibility of poverty in urban Canada is reduced because the various indicators of poverty do not necessarily overlap in the same district (Broadway 1989). For example, a cause of poverty in the cities mentioned above is the presence of a large proportion of female-headed families. This cause, however, showed only a modest correlation with other poverty indicators such as male unemployment and the presence of the elderly. But this generalization conceals considerable local variation. In CMAs that have experienced slow growth and the erosion of a traditional industrial base without significant downtown office development, the inner city has received limited reinvestment pressure, and persists as the home of a much broader grouping of poor households. In Winnipeg, Regina, and Saint John, for example (but not in Vancouver, Toronto, or Halifax), disproportionate and intensifying concentrations of the unemployed, the elderly, and female single-parent households all coexist in the same inner-city districts (Broadway 1990). Indeed, in Winnipeg's North End, which has some of the most extreme scores on impoverishment in urban Canada (Davies and Murdie in press), the geographical coincidence of poverty, female single-parent families, and low educational attainment in neighbourhoods with a high native population, together define a state of multiple deprivation that approximates the conditions identified by the under-class theorists in the United States (Willems-Braun 1989). In American cities, it has been suggested that persistent and geographically overlapping patterns of multiple deprivation may produce local cultures which encourage an intergenerational transmission of poverty.

Districts of Stability
In contrast are inner-city districts where the stability of the urban landscape suggests that the pressures for change are slight. Such areas have both a stable population and stable socio-economic status, with little land inflation and pressures for redevelopment; home-ownership rates may

well be high, and property is well maintained. The presence of a cohesive social order is indicated by the objective and symbolic indicators of community, such as strong voluntary organizations and a well-defined sense of place.

Districts such as these have attracted the title of the 'urban village', implying the existence of strong neighbourhood social networks, a complete range of local social institutions, and a tradition of mutual aid. The concept of the urban village emerged from an ethnographic study of Italians in the West End of Boston (Gans 1962a). Rather than being a slum, which the age of the district and its high densities had suggested, the West End instead had a strong sense of local community. Its social basis was a result of the chain migration that had brought immigrants of comparable socio-economic status through kin networks to the same district in the New World. There is a significant voluntary component to the map of ethnic segregation in Canadian cities, though of course these communities have unfolded within the context of (usually) below-average economic status. Ethnic segregation has not always been voluntary. Earlier in the twentieth century, racial discrimination played an important role in the residential distribution of Jewish and Asian immigrants (Anderson 1988).

The high levels of immigrant home-ownership contribute to a well-maintained housing stock, with substantial home improvement, or incumbent upgrading, completed most often by family and friends. In Vancouver's Grandview-Woodlands neighbourhood, a working-class area with a well-defined Italian presence, interviews revealed a marked sense of pride for one's home and considerable satisfaction with the upkeep practised by neighbours; indeed, without the assistance of government grants, over 90 per cent of interviewees had made major repairs in the previous five years (Mercer and Phillips 1981). The national policy of multiculturalism has encouraged such stable ethnic communities to celebrate further their identity and pride in the built environment. To the earlier ethnic icons of the parish church, the corner store, and the pool hall, some groups have added ethnic cultural centres and annual street festivals, which consolidate and celebrate a multiple identity. National backgrounds are no longer concealed. Along the main business thoroughfare of Grandview-Woodlands, an earlier ethnic modesty has given way to the amplification of ethnic symbols such as brightly-coloured shop awnings, frequently with the green, white, and red motif of the Italian flag, distinctive signs, and Mediterranean design elements (Jackson 1984).

The mutuality of identity and landscape, strengthened by the legitimating power of multiculturalism, has in some instances heightened the sense of ethnic proprietorship of neighbourhoods. This collective view of ethnic 'turf', aided by the icons of present and past cultural difference, may well be recognized by municipal councils and written into zoning and other protective by-laws (Anderson 1988). As such, ethnic interests may be favoured in land-use conflicts, a far cry from the typical experience until the late 1960s. Where older and less inclusive administrative styles persisted, however, ethnic communities continued to have a precarious status before more powerful interests; not untypical was the demolition of much of Montreal's Chinatown in the 1970s to make way for a large complex of government offices.

In recent decades, examples of stable working-class communities of British origin in the inner city have been rare (but see Crysdale 1970; Lorimer and Phillips 1971). Until the 1980s, the bastions of stable British-origin groups in the inner city have been the upper middle-class and elite districts, close to downtown, which are such a persistent feature of the Canadian city (Ley in press). In the 1970s, close to 70 per cent of Shaughnessy residents claimed British origin. This inner-city district is the wealthiest in Vancouver; it has over 70 per cent home-ownership and, until the mid–1980s, saw little turnover in population. Households were stable; indeed, many adults were living in the district they had grown up in. The landscape of the area advertises its identity; manicured, curving streets, architect-designed homes on large lots, and a supportive institutional cast of prominent Anglican, United, and Lutheran churches, private schools, and exclusive social clubs, with, on the edge of the district, a distinctive concentration of up-market shops, including galleries and specialty home-furnishing stores.

The old, elite neighbourhood is repeated across the country from the Uplands in Victoria to the South End in Halifax, and its landscapes and social groups lend a distinctive image to the Canadian city. With few exceptions, these districts have shown remarkable longevity in the twentieth century. By 1899, the southern half of Rosedale in Toronto was already a substantial elite community, and it has retained this status. In Calgary, the inner district of Mount Royal, developed before 1920 by the Canadian Pacific Railway as an exclusive neighbourhood, has upheld its social cachet. Since 1920, elite districts have expanded but they have rarely been displaced, and their locational stability is remarkable, considering urban growth and redevelopment pressures. The Toronto CMA, for example, grew six-fold from 1921 to 1981, with attendant pressures for residential redevelopment and downtown expansion, yet the inner-most Rosedale tracts have experienced very little decline in social stability.

Such stability has been accomplished through restrictive planning controls (Ley in press). In Westmount, municipal autonomy added political muscle to land-use protection, while Shaughnessy, thwarted in its efforts at political secession early this century, was nonetheless successful in acquiring protective zoning through a special act of the British Columbia legislature. Not unusual was a restrictive covenant, such as the one required of home-owners in Calgary's Mount Royal, whose terms included a prohibition on commercial land uses, minimum lot sizes and house prices, and the requirement that single family dwellings be the exclusive use. In each district, vigilant home-owners' associations oversaw the conformity of the built environment to an elite protocol.

In the acute land pressures of the 1980s, some incremental changes have influenced even elite districts. Modest infill has increased densities, although it has not diminished prices or status. More substantial is an emerging transition in the complexion of the elite population. In West-mount, francophones are replacing the departing anglophone business elite, while in Shaughnessy new Asian wealth, particularly from Hong Kong, is evident. Other in-town elite districts similarly reflect the growing reality of multiculturalism, and the growing diversity of Canada's international relations.

Districts of Revitalization

The inner-city typology identified revitalising districts as a recent phenomenon that involves small areas only (McLemore *et al*. 1975). However, from small beginnings in the 1960s, revitalization has expanded substantially in the 1970s and 1980s. The process involves 'up-filtering', the movement of middle-class households into formerly working-class or lower middle-class districts, in contrast to the 'down-filtering' found in deteriorating districts. The British term *gentrification* is commonly applied to this transition. In its original, and narrow, definition, gentrification described the renovation of older housing stock, such as has occurred in areas like Don Vale (Cabbagetown) in Toronto, Plateau Mont-Royal in Montreal, or New Edinburgh in Ottawa. However, even in these districts, renovation is associated with infill and localized redevelopment. In cities like Vancouver or Victoria, where the building material of older homes is wood rather than brick, condominium redevelopment is more often the form that revitalization takes. Whether the dominant process is renovation or redevelopment, revitalising districts are characterized by often spectacular short-term increases in land and housing costs, modest gains in home-ownership rates, and a well-educated and dominantly childless population of young professional households.

While revitalization is discernible in smaller cities like Kitchener (Bunting 1987), Saskatoon (Phipps 1983) and Halifax (Millward and Davis 1986), it is particularly evident in Canada's major cities. The rate of change quickened appreciably in the 1970s, and during that decade the level of social status gain in the inner city was four times greater than it had been during the 1960s (Ley 1981; 1988). In the five largest CMAs, a net increment of some 60,000 residents with jobs in high status, white-collar occupations occurred in inner-city neighbourhoods during the 1971–81 period. While far larger numbers were added in the rest of the CMA, in relative terms inner-city gains were more substantial, so that by 1981 the inner cities actually contained a greater proportion of these high status workers.

Figure 13.3
Social Status Change in Canadian Cities, 1971–81

a) Halifax

b) Montreal

1 Shaughnessy Village
2 Old Montreal
3 Rue St-Denis
4 Radio Canada
5 Parc Lafontaine

c) Ottawa-Hull

d) Toronto

Note:
Tracts 6 and 9
are also N/R

e) Edmonton

f) Vancouver

Index change by Quintile, 1971–1981

14.9 and more   * CBD peak land value   N/R non residential
10.0 to 14.8
6.2 to 9.9
3.4 to 6.1   0   1 km
3.3 and less   0   1 mile   SOURCE: Ley (1988).

Revitalization does not seek out districts indiscriminately, and in major cities discernible patterns occur. On the maps shown in Figure 13.3, trends in social status change are recorded by quintile; the highest rate of change shows clear tendencies towards concentration, for example, around such high-ranking cores as Don Vale, Toronto (tracts 67, 68 on Figure 13.3d), eastern Centretown, Ottawa (tract 49 on Figure 13.3c), eastern Kitsilano and False Creek-Fairview Slopes, Vancouver (tracts 48 and 49 on Figure 13.3f) and several sites in Montreal and Halifax. A correlation of increases in social status scores from 1971–81 with a range of neighbourhood attributes identifies the typical profile of a gentrifying district during that period (Ley 1988). The best predictor of revitalization was proximity to an existing elite area; in the case of Toronto, for example, six of the seven locations of early gentrification wrapped around the edge of Rosedale and the Annex, which were established higher-status districts. Typically, the process unfolds on the downtown and somewhat downmarket fringes, where down-filtering to rooming houses and cheap apartments was underway, and where, although incomes would be about average for the city, dwelling values and rents would be above average. At the same time a revitalising neighbourhood would have distinctive residential architecture, be near a university and/or major hospital, and be close to parkland and/or accessible waterfront. In 1970, its population would have included a high proportion of small households, including students and the elderly, but with relatively few blue-collar workers or non-English speakers. A number of neighbourhoods undergoing revitalization during the 1970s shared many of these attributes: Kitsilano and Fairview Slopes in Vancouver; the Annex and Don Vale in Toronto; Centretown and Sandy Hill in Ottawa; lower Outremont, Milton-Park, and the St-Denis Corridor in Montreal; and the South End in Halifax.

Particularly where the renovation (rather than redevelopment) of older houses is the dominant process, gentrification commonly takes place in stages (Gale 1980). In the initial stage, existing residents are joined by pre-professionals (students), artists, media groups, and certain other professionals, who are generally liberal or radical in their life-style and politics. This picture describes the character of Kitsilano and Cabbagetown in 1968–72 and Toronto's Queen Street West and Montreal's Rue St-Denis a decade later. These households are attracted by the social and cultural diversity of the inner city and its affordable housing. Careful research in Montreal has pointed out that this cohort is not gender-neutral— professional women play an important role—in particularly the early, but also the later, stages of gentrification (Rose 1984; 1987; Dansereau and Beaudry 1985). While the incomes of early gentrifiers are modest, they help redefine the character of a district, and prepare the way for its commercialization and more substantial transition. As the neighbourhood is discovered, subsequent purchasers buy into an inflating market as the neighbourhood's image changes. Later buyers include wealthier professionals, such as doctors and lawyers, who tend to be more sensitive and protective concerning their investment; the social mix favoured at an earlier stage is now regarded more ambivalently or resisted altogether. At this stage, pioneering professionals shift their focus to other districts, usually nearby, and a spatial diffusion of gentrification may be observed.

In Toronto, for example, escalating prices in Don Vale (tracts 67, 68 in Figure 13.3d) have caused middle-class demand to spill over to Riverdale to the east (tracts 69–71) (Dantas 1988).

The local impacts of gentrification are multi-faceted, and include the transformation of retailing (Tunbridge 1986) and institutions such as schools and churches (Martin 1989). But the most dramatic impact is in the housing market, where in extreme cases prices have doubled in only two years (Don Vale 1979–81; Fairview Slopes 1980–1). There has been a predictable increase in home-ownership, resulting in displacement of tenants from affordable housing (Ley 1981; 1985). Relocation occurs, if possible, nearby, though tenants typically pay higher rents for smaller units. The loss of affordable housing in the inner city has been precipitous. In Vancouver, some 7,500 rental units were demolished between 1973 and 1981, primarily in districts undergoing condominium redevelopment. The Toronto situation is even more serious; 18,000 tenancies were lost in the deconversion of joint owner-tenant properties back to single-family use in the 1976–85 period, while from 1981 to 1986 over 9,000 rental apartments were lost through various forms of upgrading (Howell 1986). Housing at the bottom end of the market, including rooming houses and residential hotels, has been most vulnerable, and though gentrification is not the only factor implicated, it does play a major role. Thus in Ottawa, 40 per cent of the city's rooming-house units disappeared in only three years, from 1976–9. Predictably, 70 per cent of these losses took place in Sandy Hill and Centretown, the wards where gentrification was the most marked.

Areas of Massive Redevelopment

The more subtle landscape changes of gentrification in the 1970s and 1980s were in many ways a reaction against the massive urban redevelopment that took place in a number of inner-city districts in the 1950s and 1960s. In that earlier period housing stock was ageing, while downtown employment growth sustained a lively demand, and permissive zoning maps allowed extensive apartment construction. Simultaneously, the public sector, acting on the basis of its stigmatized perception of urban slums (discussed earlier), was activating a significant slum clearance and urban renewal program across the country.

Massive redevelopment entailed population growth, but in private-sector building, this was accomplished by a changing household composition. In districts like Vancouver's West End or St James Town in Toronto, high-rise rental construction led to a loss of families and their replacement by small one- and two-person households of a somewhat higher social status than those who were displaced. While the housing units were generally of good quality, high densities from a concentration of projects did not enhance cohesive social organization, particularly with rapid tenant turnover. In St James Town, following the creation of the highest density precinct in Canada in the 1960s, the 1971 census showed a population increase of 32 per cent, and that 71 per cent of residents (almost all tenants) had lived in their units less than two years. The impersonality of such transience and massive change permitted social problems to emerge in an unregulated environment, including prostitution in Vancouver's West End and in Oliver (Edmonton).

The location of apartment development, particularly high-rise development, was strongly site-specific. In Toronto, apartments were built in nodes with good access to the CBD, close to environmental amenities, and biased towards higher income sectors (Bourne 1967). This trend was maintained in other cities also, particularly for high-rise development. The West End, adjacent to Stanley Park and the English Bay beaches, had been Vancouver's first elite district, as had Parliament Hill and Oliver in Edmonton, the sites of that city's major concentration of rental high-rise apartments (McCann 1975). Even in smaller cities like Victoria, high rises have been drawn to in-town locations with generous amenity (such as parks, waterfronts, and attractive architectural features); despite above-average rents, waterfront settings show the lowest vacancy rates in the city, while developers have neglected lower-cost (but lower status) sites (Murphy 1973). The distribution of apartments constructed during the 1968–71 building boom in Victoria demonstrates each of the spatial regularities found in larger cities. A third of new units were built within a mile of the main downtown traffic intersection, while outlying concentrations tended to be built on major arteries. A strong bias south of downtown abutted ocean frontage and Beacon Hill Park, while the disproportionate concentration on the sector leading east to Cadboro Bay Road runs through the old, elite, Rockland district and towards the present high-status areas of Oak Bay.

Public sector redevelopment showed a predictably different pattern. While population densities generally rose, there was not necessarily a decline in the proportion of family households. Nor was there an increase in socio-economic status. High levels of unemployment and poverty in concentrated locations rarely led to a positive social environment. Government-funded slum clearance was empowered in the National Housing Act of 1944, and its first project was the clearance and redevelopment of Regent Park North, east of downtown Toronto (Moore and Smith in press). The 1,300, mainly medium-density units that were built were joined ten years later by more than 700 additional units in row houses, low-rise apartments, and five high-rise projects in Regent Park South. The result is a massive and demoralizing concentration of poverty, an outcome repeated in the vast Jeanne Mance project in Montreal, the North End of Halifax, the Raymur project in Vancouver, and elsewhere. Better than most of these projects is Lawrence Heights, a public-housing complex of 2,500 people constructed in a middle-class district of North York, just outside the City of Toronto, in 1957. A 1970 survey showed that most of the men in this family-oriented environment were labourers and most of the women were home-makers (Delegran 1970). This was a population of the working poor, and family units were more stable than in many public housing projects; 75 per cent of families had both parents present. As a physical environment it was satisfactory, but there were many complaints concerning the social environment, particularly for raising children. The stigma attached to the project by outsiders was especially debilitating.

The scale of urban renewal involved massive dislocation of existing land uses and residents. In Montreal, some 15,000 inner-city dwellings were demolished by the city from the mid–1950s to the mid–1960s. Relocation problems were often severe, and there was considerable reluctance to move. Some of these difficulties were well-illustrated by the Rose-Blanshard renewal project in Victoria, which displaced 157 poor households (Robertson 1973). The city's relocation officer identified these difficulties in correspondence with city hall in the autumn of 1967. Among the tenants, he found 'many problem family units . . . the matter of relocating these persons will present a most formidable difficulty'. But there were also obstacles to be faced in purchasing from some owners (Robertson 1973, 55):

> With regard to the holdout realty owners still on the site, the majority of these are occupants who will not sell until they are offered sufficient money to be able to purchase comparable accommodation elsewhere. They cannot do this with the sums of money I am authorized now to pay them. This group of owners are [sic] unlikely to be intimidated by any means the Urban Renewal Authority can employ . . .

The high-handed hint of intimidation was not unusual in relations between renewal officials and the poor. A renewal document published by the City of Vancouver in 1956 observed that the Chinese residential quarter to the east of Main Street was currently significant only to the people who lived there (Anderson 1988). This was an insufficient reason for its survival, and large areas were bulldozed in an urban renewal program that displaced 3,300 residents. The insensitivity of slum clearance and the community mobilization it engendered, together with the social and design failure of massive renewal housing projects led eventually to the suspension of these schemes. As is reported in Chapter 14, in 1969 a federal task force reported sternly on the public-housing projects that were a common outcome of urban renewal, calling them 'ghettos of the poor' and places of 'stigma' and 'alienation'. During the 1970s, federal policy shifted decisively away from large-scale clearance and rebuilding to more incremental policies of housing rehabilitation and neighbourhood enhancement; whereas in 1970 all federal monies were committed to renewal, by 1979 the ratio of rehabilitation and improvement funds to renewal was fifty to one.

This is not to say that publicly-inspired residential redevelopment did not occur in the inner city in the 1970s and 1980s. Large schemes, housing hundreds or even thousands of residents, were undertaken in a number of cities, including Toronto (St Lawrence, Harbourfront), Vancouver (False Creek South) and Ottawa (LeBreton Flats). But there were significant departures from the 1950s and 1960s: densities were considerably lower, there was a social mixing of income groups, design standards were much higher, and, most important, the construction was on former industrial land, which obviated the need for resident displacement (Hulchanski 1984; Ley 1987).

THE INNER CITY: EXPLAINING A CHAOTIC CONCEPT

We have seen that the inner city becomes more diffuse as an object of study as we approach it empirically. There are no unequivocal grounds for delimiting it as a geographical region, and while we may set out objective or subjective indicators to establish a profile, both a statistical and a perceptual overview obscure important internal diversity between districts, and also overlook the dynamic elements of sometimes rapid urban change. Moreover, a variety of transitional processes occur within the same city. Over a few square kilometres in inner Halifax, decline, stability, incumbent upgrading, and gentrification have been identified as present simultaneously in the single-family housing stock. Nor is there any necessary relationship between household change and change in the housing stock; renovation, for example, occurs both in gentrifying and non-gentrifying districts.

There are nonetheless brave souls who have sought to contain this diversity within a single explanatory account. The Chicago School referred to such ecological processes as invasion and succession to account for the concentration of social groups within 'natural areas' of the city. The principal sorting process was the competitive bidding of different residents for urban land. This perspective of consumer sovereignty characterized the neoclassical models of urban land economics, which explained the inner-city landscape in terms of a set of preference curves. But both the Chicago School and the neoclassical theorists had a simple view of the inner city as consisting of undifferentiated poorer residents living at high densities, while the middle class opted for more space in the suburbs. In contrast, a more recent marxist interpretation emphasizes supply rather than demand functions. Accounts of the inner city are bound to relations between the basic categories of capital and labour and the unequal power each holds; consumer sovereignty is devalued before the agency of capital to mould landscapes according to its own purposes.

Other explanations resist the dominantly, or even exclusively, economic emphasis of these perspectives. It is argued that the market-place does not comprise the only dimension along which urban land is valued. How can one account for the location of Stanley Park in Vancouver on potentially the most desired residential setting in the city, without referring to more plural values including amenity, recreation, and a broader public interest? Or how to explain the survival of Shaughnessy as an in-town elite area, with aberrant low densities, without an understanding of the symbolic power of this old elite district? The symbolic value of Shaughnessy has been translated into vigorous politics of neighbourhood defence, and the same politics of turf has been exercised in poorer districts, with varying results. Urban politics implicates legal as well as political process, and introduces a set of public and private institutions (the state, the courts, financial institutions, land development corporations) which, with residents, together engage in a set of negotiations, the outcome of which is an often unpredictable urban landscape (Ley 1983).

Explanatory accounts of inner-city neighbourhoods, then, recognize both the diversity of places, and the range of processes that act upon them. An assessment of reasons for inner-city decline identified nine more or less competing explanations (Table 13.4). A convincing case could be made for the salience of any of these explanations, while at different periods they have risen or fallen in importance. Moreover, there is a geographic specificity to the incidence of these processes; regionally, for example, we cannot expect cities to share a common age or economic structure; nationally, the explanations require certain institutional and inter-group relationships which are not constant, not even between Canada and the United States (see Chapter 3). We should expect inner-city decline at a certain period in a particular place to be contingent on the intersection of a range of processes, some local, some national, some international.

Theoretical explanations are not necessarily geographically portable; an attempt to assess recent inner-city trends in Canada using primarily American literature, which discusses centrifugal (suburbanization) versus

Table 13.4
A Typology of Explanations of Inner-City Decline

Explanation	Dominant Process(es)
Natural evolution	Urban growth, ecological succession, down-filtering
Preference structure	Middle-class flight to the suburbs
Obsolescence	Ageing of built environment and social infrastructure
Unintended effects of public policy	Suburban subsidies, including construction of freeways and aids to new single-family home-ownership
Exploitation (1)	City manipulated by more powerful suburbs
Exploitation (2)	Institutional exploitation: redlining by financial institutions; tax concessions; suburbanization of factories
Structural change	Deindustrialization and economic decline
Fiscal crisis	Inequitable tax burden; high welfare, social, and infrastructure costs
Conflict	Racial and class polarization

SOURCE: Adapted from Bourne (1982).

centripetal (inner-city revitalization) processes, concluded that these competing models lose much of their explanatory power when faced with the Canadian city as an object of study (Filion 1987). A related study came to the same conclusion: that great regional and intra-urban diversity remains. No one model of city structure is sufficient to capture this diversity (Bourne 1987). A statistical comparison of four different explanations of inner-city revitalization concluded that each of them was of some relevance (Ley 1986).

THE INNER CITY IN SOCIETAL CONTEXT

The relative failure of any individual account to provide an adequate explanation of the inner city suggests the wisdom of an integrated perspective, while the fact that the profile of the inner city is geographically and historically contingent (that is, influenced by specific geographical and historical contexts) indicates the necessity for fully contextual interpretation. Integration—which concerns features common to all inner cities—and contextualization—which focuses on historical and locational particularities—together prescribe a distinctive regional geography of the Canadian inner city.

What would that regional geography look like? (see also Bunting and Filion 1988). It would recognize at first the nineteenth-century origins of the inner city in a rapidly industrializing and urbanizing society. Over this period the inner city was affected by a domination of industrial land, limited mass transit, down-filtering of housing to workers wishing to live close to work, regular inflows of immigrants, and inadequate housing and environmental standards.

The elite withdrew a mile or two from these conditions, by putting down roots in neighbourhoods such as Shaughnessy or Rosedale or, taking advantage of elevation, in the city above the hill in Montreal. These high-status neighbourhoods were quickly leapfrogged by the middle class and even the respectable working class in the new territory opened up by the electric streetcar. Mass production of the motor car had, by the 1920s, reduced still further the tyranny of distance from work for a significant segment of the work-force. Following the Progressive era of municipal reform in the early decades of this century, a more active local state, with the tool of zoning, began the regulation of urban land use, and for privileged districts provided the means for ensuring protection against undesirable change. But urban boosterism—a commitment to unrestricted urban growth—remained the dominant ethos, and over much of the city, pro-development decisions came naturally to politicians who were also businessmen and who shared a common growth ideology.

In the post-war era, the societal contexts impacting the inner city in Canada became more complex. Both the suburbanization and the closure of old industries in the zone in transition around downtown was part of a restructuring of the central-city economy. The other element was the explosive growth of the service sector, and (in the terminology of central place theory, see Chapter 7) the development of the CBD as the highest-order centre in the regional and national space-economy, the preferred location of the corporate complex of head offices and producer services, including finance and business services. Equally important was the burgeoning public sector and related non-profit professions, notably teaching and health care. These employment trends have been faithfully translated into the downtown office boom, which first became discernible in the late 1960s; since then a tripling of downtown office space in major cities is testimony to the employment growth.

The occupational profile of the (highly diverse) service sector raises further issues. First, about a quarter of its jobs are in well-paying managerial, professional, and related fields, the so-called quaternary sector. Second, in its vast clerical, secretarial, and retailing branches, the service economy offers unprecedented openings that have been filled largely by women; women are also rapidly entering the quaternary occupations. These labour market changes are intimately bound up with the recent transition in the inner-city housing market. Blue-collar workers were already a disappearing minority in many inner-city neighbourhoods by 1970; it was often groups outside the labour market, including students and the elderly, who were displaced by gentrification, together with poorer segments of the service class. In six of Canada's major cities, some 60,000 residents with quaternary occupations were added in inner-city neighbourhoods between 1971 and 1981 (Figure 13.3); some 160,000 residents with non-quaternary occupations moved out. The in-migrants to the inner city had the financial freedom to move to the suburbs, as did many of their contemporaries, but chose not to. Non-traditional family relations have been an important element in a positive valuing of the gentrified inner city (Mills 1989). It is close to work and to downtown adult attractions accessible to a childless household with discretionary income and with time freed from home maintenance and child-rearing.

This new middle class of professional and administrative workers has provided the key social group in the restructuring of parts of Canadian inner cities in the past twenty years. Through infill housing it has consolidated the status of the old elite districts, and from these bastions its more adventurous and non-conformist members have contributed to ever-advancing waves of residential renovation and redevelopment. As well as the housing stock, neighbourhood social infrastructure has been transformed; churches, schools, and thrift shops are neglected, to be replaced by leisure and fitness centres, pubs and restaurants, and shops oriented to purchasers with an eye for specialized and designer products.

The transformed retail landscapes of Spring Garden Road in Halifax, Rue St-Denis or Ste-Catherine in Montreal, Yorkville or Harbourfront in Toronto, and Granville Island or Fourth Avenue in Vancouver are all

Figure 13.4
Sites of Land Use Conflict, City of Vancouver, 1973–1975

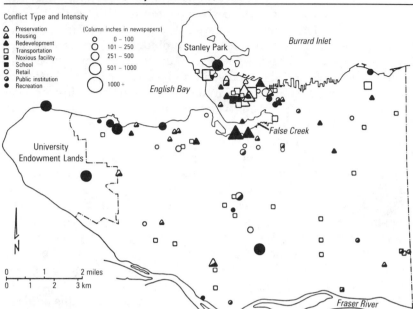

Conflict Type and Intensity

△ Preservation	(Column inches in newspapers)
▲ Housing	○ 0 – 100
▲ Redevelopment	○ 101 – 250
□ Transportation	○ 251 – 500
▣ Noxious facility	○ 501 – 1000
■ School	
○ Retail	○ 1000 +
◑ Public institution	
● Recreation	

SOURCE: Ley and Mercer, 1980.

part of a broader transition towards the construction of landscapes of consumption in the inner city. In Toronto, a concentrated leisure and recreational landscape runs continuously from Ontario Place and Exhibition Park through the public facilities of Harbourfront and the Toronto Islands' park, to the new Skydome stadium, the CN Tower, and Roy Thomson Hall. New parks, new museums, refurbished theatres, concert halls and historic districts, the cycle of annual festivals and the periodic infusion of an Expo, the Olympics, or Commonwealth Games—all have transformed parts of the inner city into a consumption cornucopia (Ley 1980; 1987). And in these landscapes, which proclaim so eloquently the power of the pleasure principle, the state is fully implicated. In the early 1980s, Vancouver's planning director declared with considerable awe that major inner-city projects presented to senior governments for funding—a trade and convention centre, a domed stadium, a light rapid transit line, an international exposition, and several smaller projects—bore a combined price tag of almost $2 billion. A decade later all have been built. Arguably, the state is the most powerful single actor in the construction of the contemporary inner city.

At the municipal scale, civic politics underwent considerable change in the early 1970s in a number of major cities. The political power of the new middle class was expressed in their defence of neighbourhoods before the encroachment of freeways and high-density redevelopment. Local

Table 13.5
Variations in Household Income, Toronto CMA, 1986

Municipality	Population 1986 ('000s)	Household Income ($) Average	Household Income ($) Median	Per cent Low-Income Families[1]	Index of Income Disparity[2]
Toronto CMA	3427	43,025	36,890	10.6	16.6
Older central municipalities					
City of Toronto	612	39,118	29,177	16.5	34.1
East York	101	34,828	29,970	11.8	16.2
York	135	32,418	27,799	15.6	16.6
Older suburbs					
Etobicoke	303	44,058	37,589	9.6	17.2
North York	556	43,258	34,797	12.9	24.3
Scarborough	485	41,010	37,840	11.7	8.4
Newer suburbs (population over 40,000)					
Oakville	87	53,205	47,479	4.7	12.0
Mississauga	374	46,781	42,204	7.5	10.8
Brampton	188	45,289	43,196	6.5	4.8
Vaughan	65	55,060	48,329	6.1	13.9
Richmond Hill	47	49,986	44,258	5.2	12.9
Markham	115	60,407	52,625	4.3	14.8
Pickering	49	50,824	48,306	5.9	5.2

[1]Using Statistics Canada's definition of the minimum income needed to sustain a family.

[2]An index of income skewness (I), where $I = \dfrac{(Average - median\ income)}{Median\ Income} \times 100$

SOURCE: Bourne (1990), unpublished table.

councils rezoned inner-city districts to lower densities, and senior government responded by abandoning urban renewal for policies of neighbourhood conservation and rehabilitation. Inner-city districts faced the brunt of land-use change; here locational conflict was most acute (Figure 13.4). Pro-development councils were challenged, and urban politics and land-use decision-making entered a more plural and combative phase.

Reform politics in the cities contained a significant environmental and social justice edge, but in the 1980s these gains have often been eroded as the federal and most provincial governments have withdrawn from their earlier involvement. The result is a growing polarization in the inner city, when one compares the new middle class and its consumption landscapes with the less visible poverty of close to 20 per cent of the families in the central city. The 1986 census showed that 19.4 per cent of families in the City of Vancouver fell below the poverty line established by Statistics Canada, almost one-third above the metropolitan average. Further analysis of the data for the Toronto CMA (Table 13.5) also reveals the same above-average incidence of low-income families in the City of Toronto. Moreover, we can derive a rough measure of economic disparity by comparing mean and median incomes. The disparity index in Table 13.5

reveals that income variation is modest in the new suburbs, is higher in the older municipalities, and reaches by far its highest level in the City of Toronto itself.

So the contemporary Canadian inner city includes a confusing mix of wealth and poverty: extremes of half-a-million dollar condominiums and renovated houses against the homelessness of at least 130,000 urban Canadians, perhaps a third of them mental patients released from institutions by cost-cutting governments. Another growing and vulnerable homeless subculture are teenage runaways; a Winnipeg study revealed that half of them had suffered sexual abuse at home, while a third had contracted a sexually transmitted disease (IUS 1990). For the poor, the ongoing gentrification of the inner city is translated into acute problems of affordability, with (as discussed earlier) the severe contraction of housing at the bottom end of the market.

Above the homeless on the housing ladder is a much larger group of poverty families, including single parents, the unemployed, the elderly, and recent immigrants, including refugees. Within (but not limited to) this group in the late 1980s is reported an alarming incidence of social pathology including child abuse, drug addiction, prostitution, and juvenile delinquency. While media accounts are invariably sensationalized, qualitative social changes are occurring in phase with the free enterprise spirit of the times. Toronto and Vancouver have their much publicised drug epidemics linking affluent and poor buyers and sellers, while for the first time teenage gangs have become a major problem among disadvantaged groups (*Maclean's* 1989). Reviewing the immigrant districts of the Lower East Side in New York in the 1880s, Jacob Riis observed that 'The gang is a distemper of the slums; a friend come to tell us that something has gone amiss in our social life' (cited in Thrasher 1963, 342). The escalating gang activity in Canadian inner cities a century later conveys the same message, as the social polarization accompanying a less regulated economy bears the same bitter harvest.

NOTES

1. These early twentieth-century students of the city are generally referred to as human ecologists. Most of them were associated with the University of Chicago under the tutelage of Robert Park. For further detail on this early work see: Hartshorn 1980; Ley 1983; Michelson 1976; Theodorson 1961.

FURTHER READING

ANDERSON, K. 1988 'Cultural Hegemony and the Race-definition Process in Chinatown, Vancouver: 1880–1980', *Society and Space* 6, 27–149

BOURNE, L. 1982 'The Inner City' in C. Christian and R. Harper eds *Modern Metropolitan Systems* (Columbus, Ohio: Charles Merrill)

BUNTING, T. and FILION, P. eds 1988 *The Changing Canadian Inner City* (Waterloo, Ont.: University of Waterloo, Department of Geography, Publication Series No. 31)

DANSEREAU, F. 1988 'Les transformations de l'habitat et des quartiers centraux: singularités et contrastes des villes canadiennes', *Les Cahiers de Recherche Sociologique* 6, 95–118

DEAR, M. and WOLCH, J. (in press) 'Homelessness in Canada' in L. Bourne and D. Ley eds *The Social Geography of — Canadian Cities* (Montreal: McGill-Queen's University Press)

HOWELL, L. 1986 'The Affordable Housing Crisis in Toronto', *City Magazine* 9, 25–9

MILLS, C. 1988 'Life on the Upslope: the Postmodern Landscape of Gentrification', *Society and Space* 6, 169–90

MILLWARD, H. and DAVIS, D. 1986 'Housing Renovation in Halifax: Gentrification or Incumbent Upgrading?', *Plan Canada* 26, 148–55

ROSE, D. 1987 'Un aperçu féministe sur la restructuration de l'emploi et sur la gentrification: Le cas de Montréal', *Cahiers de Géographie du Québec* 31, 205–24

ROWLEY, G. 1978 'Plus ça Change . . . A Canadian Skid Row', *Canadian Geographer* 22, 211–24

S. HASSON and D. LEY (in press) *Neighbourhood Organizations and the Welfare State* (Cambridge: Cambridge University Press)

LEY, D. 1981 'Inner City Revitalization in Canada: A Vancouver Case Study', *The Canadian Geographer* 25, 124–48

———— 1983 *A Social Geography of the City* (New York: Harper and Row)

———— 1987 'Styles of the Times: Liberal and Neoconservative Landscapes in Inner Vancouver, 1968–1986', *Journal of Historical Geography* 13, 40–56

———— 1988 'Social Upgrading in Six Canadian Inner Cities', *Canadian Geographer* 32, 31–45

———— (in press) 'Past Elites and Present Gentry: Neighbourhoods of Privilege in Canadian cities' in L. Bourne and D. Ley eds *The Social Geography of Canadian Cities* (Montreal: McGill-Queen's University Press)

REFERENCES

ALLEN, R. 1972 'An Introduction' in J.S. Woodsworth *My Neighbour* (Toronto: University of Toronto Press)

AMES, H. 1972 (1897) *The City Below the Hill* (Toronto: University of Toronto Press)

ANDERSON, K. 1987 'Chinatown as an Idea: The Power of Place and Institutional Practice in the Making of a Racial Category', *Annals, Association of American Geographers* 77, 580–98

———— 1988 'Cultural Hegemony and The Race Definition Process in Chinatown, Vancouver: 1880–1980', *Society and Space* 6, 127–49

BOOTH, W. 1890 *In Darkest England and the Way Out* (London: The Salvation Army)

BOURNE, L. 1967 *Private Redevelopment of the Central City* (Chicago: University of Chicago, Department of Geography, Research Paper No. 112)

—— 1987 'Evaluating the Aggregate Spatial Structure of Canadian Metropolitan Areas', *Canadian Geographer* 31, 194–208

—— 1990 'Worlds Apart: The Changing Geography of Income Distributions Within Canadian Metropolitan Areas' Presented to the annual meeting of the Canadian Association of Geographers, Edmonton

BRIGGS, A. 1965 *Victorian Cities* (New York: Harper and Row)

BROADWAY, M. 1989 'A Comparison of Patterns of Urban Deprivation Between Canadian and U.S. Cities', *Social Indicators Research* 21, 531–51

—— 1990 'Social Upgrading and Inner City Deprivation: An Analysis of Seven Canadian Cities' Presented to the annual meeting of the Association of American Geographers, Toronto

BROWN, P. and BURKE, D. 1979 *The Canadian Inner City: A Statistical Handbook* (Ottawa: Canada Mortgage and Housing Corporation)

BUNGE, W. and BORDESSA, R. 1975 *The Canadian Alternative: Survival, Expeditions and Urban Change* (Downsview, Ont.: York University, Geographical Monographs No. 2)

BUNTING, T. 1987 'Invisible Upgrading in Inner Cities: Homeowners' Reinvestment Behaviour in Central Kitchener', *Canadian Geographer* 31, 209–22

—— and FILION, P. 1988 eds *The Changing Canadian Inner City* (Waterloo: University of Waterloo, Department of Geography Publication Series No. 31)

CRYSDALE, S. 1970 'Family and Kinship in Riverdale' in W. Mann ed. *The Underside of Toronto* (Toronto: McClelland and Stewart)

DANSEREAU, F. 1988 'Les transformations de l'habitat et des quartiers centraux: singularités et contrastes des villes canadiennes', *Les Cahiers de Recherche Sociologique* 6, 95–118

—— and BEAUDRY, M. 1985 'Les mutations de l'espace habité montréalais: 1971–1981', *Les Cahiers de l'ACFAS* 41, 283–308

DANTAS, A. 1988 'Overspill as an Alternative Style of Gentrification: the Case of Riverdale, Toronto' in T. Bunting and P. Filion eds *The Changing Canadian Inner City* (Waterloo: University of Waterloo, Department of Geography Publication Series No. 31)

DAVIES, W. 1975 'A Multivariate Description of Calgary's Community Areas' in B. Barr ed. *Calgary: Metropolitan Structure and Influence* (Victoria: University of Victoria, Western Geographical Series Vol. 11)

—— and MURDIE, R. (in press) 'Measuring the Social Ecology of Canadian Cities' in L. Bourne and D. Ley eds *The Social Geography of Canadian Cities* (Montreal: McGill-Queen's University Press)

DEAR, M. 1976 'Abandoned Housing' in J. Adams ed. *Urban Policymaking and Metropolitan Dynamics* (Cambridge, Mass.: Ballinger)

―――― and WOLCH, J. (in press) 'Homelessness in Canada' in L. Bourne and D. Ley eds *The Social Geography of Canadian Cities* (Montreal: McGill-Queen's University Press)

DELEGRAN, W. 1970 'Life in the Heights' in W. Mann ed. *The Underside of Toronto* (Toronto: McClelland and Stewart)

FILION, P. 1987 'Concepts of the Inner City and Recent Trends in Canada', *Canadian Geographer* 31, 223–32

GALE, D. 1980 'Neighbourhood Resettlement: Washington D.C.' in S. Laska and D. Spain eds *Back to the City* (New York: Pergamon)

GANS, H. 1962a *The Urban Villagers* (New York: Free Press)

―――― 1962b 'Urbanism and Suburbanism as Ways of Life' in A. Rose ed. *Human Behaviour and Social Processes* (London: Routledge and Kegan Paul)

GOHEEN, P. 1970 *Victorian Toronto, 1850 to 1900* (Chicago: University of Chicago, Department of Geography, Research Paper No. 127)

HANNA, D. 1986 'The Layered City: A Revolution in Housing in Mid-nineteenth Century Montreal', (Montreal: McGill University, Department of Geography, Shared Spaces No. 6)

HIEBERT, D. 1987 *The Geography of Jewish Immigrants and the Garment Industry in Toronto, 1901–1931* (Toronto: University of Toronto, Department of Geography, unpublished dissertation)

HOLDSWORTH, D. 1979 'House and Home in Vancouver: Images of West Coast Urbanism, 1886–1929' in G. Stelter and A. Artibise eds *The Canadian City: Essays in Urban History* (Toronto: Macmillan)

HOSKINS, R. 1987 'An Analysis of the Point St. Charles Shops of the Grand Trunk Railway' (Montreal: McGill University, Department of Geography, Shared Spaces No. 8)

HOWELL, L. 1986 'The Affordable Housing Crisis in Toronto', *City Magazine* 9, 25–9

HULCHANSKI, D. 1984 'St. Lawrence and False Creek: A Review of the Planning and Development of Two New Inner City Neighbourhoods' (Vancouver: University of British Columbia, School of Community and Regional Planning)

INSTITUTE OF URBAN STUDIES (IUS) 1990 'Needs Assessment on Homeless Children and Youth', *IUS Newsletter* 30

JACKSON, B. 1984 *Social Worlds in Transition: Neighbourhood Change in Grandview-Woodland, Vancouver* (Vancouver: University of British Columbia, Department of Geography, unpublished thesis)

JACOBS, J. 1961 *The Death and Life of Great American Cities* (New York: Random House)

―――― 1971 *City Limits* (Ottawa: National Film Board)

JOSEPH, A. and HALL, B. 1985 'The Locational Concentration of Group Homes in Toronto', *Professional Geographer* 37, 143–54

LEWIS, R. 1985 'The Segregated City: Class and Occupation in Montreal, 1861–1901' (Montreal: McGill University, Department of Geography, Shared Spaces No. 3)

LEY, D. 1974 *The Black Inner City as Frontier Outpost: Images and Behaviour of a Philadelphia Neighbourhood* (Washington, D.C.: Association of American Geographers, Monograph Series No. 7)

——— 1980 'Liberal Ideology and the Postindustrial City', *Annals, Association of American Geographers* 70, 238–58

——— 1981 'Inner City Revitalization in Canada: A Vancouver Case Study', *Canadian Geographer* 25, 124–48

——— 1983 *A Social Geography of the City* (New York: Harper and Row)

——— 1985 *Gentrification in Canadian Inner Cities: Patterns Analysis, Impacts and Policy* (Ottawa: Canada Mortgage and Housing Corporation)

——— 1986 'Alternative Explanations For Inner City Gentrification: A Canadian Assessment', *Annals, Association of American Geographers* 76, 521–35

——— 1987 'Styles of the Times: Liberal and Neoconservative Landscapes in Inner Vancouver, 1968–1986', *Journal of Historical Geography* 13, 40–56

——— 1988 'Social Upgrading in Six Canadian Inner Cities', *Canadian Geographer* 32, 31–45

——— 1990 'Social Polarization and Community Response: Contesting Marginality in Vancouver's Downtown Eastside' Presented to the conference, The Changing Canadian Metropolis, York University

——— (in press) 'Past Elites and Present Gentry: Neighbourhoods of Privilege in Canadian Cities', in L. Bourne and D. Ley eds *The Social Geography of Canadian Cities* (Montreal: McGill-Queen's University Press)

LORIMER, J. and PHILLIPS, M. 1971 *Working People: Life in a Downtown City Neighbourhood* (Toronto: James Lewis and Samuel)

MACLEAN'S 1989 'Gang Terror' 22 May

MANN, W. 1970 'The Lower Ward' in W. Mann ed. *The Underside of Toronto* (Toronto: McClelland and Stewart)

MARTIN, B. 1989 *Faith Without Focus: Neighbourhood Transition and Changing Religious Belief in Inner City Vancouver* (Vancouver: University of British Columbia, Department of Geography, unpublished thesis)

MCCANN, L. 1975 *Neighbourhoods in Transition* (Edmonton: University of Alberta, Department of Geography, Occasional Papers No. 2)

MCLEMORE, R., AASS, C., and KEILHOFER, P. 1975 *The Changing Canadian Inner City* (Ottawa: Ministry of State for Urban Affairs)

MERCER, J. and PHILLIPS, D. 1981 'Attitudes of Homeowners and the Decision to Rehabilitate Property', *Urban Geography* 2, 216–36

MILLS, C. 1989 *Interpreting Gentrification: Postindustrial, Postpatriarchal, Postmodern?* (Vancouver: University of British Columbia, Department of Geography, unpublished dissertation)

MILLWARD, H. and DAVIS, D. 1986 'Housing Renovation in Halifax: Gentrification or Incumbent Upgrading?', *Plan Canada* 26, 148–55

MINISTRY OF STATE FOR URBAN AFFAIRS 1977 *Canadian Urban Trends, Vol. 3* M. Ray ed. (Toronto: Copp Clark)

MOORE, P. and SMITH, P. (in press) 'The Role of Planning in Urban Spatial Structure and Change' in L. Bourne and D. Ley eds *The Social Geography of Canadian Cities* (Montreal: McGill-Queen's University Press)

MURDIE, R. 1969 *Factorial Ecology of Metropolitan Toronto, 1951–61* (Chicago: University of Chicago, Department of Geography, Research Paper No. 116)

MURPHY, P. 1973 'Apartment Location: The Balance Between Developer and Community' in C. Forward ed. *Residential and Neighbourhood Studies in Victoria* (Victoria: University of Victoria, Western Geographical Series No. 5)

OLSON, S., THORNTON, P., and THACH, Q. 1987 'A Geography of Little Children in Nineteenth-century Montreal' (Montreal: McGill University, Department of Geography, Shared Spaces No. 10)

PHIPPS, A. 1983 'Housing Renovation by Recent Movers Into the Core Neighbourhoods of Saskatoon', *Canadian Geographer* 27, 240–62

RAM, B., NORRIS, M., and SKOF, K. 1989 *The Inner City in Transition* (Ottawa: Ministry of Supply and Services, for Statistics Canada)

RIIS, J. 1971 (1890) *How the Other Half Lives* (New York: Dover)

ROBERTSON, R. 1973 'Anatomy of a Renewal Scheme' in C. Forward ed. *Residential and Neighbourhood Studies in Victoria* (Victoria: University of Victoria, Western Geographical Series No. 5)

ROSE, D. 1984 'Rethinking Gentrification: Beyond the Uneven Development of Marxist Urban Theory', *Environment and Planning D* 1, 47–74

———— 1987 'Un aperçu feministe sur la restructuration de l'emploi et sur la gentrification: Le cas de Montréal', *Cahiers de Géographie du Québec* 31, 205–24

ROWLEY, G. 1978 'Plus ça Change . . . A Canadian Skid Row', *Canadian Geographer* 22, 211–24

RUTHERFORD, P. 1972 'An Introduction' in H. Ames *The City Below the Hill* (Toronto: University of Toronto Press)

SUTTLES, G. 1968 *The Social Order of the Slum* (Chicago: University of Chicago Press)

THRASHER, F. 1963 (1927) *The Gang* (Chicago: University of Chicago Press)

TUNBRIDGE, J. 1986 'Of Heritage and Many Other Things: Merchants' Location Decisions in Ottawa's Lower Town West' (Carleton University, Department of Geography, Discussion Papers No. 5)

WARD, D. 1976 'The Victorian Slum: An Enduring Myth?', *Annals, Association of American Geographers* 66, 323–36

———— 1984 'The Progressives and the Urban Question: British and American Responses to the Inner City Slums 1880–1920', *Transactions, Institute of British Geographers N.S.* 9, 299–314

WHITNEY, K. 1970 'Skid Row' in W. Mann ed. *The Underside of Toronto* (Toronto: McClelland and Stewart)

WILLEMS-BRAUN, B., 1989 'Winnipeg Inner-city Natives and the Underclass Thesis' (Vancouver: University of British Columbia, Department of Geography, unpublished paper)

WOODSWORTH, J. 1972 (1911) *My Neighbour* (Toronto: University of Toronto Press)

PART FOUR

URBAN FUNCTIONS

14

Housing

RICHARD HARRIS

Housing makes up a large part (about 30 per cent of the land area) of Canadian towns and cities. As a result, houses help to define the character of different places: the urbane row plexes of Montreal, the graceful limestone homes of old Kingston, the easy-going bungalows of Vancouver, and the ambitious condominiums of Toronto. For their occupants, dwellings such as these have all kinds of significance (Adams 1987; Harris and Pratt 1991). Housing is the most costly item in most people's budget; if furnishing and household expenses such as heat and property taxes are included, it absorbs, on average, almost 25 per cent of household income.[1] For homeowners, the dwelling generally is the household's largest capital asset. Most Canadians value highly the comfort, privacy, and personal autonomy, that housing provides. But sometimes four walls hide the private misery of loneliness and, for too many women and children, the daily degradation of battery and abuse. For better or worse, we spend most of our lives at home and we care a lot about how we are housed.

This chapter reviews how Canadians are housed. It considers the changing ways in which housing has been produced and sold, the different uses and the different groups of people who occupy housing. It highlights geographical variations at both the regional and local levels, variations that are important in themselves and for the development of public policy.

This chapter does not deal in detail with the inflationary trends in house prices that have plagued Canadians over the last decade. The reader is referred to Chapter 8, where the issue of house prices is discussed in conjunction with the high rates of growth in the Windsor-Quebec City corridor. Appendix 4, which appears at the end of this volume, outlines and comments on major sources of data on housing in Canada. Before looking at the substantive issues, however, it is important to consider the various ways in which housing can be viewed.

PERSPECTIVES ON HOUSING

Housing has been studied by academics with very varied points of view. For present purposes it is useful to identify four major traditions of thought.[2]

Neo-classical Economics
In our society, housing is like any commodity: being useful, it has a price. As such, it is a matter of concern to economists, most of whom take a neo-classical viewpoint (Goldberg 1983). Economists analyse housing in terms of supply and demand, with consumer demand leading the market. The many suppliers of housing, including builders, are supposed to respond to the changing demands of consumers. If more people want housing, these potential consumers bid up prices. Contractors, seeing an opportunity to make a profit, build more. Thus it is possible to explain the surge of post-war construction in terms of immigration, the baby boom, and rising prosperity. The latter enabled young singles and couples to form their own households instead of having to stay at home with their parents. Miron (1988) argues that this trend played a large part in increasing the number of households in Canada in the post-war years. It was associated with a demand for small rental units, and it underlay the apartment boom of the 1960s. In this manner changing patterns and levels of demand called forth an appropriate response from the suppliers of housing. On the other hand, neo-classical economists point out that if demand flags, so do prices, profits, and the rate of construction. Thus it is possible to explain the construction downturn of the early 1980s in terms of an economic recession that was coupled with high interest rates. Demand was stifled, and supply almost dried up.

Changes in the types of units built are also thought to be demand-led. Condominiums illustrate the point. Condominiums are a new form of multi-unit homeownership in which the household owns a dwelling unit but not the land on which it sits (Hulchanski 1991). Typically, condominium owners share the costs of paying maintenance for the building. A neo-classical explanation of condominium growth would emphasize the recent emergence of growing numbers of elderly households and of DINKs ('*Double Income, No Kids*'), who can afford property ownership but do not want the responsibilities of home maintenance. As consumers express new preferences, and make new choices, suppliers respond.

From this neo-classical point of view, the 'hidden hand' of a self-regulating market is the most efficient means of co-ordinating the actions of thousands of businesses and households. Since the price mechanism is seen to be vital to this process, attempts to interfere with prices are criticized. Rent controls, for example, are attacked on the grounds that, by artificially depressing prices, they inhibit new construction of rental units, and soon create a shortage that benefits no one (Goldberg 1983, 67–8). Proponents of this view argue that the housing industry in Canada has provided good housing to most Canadians, and that significant problems are faced by only a small minority of households, namely those on very low incomes (Goldberg 1983, 88–91). Therefore governments should concern themselves with the housing of this minority only, and in general leave the task of supplying housing to the private sector.

This approach has yielded many useful insights. It offers plausible answers to policy questions such as the effect rent controls have had upon the housing market in a specific city. It has given us tools to help us understand how households trade the convenience of access to work against the advantages of a larger home on a larger lot (Bassett and Short 1980, Chapter 3). However, the assumption that consumers of housing make free choices gives insufficient weight to the ways that the housing industry can shape demand. More generally, it makes no serious attempt to explain how housing markets are shaped by the wider society.

Socio-Political

In contrast with neo-classical economists, a number of writers have developed a socio-political view that emphasizes the existence within the housing market of a variety of interest groups (Form 1954; Bassett and Short 1980).[3] These groups, which are sometimes referred to as 'actors' or 'institutions', include builders, developers, realtors, mortgage lenders, landlords, and local governments.

All groups are seen to wield some degree of economic and political power. Lenders have the power of granting or denying mortgage credit. This is important because the great majority of home buyers need a mortgage. In 1986, a large minority (48 per cent) of homeowners owned their home outright, but most of these would have obtained a mortgage at the time of their initial purchase.[4] Local governments have the power to zone land, and hence to exclude types of housing (and, by extension, types of households) that may be perceived to be undesirable. The most common targets for restrictions are low-income households, who pay little in the way of property taxes but make relatively heavy demands on municipal services. Landlords can refuse to rent to people whom they perceive to be undesirable. Common targets have included single parents and visible minorities (racial discrimination is illegal, but difficult to identify and prove). Real-estate developers, who create and market whole subdivisions, also determine what types of residential environments are available (Lorimer 1978; 1983). In the process, arguably, they shape people's preferences. Again, condominiums can be used as an example of this.

It has been said that the demand for condominiums has been created and fostered by large developers and promoters who saw the chance to make large profits. Perhaps the most successful promoter in Canada has been Martin Atkins. In 1985 alone, he helped sell 1,006 of the 1,865 condo units sold in Toronto. Journalist Ian Brown (1986, 50) observed that 'Atkins is the man responsible not only for Toronto's current bout of condo fever, but for making real an entirely new conception of what urban life ought to be . . .'. From this point of view, consumer demand is something that, to a significant degree, is constrained and even shaped by actors on the supply side of the housing market.

The socio-political point of view introduces new dimensions to the study of housing. It is incomplete, however, because it does not set the housing market within the context of the changing structure of the economy as a whole. A third perspective is especially concerned with this issue.

Political Economy
Political economists see the social groups active within the housing market as part of a wider structure of class interests (Achtenberg and Marcuse 1986; Bassett and Short 1980; Feagin and Parker 1990). For present purposes 'political economy' will be treated as virtually synonymous with Marxism. In theory there are non-marxist forms of political economy and Marxists who do not think of themselves as political economists. In practice, the association between the two has been strong. (For discussion see Bassett and Short 1980.) Political economists agree that the housing industry has power over consumers of housing, but they stress that such power is itself circumscribed by the larger, impersonal logic of capital accumulation. Each group must act in economically rational terms or fail. In some respects this argument parallels the neo-classical economist's emphasis on the 'hidden hand' of the market. But instead of viewing this process as beneficent, political economists see it as immoral. Housing, they argue, is provided to those who can afford it, and not necessarily to those in need. In their view, capitalism creates a large group of poorly paid and unemployed workers, people who can never afford decent accommodation. Problems and crises are inherent in, not incidental to, the housing market, and will always exist. It follows that the state can never solve the housing problem until it has dealt with the structured inequalities within the wider society.

Political economists argue that the logic of capital accumulation creates a dynamic of historical change within society, and hence within the housing market. According to one interpretation, a crisis of profits in the 1930s brought on a new 'regime of accumulation' (Belec, Holmes, and Rutherford

1987). This regime depended upon allowing wages to rise so as to create and maintain demand for the products of industry. It is sometimes labelled 'Fordist' because it was heralded and exemplified by the policies of the Ford Motor Company, which in the 1920s introduced high pay-scales in order to reduce labour turn over in its new assembly-line plants. Housing played a vital role in establishing this new regime. In Canada, as in other countries, the state changed the mechanisms of housing finance. The Dominion Housing Act of 1935 was a first tentative step in this direction, and was consolidated by subsequent housing acts. These acts made it possible for many more people to afford homes. In the years after World War II, the expansion of suburban homeownership reflected and sustained economic growth through housing construction and by creating demand for a wide range of goods and furnishings. Some political economists believe that we are now living in a period of transition to a new, 'post-Fordist' regime of accumulation, one of greater social polarization and inequality. From this point of view, the condominium boom does not simply reflect a change in preferences or the activities of clever promoters such as Martin Atkins. Rather, it is an expression of a larger process of economic restructuring—one that necessarily entails, as its counterpoint, a growth in poverty and homelessness.

The recent growth of poverty has affected women more than men. It is associated with the 'ghettoization' of working women into low-paying occupations, rising divorce rates, and a parallel growth in the numbers of single-parent families headed by women. These trends have highlighted the fact that the housing experience of men and women is different (Rose and Wexler 1991). Feminism considers this perspective.

Feminism

Feminists believe that housing reflects, and helps to shape, gender relations in society as a whole. Although these relations have been changing in recent years, they are still marked by strong elements of patriarchy (male dominance). In this context, feminists note that, although the home has long been viewed as the place of women, it has typically been built and designed by men with men's interests in mind (Watson 1986). From this point of view, the suburban single-detached home, often described as the Canadian dream, is viewed with some scepticism (Hayden 1984). Although such a place may be comfortable to return to after a day in the factory or office, it is a boring, isolated work-environment for the (typically female) home-maker. Moreover, such a home does not make it easy for women to get out of the home and into the work force. Its very size makes for time-consuming housework; usually it is situated in a low-density suburb that is poorly serviced by transit (women do not have such ready access to automobiles as men [Wekerle 1985]). From this point of view, higher-density apartments or condominiums, especially those located in the inner city, are interpreted as slightly preferable alternatives. This is especially true of inner-city units, which are likely to be better serviced by transit and to have better access to a variety of social services (Rose and LeBourdais 1986). Some feminists, however, have suggested that co-operatives are better still, especially if they contain facilities such as day care, and if they involve co-operative housekeeping (Simon 1986).

The feminist point of view is the most recent and is still developing rapidly. It is currently inspiring some of the more interesting research in the field of housing, most of it focusing on the situation of women. The implication of the feminist point of view, however, is that the distinctiveness of men's experience must also be examined. There are signs that this issue is starting to be addressed. A recent article suggests that the origins of the modern suburb in the late nineteenth century lie not only in the rise of domesticity among women but also (in a different form) among men (Marsh 1988). In such ways, feminism is adding a new dimension to our understanding of housing.

These four different ways of looking at housing have sometimes been presented as incompatible alternatives. Certainly they lead to different political conclusions. In some respects, however, as the condominium example indicates, they can also be viewed as complements. A thorough explanation of the condominium boom would have to pay attention to the changing demographic structure of the population, and to changes in patterns of child-rearing. It could not ignore the actions of promoters like Martin Atkins. It would be incomplete without being interpreted as part of a larger process of social change, one that includes changes in the situation of women and men. Arguably, the political economy perspective is the most comprehensive, but each view has something to offer.

THE PRODUCTION, FINANCING, AND SALE OF HOUSING

Most Canadians are familiar with the concept of assembly-line production of goods, in which the product is moved past stationary workers. In the house-building industry, the product (i.e. dwelling) is stationary, and the tradesmen—bricklayers, carpenters, electricians—move from site to site (McKellar 1991). The industry is unusual and in some respects anachronistic. First, the rate of technological change has been slow, and increases in labour productivity more modest than in other manufacturing industries. Many attempts at innovation have fallen by the wayside. In the early 1900s, some companies (including Sears) experimented with pre-cut home 'kits'; in the 1970s, others tried European-style 'systems building' using pre-cast concrete slabs and modules. Each attempt met first with limited success, and then with failure. These failures were partly because the house-building industry is unusually cyclical. Factories are inflexible and, without regular orders, inefficient places of production.

A second distinctive feature of the residential construction industry is the small size of the average firm. In 1984, there were 8,994 registered companies in the business of making single-family homes in Canada; the following year, these companies built, on average, fewer than ten dwellings each (McKellar 1991; Clayton Research Associates 1988, 15). The contrast with the auto-assembly or home-appliance industries for example is striking. Most builders are too small to afford new technology, but they are flexible. Little capital is needed to become a builder, especially if the specialized work that requires expensive equipment (such as backhoes for digging foundations) is contracted out. As a result, this industry has, for many decades, provided good opportunities for immigrant entrepreneurs. The Sharp family is an example. In the 1920s, Max Sharp emigrated to Canada and settled in Toronto (DeMont 1989). With little in the way of capital or skills he built a family home, which he then sold for a profit. Over the next two decades he built, occupied, and sold homes at the rate of about one a year. In the 1950s, Isadore, his son, took over the now-profitable contracting business. Today, 'Izzy' Sharp owns the Four Seasons chain of hotels and is one of the richest people in Canada. For every success of this kind, there are of course innumerable failures. But this family's history highlights the unusual potential for self-made mobility and profit within the housing and real-estate industry.

Although change in the housing industry has been relatively slow, over the course of the past century, it has been considerable. Three developments are especially noteworthy. First, speculative builders (those who build first and then try to find buyers) have grown steadily in importance. A century ago it was not uncommon for affluent households to commission homes from custom builders. At the other end of the market, many low-income households built their own homes, often with the assistance of family and neighbours. In the building boom of the 1900s, about one-third of all new homes in Toronto were self-built, and in cities of the West the proportion was probably higher (Harris 1990a). Today, custom- and self-building make up a much smaller fraction of new construction.

A second change has been the growing importance, and changing nature, of housing finance. Early in this century, many households used savings to buy their first home. Those that did use credit often obtained a mortgage from friends or family, 'putting down' at least half of the purchase price from their savings. Typically, the mortgage had to be repaid within five years. In the 1930s, to encourage new construction and help pull the economy out of the Depression, the federal government passed the first in a series of housing acts which revolutionized the home finance system. After World War II, the Central (now Canada) Mortgage and Housing Corporation (CMHC) was set up, mainly to grant and insure mortgage loans. Increasingly, first-time homebuyers were encouraged to buy property on credit as soon as they were able. Mortgage terms were relaxed in stages so that 25-year mortgages on 75 to 80 per cent of the purchase price are now common. Institutional lenders (insurance companies, credit unions and caisses populaires, and more recently, trust companies and banks) have come to dominate the mortgage market, except among immigrants where personal loans are still common (Murdie 1986).

A third important change has been the emergence of the developer. A century ago, the process by which rural land was converted into urban homes was 'vertically disintegrated', in that different agents were involved at different stages. Typically, land was subdivided; sold to individual speculators; and sold again on a piecemeal basis to many small builders; homes were then built and sold with the land to the eventual owners. The result was a varied, sometimes chaotic, residential landscape in which small and large dwellings were often juxtaposed. Some housing, and some areas, are still built in this way. But, especially in the larger metropolitan areas, most housing is now built by land developers, who control the entire process from land subdivision through to the eventual sale. These developers began to emerge by the 1920s (Weiss 1987). They shaped areas like Kingsway Park in Etobicoke (Toronto) (Paterson 1984) and Westdale in Hamilton (Weaver 1978). After World War II, they were favoured by the tax system and have become very important, notably in building offices, shopping centres, apartments, condominiums, and single-family homes. From coast to coast, the characteristic result of this development is the planned and homogeneous subdivision.

Working against some of these trends is the growing importance of home renovation, much of it tied to the emergence of inner-city gentrification, as discussed in Chapter 13. In 1966, renovations to the existing stock of housing accounted for only 18 per cent of all housing investment in Canada. (The remainder was for new construction). By 1976, this proportion had increased to 23 per cent and by 1986 to 33 per cent (Fallis 1991, Table 2). If the land component of new construction is excluded, renovation expenditures began to exceed new construction expenditures in 1981 (Clayton Research Associates 1988, 6). In fact, renovation activity is even more significant than published data suggest. An unknown, but certainly high, proportion of renovation work is in the form of Do-It-Yourself (DIY). This unreported renovation work is done informally by contractors, friends, or friends-of-friends, who are paid by an exchange of services or 'under the table'. In such cases, the investment of labour is not recorded. In many ways, renovation work today is carried out in the manner of new construction in, say, 1900. As renovations become more important, the growth of large developers/contractors and of institutional lending will be slowed.

The slow change in production has been accompanied by an evolution in marketing and sales. The speculative builder is the only home builder who needs to be concerned with marketing homes: custom builders already have clients, while self-builders, by definition, are not building to sell. The rise of the speculative builder has therefore created a growing need to sell homes. In the earlier years of this century, most new homes were sold by the builders; owners of existing homes sold their own.

Typically, they relied on the classified section of the local newspaper, supplemented with a sign outside, or in the window of, the dwelling. Today most homes are sold, and some apartments are rented, through realtors. In all major cities, multiple-listing services (MLS) provide a frequently-updated listing of properties for sale in each city. This listing includes information on the price and characteristics of each dwelling. On behalf of a buyer the realtor uses the MLS to identify properties that might be of interest to the client; when acting for a seller, the realtor knows that placing a property on the MLS guarantees that the property will be brought to the attention of as many agents and potential buyers as possible. Today the majority of homes are sold through the MLS, but at a price to the seller: often a commission of about 6 per cent of the total sale price. This commission usually represents the major cost of moving for a homeowner, and is one of the reasons why homeowners move much less often than tenants.

THE OCCUPATION OF HOUSING

The household is malleable, responding to changes in economic circumstances, social mores and housing market conditions. In order to occupy the dwellings that have been produced and marketed, people form themselves into households. This process is by no means as simple as it may appear (Miron 1988; 1991). The household often corresponds to a socially distinct entity, such as an individual person or a nuclear family. But in many cases it does not. Historically, for example, it was common for families to take in single boarders or boarding families (Modell and Hareven 1973). As late as 1931, 20 per cent of all urban households in Canada contained lodgers (Harris 1989, 10). This was especially common when incomes were low, or when rapid population growth had led to a temporary shortage of dwellings. The family household itself might include the grandparents or siblings of the parents. Such family arrangements have been, and are still, most common among immigrants.

Household formation also depends upon the age composition of the population. Very high rates of household formation in the 1960s and early 1970s were due, in part, to economic affluence and the ability of a growing proportion of young people to set up separate households. Miron (1988) has estimated that as much as one-third of the increase in households from 1951 to 1981 was due to the changed living arrangements that affluence made possible. This increase was also because the post-war baby-boom generation was reaching adulthood. As this age group entered the housing market, they first sought rental accommodation and helped to fuel the apartment boom of the 1960s. As they got jobs, saved money, and had children, they started to buy homes and helped to keep home-ownership rates relatively high, even during the price booms of the 1970s and 1980s.

Filtering and Neighbourhood Change
Newly-formed households do not usually occupy newly-built housing. New households are typically made up of young people with modest incomes and little in the way of savings. Relatively little housing is built for those on low, or even moderate, incomes. Today, and especially in the larger urban centres, apartments are being built mainly (and in some cases only) for the 'top' end of the market. New homes in these centres cost at least as much as the existing average home. In 1986, for example, a new single-detached home in Canada cost on the average $85,300, while existing homes sold at $65,400, which was notably cheaper.[5] The cheapest homes and apartments are generally older, lack some modern conveniences, and may be deteriorated. It is this older accommodation that is typically occupied by new households and lower-income households in general.

For many years, it was assumed that the housing market worked in a fairly orderly way to provide housing for new and low-income households. The relatively expensive, new homes would be occupied by the affluent. The older, but still-adequate, homes vacated by the affluent would be taken over by those on more moderate incomes, who in turn would leave the most modest homes for the poor. In this manner, a new home in an expensive suburban subdivision would generate a 'chain' of moves. Each household in this chain would be moving up the housing market, while the housing units themselves would be 'filtering' down, being occupied by increasingly poorer households over time (Bourne 1981, 149–60). The concept of filtering (although not the term itself) was used by Burgess (1925) as long ago as the 1920s in his classic concentric zone model of the changing structure of the city. Burgess' model was complicated by the presence of many first-generation immigrants. He argued that these immigrants, who were for the most part quite poor, occupied housing that had 'filtered down' from the more affluent native-born. Since the older and cheaper housing was concentrated in the inner city, it was there that most immigrants first settled.

Over the years, the filtering model has provided a more accurate description of housing-market processes in the US than in Canada. Even so, and until the 1970s, it is clear that filtering was common in many Canadian cities. As a result, most inner cities came to house a disproportionate number of low-income people and first-generation immigrants. The Chinatown and east-side districts of Vancouver, the Kensington-Spadina neighbourhoods of Toronto, and the St Urbain corridor in Montreal, exemplify this process. But the recent gentrification of many inner-city areas, including those listed, has halted and reversed the process. As is discussed in Chapter 13, many affluent households are buying old homes and, through renovation, making them 'new' (Ley 1986). The most serious consequence has been the loss of cheap rental housing which has resulted in the displacement of immigrant workers' families and others on low incomes (City of Toronto 1986). To some extent, the demand for cheaper housing is still being met by the filtering down of older housing that is less fashionably designed or less conveniently located. Bungalows and apartments built in the 1920s, low- and high-rise apartments built in the 1950s and 1960s, are increasingly the source of accommodation for lower-income households. Toronto's St Jamestown is an example. But, as the growing ranks of the homeless can testify, this supply is insufficient. Reverse-filtering, or 'filtering up', has seriously disrupted what was always a fragile mechanism for providing housing to the poor.

Residential Mobility and Neighbourhood Change

Households move when they perceive their existing dwelling to be undesirable, or at least less desirable than an alternative. Many different factors can contribute to the feelings of stress or dissatisfaction that prompt a move (Brown and Moore 1970; Rossi 1955). Among the most important are job relocation, changes in family size (in either direction, but especially upwards), changes in income (again, in either direction), or a deterioration in the character of the existing neighbourhood of residence (Barrett 1973). In these terms, the mass movement of families into single-detached suburban homes in the late 1940s and 1950s represented an attempt to move closer to suburbanizing jobs, and to gain access to larger homes on larger lots that growing families may need and that rising incomes could support (Clark 1966). The slow but continuing deterioration, and the growing congestion, of inner-city neighbourhoods also seem to have contributed to this broadly popular movement to the suburbs.

The more recent trend towards residential gentrification may also be interpreted primarily in terms of job location and household structure. The more visible aspects of gentrification—singles and gay bars, up-scale specialty stores, cosmopolitan restaurants, and so forth—speak of a new life style of eclectic and discriminating consumerism. Supporting, and in many ways determining, these patterns has been the growth of new types of office employment in central-city areas, coupled with the desire of employees to live fairly close to their (new) work places (Ley 1986). Changes in household structure have caused a new generation of households to evaluate inner-city living more favourably than did their parents. Many more households now consist of two earners with or without children. In such cases, a central location may make sense even if the earners do not work downtown. It may be a compromise location for those couples who work at opposite ends of the city, and may offer the best opportunity for alternative employment should one or other lose their job. A central location also makes sense for the growing number of single persons and single parents, since inner areas are better served by transit and the kinds of community services (notably day care) that such households need (Rose 1989; Rose and LeBourdais 1986; Wekerle 1985).

The growth of two-earner families has complicated the process of residential mobility, and created a significant difference in commuting behaviour between men and women. With two wage-earners or more, and usually two work places outside the home, the adults in the household have to reach some sort of compromise about where to live. It seems that women compromise more than men. A relatively high proportion of women are employed part-time and in jobs, such as clerical work, that are available in many locations (Armstrong and Armstrong 1984). Many households still decide where to live mainly on the basis of where the man works. The woman then seeks employment close by, partly because she often does not have access to a car, and partly so as not to interfere too much with her responsibility for housework and child rearing (Michelson 1984).

A growing number of women now have full-time work or careers, often in the CBD. Whether single or married, they have a strong incentive to live close to work. Lacking a 'wife' at home, they have a particular need to minimize commuting time so as to leave time for household chores. In this context, easily-maintained downtown condominiums or apartments have a particular attraction for women (Rose 1989). For a variety of reasons, then, whether they are part-time workers seeking work close to home, or whether they have careers that encourage them to find a home that is close to work, women do not commute as far as men (Gera and Kuhn 1978; Madden 1981).

Social Differences in Housing Occupancy
Social groups differ considerably in the type of housing that they occupy. The major social groups in Canada are those defined on the basis of class (or socio-economic status), ethnicity, and gender. A person's class, ethnicity, and gender are likely to be a major factor in determining his or her housing situation. To a large extent the housing situation is a function of income. Middle-class professionals, for example, earn more than clerical workers, and a male professional more than his female counterpart (Armstrong and Armstrong 1984). Some publicly subsidized housing is provided to the needy, but the private market allocates housing on the basis of price. Differences in household income and wealth are therefore critical in determining what type of housing—and in what location—a person can afford.

In Canada, as in many countries, there are strong tax incentives for households to own their own home. For example, unlike almost any other type of asset, homes are exempt from capital gains tax.[6] Dowler (1983) has calculated that tax breaks of this kind are currently about three times as large as the amounts that have been channelled to public and 'social' housing.[7] Except for those who do not want the responsibility of maintaining a home, most households would buy rather than rent their dwelling if they could afford to do so. Since their incomes are generally more than sufficient to purchase and maintain a home, most business owners and managers and, to a lesser extent, middle-class professionals, are home-owners living in large and well-equipped homes (Harris and Hamnett 1987). Housing conditions are generally poorer among blue- and lower-echelon white-collar workers. Levels of working-class home-ownership are also lower, although higher than might be expected on the basis of their income. It seems that blue-collar workers have especially strong aspirations to own their own home. The reasons are unclear, although it has been suggested that, for a class of people who are susceptible to lay-off and who have little control over their work environment, owner-occupation offers financial security and a place of personal autonomy (Harris 1989). Those with the lowest incomes, including unskilled workers and the welfare-dependent poor, occupy the worst, typically rental, accom-modation. Some districts of poor-quality rental housing are badly deterio-rated. Slums that result in the actual abandonment of housing, however, are much less common in Canadian than in US cities. This is because disparities between the rich and poor are not as great in Canada, in part because social services are slightly more generous.

Differences in the housing situation of men and women have probably grown in recent years (McClain and Doyle 1983). In the 1950s, when a high proportion of adults lived in husband-wife households, men and women occupied the same dwellings. The home may have meant different things to the woman than to the man; she was more likely to view it as a work place and perhaps a show place for her home-making talents, while he viewed it more as a haven from work (Harris and Pratt 1991). With rising divorce rates and the increase in single-parent households, most of whom are headed by women, this is no longer true. An increasing propor-tion of households living below the poverty line, typically in poor-quality rental housing, are headed by women (Rose and Wexler 1991; Watson 1986).

Little has been written about ethnic differences in housing occupancy in Canada. In the past, although not so clearly in the present, immigrants of all nationalities tended to have low incomes and to live in modest housing. Perhaps because they brought with them a strong desire to establish themselves in their adopted country, however, they generally tried hard to improve their situation and to acquire their own homes. In the short run they were often willing to live in very crowded conditions, perhaps taking in boarders so as to save capital (Kirk and Kirk 1981). In some respects, however, it may be misleading to generalize about immi-grant housing. Although research is lacking, not all cultures seem to attach equal value to home-ownership. Italians and Portuguese, for example, appear to value it very highly; the same may not be true of the Chinese and Vietnamese. It has been suggested that one reason why Montreal has a lower rate of home-ownership than Toronto is that French-Canadians attach less value to owning a home. Recent research has cast some doubt on this interpretation (Choko and Harris 1990). In general, however, it is clear that cultural, as well as economic, factors influence the types of housing that people aspire to and occupy.

THE USES OF THE HOME

The home is used by its occupants on a daily basis and for many purposes. Over the past century, the home has become more important for recreation. As employees have had to spend less time at work, they have had more time to spend at home. The increase in the number of gas barbeques and in-ground swimming pools testifies to the recreational uses of the backyard. Perhaps even more strikingly, the invention of the phonograph, radio, television, and audio and video-cassette technology, has increased the attraction of the home as a place of recreation. Homes have developed new rooms, in part to house this new technology, with many consequences for the character and quality of daily life (Simon and Holdsworth 1991).

Unpaid Work
The home has always been, and still remains, an important work place (MacKenzie and Rose 1983). The daily maintenance of all households, even those that are blessed with the very latest in home technology, requires a great deal of labour. People, clothes, floors and dishes have to be kept (fairly) clean. Food has to be bought and cooked. The presence of children creates a host of other tasks: changing diapers, teaching and consoling. It is often assumed that technology has reduced the amount of housework done in the average home. Certainly, doing the wash by hand, or fetching water from a well, were very time-consuming tasks. But the differences between past and present is usually overrated (Cowan 1983). Appliances have been used as much to raise standards—of cleanliness and culinary expertise—as to save work. And while they have reduced the time spent on old work they have created new. After all, washers, blenders, microwaves and so forth must be bought and maintained. New low-density suburbs have forced people to buy, use, and maintain cars in order to get to work, shop, and attend school. Today we spend less time than our grandparents on cleaning, but more time on shopping. The net effect on the amount of work done is unclear. As we have seen, unpaid work is not only carried out within the home it is also performed on the home. This is the case of self-building, where the owner invests 'sweat equity' instead of hiring labour or buying the finished dwelling. More common today is do-it-yourself (DIY) home maintenance and renovation.

Paid Work
The home is used by many as a source of income. Historically, many households earned income from the home itself by taking in lodgers. In 1901, almost 10 per cent of the income of all urban households in the

United States (and probably also in Canada) was obtained from boarders (Harris 1989, 9). Although lodging, as a source of income, has long been declining, other types of home employment seem to be on the increase. In recent years, there has been an especially rapid growth in the proportion of mothers of young children in the labour force. Since the number of institutional day-care spaces has not kept pace with this trend, an increasing number of young children have been looked after informally in private-home day-care. The women providing this service use their homes to obtain a modest but (usually) tax-free income (MacKenzie and Truelove 1991). There also seems to have been a resurgence of industrial 'home-work', that is, of people employed typically in piece-work labour at home. This is especially apparent in the garment industry in Toronto and Montreal (Johnson and Johnson 1982). Recent innovations in computing and telecommunications technology have made possible a new type of home employment. The early 1980s saw an increase in the numbers of small businesses using this technology, many of which were run out of people's homes; people were also being employed to work at video terminals located in their own homes. As yet, the numbers involved seem to be quite small, and it is too soon to say whether, as some people argue, this is the beginning of a major social trend.

Work done at home is still part of a marked gender division of labour. Recent surveys show that women do a disproportionate amount of housework, even in households where both the man and the woman work full-time (Armstrong and Armstrong 1984; Michelson 1984). This is part of a legacy of patriarchy that influences most aspects of social life, but is especially apparent in the use of the home (Women and Geography Study Group 1985).

A GEOGRAPHICAL PERSPECTIVE

Canadians are among the best-housed people in the world. On the average, our homes are larger than those of Western Europeans, far larger than Japanese homes, and broadly comparable with those in Australia and the US. Almost all urban dwellings are structurally sound, and have the basic conveniences needed in a northern climate: piped water, electricity, and central heating. The neighbourhood settings of Canadian homes are not as well-designed as those in some European countries, notably Sweden, which are more supportive of the needs of children and the poor (Popenoe 1977). But they do not include desolate areas of derelict and abandoned housing, which litter too many cities in the US. In terms of housing, then, we are on the whole fortunate and even profligate.

The Uniqueness of Each Place
No generalization about housing in Canada is valid for every community. The size of the country almost guarantees that housing conditions will vary

Figure 14.1
Average House Price ($ thousands)

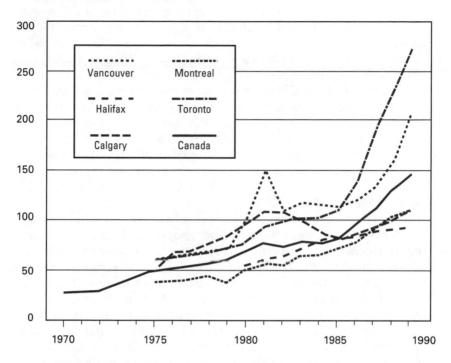

enormously from place to place (Bourne and Bunting 1991). A shortage in one place cannot be met by a surplus elsewhere, unless the places in question happen to be within easy commuting distance. The major areas of settlement in Canada, however, are strung out like islands in an archipelago over a distance of three thousand miles. The major urban housing markets are largely independent of one another. During the OPEC-induced oil boom of the late 1970s, for example, house prices rose rapidly in Calgary and Vancouver (where there was much speculation in real estate in 1980/81), but rose more slowly in Halifax, Montreal, and Toronto (Figure 14.1). With the crisis in the oil industry in 1981, housing prices dropped in the western cities. The long economic boom of the 1980s was concentrated in southern Ontario. By the beginning of the 1990s, the boom, coupled with the migration of people and capital from Hong Kong, had pushed average house prices in Toronto and Vancouver to unprecedented levels. Although company- and single-industry towns have the most volatile housing markets in the country, it is evident that even the larger cities are profoundly affected by shifts in capital investment.

The extended history of European settlement, moving from east to west, has also helped to distinguish local housing markets. Eastern cities, being the oldest, have the highest proportion of older housing, and generally have a higher proportion of dense, multi-occupancy housing stock that has been associated with relatively high levels of tenancy. In contrast, in cities like Calgary and Vancouver that grew up in the age of the streetcar and the automobile, neighbourhoods of single-detached homes may be found quite close to the CBD. Moreover, as each city was developed by different types and generations of immigrants, different architectural styles came to predominate. Nineteenth-century Montrealers favoured 'plexes', superimposed dwellings with separate exterior entrances; Torontonians preferred gabled row-houses in a late-gothic style, while twentieth-century Vancouverites have drawn heavily upon California bungalow and British 'Tudorbethan' models (Hanna 1986; Holdsworth 1977). The historical geography of the country has helped to create a unique housing stock and very different housing markets in each urban centre.

Generic Differences between Places

A geographical perspective on housing involves more than the reasonable assertion that each place is unique. Some geographical variations in housing are generic in character: that is to say, they are specific to certain *types* of places. Perhaps the most basic difference is that between rural and urban. Land and housing in urban centres is much more expensive, and more tightly regulated, than in rural areas. As a result, urban housing takes up a relatively high proportion of residents' incomes, is less likely to be owner-built or occupied, and contains a relatively high proportion of attached, multi-family dwellings (Steele 1991). In 1981, for example, the homeownership rate in urban areas (56 per cent) was almost 30 per cent points lower than the rate in rural areas (84 per cent).

Urbanization has had a significant impact upon the types of housing that Canadians occupy. It has increased the proportion of people living in multi-unit structures, notably after the apartment construction booms of the 1920s and 1960s. It has also helped to depress the level of owner-occupation. Since the 1940s, this effect has been roughly counterbalanced by a growth in real incomes (Harris 1986). Thus, in Canada as a whole, the proportion of households that owned their home fell from 65.6 per cent to 62.1 per cent between 1951 and 1981, partly because of a rapid rate of urbanization that did not taper off until the 1970s (Bourne 1991). The rate among urban areas fluctuated, but over the period as a whole held steady at 56 per cent. Trends in housing, then, must be understood in the context of the changing character of population settlement.

Recent forms of urban development seem to be obliterating the unique character of housing in each place. This process is most obviously at work in the suburbs. The postwar suburbs of most Canadian cities—and indeed most smaller centres too—look much the same (Carver 1978; Relph 1987). The trend toward homogenization has depended in part upon the growth and standardization of municipal planning, the emergence of large land-developers, and the popularity of international, and specifically modernist, architectural styles. The rise of post-modernism and a new vogue for the vernacular has seen the rediscovery of local and regional housing types. This is particularly the case in Quebec, where the style of many new suburban single-family homes is inspired by French Regime farm houses. The newest neighbourhoods in the major cities are again fairly distinctive. Following the recent construction boom in Toronto, for example, it is probable that more gabled 'Victorian' homes now date from the 1980s than from the nineteenth century. With such, possibly significant exceptions, the long-term trend has been towards a greater standardization of urban housing across the country.

HOUSING AND THE STATE

In Canada, housing is produced by the private sector, and is for the most part owned and used by private corporations or individuals. The processes of production, occupation and use, however, are profoundly influenced by the state. The 'private' tenure categories of 'owner-occupation' and 'tenancy', for example, are defined by property law. Their meaning changes in response to political pressure for legislation such as rent controls (Hulchanski 1991). Although all sectors of the economy are influenced by the state, this influence seems to extend particularly to housing.

The Growth of Government Activity
All three levels of government have played a growing role in the housing market over the past century. Municipalities were the first to get involved. The rise of industry in the late nineteenth century helped to concentrate unprecedented numbers of people in large and growing urban centres such as Montreal, Toronto, and Hamilton. Workers' wages were low and their living conditions were poor. Overcrowding and poor sanitation encouraged the spread of infectious diseases, threatening the health of workers and all city dwellers. High densities, coupled with the prevalence of wood-frame construction, were hazardous and led to serious fires. Increasingly, local municipalities recognized that one of the requirements of city life was the regulation of the built environment, and notably housing. Through local housing-health by-laws, they began to exert control over how houses were built, maintained, and occupied (Hodge 1986).

In the twentieth century, local governments have also taken control over land use. In the late nineteenth-century it was typical for parcels of land in cities to be developed in a piecemeal fashion. Stores or small factories might be built in the middle of an otherwise residential street. Investment in property was an uncertain proposition. A prosperous merchant might build a substantial brick home at the suburban fringe, only to have his investment threatened by a labourer building a shack next door. Beginning around the turn of the century, land subdividers began to realize that there was a potential demand for regulated subdivisions in which less desirable, or noxious, land uses would be prohibited. At first, they enforced regulations privately through the use of legal covenants that prevented or mandated certain types of land use. Other covenants limited the types of people that were allowed to live in a property. These covenants were sometimes directed at a particular group, but were often indiscriminate. In Westdale, a suburb of Hamilton that was developed mainly in the 1920s and 1930s, a typical covenant specified that 'none of the lands described . . . shall be used, occupied by, or let or sold to Negroes, Asiatics, Bulgarians, Austrians, Russians, Serbs, Rumanians, Turks, Armenians, whether British subjects or not, or foreign-born Italians, Greeks or Jews' (Weaver 1978, 421).

At the time that Westdale was being developed the task of land use regulation was passing to local government. Today municipal planning departments control land use through zoning plans that specify the use to which each piece of land should be put (Hodge 1986). Zoning cannot discriminate overtly against social groups, but it can prevent the access of lower-income households by specifying the types of dwelling allowed into an area. These plans are not always followed to the letter. In any area of the city, zoning can be changed in response to pressure from developers or local residents. In many provinces, such changes have to be brought before a public hearing, and today re-zoning hearings are an important element in local politics.

With minor exceptions, provincial and federal involvement in housing dates from the 1930s (Bacher 1987; Belec, Holmes, and Rutherford 1987). During the Depression, very little housing was built; many home-owners lost their homes because they were unable to maintain payment on their mortgages. Here was a national housing problem. As a make-work project, the federal government provided assistance to home-owners to undertake home renovations (Hobbs and Pierson 1988). More importantly, the federal government consolidated its influence in the housing field by providing mortgage assistance through the previously described housing acts and CMHC (Poapst 1991).

Mortgage assistance was justified in part in terms of the supposed filtering down of benefits to lower-income groups. However, this process did not produce visible or immediate effects. After World War II, and reaching a peak in the late 1960s, the federal and provincial governments undertook a program of public-housing construction that was directed at the poor. The developments that were intended to house senior citizens were relatively uncontroversial, but 'family' projects ran into a great deal of opposition from local residents. This opposition, coupled with a rapid increase in subsidy costs in the late 1960s, prompted the federal government virtually to abandon its program of construction for families and to cut back on building for seniors (Hannley 1991). From the early 1970s to the present, the federal government has directed more modest amounts of money towards housing for low-income groups (now referred to as 'social' housing). It has taken the form of municipal non-profit or of co-operative housing. Co-operatives take different forms, but in general the ownership is shared among the residents. These units also differ from public housing in that, at least at the beginning, they must be mixed in terms of household income. Income mix has helped co-operatives avoid the kind of social stigma that public housing attracted. Unfortunately, and inevitably, it has also reduced the number of low-income households that have been housed (Harris 1991; McAfee 1984, 97–104). In these terms, the pros and cons of co-operatives are still being very actively debated.

Provincial governments have generally played the minor role in housing. They participated to a variable extent in the federal public housing program, and with rather more consistency with federal co-operative programs (McAfee 1984). The Quebec government has been the most active, especially since the establishment of the Quebec Housing Corporation in 1966. In the 1970s, other provinces took significant initiatives. Ontario, for example, developed a program to help moderate-income households buy homes, and more recently Quebec has been very active in this area. In general, however, probably the most significant provincial activity has been the regulation of rents. Following the introduction of federal wage and price controls, by 1976 every province had some form of rent regulation. Most still do. Typically, rent increases are limited to a fixed amount each year, although the rate of increase has sometimes been allowed to vary from year to year with inflation, and appeals procedures allow for exceptional cases. There has been a great deal of debate about the effects of controls (Miron and Cullingworth 1983). In general, it is clear that they have helped sitting tenants (that is tenants who already occupy an apartment) and reduced landlords profits. Although the evidence is not conclusive, it seems that controls have also reduced the level of apartment construction, and therefore the supply of rental accommodation. Vacancy rates have reached new lows in recent years. As a result, migrants and new households looking to rent a dwelling may have been at a disadvantage. Rent controls are not the only culprit in creating the current apartment shortage, but they almost certainly have played some role.

The Changing Activities of the State
Over the course of the twentieth century, four broad policy shifts in the state's role in the housing market have occurred. First, there has been a steadily growing concern for the price, as opposed to the quality, of housing. Local housing reformers at the turn of the century were preoccupied by the health- and fire-hazards of poor-quality inner-city housing. Their efforts to regulate housing helped to raise standards of construction and squeeze out the shoddy 'jerry-builder'. Today, the key issue for local planners and federal policy-makers is that of affordability, usually defined in terms of the proportion of household income that must be spent on housing (Streich 1991). Over the past twenty years, rapid price increases

in many local housing markets has raised increasing concerns about the ability of young households to afford their own home. It is probable that only the increased participation of women in the labour force, and a growing willingness to purchase smaller condominium dwellings has prevented ownership rates from falling. The most serious problems of affordability, however, are experienced by renters (Filion and Bunting 1989). The growing problem of homelessness in Canada stems in part from the fact that an increasing number of people are simply unable to afford the accommodation that is on the market.

A number of factors have caused the growth of homelessness. As discussed in Chapter 20, the increasing polarization of incomes in modern society, the loss of cheaper housing stock with the gentrification of the inner city, and new policies that have left more mentally-ill people to fend for themselves, have all played a part. But, ironically, among these causes must be included the activities of government itself. Around the time of World War I, many of the poorest households found shelter by building their own modest home in the suburbs (Harris 1990b). In raising standards of housing construction and maintenance, municipalities have helped to eliminate this possibility, while raising the cost of housing to those that buy or rent a finished dwelling. For a complex combination of reasons, then, affordability has become the overriding housing policy issue of our time.

There has also been a slowly-growing recognition that the usefulness of any house depends greatly upon its geographical setting. At the municipal level, as we have seen, the importance of externalities came to be recognized quite early in the control of land use. This recognition came later, and then only haltingly, at the federal and provincial levels. The first national program of public housing construction occurred in the early 1940s to house workers employed in war industries. Many wartime housing projects were thoughtfully designed to include a range of social supports, such as day care (Bacher 1988). By the late 1940s, however, public housing projects were being designed with little attention to such matters. Large and isolated, many projects were easily stigmatized; the locations made many daily activities, including shopping, a major chore for their residents. Fortunately, following much public criticism, the important lessons seem to have been learned (Dennis and Fish 1972; Patterson 1991). The social-housing and neighbourhood-improvement programs of the 1970s and 1980s have paid much greater attention to the placement of new housing in relation to existing housing and community services.

Beginning in the 1970s, rates of urbanization and of young household formation began to slow. By the end of the decade, new dwelling construction was declining. At the same time, and especially as gentrification gathered momentum in many cities, resources devoted to the maintenance and rehabilitation of the existing stock grew. Accordingly, a third and more recent change is that planners and policy-makers are becoming increasingly concerned with how to monitor, manage, and adapt existing dwellings rather than with building anew (Moore and Skaburskis 1991). The challenge is greatest in the rental sector. Many of the apartments built during the construction booms of the 1920s, 1950s and even the 1960s have reached a fairly advanced stage of deterioration. Rehabilitation is expensive and might entail the loss of an already endangered stock of cheap rental housing. In the context of serious affordability problems for renters, the management of this ageing rental stock is, and will remain, a key policy issue (Fallis 1991).

A fourth policy shift has concerned the types of households that are housed. Home-improvement grants in the 1930s were designed to make the home more attractive and functional for raising children (Hobbs and Pierson 1988). In the immediate post-war years, the main thrust of CMHC activity was to house conventional nuclear families. In recent decades, however, family and household structures have become more diverse, and so has the demand for housing (Carver 1978; Rose and Wexler 1991). The private sector has been able and willing to meet some of this demand, for example, by providing condominiums for empty nesters and younger childless couples. But other households, especially those with limited incomes, have been poorly served. The elderly and single-parent families are numerically the most important although, because of the adoption of new health policies, increasing numbers of mental patients are also having to find their own housing (McClain 1991). These groups rely heavily upon convenient access to community services, and public transit, which provides good service only to inner-city districts. There is a particular need for public policy to address the complex and growing needs of these groups.

The Purposes and Consequences of State Activity
It has been said that Canada has housing programs but no housing policy (Dennis and Fish 1972). There is some truth to this. At the federal level, programs have not been conceived or implemented so as to achieve a specific national purpose. Provinces have sometimes followed the federal lead, but rarely with consistency across the country. Municipalities, constrained by upper levels of government, have responded differently to local circumstances. Often, intervention has failed to achieve what was intended, while it has not been uncommon for one action to work against another. The overall picture, then, seems to be made up of incoherent activity.

But, when viewed in historical perspective, a consistent (if changing) pattern does emerge. This is especially true when we examine the effects, as well as the stated goals, of state activity. In general, the effect of state activity in the field of housing has been to facilitate the emergence within Canada of a mature corporate, capitalist society. One of the main reasons for federal government involvement in the housing market was better management of the economy as a whole (Dennis and Fish 1972, 3–4). There are several links between the state of the economy and the housing industry. House construction is labour-intensive; by assisting the housing market, unemployment is reduced. In addition, new construction has a large economic 'multiplier' effect: the occupants of new units are likely to need new appliances, cars and so forth, thereby stimulating aggregate consumer demand. Moreover, since most new homes are mortgaged, and since mortgages account for a large part of all consumer debt, housing finance is a convenient tool of monetary policy. Altogether, then, the state's intervention in housing is an important part of its overall economic role as manager of the developing corporate economy.

Within this context, there has been a consistent bias towards capitalist forms of housing production. Speculative builder-developers and institutional mortgage-lenders have been assisted at the expense of self-builders and the state itself (Lorimer 1978; Weiss 1987). This is, at best, a mixed blessing. On the one hand, it has led to the production of safe and roomy housing for the majority of Canadians. On the other, it has helped create many monotonous neighbourhoods, and has not directly helped those who are relatively poor.

A similar bias may be found in terms of housing occupancy. Governments have consistently encouraged owner-occupation by individual households at the expense of private or public rental. In recent years, for example, tax subsidies to owner-occupiers have far outweighed the monies spent on 'social housing' (Dowler 1983; Steele 1991). The immediate effects are socially regressive: owners are generally more affluent than tenants, while the most affluent, living in the largest homes, have received the greatest subsidies of all. For both reasons, the poor are, in effect, subsidizing the rich. The larger effect of promoting home-ownership has been to bolster the developing consumer economy by boosting the demand for goods and credit (Belec, Holmes, and Rutherford 1987).

The biases of government policy are likely to continue, and for two reasons. First, the powerful interests that have shaped housing policy in the past still hold sway at both the federal (Bacher 1987; Lorimer 1978; Patterson 1991) and local levels (Harris 1988; Lorimer 1983). There is certainly a lobby for various forms of publicly-subsidized rental or cooperative housing, but the disadvantaged groups in this lobby have few political resources in comparison with the real-estate development lobby, which is strongly committed to building owner-occupied homes. Second, the past bias in favour of home-ownership has created its own inertia. Today, the majority of Canadian households own their home. They constitute a large, relatively affluent, and therefore powerful electorate that would resist any attempt to reduce the tax subsidies that they currently enjoy. In this context, and in the current political climate, 'social housing' programs will not be expanded much beyond their present, rather restricted, status.

The immediate challenge faced by policy-makers, then, is to make what little money there is go as far as possible towards solving housing problems.

NOTES

1. Statistics Canada, 1989 *Family Expenditure in Canada 1986* (Ottawa: Minister of Supply and Services, Table 1). This proportion varies greatly with household income.

2. This section emphasizes the main features of these points of view. For details, see the references cited in the text. For an overview see Bassett and Short (1980).

3. Many, but not all, of these writers draw upon the sociological ideas of Max Weber. In the 1970s they were referred to as 'managerialists'.

4. Statistics Canada, 1990 *Canada Year Book* (Ottawa: Minister of Supply and Services, 7.7).

5. These figures relate only to homes sold and financed under the provisions of the National Housing Act. In general, NHA homes are a little cheaper than the average. These, and comparable data for specific cities, are reported in Canada Mortgage and Housing Corporation, *Canadian Housing Statistics 1986*, Tables 86 and 87.

6. This exemption applies only to the household's principal residence and not, for example, to a summer cottage. Note that, under current tax law, every adult is entitled to a lifetime capital gains exemption of $100,000, from any source.

7. 'Public' housing is owned by government agencies and rented primarily to those in greatest need. 'Social' housing is a more inclusive term and refers to all housing that receives a public subsidy and is intended to provide assistance to low-income households. In recent years, most social housing has taken the form of housing co-operatives, which typically contain households with incomes that range from low to middle.

FURTHER READING

BASSETT, K. and SHORT, J. 1980 *Housing and Residential Structure: Alternative Approaches* (London: Routledge and Kegan Paul)

BELEC, J., HOLMES, J., and RUTHERFORD, T. 1987 'The Rise of Fordism and the Transformation of Consumption Norms: Mass Consumption and Housing in Canada, 1930–1945' in R. Harris and G. Pratt eds *Social Class and Housing Tenure* (Gavle, Sweden: National Swedish Institute for Building Research)

BOURNE, L.S. 1981 *The Geography of Housing* (London: Edward Arnold)

BRATT, R., HARTMAN, C., and MEYERSON, A. eds 1986 *Critical Perspectives on Housing* (Philadelphia: Temple University Press)

GOLDBERG, M. 1983 *The Housing Problem. A Real Crisis?* (Vancouver: University of British Columbia Press)

HAYDEN, D. 1984 *Redesigning the American Dream: The Future of Housing, Work and Family Life* (New York: W.W. Norton)

MIRON, J. ed. 1991 (forthcoming) *Housing Progress in Canada since 1945* (Ottawa: Canada Mortgage and Housing Corporation)

REFERENCES

ACHTENBERG, E.P. and MARCUSE, P. 1986 'The Causes of the Housing Problem' in R. Bratt, C. Hartman, and A. Meyerson eds *Critical Perspectives on Housing* (Philadelphia: Temple University Press)

ADAMS, J.S. 1987 *Housing America in the 1980s* (New York: Russell Sage Foundation)

ARMSTRONG, P. and ARMSTRONG, H. 1984 *The Double Ghetto* (Toronto: McClelland and Stewart)

BACHER, J. 1987 'One unit was too many: The failure to develop a Canadian social housing policy in the Great Depression', *Journal of Canadian Studies* 22, 50–61

——— 1988 'Too Good to Last: The Social Service Innovations of Wartime Housing', *Women and Environments* 10, 10–13

BARRETT, F. 1973 *Residential Search Behaviour* (Toronto: York University)

BASSETT, K. and SHORT, J. 1980 *Housing and Residential Structure: Alternative Approaches* (London: Routledge and Kegan Paul)

BELEC, J., HOLMES, J., and RUTHERFORD, T. 1987 'The Rise of Fordism and the Transformation of Consumption Norms: Mass consumption and Housing in Canada, 1930–1945' in R. Harris and G. Pratt eds *Social Class and Housing Tenure* (Gavle, Sweden: National Swedish Institute for Building Research)

BOURNE, L.S. 1981 *The Geography of Housing* (London: Edward Arnold)

——— 1991 (forthcoming) 'The Changing Settlement Environment of Housing' in J. Miron ed. *Housing Progress in Canada since 1945* (Ottawa: Canada Mortgage and Housing Corporation)

——— and BUNTING, T. 1991 (forthcoming) 'Housing Provision, Residential Development and Neighbourhood Dynamics' in L.S. Bourne and D. Ley eds *The Social Geography of Canadian Cities* (Montreal and Kingston: McGill-Queen's University Press)

BROWN, I. 1986 'The Apprenticeship of Marty Atkins', *Toronto* 1, 50–57

BROWN, L.A. and MOORE, E.G. 1970 'The Intra-Urban Migration Process: A Perspective', *Geografiska Annaler* 28, 1–13

BURGESS, E.W. 1925 'The Growth of the City' in R.E. Park, E.W. Burgess, and R.E. MacKenzie eds *The City* (Chicago: University of Chicago Press)

CARVER, H. 1978 'Building the Suburbs: A Planner's Reflections', *City Magazine* 3, 40–5

CHOKO, M. and HARRIS, R. 1990 'The Local Culture of Property: A Comparative History of Housing Tenure in Montreal and Toronto', *Annals of the Association of American Geographers* 80, 73–95

CITY OF TORONTO PLANNING AND DEVELOPMENT DEPARTMENT 1986 'Trends in Housing Occupancy', *Research Bulletin No.26* (Toronto: Planning and Development Department)

CLARK, S.D. 1966 *The Suburban Society* (Toronto: University of Toronto Press)

CLAYTON RESEARCH ASSOCIATES 1988 *The Changing Housing Industry in Canada, 1946–2001* (Ottawa: Canada Mortgage and Housing Corporation)

COWAN, R. 1983 *More Work for Mother: The Ironies of Household Technology from the Open Hearth to the Microwave* (New York: Basic Books)

DEMONT, J. 1989 'Sharp's Luxury Empire', *Macleans* 102, 30–3

DENNIS, M. and FISH, S. 1972 *Programs in Search of a Policy* (Toronto: Hakkert)

DOWLER, R. 1983 'Housing-Related Tax Expenditures: An Overview and Evaluation', Major Report No.22 (Toronto: Centre for Urban and Community Studies, University of Toronto)

FALLIS, G. 1991 (forthcoming) 'Postwar Changes in the Supply-Side of Housing' in J. Miron ed. *Housing Progress in Canada since 1945* (Ottawa: Canada Mortgage and Housing Corporation)

FEAGIN, J.R. and PARKER, R. 1990 *Building American Cities: The Urban Real Estate Game* (Englewood Cliffs, N.J.: Prentice-Hall)

FILION, P. and BUNTING, T. 1989 'Affordability of Housing', *Focus on Canada* (Ottawa: Statistics Canada)

FORM, W. 1954 'The Place of Social Structure in the Determination of Land Use', *Social Forces* 32, 317–23

GERA, S. and KUHN, P. 1978 'Occupation, Locational Patterns and the Journey to Work', Discussion Paper No. 121 (Ottawa: Economic Council of Canada)

GOLDBERG, M. 1983 *The Housing Problem: A Real Crisis?* (Vancouver: University of British Columbia Press)

HANNA, D. 1986 'The Layered City: A Revolution in Housing in Mid-Nineteenth Century Montreal' (Montreal: McGill University, Department of Geography, Shared Spaces No.6)

HANNLEY, L. 1991 (forthcoming) 'The Substandard Housing Problem' in J. Miron ed. *Housing Progress in Canada since 1945* (Ottawa: Canada Mortgage and Housing Corporation)

HARRIS, R. 1986 'Home Ownership and Class in Modern Canada', *International Journal of Urban and Regional Research* 10, 67–86

—— 1988 *Democracy in Kingston: A Social Movement in Local Politics 1965–1970* (Montreal and Kingston: McGill-Queen's University Press)

—— 1989 'The Family Home in Working-Class Life', Research Paper No.171 (Toronto: Centre for Urban and Community Studies)

—— 1990a 'Household Work Strategies and Suburban Homeownership in Toronto, 1899–1913', *Environment and Planning D. Society and Space* (forthcoming)

—— 1990b 'Self-Building in the Urban Housing Market: A Method and Case Study' Unpublished paper, McMaster University, Hamilton

—— 1991 (forthcoming) 'Social Mix, Housing Tenure and Community Development.' in J. Miron ed. *Housing Progress in Canada since 1945* (Ottawa: Canada Mortgage and Housing Corporation)

——— and HAMNETT, C. 1987 'The Myth of the Promised Land: The social diffusion of home ownership in Britain and North America', *Annals of the Association of American Geographers* 77, 173–90

——— and PRATT, G. 1991 (forthcoming) 'The Home, Home Ownership and Public Policy' in L. S. Bourne and D. Ley eds *The Social Geography of the Canadian City* (Montreal and Kingston: McGill-Queen's University Press)

HAYDEN, D. 1984 *Redesigning the American Dream: The Future of Housing, Work and Family Life* (New York: W. W. Norton)

HOBBS, M. and PIERSON, R.R. 1988 'A Kitchen That Wastes No Steps: Gender, Class and the Home Improvement Plan, 1936–1940', *Histoire sociale/Social History* 21, 9–37

HODGE, G. 1986 *Planning Canadian Communities* (Toronto: Methuen)

HOLDSWORTH, D. 1977 'House and Home in Vancouver: Images of West Coast Urbanism, 1881–1929' in G.A. Stelter and A.F.J. Artibise eds *The Canadian City: Essays in Urban History* (Toronto: McClelland and Stewart)

HULCHANSKI, J.D. 1991 (forthcoming) 'New Forms of Owning and Renting' in J. Miron ed. *Housing Progress in Canada since 1945* (Ottawa: Canada Mortgage and Housing Corporation)

JOHNSON, L. and JOHNSON, R.E. 1982 *The Seam Allowance: Industrial Home Sewing in Canada* (Toronto: Women's Press)

KIRK, C.T. and W.K. KIRK 1981 'The Impact of the City on Home Ownership: A Comparison of Immigrants and Native Whites at the Turn of the Century', *Journal of Urban History* 7, 471–87

LEY, D. 1986 'Alternative Explanations for Inner-City Gentrification: A Canadian Assessment', *Annals of the Association of American Geographers* 76, 521–35

LORIMER, J. 1978 *The Developers* (Toronto: James Lorimer)

——— 1983 'Citizens and the Corporate Development of the Contemporary Canadian City', *Urban History Review* 12, 3–10

MCAFEE, A. 1984 'Four Decades of Geographical Impact by Canadian Social Housing Policies' in B. Barr ed. *Studies in Canadian Regional Geography: Essays in Honour of J. Lewis Robinson* (Vancouver: Tantalus)

MCCLAIN, J. 1991 (forthcoming) 'Housing as a Human Service: Accommodating Special Needs' in J. Miron ed. *Housing Progress in Canada since 1945* (Ottawa: Canada Mortgage and Housing Corporation)

——— and DOYLE, C. 1983 *Women and Housing* (Ottawa: Canadian Council on Social Development)

MCKELLAR, J. 1991 (forthcoming) 'Building Technology and the Production Process' in J. Miron ed. *Housing Progress in Canada since 1945* (Ottawa: Canada Mortgage and Housing Corporation)

MACKENZIE, S. and ROSE, D. 1983 'Industrial Change, the Domestic Economy and Home Life' in J. Anderson et al. eds *Redundant Spaces in Cities and Regions* (London: Academic Press)

———— and TRUELOVE, M. 1991 (forthcoming) 'Access to Public Services: The Case of Day Care' in L. S. Bourne and D. Ley eds *The Social Geography of the Canadian City* (Montreal and Kingston: McGill-Queen's University Press)

MADDEN, J. 1981 'Why Women Work Closer to Home', *Urban Studies* 18, 181–94

MARSH, M. 1988 'Suburban Men and Masculine Domesticity, 1870–1915',*American Quarterly* 40, 165–86

MICHELSON, W. 1984 *From Sun to Sun: Daily Obligations and Community Structure in the Lives of Employed Women and their Families* (Totowa, New Jersey: Rowman and Allanheld)

MIRON, J. 1991 (forthcoming) 'Demographic Change, Household Formation and Housing Demand: Canada's Postwar Experience' in J. Miron ed. *Housing Progress in Canada since 1945* (Ottawa: Canada Mortgage and Housing Corporation)

———— 1988 *Demographic Change, Household Formation and Housing Demand: Canada's Postwar Experience* (Montreal and Kingston: McGill-Queen's University Press)

———— and CULLINGWORTH, B. 1983 *Rent Control: Impacts on Income Distribution, Affordability and Security of Tenure* (Toronto: Centre for Urban and Community Studies, University of Toronto)

MODELL, J. and HAREVEN, T. 1973 'Urbanization and the Malleable Household: An Examination of Boarding and Lodging in American Families', *Journal of Marriage and the Family* 35, 467–79

MOORE, E.G. and SKABURSKIS, A. 1991 (forthcoming) 'Measuring Transitions in the Housing Stock' in J. Miron ed. *Housing Progress in Canada since 1945* (Ottawa: Canada Mortgage and Housing Corporation)

MURDIE, R.A. 1986 'Residential Mortgage Lending in Metropolitan Toronto: A Case Study of the Resale Market', *The Canadian Geographer* 30, 98–110

PATERSON, R. 1984 'The Development of an Interwar Suburb: Kingsway Park, Etobicoke', *Urban History Review* 13, 225–35

PATTERSON, J. 1991 (forthcoming) 'Housing and Community Development Policies' in J. Miron ed. *Housing Progress in Canada since 1945* (Ottawa: Canada Mortgage and Housing Corporation)

POAPST, J. V. 1991 (forthcoming) 'Financing of Postwar Housing' in J. Miron ed. *Housing Progress in Canada since 1945* (Ottawa: Canada Mortgage and Housing Corporation)

POPENOE, D. 1977 *The Suburban Environment* (Chicago: University of Chicago Press)

RELPH, E. 1987 *The Modern Urban Landscape* (Baltimore: Johns Hopkins University Press)

ROSE, D. 1989 'A Feminist Perspective on Employment Restructuring and Gentrification: The Case of Montreal' in J. Wolch and M. Dear eds *The Power of Geography: How Territory Shapes Social Life* (Boston: Unwin Hyman)

——— and LEBOURDAIS, C. 1986 'Changing Conditions of Female Single Parenthood in Montreal's Inner City and Suburban Neighborhoods', *Urban Resources* 3, 45–52

——— and WEXLER, M. 1991 (forthcoming) 'Post War Social and Economic Changes and Housing Adequacy' in J. Miron ed. *Housing Progress in Canada since 1945* (Ottawa: Canada Mortgage and Housing Corporation)

ROSSI, P. 1955 *Why Families Move* (New York: The Free Press)

SIMON, J. 1986 'Women and the Canadian Co-op Experience: Integrating Housing and Economic Development', *Women and Environments* 8, 10–12

——— and HOLDSWORTH, D. 1991 (forthcoming) 'Housing Form and Use of Domestic Space' in J. Miron ed. *Housing Progress in Canada since 1945* (Ottawa: Canada Mortgage and Housing Corporation)

STEELE, M. 1991 (forthcoming) 'Incomes, Prices and Tenure Choice' in J. Miron ed. *Housing Progress in Canada since 1945* (Ottawa: Canada Mortgage and Housing Corporation)

STREICH, P. 1991 (forthcoming) 'The Affordability of Housing in Postwar Canada' in J. Miron ed. *Housing Progress in Canada since 1945* (Ottawa: Canada Mortgage and Housing Corporation)

WATSON, S. 1986 *Housing and Homelessness: A Feminist Perspective* (London: Routledge and Kegan Paul)

WEAVER, J. 1978 'From Land Assembly to Social Maturity: The Suburban Life of Westdale (Hamilton), Ontario, 1911–1951', *Histoire sociale/Social History* 11, 411–40

WEISS, M. 1987 *The Rise of the Community Builders* (New York: Columbia University Press)

WEKERLE, G. 1985 'From Refuge to Service Center: Neighbourhoods that Support Women', *Sociological Focus* 18, 79–95

WOMEN STUDY GROUP OF THE INSTITUTE OF BRITISH GEOGRAPHERS 1985 *Geography and Gender: An Introduction to Feminist Geography* (London: Hutchinson)

15
The Urban Retail Landscape

KEN JONES

The retail landscapes of urban Canada reflect the immense diversity of social classes, incomes, ethnicities, and lifestyles that comprise our cities. Arterial strips, neighbourhood shopping streets, suburban plazas, downtown shopping areas, and revitalized boutique districts are some of the most visible, volatile, and prominent elements of the metropolitan landscape. The Canadian retail environment is also a product of two distinct and competing retailing systems: the planned shopping-centre hierarchy; and the remaining unplanned retail areas. As well, there are combinations of these two systems, such as the forms of retailing found in revitalizing central business districts (CBDs). Chain stores dominate the planned shopping centres, while independent retailers normally are restricted to unplanned central-city or retail-strip locations.

The retail system is a major component of the Canadian economy. In 1988, total retail sales measured $173.2 billion or 29.9 per cent of the GNP (Statistics Canada 1988); 1,800,000 or 18.4 per cent of the Canadian workforce are employed in trade and commerce (Statistics Canada 1989). In our society, retailing is pervasive. For many, shopping is a major leisure activity. Retail sales absorb approximately one-third of our disposable income; and the image of our cities is shaped in large part by the nature and vibrancy of their retail environments.

This chapter describes and interprets the various elements that shape and comprise our urban retail system. First, a brief review of the literature associated with intra-urban retailing will be presented. This section familiarizes the reader with the basic structure of urban retailing, and comments on the factors that relate to urban retail development and change. Second, an examination of the evolution of the Canadian intra-urban retail system is provided. This part focuses on the development of the shopping centre, the rebirth of the central city, and the emergence of the specialty retail area. Next, a general morphology of the contemporary urban retail structure is introduced. This discussion addresses both the functional and market characteristics that make up the various components of the urban retail fabric. The chapter concludes by presenting an integrated framework for evaluating the intra-urban retail system, and outlines a series of trends that relate to the future disposition of urban retailing in Canada.

INTRA-URBAN RETAILING: A REVIEW

The geographic literature related to urban retailing can be grouped into four research perspectives. The first focuses on both the *identification and classification* of various structural elements of the retail landscape. The second explores the *spatial dynamics* of retail change.The third emphasizes an *understanding of the development and operation* of various retail structures—shopping centres, central-area retail districts, retail strips, and specialty retail areas. The fourth is directed towards *applied research investigations*. Here, geographers assess new retail locations for major retail firms, and utilize various spatial models to analyse shopping centre impacts.

The development of a systematic classification of retail structures is based to a large extent on the pioneering works of Proudfoot (1937) and Berry (1963). These studies differentiated shopping environments on the basis of their locational and functional characteristics, and provided a framework for interpreting the retail structure. Proudfoot's work described the existing retail pattern for the pre–1945 North American city. It identified five types of retail structure: the CBD; outlying business centres; principal shopping thoroughfares; neighbourhood shopping streets; and isolated store clusters, such as the old-fashioned corner store. Berry's well-known classification of the retail hierarchy summarized the post-war city. It was primarily based on studies carried out in the city of Chicago. Here, the dominant business elements of shopping centres (planned and unplanned), ribbons or strips, and specialized areas, such as used-car rows, exotic markets, or furniture districts, are interpreted in terms of central place postulates (see this book's Chapter 7 for a definition of central place theory). More recently, Davies (1976) developed an integrated model of urban retail form that was based on the simultaneous overlapping of nucleations, ribbons, and specialty retail area characteristics. According to Davies, the retail pattern of the city centre can be viewed in broad terms as a nucleation that is structured in a series of zonal belts of retail activity. Finally, Jones (1984) provided a reworking of the Berry model. In this interpretation, the urban retail system is subdivided into two structural forms—strips and centres. Each of these forms is then further differentiated according to its location in either inner-city or suburban environments.

The literature related to urban retail change can be traced back to the empirical work carried out by Simmons (1966) in the Toronto metropolitan area. Simmons' conceptual model of retail change examined how socio-economic conditions and elements of urban growth influence the development of the intra-urban retail system. In this model, temporal and spatial variations in urban demographic change, income, and technological development affect consumer mobility and preferences. Eventually these variations cause an adjustment in the nature and distribution of retail structures. In Britain, the works of Shaw (1978) and Sibley (1976) examined the long-term patterns and evolutionary processes associated with retail change. They concluded that changes in retail pattern were the outcome of the aggregate adaptive behaviours of independents and multiple-unit chains. More recently, changes in the retail system have been examined from the perspective of the supply side (Laulajainen 1987). In these analyses, the final disposition of the retail system is viewed as the outcome of the spatial strategies and interplay between developers, retailers, and planners—the actors that ultimately shape the future form of the urban retail landscape.

Retail structural analysis has had a long tradition in urban geography. In the 1950s and 1960s, North American studies of retail structure dominated the literature. These studies explored suburban retail strip development, retail mix and usage patterns, inner-city retail decline, the emergence of the shopping centre, and the specialty retail phenomenon. In the 1970s and 1980s, the interest in retail studies shifted to the United Kingdom. British geographers, in an attempt to formulate responsive retail planning policies, studied a wide variety of urban retail issues. These included inner-city blight, retail decentralization, the quality of the inner-city retail areas, the impact of hypermarkets (very large stores with a wide selection of goods that generally include food), and the future role of planned regional shopping centres.

Finally, applied studies have tended to focus on particular elements or projects associated with the retail system. Because of their nature, most of these studies adopt a micro-based, case-study approach. Typically, these analyses are undertaken to provide advice to retail corporations concerning the investment potential of particular locations, or to aid government agencies in assessing the social, economic, or environmental impact of a specific development. In the literature, the works of Applebaum (1968), Davies and Rogers (1984), and Lea (1989) illustrate these forms of study.

In the private sector, because of disclosure problems, most of this literature remains hidden, but numerous consulting and planning reports documenting the role of the applied retail geographer in assessing and planning the course of urban retail development exist in the public domain.

EVOLUTION OF THE CANADIAN URBAN RETAIL SYSTEM

The current retail landscape of urban Canada is the product of a series of complex structural changes. The entry rate and exit rate of retailers into and out of the marketing system is highly volatile. A recent study of London, Ontario (Beveridge 1985) that measured stores going out of business, relocating, or changing ownership suggested that the retail turnover rate for the city between 1978 and 1981 was an incredible 23.8 per cent. Very minor shifts in the income, demographic, or lifestyle characteristics of an area will lead to quite rapid changes in both form and structure of the retail environment. Conceptually, the retail fabric of our cities has been created in response to the dynamic interplay of demographic, technologic, behaviourial, and entrepreneurial change (Figure 15.1).

At the most basic level, retailers locate in response to market conditions. If the population/income mix or market potential is appropriate, retail development will occur. The spatial pattern that retail groupings take relates in large part to the technology of the time. When mobility is low, as in the pre-World War II period—the heyday of central business districts—retail activities concentrate; when mobility increases, the distribution of retail activities tends to disperse. At a more specific level, consumer and entrepreneurial decisions can determine which retail areas grow and which areas decline. Consumer preferences for both retail goods and destinations can reflect a whole set of considerations that can be broadly defined as lifestyle-related. Certain urban shopping areas move in and out of fashion for particular consumer groups. At the supply side, investment decisions are based on the entrepreneur's assessment of the future disposition of the retail system. Will a certain downtown redevelopment project be successful? How will the competition react? What will be the demographic composition and demands of the community in ten years?

The Pre-World War II System
The intra-urban retail system has undergone at least three transformations in the last sixty years. These eras are termed the pre-automobile city era, and the automobile city era, and the specialized era (see Chapters 11 and 12 for a discussion of the inter-relation between transportation and urban form). In the pre-World War II city, i.e. the pre-automobile city, both aggregate consumer mobility and car-ownership were low. As a result, many consumers shopped daily for food and 'going downtown to shop' was viewed as a normal activity. An examination of the pattern of retail

Figure 15.1
The Determinants of Retail Structure

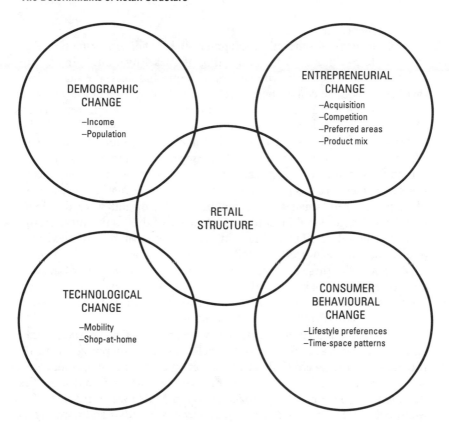

activities in urban Canada prior to 1950 reflected this reality. Nearby corner stores were a necessity, and downtown retailing flourished. It was the 'age of the department store'. In 1930, all divisions of the T. Eaton and Robert Simpson companies controlled a substantial 10.5 per cent of total retail sales in Canada (Royal Commission on Price Spreads 1935). Inner-city retail strips were a significant element in the retail landscape. These strips extended into the residential portions of the city, and consisted of almost continuous rows of shops that served essentially local convenience-oriented needs. Bloor Street and St. Clair Avenue in Toronto are good examples of retail strips that developed along major street-car lines.

As Jones and Simmons (1987, 191–2) have noted 'the low overall mobility led to relatively steep, often asymmetrical, travel-time gradients around each household. The result was an intraurban hierarchy similar in many ways to the one observed in the settlement system. Throughout the urban area, a number of retail nodes could be identified, ranging in size from the corner store to the downtown shopping district. The mix of stores was directly linked to the size of the centre and served a relatively well-defined spatial market proportional to its size.'

The Shopping Centre

In 1950, the next era of retail development in the then emerging Canadian automobile city began with the opening of Park Royal Shopping Centre in Vancouver. Since then, the shopping centre has been the major force that has shaped the contemporary retail structure of urban Canada. From the mid–1960s, it has accounted for almost all the growth in retail goods activity in the country. Shopping-centre development in Canada has undergone four periods of evolution since its inception. In the 1950s, shopping centre developers adopted a *consequent* development strategy. In this environment, the shopping centre was constructed after the housing stock in a given area was in place and the details of the market were known. Most plazas were small and automobile-oriented, and were developed independently to serve the convenience needs of the community. During this early period, retail planning controls were in most cases non-existent; often a form of uncontrolled retail sprawl development resulted. A major factor that led to these patterns was the reluctance of the major Canadian department-store chains to move to the suburbs. Both Eaton's and Simpsons adopted a wait-and-see attitude, and were content to remain securely located in the downtown cores of Canadian cities.

The 1960s saw a shift in this attitude with the emergence of *simultaneous* shopping-centre development. In this stage, both the shopping centre and the housing stock were built at the same time, and the shopping centre was viewed as the centre of the 'planned' community. In Canada, the first development to adopt this approach was Don Mills Plaza built in 1959 in Metropolitan Toronto. The linkage between residential and commercial land-uses helped to foster the emergence of several large development companies. These included Cadillac Fairview, Bramalea, and Trizec. The philosophy of simultaneous development became accepted at all levels of retail development, from the large regional complexes (e.g., Fairview Mall, Bramalea City Centre, and Scarborough Town Centre in Metropolitan Toronto) to the small neighbourhood plazas that form the centre of small residential communities. It is also interesting to note that during this period the shopping centre became an institution. The shopping-centre industry in Canada established both policies and procedures such as the percentage lease. A host of specialties emerged to deal with a variety of shopping-centre concerns—design, law, leasing, landscaping, parking, tenant mix, energy conservation, and lighting. In effect, an entire industry was created.

By the end of the 1960s, the shopping-centre industry in Canada was well established, and a level of corporate control over the prime shopping-centre locations in Canada had been assured. Table 15.1 depicts the current list of major shopping-centre developers in Canada that are the legacy of this period. These developers are arguably the most important players in determining the spatial structure of the retail distribution system in Canada. It is important to note that the shopping-centre system that emerged from the 1960s was essentially homogeneous in nature. One shopping centre at any one level of the hierarchy looked much the same as the next. It had a similar atmosphere, layout, and design; it 'felt' the same. It offered a similar range of goods, services, and tenants in a similar sterile environment.

In large part, this sameness was the product of the 'corporatization' of the shopping centre. Beginning in the early 1960s, a synergy developed between chain-retailer corporations and shopping-centre developers that continues to the present. Throughout North America, the planned shopping centre provided the principal vehicle for the entry and ultimate dominance of the retail chain in the urban market-place (Doucet, Jacobs, and Jones 1988). By 1986, slightly more than half of all retail chains and department stores in Canada—51.7 per cent or 17,795 outlets—were located in shopping centres. Certain types of retail chains were more shopping-centre oriented. In terms of total sales, the retail activities that showed the greatest propensity for shopping centre locations were women's clothing (91%), luggage and leather goods (89%), children's clothing (87%), jewellery stores (85%), and shoe stores (83%).

The relationship between the retail chain and the shopping centre is reflected in the redistribution of retail space in many metropolitan environments. For example, in Metropolitan Toronto (which has kept an inventory of retail space since 1953), the share of the total retail space found in planned shopping facilities rose from 2.4 per cent in 1953, to 40.8

Table 15.1
Major Canadian Shopping Centre Developers, 1989

Developer	Headquarters	Total Tenants	Gross Leasable Area (000 sq. ft.)	Total Number of Centres	Number of Centres by Size (000ft²)			
					>999	999–500	499–250	<250
Cadillac-Fairview	Toronto	5148	517	46	2	18	17	9
Cambridge S.C.	Toronto	4023	448	39	1	12	19	7
Trilea (Trizec/Bramalea)	Calgary	3292	377	38	3	7	11	17
Markborough (H.B.C.)	Toronto	2526	472	23	—	9	7	7
Ivanhoe (Steinberg's)	Montreal	1698	213	36	—	3	5	28
Marathon (C.P.R.)	Toronto	1726	326	23	2	3	9	10
Westcliff Management	Montreal	1833	269	24	—	4	4	16
Atlantic S.C. (Sobey's)	Stellarton	1024	227	28	—	3	5	20
Campeau	Toronto	1472	270	22	—	2	10	10
Triple Five Inv.	Edmonton	1108	1297	4	1	2	—	1
Burnac Leaseholds	Toronto	710	193	20	—	—	7	13

SOURCE: *Canadian Directory of Shopping Centres, 1989,* Toronto: Maclean-Hunter, 1988.

Table 15.2
Major Downtown Redevelopment Projects in Canada

Project	Major Tenant	Location	Size (000 sq. ft.)	Date/Renovation	Developer
1. Galleria London (Wellington Square)	Eaton's	London	800	1969 (83) (89)	Campeau
2. Place Ville Marie	———	Montreal	184	1962 (85) (87)	Trizec
3. Place Bonaventure	———	Montreal	200	1967	Place Bonav.
4. Place Alexis Nihon	———	Montreal	424	1967	Alexis Nihon
5. Highfield Square	———	Moncton	286	1968	Atlantic S.C.
6. Scotia Square	Woolco	Halifax	350	1969	Halifax Dev't
7. Toronto Dom. C.	———	Toronto	200	1969 (74) (84)	Cadillac Fairview
8. Midtown Plaza	Eaton's/Sears	Saskatoon	575	1970 (72)	Midtown Plaza
9. City Centre	Eaton's/Towers	Sudbury	400	1971 (75) (80) (86)	JDS/Canapen
10. City Centre	———	Thompson	168	1971	Thompson Mall
11. Pacific Centre	Eaton's	Vancouver	900	1971 (75) (85)	Cadillac Fairview
12. Lloyd Jackson Sq.	Eaton's	Hamilton	620	1972 (83) (88)	Yale Properties
13. Royal Centre	———	Vancouver	92	1973	Trizec
14. Manulife Centre	Bretton's	Toronto	276	1973 (88)	Manuf'ers' Life
15. Station Mall	Sears	Sault Ste. Marie	367	1973 (81) (86)	Algocen
16. Market Square	Eaton's	Kitchener	318	1974	Cambridge
17. Cumberland Terr.	———	Toronto	150	1974	Hammerson
18. Kesfus Mall	Eaton's	Thunder Bay	217	1974 (80) (84)	Park St. Plaza
19. Place Québec	———	Quebec City	155	1974	Trizec
20. Edmonton C.	Woodwards/Holt	Edmonton	800	1974 (84)	Oxford
21. Peterborough Sq.	Eaton's	Peterborough	250	1975 (84)	Marathon
22. Lethbridge C.	Woodwards	Lethbridge	531	1975 (88)	Cambridge
23. Hudson Bay C.	The Bay	Toronto	425	1975 (82)	Bramalea
24. Eaton Centre	Eaton's/Simpsons	Toronto	3,200	1977 (79) (89)	Cadillac Fairview
25. Toronto Dom. Sq.	Eaton's/The Bay	Calgary	1,220	1976	Eaton's/Oxford
26. Scotia Fashion C.	———	Calgary	86	1976	Trizec
27. Brunswick Sq.	———	St.John	152	1977 (87)	Brunswick Sq.
28. First Can. Pl.	———	Toronto	300	1978 (83)	Olympia-York
29. Place du Centre	———	Hull	177	1978	Westcliff
30. Cornwall Sq.	Sears	Cornwall	257	1979	Cadillac Fairview
31. College Park	———	Toronto	172	1979 (83)	Tor. College St.
32. Eaton Place	Eaton's	Winnipeg	960	1979	Bardero
33. Holt Renfrew C.	Holt Renfrew	Toronto	213	1979	Pension Fd. Real.
34. Brandon Gallery	Eaton's	Brandon	235	1980	Cambridge
35. King Centre	Robinsons	Kitchener	255	1980	Marathon
36. Algo Centre	Woolco	Elliot Lake	179	1980	Algocen
37 Gateway Mall	Eaton's/Sears	Prince Albert	405	1981	Marathon
38. Cornwall C.	Eaton's/Sears	Regina	590	1981 (83)	Cadillac Fairview
39. Atrium on Bay	———	Toronto	135	1982	Trizec
40. Chatham C.	Sears	Chatham	235	1982 (83)	Cambridge
41. Sarnia Eaton C.	Eaton's	Sarnia	256	1982	Cadillac Fairview
42. Rideau Centre	Eaton's/Ogilvy's The Bay	Ottawa	1,175	1983	Viking/Rideau
43. Market Square	———	St. John	150	1983	Market Sq. Dev.
44. Guelph Eaton C.	Eaton's	Guelph	223	1984	Chartwood
45. Manulife C.	Holt Renfrew	Edmonton	110	1984	Manuf'ers' Life
46. Eaton Market Sq.	Eaton's	Brantford	250	1986	Campeau
47. Le Faubourg Ste-Catherine	———	Montreal	293	1986 (87)	Multidev/ Immobilia
48. Portage Place	———	Winnipeg	274	1987	Cadillac Fairview
49. Edmonton Eaton C.	Eaton's	Edmonton	520	1987	Triple-Five
50. Les Cours Mont-Royal	Simpsons	Montreal	685	1988	Soc. en Commandite
51. Eaton Centre	Eaton's	Montreal	1,296	1988	York-Hannover
52. Promenades de la Cathedrale	Eaton's/The Bay	Montreal	161	1988	Westcliff
53. Park Place	Eaton's/Sears	Lethbridge	429	1988	Cadillac Fairview
54. Victoria Eaton C.	Eaton's	Victoria	434	1989	Cadillac Fairview

SOURCE: *Canadian Directory of Shopping Centres, 1989.* Toronto: Maclean-Hunter, 1988.

per cent in 1971, and to 54.5 per cent in 1986 (Metropolitan Toronto Planning Department 1987).

The early 1970s saw a gradual shift to a third stage in some larger metropolitan markets—the *'catalytic'* shopping centre. In this case, the shopping centre was viewed as a growth pole that would stimulate future residential development. In a typical case, a super-regional shopping centre was built in a 'greenfield' location at the intersection of two major expressways, and preceded residential development by three to five years. Scarborough Town Centre and Mississauga Square One are prime examples of this trend in the Toronto region. In part, these developments were in keeping with the 'bigger is better' philosophy that permeated North American business decision-making in this period. The success of these centres was also contingent upon large development companies with extensive land banks, and the willingness and ability of national chains to enter a location and wait for the market to develop.

The 1970s also were characterized by the commercial revitalization of central cores. These downtown areas became a prime focus for shopping-centre development. In Canada, the first attempt at a downtown shopping centre was in London, Ontario, where Wellington Square was built in 1960. By the end of the 1970s, most major cities in Canada had an enclosed shopping facility in the downtown core. In most cases, these developments were joint ventures that involved the developer, a major department store (often Eaton's), and a major financial institution. To date, over thirty city centres in Canada have experienced this form of development, which has reshaped the map of urban retailing. These projects are listed chronologically in Table 15.2.

The end of the 1970s saw the saturation of the market for shopping centres in Canada. Developers pursued a series of alternative growth strategies. First, a number of selected shopping centres were rejuvenated. This process generally involved the enclosing and 'remixing' of first-generation, regional shopping centres that had been constructed in the period of 1960 to 1965. Second, through a strategy termed 'infilling', a number of smaller towns became targets for enclosed regional- or community-malls on their periphery. As a consequence, a number of downtown cores in these smaller communities experienced severe decline. A third option adopted by major developers such as Cadillac Fairview, Olympia and York, Bramalea, Oxford, Cambridge, Trizec, and Daon was to become active in the high-growth markets of the United States. It became commonplace for Canadian retail-commercial developers to become major players in Los Angeles, New York City, Dallas, Minneapolis, and Denver.

The 1980s saw the emergence of a fourth form of shopping-centre development—the shopping centre as an entertainment or tourist attraction. The overt mixing of retailing and recreation in a major shopping centre is an innovation particular to Canada. By far the most ambitious example of this type of mega-project is the 3,800,000 square foot West

Edmonton Mall with its dozens of tourist attractions. These include an ice-skating rink, wave pool, submarine rides, marineland, aviary, Fantasyland Hotel, children's amusement park, and a mock 'Parisian' shopping boulevard. In these environments, retailing often appears secondary. Also in the 1980s, many inner-city shopping centres and redeveloped waterfront properties have been targeted partly at tourists and recreational shoppers. The Eaton Centre, recognized as Toronto's most popular tourist attraction, illustrates this phenomenon.

By far the most active form of shopping-centre development in Canada during the 1980s has been the revitalization of existing properties. Developers have found that shopping centres have a distinct lifecycle. After approximately 10 to 15 years, most centres are in need of renovation. Since their initial construction, the demography and income level of their trade area has changed, their competitive environment has been altered, and their 'book value' has been depreciated to zero. As Dawson and Lord (1985) have observed, revitalization offers a number of advantages to the developer. Existing shopping centres are well situated in a known market; they experience fewer zoning or environmental regulatory problems; and typically they incur lower construction and financial costs. Most of these renewal projects involve the re-tenanting of the centre, and result in an increase in the total number of retail units. Even if no additional retail space is added, because of the reduction in the space requirements of most retailers, the actual number of stores in a centre can increase dramatically. Revitalization has taken a number of forms. These include expansions, enclosures, re-tenanting, renovations, or various combinations of the above.

Figure 15.2 illustrates the process whereby shopping-centre maturation contributed to major shifts in the growth of new retail forms. In essence, the intra-urban shopping-centre hierarchy that was developed between 1950 and 1970 led to a dichotomous retail system. On the one hand, there was the new suburban system, which was planned, functionally homogeneous, and the domain of the retail chain. In contrast, the older inner-city areas remained unplanned and were dominated by independent merchants. By the mid–1970s, shopping-centre developers recognized that they had created a series of standardized, often sanitized, shopping environments. Their response was threefold. First, through shopping-centre renovation, they instituted new, up-scale design features in many of their major centres. Second, they began to experiment with new marketing approaches, such as the shopping centre as an entertainment vehicle. Third, they returned to the inner city, often with the assistance of local government authorities, to develop planned central-city shopping centres (e.g., Pacific Centre, Vancouver), festival retail developments in waterfront locations (e.g., Market Square, St. John) or historic properties (e.g., Le Vieux Port, Montreal, and the Warehouse District, Winnipeg).

Figure 15.2
Shopping Centre Maturation and Urban Retail Change

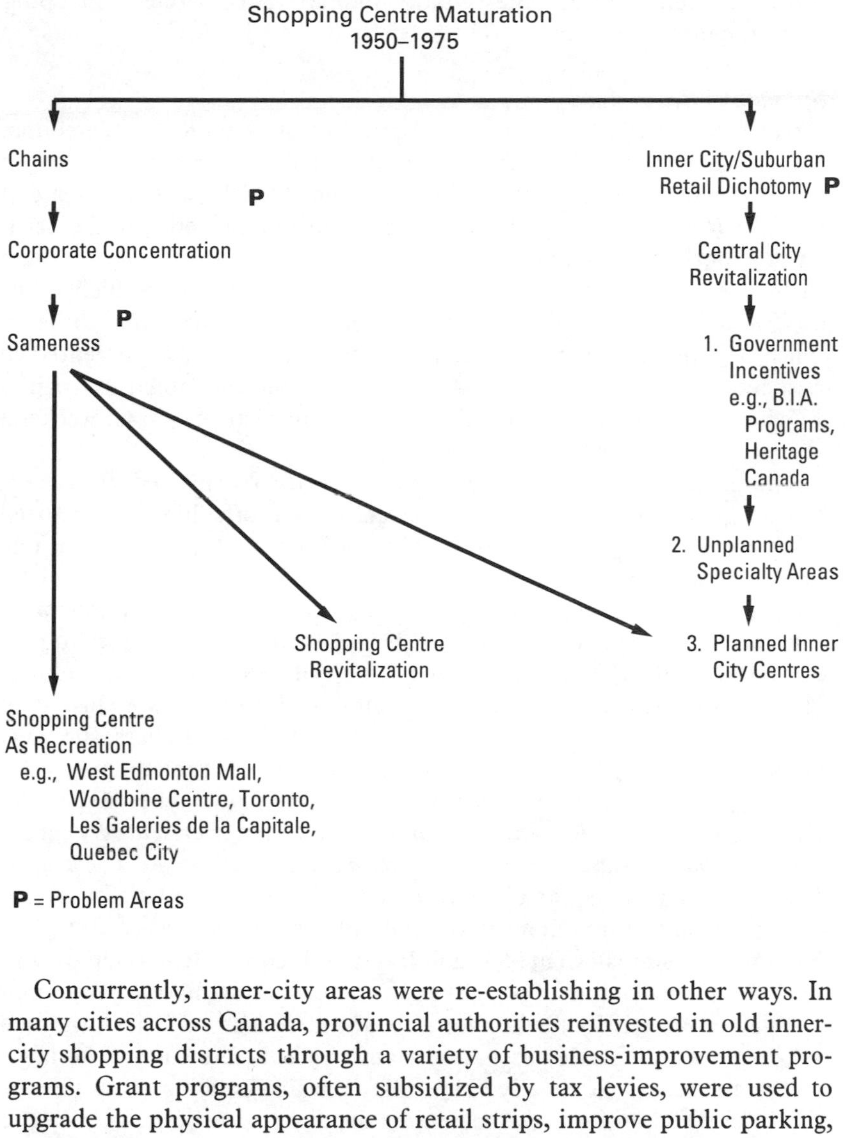

Shopping Centre Maturation
1950–1975

Chains

P

Corporate Concentration

P

Sameness

Shopping Centre
As Recreation
e.g., West Edmonton Mall,
       Woodbine Centre, Toronto,
       Les Galeries de la Capitale,
       Quebec City

Shopping Centre
Revitalization

Inner City/Suburban
Retail Dichotomy **P**

Central City
Revitalization

1. Government
   Incentives
   e.g., B.I.A.
   Programs,
   Heritage
   Canada

2. Unplanned
   Specialty Areas

3. Planned Inner
   City Centres

P = Problem Areas

Concurrently, inner-city areas were re-establishing in other ways. In many cities across Canada, provincial authorities reinvested in old inner-city shopping districts through a variety of business-improvement programs. Grant programs, often subsidized by tax levies, were used to upgrade the physical appearance of retail strips, improve public parking, and provide assistance for a wide range of business activities such as advertising, marketing, and financial management (Holdsworth 1985). In part, these programs were used to offset some of the problems that traditional retail areas experienced from shopping-centre competition. In other cases, inner-city areas rejuvenated naturally. In this scenario, selected inner-city strips in major metropolitan areas developed a specialty focus.

These areas provided an alternative shopping environment to the shopping centre. They stressed assortment and quality of merchandise, merchant expertise, and offered the vitality of an uncontrolled shopping environment.

Specialized Retail Areas

There have always been specialized retail clusters within metropolitan areas. It is the growth in the importance of these types of districts in recent years that is new. Several reasons account for the recent increase in specialty retailing. These include a general consumer reaction to the sterility of suburban plazas; an expansion of consumer demand; and changes in the demographics and lifestyles of the 1980s that have fuelled the explosion in leisure-based shopping. Specialty retailing tends to be an inner-city phenomenon, and is often spatially associated with gentrified residential areas or waterfronts—elements that are also noted in Chapter 13 which deals with the inner city. These retail districts attract weekend shoppers from all over the region.

The pattern of specialty retailing can be either dispersed or concentrated. The former pattern includes merchants who offer highly specialized products (e.g., model trains, comic books, historical documents) and rely on consumer motivations that can be described best as esoteric. These retailers have no need to form specialty clusters since they offer one-of-a-kind merchandise and their customers will travel long distances to purchase the product. The concentrated group of specialty retailers cluster in order to reach a certain set of consumers. These include clusters of antique and art dealers, furniture stores, high-fashion retailers, suppliers of electronic equipment, restaurants, and automobile showrooms.

Jones and Simmons (1987) have identified five distinct types of specialty clusters. These include *specialty-product areas, fashion centres, factory outlets/ off-price centres, historic* or *theme developments,* and *ethnic strips.* These areas can be either planned, or unplanned and serve four distinct sets of consumer demands. First, they cater to individuals who have a preference for high-quality, status-oriented, brand labels and tend to demand high-cost, exclusive goods. Second, they serve consumers who are bargain-conscious and have a propensity to shop for discount merchandise. Third, they are associated with lifestyle purchases that can be linked to cultural heritage, peer-pressure, or age. Finally, they satisfy certain shopping needs that are purely esoteric and are predicated on the need to acquire or collect a particular item.

Specialty-product areas provide an environment for comparison shopping, in which consumers are attracted by the variety offered by a group of stores selling similar goods. Some areas serve an entire metropolitan market (e.g., Granville Island Market, Vancouver; Harbourfront Antiques, Toronto) others serve a smaller portion of it. Those areas that serve the whole metropolitan market tend to locate near the city centre, although automobile showrooms and furniture districts, because of their space requirements, tend to locate at the edge of the urban area in low-rent areas. The neighbourhood specialty strip is typically found in older residential areas that have experienced gentrification (e.g., The Beaches, Toronto; Rue St-Denis, Montreal; Old Strathcona, Edmonton). It provides high-quality food and fashion goods and new forms of personal services, such as health clubs.

Fashion centres and factory-outlet centres are on the opposite sides of the spectrum. Fashion centres deliver designer products in an up-scale environment (e.g., Bay-Bloor/Yorkville, Toronto; Crescent Street, Montreal); factory-outlet centres provide products similar to the fashion centres, perhaps last year's styles or imitations, in low-overhead stores. Both forms of retail development attract the recreational shopper. Fashion streets are often the most expensive and visible shopping locations within the metropolis (e.g., Fifth Avenue, New York City; Michigan Avenue, Chicago) with close links to the high-income sectors and/or to executive employment locations. These high-fashion streets have been particularly attractive to European chains, and, in a number of instances, these retail environments have been incorporated into mix-use projects that integrate offices, hotels, and entertainment. The factory outlet, or off-price centre, is the most recent variant in the evolution of the suburban shopping centre. In these locations, costs are reduced by strategies such as less-glamorous mall design, reduced customer service, minimal mall/store fixturing, and a reliance on merchandise that are end-of-the-line, over-runs, or seconds. In Canada, these centres are not as prominent as in the United States.

Historic redeveloped properties, or theme malls have become a feature of revitalization in older parts of the city, especially in waterfront and warehouse districts. The Historic Properties in Halifax, Quebec City's Lower Town, Toronto's Queen's Quay Terminal Warehouse, and Winnipeg's Warehouse District suggest that a variety of developments are possible. Historic or architecturally important buildings provide the focus. In some developments existing building stock is used, and in others new structures are created. In each case, these environments take on the features of planned shopping centres.

In the United States, these forms of inner-city shopping areas have become commonplace, and have added a new, up-scale dimension to the retail fabric of central cities. One developer, James Rouse, has been prominent in this form of retail renewal. Examples of the 'Rouse Model' include: Faneuil Hall, Boston; the South Street Seaport, New York City; HarborPlace, Baltimore; and The Gallery on Market Street East, Philadelphia. In other cases, a property of some importance is renovated as a specialty theme mall. Examples of these forms of development include:

Trolley Square, Salt Lake City; Union Station and Georgetown Park, Washington D.C.; Jax's Brewery, New Orleans; Old Colony Mill, Keene, N.H.; and Ghirardelli Square, San Francisco.

Unplanned versions of these recreational retailing clusters have also emerged in smaller communities: examples are found in Niagara-on-the-Lake and Elora in Ontario, or Knowlton in Quebec. These retail environments are largely seasonal, and are comprised of independent merchants, although in certain instances land costs/rental rates have put extreme pressure on the traditional character of these areas.

Ethnic strips are normally associated with the point of entry of an ethnic group within a city. At first, the retail component expands to serve the needs of the customers in the immediate neighbourhood, often providing service in the native language. In this phase, certain types of stores and services dominate, in particular, food and fashion retailers, restaurants, and personal services that are linked to the cultural heritage of the community. Eventually, the strip evolves to cater to members of the ethnic group throughout the metropolitan area. In time, these areas may also become tourist attractions as is the case with Kensington Market in Toronto.

The rapid growth of specialty retailing areas has added a new aspect of competition within the urban retail system. The addition of specialty shops and services to the retail strip presents the consumer with an alternative to the conventional shopping centre. It also has created a series of negative externalities for near-by residents, based on the growing retail traffic in certain inner-city neighbourhoods. Independent merchants have normally satisfied specialty retail demands, but more specialized chains now are taking aim at the market niches that such unplanned street environments and theme malls provide. In response, the conventional malls are attempting to develop more distinct images. A new level of complexity has been added to both the geography of urban retailing and the retail location decision.

Downtown

The central business district of a city combines almost all the retail clusters described above. It is the highest-order unplanned centre and it serves the entire metropolitan region. The classic studies of US downtowns that were carried out in the 1950s tended to focus on this component of CBD functioning (see, for example, Murphy 1972). Usually, it incorporates a series of diverse retail areas. These can include skidrow retailing that features bars, cheap restaurants, and adult entertainment; high-fashion streets; major inner-city shopping centres; entertainment districts; traditional shopping streets; underground retail concourses or ancillary malls associated with mixed-use developments; and historic redeveloped specialty retail areas.

Downtown provides a distinct shopping environment. In many major US cities, and in many smaller centres in Canada, this environment has been threatened by the continued development of suburban shopping centres within an essentially 'no-growth' market. In other centres, including most major Canadian metropolitan areas, the downtown is expanding, with new construction and redevelopment. In a retail context, Eaton's has been the major player in the retail redevelopment of over twenty Canadian cores (Table 15.2).

In both Canada and the US, the key to downtown survival is the vibrancy of the economic base of the community or region as a whole. The downtowns of 'blue-collar' industrial cities (e.g., Hamilton, Sudbury, Windsor) are most vulnerable. Downtowns are more successful in cities such as London or Saskatoon that act as regional service centres. Obviously a number of factors contribute to the success of downtown retailing. These include a strong public transit system that focuses on the core; a concentration of office/government employment in the downtown area; inner-city high-rise apartment or condominium developments; a safe, unthreatening inner-city environment; and the willingness of major retailers (normally department stores), developers, and financial institutions to invest in the central area.

TOWARDS A CLASSIFICATION OF THE URBAN RETAIL SYSTEM

This section will suggest a classification system for urban retailing. This attempt to generalize should be balanced by the realization that the retail landscape within metropolitan areas is difficult to categorize. Neighbourhoods change, access patterns evolve, consumer preferences are modified, and new retail forms are developed. In effect, new retail typologies emerge daily. Many retail stores and districts are continuously undergoing change. If a store does not work with one type of product, the retailer can shift the product mix, or alter the image or advertising. It is not uncommon for the same location to go through dozens of variations in function and/or form over a twenty year period.

Four different approaches have been taken to produce a taxonomy of the urban retail structure. These relate to the *morphology* or spatial form of the cluster, the *functional composition* of the business types in the cluster, the *composition of the market* that the cluster serves, and the *ownership* patterns that differentiate planned and unplanned centres. Most taxonomies include each of these characteristics to some degree.

The visibility and familiarity of retail activities led early researchers to focus on the shape and boundaries of retail conformations. Where was the edge of the central business district? How was it spatially defined? Were the shopping districts in a city node, or were they linear, stretching along major streets with no apparent internal organization? In these studies, what becomes apparent is that the inner-city and suburban retail systems are distinct on a number of morphological dimensions. Functional studies examine the types of businesses within the retail cluster. Does the area satisfy shopping or convenience needs? Are the goods sold in a certain retail area, high- or low-order? Where does the retail centre fit within the retail hierarchy? Market composition differentiates those specialized clusters that have apparently similar functions (bars, restaurants, and fashion shops), but serve distinct market segments. The contemporary urban retail landscape mirrors a society that has become increasingly segmented. Retail areas have emerged that cater to particular market or lifestyle groupings—Italians, Chinese, inner-city urban professionals, 'punks', or young families. Finally, ownership distinguishes unplanned clusters from the major post-war innovation in the retail structure—the planned shopping centre. Over the past thirty years, the shopping centre and the retail chain have become inextricably linked. The planned shopping centre provides the retail chain with a controlled environment, a known market, a fixed traffic flow, and in Canada, because of zoning protection, a form of spatial monopoly. Conversely, the retail chain assures the developer of a known and successful product-mix and type of operation, a 'triple A' tenant, and a track record for generating known levels of sales. For both parties, the arrangement minimizes uncertainty.

In this chapter, a revised version of the taxonomy developed by Jones and Simmons (1987) is presented (Figure 15.3). The system considers five criteria for classifying urban retailing. Retail areas are differentiated according to their morphology, location, structural environment, and market size and type. In constructing the system, each urban retail area initially is defined as either a centre or a strip. Then, in sequential stages, all areas are placed into either inner-city or suburban categories; centres are further subdivided into planned or unplanned classes. Within the system, each retail area then is assigned a position in the intra-urban retail hierarchy that reflects the size of market it serves, and is defined further as satisfying either spatial or specialized markets.

Inner-city retailing has been dominated historically by the unplanned shopping area. In this classification, three unplanned forms are possible—the CBD; specialty product areas; and major retail clusters at major intersections served by public transit. The first two serve metropolitan markets; the latter, more regional demands. Planned inner-city shopping areas are a recent phenomenon, and have become a common feature in urban Canada since the mid–1970s. In the downtown core, two types of planned centres have emerged—the central-city fashion mall, that often has been the focus of major urban-revitalization projects; and the ancillary retail complex that has become the normal underground use in major office, hotel, or condominium developments in Montreal and Toronto.

Since the 1970s, four other planned-centre types have emerged in the inner city. These include theme malls; infill shopping centres; retail mall developments at major intersections; and superstores or hypermarkets. Theme malls are a recent phenomenon, and normally are tourist-oriented,

Figure 15.3
A Typology of the Contemporary Urban Retail System

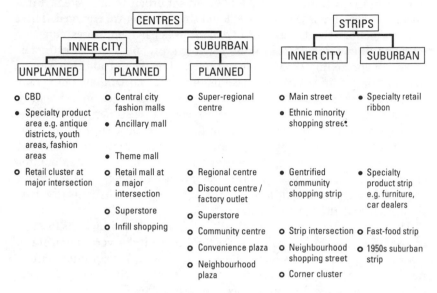

NOTE: In this classification the term 'planned' refers to a retail environment that is developed, designed, and managed as a unit and where the tenancy and common areas are under corporate control.

Items marked: o serve spatial markets;
• serve specialized markets.

occupy waterfront locations, and promote a distinct specialty-product theme and atmosphere. The infill centre is a typical suburban shopping centre that has been transplanted in the inner city. These centres were developed when the major development firms were faced with a saturated suburban market, and new growth opportunities were restricted to neglected inner-city areas. The development of planned centres at major inner-city intersections represented a modernization of traditional retailing at these shopping nodes. These centres took advantage of the established public-transit linkages and the traditional region·al shopping-focus that such areas provided. The superstore represents the return of the major supermarket chains to previously abandoned inner-city locations. Typically, these single retail units occupy a minimum of 50,000 square feet, offer discount prices, and wide product-assortment, and rely on extensive trading areas.

The classification of planned, suburban shopping centres is essentially hierarchical, ranging from the convenience plaza to the super-regional shopping centre. Following standardized methods used in classic central-place research, this hierarchy can be measured by several criteria, such as number of stores, number of establishment types, total square footage, total selling area, number of parking spaces, customer volumes, trade area size, rental rates, and sales per square foot values. Since the 1960s, there have been three additions to the planned suburban retail system. First, during the late 1960s the super-regional shopping centre emerged. These centres, anchored by a minimum of two major department stores, comprise over a million square feet of gross leasable area, and serve an estimated market of approximately 500,000 customers. The second addition was the discount or off-price centre. These malls afford 'no-frill' shopping, and cater to a market segment that is interested in bargain-oriented shopping. This discount trend is reflected in the growth of three other retail forms— the factory outlet, the flea market, and the warehouse/superstore. More recently, other variants of the suburban shopping centre have evolved. The mega-mall/recreational complex has been launched in Edmonton (Johnson 1987), and new suburban shopping complexes are becoming increasingly directed towards distinct market segments, namely, the family market and the young urban professional.

The retail strip can be effectively differentiated according to its location in the inner city or the suburbs. In the inner city, several retail forms can be identified. Main streets (the downtown strip), strip intersections, neighbourhood shopping streets, and corner-store clusters have served essentially the same functions since the early 1900s. The main street still remains the primary focus of retail activity for most Canadian cities, although its proportion of total urban retail sales has declined. Neighbourhood retail areas continue to serve the daily needs of local populations, and reflect the cultural and life-style characteristics of the resident population of the areas that they serve. These neighbourhood strips are some of the most volatile elements in the urban retail landscape. The ethnic-minority and gentrified-community shopping strips have developed specialized retail functions. They have evolved to serve metropolitan-wide markets, particularly with respect to restaurants, fashion goods, and specialized products (e.g., art and antiques).

In the suburbs, four distinct forms of strip retailing have evolved. All reflect the dominance of the automobile. The first comprises the 1950 suburban strip-shopping-mall phenomenon (see, for example, Boal and Johnson 1965). These 'unplanned' developments represented the first stage in the retail expansion to the suburbs, and were restricted to major suburban arterial locations. Normally, they are characterized by a series of small centres, with limited parking that abuts the front of these properties. Some suburban arterials-strip-malls have taken on a specialty focus. Typically, these specialized clusters include fast-food restaurants, automobile dealers, furniture warehouses, home-improvement retailers, and discount merchandisers.

This classification provides a conceptual framework for understanding the complexity of the urban retail environment. In evaluating this typology, it should be remembered that between 10 per cent and 15 per cent of stores are classed as downtown, and perhaps another 20 per cent are located in the outlying shopping centres. In total, these major nodes, with their larger stores and chain focus, account for close to half the sales in the city. However, it should be remembered that two-thirds of urban retailers operate in a variety of shopping environments other than downtown and suburban shopping centres, and serve both specialized and convenience-oriented needs.

CONCLUSION

The intra-urban urban retail system is structurally complex. In attempting to understand this environment, three distinct approaches should be integrated (Figure 15.4). First, it is necessary to describe and develop an inventory of the basic functional characteristics and spatial distribution of the retail structure. Here, such basic dimensions as retail type, number

Figure 15.4
An Integrated Framework for the Study of the Intra-urban Retail System

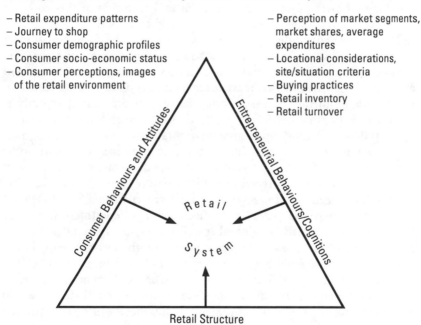

- Retail expenditure patterns
- Journey to shop
- Consumer demographic profiles
- Consumer socio-economic status
- Consumer perceptions, images
  of the retail environment

- Perception of market segments,
  market shares, average
  expenditures
- Locational considerations,
  site/situation criteria
- Buying practices
- Retail inventory
- Retail turnover

- Retail inventory
- Number of stores,
  number of establishments
- Retail square footage
- Total retail sales
- Retail employment

- Parking spaces
- Retail change
- Ownership patterns
- Degree of government
  involvement

of stores, employment, ownership, and store turn-over rates should be documented and analysed. The second and third approaches examine the retail system from the traditional perspectives of demand and supply. The geographer has been more comfortable examining the spatial aspects of demand. Here, consumer behaviour and attitudes are measured empirically in terms of retail expenditure patterns, journey-to-shop, distance-decay relationships, or images of various retail environments. Typically, the market is assessed in terms of location, areal extent, income level (market size), demographic composition, and lifestyle characteristics. The third component, retail supply, normally has been overlooked in most geographic appraisals of the urban retail landscape. But by focusing on entrepreneurial decisions, the form, spatial distribution, and dynamics of urban retailing can be better understood. Important questions to be addressed include: How do particular retailers react to specific market segments? How does the retail firm decide what retail merchandise to stock in a particular area? How are locational strategies formulated? What is the relationship between the retail chain and the shopping centre developer? What determines the retailer's ability to pay for a particular location? By conceptualizing the retail system in these terms, our ability to understand and contribute to the development and planning of this complex and volatile environment will be significantly increased.

This chapter concludes by speculating on some of the changes that most probably will affect the Canadian urban retailing system over the next decade. First, as our population ages, new retail types and forms will emerge. The growth of this market segment will place new demands on the system, requiring increased convenience, new merchandising mixes, and the growth of new specialty chains that specifically cater to the 'greying' population. Second, the degree of corporate concentration throughout the Canadian retail system will continue to increase. This will occur through acquisition, and by the arrival in Canada of major American and European retailers. This trend reflects the natural growth of an international retail system and the realities of the Canada-United States General Trade Agreement. The sectors most affected will be department stores and fashion retailers. Third, on a number of dimensions, the retail structures of our metropolitan areas are becoming increasingly schizophrenic. In the future, the dichotomy between inner-city and suburban retailing will increase. Certain areas will cater exclusively to particular market segments, and shopping environments will be developed to serve distinct lifestyle groupings, normally the affluent. Structurally, there will be a continued growth in either large, super-regional malls or small convenience centres. Similarly, at a store level, this trend will continue as fashion retailers and most shopping-mall tenants demand small square-footages, while 'stand-alone' superstores will become the preferred format for food, drug, furniture, electronics, recreation and leisure, toy, and home-improvement retailers. Finally, new issues will emerge that will influence the operation of our retail system. These may include the issue of property rights and shopping centre access, the consequences of an oversupply of stores on new retail development, the role of planning legislation on the final disposition of our urban retail future, and the impact of non-store selling, particularly mail-order, TV shop-at-home, and computer-based shopping, on the purchasing patterns of the Canadian consumer.

The retail landscape continually is washed by waves of innovation. New products, new store types, and new locations emerge, and new market segments are identified. There is a constant interplay among the actors—the retailers, the consumers, and the developers. In this system, the winners and losers are quickly identified and new retail environments constantly evolve.

FURTHER READING

DAWSON, J.A. 1983 *Shopping Centre Development* (London: Longman)

———— and LORD, J.D. 1985 *Shopping Centre Development: Policies and Prospects* (London: Croom Helm)

EPSTEIN, B.J. 1978 'Marketing Geography: A Chronicle of 45 Years', *Proceedings of the Applied Geography Conference* 1, 372–79

HOLDSWORTH, D. 1985 *Reviving Main Street* (Toronto: University of Toronto Press)

JONES, K. and SIMMONS, J.W.S. 1990 *The Retail Environment* (London: Routledge)

WRIGLEY, N. ed. 1988 *Store Choice, Store Location and Market Analysis* (London: Routledge)

REFERENCES

APPLEBAUM, W. 1968 *A Guide to Store Location Research* (Reading, Mass.: Addison-Wesley)

BERRY, B.J.L. 1963 *Commercial Structure and Commercial Blight* (Chicago: University of Chicago, Department of Geography, Research Paper No. 85)

BEVERIDGE, S.B. 1985 *Patterns of Retail Turnover and Seed-bed Activity: London, 1978–1980* (London: Department of Geography, University of Western Ontario, unpublished M.A. thesis)

Canadian Directory of Shopping Centres 1989/1988 (Toronto: Maclean Hunter)

DAVIES, R.J. 1976 *Marketing Geography: With Special Reference to Retailing* (London: Methuen)

———— and ROGERS, D.S. eds 1984 *Store Location and Store Assessment Research* (Chichester: John Wiley & Son)

DAWSON, J.A. and LORD, J.D. 1985 *Shopping Centre Development: Policies and Prospects* (London: Croom Helm)

DOUCET, M.J., JACOBS, A.H., and JONES, K.G. 1988 'Megachains in the Canadian Retail Environment', *International Journal of Retailing* 3, 5–23

EPSTEIN, B.J. 1978 'Marketing Geography: A Chronicle of 45 Years', *Proceedings of the Applied Geography Conference* 1, 372–79

HOLDSWORTH, D. 1985 *Reviving Main Street* (Toronto: University of Toronto Press)

JOHNSON, D.B. 1987 'The West Edmonton Mall—From Super-Regional to Mega-Regional Shopping Centre', *International Journal of Retailing* 2, 53–69

JONES, K.G. 1984 *Specialty Retailing in the Inner City* (Toronto: York University, Department of Geography, Monograph No.15)

—— and SIMMONS J. 1987 *Location, Location, Location: Analyzing the Retail Environment* (Toronto: Methuen)

LAULAJAINEN, R. 1987 *Spatial Strategies in Retailing* (Dordrecht, Holland: D. Reidel)

LEA, A.C. 1989 'An Overview of Formal Methods for Retail Site Evaluation and Sales Forecasting', *The Operational Geographer* 7 (2), 8–17

METROPOLITAN TORONTO PLANNING DEPARTMENT 1987 *Retailing in Metropolitan Toronto and Regional Municipalities 1987* (Toronto: Metropolitan Toronto Planning Department, Research Division)

MURPHY, R.E. 1972 *The Central Business District* (Chicago: Aldine Atherton Press)

PROUDFOOT, M.J. 1937 'City Retail Structure', *Economic Geography* 13, 425–28

Report on the Royal Commission on Price Spreads 1935 (Ottawa: King's Printer)

SHAW, G. 1978 *Processes and Pattern in the Geography of Retail Change with Special Reference to Kingston-upon-Hull* (Hull: University of Hull, Occasional Papers in Geography, No. 24)

SIBLEY, D. 1976 *The Small Shop in the City* (Hull: University of Hull, Occasional Papers in Geography, No. 22)

SIMMONS, J.W. 1966 *Toronto's Changing Retail Complex* (Chicago: University of Chicago, Department of Geography, Research Paper No. 104)

16

Manufacturing in Canadian Cities

PIERRE FILION AND
DENNIS MOCK

Industrial locations are at once a reflection and a factor of metropolitan evolution. Thus, by investigating the location of industrial activities, we consider a critical aspect of metropolitan regions' development. Industrial locations are also an important object of study because of their considerable social and environmental impacts. Social impacts stem from profound employment changes in Canadian cities' manufacturing base and the movement of plants to the suburbs, away from traditional inner-city working-class neighbourhoods but close to residential areas. Environmental consequences vary according to the location. Pollution generated by older, more obsolete central-city establishments is often painfully felt in surrounding residential neighbourhoods. Meanwhile, in the remainder of the metropolitan region the existence of newer, cleaner, better-controlled industrial parks reduces this environmental impact. But the ever increasing reliance on truck deliveries, which is associated with suburban industrial linkage patterns, is itself becoming a major source of environmental damage.

This chapter first defines 'manufacturing establishment', and then explores the different theoretical approaches to industrial location. After that, the chapter provides a brief background on industrial development in Canada; it shows that manufacturing is proportionally less important in Canada than in many other developed countries, and that Canada is presently engaged in a de-industrialization trend. This discussion of background factors then leads to a description of the evolution of intra-metropolitan industrial locations in Canada. The chapter focuses more directly on the types of industries and the features of industrial districts that are specific to three metropolitan sectors: central cities, suburbs, and outer suburbs. The discussion then moves to municipal interventions regarding industrial development, distinguishing between measures that aim at controlling development and those that attempt to stimulate industrialization. The chapter ends by considering the diverging interpretations of Canadian intra-urban industrial location that stem from the major theoretical perspectives on this phenomenon.

MANUFACTURING ESTABLISHMENTS

Simply put, a manufacturing establishment uses raw or semi-processed materials, increases their value by transforming them, and then sells them for profit. Accordingly, the activities of such establishments can be grouped in three distinct stages: procurement or input; processing; and distribution or output (Hoover 1948, 7). Each stage requires specific factors of production. First, transportation is required to assure the delivery of primary materials. Second, the processing stage depends on labour, parcels of land, space within buildings, machinery, and energy. Finally, transportation is again a necessary condition to the distribution of the firm's products. Moreover, of critical importance is capital, which is indispensable to the launching and continuation of the production process. When discussing manufacturing inputs and outputs, one must equally acknowledge the gravity of the polluting by-products of production that take the form of air emissions, liquid effluent as well as noise and occasionally radioactivity. Carriers that are responsible for moving factories' inputs and outputs are themselves major air- and noise-pollution generators. Finally, there are many forms of visual pollution such as outside storage, run-down buildings, and inappropriately-fenced facilities that pose a more subtle problem. This type of pollution is felt especially in older areas where industry conflicts with residential, commercial, and institutional uses, and in the outer fringe of cities where industries encroach on rural landscapes.

Manufacturing plants can be classified under different categories according to the nature of their production process. There are processing plants that deal with products incurring large weight losses during manufacturing. These plants generally transform raw materials. Steel mills that convert iron ore into steel are an example. Fabricating plants constitute another category. They deal with inputs that undergo minimum weight loss during the manufacturing process and create bulky, heavy outputs. Examples of such establishments are food-processing, textile, and clothing plants. Integration plants are a final category. These assemble fabricated products or component parts into finished outputs for the consumer market. This output tends to be bulky and fragile. One thinks here of automobile assembly plants (Norcliffe 1975). Some plants are dedicated essentially to standard products; others are involved in research and development to improve or modify existing products or create new ones. Moving through the chapter we shall see how differences in location patterns echo these three categories' specific requirements.

PERSPECTIVES ON INDUSTRIAL LOCATION

Industrial location patterns reflect a dynamic process of births (starting businesses), deaths (often resulting from bankruptcy or take-overs) and transfers that occur when plants change location. Also relevant is *in situ* alteration, expansion and contraction. Most investigations on industrial location concern births and transfers. Deaths, expansions, alterations, and contractions have received comparatively little attention. Explanations of manufacturing location can be grouped into three broad categories on the basis of shared assumptions.

Economic Rationality Theories

These theories are so called because they assume that industrial location decisions are guided exclusively by a desire to achieve or increase profits. Economic rationality theories also presume that decision-makers possess the information and the ability required to make the most effective location choices. These theories offer methods that attempt to identify sites that assure a balance between different factors of production in order to achieve revenue maximization and expenditure minimization. Economic rationality pertains both to deductive and normative theories. Deductive theories offer concepts based on abstractions of reality rather than modelling current location patterns; normative theories postulate the best locations for given types of establishment.

One body of economic rationality theories belongs to the least-cost approach. Alfred Weber (1929, originally published in German in 1909) launched this approach by identifying points of minimum transportation costs for different types of firms according to the nature of their inputs and outputs. He demonstrated that for processing plants the optimal location is close to the source of raw materials because of the important weight loss involved in their transformation process. On the other hand, in the case of plants where little weight is lost and where the end product is bulky (fabricating and integration plants), the optimal site is close to markets. But Weber also recognizes the existence of factors of deviation from transportation optimality. The need to take advantage of labour and agglomeration economies (see below for explanations) induces some firms to diverge from location optimalities defined solely on the basis of transportation considerations. This occurs particularly within high-value-added industries, that is industries where materials go through extensive transformation. For such firms economies accruing from other factors, such as easy accessibility to a low-cost labour force, will more than make up for higher raw-material or finished-product transportation expenses. Detailed graphical and mathematical formulation of Weber's model can be found in many contemporary texts in economic geography (see, for example, Smith 1981, 69–75).

Grounded in these same principles of location optimality, followers of Weber lengthened the list of location factors, and were responsible for variations in the importance ascribed to these different factors. For example, Hoover (1948, 89) gives considerable weight to the cost of industrial land, while Courchene (1986), a Canadian representative of the neo-classical economics tradition, explains industrial location primarily on the basis of labour costs and productivity levels. Within the least-cost tradition, Vernon (1966; 1979) has demonstrated that location requirements vary mostly according to firms' life cycle. Small, fledgling firms will tend to locate where they can interact easily with other firms, as they are particularly dependent on external economies at this early stage of their evolution. (*External economies* can be defined as savings that proceed from factors that are external to the firm, such as access to a low-cost labour force, efficient transportation and the possibility of maintaining linkages; *internal economies* are largely the result of improvements in a firm's production process.) Later, as they grow and internalize many of these external economies, firms become less dependent on contacts with other firms, and can choose among a wider variety of locations.

A consideration of urban industrial locations calls for a discussion of agglomeration economies. In cities, firms enjoy a wide variety of external economies that result from their presence in an urban setting. The accessibility to a large labour pool, the sharing of public facilities and services, economies of supply and distribution come easily to mind as examples of urbanization or agglomeration economies. Economies of supply and distribution are referred to as linkages when they consist of inter-firm transactions. Linkages can involve a movement of goods, as in the case of components reaching an assembly plant, or take the form of services, which primarily entail the movement of persons. Service linkages often include professional inputs, such as the use of a legal firm to prepare contracts, the reliance on a specialized firm to organize the marketing of a product, or more customarily, banking services (in relation to service linkages, see Bater and Walker 1977). Finally, information linkages are a form of linkage that is becoming increasingly important. This is the case of exchanges of design specifications between supply and parent companies. Information linkages may involve face-to-face contact, be delivered on a paper support, or be transmitted electronically. Chapter

Figure 16.1
Major Landowners (over 4 acres): Stockyards Industrial District

CITY OF YORK

Phantom Industries

Scrap Yard

Metro Roads Yard

Grace Meat Packers

Auto Pound

Banner Rendering

Banks Bros.

City Limit

Ontario Hydro

Reliable Transport

Coca Cola

Metro Waste Transfer Station

Feather Industries

Select Meats

Parking

Swift Eastern

Lumberking

Standard Aggregates

G & W Freight Ways

Darnigos

Old Weston Road

Levine Bros.

Shur-gain

City Limit

Packing House

Canada Packers

Edible Oils Refinery

C.N. Yards

Runnymede Road

Hunnisett

St. Clair Avenue West

Scrap Yard

Beef Terminal

Corporate Research Centre

Cattle

Trucking

Benjamin Moore Paints

Hepburn Steel

National Casing

Hogs

Canadian Dressed Meats

Ontario Stockyards

Head Office

G. Bell Arena

Hay Barns

St. Clair Poultry

Cattle

Cadet Cleaners

Former Prime Packers Site

Canadian Pacific Railways

Keele Centre

Keele Street

National Rubber

Dundas Street West

Cattle | Major Landowners and Sites

Other Meat-Packing and Related Uses

Maple Leaf Mills

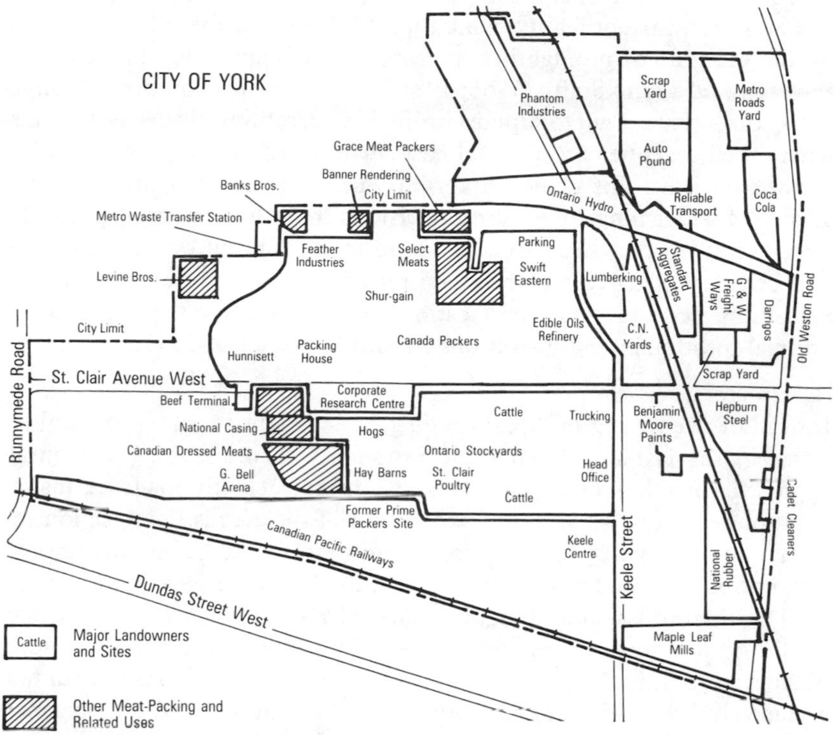

SOURCE: City of Toronto, 1984.

6 discusses in detail the impacts and potential impacts of 'high-tech' information technologies.

Returning to this chapter's spatial theme, plants that are tied together by intense linkages will tend to cluster into functional complexes so as to benefit to the fullest from agglomeration economies. Functional complexes consist of groups of firms that belong to the same sector of the economy, interact intensely with each other, and are located in the same area. The Toronto Stockyards Industrial District is a clear example of a functional complex (see Figure 16.1). Clustered within a 0.5 kilometre radius are the Ontario Stockyards, the largest public stockyards in Canada, and seventeen meat-packing firms. Meat-packing industries developed around the stockyards since the yards' inception in 1903. Proximity to the stockyards was critical because of the bulk-handling difficulties and perishable nature of meat products. In 1976, the stockyards and the meat-packing industry together employed 3,000 people in the district (City of Toronto 1984). Other examples of functional complexes are the garment industries of Montreal and Toronto.

The search for optimality, which guides least-cost theories, is relaxed by the margins of profitability approach. This approach, developed by Rawston (1958) and Smith (1966; 1981, 109–15), focuses on the full range of locations that are apt to support profitable operations, that is, operations where total revenue exceeds total cost. A firm can maintain profitability anywhere within this range or margin. Such models allow the consideration of a wider range of location decisions than the least-cost approach, which requires that such decisions tend towards profit optimization. In that sense, the margins of profitability approach is more successful at explaining existing industrial location patterns, which often depart from optimal locations (see illustrations in Smith 1981, 112–3, 116).

Behavioural Theories

Instead of attempting to explain industrial locations in pure profitability terms in the fashion of economic rationality theories, the behavioural approach considers how location decisions are actually made. A major point of departure between the two groups of theories is the rejection by behavioural theorists of the rational and omniscient 'economic person' assumption that underpins economic rationality theories (Cooper 1975, 10–1). Under this assumption, decision-makers combine a full knowledge of all location possibilities and the capacity to process this information. Furthermore, this assumption implies that location decisions are guided exclusively by pure economic interest and are unaffected by personal preferences. From the behavioural viewpoint, the 'economic person' assumption clashes with the reality of industrial location decision-making. According to behavioural theorists, there is a cost to decision-making and, more particularly, to the collection and processing of information. These costs constrain the ability to gather a sufficient quantity and quality of information to achieve full knowledge and the ability to use this information in order to reach a perfect solution (Pred 1967; 1969). It follows that to contain decision-making expenditures, managers will settle for satisfactory rather than optimal outcomes (Cyert and March 1963; March and Simon 1958; Simon 1956). A typical 'satisficing' location search will settle for the first acceptable option encountered. This contrasts with optimizing searches, which require an exhaustive assessment of all possibilities. The behavioural perspective also recognizes the influence personal preferences can have on industrial location decisions. For example, early plant-transfers from the inner city to suburbs have been partly attributed to managers' desire to reduce their commuting journey (see illustration in Smith 1981, 119).

The Transition to Post-Fordism

While behavioural theories moderate location assumptions underlying the economic rationality perspective by demonstrating that optimal locations are rarely achieved, other theorists make a clear break with these assumptions. In their view, the economy is driven by long-term trends that result from efforts to maximize or maintain profits in a constantly evolving class-struggle environment (Aglietta 1979; 1982; Houle 1983). By considering both the production and the consumption spheres, these theorists highlight the role that consumption plays in 'regulating' the economic system as a whole. They are also attentive to the international redeployment of different industrial sectors.

In this perspective, the economy of the developed world is currently transformed by the passage from the Fordist phase (named after Henry Ford, who introduced assembly-line production and higher wages for production workers) to a post-Fordist phase. Fordism was characterized by a standardization of consumer goods, mass-production techniques, and the payment of relatively high wages to industrial workers, which enabled them to partake in the consumption of mass-produced consumer goods. Production was then concentrated in the large industrial cities of First World nations. Post-Fordism, which is rapidly overtaking Fordism, grows out of a considerable transfer of production capacity from developed to less developed countries, and a tendency for large corporations to contract out more of their operations (Scott 1988). Post-Fordism is also associated with a reduced standardization of consumer goods (for example, the multiplication of food-product varieties in response to increasing market segmentation).

In developed countries, this transition has resulted in devastating losses of industrial employment, and a deterioration of industrial workers' wages and working conditions. From a spatial perspective, urban sectors such as the central city, where traditional, labour-intensive industries are concentrated, have been particularly hard hit by the movement towards post-Fordism. Smaller manufacturing cities where these kinds of industries dominate the economy also suffered. This is particularly the case of some cities surrounding the two metropolitan centres of Montreal and Toronto such as, for example, Sorel (shipbuilding), Valleyfield (textile), and Welland (textile and metals).

Within this framework, location becomes an instrument of exploitation. This is because threats to relocate constitute an important weapon that firms can deploy to discipline workers. Also, firms can intensify the exploitation of workers (and therefore of regions and communities) by locating plants where labour costs are lowest. Massey (1984) has shown that corporations segment production processes in order to take maximum advantage of the labour-skill/labour-cost balance provided by different regions and cities. Production stages that entail simple routine work settle in areas offering an unskilled labour force at a low cost, while less standardized stages locate in sectors with a skilled labour force that expects higher wages.

FROM INDUSTRIALISM TO POST-INDUSTRIALISM
IN CANADA?

This section provides a short background on industrial development in Canada. For a start, as was stressed in Chapter 5, it must be acknowledged that the Canadian economy is, to a larger extent than other developed Western economies, polarized around the primary and tertiary sectors. Canada's manufacturing sector is atrophied by comparison. In 1984, manufacturing value added accounted for 17.2 per cent of Canada's gross domestic product (GDP), which is much lower than the average 23.6 per cent for the seven most developed countries belonging to the Organization for Economic Cooperation and Development (OECD). In Germany, the OECD country that allocates the highest proportion of its GDP to manufacturing, this figure reaches 31.2 per cent (OECD 1988, 59). In the light of these figures, it is hardly surprising that in most manufacturing sectors Canada posts a deficit balance of trade, that is, the value of imported products exceeds that of exports (McFetridge 1986, 10). This underdevelopment of the Canadian manufacturing sector has been attributed to the modest size of the Canadian consumer market, which is roughly equal to that in the State of California but impractically spread along a 6,000-kilometre band. Another factor is unusually high foreign ownership. As a result, much of Canada's manufacturing has historically been carried out by branch plants, which were set up by parent companies to enter the Canadian market without paying import tariffs. In this context, foreign ownership was less than conducive to the development of new products and to a healthy Canadian manufacturing export sector (Britton 1980).

From a historical point of view, Canadian manufacturing has experienced, and is still experiencing, a decline in its proportional importance within the economy. In absolute terms, manufacturing employment grew until 1981 and then declined slightly between 1981 and 1986. As a proportion of total Canadian employment, manufacturing lost considerable ground throughout the entire period between 1951 and 1986. In 1986, this sector accounted for 16.8 per cent of total employment, while in 1951, this proportion was 24.5 per cent (Statistics Canada 1988a, Table 1).

A number of factors explain this downward trend. First, automation has long been a major cause of decline in manufacturing employment. But it is noteworthy that employment loss due to automation does not normally translate into reduced manufacturing output. To the contrary, since automation usually enhances workers' productivity levels, such employment cutbacks are accompanied by augmented outputs. Another factor of decline is a consumption pattern that is increasingly directed towards services. Expansion in the durable consumer-goods sector abates when a number of needs are satisfied (cars, appliances, clothing, etc.). Meanwhile, a growing proportion of disposable income goes towards services such as education, restaurant meals, entertainment, tourism, and fitness clubs. We can expect this trend to accelerate with an ageing population that will consume services such as tourism and health care extensively.

The greatest threat to Canadian manufacturing comes, however, from a globalization of the economy in the wake of diminished transportation costs, a lowering of tariffs, and an ongoing expansion of multinational corporations. On the one hand, new areas of development, which seriously challenge more traditional ones, have emerged on the international scene. These economies allocate a higher proportion of their resources towards non-military research and development than other industrial nations, and have evolved new organization techniques to enhance industrial productivity. The success of Japan in the automobile and electronics sector comes immediately to mind. On the other hand, standardized production plants are locating in less developed countries where labour costs are lower. For example, in 1986, iron-and-steel manufacturing hourly compensation (including salaries and benefits) was $16.50 in Canada, compared with $2.32 in Korea and $1.86 in Brazil (United Nations 1988, 245). Most vulnerable are Canadian labour-intensive manufacturing sectors, which are particularly exposed to foreign competition. Between 1966 and 1985, the average annual import-value growth rate reached 9.4 per cent in the textile sector and a staggering 15.7 per cent in the clothing sector (DRIE 1986). As expected, employment in these sectors suffered a serious decline. Between 1973 and 1983, total textile employment dropped by 26.6 per cent, while clothing endured a 13.2 per cent employment loss (Ahmad 1988).

The vulnerability of certain Canadian manufacturing sectors is further exposed by the Canada-United States General Trade Agreement (the Free Trade Deal). As tariffs are phased out, Canadian plants will be in direct competition with US establishments, some of which are located in regions where factors of production—notably transport, labour, and infrastructure—are cheaper than in Canada.

The above factors seem to point towards the disappearance of Canadian manufacturing; and towards the transition to a post-industrial society where the production and consumption of goods give way to services. We must be cautious in interpreting these trends. Although manufacturing employment is declining in relative, and, of late, in absolute terms and consumers are allocating increasing shares of their expenditure to services, the consumption of goods still holds up in absolute terms. Accordingly, the decline in manufacturing employment is not caused by a waning interest in consumer goods; it is rather a result of greater automation and an international redistribution of manufacturing capacity that has been unfavourable to Canada. Moreover, former manufacturing jobs are reclassified as service-sector jobs because firms are now more likely to subcontract tasks that support production such as building upkeep (Scott 1988). Finally, employment in the trade sector, which is mostly devoted to the handling and marketing of consumer goods, has swelled since 1951. It

Figure 16.2
Railways and Industry, 1897 and 1913

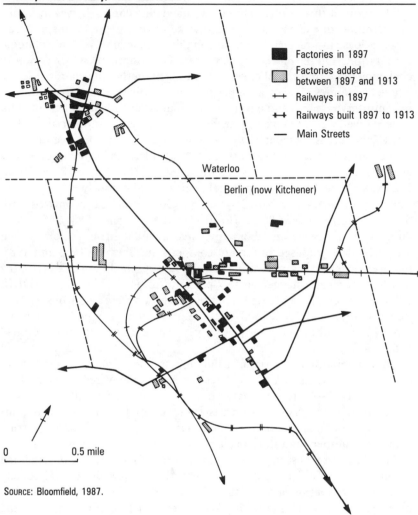

Factories in 1897

Factories added
between 1897 and 1913

Railways in 1897

Railways built 1897 to 1913

Main Streets

Waterloo

Berlin (now Kitchener)

0   0.5 mile

Source: Bloomfield, 1987.

accounted for 14.1 per cent of total employment in 1951; by 1986, this
sector employed 16.4 per cent of the Canadian work force, a proportion
that was only 0.4 per cent lower than that for the manufacturing sector
(Statistics Canada 1988a, Table 1).

THE EVOLUTION OF METROPOLITAN INDUSTRIAL
LOCATION IN CANADA

Early stages of industrialization in Canadian cities occurred in core areas.
Such locations offered proximity to harbours and canals, which were the
primary points of raw-materials access and of finished-products shipment.

In addition, by locating in cities manufacturers reaped economies of urbanization that resulted from access to a large labour pool (for the time), and the possibility of forging linkages with other establishments in related industrial sectors. Visitors to Old Montreal, Old Quebec, and the Halifax Historic Properties can see industrial buildings dating from this period.

With the advent of railways, industrial areas developed along adjoining sites, largely because the land was made available for this purpose by railway companies. Industrial areas then took a predominantly linear configuration, and radiated from the core towards the outskirts of cities along railway lines. In many cities this contributed to the establishment of a sectoral land-use alignment (discussed further in Chapters 10 and 12). In larger cities, the opening of belt lines meant to by-pass the central area somewhat modified this radial pattern. Kitchener provides a classic illustration of this first wave of industrial decentralization. Although waterways did not play a role in the early stage of industrialization in Kitchener (then named Berlin), early manufacturing firms still located in the core. They were originally to be found in lofts and in the back alleys of the commercial centre. As they expanded through the late-nineteenth century, factories relocated for a large part in an industrial zone abutting the Grand Trunk Railway tracks, half-a-mile north of the core. These factories were attracted by the availability of industrial land along tracks (see Figure 16.2 and Bloomfield 1987, 30–3).

In Canadian cities, this location pattern held on the whole until the mid- to late-1950s. After that, manufacturing firms became increasingly attracted to suburban industrial parks, which are areas zoned exclusively for industrial use and that provide the required infrastructures to industries (Hunker 1974, 179–80). Industrial parks are generally located close to major highways or expressways and often offer rail connections; they are usually at a distance from residential neighbourhoods to minimize environmental impact. The lure of these areas for industries arises from a combination of relatively cheap sites and excellent transportation connections. Again, Kitchener exemplifies these changes. In the 1950s and 1960s, the need for additional industrial space was satisfied by pockets of unused land zoned for industry. With the completion of Highway 401 in the early 1960s and of the Conestoga Parkway in the early 1970s, industrial parks developed at some of the better points of access. Most new firms located in these industrial parks; so did a number of firms relocating from the central area (see Figure 16.3 and Walker 1987). Recent statistics indicate that the secular decentralization trend is enduring. Table 16.1 shows that in the three largest Canadian metropolitan regions, between 1975 and 1985, manufacturing employment was growing most rapidly in the outer suburbs. Indeed, in Montreal, this is the only sector where manufacturing employment registered any increase.

Suburbanization of manufacturing establishments is most often explained by the impact of a transition in the technology of goods transpor-

Figure 16.3
Major Industrial Zones, 1985

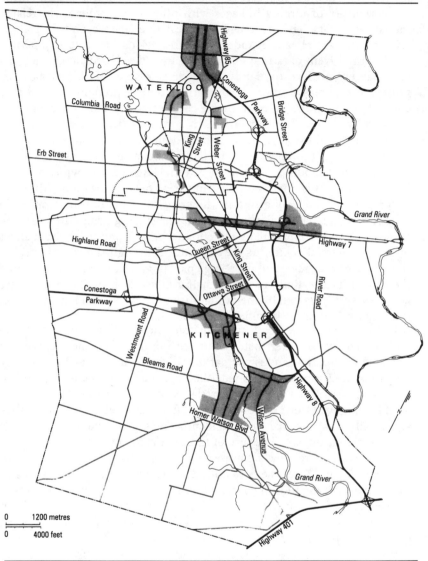

Source: Walker, 1987.

tation, and the spread of space-consuming production methods. According to this interpretation, truck transportation made suburban sites along highways and expressways attractive industrial locations. Concurrently, assembly-line production processes, which were increasingly adopted after World War II, function better in single-storey buildings and require a large ground-area per worker. This raised the appeal of cheap and plentiful

Table 16.1
Manufacturing Employment Change in Montreal, Toronto, and Vancouver, 1975–1985

	1975 Numbers	%	1985 Numbers	%	Change %
City of Montreal	146,861	52.1	108,941	43.4	− 25.8
Montreal Island (excluding the City of Montreal)	91,929	32.6	90,393	36.0	− 1.7
Remainder of the Census Metropolitan Area	43,210	15.3	51,869	20.6	20.0
Total	282,000	100.0	251,203	100.0	− 10.9
City of Toronto	79,747	24.3	66,388	18.0	− 16.8
Metro Toronto (excluding the City of Toronto)	165,157	50.4	181,700	49.3	10.0
Remainder of the Census Metropolitan Area	83,040	25.3	120,662	32.7	45.3
Total	327,944	100.0	368,750	100.0	12.4
City of Vancouver	27,961	40.6	22,678	33.5	− 18.9
Greater Vancouver Regional District (excluding the City of Vancouver)	36,925	53.6	37,452	55.4	1.4
Remainder of the Census Metropolitan Area	4,026	5.8	7,471	11.1	85.6
Total	68,912	100.0	67,601	100.0	− 1.9

SOURCE: Statistics Canada, 1979, Table 6, and Statistics Canada, 1988b, Table 6.

suburban industrial sites. Although valid, these explanations must also be seen in a broader context characterized by a more elaborate chain of events.

The concentration of ownership that is being driven by the expansion of large national and multinational corporations has led to the consolidation of national and international markets. This evolution, which is a critical element of the Fordist era, has prompted a higher standardization of consumer goods, which in turn, resulted in longer runs at the production level. This is where assembly-line production and the attendant need for large, single-storey plants favourable to suburban locations come into the picture. This form of production is particularly well adapted to the fabrication of standardized items. The need to secure easy accessibility to regional, national, and international markets constitutes a further factor of suburban industrial location. This requirement favours sites that are close to expressways and airports. Inter-regional linkages, which became more frequent as networks of exchange tied branch plants within large corporations also make these sites favourable. The industrial decentralization trend was also sustained by a suburbanization of the labour force. Industrial workers' wages increased as productivity improved throughout the Fordist phase and, in particular, in the 1950s and 1960s, and as trade unions became powerful enough to extract advantageous settlements. As a result, many of these workers gained access to a suburban life-style by buying a car, purchasing a home, or renting a new apartment.

It is important to note that causality within this chain of events does not flow in one direction only, but is the outcome of interactions between the above-mentioned factors of decentralization (as illustrated by the double arrows in Figure 16.4). For example, the cheaper products made possible by assembly-line processes were themselves conducive to an extension

Figure 16.4
Factors of Manufacturing Suburbanization

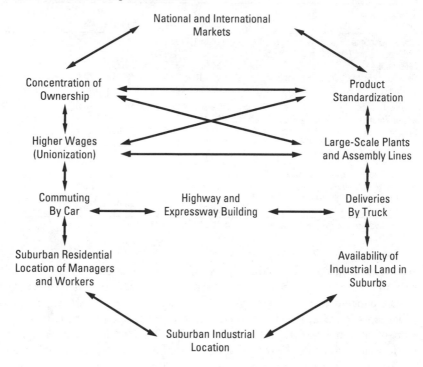

of markets and a concentration of ownership. Likewise, the very availability of large, serviced sites in easily accessible suburban locations provided an inducement to an extension of space-consuming production techniques. Discussion now turns to the industrial characteristics of different sectors within metropolitan regions.

CONTEMPORARY LOCATION TRENDS

The Central City
As Table 16.1 shows, the central city areas of Montreal, Toronto, and Vancouver, all registered an important decline in manufacturing employment between 1975 and 1985, ranging from 16.8 per cent in Toronto to 25.8 per cent in Montreal. We now turn from examining the pull factors that attract manufacturing establishments to suburban location to central-city push factors—that is, the aspects of the central city that provoke the departure of such establishments. For a start, central-city industrial buildings may themselves be a source of dissatisfaction on the part of manufacturing firms. These are often old, multi-storey structures with closely-spaced columns and rather low ceilings. Such features set limita-

tions on production techniques, and, in particular, on assembly-line processes, which function best in large single-storey structures. Moreover, the use of elevators slows down shipping and receiving. The morphology of central-city industrial areas, which reflects their unplanned development, is a further source of inconvenience for manufacturing establishments. Surveys of firms that have left the central city usually reveal that the principal relocation motive was the incapacity to expand within their central location (see in the case of Vancouver, Steed 1973). This incapacity may proceed from an unavailability of land, the high cost of central-city land, and/or the impossibility of increasing floor space within rented premises. The lack of space for parking and for the loading and unloading of trucks is another cause of irritation for many central-city firms. These areas' unplanned development is most apparent in the proximity of industrial and residential sectors and in the frequent mingling of these two types of land use. This makes for an uneasy coexistence between industries and residents. As residents become increasingly concerned with their living environment, they are less tolerant towards the noxious impact of industries. And as they mobilize and become politically active, they are often successful in forcing the closure of polluting manufacturing establishments or in bringing about legally required adoptions of pollution-control devices.

The Toronto Riverdale neighbourhood offers an example of residents' actions against industrial pollution. In a fashion that is typical of central-city land-use patterns, Riverdale industries and houses are often cheek-by-jowl (Figure 16.5). Over the 1980s, residents sent delegations to City Hall and to the Minister of the Environment to object to industrial pollution—more specifically, to lead emissions from one industrial source and sulphuric acid emissions from another. The provincial government responded by replacing lead-contaminated soil in the residential area surrounding the polluting plant and by forcing the plant to install pollution control devices.

The encroachment of industrial areas by non-industrial activities represents another cause of central-city manufacturing decline. High-density forms of land use, such as office and apartment or condominium buildings, can usually outbid industrial premises. This is particularly likely in core industrial areas, which are vulnerable to the spread of the central business district. In these circumstances, industrial firms can make a considerable profit by selling their central-city facilities. Governments may also be participants in the de-industrialization of the central city. In Montreal, for example, older industrial buildings made way for public-housing units (Filion 1988a). In Toronto, the Harbourfront Corporation, set up by the federal government, is responsible for the transformation of what used to be a port and an industrial sector into an area occupied by luxury hotels, condominium buildings, specialty stores, cultural and recreational activities, and public open space.

Figure 16.5
Land Use in South Riverdale Central Industrial District, Toronto

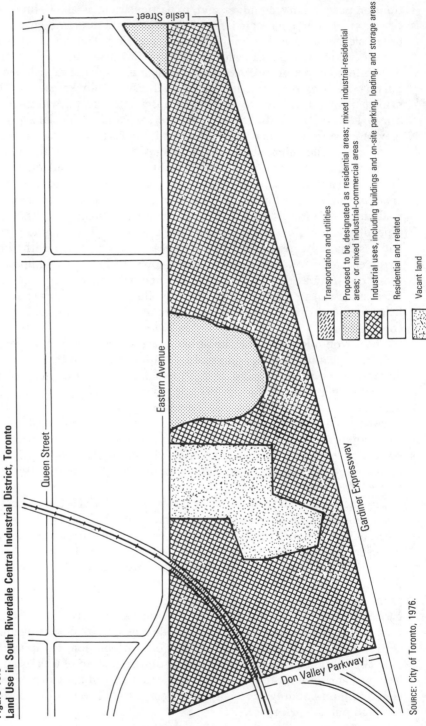

Transportation and utilities

Proposed to be designated as residential areas; mixed industrial-residential areas; or mixed industrial-commercial areas

Industrial uses, including buildings and on-site parking, loading, and storage areas

Residential and related

Vacant land

SOURCE: City of Toronto, 1976.

It would be wrong to assign the reasons for central-city industrial decline exclusively to either the pull effect of suburbs or the push effect of central areas. This decline is also due to the high contraction and closure rate of central-city manufacturing establishments. This rate derives, in part, from the presence in the central city of plants at the tail-end of their life cycle. These are plants that are labour intensive, involved in standardized forms of production, and that have been the object of little capital investment of late. Such plants are particularly exposed to inroads from foreign sources where production costs are considerably lower. The City of Montreal affords a clear example of the association between a concentration of low-productivity sectors and manufacturing employment decline. Montreal, which among the three largest Canadian central cities suffered the sharpest erosion of manufacturing employment, both in absolute and proportional terms, between 1975 and 1985, is host to many low-productivity sectors that are vulnerable to international competition. For instance, clothing industries accounted in 1985 for 35.2 per cent of the City of Montreal manufacturing labour force (Statistics Canada 1988b, Table 5; see also, Lamonde and Polèse 1985).

Manufacturing decline in central cities can result in a loss of municipal tax revenues (except in the case where manufacturing installations are replaced by more fiscally lucrative land-uses, such as large office buildings). There are also social consequences to this decline. It can dislocate ties between working-class neighbourhoods and adjacent industrial areas, and hence provoke population changes in these neighbourhoods. An example of close ties between central-city residential neighbourhoods and specific industrial areas is offered by the Toronto Stockyards Industrial district discussed earlier and the surrounding neighbourhoods. In the early 1970s, 26 per cent of the district's labour force resided within one mile of their work place (City of Toronto 1975). Central-city manufacturing decline also creates difficulties for unskilled, low-income workers who, without a car, face hardship in reaching suburban employment locations. A 1975 City of Toronto survey revealed that 29 per cent of the low-income central-city workers in plants that relocated to suburbs were dissatisfied by the move. By comparison, the dissatisfaction rate for the two higher-income groups was 4 per cent and 10 per cent (City of Toronto 1978, 127).

The City of Toronto has launched what amounts to perhaps Canada's most extensive municipal strategy to arrest central-city de-industrialization. There are three facets to this strategy. The first consists in zoning-by-law revisions adopted in 1977 that created an I-zoning category encompassing industrial and related purposes. Prior to this revision, industrial uses were included within C-zoning categories, which authorized both industrial and commercial facilities. This zoning allowed industries to be outbid by commercial establishments in the real-estate market. The I-zoning category was designed to stabilize industrial land uses, and to create a context that is more conducive to new investments in industrial buildings.[1] Another facet of the strategy is the promotion of the port as an industrial area. This area is seen as suitable to industries that contribute a large number of jobs, but that are incompatible with other sectors' land use. The final facet consists in improvements to industrial districts' public infrastructures. This includes upgrading streets, improving sidewalks, and planting trees.

The above discussion of the central-city predicament should not leave the impression that this sector is deprived of comparative advantages. We need to look beyond the generally poor appearance of central-city industrial districts to unravel these areas' economic dynamic. One central-city advantage is the presence of a harbour. Flour mills in Montreal, sugar refineries in Toronto, steelworks in Hamilton, and fish-packing plants and sawmills in Vancouver make extensive use of port installations and therefore benefit from their proximity to these facilities (Norcliffe 1981). The central city also has many more advantages to offer. Among these are: enduring functional complexes; accessibility to a wide variety of business services; the availability of flexible rental space at relatively low cost (in Kitchener, core-area industrial rents are approximately half that of rents in suburban sectors); and an easy accessibility to a low-income labour force. This labour force is often made up of immigrants and especially female immigrants. In 1981, 43 per cent of the Montreal-region female work force employed in labour-intensive manufacturing lived in the central city. The comparable figure for males was 33 per cent. Of the total female work force, 35 per cent resided in the central city (Rose and Villeneuve, forthcoming).

The more important that central-city advantages are to a firm, the more likely it is to choose or maintain a central location. This is the case of clothing and printing industries, which have been shown to be most likely to remain in the City of Vancouver from the mid–1950s to the mid–1960s (Steed 1973). In a Toronto context, Mock and Norcliffe (1986) show that communications, jewellery, and wholesalers are also likely to settle or remain in the inner city.

Central-city location advantages can be best understood by focusing on the clothing industry in Toronto and Montreal. Much of the Toronto clothing industry is located within the garment district in the Spadina Avenue area immediately to the west of the central business district. There, clothing firms benefit from relatively cheap rental space and accessibility to low-waged female employees living mostly in neighbourhoods located in the western part of the City of Toronto. Good transit connections ease commuting for workers. The district also offers tight linkage networks consisting of frequent supply deliveries using trucks as major carriers, and messengers on foot. Face-to-face contacts between firms at the different stages of the production and distribution process are also an essential part of this un-standardized production process (City of Toronto 1976). Direct links to fashion houses, designers, and major retailers of ready-to-wear clothing make it relatively easy to keep up with fads and trends that characterize the volatile clothing market. Meanwhile, clothing establishments that have relocated outside the garment district tend to be larger factories that are able to internalize external economies, thus reducing their dependence on linkages. Most of these plants have settled in the North Dufferin Industrial District, which is closer to their female employees' residential areas (Mock 1976).

An examination of the Montreal clothing industry yielded similar findings. The establishments that are concentrated downtown are characterized by their small size, frequent variations in products, high face-to-face contact requirements, and well-developed product- and information-linkages. These are generally fashion conscious clothing firms. By contrast, larger firms that are involved in a more standardized form of production have largely relocated in the north Saint-Laurent Boulevard area, which is close to sources of a low-waged immigrant work force, as is the Toronto North Dufferin District (Steed 1976). It is noteworthy that in Montreal, both the downtown and the north Saint-Laurent Boulevard clothing districts are easily accessible by subway.

More generally, there is evidence that fledgling and small firms are particularly sensitive to the advantages of central-site locations. A Kitchener survey reveals that 89 per cent of core-area firms employ less than twenty workers, and that one-half of the firms have been in the core for less than five years (Habl 1987). Again, these findings point to the attraction for certain firms of moderate rents, accessibility to a low-waged labour force, and the possibility of linkages with nearby establishments. They also suggest that central areas can have an 'incubator' potential that helps the formation and early development of new firms.

The Suburbs

While there are clearly major differences in suburban and central-city industrial trends, it is important to realize that conditions in the suburbs are not uniform. Indeed, some inner suburbs share the fate of central cities in that their manufacturing is also seriously declining. In these cases, industry is being confronted with the same adverse conditions that are being met by more centrally located establishments. For example, Lachine, a south-western inner suburb of Montreal, has lost 41.7 per cent of its manufacturing employment between 1975 and 1985—manufacturing jobs have declined from 14,687 to 8,563 over these years (Statistics Canada 1988b, Table 6). Overall, however, Table 16.1 indicates that suburbs, and particularly outer suburbs, have experienced growth in manufacturing employment. One exception is the island of Montreal (excluding the City of Montreal), which experienced a 1.7 per cent decline between 1975 and 1985. This drop is largely attributable to the metropolitan region's poor manufacturing-sector performance over this period.

Suburbs unlike central cities, tend to offer industrial parks with ample space for single-storey plants, parking, truck movement, and future expansion. Furthermore, industries are usually segregated from residential areas, thus avoiding friction between those land uses. Interestingly, there is scant evidence of linkages within industrial parks. This suggests that there is no replication in the suburban context of the functional complexes encountered in the central city (Bale 1974, 295; Mock 1976). This is due to the relaxation of spatial association requirements in suburban environments. In suburbs, industrialization has gone hand-in-hand with the use of the truck as the main mode for product linkages, and the construction of extensive highway and expressway networks. Meanwhile, electronic communication was easing long-distance information linkages. This evolution has significantly reduced transportation and communications costs, and therefore lessened the distance-decay factor as regards linkages. Add to this the absence of historical clusters of related firms predating current forms of transportation and communication, and the lack of suburban functional complexes becomes readily understandable. This same loosening of location constraints applies to accessibility to the labour force. With the growing use of the car for commuting purposes, we are moving towards an integration of the metropolitan labour market. Accordingly, it becomes less imperative for most firms to locate close to a specific labour force.

There are exceptions to the absence of suburban functional clusters. Petrochemical complexes, which are located at the mouth of pipelines or close to docks adapted to tankers (as in the case of the Montreal East complex which combines both locational determinants), constitute such an exception. Petrochemical industries also congregate because of linkages involving the movement of oil products from refineries to chemical plants. The clustering of such industries is further due to planning regulations that are attempting to minimize the impact of noxious air emissions by isolating the plants from other forms of land use and, in particular, from residential areas. For example, in 1968 the Alberta Board of Health adopted a regulation requiring a one-mile buffer zone between heavy industries generating appreciable air pollution and present or future residential areas.

Since industrial parks are the foremost suburban industrial locale, it is pertinent to look briefly at their diversity. Over time, suburban industrial parks have become more specialized. They now run the gamut from parks that predominantly include industrial malls providing cheap and flexible space to prestigious business parks. Industrial malls partly serve an incubator role. They lease or sell small industrial units at prices that often rival cheap central-city premises. A survey of a sample of firms located in Toronto-region industrial malls revealed that, on average, these firms employed 9.2 employees and occupied 4,626 square feet of industrial space (Smith and Werb 1977). At the other end of the spectrum are prestige business parks that include light-manufacturing establishments along with distribution facilities, office buildings, hotels, and recreation centres. These parks are generally developed around one or more major establishments, in the same fashion as office and retail projects. Moreover, developers (or municipalities) give close attention to such parks' appearance by burying wires, enforcing site-plan controls, and offering maximum exposure from major highways.

The Outer Suburbs and Beyond

We now turn to the periphery of metropolitan regions—outer suburbs and former self-standing cities that are gradually being absorbed within metropolitan zones of economic influence. As Table 16.1 indicates, this is where most of the manufacturing employment growth now takes place. Overall, peripheral areas offer the same advantages as all suburbs: industrial parks and good transportation links. But there are the added advantages of an abundance of land and relatively low industrial-land prices.

Two types of industrial development highlight some key aspects of industrialization within these areas. The first type is the creation of high-technology centres of development. High-technology industries are defined here as firms that devote a large proportion of their activities to research and development and whose products are both innovative and the result of a still un-standardized fabrication process. Like petrochemical establishments, high-technology industries are an anomaly in the suburbs in that they tend to cluster into functional complexes. The evolution of the two US prototypes of high-technology complexes, Silicon Valley south of San Francisco, and Route 128 surrounding Boston, indicates that emerging firms usually congregate around pioneer establishments. There are three reasons for this. First, these new firms are usually set up by engineers and professionals who were formerly employed by the pioneer companies. Second, as expected because of their un-standardized production process and their operation in fields where knowledge evolves rapidly, high-technology firms are linked together by intense flows of goods and information. High-technology firms also congregate because they share a highly skilled labour pool, which is known for gravitating easily from one firm to another. In fact, such firms' predilection for amenity-rich regions is explained by the need to attract professional workers. In addition, high-technology firms favour locations that provide excellent highway connections and easy accessibility to a major airport in order to reach markets and maintain distant linkages (Gordon and Kimball 1987; Joint Economic Committee 1982; Markusen, Hall, and Glasmeir 1986, 71–96). The presence of such industries in outer suburbs can further be explained by the coincidence between their emergence and the development of these urban areas. Also, developing urban areas offering large expanses of industrial land are more conducive to the clustering of growing numbers of high-technology establishments than are built-up areas.

In Canada, the growth of the high-technology sector within the Ottawa metropolitan region has been remarkable. From 8,145 jobs in 1976, the number of jobs in advanced technical establishments increased to 21,850 in ten years. According to Steed (1987) and Steed and DeGenova (1983), the trigger for this development came from the presence of a large number of research and development jobs in federal government agencies and at the Bell Northern Research Laboratory. In the 1970s and 1980s, many new high-technology firms developed, most of them specializing in electronics, telecommunications equipment, avionics, scientific equipment, computers, and medical instruments (Steed 1987; Steed and DeGenova 1983). As in the case of US high-technology complexes, much of the Ottawa region's high-technology industry converged on the outskirts of the agglomeration, in the developing suburb of Kanata.

Another type of industrial development throws a different light on the advantages of metropolitan regions' peripheral zones. When choosing a location, some firms aspire to combine accessibility to the metropolitan area (to maintain a high linkages-potential and market access) with a lowering of production costs. Sites at the outskirts of metropolitan regions become particularly attractive for these firms. For one, these sites are much cheaper than more central locations, such as strategically located inner-suburban industrial parks. In 1977, a square foot of land in an industrial park in Saint-Laurent, an inner suburb of the Montreal metropolitan region, sold for $2.00, which is 33 times higher than the $0.06 cost in Saint Jean, a self-standing city 25 kilometres south east of Montreal (Gouvernement du Québec 1977). But lower land costs are only a small fraction of the savings that can be realized by locating in outlying areas. Production processes can benefit from the availability of large tracts of flat land. Also, many peripheral areas offer a sufficiently large labour force within a 45-minute commuting shed. This labour force is likely to be both less expensive and more loyal than in larger centres where there is more competition for workers. Those peripheral areas that are most attractive to firms are the ones that enjoy good highway and railway access. Three new Ontario car-assembly plants have opted for sites at the periphery of metropolitan regions: in Cambridge (a medium-sized city located 75 kilometres from Metropolitan Toronto); in Alliston (a town located 55 kilometres from Metropolitan Toronto); and in Ingersoll (25 kilometres from London). All three sites offer all of the above mentioned advantages. An added benefit for the Cambridge and Alliston plants, which are non-unionized, is the sites' distance from unionized car-assembly plants paying higher wages. This distance is sufficient to prevent a pirating of the new non-unionized plants' labour force by existing unionized establishments. Research in the Quebec City economic region also supports the existence of such a centrifugal tendency. Klein (1980) has shown an inverse correlation between industrial employment growth and county income levels. Highest growth occurred in three low-income counties (Kamouraska, Frontenac, and Dorchester) at the periphery of the economic region.

Consequences of Location Trends
One of the major consequences of industrial location trends is their impact on contemporary urban form. These trends are associated with the emergence of the 'diffused' metropolis, which is characterized by a patchwork of unifunctional zones connected to each other by highways and expressways. In general, the pattern conforms to the multiple-nuclei model of urban form discussed in Chapters 10 and 12. Canadian suburban areas qualify for the most part as examples of such diffused metropolitan development. By comparison to central-city urban form, suburban areas are not structured by a strict hierarchy of space. In central cities, employment is clearly dominated by the central business district; other concentrations are comparatively modest. By contrast, the remainder of metropolitan regions is dotted with retail and employment concentrations of varying dimensions, none of which is large enough to assume a dominant position. It is noteworthy that suburban patterns of industrial location have become the norm; traditional central-city patterns with manufacturing establishments huddled along railway lines are now marginal.

This dispersion and declining transportation costs due to the use of trucks and the existence of highway networks translate into a reduction of site-specific advantages for manufacturing firms. Any location close to a major highway is suitable to the maintenance of linkage networks throughout the metropolitan region and beyond. Such locations are also easily accessible by an extensive skilled and unskilled labour force residing in the suburbs and commuting by car. This dissipation of site advantages is particularly favourable to peripheral 'greenfield' locations that provide both cheap land and easy highway connections.

There are both environmental and social drawbacks to this pattern of industrial location. On the environmental front, there is a paradox between manicured, suburban industrial parks, and the pollution and congestion generated by growing fleets of trucks criss-crossing metropolitan regions to maintain ever-extending linkages networks. In this sense, an apparent abatement of the local environmental impacts common in central-city areas has been accompanied by a worsening of manufacturing-induced noxious effects at the metropolitan level. Another environmental consequence is the loss of agricultural land that results from 'greenfield' manufacturing development and attendant residential and retail growth.

The social repercussions parallel the environmental ones. The continuing peripheral location of manufacturing establishments is conducive to higher levels of commuting by car (a form of transportation which is a major source of pollution and congestion). Because of poor or non-existent transit services in outlying industrial areas, it is difficult for low-waged workers, who often do not own a car, to reach these employment locations. Manufacturing trends are also responsible for changes affecting the social structure of Canadian cities. The relative decline of manufacturing in Canada and its absolute decline in urban sectors such as the central city is responsible for a greater income polarization. In Toronto, wages in the rapidly-growing service sector are 15 per cent lower than those paid in manufacturing establishments (Yalnizyan 1988). So incomes drop as service replaces manufacturing employment. Meanwhile, however, well-paid managerial and professional employment is on the rise in the Canadian economy, and more particularly in the central business districts of larger metropolitan centres. This trend gives rise to growing income polarization, which is particularly acute within the central city.

It is in this socioeconomic context that the gentrification phenomenon described in Chapter 13 takes root in many Canadian central cities. Gentrification is generally understood as a replacement of blue collar-workers by middle-class newcomers, the latter outbidding and therefore displacing blue-collar households. While this interpretation clearly accounts for much of the gentrification phenomenon, urban and in particular central-city industrial trends give rise to a complementary explanation: as the decline of the manufacturing sector depletes the ranks of the blue-collar working class, these workers (in the work force or retired) are less likely, when they move or die, to be replaced by people belonging to this same occupation category. Chances are that newcomers will be members of the rapidly expanding white-collar middle class.

MUNICIPAL INTERVENTIONS AND INITIATIVES

There are two aspects to municipal governments' involvement in matters of industrial development. One is the control of this development; the other is its promotion. The distribution of industrial establishments within suburbs was largely guided by strict zoning regulations, which confined these establishments to designated zones. These regulations were meant to protect residential areas from industries' noxious effects. We have seen that by contrast to its suburban use, the industrial zoning category was introduced by the City of Toronto to safeguard existing industries. Many suburban municipalities extend their control to the prohibition of certain types of installations. For example, Etobicoke excludes plants that are obnoxious because of the emission of odours, dust, smoke, noise, gas fumes, cinders, vibrations, refuse matter, or water carried waste. Kanata is even more rigid: it disallows noxious uses and uses that are detrimental in appearance or in effect to surrounding uses (Government of Ontario 1986).

In suburbs, there are moves towards a stricter control of industrial zones through the enforcement of site-plan controls. These controls are meant to improve the appearance of industrial zones. Again, Kanata's criteria are among the most stringent. Here are two examples:

—All buildings shall be designed such that the architectural features of adjacent structures are taken into account and no building design shall detract from the architecture of adjacent buildings due to its massing, proportion, location or its external material selection and placement.

—Sites not graced by an abundance of interesting topographical features shall be augmented by the judicious use of berms, mounds, tree planting and the like. (Government of Ontario 1986, 57.)

A final consideration is the oversupply of suburban industrial zones, which follows from the advantages municipalities derive from the presence of industries. Industries are an attractive source of fiscal revenues, and of course procure employment for the local population. Accordingly, municipalities that are eager to increase the number of industries within their boundaries will zone a significant proportion of their land for this purpose, much of which may remain empty for years. The Toronto metropolitan region illustrates this tendency. Within this region, industries occupy nearly 30,000 acres of land; meanwhile, 35,000 acres designated for industrial use are currently vacant (Moore 1986).

The local benefits that accrue from industrialization explain why municipalities actively encourage industrial expansion. Mainstream economic development initiatives mostly take the form of 'smokestack chasing', that is, trying to lure large, footloose plants. To achieve this goal, many cities develop their own industrial parks, and then set out to fill them by making land available at relatively low cost. Municipalities also distribute literature highlighting local comparative advantages (such as available public infrastructures, local labour skills, linkages possibilities with local firms, and accessibility potential to large markets). In this same vein, municipalities also participate in industrial fairs, and set up information offices directed at potential investors. Some cities target their industrial development strategies towards specific sectors. This is the case of Edmonton, which has set up a research park meant to attract research facilities for the petroleum industry, electrical manufacturing, aircraft components, and scientific instruments. Some municipalities attempt to revitalize older industrial areas by promoting their 'incubator' potential, which is associated with cheap and flexible rental facilities and high linkages potentials.

More recently, municipal economic development efforts have fanned out to include the attraction of service sector establishments. This is particularly the case in areas where the economy is dominated by cyclical industries. For example, the Hamilton-Wentworth regional municipality has been active in attracting offices and other forms of service employment in order to reduce the local economy's vulnerability to the sharp cycles of the steel industry. Moreover, local firms receive added attention as municipalities become aware of such firms' employment-growth potential. Figures reveal that in the average city, 80 per cent of new employment is attributable to local industries (Bureau of Municipal Research 1982, 2–3). Local entrepreneurs have become another recent object of attention for municipal development initiatives. Sudbury's development strategy, for example, gives pre-eminence to local entrepreneurs in its attempt to offset nickel industry employment decline (Filion 1988b). Municipalities have an advantage in helping local residents to become entrepreneurs, as these residents tend to set up their businesses locally. A study has shown that nearly all Vancouver entrepreneurs had been living in the region for at least eleven years (Khan and Hayter 1984).

We must, however, acknowledge that the impact of local development efforts is necessarily limited by municipalities' finite resources, and by provincial statutes that prevent them from engaging in certain types of actions (such as offering grants or tax rebates in Ontario). But the major limitation is that local comparative advantages largely elude municipal governments' spheres of influence. Indeed, industries mostly base their location choices on market accessibility and the presence of a labour force with appropriate skills at an acceptable cost; linkages are also considerations. The impact of any municipality's development efforts is also diluted by the tendency for most municipalities to adopt similar development strategies (Kitchen 1985). In these circumstances, local economic development strategies are most beneficial to municipalities that are already blessed with comparative advantages for potential industrial investors.

CONCLUSIONS

The chapter has described a secular tendency towards industrial decentralization within metropolitan regions. This tendency has simultaneously translated into the de-industrialization of central cities and of some inner suburbs, and rapid developments at the fringe of metropolitan regions. The chapter has explored the environmental and social consequences of these location trends: increased transportation requirements generated by a scattering of industrial parks translate into longer journeys and added congestion and pollution. This location pattern is also responsible for the difficulties that low-income workers experience when trying to commute to outlying industrial areas.

Each theoretical perspective discussed in the chapter throws a distinct light on these location trends. Economic rationality theories and, in particular, their least-cost variant stress the impact of reduced transportation costs. In this perspective, lower costs lessen transportation's constraining effect on location, and allow firms to place more importance on other location factors such as space requirements. Behavioural theories provide another dimension by acknowledging the effect of decision-makers' personal preferences and limited capacity to obtain and process information. According to behavioural theories, it is conceivable that the movement of firms to the suburbs can be imputed in part to managers' better knowledge of available sites that are close to their homes, as well as to their desire to reduce commuting journeys. Municipal industrial promotion efforts are consistent with a behavioural understanding of decision-making. These efforts consist in providing easily understandable data on local advantages relevant to industries and in vaunting amenities that are likely to appeal to managers. Finally, the transition from Fordism to post-Fordism helps explain the de-industrialization process that affects many developed countries entering into the post-industrial era. The chapter has shown that de-industrialization is particularly devastating in areas, such as central cities, that are dominated by traditional industries.

NOTES

1. The I-zoning classification ranges from I1 to I4. I1 allows silent and relatively clean light-industries (such as carpenters' shops, photographic studios, or small garment factories), which can be located close to homes without being a source of nuisance for nearby residents. At the other end of the spectrum, I4 applies to facilities that must be located on their own, for example, chemical plants. The purpose of the I4 category is to protect all types of urban activities (including other industries) that could be disturbed and disadvantaged by proximity to such facilities.

FURTHER READING

AHMAD, J. 1988 *Trade-Related Sector-Specific Industrial Adjustment Policies in Canada: An Analysis of Textile, Clothing, and Footwear Industries* Discussion Paper No. 345 (Ottawa: Economic Council of Canada)

BALE, J.R. 1974 'Toward a Geography of the Industrial Estate', *The Professional Geographer* 26, 291–97

KHAN, A. and HAYTER, R. 1984 'The Linkages of New Manufacturing Firms: An Exploratory Enquiry in the Vancouver Metropolitan Area', *The Albertan Geographer* 20, 1–13

MCFETRIDGE, D.G. 1986 'The Economics of Industrial Structure: An Overview' in D.G. McFetridge ed. *Canadian Industry in Transition* Volume 2 in the series of background studies for the Royal Commission on the Economic Union and Development Prospects of Canada (Toronto: University of Toronto Press)

MOCK, D. and NORCLIFFE, G. 1986 'Industry in Toronto in the Post-Industrial Era', *City Planning* 4, 30–3

SCOTT, A.J. 1988 'Flexible Production Systems and Regional Development: the Rise of New Industrial Spaces in North America and Western Europe', *International Journal of Urban and Regional Research* 12, 171–86

STEED, G.P.F. 1973 'Intrametropolitan Manufacturing: Spatial Distribution and Locational Dynamics in Greater Vancouver', *The Canadian Geographer* 17, 235–58

——— 1976 'Centrality and Locational Change: Printing, Publishing, and Clothing in Montreal and Toronto', *Economic Geography* 52, 193–205

——— 1987 'Policy and High Technology Complexes: Ottawa's "Silicon Valley North" ' in F.E.I. Hamilton ed. *Industrial Change in Advanced Economies* (London: Croom Helm)

WALKER, D.F. 1987 'Expansion and Adaptation in the Post-War Years' in D.F. Walker ed. *Manufacturing in Kitchener-Waterloo: A Long-Term Perspective* (Waterloo: University of Waterloo, Department of Geography, Publication Series No. 26)

REFERENCES

AGLIETTA, M. 1979 *A Theory of Capitalist Regulation* (London: New Left Books)

—— 1982 'World Capitalism in the Eighties', *New Left Review* 136, 3–41

AHMAD, J. 1988 *Trade-Related Sector-Specific Industrial Adjustment Policies in Canada: An Analysis of Textile, Clothing, and Footwear Industries* Discussion Paper No. 345 (Ottawa: Economic Council of Canada)

BALE, J.R. 1974 'Toward a Geography of the Industrial Estate', *The Professional Geographer* 26, 291–97

BATER, J.H. and WALKER, D.F. 1977 'Industrial Services: Literature and Research Prospects' in D.F. Walker ed. *Industrial Services* (Waterloo: University of Waterloo, Department of Geography, Publication Series No. 8)

BLOOMFIELD, E. 1987 'Building Industrial Communities: Berlin and Waterloo to 1915' in D.F. Walker ed. *Manufacturing in Kitchener-Waterloo: A Long-Term Perspective* (Waterloo: University of Waterloo, Department of Geography, Publication Series No. 26)

BRITTON, J.N.H. 1980 'Industrial Dependence and Technological Underdevelopment: Canadian Consequences of Foreign Direct Investment', *Regional Studies* 14, 181–99

BUREAU OF MUNICIPAL RESEARCH 1982 *Industrial Development: The Municipal Role* (Toronto: BMR)

CITY OF TORONTO PLANNING BOARD, INDUSTRY WORK GROUP 1975 *Industry Relocation and its Impact on Employees, Summary Report 1: A Place for Industry* (Toronto: City of Toronto)

—— 1976 *The City's Attractiveness for Industry (A Place for Industry, Tome 2)* (Toronto: City of Toronto)

CITY OF TORONTO PLANNING BOARD 1978 *Official Plan Amendments; Industrial Policy and the Central Industrial District* (Toronto: City of Toronto)

CITY OF TORONTO PLANNING AND DEVELOPMENT DEPARTMENT 1984 *Part II: Official Plan Proposals, Stockyards Industrial District* (Toronto: City of Toronto)

COOPER, M.J.M. 1975 *The Industrial Location Decision Making Process* (Birmingham: Centre for Urban and Regional Studies)

COURCHENE, T.J. 1986 'Avenues of Adjustment: The Transfer System and Regional Disparities' in D.J. Savoie ed. *The Canadian Economy; a Regional Perspective* (Toronto: Methuen)

CYERT, R.M. and MARCH, J.G. 1963 *A Behavioral Theory of the Firm* (Englewood Cliffs, N.J.: Prentice-Hall)

DEPARTMENT OF REGIONAL INDUSTRIAL EXPANSION 1986 *Commodity Trade by Industrial Sector, Historical Summary 1966–1985* (Ottawa: DRIE)

FILION, P. 1988a 'The Neighbourhood Improvement Plan: Montreal and Toronto, Contrast Between a Participatory and a Centralized Approach to Urban Policy Making', *Urban History Review* 17, 16–28

———— 1988b 'Potential and Weaknesses of Strategic Community Development Planning: a Sudbury Case Study', *Canadian Journal of Regional Science* 11, 393–411

GORDON, R. and KIMBALL, L. 1987 'The Impact of Industrial Structure on Global High Technology Location' in J.F. Brotchie, P. Hall, and P.W. Newton eds *The Spatial Impact of Technological Change* (London: Croom Helm)

GOUVERNEMENT DU QUEBEC, MINISTERE DE l'INDUSTRIE ET DU COMMERCE 1977 *Renseignement sur les parcs industriels du Québec* (Quebec City: Gouvernement du Québec)

GOVERNMENT OF ONTARIO, MINISTRY OF MUNICIPAL AFFAIRS 1986 *Industrial Trends: Implications for Municipal Planning* (Toronto: Government of Ontario)

HABL, L. 1987 'Kitchener's Inner City Industrial Zone—A Revitalization Proposal' in D. F. Walker ed. *Manufacturing in Kitchener-Waterloo: A Long-Term Perspective* (Waterloo: University of Waterloo, Department of Geography, Publication Series No. 26)

HOOVER, E.M. 1948 *The Location of Economic Activity* (New York: McGraw-Hill)

HOULE, F. 1983 'Economic Strategy and the Restructuring of the Fordist Wage-Labour Relationship in Canada', *Studies in Political Economy* 11, 127–47

HUNKER, H.L. 1974 *Industrial Development* (Lexington, Mass: Lexington Books)

JOINT ECONOMIC COMMITTEE 1982 *Location of High Technology Firms and Regional Economic Development* (Washington, DC: US Congress)

KHAN, A. and HAYTER, R. 1984 'The Linkages of New Manufacturing Firms: An Exploratory Enquiry in the Vancouver Metropolitan Area', *The Albertan Geographer* 20, 1–13

KITCHEN, H.M. 1985 *The Role for Local Government in Economic Development* (Toronto: Ontario Economic Council, Discussion Paper Series)

KLEIN, J.-L. 1980 'Formation et partage de l'espace régional: le coût du travail et le déplacement de l'industrie dans la région de Québec', *Cahiers de Géographie du Québec* 24, 429–46

LAMONDE, P. and POLESE, M. 1985 *Le déplacement des activités économiques dans la région métropolitaine de Montréal de 1971 à 1981* (Montreal: INRS-Urbanisation)

MCFETRIDGE, D.G. 1986 'The Economics of Industrial Structure: An Overview' in D.G. McFetridge ed. *Canadian Industry in Transition* Volume 2 in the series of background studies for the Royal Commission on the Economic Union and Development Prospects of Canada (Toronto: University of Toronto Press)

MARCH, J.G. and SIMON, H.A. 1958 *Organizations* (New York: Wiley)

MARKUSEN, A., HALL, P., and GLASMEIR, A. 1986 *High Tech America: the What, How, Where, and Why of the Sunrise Industries* (Boston: Allen and Unwin)

MASSEY, D.B. 1984 *Spatial Divisions of Labour: Social Structures and the Geography of Production* (London: Macmillan)

MOCK, D.R. 1976 *Agglomeration and Industrial Linkages: Case Studies of Metropolitan Toronto* (Toronto: University of Toronto, Department of Geography, unpublished Ph.D. thesis)

—— and NORCLIFFE, G. 1986 'Industry in Toronto in the Post-Industrial Era', *City Planning* 4, 30–3

MOORE, P. 1986 'From Cornstalks to Smokestacks: Planning for Industry in the Suburbs', *City Planning* 4, 37–40

NORCLIFFE, G.B. 1975 'A Theory of Manufacturing Places' in L. Collins and D.F. Walker eds *Locational Dynamics of Manufacturing Activity* (London: John Wiley)

—— 1981 'Industrial Change in Old Port Areas; the Case of the Port of Toronto', *Cahiers de Géographie du Québec* 25, 237–54

ORGANIZATION FOR ECONOMIC COOPERATION AND DEVELOPMENT 1988 *Economic Outlook: Historical Statistics 1960–1986* (Paris: OECD)

PRED, A. 1967 'Behaviour and Location: Foundations for a Geographic and Dynamic Location Theory, Part 1' *Lund Studies in Geography, Series B* 27

—— 1969 'Behaviour and Location: Foundations for a Geographic and Dynamic Location Theory, Part 2' *Lund Studies in Geography, Series B* 28

RAWSTON, E.M. 1958 'Three Principles of Industrial Location', *Transaction and Papers, IBG* 25, 132–42

ROSE, D. and VILLENEUVE, P. (forthcoming) 'Work, Labour Markets and Household Transition' in L.S. Bourne and D. Ley eds *The Social Geography of Canadian Cities* (Montreal and Kingston: McGill-Queen's University Press)

SCOTT, A.J. 1988 'Flexible Production Systems and Regional Development: the Rise of New Industrial Spaces in North America and Western Europe', *International Journal of Urban and Regional Research* 12, 171–86

SIMON, H.A. 1956 *Administrative Behavior* (New York: Macmillan)

SMITH, D.M. 1966 'A Theoretical Framework for Geographical Studies of Industrial Location', *Economic Geography* 42, 95–113

—— 1981 *Industrial Location: an Economic Geographical Analysis* (2nd ed.) (New York: John Wiley and Sons)

SMITH, J. and W.M. WERB 1977 'Industrial Malls: A Modern Home for the Service Sector' in D.F. Walker ed. *Industrial Services* (Waterloo: University of Waterloo, Department of Geography, Publication Series No. 8)

STATISTICS CANADA 1979 *Manufacturing Industries of Canada: Sub-Provincial Areas* (Ottawa: Minister of Supplies and Services)

—— 1988a *Dimensions: Industry Trends 1951–1986* (Ottawa: Minister of Supply and Services, Catalogue 93–152)

—— 1988b *Manufacturing Industries of Canada: Sub-Provincial Areas* (Ottawa: Minister of Supplies and Services, Catalogue 31–209)

STEED, G.P.F. 1973 'Intrametropolitan Manufacturing: Spatial Distribution and Locational Dynamics in Greater Vancouver', *The Canadian Geographer* 17, 235–58

—— 1976 'Centrality and Locational Change: Printing, Publishing, and Clothing in Montreal and Toronto', *Economic Geography* 52, 193–205

—— 1987 'Policy and High Technology Complexes: Ottawa's "Silicon Valley North" ' in F.E.I. Hamilton ed. *Industrial Change in Advanced Economies* (London: Croom Helm)

—— and DeGenova, D. 1983 'Ottawa's Technology-Oriented Complex', *The Canadian Geographer* 27, 263–78

UNITED NATIONS, INDUSTRIAL DEVELOPMENT ORGANIZATION 1988 *Industry and Development: Global Report 1988–1989* (Vienna: UNIDO)

VERNON, R. 1966 'International Investment and International Trade in the Product Cycle', *Quarterly Journal of Economics* 80, 190–207

—— 1979 'The Product Cycle Hypothesis in a New International Environment', *Oxford Bulletin of Economics and Statistics* 41, 255–67

WALKER, D.F. 1987 'Expansion and Adaptation in the Post-War Years' in D.F. Walker ed. *Manufacturing in Kitchener-Waterloo: A Long-Term Perspective* (Waterloo: University of Waterloo, Department of Geography, Publication Series No. 26)

WEBER, A. 1929 *Theory of the Location of Industries* (New York: Russell and Russell)

YALNIZYAN, A. 1988 *A Statistical Profile of Toronto's Labour Market, 1976–1987* (Toronto: Social Planning Council of Metropolitan Toronto)

17

Office Location

GUNTER GAD

In the larger Canadian metropolitan areas, about 50 per cent of the labour force works at office desks. The vast numbers of people employed in offices spans an incredibly wide range of occupations, ranks, and salary levels: from chief executive officers of large corporations with million-dollar salaries or 'benefit packages' to junior secretaries and mail-room clerks, who may earn less than $20,000 per annum. Human labour is at the core of office work; very few other work places, at least until recently, rely on such a large input of labour and a small input of capital, especially in the form of machinery.

The purpose of this chapter is to take a look behind the facades of office buildings and explore some of the nuances and complexities of office location in our larger cities. The first part of the chapter describes the distribution pattern of a variety of types of offices and the combination of these offices in recognizably distinct areas. A second task is to present some ideas about the circumstances which are responsible for the distribution of offices.

The chapter deals mainly with Toronto because the large size of this metropolitan region means that its office landscape is more varied than that of any other Canadian metropolis. Another reason is that office location has become such a public concern in this census metropolitan area (CMA) that governments and businesses have generated a considerable data base that can be used to aid analysis.

TORONTO OFFICES IN THE 1980s

Every summer the Metropolitan Toronto Planning Department conducts an employment survey of Metropolitan Toronto. The results of this survey are reported by major categories: offices, manufacturing/warehousing, institutions, retail, services, and other. The office category is defined as 'all jobs in which the main function is with people behind a desk'. This category includes separately located offices and all other establishments in which only office work takes place, including offices that are detached from plants, shops, etc.

In 1988, there were about 533,000 full-time office jobs in Metropolitan Toronto, accounting for 48 per cent of a total of 1.1 million full-time jobs. Office jobs are evenly split between the central district (a fairly large area centred on the Yonge Street subway line within the City of Toronto) and

Figure 17.1
Major Office Nodes in the Toronto Census Metropolitan Area

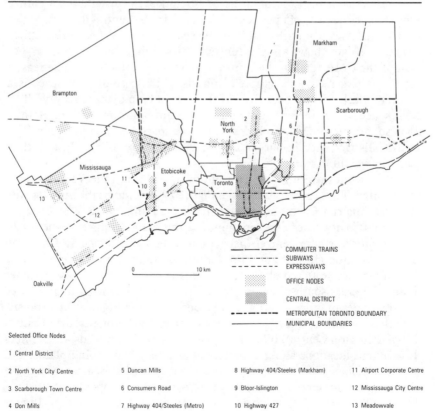

COMMUTER TRAINS
SUBWAYS
EXPRESSWAYS
OFFICE NODES
CENTRAL DISTRICT
METROPOLITAN TORONTO BOUNDARY
MUNICIPAL BOUNDARIES

Selected Office Nodes

1 Central District

2 North York City Centre	5 Duncan Mills	8 Highway 404/Steeles (Markham)	11 Airport Corporate Centre
3 Scarborough Town Centre	6 Consumers Road	9 Bloor-Islington	12 Mississauga City Centre
4 Don Mills	7 Highway 404/Steeles (Metro)	10 Highway 427	13 Meadowvale

Table 17.1
Distribution of Offices in the Toronto Census Metropolitan Area, 1988

	Employment[a] (%)		Floor space[b] (%)	
Central District	49.8	44.8	62.2	57.2
Metro Suburbs	50.2	45.1	37.8	34.8
Metro Total	100.0		100.0	
	(N = 533,000)		(N = 9.5 million m²)	
CMA Suburbs		10.1		8.0
CMA Total		100.0		100.0
		(N = 593,000)		(N = 10.7 million m²)

[a]Full-time employment only.
[b]Only buildings with 1858m² or larger; includes government-owned and other owner-occupied buildings.

SOURCE: Employment figures from Metropolitan Toronto Planning Department Report P3.52, 31 Jan. 1989; CMA Suburbs estimated. Floor space figures from Royal LePage Ltd.

the Metropolitan Toronto suburbs (see Figure 17.1 and Table 17.1). If the municipalities outside Metropolitan Toronto but within the CMA boundary, that is the CMA suburbs, are included, the distribution of office jobs changes slightly: 45 per cent of jobs are in the central district, 45 per cent are in Metro suburbs, and 10 per cent are in CMA suburbs. Office floor-space data shows a more centrally-biased distribution, with 57 per cent of the CMA total in the central district (see Table 17.1). The reason for the stronger central district emphasis in the case of floor space is a stricter definition of offices than in the case of employment surveys. The floor space survey includes only office space in buildings with more than 1858 square metres, and excludes any office space attached to plants. The central district with its larger buildings and 'pure' office clusters thus gains in weight.

Both within the central district and in the suburbs offices are unevenly distributed. The central district (see Figure 17.2) contains the high-density financial district (or inner core) centred on King and Bay Streets, the medium-density outer core surrounding the financial district, the medium-density northern central district (including the Yonge/St. Clair and Yonge/Eglinton clusters), and the central district fringe, where relatively few offices are scattered along arterial roads and in sections of the older industrial areas south of Queen Street. Outside the central district three distinct types of office location can be observed (see Figure 17.1): transit-oriented subcentres (North York City Centre, Scarborough Town Centre, Bloor-Islington Centre); office parks (for example, Don Mills, Consumers Road); and locations along commercial arteries, in shopping plazas, and in industrial areas. The node areas in the suburbs (that is, areas with more than 1,000 office employment) are strung along the Yonge Street subway-Don Valley Parkway axis. These nodes (numbers 2, 4, 5, and 6 on Figure

17.1) contain 67,000 jobs. This axis of office employment nodes coincides with Toronto's high-income sector to the north and north-east of the central business district (CBD) (see Chapter 12). Another 17,000 office jobs are found in the west of Metro along the Highway 427/Airport axis. This axis is rapidly spreading into Mississauga further to the west. In this sector too, high-income areas either overlap with or are in close proximity to office nodes. On the other hand, Metro's north-west sector, home to a high percentage of blue-collar workers and low-income groups, hosts few and small office nodes: only 8,300 jobs are located in the three nodes in this sector. Similarly, most of Scarborough has so far attracted relatively little office development.

In Table 17.2, offices are broken down into different 'sectors' or 'industries', and these are ranked according to degree of spatial concentration. Before describing spatial patterns, it is worthwhile to consider briefly the sectoral breakdown. There are various industries that are part of the service or tertiary sector of the economy, such as law firms, radio, television and

Figure 17.2
The Central District of Toronto and Sub-areas

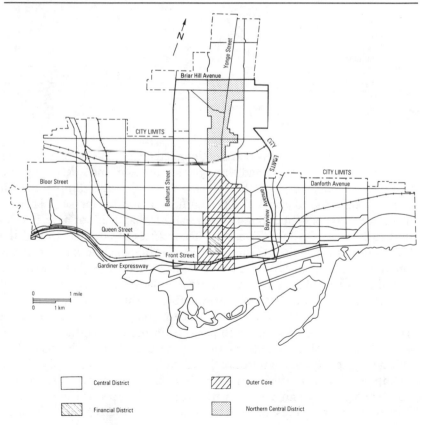

☐ Central District	▨ Outer Core
▨ Financial District	▨ Northern Central District

Table 17.2

Distribution of Offices by Economic Sector and Major Parts of Metropolitan Toronto, 1988 (ranked according to degree of concentration)

Economic Sector Ranked by Degree of Spatial Concentration of Employment	Employment[a] (rounded)		% in Central District	Number of Establishments		% in Central District
	Metro Total	Central District		Metro Total	Central District	
1. Law Firms	19,900	16,400	82.5	1,613	873	54.1
2. Radio, TV, Film	9,100	7,100	77.8	357	248	69.5
3. Banks and Trust Cos.	49,600	32,500	65.4	1,283	427	33.3
4. Insurance, Real Estate and Finance other than Banks and Trust Companies	76,100	48,800	64.1	3,384	1,205	35.6
5. Government	69,300	42,100	60.8	784	416	53.1
6. Publishing	16,900	9,600	56.7	740	424	57.3
7. Associations	15,700	8,000	50.9	1,370	629	45.9
8. Business Services other than Law Firms	84,800	42,300	49.9	9,199	3,327	36.2
9. Mining and Oil Companies	9,500	4,700	49.5	217	158	72.8
10. Transportation, Construction, Utilities	66,500	25,100	37.7	2,788	672	24.1
11. Trade/Personal Services	39,000	14,000	35.8	2,051	738	36.0
12. Technical Services	17,800	6,200	35.0	1,515	513	33.8
13. Health Services	18,900	4,200	21.9	5,571	1,170	21.0
14. Manufacturing	40,400	4,900	12.2	702	87	12.4
	533,400			31,600		

[a]Full-time employment only.

SOURCE: Metropolitan Toronto Planning Department, Report P3.52, Jan. 31, 1989.

film companies, and various kinds of financial firms. The secondary sector of the economy is represented through the offices of manufacturing and publishing companies, and the primary sector through mining and oil company offices (and even a few head offices of agri-businesses). There is hardly any facet of contemporary Canadian life that does not have an echo in the offices of Toronto. There are head offices of large banks and the head office of the United Church of Canada; the gigantic Bay Street law offices and the small law offices above shops that help clients with the sale of their family homes; the holding company offices controlling vast business empires and the fund-raising office of the Salvation Army.

If we use the distribution of all office employment in Metropolitan Toronto as a yardstick—about 50 per cent in the central district and 50 per cent in the Metro suburbs—we can see from Table 17.2 that some offices are strongly concentrated in the central district, especially law firms, the offices of radio, television and film companies; finance, insurance, and real estate offices; and government. Other industries are more evenly distributed between the CBD and the remainder of Metropolitan Toronto,

Table 17.3
Ranking by Percentage of Selected Office Activities by Degree of Concentration, and
Numbers of Establishments, Toronto, 1981

Industry	Central District	Per cent[a] Metro Suburbs	CMA[b] Suburbs	CMA[b] Total Number of Establishments
Canadian Banks	100.0	.0	.0	9
Foreign Banks	100.0	.0	.0	39
Investment Dealers	98.0	.0	2.0	68
Trust Companies	87.2	7.7	5.1	39
Insurance Companies	81.7	13.7	4.6	131
Advertising Agencies	74.2	16.7	9.0	233
Law Firms	57.4	30.0	12.6	2,245
Architects	55.6	36.3	8.1	369
Manufacturing Companies	48.6	34.7	16.9	c
Data Processing Consultants	41.2	47.6	11.2	267
Chartered Accountants	34.1	55.1	10.7	847
Engineering Consultants	29.9	51.0	19.1	418
Office Floor space	65.9	28.3	6.0	d

[a]Because percentages are rounded their sum does not always amount exactly to 100 per cent.
[b]CMA = Census Metropolitan Area (1981).
[c]Total employment in 'separately located head offices, sales offices, and ancillary units' in 1981; 40,300.
[d]Total office floor space in 1981: 6.8 million square metres.

SOURCES AND DEFINITIONS: see Gad, 1985, 336.

such as non-profit associations, business services other than law firms, and mining and oil company offices. The office employment of other industries, namely that of trade and personal service businesses, technical services (architects and engineering consultants), medical services, and office employment in manufacturing company offices, is highly deconcentrated.

This ranking masks a number of facets, especially the divergence of distribution patterns between subcategories within each industry category displayed in Table 17.2 and the differences in the size and status of offices. A further table (Table 17.3) displays another tabulation of offices, where emphasis is put on a finer industry breakdown and in some cases on major offices only.[1] With the exception of manufacturing companies and office floor space, figures refer to percentages of establishments (or offices) rather than employment (see also the three columns under the Number of Establishments heading in Table 17.2). Although the data are for 1981 and to some extent out of date, they are of value because they include the CMA suburbs and point to an ongoing deconcentration process. When only the major offices of financial businesses are considered, it becomes apparent that there is a considerable difference between the highly concentrated banks and the far less concentrated distribution of the insurance company head offices and 'chief agencies' of foreign firms. An even greater degree of difference in spatial concentration occurs within the business services group of industries: it ranges from the strong concentration of advertising agencies to the highly deconcentrated patterns of data-processing consultants and accountants. Also note the breakdown of technical services into architects, which show a fairly high degree of concentration, and engineering consultants. The latter show the greatest degree of deconcentration of any industry considered here.

A comparison of the spatial distribution of employment and number of establishments (compare column 3 and column 6 in Table 17.2, or column 3 in Table 17.2 and column 1 in Table 17.3) shows a great degree of discordance in some categories. In the case of banks and trust companies, financial services other than banks and trust companies, law firms, and business services other than law firms, the concentration of employment is much stronger than the concentration of establishments. This is a result of the pronounced cluster of large firms or large offices in the central district and especially the financial district. For instance, Toronto's largest law- and accounting-firm offices can be found in the financial district; the suburban law and accounting offices are usually quite small. Similarly, head offices of the large banks and insurance companies are located in the financial district or in the outer core of the central district. Suburban offices are often much smaller branches or subsidiary units.

Here we encounter another dimension of offices: apart from industry and size we can look at the 'status' of an office. What role does an office establishment play within an organizational hierarchy? While some offices are identical with a firm (unilocational firms), other offices fit into a hierarchy from head office down to regional office and branch office. To make matters more complex, even head offices can be broken down into executive and 'back offices'. Back offices are head office departments, such as personnel, billing, or accounting, to name a few, or new types of internal groupings such as data centres, systems development, or credit card centres, which are located separately from the main part that houses the chief executives. Implied in the term 'back office' is an inferior status, that is, the workers are at the lower end of the job spectrum. Huang (1989) has demonstrated through some case studies that back offices can vary considerably in occupational mix and that some of these are hardly inferior in status at all. Table 17.4 shows the major components of a hypothetical bank head office, including the job mix in the different spatial units (or establishments). The hypothetical head office shown here includes the bank's Toronto main branch, the Ontario regional office, and such subsidiary offices as a second general office, the main data centre, and a credit card operations office. Total employment of 5,300 is fragmented into four offices, ranging in location from the financial district to the outer core of the central district and two suburban locations. The two central district offices are quite similar in terms of occupational mix and the subsidiary general office hardly deserves the label back office. The two suburban offices are radically different from each other. In the data centre, professional and middle level technical jobs account for 85 per cent of all jobs, while in the credit card centre supervisory and clerical jobs account for

Table 17.4
Occupational Mix in a Spatially Fragmented Bank Head Office, Mid-1980s

Head Office Fragment and Location	Employees %[a]					Total No. of Employees
	Upper Level			Middle Level	Lower Level	
	Executive Senior Managers	Managers	Professionals	Technical/ Sales/ Supervisory	Clerical	
Primary General Office, Financial District	7	28	6	25	33	2,000
Subsidiary General Office, Core Area	4	33	11	23	29	1,700
Central District	6	31	8	24	31	3,700
Data Centre, Suburbs	0.5	2	26	59	12	1,200
Credit Card Centre, Suburbs	0	4	0	27	69	400
Suburbs	0.4	3	20	51	26	1,600

[a]Because percentages are rounded their sum does not always amount exactly to 100%.
SOURCE: based on Huang, 1989.

96 per cent of jobs. The credit card centre houses a very high proportion of clerical workers (69 per cent) and is the only one of the four establishments that conforms to the image of a back office as having inferior status. If one studies the effect of the spatial fragmentation of these large offices on the central district and suburban occupational mix, one sees that overall the central district has concentrations in the uppermost and lower level jobs and the suburbs in the middle level jobs.

In the late 1980s, all five of the large Canadian banks—irrespective of whether their head offices are in Toronto or not—have fragmented Toronto head or major offices,[2] although there are differences in the specific spatial configuration of each organization. These offices have grown to such an extent that a considerable deploying of fragments is occurring at the moment. The largest of the trust companies have also split their Toronto offices into two or more spatially separate units. Here, too, it does not matter whether Toronto hosts the head office or hosts only a substantial operational unit; large size seems to be a major reason for the break-up. Other large offices, especially those of insurance companies, utilities, transportation, and manufacturing companies, and even some

Table 17.5 Characteristics of Selected Toronto Office Nodes

Characteristics	Office Nodes[1]								All of Metro Toronto
	1A Financial District	1B Outer Core	1C Northern Central District	2 North York City Centre	3 Scarborough Town Centre	4 Don Mills	6 Consumers Road	7 Consumers Hwy. 404-Steeles	
Industries[2]	Percentage of office jobs								
Mining, Oil Cos.	3.1	0.3	5.0	6.1	0.0	11.4	0.3	9.9	1.7
Manufacturing	0.9	0.8	5.7	6.1	4.0	15.1	5.3	9.8	7.5
Transportation, Construction, Utilities	3.7	15.2	5.6	3.3	15.2	14.5	21.6	4.6	12.6
Banks	27.4	5.6	3.2	3.3	1.4	4.2	4.5	10.0	9.4
Finance, Insurance, Real Estate	30.1	13.4	15.9	13.9	25.2	14.0	11.4	8.6	14.3
Law Firms	13.7	2.6	1.8	2.0	0.3	0.5	0.4	0.4	3.8
Business Services	14.1	13.2	23.6	17.4	11.2	11.6	30.6	24.6	16.0
Technical Services	0.7	1.5	5.4	1.5	0.5	7.6	6.2	10.2	3.4
Radio, TV, Film	0.2	3.6	2.9	0.1	0.0	2.7	0.0	0.0	1.7
Publishing	0.4	4.2	4.0	4.0	14.5	4.8	2.8	2.5	3.2
Government	2.4	28.2	13.8	30.3	26.4	0.0	1.4	1.0	13.0
Other	3.3	11.4	12.9	10.0	1.2	13.7	15.8	18.2	14.0
TOTAL (%)*	100	100	100	100	100	100	100	100	100
TOTAL (000s)	88	114	30	16	10	15	12	8	533
Occupational level[3]	Percentage of office jobs in occupational category								
Executive, Managerial, Professional	40.9	36.0	38.9	32.9	N.A.	31.6	39.2	N.A.	37.3
Technical, Sales, Supervisory	13.9	17.1	17.6	23.3	N.A.	13.7	18.6	N.A.	16.1
Clerical	45.2	47.0	43.5	43.8	N.A.	54.7	42.2	N.A.	46.7
Gender[3]	Percentage of office jobs held by women								
	55.6	58.2	55.8	55.2	N.A.	57.8	49.4	N.A.	55.7
Commuting[3]	Percentage of office workers residing within 8 km of employment node								
	37.8	45.8	65.5	N.A.	N.A.	65.8	N.A.	N.A.	N.A.
Office Rents[4] (in $ per m² per annum)	478	278-327	270-300	347	306	215	234	205	N.A.

*Because percentages are rounded their sum does not always amount exactly to 100 per cent.

[1]For full name and location of node, see Figs 17.1 and 17.2.

[2]1988 data. Source: Metropolitan Toronto Planning Department, Report P.3.52, Jan. 31, 1989.

[3]1981 data. Source: Huang, 1989, based on special 1981 census tabulations.

[4]1988 data. Source: Royal LePage Ltd.

'professional' firms like accountants engage in the fragmentation of the main office. In some cases, this fragmentation overlaps with the more traditional hierarchical spatial fragmentation down from head office to regional office to branch. However, before the 1980s large insurance companies would not have had a different location for the company head office and the Canadian operations office. This trend is on the increase.

The various spatial patterns of industries, establishment size, status, occupations, and other aspects, such as the gender of employees or commuter patterns, combine to produce quite distinct office nodes in the Toronto area. It is tempting to see an intra-urban set of regions emerging. Table 17.5 displays a number of characteristics for eight office districts or nodes. Data from the table, as well as knowledge gained from recent interviews and more unstructured observations over the last few years, are used to characterize these nodes.

The *financial district* deserves its name, since 57.4 per cent of jobs are in the finance, insurance, real estate (including banks) subsector. Employment in law firms is also strongly over-represented. Law firms, together with the various financial and real estate activities, account for over 70 per cent of the total office employment here. There are also parts of the business services group, especially accounting and management consulting firms, that are over-represented and rapidly growing. The character of this area is determined by the large bank and trust company offices, stockbroker offices of every size, medium-size insurance companies (with fewer and fewer life insurance companies), the country's largest law and accounting firms, both very large and small mining companies, and a host of small offices of holding companies of different degrees of significance. These offices range from the tiny ones of individual speculators to those of pension fund managers and gigantic corporate empires. The latter, it must be stressed, are relatively small too, rarely occupying more than one floor, since the selling of shares or entire companies does not require large staffs. The operating companies controlled by these holding companies are usually located separately, either in the financial district, or elsewhere in Toronto, other parts of Canada, or the rest of the world.

Of all the office nodes, the financial district has the highest proportion of high-level jobs. It has also a fairly high level of clerical jobs, which are especially noticeable in the very large offices of the financial industries. As in most of the other office nodes, female employees hold the majority of the office jobs and increasingly occupy upper-level jobs, even if they are still very thinly represented at the executive levels. The financial district, with 37.8 per cent, has the smallest proportion of office workers who live in close proximity (less than eight kilometres away) to their place of work, in spite of relatively high residential densities in the city of Toronto. Long-distance commuters make up a substantial proportion of the commuters. Female clerical workers increasingly take part in long-distance commuting, while upper-level workers, especially female ones, show increasing numbers within the eight-kilometre ring, an occurrence that contradicts almost all previous observations on gender- and income-related commuting behaviour.

A tightly-knit network of personal and messenger linkages holds the financial district activities together, and prompts firms to pay extremely high rents for prestigious office space. Most of the professional and other high-ranking employees seem to consider their expensive location as essential. Forced moves out are interpreted as demotions. Companies worried about high rents and the high cost incurred by female clerical workers (in terms of commuting time, commuting expenses, housing costs in the inner parts of Toronto, and 'living' costs like lunches) attempt to move many employees out of the financial district. These companies contributed in the 1980s to the Toronto region office redistribution dynamic.

In the *outer core* of the central district, we see more government workers, architects, advertising specialists, and representatives of the media and entertainment industries. Table 17.5 shows that government, both provincial and municipal, looms large here; the government category is highly over-represented with 28.2 per cent of office employment. Radio, TV, and film, including many offices of the highly fragmented CBC organization, as well as publishing are over-represented. If the business services group is disaggregated, it becomes apparent that advertising agencies and graphic designers are also very strongly over-represented here. The transportation, construction, and utility group is also very strong, partly because of the gigantic office of Ontario Hydro (with about 7,000 employees, Ontario Hydro is Toronto's largest office), the very large offices of Bell's Ontario region, and other large offices such as Toronto Hydro. A smaller portion of employment is represented by scores of offices of the travel industry. The Bloor-Bay area especially houses not only airline ticket offices, but also regional sales offices (largely invisible to the public), travel agencies, and both provincial and foreign tourist-industry representatives. Finally, mixed in between government offices and the various media, advertising, and travel industry offices are dozens of the very largest insurance company head offices. Several of Canada's largest life insurance companies have escaped the high rents of the financial district and are housed in large office buildings or in multi-building office complexes in the outer core.

There is little evidence that the various industries of the outer core are as intimately linked together in terms of contact patterns as those in the financial district. One functionally related set of businesses, however, stands out here. Strong face-to-face linkages exist between advertising agencies, radio and television companies (either major offices or 'time' sales offices), public relations consultants, industrial designers (or graphic artists), and non-profit associations. Less intimately linked 'industries' of this cluster are market research, publishing, and federal government agencies. With the exception of federal government offices, all of these industries are over-represented in the outer core. This advertising and media network most likely also includes such non-office activities as film and television studios and commercial photographers. These are not likely to be strongly concentrated in the outer core but rather in the adjacent fringe areas of the central district. Many of the firms of this network are not found in the newer high-rise office buildings. For reasons of space cost and/or the desire to occupy buildings whose image they can control, these firms look for cheaper space in older and smaller buildings. It is no surprise that these firms, as well as architects, urban planning consultants, and also back offices of financial district firms put considerable pressure on the older industrial and even residential districts in the fringe areas of the central district. The advertising agencies have found the outer core convenient for maintaining their production or input linkages, and for access to clients. The financial institutions, the major department store and retail chain head offices, the travel industry, and a wide range of other corporate head offices are close by. Another major client, the Ontario provincial government, has most of its ministry 'head offices' in the outer core or in adjacent areas.

With a relatively small percentage (36 per cent) of higher level office workers and a high percentage (47 per cent) of clerical workers, the outer core's office jobs are more strongly biased towards the clerical end of the job hierarchy than most other office nodes. This is not surprising, since insurance, utility, and government offices are very large, with between 1000 and 7000 jobs each, and clerical labour represents an important proportion of these large public and private sector bureaucracies' work-force. Of nine office areas examined by Huang (1989), the outer core, not surprisingly, was the area with the highest percentage (58 per cent) of office jobs held by women. The commuter shed of the outer core is less far-flung than that of the financial district: 45.8 per cent of the outer core office workers live within the eight-kilometre boundary, rather than only 37.8 per cent in the case of the financial district. The outer core is extremely well positioned within the residential space of Toronto and, since it has a large percentage of unspecialized jobs, it is reasonable to expect that it can collect its huge labour force of 114,000 from within a reasonably tight commuter shed.

Rents vary considerably within this rather large sector. Areas east, west, and north of the financial district have rents in the $265 to $278 per square metre per year range (these are surpassed by rents in some suburban districts). New office stock on the waterfront just south of the financial district and along Bloor Street rents for around $325 per square metre per year and is only surpassed by rents in the financial district and narrowly by those in the North York City Centre. High rents in some sub-areas and the limited possibilities that exist for construction of new large-scale office buildings, because of tight zoning limits, are some of the reasons why many large tenants of all kinds are leaving the outer core. The provincial government of Ontario is a major source of spin-offs to the suburbs and to other cities in Ontario, while Ontario Hydro is planning to move about half of its 7000 head office employees to the North York City Centre. Until the mid–1980s, the outer core also housed three of Canada's seven integrated oil companies. By the end of the 1980s they had all gone: Shell to Calgary, Sunoco to North York, and Gulf had disappeared, swallowed up by Petro-Canada.

The industrial mix in the *northern central district* is quite similar to that of the outer core: government, both federal and provincial, publishing, and radio, television, and film are all over-represented, as are business services other than law firms. As in the outer core, advertising agencies are strongly concentrated here and so are a wide range of other business and technical services (architects and also engineering consultants). Finance, insurance, and real estate is slightly over-represented, largely due to the large number of small- and medium-sized insurance companies. The over-representation of mining and oil companies is almost exclusively because of several very large office establishments of Imperial Oil. This area includes several of the head offices of 'industrial' (that is, non-financial and non-professional businesses) Canadian giants or large companies operating in Canada: Imperial Oil, the Weston group of companies, Canada Packers, the Unicorp group, Canadian Tire, Cineplex, Union Carbide, and several others. Due to fairly high rents, very low vacancy rates, and almost no possibilities for construction of new buildings in office clusters surrounded by elite neighbourhoods, several other giants, for example, McDonald's of Canada and Procter and Gamble, have left for the suburbs in recent years.

The occupational mix is strongly biased towards the upper end of the hierarchy. Only the financial district and the Consumers Road office park have a higher percentage of executive, managerial, and professional employees. Because of its relatively small size (30,000 office workers), its up-scale employment composition, and its location surrounded by elite residential areas, this office node has a very small labour shed: 65 per cent of the office workers live within eight kilometres. Of particular interest is the observation that female high- and middle-level office workers of this district seem to have some of the most concentrated labour sheds in the metropolitan area. Eighty-three per cent of the female office workers in the highest level jobs, 97 per cent in the middle-level jobs and only 63 per cent in the clerical jobs come from within an eight-kilometre ring (Huang, 1989, 157).

The *North York City Centre* office node has gradually diversified beyond the initial reason for its existence—the municipal government of North York and its city hall. While large-scale commercial office development started at the time of the Yonge Street subway extension from Eglinton to Finch in the mid–1970s, the major development boom occurred after the early 1980s recession. The various offices of municipal government (city hall, board of education, hydro commission) have been complemented by large offices of the federal and provincial governments, and all three levels of government account for 30 per cent of office employment. Apart from the strong government component, the mix of industries is close to that for Metropolitan Toronto as a whole. The pronounced under-representation of banks and the over-representation of mining and oil companies is remarkable. However, the latter industry's stronghold depends almost entirely on the large regional office of Petro-Canada. Although the rents for class A space, that is largely new space, are comparable to those in the Bloor Street and northern central corridor areas, the North York City Centre and the Yonge-York Mills node just to the south have become popular destinations for movers from the outer core and even for some large financial district movers. The availability of large amounts of space in the late 1980s, the accessibility by public transit, and the high profile of the new high-rise townscape forcefully promoted by North York mayor, Mel Lastman, have proved to be very attractive. More companies and Ontario Hydro have plans to move there with back offices. However, these will be very expensive back offices, and one of the companies that arrived in the mid–1980s with about 600 employees is already complaining about high rents and is considering spinning-off a back office from the North York City Centre location. Since employment composition data was collected in 1981 when this office node was very small, this data is not worth too much attention. The data profile of 1981 is closest to that of the outer core and reflects the very strong government component.

Like the North York City Centre, the *Scarborough Town Centre* is also a major office subcentre in Metropolitan Toronto's official plan, and here too the development of private office space was preceded by municipal government offices. However, development proceeded more slowly than in North York and a few large office establishments, several in single-occupancy buildings, have put their stamp on the industrial mix so far. Government (municipal and federal branch offices) and insurance (one large head office and a few smaller offices), the large Toronto-East regional office of Bell Canada and the yellow pages publishing subsidiary of Bell make up the majority of office employment. Some attempts to estimate occupational mix show almost 70 to 80 per cent of workers in clerical employment and an equally high percentage of female office workers.

The remaining three office districts shown in Table 17.5 are *office parks* in the Don Valley/Highway 404 corridor (see Figure 17.1). All three office parks have low- to medium-rise buildings, mostly set in the middle of large lawns and parking lots. The parks have much lower rents than the central district subareas or the official subcentres. In their industry profiles they also have much in common: an almost complete absence of government offices and law firms, and an over-representation of technical services (especially engineering consultants). The mix of other industries, however, varies strongly and even the status of offices within industries may vary.

The Don Mills node stands out because of the strong presence of offices of companies engaged in manufacturing, mining and oil, transportation, construction and utilities, and publishing. Some of these industries or subsectors within industries are either completely or strongly represented by one or several large back offices. It seems that these and other industries with a high clerical-labour component have managed to outweigh those offices with generally low proportions of clerical work (technical services and manufacturing company head offices). Of the nine office nodes studied by Huang (1989), the Don Mills node had the second lowest percentage of high-level workers and highest percentage of clerical office workers (54.7 per cent). With 57.8 per cent, the share of office jobs occupied by women was second only to that of the outer core.

This employment mix contrasts very sharply with that of the Consumers Road office park, which is only about five kilometres north along the Don Valley Parkway. With 39.2 per cent of employees classified as high-level, the Consumers Road office park has the second highest of this ratio (following the financial district, which posts a 40.9 per cent value), but unlike the financial district it has a high percentage of medium-level workers and a very low percentage of clerical workers. Of all nine office nodes, it has the lowest share of clerical jobs: only 42.2 per cent. The different emphasis in industrial and establishment status mix compared to the Don Mills node seems to account for the difference in occupational mix. Of particular interest is the high proportion of jobs in business services, which is largely due to the strong presence of various types of computer consulting firms. Also strongly over-represented is the transportation, construction, and utilities group, which includes several construction company head offices and several utility company offices with more high-level employment than the utility company data centre and billing operations in Don Mills.

The Highway 404/Steeles Avenue office park displayed in Table 17.5 shares industrial composition features of both the Don Mills and Consumers Road parks. Business services (largely data processing firms) and technical services (predominantly engineering consultants) are very strongly over-represented and account for nearly 35 per cent of all employment. Oil companies and manufacturing companies are also strongly over-represented and this node is the only one outside the financial district that is over-represented in the bank category. The strong presence of the latter, however, is almost entirely the result of a very large data centre (with almost no clerical workers) in the Highway 404/Steeles office node.

No occupational mix data are available for this last node, but it is probably very similar to that of the Consumers Road area. Commuter shed data are only available for the Don Mills office node, and the general extent of the labour shed is very similar to that of the northern central district: 65.8 per cent live within the eight-kilometre radius. In the case of Don Mills, sharp differences in commuting patterns exist between male and female upper-level workers on the one hand and female clerical workers on the other. Only 41.8 per cent of upper-level males and 55.4 per cent of upper level females reside in the eight-kilometre zone, but 70.2 per cent of the female clerical workers do. It seems that the social geography of the surrounding area provides a large supply of female clerical workers but not the type of upper-level workers required here.

Needless to say, the office parks rely very heavily on commuting by car. In most of these parks, three quarters or more of the employees arrive by car—a situation opposite to that in the financial district, where only about 20 per cent of commuters use the car. In some of the newest office parks in the CMA suburbs of Markham or Mississauga almost everybody uses the car for the journey to work.

No in-depth examinations of the linkage patterns of offices outside the central district exist; accordingly, tentative suggestions only can be made. Many of the industries that are strongly decentralized and over-represented in the suburban office nodes have very few face-to-face contacts (especially insurance companies and manufacturing company head offices). Other types of businesses may have higher levels of face-to-face contacts, but there are strong hints that these contacts are with other companies or government offices, which are widely dispersed over the suburban and exurban area. (See Chapter 16 for similar conclusions concerning the linkages of manufacturing plants located in suburban industrial parks.) It is almost impossible in these circumstances to conduct business without a car and without reasonable parking space. Some other establishments, especially manufacturing company head and sales offices and most insurance companies, have very far-flung face-to-face communications networks. Visits to plants and branch offices, with many of these scattered over the Metro region and, indeed, over Canada as a whole, are the major type of contacts emanating from these offices; most of the travel for this type of contact within southern Ontario seems to be made by car.

BROADENING THE SCOPE: OFFICES IN CANADIAN CITIES IN THE 1980s

How similar is the distribution of offices in other Canadian cities to that in Toronto? Obviously, the sheer size of Toronto's office 'complex' and the much smaller aggregate amount of office activity in the other cities (see Table 17.6, column 1, Total Office Floor-space column) makes an extrapolation of Toronto patterns difficult. However, it can be shown that there are fairly consistent extensions of the Toronto experience, and one can expect that those cities with growing office employment will face similar prospects—and problems—as Toronto. Systematic comparisons

Table 17.6
A Comparison of Offices in Canadian Cities in the 1980s

City	Total Office Floor-space (in 000m²)	Private Sector Office Floor-space (in 000m²)	Private Sector Floor-space 'Downtown' (%)	Manufacturing Offices in Central City (%)	Advertising Agencies in Central City (%)
Toronto	10,284	7,859	49	33	71
Montreal	5,799	4,496	72	61	90
Calgary	N.A.	3,772	73	N.A.	N.A.
Vancouver	4,161	2,471	66	67	88
Ottawa	3,530	1,737	62	53	95
Edmonton	N.A.	1,672	59	N.A.	N.A.
Winnipeg	N.A.	780	N.A.	N.A.	N.A.
Halifax	929	632	62	66	100

SOURCES: *Total office floor-space* (includes government-owned space and, in some cases, space in small buildings). Toronto: Royal LePage Ltd., 1990 (1989 data); Montreal: Royal LePage Ltd. 1989 (1988 data); Vancouver: GVRD, Vancouver Perspectives, 1988 (1988 data); Ottawa: Royal LePage, personal communication (1988 data); Halifax: Nova Scotia, Department of Industry, Trade and Technology, *Survey and Inventory of Commercial Space,* 1987 (1986 data) and City of Halifax, Development and Planning, *Moving of Government Offices.* Information Report, 22.12.1986 (1986 data).

Private sector office floor-space: Financial Post, 15.2. 1989, based on figures supplied by J.J. Barnicke (realtors).

Per cent private sector floor-space 'downtown': Financial Post, 17.10.1990, based on figures supplied by J.J. Barnicke (realtors)

Manufacturing offices ('Employment in separately located head offices, sales offices and ancillary units') in Central City (major incorporated city in CMA) in per cent of CMA total: Statistics Canada, *Manufacturing Industries of Canada: Sub-Provincial Areas 1985,* Catalogue No. 31–209.

Advertising agencies: National List of Advertisers, Toronto: Maclean-Hunter, 1987.

of office location patterns in Canadian cities is not without problems, though. There are few systematic and in-depth studies and few comparable data. Employment figures are almost impossible to obtain and floor-space data, mostly collected by leasing firms, suffer from inconsistent definitions of offices and areas considered. The synopsis in Table 17.6 and below provides only a very tentative picture.

The distribution of 'aggregate' office space, that is, space not broken down by industries, shows some strong differences between Toronto and all other cities when 'private sector' space is considered. Toronto's space is much more dispersed than Edmonton's, where 59 per cent of this kind of space can be found 'downtown'. The other CMAs for which figures are available show an even greater concentration, with Montreal and Calgary proving to be CMAs with the most concentrated patterns of office development (72 per cent and 73 per cent of space 'downtown' respectively). The reasons for this strong concentration lie primarily in the importance of a 'corporate head office complex' for the private office floor-space in CMAs with more concentrated patterns. An example of this is the resource industry head office complex and its related business services function in Vancouver (Hayter 1978; Hutton and Ley 1987; Ley and Hutton 1987).

Calgary's offices are similarly dominated by the offices of the oil industry (Zieber, 1975), and Montreal's by many of Canada's largest 'industrial' corporations. These specialized office cores probably account for a high degree of cohesion and spatial inertia. High-level business services also aggregate within these cores (see Hutton and Ley 1987, 130), as can be seen in the high degree of concentration of advertising agencies in Montreal and Vancouver (see Table 17.6). Lesser concentrations of advertising agencies in Toronto may be a consequence of this city's role as Canada's primary financial centre. High CBD rents fuelled by the presence of large and opulent financial firms become an incentive for business services to take advantage of lower rents in other parts of the CMA.

Support for this notion of specialized, highly centralized clusters is also derived from two other observations: first, from a consideration of all floor-space, that is, including government floor-space; and second, from the form of office development outside the downtown cores.

Different data show a much closer relationship between the distribution of office floor-space in Toronto and in other CMAs. The addition of government floor-space to 'private floor-space' and an inclusion of smaller offices usually produce a much more deconcentrated pattern. In Toronto's case there is little change because government is a relatively small component of office activity, although, as was pointed out earlier, the inclusion of smaller offices in the employment survey produced a somewhat lower concentration rate than the space survey with a size threshold. It is very remarkable that a 1983 study of Edmonton, in which all office space was surveyed, could claim that only 50 per cent of all office floor-space in the city was 'downtown' (Edmonton, 1983). Ley and Hutton (1987, 417) mention that only 56 per cent of Vancouver's office floor-space was in the downtown peninsula, and the 'downtown' area in 1986 seems to have held only 43.5 per cent of Vancouver's office space (Coriolis Consulting Corp. 1986). Estimates for Montreal, Ottawa, and Halifax also point to a lower concentration of all office space than 'private sector' space as determined by commercial surveys.

Accordingly, government offices and small offices are more deconcentrated than the larger commercial office buildings and occupants. This deconcentration is not surprising given a number of factors: the often aggressive government decentralization policies, the political fragmentation of large urban areas producing a multitude of government offices in suburban areas, and the closeness of small offices of all kinds to final consumers (that is, households) and small businesses throughout the metropolitan area. (For a discussion of the dispersed pattern of 'local market offices' see Armstrong 1972, 97–100.) Following this pattern is the wide dispersion of offices within the metropolitan area noticed in the case of Montreal in the early 1980s (Beauregard 1981, 38–40), Edmonton of 1983 (Edmonton 1983), and Vancouver of 1986. In all cases office space was dispersed over a wide variety of nascent town centres, shopping plazas,

Table 17.7
Distribution of Industries by Major Districts, Edmonton, 1983

Industry	Percentage of Primary Office Space[a]		Total Primary Office Space (m²)
	Central District[b]	Downtown	
1. Natural Resource Extraction	90	77	51,350
2. Government	83	70	418,387
3. Transportation, Storage, Communication, Utilities	83	72	77,330
All Primary Office Space	65	50	1,395,647
4. Finance, Insurance, Real Estate	63	50	236,640
5. Manufacturing	58	N.A.	45,430
6. Business Services	52	35	350,310
7. Health, Welfare	46	N.A.	87,610
8. Retail	40	N.A.	43,360
9. Construction	14	N.A.	40,490

[a]'Primary office space' includes all space in establishments where office space equals 66 per cent or more of the entire floor space occupied by a business.
[b]Bounded by the river valley, 75th Street, 127th Avenue and 122nd Street—an area of about 3 by 3 kilometres.

Source: Edmonton, City Planning Department (1983) *Office Space, Its Use and Distribution. Commercial Development in Edmonton, 1983*. Report No. 2 (Edmonton: City of Edmonton) pp. 16 and 49.

arterial roads, various transportation nodes, and industrial parks. Unlike the Toronto developments, subcentres or office parks with concentrations of 10,000 to 20,000 office workers seem to have been lacking so far, but smaller versions of these have appeared in a number of metropolitan areas in the 1980s.[3]

When offices are disaggregated by industries, a range of concentration versus deconcentration is visible similar to the case of Toronto, although the ranking of some industries may be quite different. Table 17.7 shows that Edmonton's 'basic' industries—natural resource extraction, government, and the category including transportation, communications, and utilities—are highly concentrated in the rather large 'central district' (or inner city) and also in the relatively small 'downtown' area. Manufacturing offices, retail offices, construction company offices, and the household-oriented health and welfare offices are spread out in varying degrees. Also less concentrated are the two categories of finance, insurance and real estate, and business services. This is not surprising, since these two categories contain different sub-industries with very different location patterns.

The smaller size of central office districts of cities other than Toronto and the dispersed nature of offices outside the central districts make it less likely that the specialized, or at least distinct, office nodes that could be observed in Toronto will be found. Larger suburban nodes are mostly absent and the central districts are generally small and accommodate a wide range of offices in a mixed fashion. Sometimes a finely-grained sorting is visible, as in Edmonton, where government offices are grouped at the ends of the Jasper Avenue financial axis. Apart from concentrations of government offices, especially law court complexes and a small concentration of bank- and trust-company main offices, other offices are usually mixed in a random fashion. Montreal, however, is an exception. After the desertion of St. James Street by all types of financial offices, a new financial district took shape to the north-west in the area bounded by St. James and Sherbrooke, Beaver Hall, and Stanley. Head offices and other main offices of banks and trust companies, the Montreal Stock Exchange, and most of the stockbrokers, and other financial businesses or federal government branches are located here. Also, as in the case of Toronto's financial district, the large law firms and accounting firms share the new office towers or office complexes with financial companies, while many of the smaller, less complex law firms are still clustered near the courts at the eastern end of the old St. James Street axis. While the constellation of financial offices, law firms, and accountants' offices is very similar to that found in Toronto's financial district, Montreal's new 'financial district' is still less specialized than Toronto's. Almost all the large 'industrials' headquartered in Montreal have their head offices in this district, as have the major advertising agencies. In Toronto, these two categories of offices are only partly represented or not found at all in the financial district. Also, the St. Catherine Street retail axis cuts right through Montreal's new financial district, while Toronto's major central retail complex is peripheral to the financial district.

Given the sparseness of data and the individualistic character of Canadian cities in terms of size, industries, geography of government, and several other factors, it is very hard to make firm generalizations about the location of offices. On the other hand, it is quite apparent that offices are not randomly distributed over the space of our large CMAs. First of all, there are some features that are related to the size of an urban region and its office complex. Large amounts of office employment and floorspace are associated with a noticeable specialization of office districts. A smaller amount of office activity supports only a general central office district and a dispersed pattern of offices in the rest of the CMA. Secondly, when offices are disaggregated by industry, a range of location patterns from the highly concentrated to the strongly deconcentrated can be observed. Most cities have a particular office component—finance in Toronto, resource industries in Vancouver, oil industry in Calgary, large 'industrials' in Montreal—that seems spatially to form a highly concentrated 'corporate complex' (Hutton and Ley 1987; Ley and Hutton 1987) around which high-level business services congregate. Other types of offices—manufacturing company offices, data processing, and technical services like engineering consultants—are usually less strongly concentrated or even deconcentrated. End-consumer oriented offices, like small law firms and health care offices, are highly deconcentrated. If an urban region has a fragmented municipal government, and especially if provincial governments have followed decentralization policies, the government category shows a deconcentrated pattern of location.

LOCATION FACTORS

Needless to say, office location does not happen outside an institutional framework and a system of infrastructures such as roads and rail transit lines. It is important, therefore, to keep in mind various forms of collective actions ('planning' and 'infrastructure') and the historic concatenation of events. Every new round of office location and relocation builds on a previous urban structure and especially on a previous office location pattern.

In locating an office establishment—and in deciding whether to relocate or to spin-off a back office—decision-makers consider the cost of rental (or purchase) of space, the cost, in a broad sense, of 'linkages', the accessibility of the office for labour, which includes the owners or chief managers, the ambience of the location, and special building or site requirements.

Cost of Space or Location Rent
Normally, in a large city, office rents are not uniform between locations, and the location decision-makers have to figure out what rent they can pay. In extreme cases, offices simply cannot afford the rents being charged. The level of rents that will be paid will partially depend on the savings achieved in transportation costs or 'linkage' costs (or maybe in terms of increased levels of business or prestige gained) and partly by the surplus of revenue over production costs. Since personnel costs are such a high proportion of an office's expenses, one could simplify the picture by arguing that the ability to pay rent rests on the ability to generate professional revenues. Considerable differences in revenue levels per person and hence per unit of land can be visualized if one considers the very high incomes of lawyers versus the lower incomes of architects or urban planning consultants. In the very high-rent buildings of the financial districts or prime crossroads of the Toronto CBD one can indeed hardly find an architect or planning consultant because they are priced out.

While this differential rent-paying ability can be reasonably well-determined for professional firms, it is much harder to pin it down in the case of head offices of large firms. These head offices do not themselves primarily generate revenues; individual branches or plants are the revenue generators. One has to visualize the head office as a kind of service unit that gets a 'service fee' from its 'production' units, and uses this fee to pay for head office space, equipment, and labour. There is a major problem: since the head office is also the central unit, it can usually determine the price of the services it delivers to its 'producing' units. What usually happens is that some judgement is used to decide whether an expensive location makes more sense than a cheaper one in terms of advantages derived. Usually the head office has a great deal of latitude concerning this judgement, but, on the other hand, occasions arise when the cost calculus comes under close scrutiny. This happens when the head office has grown and needs to make a major space adjustment, when the landlord increases the rent, or under harsh business conditions when top management is under severe pressure to cut costs. In those cases, head office buildings in expensive locations are sold and cheaper space and/or locations are chosen.

Linkage Costs
Accessibility to other firms and to 'final consumers' is bought with high rents. No office has a reason to exist unless it 'sells' a product to someone. It 'sells' an 'output' to a client: a commercial client, a private person, a part of its own organization, or even an unwilling recipient, such as the branch inspector of a bank making an unwelcome visit. These office-client relationships involve the transfer of information in the form of personal contacts (visits and meetings), written contacts, or contacts over the telephone or by computer terminal. Of course, most firms require 'inputs' in order to produce and to sell outputs. In the case of offices the major inputs are not tangible goods but information. The network of information relationships, comprising input and output links, is usually referred to as the 'linkage network'. Personal meetings or face-to-face contacts have so far played a major role in the linkage network of an office, and since face-to-face meetings involve persons with high levels of pay, the cost of linkages can be very high. If a certain type of office work requires a high frequency of meetings—or many participants with resulting severe scheduling problems—the proximity between establishments, which are related through information exchange, pays off in terms of time and transportation-cost savings. There are, as Thorngren (1970) has pointed out, different levels of information exchange, some more complex, involving open-ended discussions and often several high-ranking participants (so-called orientation contacts) and some, at the other extreme, highly routinized contacts, involving the transfer of very simple information. Empirical research shows that the latter kinds of contacts can be satisfactorily performed through the mail or by telephone (Thorngren 1970; Goddard 1973).

Locations where the linkage expenses can be minimized are those where many firms forming an input-output relationship are clustered in space (for example, various financial firms in the financial district, or the advertising-media industries in the outer parts of the central office core). Central locations from which dispersed business partners can be accessed are also advantageous. Since dispersed contact partners cannot easily be reached unless a car is used, an off-centre location without congestion costs is often a preferred choice. In other words, a high frequency of face-to-face contacts or severe scheduling problems does not automatically lead to a city-centre location or for that matter to other clusters of business, if congestion is a problem in these locations.

Labour and its Accessibility

An office can benefit from a location that allows it to capture an adequate supply of the right type of labour at a relatively low cost. For some offices a city centre location with its high rents may be the best location, especially when the office relies on a mix of labour, including many different specialists as well as a major group of low-paid employees. A city centre location is advantageous when it offers reasonable access by car and a strongly focused (radial) public transit network. In these circumstances, the office at the city centre is well located to assemble a labour force scattered over a wide area and do it cheaply in terms of labour cost—including low turnover, low absenteeism, and punctuality—because the public transit system will absorb a great deal of the cost of travel (and, in this sense, subsidize wages). One special case of office location is the back office with a high or very high percentage of clerical workers. Based on research in San Francisco, Nelson (1986) argues that back offices seek a well-educated and stable, yet low wage, female labour force, which they find in the middle- and upper-income white suburbs of the San Francisco Bay Area. Since many of these suburban women are second-income earners with home responsibilities, a short journey to work limits the range where these kinds of back offices can locate. Undoubtedly these considerations apply in the case of some office location decisions. It was pointed out earlier that not all back offices employ a high percentage of female clerical labour. As a result, Nelson's explanation does not apply to all such offices.

It is quite clear that the match of places of work and places of residence is not straightforward. The selection of an office location, if only access to labour is considered, depends on the type of labour required, the spatial configuration of the labour supply as expressed in the social geography of the city, and the configuration of the transportation system.

Amenity

There are a number of factors that are less easily pinned down but which deserve some attention. Urban landscapes are imbued with symbolic meaning, and are used to communicate achievements, assurances, or simply the presence of a firm. Visibility or prestige associated with a building, a set of buildings, a street, or a district has some influence on the location of offices. The concentration of office nodes in high-income residential sectors obviously has some functional value in terms of work-residence linkages for the kind of labour required. But this concentration has another reason: the appearance of respectability. This appearance entails not only visibility in the marketable sense of tall downtown buildings or suburban expressway-oriented buildings with corporate logos; in some cases it entails a more profound feeling of well-being, if not belonging, that is important to those who occupy offices. Familiarity and trust are features that are mentioned frequently by high-level office workers in Toronto's financial district. A fiercely competitive and unpredictable work situation is being counteracted by this sense of familiarity and belonging. Apart from the assurances provided to managers and workers, assurances are also given to customers, especially investors.

Special Building or Site Requirements
Some firms choose to own their own buildings for economic reasons, or because of better control of security, such as supervision of pathways between parking lot and front door for the safety of shift workers (Matthew 1986, 29). New and smaller buildings with large parking lots are preferred to high-rise towers, and this preference exerts a strong pull away from central district or subcentre locations. Other specific requirements may be an adequate and reliable supply of electricity and telecommunications capacity to run large computer installations or special electronic trading facilities.

CONCLUSIONS

In this chapter, offices have been treated as a reflection of several facets of contemporary society. Offices are part of the system of industrial commodity production, reflecting advanced divisions of labour in this system. Financial and other offices are also part of the capital circulation system, playing a key role in speeding the process of industrial and other capital circulation and accumulation. Offices, especially in the case of government offices and the offices of public relations consultants and non-profit associations, also reflect the existence of a mixed private-public sector economy. They also reflect, to some degree, an increased 'consumption' of information, parallel to a consumption of physically tangible goods.

To reduce the vast array of offices to one common denominator, however, is not very useful and is even misleading. Offices serve a variety of markets and clients, disallowing a simple dichotomy of 'corporations' on the one hand and 'services' meeting the demands of these corporations on the other. Offices are differentiated by a wide range of linkage and labour requirements, and offices appear in quite different locations within metropolitan areas.

The spread pattern with more and more low-density office parks in an expanding urban periphery is a pattern that allows for a high degree of freedom for firms and the majority of commuters. Because of the high reliance on cars implied by this pattern, implications for energy consumption, air quality, and accessibility hardship for the carless makes the pattern hard to accept.

The concentrated pattern, with a high proportion of offices in the central district, has great advantages, but also some disadvantages. The cost of linkages is kept at its lowest level, the concentration of large numbers of employees allows for economical rail-born commuter flows, and additional high-density housing near the offices, as discussed in Toronto (Nowlan and Stewart, forthcoming), might even keep the need for commuting facilities within bounds. However, it is doubtful whether housing can keep pace with employment growth, and there is the danger that many of the current long-distance commuting trips will not disappear but rather expand in number and range. A growing central district office and high-density housing agglomeration will also disrupt the existing building and social fabric in the inner city, and might trigger the same neighbourhood opposition as that raised by privately and publicly funded urban renewal experiences of the 1960s and early 1970s.

The nodal pattern—that is, the concentration of office jobs into a number of high-density, transit-oriented subcentres—which is a compromise between dispersion and concentration, has great appeal. For a start, the nodal pattern gives an opportunity for different municipalities in a metropolitan area to share in the benefits of office development. Secondly, the average journey to work, especially in the outer edge of the labour shed, will be much shorter than in the case of the concentrated pattern. There are, however, costs to this pattern, and doubts about the feasibility of these subcentres. If the subcentres are small, say in the 5,000 to 20,000 employment range, the cost of business travel will be much higher than in the highly concentrated pattern (Clapp 1983; Code 1983; Pye 1979). It is unlikely that centres of this size can be adequately serviced by public transit, and the car will most likely be used by the majority of employees for the journey to work and most certainly for business trips. It is also inconceivable that all employees will move into homes close to their place of work, which will result in cross-commuting between these subcentres, and thus long commuting distances. If the office subcentres are much larger, say 40,000 to 100,000 employees, and if they are surrounded by higher density housing than is the case in most existing Canadian suburbs, effective and efficient public transit may be feasible, and commuter sheds smaller than those for the central district may be achievable. Needless to say, an efficient road network is still needed to allow for car trips between offices and between offices and other establishment types (factories, warehouses, shops, etc.).

The choice is by no means simple. More offices, increasing office employment, and the options available have many ramifications for urban transportation, job choice, and residential patterns. Increasing turmoil in public discussions about office location can be expected in several major urban areas in this decade.

NOTES

1. The 'major office' category is used here in order to include a firm's main office location in a metropolitan region irrespective of whether this location is the

'head office' for the entire country or not. A head office is usually where the chair and the president have their office, and where major corporate decisions are made.

2. 'Major offices' include: head offices; Canadian head offices of foreign companies; head offices of subsidiaries and divisional head offices; head office fragments when a head office is split between two cities (for example, the Royal Bank of Canada, whose head office is in Montreal but which also has a 'Toronto head office'); Toronto main branches of financial institutions; main branches together with regional offices and/or head office departments; large operation departments or divisions of a head office located elsewhere (for example, the Toronto offices of Canada Trust, whose head office is in London, Ontario).

3. Vancouver has several regional town centres, and office parks along major highways have begun to compete with these (Greater Vancouver Regional District 1987, 25). In the western parts of the city of Ottawa, several office parks have emerged along the Queensway expressway, especially at the Carling Avenue and Pinecrest/Greenbank interchanges, and others in the suburban municipality of Gloucester (Building Owners and Managers Association of Ottawa-Carleton 1988). In Montreal there are signs of office parks emerging in the vicinity of Dorval airport and especially at autoroute interchanges in the suburb of Saint-Laurent. Also clusters are beginning to be visible in some of the industrial parks of Dartmouth and Bedford in the Halifax CMA (Nova Scotia, Department of Industry, Trade and Technology 1990, 28).

FURTHER READING

GAD, G.H.K. 1979 'Face-to-face linkages and office decentralization potentials: a study of Toronto' in P.W. Daniels ed. *Spatial Patterns of Office Growth and Location* (Toronto: John Wiley and Sons)

—— and HOLDSWORTH, D. 1984 'Building for city, region, and nation: office development in Toronto 1834–1984' in V.L. Russell ed. *Forging a Consensus: Historical Essays on Toronto* (Toronto: University of Toronto Press)

GODDARD, J.B. 1973 *Office Linkages and Location. A Study of Communication and Spatial Patterns in Central London* (Oxford: Pergamon)

HUTTON, T. and LEY, D. 1987 'Location, Linkages, and Labour: The Downtown Complex of Corporate Activities in a Medium Size City, Vancouver, British Columbia', *Economic Geography* 63, 126–41

LEY, D. 1985a 'Downtown or the suburbs? A comparative study of two Vancouver head offices', *Canadian Geographer* 29, 30–43

—— 1985b 'Work-residence relations for head office employees in an inflating housing market', *Urban Studies* 22, 21–38

—— and HUTTON, T. 1987 'Vancouver's corporate complex and producer services sector: Linkages and divergence within a provincial staple economy', *Regional Studies* 21, 413–24

NELSON, K. 1986 'Labour demand, labour supply and the suburbanization of low-wage office work' in A.J. Scott and M. Storper eds *Production, Work, Territory: The Geographical Anatomy of Industrial Capitalism* (Boston: Allen and Unwin)

THORNGREN, B. 1970 'How do contact systems affect regional development?', *Environment and Planning* 2, 409–27

REFERENCES

ARMSTRONG, R.B. 1972 *The Office Industry: Patterns of Growth and Location* (Cambridge, Mass.: M.I.T. Press)

BEAUREGARD, L. 1981 *La Rue Saint-Jacques à Montréal: une géographie des bureaux* (Montreal: Université de Montréal)

BUILDING OWNERS AND MANAGERS ASSOCIATION OF OTTAWA-CARLETON 1988 *Ottawa-Carleton Office Space Directory* (Ottawa: Building Owners and Managers Association of Ottawa-Carleton)

CLAPP, J.M. 1983 'A model of public policy toward office relocation', *Environment and Planning A* 15, 1299–1309

CODE, W.R. 1983 'The strength of the centre: downtown offices and metropolitan decentralization in Toronto', *Environment and Planning A* 15, 1361–80

CORIOLIS CONSULTING CORPORATION 1986 *Commercial Centres in the Greater Vancouver Regional District* (Vancouver: Greater Vancouver Regional District, Development Services Department)

EDMONTON, CITY PLANNING DEPARTMENT 1983 *Office Space, Its Use and Distribution: Commercial Development in Edmonton, 1983. Report No. 2* (Edmonton: City of Edmonton)

GAD, G. 1985 'Office Location Dynamics in Toronto: Suburbanization and Central District Specialization', *Urban Geography* 6, 331–51

GODDARD, J.B. 1973 *Office Linkages and Location: A Study of Communication and Spatial Patterns in Central London* (Oxford: Pergamon)

HAYTER, R. 1978 'Forestry in British Columbia: A resource basis of Vancouver's dominance' in L.J. Evenden ed. *Vancouver: Western Metropolis* (Victoria: University of Victoria)

HUANG, S. 1989 *Office Suburbanization in Toronto: Fragmentation, Workforce Composition and Laboursheds* (Toronto: University of Toronto, Ph.D. thesis)

HUTTON, T. and LEY, D. 1987 'Location, Linkages, and Labour: The Downtown Complex of Corporate Activities in a Medium Size City, Vancouver, British Columbia', *Economic Geography* 63, 126–41

LEY, D. and HUTTON, T. 1987 'Vancouver's corporate complex and producer services sector: Linkages and divergence within a provincial staple economy', *Regional Studies* 21, 413–24

MATTHEW, M.R. 1986 'Decentralization of Toronto's office space', *City Planning (Toronto)* 4, 27–9

NELSON, K. 1986 'Labour demand, labour supply and the suburbanization of low-wage office work' in A.J. Scott and M. Storper eds *Production, Work, Territory: The Geographical Anatomy of Industrial Capitalism* (Boston: Allen and Unwin)

NOVA SCOTIA, DEPARTMENT OF INDUSTRY, TRADE AND TECHNOLOGY 1987 *1987 Survey and Inventory of Commercial Space: Halifax Metropolitan Area* (Halifax: Government of Nova Scotia)

———— 1990 *1990 Survey and Inventory of Commercial Space: Halifax Metropolitan Area* (Halifax: Government of Nova Scotia)

NOWLAN, D.M. and STEWART, G. (forthcoming) 'The effect of downtown population growth on commuting trips: some recent Toronto experiences', *Journal of the American Planning Association*

PYE, R. 1979 'Office Location: The Role of Communication and Technology' in P.W. Daniels ed. *Spatial Patterns of Office Growth and Location* (Chichester: John Wiley)

THORNGREN, B. 1970 'How do contact systems affect regional development?', *Environment and Planning* 2, 409–27

VANCOUVER, GREATER VANCOUVER REGIONAL DISTRICT 1987 *Challenges for a Contemporary Statement of the Livable Region Strategy* (Vancouver: Greater Vancouver Regional District, Development Services Department)

———— 1988 *Vancouver Perspectives: A Business and Investment Guide to Greater Vancouver, Canada* (Vancouver: Greater Vancouver Regional District, Development Services Department)

ZIEBER, G.H. 1975 'Calgary as an oil administrative and oil operations centre' in B. Barr ed. *Calgary: Metropolitan Structure and Influence* (Victoria: University of Victoria)

PART FIVE

SOCIAL ISSUES AND THE PUBLIC SECTOR

18

The Municipal Role in the Governance of Canadian Cities

ANDREW SANCTON

In the early 1970s, students of Canadian urban affairs assumed that the rapid growth of the country's cities, the complexity of its urban problems, and the increasing political sophistication of local elected officials would all lead to a new era characterized by the emergence of municipal government as an equal partner in a tri-level public sector (Miles, Cohen, and de Koning 1973). The creation by the federal government of the Ministry of State for Urban Affairs in 1971 and the election of David Crombie as mayor of Toronto in 1972 (Caulfield 1974) seemed to suggest that this view might be accurate. In retrospect, however, a far more significant event was the decision by Premier Davis of Ontario in 1971 to stop the construction of the Spadina Expressway linking Metropolitan Toronto's north-west suburbs to the downtown (Leo 1977, 36–7). The decision was a direct response to citizen activism and the new consciousness concerning the value of stable, mixed-use inner-city areas.

In terms of understanding city politics, the most notable feature of the Spadina decision was that it was made by the *provincial* government in direct opposition to the expressed policy objectives of the Municipality of Metropolitan Toronto as determined by a majority vote of its council. Similarly, it was the *provincial* government that ultimately decided the fate of the by-law promoted by Mayor Crombie that aimed to freeze Toronto's downtown growth until a new official plan was in place (Frisken 1988, 42–3).

Not only do provinces tightly control the activities of municipalities, they also establish and/or fund all kinds of other local bodies to deliver local public services, such as, for example, schools boards, community colleges, and hospitals. Many of these local bodies have little or no connection to the municipal government, thus making it difficult for the latter genuinely to make local policy across a wide range of governmental functions. Partly because their functions are relatively narrow, municipalities are characterized by political processes that are quite different from those found at the federal and provincial levels. Ideological conflict is less prevalent, and political parties, so important in federal and provincial politics, are generally not considered to have a legitimate role (Sancton 1983a; Peterson 1981).

In contrast to provincial governments, the boundaries and functions of municipal government are changed almost as a matter of course, sometimes with the approval of the municipalities involved, often without (Higgins 1986a, 220). Boundary changes are frequently implemented so as to make the territory of a municipality correspond more closely to the built-up area of a particular city. Rarely do the two areas ever match; when they do it is often not for long. At the municipal level, ongoing uncertainty about where boundaries will be ten years from now is common; so is uncertainty about the municipalities' role in such matters as the delivery of social services or in the regulation of Sunday shopping.

The central purpose of this chapter is to explore the unique and changing features of municipal policy-making in Canadian cities. The first section looks at the historical development of Canadian municipalities, as this level of government is the one most concerned with our built environment. It then explores the possibilities for change. Can Canadian municipal governments increase their functional scope so as to more closely approximate genuine urban governments that would deal with all areas of intervention that can be defined as urban (see Chapter 1 for a discussion of what such areas can be)? Did the reform movement of the 1960s and 1970s lead to lasting and significant changes in our local political processes? What is the prospect for political parties in our municipal politics? By briefly examining developments in Ontario, Quebec, Manitoba, British Columbia, and Alberta, the second section of the chapter looks at how our provinces have tried to adapt their systems of municipal government to the constant outward expansion of our largest cities. Is two-tier regional government—where some traditionally defined municipal responsibilities are taken over by regional governments who have jurisdiction over the territory of more than one municipality—the answer? What about annexation? What needs to be protected most in municipal reorganization?

Why? These questions cannot be answered unless we clearly understand both the constraints on municipal government and the real opportunities these governments have to shape the quality of our urban life.

MUNICIPAL GOVERNMENT: THE POLITICS OF THE BUILT ENVIRONMENT

Canada's municipal system—even in Quebec—is grounded almost entirely in British law and practice, with some later additions from the United States. In Britain, prior to the nineteenth century, the first municipal corporations were established by royal charter or Act of Parliament in order to remove partially certain defined urban territories from the control of traditional feudal authorities. By this device, urban property-holders were able to establish their own taxing system, build their own streets and public markets, and enforce their own regulations concerning local trade and commerce. In these early days, attaining municipal status was often a major victory, if not for the whole community, at least for established merchants and property-owners. During the nineteenth century, Parliament extended the municipal system throughout Britain. The central government had become increasingly strangled by hundreds of its own local boards and commissions that had been established to cope with the multitude of problems resulting from rapid industrialization. A comprehensive system of municipal government was seen as a valuable mechanism for helping finance, implement, and co-ordinate central policies at the local level (Redlich and Hirst 1970).

Reasons for establishing municipal government in Canada were similar to those that emerged over the centuries in Britain. Municipalities met the needs of both local elites and central governments. As in Britain, early Canadian municipal governments were not particularly democratic. The franchise was generally restricted to male property-owners or leaseholders. Much of the impetus to democratize Canadian local government—including the idea of holding direct elections for the office of mayor—came from the United States.

Constitutional Status of Municipalities
The Constitution of Canada[1] establishes two orders of government: federal and provincial. By Section 92 (8) of *The Constitution Act, 1867*, 'Municipal Institutions in the Province' are included as one of the 'Classes of Subject' for which 'In each Province the Legislature may exclusively make Laws'. Municipal institutions are mentioned in the 1867 Act because they were already established in the three British colonies—Canada (Ontario and Quebec), New Brunswick, and Nova Scotia—that initially comprised the Canadian federation.

The oldest incorporated municipality in Canada is Saint John, New Brunswick, which received a royal charter in 1785. The Legislature of Lower Canada incorporated Montreal and Quebec City in 1832; Hamilton and Toronto were incorporated by the Legislature of Upper Canada in 1833 and 1834 respectively. Following the unification of Upper and Lower Canada in 1840, the new Legislature established comprehensive systems of municipal government for both parts of the colony. The Municipal Corporations Act of 1849 (the Baldwin Act) was the most important legislation for what is now Ontario; the equivalent legislation for Quebec was approved in 1855 (Higgins 1986b, 40–7).

In both Ontario and Quebec, each distinct urban area was to be governed by a single municipality that was usually called a city but sometimes a town. Rural areas were to be governed by both counties and smaller units contained therein: townships or parishes, towns, and villages. This system survived intact for more than a century in both provinces. It still exists in many parts of Ontario. Other Canadian provinces have generally adopted similar systems of municipal government, except that they have generally done without counties as top-tier units of rural government (Higgins 1986b, 33–59).

When an area is incorporated as a municipality under provincial legislation, it acquires a legal personality, just as a business does when it is incorporated as a limited company. Incorporation necessarily involves the specification of three features essential to a municipality's existence: a precisely defined territory; a mechanism, usually an elected council, that allows the municipality to make legally enforceable decisions; and a list of governmental functions that are legally within its jurisdiction. Because municipalities owe their existence to provinces while the federal and provincial governments owe theirs to the Constitution, the municipal level of government in Canada is in a legally inferior position. Such a position is reflected by the fact that, legally, the federal and provincial governments are directly linked to the Crown and carry out their activities in the name of the reigning monarch while municipal corporations act legally only on their own behalf; they are not acting for the Crown (Rogers 1971, 2.1).

Municipalities in Canada can only perform functions specifically authorized by provincial statute; provinces can only delegate functions that are within provincial jurisdiction. For some controversial problems, such as the regulation of Sunday shopping and adult entertainment parlours, the exact jurisdictions of federal and provincial governments are far from clear. Courts sometimes have to determine whether provincial laws apparently authorizing various kinds of municipal activity are in fact delegating valid provincial legislative authority or whether they are impinging on matters that are properly federal. It is unconstitutional for the federal government to delegate its legislative authority to provincial legislatures or municipal councils (Dawson 1970, 79). It can, however, spend money in whatever way it wishes. Direct federal grants to municipalities were at one time quite common, but in recent years the provinces, led by Quebec, have successfully severed most of the links, financial and otherwise, between the national government and the municipalities.

Federal and Provincial Urban Influence

Just because the federal government has only limited formal contact with municipalities does not mean it is irrelevant to Canadian cities. The federal government remains as perhaps the most important institution determining the quality of our urban life. Through its monetary, fiscal, and trade policies, it plays a central role in defining the nature of urban economic activity. Its policies concerning taxation and intergovernmental transfers have much to do with determining the capacity of provincial governments to respond to municipal demands for additional funds for urban services. Federal jurisdiction over railways, ports, and airports is of crucial importance to many aspects of urban development; so is the fact that the federal government is the biggest single landowner in urban Canada. For some of our urban neighbourhoods, the most significant determinant of their future character will be federal immigration policy.

The importance of provincial governments for cities goes far beyond their constitutional responsibility for municipal government. Provinces control health care, education, and social services. Hospitals, schools and universities, and centres providing special services to the young, the old, or the handicapped are all important features of urban life. Although provinces usually do not operate such institutions directly, they have become increasingly responsible for assuring their financial survival. Provincial highways are crucial arteries for urban transportation; their extension and expansion often determines the future direction of urban development. Provincial policies for the subsidization of housing, sewage treatment, water-supply systems, public transit, and other urban services effectively determine many large-scale strategic land-use decisions which, formally at least, remain the responsibility of municipal government.

Property—the Core Municipal Function

The exact functional responsibilities of municipalities vary widely across the country (Higgins 1986b, 88–9). Even within the same province, municipalities of similar size and character often do not have the same list of functions. In Quebec, municipalities have virtually no involvement with hospitals or social services. In Ontario, municipalities operate homes for the aged, provide child day-care for low-income families, and are responsible for the delivery of short-term welfare payments. Although they have no formal responsibility for local hospitals, they are often expected to make significant contributions to their capital fund-raising campaigns. Most cities in Ontario have direct control over parks and recreation, but in London (as in Vancouver) this task is performed by a directly-elected local commission. In Quebec, local police forces are generally under the direct control of the municipality. In Ontario and other provinces, the municipalities generally pay the costs, but the forces themselves are controlled and directed by commissions not directly accountable to the municipal government (Stenning 1981).

Almost without exception, Canadian provinces have assigned the following functions to municipalities: fire protection; local roads and streets; the collection and disposal of residential solid waste; sewage systems; the taxation of land and buildings; and the regulation of local land use. The common thread in this list of functions is property. This has led many in Canada—practising municipal politicians, journalists, and academics—to conclude that municipalities are the units of government concerned with regulating, servicing, and taxing our built environment. For many politicians, other municipal functions are at best frills and at worst the unjustifiable result of provincial policies aimed at unloading costly social functions on unwilling municipalities and their overburdened taxpayers.

Special-Purpose Bodies
One of the major difficulties in attempting to describe municipal functions in Canada is that, in most cities, the municipal government does not have direct responsibility for many important functions of government that are subject in some degree to local control. Instead, such functions are under the control of what are generally known as special-purpose bodies. Exact definitions of such bodies are notoriously difficult. In their purest form they are very much like municipalities. They are established by provincial legislation; they have a defined territory; they have the right to raise their own revenues; members of their governing body are directly elected by the public. The main difference is that, while municipalities are responsible for a number of governmental functions, special-purpose bodies only deal with a particular function or set of closely related ones. School boards are the best Canadian examples.

Most other special-purpose bodies lack one or more of the characteristics listed above. They have no taxing authority or legal right to claim municipal funds; their members are appointed rather than elected; or certain of their decisions are subject to approval by municipal councils. In assessing the real political power of various special-purpose bodies, it is important not to rely exclusively on an examination of their legal status. For a wide range of reasons, municipal councils might be extremely reluctant to attempt to change police, transit, or library policies, even though in some circumstances they might be legally entitled to overrule the relevant special-purpose body.

Municipal Expenditure and Revenues
A frequent claim of municipal politicians and administrators is that municipal functions and expenditures have increased dramatically over the past few decades. There is an obvious sense in which this is true. Even using constant (1971) dollars, per capita local government expenditures in Canada increased from $163.96 in 1947 to $406.75 in 1980 (Kitchen 1984, 415). This rate of increase was greater than that of the federal government for the same period ($520.11 to $788.11, grants to other governments

excluded) but considerably less than that of the provincial governments ($194.82 to $591.26, again excluding grants to other governments, i.e. local) (Kitchen 1984, 415).

Municipal governments have added some new functions in recent years, special public-transit facilities for the disabled being one of the more obvious. However, these additions must be considered against what has been lost. Many provinces, notably Quebec, have stripped municipal governments of most or all of their traditional social-service functions (Sancton 1988, 82). The assessment of real property for local taxation purposes is now generally a provincial function rather than a municipal one. Provinces have taken over most municipal court systems (Higgins 1986b, 88–9).

While municipal expenditures have been increasing, municipal revenues from local taxes (almost exclusively related to property) and user charges have not been keeping up. In 1947, transfer payments from other governments made up 17.2 per cent of total municipal revenue; for 1978 the figure was 47.6 per cent (Kitchen 1984, 416). Only 1.1 percentage points of the 1978 figure were contributed by the federal government (Kitchen 1984, 475). Of the remaining amount, 41.6 percentage points came from the province in the form of conditional, rather than unconditional, grants. These figures indicate how closely municipal governments are tied to the provinces and how weak their links are to the federal government.

Table 18.1 presents local-government revenue and expenditure data relating to the City of London, a single-tier unit of municipal government not forming part of the political and administrative structure of any of Ontario's counties or regional governments. The table has a number of significant features. Its main object is to show, in descending order, the extent to which each of the various functions of local government in London draws on the general revenues of the municipal corporation, that is, on proceeds from the property tax and from unconditional grants from the provincial government.

Some local special-purpose bodies serve areas extending beyond London's city limits. For them it is impossible to determine the extent of their total expenditures and revenues relating only to London. What is known, and what is reported in the third column of the table, is the extent to which they are funded from London's general revenues. For purely municipal functions and for functions performed by special-purpose bodies operating only within the city boundaries, the table reports in the first column the total expenditures for each function. The second column shows the revenues—user charges and conditional grants—generated by each function. For these functions, the figure in the third column is the result of subtracting the figure in the second from that in the first.

Primary and secondary education, as provided by the public and separate school boards, makes by far the greatest demands on general municipal revenues. Although well behind education, police and fire protection are also quite significant. Roads and sewage come next, but their figures would

Table 18.1
Local Government Expenditures in Thousands of Dollars by Functions, London, Ontario 1986

Function	Total Expenditure	Revenue from Conditional Grants and User Charges	Expenditures from Property Tax and Unconditional Grants
*Education	n/a	n/a	94,843[a]T
*Police	22,372	412	21,960
Debt Charges, Capital Levy and Contribution to Reserves	20,840	0	20,840
General Municipal Government	17,735	643	17,092[b]T
Fire Protection	15,674	73	15,601
Roads, Traffic, Parking and Street-Lighting	14,866	5,624	9,241[c]T
Sewage Collection and Treatment	10,796	1,695	9,101
Income Maintenance	25,727	19,853	5,874
*Library	6,948	1,151	5,814
Solid Waste Disposal	6,215	1,280	4,935
*Recreation	6,210	3,152	3,058
*Public Transit	20,638	18,457	2,182
*Parks	2,204	105	2,059
*Public Health	n/a	n/a	1,670
Services for the Elderly	8,255	6,979	1,276[d]T
*Child Protection	n/a	n/a	1,208
Economic Development and Promotion	1,665	19	1,645[e]T
Land-Use Planning	898	34	863
Animal Control	664	194	470
*Art Gallery	n/a	n/a	429
*Watershed Conservation	n/a	n/a	389
Child Day-Care	1,347	1,078	269
Grants to Cultural and Educational Institutions	229	0	229
Services for the Handicapped	606	410	196[f]T
Community Support Services	186	9	177[g]T
Centennial Hall	352	199	153[h]T
Housing	284	131	153
*Eldon House	112	13	99[i]T
Emergency Planning	26	19	7
*Electricity	107,842	107,842	0[j]T
*Water	23,056	23,056	0[k]T
Licensing and Vital Statistics	193	384	(191)
Building Controls	1,661	2,843	(1,182)

*Indicates this function is not under the direct control of city council but rather under the control of a local special-purpose body of one type or another.

n/a Indicates that expenditures and revenues relating only to the City of London are not available because the relevant special-purpose body operates beyond the city's boundaries.

[T]Indicates that these notes are included under endnote 2 at the end of the chapter.

SOURCES: City of London, *1987 Program Plan and Budgets,* loose-leaf dated March 4, 1987; City of London, *1986 Financial Report* (London, 1987); and City of London, Public Utilities Commission, *1986 Annual Report* (London, 1987).

be significantly higher if the cost of debt charges and capital levies could be accurately attributed to particular functions. This is because a large proportion of any municipality's capital borrowing is for roads, sewers, and sewage treatment.

Income maintenance (what is known in Ontario as General Welfare Assistance) and public transit cost a lot of money, but both attract high proportions of offsetting revenue from the province. The same is true of services to the elderly and child day-care. The general message from these numbers (excluding education) is that it is the so-called 'hard' services relating to property that make the greatest demands on general municipal revenues. Once again the evidence suggests that municipal government is primarily about property (Peterson 1981). Costs for the provision of electricity, and to a lesser extent water, are very high but, because they are all covered by user charges, the demands on general municipal revenues are nil. Finally, two functions—licensing and building controls—actually provide a profit for the city.

Land-use Planning

Despite its obvious importance, land-use planning is not shown in Table 18.1 as a significant consumer of municipal funds. This is because planning is implemented not by spending money but rather by making legally enforceable regulations about how owners of property can use their land. Municipal governments are the main regulators of land use in Canada. The federal government controls land use only to the extent that such use is directly related to explicit or implicit federal constitutional responsibilities, for example, airports and the role of the Ottawa-Hull region as the national capital. Apart from their inability to control land owned by the federal government or used for purposes under federal jurisdiction, Canadian provinces are virtually untrammelled in their legal authority to regulate land use. For most land in populated parts of the provinces, this authority is delegated to municipalities. A notable exception is Quebec's Act to Preserve Agricultural Land, which provides that municipalities cannot allow development on land designated by the province as agricultural (Rogers 1973, 4.2). (For more details on rural land preservation, see Chapter 9.)

It is almost impossible to generalize about land-use planning procedures in the various provinces. All provinces provide for municipal adoption, in one form or another, of an overarching plan that is supposed to provide a framework for future development and detailed land-use regulation (Hodge 1986, 201–16). Similarly, they all provide for some form of municipal control on the subdivision of land for new development and on the uses to which land can be put. However, the degree of provincial control over these processes varies widely. In Ontario, for example, all official plans and their amendments require the explicit approval of a provincial minister. In Quebec there is no formal provincial approval; a designated minister intervenes only if a county development plan is seen to be in conflict with the aims of the provincial government. In some provinces, such as Quebec, the main focus of overall development planning is at the county or regional level; in Ontario, all municipalities including regions, counties, cities, and townships are authorized to adopt official plans (Rogers 1973, 3.3).

Regardless of legal arrangements in the various provinces, the political agenda of municipalities throughout the country is dominated by land-use issues. In the real world of inter-municipal competition for investment, and provincial regulations that may be aimed at ensuring affordable housing or co-ordinating the development of large-scale infrastructures, there is little room for radical differences in land-use policies among municipalities that share similar characteristics within the same province. Nevertheless, there are important decisions to be made in each locality about such matters as the number, size, and location of suburban shopping malls; the preservation of heritage buildings and streetscapes; the extent to which downtown business and commercial functions will be allowed to spread into adjoining residential neighbourhoods; the timing and density of new suburban development. All these matters relate to land-use planning. They are at the heart of Canadian municipal politics. (For a fuller discussion of planning in Canada, see Chapter 19.)

Beyond Property Functions?
Issues relating to the servicing and regulation of property so dominate the Canadian municipal political process that in some respects our municipal councils can most accurately be seen as special-purpose bodies in charge of property (Magnusson 1985, 586–9). In this view, other municipal functions are so insignificant or so tightly controlled by the province that they need not be taken seriously. In general, Canadian municipal politicians and officials have done little to urge that municipal governments become directly responsible for the full range of locally controlled public services. Ever since the Great Depression, they have been reluctant to take on new social-service responsibilities, fearing that the costs of such services are beyond their limited fiscal resources. But this reluctance to expand functionally is not restricted to social services.

Municipal politicians, especially in Ontario, seem not to believe that they are best suited to make decisions about Sunday shopping in their communities. They complain about having to pay the bills for school boards and police commissions from property tax revenues, but the case for placing these functions under direct municipal control is more often made by academics and other outsiders than it is by practising municipal politicians. Municipal reluctance to make the case for increased authority is one of the reasons why Canadian city governments are relatively weak. It is not the only reason.

Interest groups—especially professional groups—connected to various local governmental functions are generally reluctant to be under direct municipal control. Teachers support independent school boards; police support police commissions; social workers support agency links to the provincial rather than the municipal government; librarians support library boards; land developers want to make sure municipal planning decisions can always be appealed. Government bureaucrats at the provincial level charged with supervising and improving the delivery of these local services provide complementary support for special-purpose bodies and/or limitations on municipal autonomy. Their jobs are made easier if they have direct regulatory control, or if they can deal directly with local agencies having an exclusive concern with their service. By contrast, it is harder to operate through a municipal department that is just one of many and which might be subject to strong local direction from either politicians or senior municipal general managers (Dupre 1981, 159). In the absence of a clear societal commitment to municipal government as the main local regulator and allocator of available local resources, provincial governments are likely to pay close attention to the interests of people directly involved in the delivery or consumption of a particular service. If these people are opposed to direct municipal control, they are unlikely to be overruled.

Opposition to direct municipal control by providers of certain kinds of local public services is not irrational. There are good reasons to expect municipal governments to have an inherent tendency to want to cut expenditures on items not directly contributing to the economic development of the community (Peterson 1981). When American liberals opposed policies of the Reagan Administration to turn over various federally supported programs to municipalities, they were acutely aware that, though these decentralizing policies were publicly justified by arguments about the virtues of local control, the real objective was to place them in open competition with other programs at the local level so that they would inevitably be cut.

In Britain, many municipal councils in major cities are controlled by strong left-wing political parties (local branches of the Labour Party). That is precisely why Prime Minister Thatcher, unlike President Reagan, has removed authority from municipal governments. In Canada, the only strong left-wing municipal political party is found in Montreal. To fully implement its program, the Montreal Citizens Movement needs more jurisdiction over such functions as social services, housing, and public health (Milner 1988, 8). So far, however, it has found enough to do within the limits of the city of Montreal's present jurisdictions. In other Canadian cities, more traditional municipal politicians are even less likely to raise such issues. Instead, they battle with each other about who is more likely to attract development and help the city grow.

Reform Movements in the 1960s and 1970s
During the 1970s in many Canadian cities it looked as though municipal politics was going through a period of fundamental change. Citizen groups were mobilizing against developers, and were often winning their battles to protect neighbourhoods and green space. Their political representatives were being elected to council and were occasionally in control. Although adherents of the so-called 'new reform movement' might have had a relatively clear conception of the ideal urban environment, they had no common view concerning the role of municipal government in bringing it about. Some were genuinely committed to various forms of neighbourhood self-government. Others wanted to use local issues primarily as a way of mobilizing the working class for larger and more important battles to be fought in the national arena. Most were concerned only with the particular issues at hand, and became involved in municipal politics simply because it was the municipal government, in the first instance at least, that would be making the relevant decisions (Caulfield 1988). Nobody in the new urban reform movement argued in favour of the principle that decisions by municipal governments should be considered final and should not be appealed to provincial supervisory bodies. Nobody articulated a vision of a genuinely multi-functional municipal government, the control of which would be contested at election time by competing political parties. Such views were more often expressed by academics (Plunkett and Betts 1978, 147–52) and authors of provincially-sponsored reports (Manitoba 1976, 61–7). In fact, many new urban reformers seemed profoundly suspicious of any political institutions, including municipal governments and local political parties, that would have the potential to overrule the expressed preferences of local neighbourhoods and their leaders (or delegates).

The new urban reformers were successful in changing the way many Canadians viewed their cities. They were responsible for the implementation of elaborate new mechanisms to insure that individuals and citizen groups had ample opportunity to express their views about proposed changes to the physical environment in their areas. They helped change the style of the municipal political process so that sensitivity to neighbourhood concerns became an avowed objective of just about everybody, including municipal managers and engineers. But the functions and capabilities of municipal government changed very little. If anything, new provincial regulations relating to such matters as environmental assessments had the effect of reducing the capacity of municipal governments to manage their own affairs.

Political Parties in City Politics
Sharp divisions between new reformers and old-guard pro-development municipal politicians are now hard to find. This means that we seem

further away now from municipal party politics in Canada than we were in the 1970s. Apart from cities in Quebec, Vancouver is the only major Canadian city whose council is in any way controlled by a political party. Because of Vancouver's at-large election system (where councillors are elected at the scale of the city as a whole rather than at that of specific wards as in most other cities), the 'right' organizes itself as the Non-Partisan Association (NPA) in order to finance expensive city-wide contests and present a complete slate of candidates. In the 1988 municipal elections, the NPA won seven of the eleven council seats while the left-wing Committee of Progressive Electors (COPE) won three (Lee 1988). The NPA is no longer the unreservedly pro-development organization it once was. According to Donald Gutstein, NPA mayoralty candidate Gordon Campbell, despite his obvious personal links to development interests, was successful in his first campaign in 1986 because he was 'able to convince four-fifths of the centre voters that he was a moderate and could represent their interests' (Gutstein 1986–87, 30).

In Winnipeg, an organization similar to the NPA, the Independent Citizens Election Committee (ICEC), has disbanded. Its former members still effectively control the council—their opposition after the 1986 municipal elections was only two New Democrats (Gerecke 1986–87, 35). New Democrats hold six of seventeen council seats in the City of Toronto following the 1988 elections there. Three other councillors are 'reformers', thereby creating a reform majority. To what extent this group works together so as to implement coherent alternative policies is far from clear (Taylor 1988).

In Montreal, a municipal party system has been in place since the mid–1950s. The most successful municipal political party in Canadian history is Jean Drapeau's Civic Party, which completely controlled Montreal city council from 1960 to 1986 (Sancton 1983b). By embodying Montrealers' intense civic pride, Drapeau remained firmly in control through the turbulent late 1960s and early 1970s. By the time the Montreal Citizens Movement (MCM) took over in 1986, the provincial legislature had amended municipal election law to provide for public funding of recognized municipal political parties, and to allow the printing of their names on the ballot.

The MCM victory in 1986 was by no means a victory for the urban radicals who had been prominent in the party since its initial electoral breakthrough in 1974. In preparing to succeed Drapeau, most members of the party had increasingly moderated their political positions. The others either drifted away altogether or found themselves on the margins of party decision-making (Milner 1988). One of the many ironies of the MCM victory was that it was as massive (54 of 57 council seats) as most of Drapeau's. Only three opposition councillors were elected: one from the Civic Party, one from another political alignment, and one independent. The real opposition to the current MCM administration is within the MCM itself, as became clear in late 1988 when three dissident councillors quit the MCM caucus to sit as independents (Poirier 1988). Despite appearances to the contrary, the municipal political party system is not alive and well in Montreal.

During the 1960s and 1970s, there was a widely-held belief that the emergence of political parties at the municipal level in Canada was both desirable and inevitable (Masson and Anderson 1972). At the end of the 1980s, it is clear that increasing urbanization and the complexity of urban problems do not themselves create and nurture local political parties. We are no closer to having established party systems in our major cities now than we were fifteen years ago. Why were the earlier expectations never realized?

The answer seems to lie in the fact that, notwithstanding the growing importance of cities and their problems, municipal government remains limited in its functions and autonomy (Peterson 1981). The great societal issues that create and sustain political parties in our national politics— building the Canadian nation on the basis of the National Policy for the Conservatives, establishing our independence from Britain and bilingual identity for the Liberals, and building the welfare state in response to the Great Depression for the C.C.F./N.D.P.—are not present in local politics.

This is not to say that there are no divisive issues in local politics. In the 1980s, we have become increasingly familiar with the NIMBY syndrome—Not In My Back Yard. Residents of particular areas fight bitterly with municipal governments and other public and private institutions that try to build potentially dangerous, noisy, disruptive, or ugly installations in their immediate areas. Citizens rarely become more aroused politically than when someone wants to turn their quiet neighbourhood street into a multi-lane thoroughfare or the nearby vacant field into a landfill site. Important as such issues are at the time, they are rarely capable of building an ongoing city-wide coalition of like-minded people sharing similar interests and political priorities. Without such coalitions there can be no indigenous local political parties. Whether Progressive Conservatives, Liberals, or New Democrats decide to become more openly involved in local politics will probably have more to do with the exigencies of national and provincial politics than with their assessments of the need for change in our municipalities.

There is every reason to believe that municipal politics in Canada will continue to focus on issues relating to the use and development of land. Depending on the economic circumstances of the particular community in question, there will be more or less pressure to accommodate the wishes of particular developers who invariably will promise that their proposed projects will improve the community, attract further investment, and provide jobs. In prosperous economic times, citizen groups opposing particular developments are in a relatively strong position (as they were in Toronto in the early 1970s and the late 1980s); in times of economic downturn, the pressures for growth and development are irresistible and the political leverage of citizen groups all but disappears.

IS THERE A FUTURE FOR MUNICIPAL REORGANIZATION?

Major Canadian municipalities such as Montreal, Toronto, and Vancouver were originally incorporated as a result of specific legislation relating only to them. Montreal and Vancouver remain legally isolated from the general municipal systems subsequently established in their provinces. The more common arrangement was for cities to be incorporated according to procedures outlined in such general legislation. The important point, however, is that cities in Canada, until the 1950s at least, were not linked in any legal or political way to the towns, villages, and countryside that surrounded them. Conventional wisdom held that city problems and rural problems were different. Arrangements for municipal government were structured accordingly.

Emergence of Two-tier Systems
In the early twentieth century, Montreal was unquestionably Canada's pre-eminent city. Municipal incorporation in parishes surrounding the City of Montreal was relatively easy. As the residential and industrial property market boomed, new municipalities sprang up by the dozens. As many sank into bankruptcy (in some cases by design), they were annexed by the city of Montreal. The territory of the central municipality grew dramatically; so, too, did its debt, because the standard condition of annexation was that the city absorb all outstanding financial obligations of its new component parts. In 1920, when four more suburban municipalities were in desperate financial straits, the city refused to solve the crisis through annexation. As a result, the provincial legislature established Canada's first metropolitan government, the Island of Montreal Metropolitan Commission. The Commission's main initial function was to control the borrowing of the member suburban municipalities. Optional functions were added later, including the building of a 'metropolitan boulevard', but most municipalities resisted this encroachment on their jurisdictions and progress was virtually non-existent (Sancton 1985, 26–30).

As in Montreal, the city of Toronto's boundaries also grew dramatically as a result of annexation in the early twentieth century. But in Ontario the provincial government itself moved in to control the problem of excessive borrowing by the remaining Toronto suburbs as well as for all Ontario municipalities. Toronto did not get metropolitan government until 1953 with the creation of the Municipality of Metropolitan Toronto. The metropolitan level of government in Toronto soon became much more important than its equivalent in Montreal. Metropolitan Toronto was charged with providing the roads, sewers, water supply, and overall planning for the gigantic suburban expansion of the 1950s and 1960s. It did its job well, and became known world-wide as a Canadian success story (Rose 1972). In 1960, the Manitoba legislature implemented its version of metropolitan government by creating the Corporation of Greater Winnipeg (Brownstone and Plunkett 1983, 21–5). In 1969, the Quebec legislature greatly strengthened and enlarged Montreal's system of metropolitan government by creating the Montreal Urban Community (Sancton 1985, 116).

The essentials of the metropolitan government systems in Montreal, Toronto, and Winnipeg were the same. The central city and surrounding municipalities kept their existing boundaries. They each gave up some of their functions to the new level of government, which was controlled by its own council. In Montreal and Toronto (until 1988) members of the metropolitan council came from the local councils, while in Winnipeg they were directly elected. Costs of the new metropolitan functions were apportioned to each member municipality in proportion to its share of the total taxable property assessment in the area covered by the metropolitan authority.

Constituent municipalities in the metropolitan authorities surrendered the relevant functions with varying degrees of reluctance. Some of them correctly calculated that a modest loss of authority was a small price to pay to maintain their existence and their ability to continue to control such matters as local zoning, streets, and parks and recreation. Rapidly growing areas, especially in suburban Toronto, experienced real gains from metropolitan government. Infrastructure to support new development was built on a scale far surpassing the financial capabilities of the municipality itself. Using the established tax base of the central city, Metropolitan Toronto effectively created vast portions of what are now the cities of North York, Scarborough, and Etobicoke.

Reasons for Municipal Reorganization

Starting in the mid–1960s, there were two new developments concerning metropolitan government in Canada: (1) many more were being created, especially in Ontario, British Columbia, and Quebec, and (2) existing municipal boundaries began to be radically altered (Higgins 1986b, 168–231). Both phenomena occurred in Ontario with the launching of the regional government program. In Winnipeg in 1970 the boundaries of the twelve constituent municipalities of the Corporation of Greater Winnipeg were abolished and one 'Unicity' was created in its stead (Brownstone and Plunkett, 1983).

Policy-makers justified this dramatic assault on traditional structures for municipal government on three main grounds. First, they argued that, especially in fast-growing areas, a local political authority was needed to plan future development around existing population centres. The main implication of this belief was that, contrary to previous practice, city and countryside, at least for planning functions, would now have to be joined.

Second, they believed that there were economies of scale to be captured both by moving services from lower-tier municipalities to the regional or metropolitan level, and by merging lower-tier municipalities into larger units so that even the most local of services could be delivered by larger units. Associated with this belief was the argument that more highly-trained administrators were needed at the municipal level, and that the inevitably large salaries these personnel would command could only be paid by relatively large units.

Third, many policy-makers in this field were convinced that larger municipal units would increase equity as measured both by relative tax burdens and levels of service. Municipalities that benefited from abnormally high concentrations of revenue-producing industrial and commercial property would now have to share their good fortune. Those that may have been unable to afford such items as sophisticated sewage treatment facilities or good public libraries would find their service levels upgraded, probably to the standards in place in the best-served community with which they had been merged.

Problems in Merging City and Countryside
Unfortunately, each of these arguments was flawed which caused serious problems when the policies they supported were implemented (Sharpe 1981). The merging of city and countryside caused significant problems for both sides. If the central city was relatively strong within the new region, as it is in the Regional Municipality of Hamilton-Wentworth, outlying areas felt that effective regional government inevitably served the city's interests and not theirs. If suburban areas seemed to be politically stronger, as was the perception in Winnipeg's Unicity, then the central city felt its concerns always took second place after those of suburban shopping centres or new residential subdivisions. If the boundaries for the region extend far into the countryside, as they do for the Regional Municipality of Ottawa-Carleton, the different concerns of city and countryside are all too obvious. If boundaries are tightly drawn around largely built-up areas, which is now the case for Metropolitan Toronto, then genuine regional planning becomes impossible.

This is not to suggest the total absence of a solution to this problem. The point is simply that *no* structural arrangement is likely to mitigate the inherently different interests of city, suburb, and countryside; hence democratic regional planning is likely to be exceptionally difficult regardless of the structural arrangements. There are obvious problems with the traditional municipal system in Canada in which city and countryside are kept separate. But this system at least has some inherent flexibility in that both sides recognize the inevitability from time to time of annexations of rural land to the city for purposes of new urban development.

In Ontario, annexations no longer take place in areas covered by regional government. Because the regional government provides the major infrastructure, all municipalities are seen as having the potential to support at least some significant urban development. But what about the boundaries of the regions themselves? Since the first regional government in Ontario was introduced, not a single one has experienced any external boundary change. Recent review commissions for individual municipal governments have been specifically mandated *not* to contemplate any boundary changes, either in relation to the constituent municipalities or to the region itself. Meanwhile, in the Golden Horseshoe area around Toronto, public transit issues now completely submerge the existing regional boundaries (Ontario 1987). This does not mean that all the regional governments in the area should be merged into one. It does mean that establishing regional government is no more of a final solution to the boundary problem than is a single annexation to a particular city.

Arguments about efficiency and equity turn out to be closely connected to each other. What little evidence there is about the relative costs of regional government in relation to the traditional system, seems to suggest that there is not much difference (Ontario 1979, 11–26). This finding does not necessarily mean, however, that there are no economies of scale. It is undoubtedly the case that some areas covered by regional government have seen their levels of service rise to match the levels in nearby (possibly more affluent) areas. From this perspective, efficiency gains have not led to decreased costs but to increased levels of service to some areas, resulting in a greater degree of overall equity.

Two problems remain, however. Perhaps people in areas with upgraded services resulting from regional government had no particular desire for such improvements. If they were given a choice about how to use resources channelled to them from elsewhere, perhaps they would have chosen lower tax rates rather than a larger police force or municipally subsidized day-care spaces. When regional government was imposed, they were given no choice. In the case of such services as sewage treatment, however, there is an argument to be made that, from the perspective of the welfare of society, small groups should not be allowed to make choices that result in negative consequences for those living elsewhere.

Another problem is that alleged higher levels of service for the region as a whole do not necessarily translate into higher levels of satisfaction with such services in each and every part of the region. The closing of a local village hall and establishment of a much larger town or regional civic centre many miles away is not a great gain for the village, notwithstanding the sophisticated features of such new facilities. Similar arguments can be made about any facility or service that is consolidated to serve a larger area. A wider range of services provided by better qualified professionals theoretically becomes available to everybody included in the formally designated catchment area. Whether such services are genuinely available to the less mobile citizens not physically close to the point or points at which the services are provided is a quite different issue (Sharpe 1981, 384).

Problems with Two-tier Systems

The biggest problem with two-tiered regional governments has nothing to so with the efficient or equitable provision of services. It is a political problem. The case has already been made that Canadian local government is badly fragmented by the existence of too many special-purpose bodies. Two-tiered regional government fragments it even more by splitting already weak municipal governments into two distinct levels. For reasons outlined by Paul Peterson (1981, 109–30), most citizens have enough difficulty becoming involved in the affairs of a single municipal tier. Adding another makes it doubly difficult.

Most Canadian two-tier systems have been structured so that all members of the top-tier council are also members the bottom-tier councils. The advantage of this system has been that the top-tier has had to be extremely responsive to the expressed desires of the politicians who run the constituent units. The potential for jurisdictional squabbles between the two tiers is reduced, at the political level if not at the bureaucratic. The main disadvantage has been that politicians and voters have focused most of their attention at the bottom tier, leaving the regional bureaucrats and, in some cases, the indirectly elected chairperson (who is selected by the regional council from its members) very much in control and not particularly accountable.

Conventional wisdom offers a standard solution to the accountability problem: provide for the direct election of top-tier councillors who will sit only at that level. Such was the electoral system for the two-tier Corporation of Greater Winnipeg, which existed from 1960 to 1971 prior to Unicity. It has also been the system in the Regional Municipality of Niagara since its creation in 1968. It was introduced for the first time in Metropolitan Toronto in 1988. Twenty-eight directly elected Metropolitan councillors are joined by the mayors of the six constituent municipalities, who are the only municipal politicians sitting at the regional level. Also beginning in 1988, the Regional Municipality of Hamilton-Wentworth became the first metropolitan or regional municipality in Canada to have its chair directly elected by all municipal voters within its territory. These electoral changes are designed to make the top tier more politically visible and accountable (Ontario 1986). In the longer term, they will also likely lead to an increase in the political strength of the top tier in relation to the bottom. The municipal governments of cities and towns will become weaker still. Unless the top-tier governments get more functions to match their new political importance, the fragmentation of government at the local level will become more apparent, not less.

Annexation and Special-purpose Bodies
Winnipeg's Unicity was created in 1971 so as to avoid the problems of two-tier municipal government by amalgamating all the municipalities in the metropolitan area into one (Brownstone and Plunkett 1983, 39). Such might well be the end result for some of Ontario's two-tier systems as well. But whenever total amalgamation is seriously proposed for the Municipality of Metropolitan Toronto, City of Toronto politicians inevitably point out that there is nothing City residents should fear more than a metropolitan council having the unfettered authority and fiscal resources to connect the suburbs to downtown offices by building expressways running through inner-city neighbourhoods.

Tinkering with municipal structures in Canadian metropolitan areas is likely to continue. A return to the large-scale metropolitan and regional reorganization schemes of the 1960s and 1970s seems most unlikely. If any metropolitan area requires such restructuring, it is Toronto. The Ontario government, however, has been quite explicit in stating that Metropolitan Toronto and the surrounding regional municipalities of Halton, Peel, York, and Durham are here to stay and that their boundaries are not being reconsidered.

Inter-regional problems in the Toronto area are to be dealt with by provincial agencies and *ad hoc* local bodies created to deal with particular problems. Such an approach is surely an acknowledgment that there is no final structural solution to the metropolitan problem. Boundaries suited to one period of urbanization are quickly transcended in the next. If two tiers seem appropriate for metropolitan areas of one or two million people, why are three or four tiers not appropriate when the population doubles or triples?

The shortcomings of two-tier systems of municipal government for urban areas and (arguably) of dramatic amalgamations such as Winnipeg's Unicity should cause students of municipal organization to look more closely at those metropolitan areas dominated by a single city-government whose boundaries have expanded as a result of multiple annexations over a long period of time. Edmonton, Calgary, and London, Ontario, are the most notable examples, although the first of these cities has suffered by attempting too ambitious an annexation in the early 1980s (Masson 1985, 72–3). Annexation is a difficult, time-consuming, and politically delicate process, but it allows for evolutionary change, maintains a one-tier municipal system for urban areas, and adapts to unpredictable patterns of urban growth.

Annexation cannot solve all metropolitan problems, particularly when more than one urban municipality already exists in an area and when it is clear that the most appropriate catchment areas for some metropolitan services are different from others. In these circumstances the much-maligned special-purpose body is the answer. In such circumstances, special-purpose bodies would be established not because municipal *politicians* were deemed inherently incapable of dealing with a certain kind of local service but because municipal *boundaries* were seen as inherently unsuitable for its delivery. Different special-purpose bodies would have different boundaries. The anchor for the system would be the one-tier urban municipality, the unit of local government that would be most visible to most citizens and hence the main (and preferably only) arena for local electoral politics.

CONCLUSION

In exercising his authority in 1971 to stop Toronto's Spadina Expressway, Premier Davis vividly demonstrated the power of provincial governments in relation both to their respective municipal governments and to urban policy-making. Since that date, provincial power in relation to our cities has probably increased. Although various reorganization schemes—including Ontario's program of regional government—were in part justified on the grounds that they would enable more decentralization of provincial authority to restructured municipalities, there was in fact very little decrease in provincial control. Furthermore, most provinces, led by Quebec, collaborated in helping prevent the Ministry of State for Urban Affairs from establishing effective direct links to city governments (Goldbloom 1988). Such links might have enabled skilful city governments to play one level off against the other, thereby enhancing their own political position and creating a more genuinely tri-level system of Canadian government.

Students of urban politics can perhaps be excused for not understanding why and how provincial power was to increase in relation to federal power. What is less excusable was their exaggerated belief in the potential importance of municipal government. We have seen that increases in urban population and the complexity of urban problems have not led to a concomitant increase in the relative importance of municipal government. If anything, the opposite trend occurred, and for quite understandable reasons. As provincial governments tried to orient their economies away from various forms of primary production, their cities became increasingly important as the places in which diversified economies could take shape. How in such circumstances could we ever have expected that municipal autonomy would be fostered?

Listing the limitations of municipal governments is not sufficient to understanding their role. Trying to imagine how our cities could be run without them is likely to give us a more accurate view of their overall importance for the quality of urban life. The capacity of all governments, particularly perhaps Canadian ones, is circumscribed by forces over which they have only limited control. The fact that local governments are more limited than other levels of government does not mean they are unimportant. Their importance will not be determined, however, through the analysis of institutional changes, local election results, or even the changing tides of citizen activism. What we need from local political research is a deeper understanding of the complex processes whereby changing economic, political, and social forces act on local politicians, bureaucrats, and citizens so as to produce new public policies for controlling the built environment and providing the collective goods that make cities work. Only when such research is seriously attempted will we have some genuine knowledge of the municipal role in the governance of Canadian cities.

NOTES

1. The Constitution of Canada is defined (partially at least) in Section 52 (2) of *The Constitution Act, 1982*.

2. Notes relating to Table 18.1:

a) The figure represents the total property tax revenues collected by the City of London for the two school boards covering its territory: The Board of Education of the City of London and the London Middlesex Separate School Board. The territory of the latter board extends beyond the City of London.

b) Includes the following items: the City Administrator's Department excluding fire services and emergency planning; the Finance Department excluding parking enforcement; the Clerk's Department excluding licensing and vital statistics; all costs associated with elected officials and the Legal Department; departmental management costs of the Social Services Department; various general management costs in the City Engineer's Department totalling about $4 million; and various financial management charges, including tax-revenue write-offs and insurance charges, totalling about $5 million.

c) Includes the following items: road design and maintenance, street-lighting, traffic safety devices, traffic engineering management charges, and parking enforcement.

d) Includes the following items: Dearness Home for the Aged, reduced fares for the elderly on public transit vehicles, and services for the elderly included in the budget of the community support services program of the Social Services Department.

e) Includes the following programs from the Economic Development Department: development strategy and initiatives, and visitors and convention services.

f) Includes transportation services for the physically disabled, free public transit for the blind, and grants to various community organizations providing services to the handicapped.

g) Includes the following items: the community support services program of the Social Services Department, excluding direct costs of child day-care and services to the elderly and various direct grants to various community organizations.

h) A multi-purpose hall owned and operated by the City.

i) A historically important residence operated primarily as a tourist attraction by the London Public Library Board.

j) The Public Utilities Commission purchases electricity from Ontario Hydro, owns and operates the electricity distribution system within the City of London, and retails electricity at cost to London consumers. Annual operating deficits or surpluses are retained within the P.U.C. electricity accounts.

k) As for electricity above, except that the wholesaler of water is the Ontario Ministry of Natural Resources, which pipes water to London from Lake Huron.

FURTHER READING

BIRD, R.M. and SLACK, N.E. 1983 *Urban Public Finance in Canada* (Toronto: Butterworths)

BOSSONS, J., MAKUCH, S.M., and PALMER, J. 1984 *Regulation by Municipal Licensing* (Toronto: University of Toronto Press, Ontario Economic Council Research Studies)

FILION, P. 1988 'The Neighbourhood Improvement Plan, Montreal and Toronto: Contrasts between a Participatory and Centralized Approach to Urban Policy Making', *Urban History Review*, 17 16–28

FRISKEN, F. 1988 *City Policy-Making in Theory and Practice: The Case of Toronto's Downtown Plan* Local Government Case Studies #3 (London, Ont.: University of Western Ontario Department of Political Science)

HARRIS, R. 1988 *Democracy in Kingston: A Social Movement in Urban Politics, 1965–1970* (Kingston, Ont.: McGill-Queen's University Press)

HIGGINS, D.J.H. 1986 *Local and Urban Politics in Canada* (Toronto: Gage)

KITCHEN, H. 1985 *The Role for Local Governments in Economic Development* (Toronto: Ontario Economic Council)

MAGNUSSON, W. 1981 'Metropolitan Reform and the Capitalist City', *Canadian Journal of Political Science* 14, 557–85

———— 1985 'The Local State in Canada: Theoretical Perspectives', *Canadian Public Administration* 28, 575–99

———— and SANCTON, A. eds 1983 *City Politics in Canada* (Toronto: University of Toronto Press)

MAKUCH, S. 1985 'Urban Law and Policy Development in Canada: The Myth and the Reality' in I. Bernier and A. Lajoie eds *Labour Law and Urban Law in Canada* Volume 51 in the Research Studies of the Royal Commission on the Economic Union and Development Prospects for Canada (Toronto: University of Toronto Press)

SEWELL, J. 1985 *Police: Urban Policing in Canada* (Toronto: James Lorimer)

REFERENCES

BROWNSTONE, M. and PLUNKETT, T.J. 1983 *Metropolitan Winnipeg: Politics and Reform of Local Government* (Berkeley: University of California Press)

CAULFIELD, J. 1974 *The Tiny Perfect Mayor: David Crombie and Toronto's Reform Aldermen* (Toronto: James Lorimer)

―――― 1988 ' "Reform" as Chaotic Concept: The Case of Toronto', *Urban History Review* 17, 107–11

DAWSON, R. MACG. 1970 *The Government of Canada* revised by N. Ward (Toronto: University of Toronto Press)

DUPRE, J.S. 1981 'Intergovernmental Relations and the Metropolitan Area' in L.D. Feldman ed. *Politics and Government of Urban Canada* (Toronto: Methuen)

FRISKEN, F. 1988 *City Policy-Making in Theory and Practice: The Case of Toronto's Downtown Plan* Local Government Case Studies No. 3 (London, Ont.: University of Western Ontario Department of Political Science)

GERECKE, K. 1986–87 'Winnipeg Hits Bottom', *City Magazine* 9, 35

GOLDBLOOM, V. 1988 'Recollections from a Provincial Perspective' in H.P. Oberlander and A.L. Fallick eds *The Ministry of State for Urban Affairs: A Courageous Experiment in Public Administration* (Vancouver: University of British Columbia Centre for Human Settlements)

GUTSTEIN, D. 1986–87 'Vancouver Voters Swing Right', *City Magazine* 9, 30–32

HIGGINS, D.J.H. 1986a 'The Process of Reorganizing Local Government in Canada', *Canadian Journal of Political Science* 19, 219–42

―――― 1986b *Local and Urban Politics in Canada* (Toronto: Gage)

HODGE, G. 1986 *Planning Canadian Communities* (Toronto: Methuen)

KITCHEN, H. 1984 *Local Government Finance in Canada* (Toronto: Canadian Tax Foundation)

LEE, J. 1988 'Campbell and NPA Returned to Power', *Vancouver Sun* 21 November

LEO, C. 1977 *The Politics of Urban Development: Canadian Urban Expressway Disputes* (Toronto: Institute of Public Administration of Canada)

MAGNUSSON, W. 1985 'The Local State in Canada: Theoretical Perspectives', *Canadian Public Administration* 28, 575–99

MANITOBA, GOVERNMENT OF 1976 *Committee of Review, City of Winnipeg Act, Report and Recommendations* (Winnipeg: Government of Manitoba)

MASSON, J. 1985 *Alberta's Local Governments and Their Politics* (Edmonton: Pica Press)

―――― and ANDERSON J.D. eds 1972 *Emerging Party Politics in Urban Canada* (Toronto: McClelland and Stewart)

MILES, S., COHEN, S., and DE KONING, G. 1973 *Developing a Canadian Urban Policy: Some Problems and Proposals* (Toronto: Intermet)

MILNER, H. 1988 'The Montreal Citizens' Movement, Then and Now', *Quebec Studies* 6, 1–11

ONTARIO, GOVERNMENT OF 1979 *Report of the Waterloo Region Review Commission* (Toronto: Ministry of Intergovernmental Affairs)

—— 1986 *Analysis and Options for the Government of Metropolitan Toronto* (Toronto: Ministry of Municipal Affairs)

—— 1987 *Crossing the Boundaries—Coordinating Transit in the Greater Toronto Area: Report of the Transit Advisory Group to the Minister of Transportation for Ontario* (Toronto: Ministry of Transportation)

PETERSON, P.E. 1981 *City Limits* (Chicago: University of Chicago Press)

PLUNKETT, T.J. and BETTS, G.E. 1978 *The Management of Canadian Urban Government* (Kingston, Ont.: Queen's University Institute of Local Government)

POIRIER, P. 1988 'Montreal Councillors Quit Dore's Caucus', *The Globe and Mail* 22 December

REDLICH, J. and HIRST, F.W. 1970 *The History of Local Government in England* with an Introduction and Epilogue by B. Keith-Lucas (New York: Augustus M. Kelley)

ROGERS, I. MacF. 1971 (with loose-leaf updates to 1988) *The Law of Canadian Municipal Corporations* (Toronto: Carswell)

—— 1973 (with loose-leaf updates to 1988) *Canadian Law of Planning and Zoning* (Toronto: Carswell)

ROSE, A. 1972 *Governing Metropolitan Toronto: A Social and Political Analysis, 1953–1971* (Berkeley: University of California Press)

SANCTON, A. 1983a 'Conclusion: Canadian City Politics in Comparative Perspective' in W. Magnusson and A. Sancton eds *City Politics in Canada* (Toronto: University of Toronto Press)

—— 1983b 'Montreal' in W. Magnusson and A. Sancton eds *City Politics in Canada* (Toronto: University of Toronto Press)

—— 1985 *Governing the Island of Montreal: Language Differences and Metropolitan Politics* (Berkeley: University of California Press)

—— 1988 'Social Service Delivery at Relevant Government Levels' in H. Symonds and H.P. Oberlander eds *Meech Lake: From Centre to Periphery* (Vancouver: University of British Columbia Centre for Human Settlements)

SHARPE, L.J. 1981 'The Failure of Local Government Modernization in Britain: A Critique of Functionalism' in L.D. Feldman ed. *Politics and Government of Urban Canada* (Toronto: Methuen)

STENNING, P.C. 1981 'The Role of Police Boards and Commissions as Institutions of Municipal Police Governance' in C.D. Shearing ed. *Organizational Police Deviance* (Toronto: Butterworths)

TAYLOR, P. 1988 'Reformers to Brake Toronto Development', *The Globe and Mail* Nov. 16

19

Planning and Development in Canadian Cities

WILLIAM T. PERKS AND WALTER JAMIESON

This chapter provides a historical overview and some outlines of the contemporary nature and role of urban planning in the development of Canadian cities. There are conflicting views about the purposes, the social meanings, and the efficacy of planning cities. At one end of a spectrum, planning is seen as a desirable and necessary regulatory function of municipal administrations. At the other end of the spectrum, planning will be seen as a costly, counter-productive intrusion into the market-place of land and building, and business affairs in general. In this perspective, planning is believed to impose untenable restraints on individual and corporate property rights.

Urban planning in Canadian cities is today a firmly established social-political institution.[1] Its workings are governed by provincial statutes and municipal by-laws, administrative regulations, and negotiations and business relations. These negotiations and relations variously involve entrepreneurs, planning and architectural-design professionals, community groups, politicians, and municipal officials. Our task is to outline the terms and the contexts of urban planning as it is practised in Canadian cities—how planning ideas took shape, how planning contributes to the form and quality of city environments, what planners do, and how the planning system operates. Two periods, pre–1960s and post–1960s, with illustrative reference to Toronto and Calgary, provide a framework. The time periods reflect two major stages. In the post–1960s, for example, planning made a significant shift from the practice of comprehensive plan-making and regulated land use, to a system in which pragmatic working relationships between municipal administrators and private developers emerged; partnerships between the private sector and the public sector begin to figure more prominently. It is a period, too, of expansion and diversification of the roles played by planners.

We adopt the perspective that sees *planning and property development as interlocking institutions and professional practices.* Therefore, we begin with an account of what makes up a city's development and what it is that planners do. We then discuss the formal terms of planning that were adopted from abroad and adapted to Canadian circumstances. The chapter concludes with some thoughts about what lies ahead for urban planning.

CITY AS ARTIFACT: PLANNING AND DEVELOPMENT AS IT NOW IS

The Artifact: City Form and Planning

The built environment is what gives the city its form and its visual character. In one sense, the form of the city can be understood as a two-dimensional artifact, as a 'flat-surface' composition, a subdivision of land into streets and their contiguous parcels of land. A typical illustration of this form is the gridiron pattern of streets and properties laid out in the surveyors' plans of Calgary in the 1870s, and Toronto (York) in 1788. In one important respect, this is what planning cities is about—predetermining the two-dimensional pattern of the overall city, or the pattern of some new suburban neighbourhood. But in reality, a city has three-dimensional form. It is a composite of buildings and other artifacts that rise upwards from the ground. The three-dimensional (architectural) form creates the visual character of our environment and determines the comforts, excitements, and pleasures of living and working in urban places. Human behaviour, health, and social activity can also be very much influenced by the three-dimensional composition of our environments. In its essentials, the real form of the city is made up of buildings and spaces adapted or fitted in particular ways to the landscape and climatic settings of the city. It is here that planning and architectural design come together. Thus, composing cities with a view to creating satisfactory public spaces and environments for living and working constitutes another preoccupation of city planning. However, this preoccupation has not been pursued with constant purpose by Canadian planners, architects, and politicians. Indeed, the general appraisal of Canadian city form and space is one of disappointment and missed opportunities (Kemble 1989).

The Composite Artifact: Building and Planning

The city, then, is a *composite artifact*. It is made up of land that has been divided up and designated for use in specified ways. Some of the bits of land are very small, while others can be very large. The corner store in an old neighbourhood of Calgary may sit on a 250-square metre plot of land; High Park in Toronto extends over 137 hectares.

On and under the bits of land, we build. We build houses, apartment buildings, condominiums, day-care centres, office buildings, manufacturing plants, retail stores and shopping malls, industrial parks, recreation parks, and ornamental gardens. We build public buildings: city hall and government offices; hospitals and airports; buildings for worship, for the performing arts, amusements, and exhibitions; for education and sports. We also build an infrastructure of roads, sewers, water-mains, and other utilities to support and service these buildings and places.

On the streets and in the parks we build bus shelters, telephone booths and benches, traffic lights, bicycle paths, and pedestrian malls. We plant trees, we shape the contours of the land, and we rechannel rivers and streams. We create special places to erect monuments for our history and sculptures for the fun of it. We put up signs to advertise, to tell us where we are, or where not to be, and where to go and turn and park.

In the most elemental sense, planning has to do with anticipating all of these many land-use needs, then 'assigning' them to various locations within the city. Through this process, communities and their municipal governments determine where various types of buildings or uses of land can be most appropriately located, and how they will be connected together by transportation and other services. The process also determines those locations where specified building developments or uses of land will *not* be allowed. That is the anticipatory aspect of planning. But city planning today also embraces the concept of development control; that is, determining when land and building developments will occur and, generally speaking, setting out the precise conditions by which a building is to be laid-out on its site and what its architectural design will be.

Within this conception of planning and development, there are also those activities that have to do with renewal and redevelopment, for example, rearranging or widening streets, reclassifying allowable land uses, the demolition and reconstruction of properties, and rehabilitating heritage properties. Planning authorities may also set aside environmentally sensitive lands for protection from building developments and for use as public open space.

Provincial planning statutes give force to those aspects of planning practice thus far described, and they legitimate the premises upon which urban plans are drawn up: 'Planning laws limit an owner's rights in private property in order to secure benefits for the community as a whole. These benefits include such things as the safety and health of persons; convenience, amenities and agreeable environments for the public; and reasonable burdens of public expenditures that have to be incurred when developments occur . . .' (Perks and Smith 1988, 2229).

Planning Practice and the Roles of Planners

Planning can be seen, therefore, as a process of thinking ahead to accommodate a city's growth and renewal, and then regulating developments as they are about to occur. To meet these objectives, planners engage in a variety of roles. Some will actually do the controlling, employing their specialized knowledge to ensure that land- and building-development projects conform to the goals and conditions set out in the city's general plan, or in one of its special area plans; for example, an area redevelopment plan. These 'Official Plans' are typically a compendium of forecasts, analyses of issues and concerns, studies of social and environmental impacts to be anticipated, goal statements, maps and illustrations, and development standards and regulations. The tendency is to call planners involved in preparing such plans *policy planners*.

Implicit in the practice of planning is the notion of betterment, of creating physical environments that satisfy not only a need for orderly development and the convenience of people as they go about their daily lives but creating beauty and enjoyment as well. 'An intrinsic part of . . . community planning efforts involves the consideration of ideal situations, of desirable conditions.' (Hodge 1986, 10.) Planning practice is infused with theories about the 'good' form that cities should take, and with ideal conceptions about the spatial composition of physical environments— the buildings, streets, landscapes, and so on—taken together as a whole. Planners seek to integrate ideals of sociability and social equity, the public interest, equality of access to public services and amenities, beauty in the environment, and other factors.

When planners try to create a unifying composition of the city artifacts, whether it be at the level of a street block, a neighbourhood, or a downtown district, they 'design' (van Ginkel 1988). The main objective of design is the creation, by use of drawings or models, of images that illustrate how the many parts ought to be brought together in harmony, and what the appearances and social activities of the urban spaces will be like. Planners engaged in these activities are commonly referred to as *urban designers*. Urban designs might be further elaborated into documents that stipulate the rules and the architectural standards by which developers should or shall build on their properties. Plans of this type will likely be promulgated using a development by-law or urban-design guidelines.

Planners now play an influential part in managing a public planning process. In all jurisdictions of Canada, public participation in planning is now required, although prior to the 1960s, planning was mostly left to city politicians and their expert staffs. Canadian communities have been very successful in assuring that all parties with an interest in planning issues or development proposals can make known their desires and objections. Public participation typically continues throughout the 'life' of the plan-making project. Community groups have been known to exercise decisive influence over the final outcomes of a plan or property development proposal.

In the larger perspective, the planners' roles can be seen to embrace land-use plans and regulation, urban design, the phasing, coordination, and integration among and between property developments, and the management of public participation in the process of city development. Beginning in the late 1970s, the roles of the public planner were expanded and further differentiated. Within the municipal system planners are involved in decisions on planning ventures that depart from an exclusively land-use focus—for example, economic development strategies; tourism plans; festivals and events programming; financial negotiations on land development deals; business district 'revitalization' schemes; the management of joint venture projects between public authorities and the private sector (Perks 1985b; Perks and Robinson 1979).

Planning Decisions
In essence, what drives the planning system is the market place. A common misconception is that planners are the determinant agents; that they are responsible for everything—good, bad, or mistaken—that happens to a city. However, and certainly where the major, instrumental planning policies are concerned, decisions about plans and development are first and foremost market decisions, and ultimately political decisions. Political decisions are, in turn, as much influenced by the temper of the marketplace as they are by the politicians' sensitivity to the aspirations of communities and ordinary city residents. Indeed, during episodes of intense economic growth and city expansion—as in Metropolitan Toronto, in the mid-1980s—planning and development matters will typically dominate city council agendas.

Planners are mostly regulators, and seldom the creators of plans. Their role is mainly development control, and the powers they bring to that task are limited. For developers, the profitability of the project will be the pivotal condition. Generally speaking, profitability rises with the density or bulk of building to be allowed on a given parcel of land. Municipalities will offer the developer density bonuses above zoning specifications to extract public benefits such as plazas and gardens, public parking facilities, spaces for day care or public service departments, retail shops at street level, building of plus–15 bridges (a system of pedestrian walkways linking central Calgary buildings and thus creating an integrated shopping environment), etc. Canadian public planners have, in the last two decades, shown themselves to be particularly skilful, and often imaginative in this practice of development control and bargaining with the property industry. But the general experience, however, is that municipal administrations give more than they get. Most frequently, what is gained for the public implies investments of public funds in shared-cost or trade-off arrangements with the property developer. Certainly, the allowances and public investments committed by the planners in return for public benefits are decisions ultimately sanctioned by politicians, but these politicians for the most part who, it is frequently argued, depend for their electoral financing upon the property industry.

Planning in cities is tied to municipal financial planning; that is, it attempts to ensure public investment in infrastructure well in advance of land developments. These strategies create a kind of 'fiscal zoning', by which private-sector agencies can, to a degree, gauge the potential profitability and success of their private plans. Here, too, a municipality's plans can be made to bend under the persuasive political influence of the property industry. Instances of this kind of influence can be seen in the downtown high-rise building booms that swept through Calgary in the 1970s and through Toronto, first in the late 1960s, and then more voraciously in the mid–1980s.

PLANNING AND DEVELOPMENT TO THE 1960s

Roots and the Planning Movement

The idea that the development of cities ought to be subject to planning by public authority drew its impetus from five interconnected movements: (1) public health; (2) affordable and decent housing; (3) reform of municipal government; (4) civic art and the late-nineteenth century revival of artistic principles in city building; and (5) conservation. With degrees of expression and intensity of purpose that varied from country to country, these movements originated in the urban-industrial environments of continental Europe, Britain, and the eastern United States in the mid- to late-nineteenth century. By the first decade of the twentieth century, they had made their appearances in Canada (Hodge 1986, 86–95; McAfee 1988, 1016–17; Perks and Smith 1988, 2228–9; Rutherford 1974; Weaver 1988, 2232).

Up to 1920, no more than a handful of Canadian cities had committed themselves to the preparation of city development plans; among these were Toronto (1911), Calgary (1912–14), Ottawa (1915), and Berlin (now Kitchener) (1914). Part of the early Toronto plan is outlined in Figure 19.1. This can be explained by the state of maturity of Canadian political and economic institutions. A smaller proportion of Canadians lived in cities than did people in Britain and the eastern United States. There were few urban centres of substantial size that might demand urban planning services.

Though it lacked a unitary conception, the early Canadian planning movement profited from and asserted itself in concert with the moderniza-

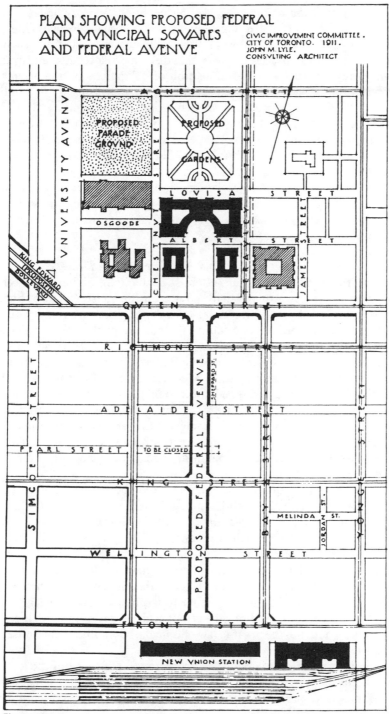

Figure 19.1

SOURCE: Environments, 1985, 17, 2.

tion and expansion of the state. As the twentieth century opened, state intervention had been firmly established in two main forms: 'One was the direct provision by public authority of common facilities such as thoroughfares, drains, sewers, water and ... gas, electricity and public transport. The other was the imposition of obligations on the owners of urban property and, to a lesser extent, on those who used it' (Sutcliffe 1981, 5.) Canada, preoccupied with nation-building, immigration, the layout of settlements and infrastructure, rapid expansion of cities, and the management of resources development, inclined quite naturally to these imperatives of modernity. Thus it was that the federal state gave birth to Canadian planning institutions.

We draw attention to three landmark events: the establishment of a commission of conservation; the 1914 Toronto conference on town planning; and the arrival in Canada of Thomas Adams, a British publicist and practitioner of planning.

Planning Doctrines Outlined ... And Artistic Principles Denied
In 1909, the federal government established the Commission of Conservation to provide governments with advice on the conservation of human and natural resources (Smith 1988, 465). Among the seven topics on the Commission's agenda were agricultural lands and public health. Concerns about public health centred on the established urban centres where disease was patently evident. Disease could be linked to unsanitary conditions in housing and the environment, to a deficiency of infrastructure, and to *laissez-faire* land speculation, all of which placed immense strains on municipal administrations. Questions concerning the use of agricultural lands were of a different order, namely: How should land be managed for optimal productivity and conservation? How could improvements be made in the method of planning and subdivision of rural farm communities?

These two broad areas of inquiry ushered the federal authority into urban planning. In 1914, with financing from the government of Canada, the Commission of Conservation hosted—in Toronto—the first Town Planning Congress ever held in Canada.[2] The Commission's practical objectives were clearly stated by its chairman, Sir Clifford Sifton.[3] Acknowledging that some form of planning laws had been passed in some of the provinces, Sifton pronounced these 'insufficient for the necessities of the case'. He wanted the conference to '... help us promote legislation which we can recommend to the various legislatures of the provinces ... and make it a part of the organic law of Canada' (Commission of Conservation 1915, 238.)[4]

The governor general opened the conference. He spoke of the 'evil' of slums and the 'physical, mental and moral decadence' they engendered. He emphasized three domains for urban planning: the provision of parks and playgrounds, the creation of main thoroughfares in cities, and the securing of proper and adequate housing conditions.

Equally or more significant, in his opening and closing speeches Clifford Sifton discoursed on the moral and utilitarian arguments for planning and public intervention. Sifton's speeches were eloquent yet reserved. On the one hand, he acknowledged the environmental and human degradations that evidently accompanied the 'progress' of capitalist industrial societies and science itself. On the other, Sifton rejected the radical remedies to be found in such programs as 'government ownership of utilities', 'socialism', and 'single (land) tax'. The new professional planners, Sifton insisted, were not called upon to deal with the economic *causes* of the evils of city living. Rather they would need to study and understand the economic *conditions* under which they had to work. Planning would need to be an economical proposition: a proposition to save money, and to get good value for money. As for the *art* of city building, Sifton was pointedly silent on the subject.

Sifton had categorically set out the Canadian framework and the state's terms for advancing urban planning: do not tamper with the economic and property system; make efficiency the central objective of plan-making; do not be concerned with aesthetics; use scientific methods and means. Planning was to be only meliorative in its socio-economic intentions. These were the doctrines that the practice of urban planning adopted and perfected over the next half century and more. They would first be championed and codified by an Englishman, Thomas Adams, Sifton's appointee to the post of Town Planning Adviser at the Commission of Conservation.

When recruited in October 1914, Thomas Adams was one of the half-dozen or so leading practitioners of the new planning profession in Britain.[5] He was also the first person to have held a public service position under the pioneering Housing and Town Planning Act adopted there in 1909. Adams was also an organizer, writer-publicist, and political conciliator *par excellence*. Yet he was a man of limited imagination, with only meagre talents in composing urban environments on plans. Outwardly receptive to a role for architects but inwardly resentful of the fact that most urban development plans of the time were being drawn up by architects for private sector clients, Adams developed two important positions on urban planning. First, planning schemes must be made compulsory in law and be drawn up on the authority of the municipality; they should be comprehensive—that is, they should embrace the whole of the municipal territory and all of its future land use needs. Second, '... the work to be performed will fall for the most part into the hands of the engineers and surveyors' (Simpson 1985, 65; Perks 1985a). Adams's antipathy towards the architectural profession grew during his mission to Canada, a factor of no small consequence in the development of a professional ideology devoid of artistic principles that Adams formed and his disciples later furthered.

The Gradual Institutionalization of Planning: Character, Style and Experimentation

With the assistance of two Canadians, George Ross and Horace Seymour,[6] Adams produced a rebuilding plan for the Richmond district in Halifax after the devastating explosion of December 1917; he designed the Lindenlea Garden Suburb in Ottawa under the auspices of the Ottawa Housing Commission (1919–20); he produced a complete, new-town plan at Temiskaming in northern Quebec (1917). These were modest demonstrations of what the novel idea of town planning meant, but they were scarcely, or not at all, sensitive to the peculiarities of the Canadian setting. Lindenlea was in its own time described as 'an ordinary real estate development' (Simpson 1985, 107–108). The Temiskaming plan imitated a style introduced in the Letchworth Garden City project in England, a style not particularly in harmony with Laurentian Shield conditions and human needs. The street layout ignored orientations to sun that could mitigate winter exposures; the plan was devoid of house forms, and open space arrangements appropriate to cold climate living. In other respects, too, Adams's mission to Canada was not a great success. Canadian legislatures did not respond favourably to the 'sophisticated British legislative and institutional framework' that Adams urged upon them (Simpson 1985, 117), and Adams himself was unresponsive to the pleas of Canadian urban reformers that a government-backed housing program be linked to urban planning. In effect, the economic recession of 1913, the resistance of industrialists and land speculators, and World War I (1914–18) combined to retard the planning movement. Not until the buoyant 1920s did municipalities return to the issues of unfettered land development. The revival was short-lived; advances made in public planning were arrested by the Great Depression and World War II (1939–45). These events stopped land developments, taking the expansion pressures off municipalities, prompting the dissolution of the Town Planning Institute of Canada (TPIC), a proto-professional association that Adams had organized. The dissolution of the TPIC was also due to mounting hostility on the part of government and business to 'planning', an attitude occasioned by the spectre of socialist politics that had risen in Canada.

Planning Doctrine from Planning Practice

The period of the 1920s was one of episodic municipal ventures into plan-making. Plans were drawn up not by municipal officials but by consultants. The plans were of three types: small-area plans for private housing projects or the subdivision in innovative fashion of tracts of suburban land; zoning plans; comprehensive master plans. The latter two are of importance, for it was out of these experiments that the central practice of urban planning after World War II evolved. Comprehensive plans and zoning were urged upon municipal councils by civic-minded pragmatists and planners alike. It was from these local and national 'movers' that the US practice of setting up politically-independent planning commissions or boards came into being, a device intended to remove planning from 'politics' and give it an aura of 'scientific' urban technology.

Most of these early comprehensive plans were either pigeon-holed or only loosely respected as regulatory devices. Sometimes because of economic reversals, as with the Calgary Plan drawn up by Thomas Mawson just as the real-estate collapse of 1913 set in; and sometimes because of political incompatibility (or incomprehension), as with the Kitchener-Waterloo Plans of 1915 and 1923 (Perks 1985a; Bloomfield 1982). Active and experimental though cities were in the 1920s, planning and development control were not systematically incorporated into municipal government. Among the notable exceptions were Calgary, Edmonton, and Toronto where zoning, highways planning, slum clearance, and public housing schemes were variously set afoot. (Simpson 1985, 116).

The achievements and the temper of planning in the pre-World War II period were few and only mildly reformist, though not without significance for the manner in which planning thought and practice would eventually become institutionalized. Cities in Canada began to implement zoning by-laws in selected city districts (e.g., Calgary, 1926); and a definitive style for the comprehensive master plan was established, for example, that of Vancouver (1928), prepared by an American consulting firm—was established. It is important to note that impressive advances were made in the 1920s through the 1930s in the acquisition of urban parks for municipally-run recreational services; these were largely made possible by the deflation of land values and tax-defaulting land owners. The dual themes of parks and recreation programs addressed concerns for city liveability and social health, especially with respect to the poor and disadvantaged living in crowded, substandard housing districts. On the other hand, the push for parks served to divert municipal and senior governments from the nagging question of housing conditions (see, for example, Chapter 14). Thomas Adams and the authors of the Vancouver Plan renounced housing as a subject proper for public planning intervention. Also subdivision plans of this period integrated many of the elements that were to guide the development of the post-World War II suburb. This is illustrated by Seymour's plan for the Slattery Estate in Ottawa reproduced on Figure 9.2.

National Strategy and the Consolidation of Public Planning: 1949 to the 1960s

When planning eventually 'returned' in the 1950s, it once again enjoyed the patronage of federal authority. This time, the focus was housing, and the deployment of resources was strategic. The Depression and the war years had left Canadian cities with serious shortages in housing stock. Slums had burgeoned with the migration of workers from farms to factories, and cities were expanding under the pressures of immigration and a

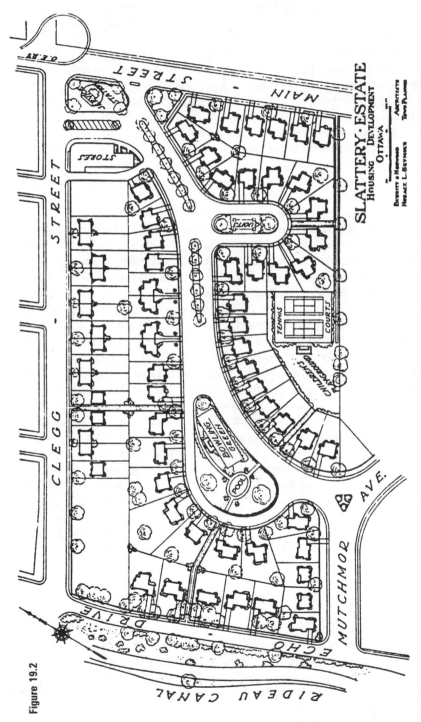

Figure 19.2

Seymour's subdivision plan for the Slattery Estate, Ottawa, 1936, has most hallmarks of progressive housing development layouts in the interwar period.
(Source: Original Seymour Paper, PAC, MG30. B 39, Vol. 11, File 4.) Source: Bloomfield, 1985, 38.

movement of middle-class families to the city outskirts. The drama of growth that unfolded can be gauged by a few statistics: 'Between 1941 and 1951, Canadian urban centres grew by three million people or an astounding 51%. . . . Another five million were added . . . in the succeeding decade, 1951–1961, and two thirds of this went into the largest cities.' (Hodge 1986, 68.)

Beginning in 1935 with the passage of the Dominion Housing Act, the federal government was to assume almost exclusive responsibility for housing programs. Subsequently, 'housing for all' (that is, the right of all Canadians to decent, comfortable houses and neighbourhoods) and the planning of new neighbourhood communities were given powerful effect in the combined passage of the 1946 National Housing Act (NHA) and the creation of Central Mortgage and Housing Corporation (CMHC; now Canada Mortgage and Housing Corporation).[7]

The 1949 amendments to the Housing Act transformed the CMHC into a promoter of community planning. In the amendments, the NHA allowed the CMHC to dispense research funds; these funds would support a modernization of the Canadian housing industry and improvements in architectural design and land development standards, and make possible the establishment of 'professional' planning education in Canadian universities. The Act also funded public housing for low-income families, seniors, and the disabled. From 1947 to 1986, 250,000 public housing units were built. Finally, CMHC expert assistance and funding went into the creation of community planning associations across the country.

The major challenges that unfolded in the 1950s were how to accomplish three tasks: (1) the organization and layout of housing subdivisions and neighbourhood communities at the periphery of cities; (2) the eradication of slums in city centres and the subsequent reconstruction of these districts; and (3) an expansion of roadway systems, including extension outwards to the suburbs and radical enlargements along selected corridors within already built-up areas.

When, in 1954, CMHC was empowered to insure privately-arranged house mortgage loans against borrower default, the corporation was handed a strategic instrument for advancing the community planning movement across the whole of the country. This allowed CMHC to impose planning over the heads of the provinces who, in a repeat of history, were dilatory in implementing regulations commensurate with the scale and pace of the development boom. CMHC made it a condition of insurance that proposals to build houses were part of a city plan, regardless of whether the plan was drawn up by the municipality or by private-sector agents on a project-by-project basis. These exigencies soon propelled municipalities into preparing comprehensive, city-wide master plans and zoning measures. At first, the cities called on planning and engineering consultants to do the job. As city plans came into effect, planners in the employ of the municipality were needed to monitor and revise these plans, and to administer development control regulations. Eventually, as provincial planning statutes came into being, full-time municipal planning staffs took over the preparation of long-term master plans.

During the 1950s, CMHC introduced the funding of municipal land assemblies. These brought large tracts of land that could be planned comprehensively and used for locally-designed, market-assisted housing projects into public ownership. By the late 1950s, virtually all major cities were receiving CMHC funds for urban renewal. And, in the 1960s, CMHC was giving financial assistance to municipalities for infrastructure, particularly where major sewage-treatment facilities were needed.

What can be said of the 'styles' and the achievements of the new planning system? Master plans, transportation planning, and urban renewal dominated. With partial exception in the case of renewal, all three modes of planning were founded in the doctrines of technical functionalism and economic efficiency. Further, the system developed in Canada was predicated on the political proposition that, through its control and regulation of land development, public authority would direct change—and even social betterment—in significant and meaningful ways. Tied to this conception was an implicit understanding that public authority held a legitimate monopoly on planning wisdom. This, in turn, embraced the belief that public authority would possess the necessary imagination and the creative, persuasionary, and coercive powers to articulate ideals and bring them to fruition.

By bringing order and coherency to the land development process and its correlate, municipal fiscal programming, the system worked. For visionary design of the three-dimensional, spatial form of city environments, the system was ill-equipped, if not ill-conceived. Equally, the planning system lacked the political will to demand of the property industry a humanistic, aesthetically-enriching enterprise. Even when public planners were handed the opportunities of inner-city renewal projects, planned and managed entirely under public authority, they were found to be no less unimaginative. In short, the Canadian public planning system lacked consensus and will in the matter of vision and in the application of high 'design' standards. The form of cities shaped in the period were subject to popular as well as intellectual criticism, and even ridicule. The suburban plan, for example, it could be argued, was the epitome of inefficiency, and it created a social desert and an aborted Garden City design.

It must be acknowledged, however, that by the mid–1960s a public planning system was in place. A systematic regulation of the property industry had now been implemented; there could be no turning back. The unprecedented post-war forces of city growth and expansion were for the better part contained and channelled in generally beneficial ways.

The Neighbourhood and The Positioning of Planning Practice

The neighbourhood became the basic organizing principle for planning in the new suburbs. A concept that was first publicized in the New York Regional Plan of 1929, a neighbourhood consisted of an area of 160 acres (64 hectares) with a population of 1,500 or so families, a number thought sufficient to support one elementary school. Two or more neighbourhoods would form the basis for a high school. Heavy traffic routes defined the outer edges of neighbourhoods and housing was laid out so that the school and other community facilities were within walking distance for children (1/4-mile/500 metres). Within the confines of the neighbourhood, street layouts discouraged 'through traffic', a device that led to culs-de-sac and curvilinear streets.

The first, fully-planned neighbourhoods appeared in eastern cities. Depending on the local conditions of land development and property ownership patterns, they ranged in size from 3,000 to 5,000 persons. In the West, the mile-square farmland grid—onto which city arterial traffic routes could be conveniently extended—and public policies favouring low-density, single-family housing came to define the neighbourhood, some of which had populations eventually reaching 20,000 or more. Housing was almost exclusively of the single-family type, while land-use densities were designed to be much lower than those found in pre-World War II city communities. In Calgary, for instance, new neighbourhoods were laid out for as few as 18 persons per acre.

A logical extension of the neighbourhood concept was to design 'complete' new communities, such as the pioneering Garden Cities and post-World War II new towns in England, or the Greenbelt Cities of the 1930s, launched under the New Deal in the USA. These were communities in which office and industrial employment could be located, along with commercial-retail services, and a range and choice of housing types and densities for all income classes. New communities of this order would be more convenient for residents, more economic to service, and could save on construction of roadway systems otherwise required to link distantly-spaced homes and work places. Only a few but notable experiments of this kind were undertaken, for example, Strathcona Park near Edmonton, and Don Mills and Ajax outside of Toronto. Our failure to create complete communities can be attributed to the fragmentation of the property industry into many small companies at the time. Very few had the capacity and resources to assemble the extensive tracts of land required; and those who could, would not risk building beyond the assured market for houses alone. For its part, the public planning system was as yet too weak in its convictions and too insecure in its powers to compel initiatives from the private sector that could have rendered a more sociologically—and economically—satisfactory development of community in the expanding city.

Instead, planning of the suburbs evolved into a four-part specialization: first, planning and engineering design of the major street systems that, in turn, generally determined the city-wide configuration of neighbourhoods; second, the demographic sizing and land-subdivision of neighbourhoods themselves; third, the locating, sizing, and zoning of shopping centres on major thoroughfares and in proximity to the consumer markets defined by the new neighbourhoods; and four, the locating, sizing, zoning, and subdivision of industrial and commercial office 'parks'. In this characteristic process of the 1950s and 1960s, the driving forces were strong demand for home-ownership pumped by federal and provincial programs, rising automobile ownership, an explosive mobility of middle-class families, and virulent land speculation. Private land developers and home-builders were the primary initiators in the system, while public planners became re-active, regulatory agents.

Urban renewal was a different story. Here, public planning was more proactive: federal, provincial, and municipal funds, (shared 50/25/25 per cent respectively) were channelled into the acquisition of run-down, inner-city properties that were placed in the hands of the municipality to re-plan and rebuild; planning and implementation of the schemes were entirely under the control of public authority. In the mid–1950s, 900,000 housing units across Canada were fifty- or more years-old, and classed as 'sub-standard'. Abandoned or unsightly industrial properties were commonly mixed in among the 'blighted' residences. CMHC's urban renewal program anticipated that municipalities would 'clear' these areas and, either within the area or on other sites, build new housing for the residents.

Renewal was a mixed success, if not an unpopular venture. Inner-city communities were destroyed or fragmented beyond the possibility of restoration. An insignificant number of the displaced residents were actually rehoused in public housing, while the captured downtown sites were mostly deployed for the construction of commercial buildings and large public institutions. Moreover, for decades, vacant or decaying properties awaiting some planning resolution were conspicuously left to induce yet another form of blight in the downtown fabric. The re-active, regulative, and two-dimensional planning style adopted over the 1950s proved a rather inept model for dealing with the intensive redevelopment of down-towns and inner-city communities that was to occur in the mid–1960s. This period needed architectural/urban design schemes that would delineate redevelopment projects, with attention to social sensitivity and community continuity, respecting history, and the established contextual fabric in the city, and allocating public spaces fitted for human enjoyment. But by this time the architectural design traditions of urbanism had been thoroughly flushed from planning doctrine, while the practice of Canadian architecture itself had capitulated to modernism.[8] Further, in the determination of overall city form and quality of environments, the planners had, in the final analysis, too little influence by comparison with transportation planners (see Chapter 11 for a discussion of the role of the transportation planner and a description of transportation planning's techniques and processes). When transportation and community planning were eventually performed with some attention to integration, it was the 'even-handed truth' of computer simulations, efficiency, and engineering logic that triumphed.

Such was the state of transportation/land use planning that no sooner were four- and six-lane expressways built than they were filled to capacity, and transportation departments began planning the next series of 'improvements'. Major roadways and expressways frequently produced destructive effects on the fabric and social coherency of existing communities. Meanwhile, the mounting number of cars on the road soon contributed significantly to the environmental pollution that would eventually seize the attention of governments in the 1970s. Moreover, the provincial urban road programs of the 1950s and 1960s tended to impoverish public transport facilities in all Canadian cities. This proved to be a factor of no small importance to low-income groups (some now dispersed and scattered by urban renewal) who became constrained in their choices of work place and residential community, and in their access to cultural, social, and retail facilities.

The end result of suburban neighbourhood planning and transportation planning was a radical transformation of Canadian cities into low-density, spread-out forms with enormous proportions of space dedicated to vehicular movement. In this condition, dependency on the private automobile became the dominant preoccupation in the planners' and the politicians' conceptions of a modernizing urbanism. It is questionable, however, whether public planning in Canada could have established itself much differently given the economic and technological revolution that put private means of transportation, namely, the automobile, in reach of virtually everyone, and turned the disposition of Canadians to consumerism and freedom of choice.

By the mid-1960s, the institutionalization of a public planning practice had been completed. Cities were now organized for plan-making in the styles we have described. The Town Planning Institute of Canada was revived (since renamed Canadian Institute of Planners). From fewer than thirty members in 1951, the corps of Canadian professional planners rose to some 600 in the mid-1960s. Most municipalities with a population over 25,000 employed full-time planning staffs. Four universities were offering professional education programs in the 1950s; the number rose steadily to eleven programs in 1972. By the mid-1980s, the corps of Canadian planners numbered over 3,500.

POST 1960s : CRITIQUE AND SEARCH FOR QUALITY, DIFFERENTIATION, AND PUBLIC PARTICIPATION

By the 1970s, critiques of planning practices that had evolved over the post-war years grew, and the planning system itself came under attack. The critique of the planning system in cities had five main themes: (1) the suburbs were sterile and cried out for more diversity of both environments and human activities; (2) the people most affected by major development ventures in the older, residential parts of the city had been ignored and were given no voice in planning decisions; (3) the vitality and security of city neighbourhoods was being destroyed by a narrow and regulatory, technocratic planning system that had seemingly been co-opted by business- and property-interests; (4) planning paid too little attention to concerns for environmental degradation; and (5) a generalized indifference among planners, architects, and politicians was abetting the destruction of historic places. The last-mentioned critique was influential in renewing an interest in visual and amenity qualities, or the art of city design (Carver 1962; Falkner 1977; Goodman 1971; Harvey 1973; Jacobs 1961; Sennett 1970; Spurr 1976).

In response to the critique, and to shifting societal values in the 1970s, the roles played by public planners underwent reformulation and differentiation. Changes in planning practice were not, however, attributable exclusively to the critique. In the 1970s and 1980s, newly-conceived opportunities and new demands for municipal services and public goods arose from several factors: expansion and change in the economy of Canada and its regions; the energy 'crisis' of the 1970s; re-defined markets in the property industry; and a flourishing of cultural and tourist-related pursuits.

An Outline of Change

The planned suburbs of the 1950s and 1960s grew and expanded. Many of them became towns and cities in their own right. As they matured and competed for their share of an ever-expanding market in 'homes', the planners began to give more attention to the quality of suburban environments, most notably in the creation of community or city centres (for example, Scarborough and North York). More call was made upon the arts of urban design and landscape design. In this shifting disposition of planning towards qualitative as opposed to uniquely-functional characteristics of urban environments, we can discern the beginnings of a response to the critique.

But still, the 'scientistic' land-use planning- and zoning-system perfected since the time of Thomas Adams dictated that one travelled 'downtown' or 'across town' to work, one drove to the 'mall' to shop, and so forth. The incompatibilities of this system with the longer-established lifeways of the city were slow to be recognized. In effect, zoning denied and progressively destroyed the traditional intermingling of work, manufacture, home, play, leisure activity, and retail trade that gave coherency, social meanings, and a sense of stability and place to urban communities.

Meanwhile, redevelopment/reconstruction gained momentum. Five key forces were at work. First among these was the relocation of existing industries to outer areas, where larger parcels of land next to rapid communications systems could be readily obtained. Two other development forces—corporate office-retail building and high-rise housing—defined the most profitable opportunity fields in which the property industry would operate from the early 1970s onwards. The demand for high-density housing and high-rise office sites was partly targeted at the lands traded by industries in their flight from city centres. It was also directed at established inner-city neighbourhoods where bargain-priced properties were abundant and resident populations were powerless to resist the intrusions. Fourth among the forces was urban transportation. Automobile ownership continued its rise, while the transportation of goods by railway was superseded by truck transport. From a strictly engineering 'logic', the routes penetrating and crossing the inner city, whether 'upgraded' streets or new expressways, needed to be immensely larger to carry goods and suburban commuters. And fifth, within the decade of the 1970s, the Canadian property industry was transformed to become a few, very large land development corporations.

Influential Changes and Responses in the Planning System

By far the most influential trends to occur in the 1970s and 1980s were the rise of citizen participation, the creation of large, powerful, pan-Canadian property-development corporations, and a differentiation of roles for the public planner. The 'urban protests' begun in the major cities in the 1960s carried through into the 1970s with increasing effect. Citizen groups first fought against urban renewal schemes that demolished old neighbourhoods and rooted people out. Neighbourhood groups were formed to battle against 'up-zoning'—the rezoning of inner-city residential properties from their low-density status to high-rise apartment or commercial buildings that would destroy community stability and established lifeways. Expressway construction schemes were fought, and notable victories were eventually won, such as the halting of the Spadina expressway in Toronto and the Bow River expressway in Calgary.

In these urban actions, we see the emergence of advocacy planning, a type of activism by which planners worked for citizen groups and community associations. These planners then pitted their expertise and insights against those of the planners at city hall, and against politicians and developers. The techno-bureaucratic planning doctrines of the 1950s were now challenged, and eventually a formal incorporation of citizen participation into the Canadian public planning system was obtained. It was no longer sufficient, or legitimate, for planners to produce plans and present them *fait accompli* to the public; urban residents were heard and allowed to provide direction to the development policies that affected their neighbourhoods and the city in general.

Until well into the 1960s, the land development and house-building business was mostly in the hands of small and independent, locally-based entrepreneurs. The power to regulate development and determine the nature and character of plans throughout the city and the suburbs rested comfortably with the public planners and the simple devices of zoning and master plans. During the late 1960s and 1970s, however, national corporations, such as Cadillac-Fairview, Trizec, and Olympia and York, came into being. They operated variously in the suburban arena and the 'ripe-for-reconstruction', inner-city districts. And they were now offering many types of products—shopping centres, retail and commercial office buildings, as well as housing.

What these new corporations brought into the planning system was a highly-integrated financial and production industry with the power to undertake development projects of a scale and complexity hitherto not encountered by municipal administrations. As a result, the public planners were increasingly forced to negotiate. Their ideals and visions, together with official standards and regulations, would now be placed on a bargaining table as official zonings were regularly abrogated by city councils eager to accept the blandishments of progress and investment proffered by the 'new' developers. In negotiations, public planners faced highly-trained and politically-sophisticated business teams possessed of immense financial power and influence. 'More than a dozen firms with assets of $100 million or more had emerged. . .'. (Lorimer 1988, 590.) By and large, planning principles came to play little part in the new field of *ad hoc*, negotiated development schemes. Eventually, many of our traditional planning doctrines, such as absolute public authority in plan-making and the idea of comprehensive city planning, were abandoned.

In essence, the expansionary-redevelopment period of the 1970s was one of crisis-management, and also a time for differentiation and further specialization of the roles played by planners. Managerial and business negotiation skills, financial and public administration know-how, and sophisticated technical skills in the packaging of development agreements between private and public-sector agencies had to be learned. Provincial governments were now active interventionists in urban development, particularly through housing, environment, energy, conservation, and cultural-heritage programs. Here too, managerial and policy-type planners with specialized skills came into demand. And, from the other side of the system, the communities and other non-governmental interest groups initiated demands for a type of planner who could facilitate a process of participation, mobilization of resources, and community decision-making. This type of planner was also to become an effective political operative for the advancement of community interests in a kind of counterpoise to the power and influence of the property industry.

As the 1980s proceeded, virtually all of the cities of Canada showed concerns for economic development or economic renewal. 'Strategic'- and 'economic'-type development plans made their appearance, while programs and legislative measures to make possible the revitalization of failing business districts were introduced. Legislation and funding programs made it possible and convenient for urban administrations to bring their planning resources to bear on tourism, festivals, and other cultural projects. Coincidentally, it was becoming evident that planning could no longer operate on the assumption of a unitary 'public interest' and a unitary value system among urban residents. Urban Canada had become multicultural; and a new pluralism of values and life styles had to be accounted for—both in the way that planning worked, and in the nature and appeal of community plans and urban designs.

By the middle of the decade, concerns for economic growth and development had effectively supplanted earlier concerns about energy conservation and the environment. Many of the planning departments that once were dedicated exclusively to making plans and administering by-laws were restructured as planning *and* development departments. The idea behind this reorganization was that local governments would themselves have a proactive role to play in developing strategies and implementing developments, and in delivering certain cultural and leisure services. Many cities had established urban design and architectural departments wherein city-initiated projects and/or partnership projects with private sector developers would be implemented. Only in the late 1980s was the environment *per se* again on the public agenda—although, we should note, without any clear direction on how to incorporate into urban affairs the notion of 'sustainable development', or how to respond to the 'greenhouse effect'.

As the 1980s came to a close, the planning system could no longer be identified solely with the regulatory land-use preoccupations of twenty years earlier. 'Planning' and 'development' are now very much less ideologically-oppositional terms than they once were. This is not to say that the confrontation of community-held values with the urban property industry and the commercialization of urban space is fully resolved. It is not—and never will be—in the liberal market-economy that Canadians have defined for themselves. The remarkable fact of urban planning as it evolved through the 1970s and 1980s is its resilience, its adaptability to shifting terms of the Canadian political economy, and its growing receptivity to the sensitivities of people at the level of local communities.

Urban Renewal and Neighbourhoods
In the 1970s changes were introduced in response to widespread resident protests against urban renewal and dissatisfaction with the type of replacement housing offered. Also, studies had shown that, contrary to the beliefs of planners and politicians, the 'slums' more frequently than not had significant social and cultural values for the community and the people

who inhabited them. These unmeasurable, non-monetized values could often outweigh or transcend the 'substandard' physical conditions of the housing itself. Public policy aimed at addressing these problems first came in the federal Neighbourhood Improvement Program (NIP) and the Residential Rehabilitation Assistance Program (RRAP). NIP and RRAP provided, for the first time, significant amounts of funding and professional services support for the restoration and improvement of older neighbourhoods.

Conservation-based strategies rather than demolition were now seen as desirable; funding could be channelled directly to neighbourhood associations, thus allowing them to plan and design improvement schemes in their own terms. 'Homeowners and landlords used the home improvement and rehabilitation funding to upgrade over 315,000 homes between 1974 and 1986.' (McAfee 1988, 1017.) In 1974, amendments to the National Housing Act allowed for new social housing to be built by municipalities, non-profit organizations, and co-operatives; some 110,000 assisted family homes and a comparable number of senior-citizens housing came into being during the next decade.

In these neighbourhood/home-improvement schemes of the mid-1970s through the 1980s, traditional planning doctrines were altered. Wholesale renewal and comprehensive city plans were put aside. Other significant changes were brought about: planners (and politicians) learned to work more closely with the people, allowing them decisions in the way their homes and neighbourhoods would be designed and improved; planning now recognized that modern urban society could not be addressed with 'homogenizing' policies and programs, zonings and regulations; and principles of orderly and efficient development in residential communities began giving way to a 'messier', more time-consuming participatory process of planning. This process involved first coming to understand the cultural and social life of individuals and neighbourhoods, and then dealing with redevelopment or environmental improvements according to the residents' own expectations and desires.

In many instances, city councils were compelled to down-zone selected inner-city areas so that their existing character and social fabric might be preserved. This spurred a significant level of privately-financed housing improvement and tended to stabilize (in at least a physical environment sense) large parts of the inner city. The Annex in Toronto and the Hillhurst-Sunnyside and Inglewood communities in Calgary are good examples. Stabilization occurred through several mechanisms: homes that had been divided up into rental suites were converted back to single-family homes; tenanted properties were sold to new resident-owners; and infilling of vacant or demolished lots with new housing brought investment and a fresh generation of families to the older communities. But the results were two-sided. If communities were stabilized and economically revitalized, they were no less eventually changed. Tenants were eased out as the communities became desirable for home-ownership, while property values increased, resulting in an exodus of lower-income families (an occurrence also abetted by the rising costs of housing through the period). This process of 'gentrification' could be only marginally mitigated by planning policies. (Chapter 13 offers a detailed outlook on inner-city change and gentrification.)

Historic Preservation

The changes in housing programs, together with the new approaches to planning in older residential communities, were accompanied—and oft-times supported—by changing public perceptions and attitudes about the historical/architectural fabric of cities. The first significant project came about by federal government fiat in the early 1960s: Prime Minister Diefenbaker's declaration of the 'Mile of History', a designation of Sussex Drive in Ottawa that included funding to the National Capital Commission for carrying out the property acquisitions and restoration works. This initiative was emulated in Victoria and Quebec City where resources were allocated by the provincial governments. However, as the historic preservation movement gathered momentum throughout the 1960s, governments wavered in their support for a generalized program; for it was clearly evident that in all cities, historic properties stood squarely in the path of the entrepreneurs' ventures in central-city redevelopment.

The procedures and policies introduced for historic preservation have helped to reshape our approaches to community planning and city development policies, and our educational programs for planners. They induced an assimilation into planning practice of a number of new technical skills, a renewed appreciation of architectural and urban design matters, and the innovative use of transfer of development rights, tax breaks, joint public-private sector projects, and new techniques of land use control. By the mid-1980s all of the major cities were hiring 'heritage planners' and 'heritage architects'.

Significant accomplishments have been made, most particularly in the cities of the Maritime Provinces and central Canada, where the presence of historic properties is pronounced compared to west of Winnipeg. Many cities use zoning and development control powers for historic preservation areas or sites. In a number of instances, whole districts are protected (the 'old' Montreal district, the historic, lower- and upper-town districts in Quebec City, Gastown in Vancouver, and areas of Halifax, Ottawa, and Victoria). The criteria for identifying important areas also underwent changes, from concerns for areas of the highest (or 'deepest') historical-architectural significance to interest in areas that contain buildings that are vernacular in nature and represent an everyday history (Jamieson 1984).

Increasing municipal activity in tourism is already posing challenges to the 'success stories' of historic preservation. Historic properties hold intrinsic value for tourism, but development projects that aim to attract tourists too frequently arrive in commercial packages that run counter to preservationist goals. The lower-town historic area of Quebec City is a case in point; one's image of the area is largely defined by T-shirt stands and ice-cream shops. How to respect the historic fabric of an area and at once cultivate its indigenous social character and economic dynamic is a dilemma facing heritage planners. One possible response is to adapt by-laws that prescribe in detail the uses and the type of occupancies of the buildings preserved. However, such measures would be highly interventionist and an administrative nightmare to implement.

Downtown Developments

As measured by the goal of producing human-scale, liveable city environments, the episode of downtown redevelopment cannot be rated much of a success. No provincial capital, however 'sleepy', and none of the major commercial or industrial cities escaped extensive downtown reconstruction. Even the most enlightened municipal bureaucracies and politicians appeared unable to deal with the tremendous power of the property industry. Provincial and federal governments were substantial players as well, often pursuing redevelopment schemes jointly with entrepreneurs, and invariably with immunity from local planning goals and regulations. The downtowns of virtually all cities were dramatically altered in character and form (see Lorimer 1978; 1988; Kemble 1989; and Mertins 1989).

While planners could claim successes in controlling change in selected inner-city residential areas, downtown cores were, generally speaking, transformed into densely-packed, homogenized zones of 'international'-style towers, convention centres, performing arts halls, and car parks. Many of these schemes destroyed the traditional street—as architectural facade, as a pedestrian movement system, and as a retail-commercial environment with diversity and multiple opportunities for choice. Streets were confined by block-long, 'impermeable' walls, sterile in appearance and in the social experience of being on them. Downtown developments took the public realm of the city indoors, sometimes underground, sometimes fifteen and more feet up, 'climatized' it, vegetated it with exotic plants, and appropriated it to commercial marketing ends. The blessings were decidedly mixed. Moreover, downtown became the place where ordinary families with children could no longer live for want of community facilities, amenities, or affordable housing.

No city council or planning department had the will or capacities to produce a visionary urban-design conception of public spaces, and an architecture that moves beyond private developers' standardized models. By the beginning of the 1970s, when central-city reconstruction took off, senior management of the public planning system had passed completely into the hands of the land-use processors and policy-type planners. Hardly anywhere was a city planning and development operation headed by persons with capacities in the art of city design. And the few urban designers actually in the service of planning departments were scarcely heeded.

Housing and Sociable Communities

Current housing problems attest to a failure on the part of the public planning system to achieve genuinely sociable communities, and to maintain or promote social equity and affordable choice. On the one hand, the social reform goals of the planning movement after World War II have largely given way to the middle-class NIMBY syndrome (*Not In My Back Yard*) and 'market economies' ethos of the present era. Some would argue further that the institutionalization of the planning movement, predicated as it was on a technocratic regulatory process led to the co-opting of 'planning' by a property industry that was unsympathetic to planning. There is truth in both assertions, a truth that serves to remind us how intertwined are politics and planning. In the matter of housing, it is senior government policies and fiscal priorities—not municipal administrative planning policies—that explain in the final analysis housing-community problems outlined here and in Chapter 14.

Planners in municipal administrations can, however, conceivably make some impact on the situation. There is no reason why they should not introduce into the development system affordable community designs and regulatory policies for new residential areas that compel rather than simply suggest social integration. In some jurisdictions, this is beginning to happen, with the imposition of specified percentages of affordable houses that have to be included in a development project. Another avenue could be a process of plan-making for existing communities that anticipates gentrification, and mobilizes communities towards solving their problems at the local level. Such programs would educate residents to become more receptive to the introduction of social housing in their neighbourhoods. The St. Lawrence Neighbourhood, a project of the 1970s situated in the east-downtown of Toronto, affords an excellent example of how various house designs, diverse forms of housing tenure, and a community-wide urban design/community design approach can be combined to achieve sociability and equitable opportunities.

Public-Private Partnerships

Public-private partnerships in city development projects blend together planning, design, and management resources of public- and private-sector agents; sometimes they blend public lands with private lands and capital, and commonly, capital funds from both partners. Partnerships represent one of the key developments in the planning field in the 1970s. They gained political popularity in North America as a way of remedying the inherent contradictions of a private-public 'split' (that is, the public authority plans and regulates, while private agents are expected to invest in and implement what the municipality plans). Partnerships most commonly make their appearance in downtown commercial building projects, for example, projects such as stadia and golf courses, hotels connected to convention centres, and waterfront redevelopments. The partnership approach seeks a compromise of objectives, and it provides for the resources of each party to be pooled. The purpose is to produce projects of a quality that could not be obtained by regulatory devices alone.

Whether the product of partnerships always meets this high purpose or satisfies at acceptable and reasonable cost the public's goals is open to serious question, as is the political morality of the practice! However, the practice is a significant innovation within public planning and is unlikely to be rescinded. It is difficult to balance public good with the need for the development industry to make a profit. In negotiations, planners require the skills to ensure that the private agents maintain their interest in participating in the project, and that public objectives are achieved at acceptable public costs. Most often, it appears, private goals have taken precedence. While public-private partnerships have been commonly used in the United States to attack housing needs, they have not been employed for that purpose in Canadian cities. There is no reason to believe, however, that such partnerships could not be made to work here.

Economic Revitalization

Initiatives have been taken in several cities to revitalize commercial areas, or in some cases, the economy of the city as a whole. Economic development 'strategy'-making and downtown revitalization projects represent quite recent adjuncts to the roles played by city planners. They are significant for the way in which they have altered our conception of what public-planning doctrine is or ought to be. They invariably imply a proactive rather than re-active, regulatory, and meliorative role for planners and city councils. Cities are now keen rivals in the search for business and industrial enterprises. To succeed, they must upgrade and up-scale the quality of their public environments, downtown amenities, and community and leisure services. As has been pointed out in Chapter 15, Business Improvement Areas (BIA) in Ontario and Business Revitalization Zones (BRZ's) in Alberta have been successful in revitalizing a number of city areas. Good examples are Bloor Street West in Toronto and the Uptown 17th Avenue area of Calgary. In these and similar projects elsewhere, a combination of merchants' organizations, integrated business promotions, streetscape improvements, and recruitment of new businesses to the areas have demonstrably helped to reverse or forestall business decline.

To these ends, public-private partnerships of one form or another are called into play: for implementing public works to embellish the environments of commercial districts and to provide public space amenities; to engage in marketing and promotions; to offer tax-relief incentives to attract new enterprises, etc. The public-private negotiations on development conditions for the Vancouver EXPO 86 lands in the late 1980s illustrate this kind of partnership; the linking together of economic development strategy-making and public environment improvements in development plans formulated in the 1980s for Hamilton, Sudbury, Saint John, Calgary, and other cities are other examples. In effect, the city planning system now incorporates the notion of 'public entrepreneurship', with all that this implies for altering the traditional tenets of 'good' public planning.

THE FUTURE OF PLANNING FOR CANADIAN CITIES

Planning Enters the 1990s

As we enter the 1990s, the function of planning in cities is being broadened in scope. The roles played by planners are becoming differentiated and specialized in response to enlarged municipal agendas. Planners' roles now embrace extensive community level plan-making with residents' participation, cultural-heritage projects, and special-place development schemes such as waterfronts and derelict industrial lands. This new breadth and differentiation assuredly reflects certain planning priorities founded in exigencies and opportunities of the present. But what of the challenges and choices that lie in the future?

Current demographic forecasts and economic prospects suggest that, with few exceptions, Canadian city-planning regimes will not be overwhelmingly preoccupied with the problems engendered by high-growth pressure. On the contrary, most of our urban communities will be actively involved in proactive, economic development planning—that is, in creating new job opportunities and devising strategies to retain present ones. In this respect, city planning and local economic development and promotion (marketing) are finding common ground. Already many cities are setting up 'task forces' of business and industrial representatives, politicians, and municipal planning officials to engage in strategic development planning and 'visioning' the future. For example, in 1989, in the City of Calgary, citizen committees, business representatives, and the Calgary Economic Development Authority jointly engaged in producing two visionary documents: *Vision 2020*, an outline of the city's future social and physical environments, and *A Strategy for Economic Development*.[9] Task groups related to the latter project continue to work on detailed sectoral planning for tourism, finance and management, high-tech industries, and other areas.

While environmental protection is for the most part a management and regulatory function of senior governments, there is little doubt that local governments will be increasingly drawn into both conservation and protection initiatives. Clean environment and amenity will be a new factor of competition in city programs for attracting new economic enterprises, which, for the most part, will be freed of the classical location dependencies of labour and markets. Contracted household budgets will combine with the mounting sensitivity of Canadians to environmental and conservation issues. One can expect what might be called a 'social reorientation'—such as demands for shorter work trips that would reduce household expenditures on transportation; user fees for water consumption and refuse collection at the doorstep, and planning regulations that allow certain forms of refuse composting and disposal in the neighbourhood and at the home site. At the same time, designing urban developments with greater attention being given to harmony with nature's processes and with sustainable development principles, will steadily make its way into planning practice. This environmental side of the changing urban-planning doctrine has been steadily growing in importance since the early 1970s. It flows from a number of sources: from the introduction of environmental sciences, environmental impact studies and resource management into planning-education programs; from the enormous expansion of city parks departments, and the capacities of these departments to plan, acquire, and develop extensive 'open space' lands; from political priorities that Canadians now give to environmental issues; and from the research and theory that has emerged in the last two decades.[10]

More significantly for the general issue of conservation-driven land use and city form, we should expect to see contracted budgets—both consumer and government—produce a downward shift in land consumption per household and housing-space standards. The challenge for public-planning agencies will be to produce, under their own authority, prototype urban design schemes and community management programs that compel entrepreneurs to build affordable communities—communities that cost less to 'enter' and less to maintain, and in which residents will play a role in providing collective services to themselves.

Uncertainties and Choices
If Canadian planners have learned anything in the past several decades, it is that there are multiple futures—multiple possibilities and choices. Moreover, most of the important forecasts produced in urban planning in the past two decades have been either wrong or thwarted by those who control the urban development process. And planning forecasts have frequently led to distorted public policies. For example, in Calgary, forecasts of very high population growth in the early 1980s (since proven wrong), spurred a municipal spending program out of proportion to present affordability. Forecasts and projections, we have learned, depend for their value on stable systems, on 'models' of the world that portray patterns of behaviour that do not change appreciably over time. But it was uncertainties, not stability, that characterized the period of the mid–1970s through the 1980s; and uncertainties will characterize the 1990s.

What we are only just learning is that the future can be willed. The future need not be determined exclusively by forces at work in the present. There are choices to be made; there is collective will to be exercised. As scientism and techno-rationality relax their grip on planning practice, urban planners will have to look to new and inventive, even 'opportunistic', styles of thinking about the future. They will have to become more strategic thinkers and doers. And should they not also become mobilizers of a political will to assert a visionary and directive rather than a solely adaptive, meliorative role? Within the larger visionary frame, planning will have to become more proactive, responsive to the quick turn of events, and more inventive in public-private partnership deals. And planners will have to focus more emphatically on designs for creating collective, as opposed to private, urban spaces. This task necessarily compels a new mode of thinking about how to build better the composite artifact we call 'city'; it calls for a mutual accommodation, a revived artistry, between planning and architectural philosophies, and their respective practices.

NOTES

1. For descriptive and normative accounts of public planning theory, a major treatise is offered in Friedmann (1987). Hodge (1986) provides a text on Canadian community planning as it is typically practised. Cullingworth (1987), Perks and Robinson (1979), Perks and Smith (1988), and Perks (1985b) can be usefully consulted for contemporary and historical accounts of planning in Canada. Kemble's (1989) extensively illustrated, critical commentary is the only book that specifically addresses urban design and the qualities and character of Canadian city spaces. Whittick (1974) is an excellent reference for synoptic accounts of persons and movements, countries, theories, and practices.

2. This congress was in fact a meeting of the National Conference on City Planning, a US organization that rallied all persons and interest groups participating in the planning movement in North America. The work of the National Conference was eventually taken over by professional associations of planners established in the United States and in Canada.

3. Sifton had earlier served as Minister of the Interior in Sir Wilfrid Laurier's government and continued to exercise influence in federal affairs.

4. The conference was addressed by proto-planners and politicians from Canada, the USA, and Britain. Topics covered a variety of preoccupations; for example: proposals for planning legislation in Canada; the introduction of 'zoning' in the USA and 'districting' in Germany; public transportation systems; playgrounds and parks; waterfront development in Toronto; and municipal financing and city planning.

5. Thomas Adams held his appointment at the Commission of Conservation from 1914 to 1921. He subsequently worked as a private consultant in Canada until 1923, then moved on to the directorship of the New York Regional Plan. See Simpson's (1985) authoritative biography; Chapters 4 and 5 of Simpson's book provide a detailed account of Adams's Canadian years.

6. Horace Seymour was to become Canada's leading planning practitioner of this early period and into the 1940s. He figured as project leader in the Vancouver Plan (1926–8) produced by the Harland Bartholomew consulting firm from the USA; he served as Alberta's first provincial director of planning

in the 1930s; and, as assistant to Adams at the Commission and later a consultant, he worked on many comprehensive plan projects for cities in Eastern Canada. See Bloomfield (1985).

7. The CMHC story is partly told in Humphrey Carver's autobiography, *Compassionate Landscape* (1975). See also his *Cities in the Suburbs* (1962).

8. Among the nefarious effects of the Modern movement was the treatment of the design of buildings as objects in space, not as elements composing an urban fabric or intended to contribute to the composition of urban spaces. A succinct critique of this and the impacts on modern planning and city building can be read in Roger Trancik, *Finding Lost Space* (1986). Kemble (1989) expands on this critique with reference to Canadian cities.

9. Calgary 2020 presents a vision in words of the future city. The text touches upon every conceivable sector of life and portrays, indirectly, current issues and problems in the city by depicting their resolution 'by the year 2020'. It is a promotional and marketing 'plan', written in the style of scenario. Hundreds of Calgary residents were divided into working groups to draft parts of the composite picture. The project was financed under the province's 'Vision 2020' program.

10. See, for example, Michael Hough (1984), Dorney and Rich (1979), and Robert Dorney (1989).

FURTHER READING

ARTIBISE, A.F.J. and STELTER, G.A. 1979 *The Usable Urban Past: Planning and Politics in the Modern Canadian City* (Toronto: Macmillan)

FRIEDMANN, J. 1987 *Planning in the Public Domain: From Knowledge to Action* (Princeton, N.J.: Princeton University Press)

HARVEY, D. 1973 *Social Justice and the City* (Baltimore: Johns Hopkins University Press)

HODGE, G. 1986 *Planning Canadian Communities* (Toronto: Methuen)

KEMBLE, R. 1989 *The Canadian City, St John's to Victoria: A Critical Commentary* (Montreal: Harvest House)

LORIMER, J. 1978 *The Developers* (Toronto: James Lorimer)

PERKS, W.T. and ROBINSON, I.M. eds 1979 *Urban and Regional Planning in a Federal State: The Canadian Experience* (Toronto: McGraw-Hill)

STELTER, G.A. and ARTIBISE, A.F.J. eds 1982 *Shaping The Urban Landscape: Aspects of the Canadian City-Building Process* (Ottawa: Carleton University Press)

REFERENCES

BLOOMFIELD, E. 1985 'Ubiquitous Town Planning Missionary: The Career of Horace Seymour', *Environments* 17, 29–42

——— 1982 'Reshaping The Urban Landscape?: Town Planning Efforts in Kitchener/Waterloo, 1912–1926' in G.A. Stelter and A.F.J. Artibise eds *Shaping the Urban Landscape: Aspects of the Canadian City-Building Process* (Ottawa: Carleton University Press)

CARVER, H. 1962 *Cities in the Suburbs* (Toronto: University of Toronto Press)

──── 1974 *Compassionate Landscape* (Toronto: University of Toronto Press)

COMMISSION OF CONSERVATION 1915 'National Conference on City Planning: Toronto, May, 1914', *Annual Report, Appendix 1*

CULLINGWORTH, J.B. 1987 *Urban and Regional Planning in Canada* (New Brunswick, N.J.: Transaction Books)

DORNEY, R.S. 1989 *The Professional Practice of Environmental Management* (New York: Springer-Verlag)

──── and RICH, G. 1979 'An Ecosystems Framework for Urban Design' in B. Perks and I. Robinson eds *Urban and Regional Planning in a Federal State: The Canadian Experience* (Stroudsberg, Pa.: Dowden, Hutchinson, and Ross)

FALKNER, A. 1977 *Without Our Past?* (Toronto: University of Toronto Press)

FRIEDMANN, J. 1987 *Planning in the Public Domain: From Knowledge to Action* (Princeton, N.J.: Princeton University Press)

GOODMAN, R. 1971 *After The Planners* (New York: Simon and Schuster)

HARVEY, D. 1973 *Social Justice and the City* (Baltimore: Johns Hopkins University Press)

HODGE, G. 1986 *Planning Canadian Communities* (Toronto: Methuen)

HOUGH, M. 1984 *City Form and Natural Process* (New York: Croom Helm)

──── 1985 'Changing Roles of Urban Parks—An Environmental View', *Environments* 17, 84–94

JACOBS, J. 1961 *Death and Life of Great American Cities* (New York: Random House)

JAMIESON, W. 1984 'Conservation as an Approach to Urban Renewal', *Plan Canada* 24(2), 44–54

KEMBLE, R. 1989 *The Canadian City, St John's to Victoria: A Critical Commentary* (Montreal: Harvest House)

LORIMER, J. 1978 *The Developers* (Toronto: James Lorimer)

──── 1988 'Development Industry' *The Canadian Encyclopedia* 2nd ed. (Edmonton: Hurtig Publishers)

MCAFEE, A. 1988 'Housing and Housing Policy' *The Canadian Encyclopedia* 2nd ed. (Edmonton: Hurtig Publishers)

MERTINS, D. ed. 1989 *Metropolitan Mutations : The Architecture of Emerging Space* RAIC Annual 1 (Toronto: Little, Brown & Co.)

PERKS, W.T. 1985a 'Idealism, Orchestration and Science in Early Canadian Planning' *Environments* 17, 1–28

──── 1985b 'Canada' in N. Patricios ed. *International Handbook of Land Use Planning* (New York: Greenwood Press)

──── and ROBINSON I.M. eds 1979 *Urban and Regional Planning in a Federal State: The Canadian Experience* (Toronto: McGraw-Hill)

──── and SMITH, P.J. 1988 'Urban and Regional Planning' *The Canadian Encyclopedia* 2nd ed. (Edmonton: Hurtig Publishers)

RUTHERFORD, P. ed. 1974 *Saving the Canadian City* (Toronto: University of Toronto Press)

SENNETT, R. 1970 *The Uses of Disorder* (New York: Alfred A. Knopf)

SIMPSON, M. 1985 *Thomas Adams and the Modern Planning Movement: Britain, Canada and the United States, 1900–1940* (New York: Mansell)

SMITH, P.J. 1988 'Commission of Conservation' *The Canadian Encyclopedia* 2nd ed. (Edmonton: Hurtig Publishers)

SPURR, P. 1976 *Land and Urban Development: A Preliminary Study* (Toronto: James Lorimer)

SUTCLIFFE, A. 1981 *Towards The Planned City: Germany, Britain, the United States and France, 1780–1914* (Oxford: Basil Blackwell)

TRANCIK, R. 1986 *Finding Lost Space: Theories of Urban Design* (New York: Van Nostrand Reinhold)

VAN GINKEL, B. 1988 'Urban Design' *The Canadian Encyclopedia* 2nd ed. (Edmonton: Hurtig Publishers)

WEAVER, J. 1988 'Urban Reform' *The Canadian Encyclopedia* 2nd ed. (Edmonton: Hurtig Publishers)

WHITTICK, A. 1974 *Encyclopedia of Urban Planning* (Huntington, N.Y.: Robert E. Krieger Publishing Co.)

20

People, Urban Space and Advantage

BETH MOORE MILROY

This chapter concerns social problems and policy for cities. It explores the theme that the advantages and disadvantages that cities convey to different people depend upon who these people are and what they do. With rare exceptions, the more tenuous one's relationship to money, social norms and legal codes, the harder it is to make a city work to one's advantage. This chapter is intended to help readers to become more aware of: (1) the way that urban spatial development affects the capacities of individuals to use cities to their advantage; (2) how those who are best endowed dominate urban space while those already most disadvantaged are buffeted around in Canadian cities; and (3) how land use, social groups, and city planning are interrelated in complex ways.

To achieve these three objectives we review history to show that groups have congregated in cities in a variety of patterns, and that the patterns we see today are neither inevitable nor fixed. As well, we look at how social services became an axis of reform as industrial capitalism increasingly took hold from the latter part of the nineteenth century.

We turn next to theories that examine some recent descriptions of people's relationships to space. Here we consider five types of theories that people have used to understand why certain groups occupy or move away from particular parts of cities.

In the subsequent section, some of the social groups found in Canadian cities are described. The basis for the groupings used here is not only what separates one group from another such as age, ethnicity, or gender, which are commonly employed. Distinctions are also based on the varying degrees of power people enjoy.

The next section deals with actions, that is the policies, planning, programs, and practices, that are directed towards solving the problem of cities being differentially advantageous for people. This is dealt with principally in a short case-study describing one city's experience regarding housing.

The paper concludes with a sketch of some of the current debates in the field of urban social groups and the underlying issues that need further study.

HISTORY

Industrialization and Urbanization

Canada in the nineteenth century was predominantly rural; its people were also engaged in the extraction and shipping of raw materials. Midway through the 1800s it was beginning to urbanize rapidly. (McCann and Smith provided details of this process in Chapter 4.) The process was dramatic. Ten-year growth percentages of urban centres reached as high as 81 per cent. While the decades of greatest growth varied across the country (for example, the early years of this century were the most dramatic for Winnipeg compared to Toronto's growth in the previous century), overall the country was rapidly moving from an agrarian to an urban society.

The towns and cities of the early part of the nineteenth century were characterized by small, locally-owned businesses (Katz 1977, 233). These urban centres did not specialize in the production of any one item, but rather produced a wide range of goods for local consumption; home and work place were usually integrated or close to one another; and little or no 'ghettoization' by income or special group existed (Katz 1977, 233; Careless 1977, 136). This was the pre-industrial Canadian city and, as Katz observes, if the extent of home- and work-place integration is an indicator of non-industrialization as some claim, then Canadian cities were only modestly industrialized if at all (Katz 1977, 232). As industrialization advanced, homes and work places were increasingly separated. This meant a complete shift in the functioning of family units from one in which most of what was needed was provided from the home to one that depended more on purchased goods and services and which emphasized men's labour outside and increasingly, women's labour inside the home. Apart from poorer women who worked in manufacturing (more particularly in the textile and garment sector), women's work was geared almost exclusively to reproducing and caring for families. In this sense, women can be said to have reproduced the country's labour force, generation after generation.

Not only were industrial cities marked by a complete split between home and work place, but in Canada they saw the richer and more stable working-class families gradually move out from the city centre towards the periphery. This movement began in the period of 1860 to 1880. One or two upper-class areas tended to remain very near but not in the core of the Canadian cities; classic examples are Rosedale in Toronto and Westmount in Montreal. The poorest, unskilled workers and all those least able to manage the new industrial way of life remained in the core (Goheen 1970, 194). As Artibise notes, the rich and poor were residentially (and in all other respects) isolated from one another. Further division by ethnicity marked cities such as Winnipeg, with its non-British immigrants, mainly Slavs and Jews, focused in the north end and the so-called 'charter-group' immigrants of British stock located in the south and west of the city (Artibise 1977, 312). A relatively undifferentiated residential pattern in early cities was thus supplanted by a pattern increasingly differentiated by income, ethnicity and compliance with social and legal norms.

Several distinct population groups defined in terms of age, gender and ethnicity emerged in industrial cities. For example, young women were attracted to Montreal and Quebec City as places to find work in manufacturing and domestic service, and migrated there in numbers considerably exceeding men (Cross 1977, 256). By contrast, men dominated resource centres like Winnipeg and became a noticeable population group, haunting bars and generally pursuing frontier-style living patterns. Immigrants represented 70 per cent of Winnipeg's population increase between 1881 and 1921. In 1881 Winnipeg's foreign-born population was about 33 per cent of the total, in 1911 56 per cent, and in 1921 48 per cent. In Winnipeg these immigrants were largely non-Anglo-Saxon, which led to more difficult integration for the new arrivals.

Families found themselves in the predicament of trying to coordinate production needs and reproduction needs (that is, needs associated with the basic physical and social requirements of human existence such as food, shelter, nurturing, the rearing of children . . .) in new ways as a result of the separation between work places and homes (Mackenzie 1980). Increasingly, families came to depend upon waged work—work from which one derives an income—and needed to acquire the skills, attitudes, schedules, education, and so on that industrial capitalism demanded. Education, which had previously taken place largely within the home and was geared towards the integrated home/work-place mode of life, was now provided largely by the state in order to inculcate those habits and attitudes appropriate to capitalist enterprise. Parts of food production and health services also moved outside the home, which could no longer be depended upon to provide these, especially if the wife-mother was also engaged in waged labour typical of the poorer families. In middle- and upper-class homes, the separation of waged work and home increasingly assigned housework and child-rearing work to women. As a result, two new social groups emerged: full-time housewives (Mackenzie 1988) and non-productive children, neither of whom contributed, in theory, to production, but instead were full-time consumers.

A further group can be identified, although not for the first time in a historical sense. This group was made up of the outcasts: the insane, the destitute, and the chronically ill. For these people, asylums were built. In Ontario, asylums tended to be built on the periphery of cities because treatment deemed peace and tranquillity as important for recovery. These buildings which were once on the outskirts, have been surrounded by urban development and are now in the inner cities. Today they are often the sites of out-patient services and the continuing hubs of service for populations which seek to stay in city cores.

Reforms

Let us now consider some of the actions undertaken to resolve the growing problems associated with a new form of economic production developing in an old urban landscape and in old social structures. Publicly, the problem was articulated as how best to help the poor, sick, unemployed, and insane. In a larger context, it must be seen as an effort to adapt people to new ways of production and changing urban conditions, or to modify the conditions so that urban society was not threatened by social upheaval and revolution (Rutherford 1977, 375).

It was recognized that not all poverty and ill-health was the fault of individuals' negligence: the city and socio-economic processes played a role in peoples' fates (Artibise 1977, 325; Rutherford 1977, 372). Reformers examined the physical and administrative conditions in cities, and found, for the most part, that they were deplorable. Housing and sanitation were particularly inadequate, contributing to the spread of contagious diseases. A better understanding of how diseases are spread led to the realization that disease could not be confined to a particular sector of a city or population. This appears to have supplied a prod to reform, according to several scholars who have identified self-interest rather than mercy as the spur that led to urban reforms (Copp 1974, 140; Weaver 1977, 406; Fingard 1977, 347).

The number of charitable organizations rose significantly in the early period of reform. For example, organizations that formed in Montreal around the turn of the century included the Montreal Parks and Playgrounds Association, the Victorian Order of Nurses, and the Charity Organization Society, an umbrella organization for a number of charitable groups (later called the Family Welfare Association and the Council of Social Agencies). Wolfe and Strachan (1988) provide a glimpse of how the city's elite formed organizations in response to civic problems, how the organizations were run—often with men forming the Board of Directors and women doing the hands-on work—and how this charitable work offered a social network, particularly for upper-class Montreal women.

Charitable organizations most readily helped the 'worthy' poor—those who had fallen upon hard times because of unemployment or illness. The 'unworthy' poor—those tempted by drink, prostitution, sloth, vagrancy, or other signs of wilful non-compliance with social norms—had to fend for themselves, or be prepared to take a lesson in morality along with the charity.

Modern urban planning began in this period. Overall, the effect was to expand the scope of civic bureaucratic work, as well as provincial and federal involvement in municipal matters. Zoning schemes were proposed to protect residential areas; suburbanization was recommended to relieve city centre-congestion. More aspects of civic life were regulated by reference to codes of minimum compliance in water, sanitation, housing, health, or buildings. However, as Weaver (1977, 408–9) pointed out, regulation did not benefit all sectors because it derived in part from prejudice, self-interest, and property value protection. A new set of conditions involving welfare, zoning and minimum standards had been laid down to permit the continuation of capitalist industrialism in a relatively tranquil social environment. This was maintained by adding formal state welfare measures when necessary through the 1920s to the early 1970s (Moscovitch and Albert 1987).

THEORY

In this section we look at five types of theories that have been used to describe and explain the location in cities of social groups. Table 20.1 provides a succinct outline to these five theoretical approaches.

The first and most influential of the theory types are *spatial competition* theories. These have been common in both geography and sociology. The

Table 20.1
Approaches to Understanding People's Clustering in Cities

	Household Preference	Public Decisions	Class[a]	Gender	Social Values
Spatial Competition	●				
Socio-spatial Management	●	●	○		
Class Competition		○	●		
Gender Relations			○	●	
Social Use			○		●

● Principal focus

○ Other foci explicitly taken into account

[a]Class may refer to one's role in an economic production system; alternatively, it may be a surrogate for income, race, ethnicity, handicap, minority or majority status, or any combination of these.

idea of using spatial competition to explain the location of social groups in urban space was initially borrowed from the biotic process of invasion and succession identified in ecology. Students of urban change saw this process as being analogous to the gradual movement of groups of people in cities moving outwards from the core to outer areas in succession. These theories of the Chicago School and, later, of Amos Hawley, were widely employed by sociologists and urbanists. A later version substituted economic variables for the ecological ones (Okraku 1987, 434). Spatial competition theories derived both from ecology and economics are covered extensively in texts such as Bourne's (1982) and critically assessed in several places (Saunders 1981 and Cooke 1983, 132–138).

There are two central problems with spatial competition theories in terms of their capacity to explain the location of groups in cities. One is that they place inordinate weight on the likelihood that people in cities will be able, within the constraints of budget, to live where they choose. In fact, most of us 'choose' where we live within highly constrained fields governed by such things as what housing space is unoccupied, what kind of housing is built, where we feel safe, what our aspirations are (see, for example, Michelson 1977). The key assumption that cities reflect expressed preferences is only partially supported empirically. A second problem with spatial competition theories is that they describe rather than explain where people reside. This is because social status (expressed as preferences constrained by budget) serves as both the cause of segregation and its effect (Cooke 1983, 135).

The remaining four types of theories either draw on spatial competition theories or have had less effect on urban-development thinking in Canada. The *socio-spatial management theories* are based on the economic version of spatial competition, but with one major difference. In the economic model public decisions that affect the development of cities are not considered explicitly. In socio-spatial management theories the selection of a location is presumed to take place in urban spaces that are already regulated to achieve publicly sanctioned goals (including certain housing densities, housing price ranges, or separation of industry from housing); and planned to accommodate public goods (such as parks, subways, or hospitals). These regulations and plans exist because without them the goals and goods thought beneficial to a city and its people (so-called 'public goods') would not be produced by the operations of the private sector 'market' economy. We therefore 'buy' them with public money (for instance, parks) or tease them from developers (for example, a prescribed number of housing units per hectare). These public decisions affect how land will be developed and, therefore, where specific groups will be able or willing to locate. For instance, the public decision in the 1970s not to build an expressway in Vancouver that would have passed through residential areas east of the city core, served to guide subsequent decisions concerning land development. Low-cost housing in its proposed pathway was not torn down. But these properties greatly appreciated in value in the ensuing years because, by keeping the access to the inner-city areas at the same level while the Greater Vancouver Region's population was increasing, these areas were sought after by more and more people who prized short commuting distances. Some ramifications of public decisions taken in the interests of socio-spatial management are described in Goldberg and Mercer (1986). For instance, one effect of appreciating values is to reduce the amount of housing available at the lower end of the market, assuming no countervailing action is taken.

Class competition theories offer a completely different perspective. In this case, development is said to result from competition for space among social classes, as well as among fractions of a class such as landholders, developers and industrialists (which are all fractions of the capitalist class). These struggles determine who will be able to locate where in urban space, and to what advantage. Ultimately, it is claimed, people locate according to the opportunities provided by their class membership, that is, their capacity to exert their power over the production of space; and they do so in cities in which capital is already accumulated in buildings, at nodes in transportation networks, and therefore in patterns that reflect the values of a capitalist economy.

Classic struggles occur when capitalists want a parcel of land for production and citizens want the same space for housing or other social uses. One of many illustrations of such a struggle is captured in Helman's (1987) description of the battle for central city-housing in the Milton-Parc area of Montreal. Developers wanted to demolish six city blocks of low-cost, low-rise housing and small shops. They planned to increase the capital return from the land by intensifying its use with high-rise apartments, commercial space, and a hotel. The financiers and developers bought up the land and housing, and received approval of their scheme from the City of Montreal, as well as public assistance in several forms, including massive upgrading of water and other services in the area. Helman describes the inter-class battle that ensued. A citizens' organization was formed, and through sustained and often very imaginative protest, succeeded in derailing some of the developers' plans. They saved many of the century-old, two- and three-storey greystone residences in the area from demolition, established nearly six hundred co-operative and non-profit housing units, and kept hundreds of other low-cost units from disappearing.

Theories of gender relations propose that peoples' location in cities reflects the state of the relationship between men and women in a specific era and place. Primary attention is paid to gender relations, an element that is missing from the other theories. Theorists in this group claim that, although the explanations of urban structure and residential location found in the three previous groups of theories are useful, they obscure the basic activity every community must have, which is 'reproducing' ourselves—procreating, caring for and nurturing ourselves. They argue that the way in which the two main activities—nurturing and goods production—are organized (as between men and women, within families, shared partially by families and by the state, or shared in other ways) will have implications for urban structure. (See Moore Milroy, forthcoming, for fuller discussion of these points.) For example, the separation between homes and work places in cities since the nineteenth century, makes it difficult for a person to engage in both production and domestic functions. A contemporary shift in urban structure and residential location is being signalled now because, with the majority of women in the labour force, more compact home/employment arrangements are being sought. It is theorized that the way in which these arrangements are defined will influence the structure of a city and its social group distribution.

The fifth group of theories draws mainly on *sociological traditions*. Here, other researchers look at social segregation from the point of view of how social groups *use* space rather than how they acquire it. For example, the use of urban space by ethnic minorities and low-income groups has been researched extensively (Chimbos and Agocs 1983; Gans 1962; Suttles 1968). These studies examine the advantages and disadvantages of clustering to certain groups: do similarities among people provide a supportive environment on balance, are these groups attempting to maintain their difference from others? Frequently these studies describe in great detail how people order their social relationships within quite small geographic areas—a street corner, a few blocks, a neighbourhood. These studies' focus on the ways in which social values are expressed in space suggests people voluntarily decide these values, and seems to ignore the ways in which economics, politics, and culture help to shape them.

Nonetheless, these sociological studies are salutary in comparison to the economic models of utility maximization. This group of sociological studies offers a glimpse at the rich relationships among gender, ethnicity, class, handicap, income, and rejection of norms on the one hand, and urban location on the other. People from different social groups evidently use city space differently because they experience it differently.

TYPES OF SOCIAL GROUPS WITHIN THE CITY

A Typology

We now want to describe some types of groups found in cities using a framework that helps explain their distribution in space in relation to one another. One way to approach this is to investigate what serves to set the distance between being powerful and powerless, and the processes by which this happens. Winchester and White (1988, 37) categorize groups using their relationships to 'economic standards, social norms, and legal codes'. These relationships determine the extent of power different groups enjoy. This discussion will consider in turn the impact of these three types of relationships on social groups.

Economic standards refer to the ability to maintain an 'adequate' standard of living ('adequate' is relative to other groups in the society rather than absolute). Employment is an important factor for most in fulfilling at least basic food, shelter, and clothing needs. For some, access to money through family connections or pensions may moderate the influence of employment status. One's relationship to economic standards will significantly influence one's tenure, the amount of space one can occupy, one's type of dwelling structure, and where one can reside locationally within a city that is organized around a competitive real property market.

Relationship to *social norms* describes the degree of adherence to acceptable behaviour and attitudes. What is socially acceptable is determined by the attitudes and behaviour favoured by political and economic elites (Winchester and White 1988, 38). The behaviour and attitudes of some groups may be considered unacceptable or potentially threatening (for example, homosexuals, political radicals, street gangs, beggars, panhandlers); other groups may be all but invisible (e.g. the 'worthy' poor).

Thirdly, *legal codes* establish a range of behaviours that are determined by people in authority. Some of these behaviours are illegal, and some are criminalized by imputation. Street people, including a wide range of subgroups who reject mainstream social behaviour, often find themselves in an 'isolated social position, accentuated by the absence of normal labour and housing market participation. Illegality comes about through vagrancy and through activities such as squatting, trespass, begging, petty pilfering, or aggression that result in imputed criminalization'. (Winchester and White 1988, 41.)

There are, then, sets of unwritten social conventions within which individuals conduct their daily lives. These conventions establish ranges within which we are able, as a society, to read the degree to which an individual has achieved or adheres to the behaviours and attitudes that are sanctioned by the society at a given time. The actual dimensions of these economic, social and legal standards change with time.

One or more of these aspects—economic, social and legal—may simultaneously characterize a group. For example, Winchester and White (1988, 40) classify the unemployed and especially the long-term unemployed, impoverished elderly, students, and single parent (mainly single-mother) families as economically marginal. Among those who are both economically and socially marginal are ethnic minorities and people with mental or physical handicaps or disorders. Still other groups combine legal marginalization (whether formally or by imputation) with some economic or social aspects, or both. Examples are illegal immigrants, street people, criminals, prostitutes, and homosexuals.

The classification of groups in this way is not meant to reduce the very real complexities of people's lives, but rather to provide a way to visualize the perpetual marginalizing and mainstreaming processes played out in cities. The processes by which people come to feel powerless and set apart from others in their community need to be understood if the nature of social-group disparities is to be grasped.

The Economically Marginal

The numbers of unemployed, underemployed, and working poor have shifted dramatically over the 1970s and 1980s. In 1988, every sixth child in Canada was growing up in poverty (National Council of Welfare 1988); one-quarter of Canadian households could not afford adequate housing. Riches reported in 1987 that 75 soup kitchens serving the unemployed and the working poor were operating from Nova Scotia to British Columbia (Riches 1987), a number that had risen to 180 by late 1989 (CBC 1989). Labour income, which had increased in dollars by 140 per cent from 1975 to 1987 represented only a real increase of 1.5 per cent after adjustment for inflation. In fact, wages and salaries fell by 1 per cent in real terms; the 1.5 per cent increase was solely the result of increases in employee benefits (Wong 1988). A large percentage of the labour force does not have access to those benefits, especially part-time workers. The proportion of part-time workers who said they would prefer full-time work increased 374 per cent between 1975 and 1986 (Akyeampong 1987), with the highest rates among women (Armstrong and Armstrong 1987).

Long-term unemployed people as their resources are depleted, must seek very low-cost accommodation, usually in older housing that has been converted from single-family dwellings to multiple dwellings, and found in city centres. As unemployment insurance payments are exhausted, the next line of defence is social assistance. In Ontario, as one example, those transferring from federal unemployment insurance payments to provincially funded General Welfare Assistance (which is short-term aid for employable people) experience a substantial drop in income (see National Council of Welfare 1986). Those renting in the private market and living on General Welfare Assistance or Family Benefits (long-term support for families and disabled) often pay 60 per cent to 80 per cent of their incomes on housing, and must depend on soup kitchens, purchases from secondhand stores, and donations for other basic necessities. The inadequacies of Ontario's social assistance principles and programs are detailed in a report prepared for the Ministry of Community and Social Services (1988).

The impoverished elderly are primarily women. This is partly because these women depend heavily on government pensions as they do not have private retirement plans derived from a lifetime of paid employment, and partly because they live an average of six to seven years longer than men. They are principally urban dwellers, often in homes they own outright but are barely able to maintain.

Single-parent families represent the fastest growing group of poor Canadians. There are over 700,000 single-parent families with children under 18 years of age living at home. In 67 cases out of 100 the reason for single parenting is divorce, separation, or the death of a spouse (Moore 1988, 41). In about 85 per cent of the cases the parent is female. Mother-led families are the poorest; their incomes averaged less than half that of two-parent families in 1985. The combination of poverty and family encumbrances makes these families highly vulnerable to discrimination in the private housing market. They are the most in need of residential locations that offer a range of educational, health, recreational, and retail services as well as employment within short distances—in areas that are physically safe for women and children (Klodawsky and Spector 1988; Wekerle 1985).

Economically and Socially Marginal

Individuals belonging to ethnic and racial minorities, especially if they are visibly distinct from the majority, will likely be in the economically and socially marginal category. Balakrishnan (1982, 101) found that in the largest metropolitan areas of Canada (excluding Montreal) 'residential segregation between ethnic groups closely follows patterns of "social distance" between them', and the pattern is based on increasing social distance from Anglo-Saxons.

Other groups that experience a combination of economic and social marginalization are those with various physical and mental disorders. The total numbers of people who might be classified in these categories are imprecise. This is not surprising, since the count includes only those who describe themselves in these terms, appear at public agencies for assistance, or are known to advocacy groups. However, attempts to estimate the sizes of these populations in Canada and the United States have been made. According to Dear and Wolch's assessment of these studies, approximately 3 per cent of the population may be physically disabled (1987, 259), and another 3 per cent may be mentally retarded, although no more than 1 per cent will probably be classified as such. Moreover, at any given time, nearly 20 per cent of adults is estimated to be affected by a definable psychiatric disorder. Besides these, 'a further (unknown) proportion of undeclared mental illness exists among persons whose behaviour is socially "undesirable", including alcoholics, drug abusers, homeless persons, and parasuicides' (Smith and Giggs 1987, xvii). Sufferers from AIDS may also find themselves economically and socially stigmatized by being denied employment, shelter, and freedom to move about in a community (see, for instance, Goodman 1988; Kimble and Labonte 1987; Quaggin 1987).

Legal Plus Economic and/or Social Marginalization

Data are not available for all these groups, especially with respect to their location and overall numbers in a given city. For example, data are scant for both male and female prostitutes (Symanski 1981, 10–12), homosexuals, criminals, participants in drug cultures, and illegal immigrants. These groups generally seek anonymity. This is not, however, universally the case. Winchester and White give an interesting example of the different

Table 20.2
Number of Shelters Identified and Capacities by Type of Clients

Location	Men & Women[a]		Women		Men		Youth		Battered Women[b]		Total	
	No.	Capacity	No.	Capacity	No.	Capacity	No.	Capacity	No.	Capacity	No.	Capacity
Newfoundland	3	29	2	36	1	40	1	14	6	87	13	206
P.E.I.	0	0	0	0	0	0	0	0	1	16	1	16
New Brunswick	2	60	3	60	2	59	0	0	10	193	17	372
Nova Scotia	2	75	1	18	2	166	1	10	6	95	12	364
Quebec	16	391	6	67	16	827	8	47	69	1,227	115	2,559
Ontario	12	613	20	326	27	2,401	14	187	98	1,752	171	5,279
Manitoba	2	76	3	197	4	585	0	0	10[c]	43	19	901
Saskatchewan	0	0	2	28	2	143	0	0	9	205	13	376
Alberta	8	296	3	105	8	1,015	2	48	24	518	45	1,982
B.C.	10	257	5	239	6	559	2	22	35	492	58	1,569
Yukon	0	0	0	0	0	0	0	0	1	16	1	16
N.W.T.	2	98	0	0	0	0	0	0	5	59	7	157
Total Canada	57	1,895	45	1,076	68	5,795	28	328	274	4,703	472	13,797

NOTES: [a]Includes shelters for families.
[b]Includes women and children. Capacity was estimated for 104 of the shelters for battered women.
[c]Includes safe homes.

SOURCE: McLaughlin 1987, 3.

strategies employed by homosexuals in Paris: male homosexuals take an out-in-the-open approach while females tend to be relatively covert (1988, 48–9).

Another group in this category is the homeless. Homelessness grew substantially in the 1980s. On the night of 22 January, 1987 efforts were made in Canada to count the homeless (McLaughlin 1987). The best estimate was that about 10,000 found a place to sleep in one of the 472 shelters across the country that night. This compares to an estimated 100,000 who had used shelters during the entire preceding year. Table 20.2 shows the total number of shelters and beds in Canada by group served, and Table 20.3, the number and capacity of shelters that answered the 1987 survey as well as their occupancy rate. A range somewhere between 130,000 and 250,000 is a conservative estimate of people currently homeless in Canada, given that not all of the homeless use shelters on a given night. Over and above that figure, thousands more are near-homeless, living in temporary or seriously inadequate housing.

Canada's homeless are not the stereotypical elderly, alcoholic men or 'tramps'. Sixty-one per cent of the people who stayed in shelters were men, 27.5 per cent were women, and 11.5 per cent were children under age 15. The 1,271 women and children who stayed in shelters for battered women represented 16.4 per cent of the total number of people in shelters. Over half were receiving social assistance, but still were unhoused. Table 20.4 gives further information about the people sheltered.

Parolees and those under mandatory supervision make up another group in the legal, economic, and socially marginalized category. In Canada, there

Table 20.3
Shelter Bed Counts for 22 January 1987

Location	No. of Shelters Reporting[a]	Capacity	No. of People	Occupancy Rate (%)
B.C.	41	1,231	715	58.1
Alberta	31	1,751	1,118	63.8
Saskatchewan	11	348	259	74.4
Manitoba	10	756	587	77.6
Ontario	95	3,677	3,268	88.8
Quebec	62	1,461	1,360	93.1
P.E.I.	1	16	0	0.0
Nova Scotia	10	306	188	61.4
New Brunswick	12	262	147	56.1
Newfoundland	8	151	94	62.3
N.W.T.	1	44	9	20.4
Yukon	1	18	6	33.3
CANADA	283	10,021	7,751	77.3

[a]Includes shelters that have answered the questionnaire.
SOURCE: McLaughlin 1987, 4.

Table 20.4
Personal Situations of People Who Sought Shelter on 22 January 1987

Situation	People	Per Cent of Sample
Unemployed	4,239	54.7
Current or ex-psychiatric patient	1,556	20.1
Receiving social assistance	3,995	51.5
Evicted	726	9.4
Alcohol abuser	2,580	33.3
Drug abuser	1,163	15.0
Physically handicapped	237	3.1

SOURCE: McLaughlin 1987, 5.

are over 130 community-based residential centres specifically directed to parolees; of these, 15 are for women and 13 serve both women and men. These centres range in size from three beds to over one hundred, but most are in the smaller range. About 46 per cent have 15 beds or less, and another 36 per cent have 16 to 25 beds (estimated from Correctional Services of Canada 1985). The community correctional centres are scattered across the country, but just over half of them are in census metropolitan areas.

Location and Concentration
Core areas of cities are highly contested territories because many different social groups want space in them. In the 1950s and 1960s, divestment from central-city real estate was a major social and planning concern (Drover, Wolfe, and Skelton 1980). Areas were 'redlined'—that is, financiers would not provide mortgages and fire insurance was hard to obtain in these areas. As a result, repairs were withheld. This situation shifted rapidly to super-investment in the early 1970s (see Ley, Chapter 13, and Harris, Chapter

14). In both cases, the movement of private capital resulted in the same public problem: how to provide adequate housing and services for vulnerable people for whom these areas of relatively high density were advantageous. Of course, the actions differed. In the following section, the actions of one city in the throes of super-investment in central-city housing will be described.

Considerable attention has been given to the locations of those who are service-dependent, whether in housing, income support, drug therapy, sheltered day programs, permanent lodging for the chronically ill, and so on. Dear and Taylor (1982), Dear and Wolch (1987), and Taylor (1988) explain city-centre concentrations of group homes and services for the mentally ill in Ontario partly in terms of the historical development of the original health centres built in the nineteenth century. Dear and Wolch (1987) describe this trend specifically for Toronto. They show that group homes for ex-psychiatric patients in Toronto are concentrated in the Parkdale area west of the city core near the Queen Street Mental Health Centre, which was established in 1850. Similar concentrations of service-dependent populations are found, for example, in and very near the downtown core of Ottawa (The Regional Municipality of Ottawa-Carleton Social Services Department 1984). Residential areas there are characterized by old houses converted to several small units, and buildings that combine retail, small businesses and dwellings. Gradually, these old houses are bought and redeveloped, displacing service-dependent people and attracting wealthier occupants. Common social services and land-use planning concerns can be identified through such mapping, as well as showing the need for community planning so that these people have options.

Some recent studies have looked at how gender relations influence location of groups in cities. In particular, Rose and Villeneuve (1988) and Rose (1989), in their study of inner-city areas of Montreal, related changes regarding where employed women reside with the types of jobs available in nearby areas and alterations to neighbourhood services. They suggest that inner-city gentrification is partly influenced by changes in women's employment situation (which is itself influenced by alterations to other aspects of gender relations); and that gender-sensitive studies are needed to understand how gentrifiers use the housing stock and alter neighbourhood services (Rose 1989, 133).[1]

The typology shown in Table 20.1 and discussed here lends some coherence to the complex web of relations that links money, social norms, and legal status to urban segregation. Let us now consider actions taken to deal with the differences in various groups' needs.

ACTIONS

In Canada there is substantial inequality of income and opportunity. We expect public policy-makers to act to ameliorate, if not resolve, the effects of poverty, unemployment, and disability.

Drover and Moscovitch (1981, 5–6) discuss approaches that public policy-makers take to solving the problems of social inequality, arguing that in Canada we tend to view solutions in terms of some mix of: (1) conservative individualism in which individuals are supposed to maximize their own welfare; (2) liberal intervention by the state to moderate the excesses of industrial capitalism; and (3) institutionalized redistribution on the basis of need as in the social democratic tradition. In any city, a range of views broadly reflective of these three positions will be expressed whenever there is pressure to deal with needs. It might appear that very different actions are suggested by the various ideological positions but in the end it does not seem to make all that much difference. This at least is the view of Schmidt (cited in Banting 1987, 311) who says that 'the combination of a capitalist economic structure and democratic political arrangements seems compatible with widely divergent policy stances'.

An income-security system made up of transfer payments and tax programs was introduced gradually from the 1920s to 1970s, along with a wide range of specific programs in areas such as health, education, and housing. From time to time, explicit pressure is exerted by business and industry to reduce and eliminate programs, and countervailing pressure is brought to bear by citizens' organizations to retain and expand them. Banting (1987) and others have shown that the Canadian welfare system is very modest compared with those in other OECD countries. The impact of public expenditure and taxation in Canada appears to have been only mildly redistributive, if at all, when one considers that income shares by quintile have barely changed after a half-century of programs, and that home-ownership, which used to be widely accessible across quintiles, is increasingly reserved for the upper two-fifths (Hulchanski and Drover 1987).

A snapshot case-study of Ottawa in the mid–1980s conveys some sense of how policies, plans, programs, and practices can develop in one locality around one area of social provision, in this case—housing. Housing has been chosen as an example because it is one of the most important areas in which municipalities contribute to redistributing resources and opportunities among social groups.

Background

The City of Ottawa, with a population of about 305,000 is the urbanized centre of the Regional Municipality of Ottawa-Carleton (population about 585,000). The Region is an administrative unit in Ontario. In all regions, provision of municipal services are made the responsibility either of the regional government or of the municipalities within the region. Functions such as public transit, police, the maintenance and building of major transportation routes, and social welfare services tend to be regional undertakings, while libraries, local roads, parks, and most housing matters tend to fall to municipalities. Land-use planning is undertaken at both levels, and municipal plans must be compatible with those at the higher level. In the case presented here, because social-services planning and some aspects of housing (e.g. emergency housing) are handled by the Region (or RMOC), we will frequently refer to this level of government although the City of Ottawa remains the principal focus.

The RMOC is comprised of eleven municipalities and townships, covering more than 2,700 square kilometres. The population, which is 90 per cent urban, is growing, showing a 5.1 per cent increase from 1976 to 1981 and a 10.9 per cent increase from 1981 to 1986. The age structure of the population is changing: there are considerably fewer children under 14 years of age and many more people in the age range of 25 to 44 than in 1976.

The Region is located south west of the Ottawa River. Several bridges connect it to Hull, Quebec, and people move readily between the two

Table 20.5
Ottawa: Actors and Actions Related to Housing

INFORMATION/ EDUCATION	— Series of reports prepared about losses of low-cost housing. — Consultants hired to develop a 'housing strategy'. — Mayor's Task Force on Housing formed in 1985. — Housing data base developed. — Policy-making regarding affordable housing strengthened.	— Federal rehabilitation program prepared. — Reports on women's problems in housing market prepared. — Conference on housing and disabled held. — Permanent housing committee for generating and diffusing information was active.
SERVICE PROVISION	— Built and acquired low-cost housing through City Living, Ottawa's municipal non-profit housing corporation. — Managed public housing using Ottawa-Carleton Regional Housing Authority.	— Used government programs to build, acquire, and maintain housing for service dependent groups.
LAW	— By-laws passed to restrict conversions to condominiums.	— Pressure exerted for laws to restrict losses of low-cost housing.
SOCIAL ACTION	— Pressured the provincial and federal governments for more money and better programs.	— Marches — Teach-in — Media stunts — Community education furthered through media meetings. — Forced political debate, e.g. on the revision of the Regional Plan.
COMMUNITY DEVELOPMENT	— Participated with other municipalities on housing concerns (Association of Municipalities of Ontario; Federation of Canadian Municipalities). — Assisted non-profit housing and co-operatives organize to find land or buildings, etc.	— Built co-operative and non-profit housing. — Formed organizations around poverty, landlord and tenant issues, food banks. — Neighbourhood associations and groups investigated housing in their areas.

centres for work, shopping and entertainment. Together, Ottawa-Hull forms the urban core of the census metropolitan area and, as well, the urban core of the National Capital Region.[2]

Politics
Ottawa was tending towards a liberal-social democratic ideology with respect to social well-being in the mid–1980s. It had a relatively activist city council and mayor, some of whom had been elected to office in the 1970s when that city, like so many others in Canada, the United States, and Western Europe, was the site of repeated protests about the forms of urban development that politicians and planners were promoting, or at least permitting. Sparked by this unrest, Ottawa had had a ten-year neighbourhood planning process that had helped to develop a number of citizens' groups and local leadership skills (Andrew and Moore Milroy 1986).

Social problems were interpreted largely as the effects of economic activity rather than as problems that individuals brought upon themselves through sloth or carelessness. They were believed to be exacerbated by the rapid recapitalization of central areas, resulting in the least able citizens being squeezed out to make room for the most able. These problems were seen to be resolvable by a combination of public-spending policies and legal clout with private goodwill and good sense.

The Social Planning Council of Ottawa-Carleton, a quasi-public body funded jointly by the United Way and local governments, documented the many areas of concern in a report called *Trends 1985*. The report was published just before the municipal elections of that autumn so as to draw attention to the extent to which twelve basic needs of nine, particularly vulnerable, social groups in the community were being met. The identified needs included, among others, income, employment, health, housing, food, transportation, and child care. The particularly vulnerable populations included children, youth, street people, seniors, disabled people, and ethnic and racial minorities. We concentrate here on housing, the need that the study identified as the Region's most pressing concern.

Sectors and Actions
Let us consider the range of actions that people in Ottawa in the mid–1980s took to improve the housing situation for special groups in the face of an increasingly acute shortage of affordable housing. Table 20.5 shows a selection of undertakings by citizens and the governments of Ottawa and the RMOC.

Certainly there was a substantial and sustained involvement. Beginning in the late 1970s, research reports began to show the loss of low-cost housing in the central areas that resulted from a number of initiatives (Ottawa 1979a; 1979b; 1981; Moore Milroy et al. 1982; Barton 1983). One of these was the federal Residential Rehabilitation Assistance Program for rental units (discussed earlier in Chapter 14). About one-quarter of the tenants were estimated to have been displaced because of the way units were rehabilitated under this program. Rents charged to incoming tenants were significantly higher than those paid by displaced tenants. Research also showed the loss of rooming houses (57 per cent of the stock lost from 1976 to 1985); losses from severing rental (often row-housing) units to convert them to ownership tenure (lost at an average rate of 360 units a year in the early 1980s); and the losses from conversions of rental units to condominium tenure. In the late 1970s, the City prohibited condominiums conversions, and put legal barriers in the way of demolition. The Region prepared a housing statement in 1984 (funded by the province) that detailed virtually every aspect of the housing situation in its jurisdiction (RMOC 1984). The City also hired consultants to examine the housing situation and to develop a 'housing strategy' (Peter Barnard Associates 1984). In addition it commissioned a special Mayor's Task Force in 1985 to develop and recommend solutions to the housing problem.

Meanwhile, City Living, Ottawa's municipal non-profit housing corporation, continued to build, acquire, and manage units, making use of all the provincial and federal programs it could. It gave assistance regarding land acquisition to 'third sector', or mixed public- and private-housing groups that were building projects under private non-profit and co-operative programs; tried to maximize the number of units for handicapped people built into municipal non-profit units; and used City equity-financing to acquire a six-door row-housing structure that it converted to a 46-room rooming house (City Living 1985). Two more rooming houses were opened by the City soon afterwards.

The Social Planning Council of Ottawa-Carleton had a permanent housing committee that served as a point of contact and information dispersal for all those interested in housing issues in the Region. Various initiatives were promoted by interested parties who met through that organization. The strategy was loosely defined as a community-development approach, making facilities, contacts, and information available to encourage people to lobby and undertake community-building initiatives.

The new notion of empowerment was embraced within some of the organizations dealing with de-institutionalized people. Service workers tried to give individuals support while enhancing their sense of efficacy and self-determination. Others were pursuing, with some success, educational campaigns to heighten the general public's awareness of mental and physical disabilities, and trying to organize seniors.

Citizen participation and pressure were important. For instance, when the Region's official plan was being reviewed in the mid–1980s, a number of neighbourhood and other organizations (including the Social Planning Council) banded together to try to convince the Region's Planning Department and councillors of several concepts. One of these was that land use and individual well-being are related, in the sense that where one lives within an urban-centred region has an effect on one's ability to pursue activities within the city, in particular if one is disadvantaged relative to the majority.

Sectors and Groups

Housing may be provided by various sectors, alone or in combination. These sectors are: the state; the voluntary service sector; neighbourhood exchange or barter; the household; or the market. Combinations are frequent, such as state/household pairing for foster-care programs, and state/voluntary-sector liaisons to support private non-profit housing corporations. Changes in economic and family structures will affect the amounts of shelter provided by each sector, its location in urban space and the time-space budgets of city dwellers. It is most important to realize that we speak here of shelter which absolutely must be provided for everyone somehow. If the market does not produce it, it must still be provided by another sector. Appendix 5 which is located at the back of the book describes in detail the housing available for particular groups by the sector providing it.

In Ottawa, untold numbers of volunteer hours are spent developing, funding, and running housing for special groups. As well, all levels of government are involved in producing an array of housing. The municipal level encourages housing development in Ottawa through its housing department and its wholly-owned municipal non-profit housing corporation, City Living. The Region operates through its housing department, as well as through its social services department, which issues various welfare benefits, that include special housing subsidies to some clients. The province of Ontario is involved through the Ministry of Housing and the Ministry of Municipal Affairs because of its direct and joint provision and management of certain housing forms (especially municipal non-profit housing, public housing management, rent supplements and, since 1986, private non-profit housing) as well as through the ministries of community and social services and health, which provide so-called 'programing dollars' to pay for the assistance given to individuals in group homes and certain other facilities.

Approximately 15 per cent of households are served in this way in the RMOC. There are always waiting-lists of families and individuals in need of the housing units provided within these programs. In Ottawa, there would commonly be two lists, each with about 2,000 names on it. Beyond the 15 per cent of households provided for, at least another 10 per cent is in poverty. These people must manage by staying with relatives or friends, live on the streets, have one of the few low-cost rental units available in the city, or live in inadequate housing.

The actions directed towards special groups have brought their plight to the public's awareness, and some hardship has been alleviated. But the systemic basis of that marginalization has barely been questioned—that is, its roots in the economic, social, and legal norms discussed in connection with the typology above. Lack of housing is treated mainly as a misfortune befalling some individuals who are inadvertently caught in a housing market temporarily ill-attuned to their needs. Despite tremendous effort on the part of thousands, Ottawa, like other cities, has a homeless, near homeless, and low-income population repeatedly squeezed out of housing options. This is not a problem that is being solved.

DEBATES

The assumption underlying public policy, including planning, is that public actions will serve the public good. A corollary is that public actions will tend towards evening out the distribution of wealth rather than the reverse. One would expect, then, from decades of public intervention that trends in the distribution of income and opportunity would be less uneven than they are. However, as seen, the long-term trends show that income distribution is essentially static (Banting 1987; Prager 1988; Wolfson 1986), while opportunity for home-ownership is falling off for those in lower income groups (Hulchanski and Drover 1987). Indeed, polarization is increasing along tenure and income lines, a phenomenon also noted in other countries (e.g. Hamnett 1984). No advantage for the poorest groups has been realized, other than the negative one of not falling further behind according to certain income indicators. We must surely question public actions that merely rearrange disadvantages in urban space.

A second theme is how groups exercise power, especially concerning the siting of affordable housing and various public facilities. Opposition to these kinds of buildings is not a new phenomenon. Dear and Wolch (1987, 21) cite T.J.W. Burgess who, in 1898, made these observations about the siting of an asylum in the Montreal area:

> The chief grounds on which the plaintiffs based their opposition to the new asylum were: that the erection of the building and the maintenance and carrying on of an asylum on the site chosen constituted a public nuisance, and was a source of injury and damage to them, decreasing the value of their property, especially as sites for villas and elegant dwellings; and that they, the plaintiffs, would be exposed to constant annoyance, inconvenience, and danger, with great risk of disease through the contamination of the air and the pollution of the Rivers St. Lawrence and St. Pierre by the sewage from the hospital.

The reasons given today for opposing all types of non-market housing are similar: decreasing property values, increasing traffic, and lack of safety. Similarly, these issues are raised in cases of locating disposal sites for society's wastes, expanding facilities like hospitals, or developing urban-transportation corridors.

Some professionals accuse property owners of narrow-mindedness because they refuse to have any public good 'in their backyards'. However, the resistance to public facilities could be interpreted as an effort by property owners to keep some control over their immediate environment. The effects of these disputes are to harden the lines between the haves and the have-nots, erode goodwill, and reduce the location options available to those who already have least.

The process of de-institutionalizing developmentally delayed and psychiatrically handicapped individuals from large facilities to community settings is a third theme. The underlying philosophy of integrating these people in communities as opposed to separating them in institutions is fully supported. However, neither sufficient money nor adequate supportive arrangements have been made available to carry out the process (Lord and Hearn 1987). Therefore, the level of integration achieved is minimal. Group homes may be little more than institutions without walls. They also tend to be clustered in so-called 'urban service ghettos' where a range of social services facilities are concentrated, such as around the Queen Street Mental Health Centre in Toronto. This is a new phenomenon in cities, aggravated by the two previous themes of poverty/dependency and battles to control land uses.

Finally, feminists challenge the weight urban planners give to economic efficiency in deciding public actions. Investment in the development of residential neighbourhoods separated from production centres, and in private transportation spatially disadvantaged women more than it concerns men. Women are poorer, less mobile, and far more frequently encumbered by family responsibilities. This is a structural, or systemic problem. Women are pressing for more mixed land uses that place employment, homes, day-care centres, retail and services within close proximity.

There seem to be two main avenues for resolving these debates. One would make cities in which all women and men could be equally efficient and productive. The other, more radical, alternative would question whether efficient production is a legitimate aim, and is the appropriate guide for city building. Efficient production does not, after all, deal with care and nurturing, which are also important activities in our lives. An alternative paradigm would emphasize inter-subjectivity, relationships, and association. Cities would have to be conceptualized as places for inter-subjective experiences, only some instances of which would relate to production. In a world of material limits, made all too obvious by degraded physical environments, it would make sense to redirect some of our energy from making objects to learning how to associate in ways that do not create redundant people shoved to the margins of social existence. Neighbourhoods in such a vein would accommodate both productive and nurturing work; and in the symbiosis implied by those activities, would also make room for more heterogeneous populations.

NOTES

1. Labour force participation by women has increased steadily since the end of World War II, when it was about 24 per cent, to 55.9 per cent in 1986. According

to the 1986 census, women in the younger age brackets participated at very high rates (20- to 24-years, 80 per cent; 25- to 34-years, 73 per cent). A high rate (61.2 per cent) was also recorded for married women with children at home, who were living with their spouses (Statistics Canada 1988, 7–8).

2. There are three levels of planning in most southern Canadian urban areas: municipal, regional and provincial. This is the case for Ottawa; however, being the nation's capital, a further federal level, the National Capital Commission, administers the National Capital Region. Yet another federal involvement in the city's physical planning is through the Department of Public Works, which administers the Parliamentary Precinct (mainly the Parliament Hill area and south across Wellington Street to Sparks Street). Federal initiatives are excluded in this chapter except as they occur in housing under the National Housing Act, which is administered by Canada Mortgage and Housing Corporation.

FURTHER READING

ANDREW, C. and MOORE MILROY, B. 1986 'Making Policies and Plans for Neighbourhoods: Ottawa's Experience', *Plan Canada* 26, 34–9

BALAKRISHNAN, T.R. 1982 'Changing Patterns of Ethnic Residential Segregation in the Metropolitan Areas of Canada', *Canadian Review of Sociology and Anthropology* 19, 92–110

CHAN, K.B. 1986 'Ethnic Urban Space, Urban Displacement and Forced Relocation: the Case of Chinatown in Montreal', *Canadian Ethnic Studies* 18, 65–78

DEAR, M.J. and WOLCH, J.R. 1987 *Landscapes of Despair: From Deinstitutionalization to Homelessness* (London: Polity Press)

MCLAUGHLIN, M.A. 1987 *Homelessness in Canada: The Report of the National Inquiry* (Ottawa: Canadian Council on Social Development)

MOSCOVITCH, A. and ALBERT, J. eds 1987 *The 'Benevolent' State: the Growth of Welfare in Canada* (Toronto: Garamond Press)

SMITH, C.J. and GIGGS, J.A. eds 1987 *Location and Stigma: Contemporary Perspectives on Mental Health and Mental Health Care* (Boston: Unwin Hyman)

REFERENCES

AKYEAMPONG, E.B. 1987 'Involuntary Part-time Employment in Canada, 1975–1986', *Canadian Social Trends* (Autumn), Statistics Canada Catalogue 11–008E

ANDREW, C. and MOORE MILROY, B. 1986 'Making Policies and Plans for Neighbourhoods: Ottawa's Experience', *Plan Canada* 26, 34–9

ARMSTRONG, P. and ARMSTRONG, H. 1987 'The Conflicting Demands of "Work" and "Home"' in K.L. Anderson et al. *Family Matters: Sociology and Contemporary Canadian Families* (Toronto: Methuen)

ARTIBISE, A.F.J. 1977 'Divided City: The Immigrant in Winnipeg Society, 1874–1921' in G.A. Stelter and A.F.J. Artibise eds *The Canadian City* (Toronto: McClelland and Stewart)

BALAKRISHNAN, T.R. 1982 'Changing Patterns of Ethnic Residential Segregation in the Metropolitan Areas of Canada', *Canadian Review of Sociology and Anthropology* 19, 92–110

BANTING, K.G. 1987 'The Welfare State and Inequality in the 1980s', *Canadian Review of Sociology and Anthropology* 24, 309–38

BARTON, D. 1983 *Housing in Ottawa-Carleton: A Women's Issue* (Ottawa: Elizabeth Fry Society)

BELL, C. and NEWBY, H. 1972 *Community Studies: An Introduction to the Sociology of the Social Community* (New York: Praeger)

BOURNE, L.S. ed. 1982 *Internal Structure of the City* (New York: Oxford University Press)

CARELESS, J.M.S. 1977 'Aspects of Urban Life in the West, 1870–1914' in G.A. Stelter and A.F.J. Artibise eds *The Canadian City* (Toronto: McClelland and Stewart)

CBC 1989 'Open House', November 26

CHIMBOS, P. and AGOCS, C. 1983 'Kin and Hometown Networks as Support Systems for the Immigration and Settlement of Greek Canadians', *Canadian Ethnic Studies* 15, 42–56

CITY LIVING 1985 *Somerset Street Rooming House: An Evaluation* (Ottawa: City Living)

COOKE, P. 1983 *Theories of Planning and Spatial Development* (London: Hutchinson)

COPP, T. 1974 *Anatomy of Poverty: The Conditions of the Working Class in Montreal, 1897–1929* (Toronto: McClelland and Stewart)

CORRECTIONAL SERVICES OF CANADA 1985 *Directory of Community-based Residential Centres in Canada 1985–86* (Ottawa: Ministry of Supply and Services)

CROSS, S. 1977 'The Neglected Majority: the Changing Role of Women in Nineteenth Century Montreal' in G.A. Stelter and A.F.J. Artibise eds *The Canadian City* (Toronto: McClelland and Stewart)

DEAR, M.J. and TAYLOR, S.M. 1982 *Not on Our Street* (London: Pion)

────── and WOLCH, J.R. 1987 *Landscapes of Despair: from Deinstitutionalization to Homelessness* (London: Polity Press)

────── and MOSCOVITCH, A. 1981 'Inequality and Social Welfare' in G. Drover and A. Moscovitch eds *Inequality* (Toronto: University of Toronto Press)

DROVER, G., WOLFE, J.M., and SKELTON, I. 1980 'Inner City Real Estate Activity in Montreal: Institutional Characteristics of Decline', *The Canadian Geographer* 24, 349–67

FINGARD, J. 1977 'The Relief of the Unemployed: the Poor in Saint John, Halifax, and St John's, 1815–1860' in G.A. Stelter and A.F.J. Artibise eds *The Canadian City* (Toronto: McClelland and Stewart)

GANS, H. 1962 *The Urban Villagers* (New York: The Free Press)

GOHEEN, P.G. 1970 *Victorian Toronto, 1850 to 1900: Patterns and Process of Growth* (Chicago: Department of Geography, University of Chicago)

GOLDBERG, M.A. and MERCER, J. 1986 *The Myth of the North American City* (Vancouver: University of British Columbia Press)

GOODMAN, E. 1988 'The Trials of Eric Smith', *New Maritimes* 7, 14–24

HAMNETT, C. 1984 'Housing the Two Nations: Socio-tenurial Polarization in England and Wales 1961–81', *Urban Studies* 21, 389–405

HELMAN, C. 1987 *The Milton Park Affair: Canada's Largest Citizen-Developer Confrontation* (Montreal: Vehicule Press)

HULCHANSKI, J.D. and DROVER, G. 1987 'Housing Subsidies in a Period of Restraint: The Canadian Experience' in W. Van Vliet ed. *Housing Markets and Policies under Fiscal Austerity* (New York: Greenwood Press)

KATZ, M.B. 1977 'The People of a Canadian City, 1851–1852' in G.A. Stelter and A.F.J. Artibise eds *The Canadian City* (Toronto: McClelland and Stewart)

KIMBLE, E. and LABONTE, R. 1987 'Better Ways of Living, Better Ways of Dying', *New Internationalist* 15, 24–5

KLODAWSKY, F. and SPECTOR, A. 1988 'New Families, New Housing Needs, New Urban Environments: the Case of Single Parent Families' in C. Andrew and B. Moore Milroy eds *Life Spaces: Gender, Households, Economy* (Vancouver: University of British Columbia Press)

LORD, J. and HEARN, C. 1987 *Return to the Community: The Process of Closing an Institution* (Kitchener, Ont.: Centre for Research & Education in Human Services)

MACKENZIE, S. 1980 *Women and the Reproduction of Labour Power in the Industrial City: a Case Study* (Working Paper 23, Urban and Regional Studies, University of Sussex)

———— 1988 'Building Women, Building Cities: Toward Gender Sensitive Theory in the Environmental Disciplines' in C. Andrew and B. Moore Milroy eds *Life Spaces* (Vancouver: University of British Columbia Press)

MCLAUGHLIN, M.A. 1987 *Homelessness in Canada: The Report of the National Inquiry* (Ottawa: Canadian Council on Social Development)

MICHELSON, W. 1977 *Environmental Choice, Human Behaviour, and Residential Satisfaction* (Oxford: Oxford University Press)

———— 1985 *From Sun to Sun: Daily Obligations and Community Structure in the Lives of Employed Women and their Families* (Totowa, New Jersey: Rowan and Allanheld)

MOORE, M. 1988 'Female Lone Parenthood: the Duration of Episodes', *Canadian Social Trends* Autumn 40–2, Statistics Canada Catalogue 11–008E

MOORE MILROY, B. et al. 1982 *A Study of Tenant Displacement Associated With the Residential Rehabilitation Assistance Program* (Ottawa: School of Urban and Regional Planning, University of Ottawa)

———— forthcoming 'Planning, Space and Gender: Taking Stock', *Journal of Planning Literature*

MOSCOVITCH, A. and ALBERT, J. eds 1987 *The 'Benevolent' State: The Growth of Welfare in Canada* (Toronto: Garamond Press)

NATIONAL COUNCIL OF WELFARE 1986 *Progress Against Poverty* (Ottawa: National Council of Welfare)

—— 1988 *Child Care: A Better Alternative* (Ottawa: National Council of Welfare)

OKRAKU, I.O. 1987 'Age Residential Segregation in Canadian Cities', *Canadian Review of Sociology and Anthropology* 24, 431–52

ONTARIO MINISTRY OF COMMUNITY AND SOCIAL SERVICES 1988 *Transitions: Report of the Social Assistance Review Committee* (Toronto: The Ministry)

OTTAWA, CITY OF, COMMUNITY DEVELOPMENT DEPARTMENT 1979a *Instability and Tenant Displacement Within the Inner City Rental Market* (Ottawa: The City)

—— 1979b *Public Funding of Private Renovations in Ottawa* (Ottawa: The City)

—— 1981 *Rental Housing Crisis in Ottawa* (Ottawa: The City)

PETER BARNARD ASSOCIATES 1984 *City of Ottawa Strategic Housing Study: Phase 1 Report* (Toronto: P. Barnard Associates)

PRAGER, C.A.L. 1988 'Poverty in North America: Losing Ground?', *Canadian Public Policy* 14, 52–65

QUAGGIN, A. 1987 'Home Care of AIDS Patients Will Remain Rare', *Canadian Medical Association Journal* 15, 867

REGIONAL MUNICIPALITY OF OTTAWA-CARLETON, PLANNING DEPARTMENT 1984 *Regional Housing Statement Update* (Ottawa: The Region)

RICHES, G. 1987 'Feeding Canada's Poor: The Rise of the Food Banks and the Collapse of the Public Safety Net' in J.S. Ismael ed. *The Canadian Welfare State* (Edmonton: University of Alberta Press)

ROSE, D. 1989 'A Feminist Perspective of Employment Restructuring and Gentrification: The Case of Montreal' in J. Wolch and M. Dear eds *The Power of Geography* (Boston: Unwin Hyman)

ROSE, D. and VILLENEUVE, P. 1988 'Women Workers and the Inner City: Some Implications of Labour Force Restructuring in Montreal, 1971–81' in C. Andrew and B. Moore Milroy eds *Life Spaces* (Vancouver: University of British Columbia Press)

RUTHERFORD, P. 1977 'Tomorrow's Metropolis: The Urban Region Movement in Canada, 1880–1920' in G.A. Stelter and A.F.J. Artibise eds *The Canadian City* (Toronto: McClelland and Stewart)

SAUNDERS, P. 1981 *Social Theory and the Urban Question* (London: Hutchinson)

SMITH, C.J. and GIGGS, J.A. eds 1987 *Location and Stigma: Contemporary Perspectives on Mental Health and Mental Health Care* (Boston: Unwin Hyman)

SOCIAL PLANNING COUNCIL OF OTTAWA-CARLETON 1985 *Trends 1985* (Ottawa: The Council)

STATISTICS CANADA 1988 'The Daily' (Tuesday March 1, 1988) Cat. no. 11–001E (Ottawa: Statistics Canada)

SUTTLES, G.D. 1968 *The Social Order of the Slum* (Chicago: University of Chicago Press)

SYMANSKI, R. 1981 *The Immoral Landscape: Female Prostitution in Western Societies* (Toronto: Butterworths)

TAYLOR, S.M. 1988 'Community Reactions to Deinstitutionalization' in C.J. Smith and J.A. Giggs eds *Location and Stigma: Contemporary Perspectives on Mental Health and Mental Health Care* (London: Unwin Hyman)

WEAVER, J.C. 1977 'Tomorrow's Metropolis Revisited: A Critical Assessment of Urban Reform in Canada 1890–1920' in G.A. Stelter and A.F.J. Artibise eds *The Canadian City* (Toronto: McClelland and Stewart)

WEKERLE, G. 1985 'From Refuge to Service Center: Neighbourhoods That Support Women', *Sociological Focus* 18, 79–95

WINCHESTER, H.P.M. and WHITE, P.E. 1988 'The Location of Marginalized Groups in the Inner City', *Environment and Planning D: Society and Space* 6, 37–54

WOLFE, J.M. and STRACHAN, G. 1988 'Practical Idealism: Women in Urban Reform, Julia Drummond and the Montreal Parks and Playgrounds Association' in C. Andrew and B. Moore Milroy eds *Life Spaces* (Vancouver: University of British Columbia Press)

WOLFSON, M.C. 1986 'Stasis Amid Change—Income Inequality in Canada 1965–1983', *Canadian Statistical Review* 24, vi–xxvii

WONG, F. 1988 'Trends in Labour Income' in *The Labour Force* Cat. no. 71–001 monthly (Ottawa: Statistics Canada)

APPENDIX 1: URBAN DEFINITIONS, STATISTICS CANADA, 1986

CENSUS AGGLOMERATION (CA)

Concept and General Criteria

The general concept of a census agglomeration (CA) is one of a large urbanized core, together with adjacent urban and rural areas which have a high degree of economic and social integration with that core.

A CA is defined as the main market area of an urban area (the urbanized core) of at least 10,000 population, based on the previous census. Once a CA attains an urbanized core population of at least 100,000, based on the previous census, it becomes a census metropolitan area (CMA).

CAs are comprised of one or more census subdivisions (CSDs) which meet at least one of the following criteria:

(1) the CSD falls completely or partly inside the urbanized core;

(2) at least 50% of the employed labour force *living* in the CSD *works* in the urbanized core; or

(3) at least 25% of the employed labour force *working* in the CSD *lives* in the urbanized core.

Regular and Consolidated CAs

In some parts of the country, adjacent CAs are socially and economically interrelated. When this occurs, they are grouped into a single consolidated CA. A regular CA, on the other hand, is free-standing. It is either not adjacent to another CA or not sufficiently related to another CA to be consolidated.

To be eligible for consolidation, the total community interchange between the adjacent CA must be equal to at least 35% of the labour force living in the smaller CA. After consolidation, the original CAs become subregions (called *primary* CAs) within the consolidated CA.

CENSUS METROPOLITAN AREA (CMA)

Concept and General Criteria

The general concept of a census metropolitan area (CMA) is one of a very large urbanized core, together with adjacent urban and rural areas, which have a high degree of economic and social integration with that core.

A CMA is defined as the main labour market area of an urban area (the urbanized core) of at least 100,000 population, based on the previous census. Once an area becomes a CMA, it is retained in the program even if its population subsequently declines.

Smaller labour market areas, centred on urbanized cores of at least 10,000 population, are included in the census agglomeration (CA) program.

CMAs are comprised of one or more census subdivisions (CSDs) which meet at least one of the following criteria;

(1) the CSD falls completely or partly inside the urbanized core;

(2) at least 50% of the employed labour force *living* in the CSD *works* in the urbanized core; or

(3) at least 25% of the employed labour force *working* in the CSD *lives* in the urbanized core.

Regular and Consolidated CMAs

In some parts of the country, adjacent CMAs and CAs are socially and economically interrelated. When this occurs, they are grouped into a single consolidated CMA. A regular CMA, on the other hand, is free-standing. It is either not adjacent to another CMA or CA, or is not sufficiently related to another CMA or CA to be consolidated.

To be eligible for consolidation, the total commuting interchange between the adjacent CMAs and CAs must be equal to at least 35% of the labour force living in the smaller CMA or CA. After consolidation, the original CMAs and CAs become subregions (called *primary* CMAs and CAs) within the consolidated CMA.

URBAN AREA

Refers to a continuously built-up area having a population concentration of 1,000 or more and a population density of 400 or more per square kilometre, based on the previous census. To be considered as continuous, the built-up area must not have a discontinuity exceeding two kilometres.

In addition to the above, many other commercial, industrial and institutional land uses may be considered as urban even though they do not meet the population and density requirements. Examples include commercial and industrial areas, railway yards, airports, parks, golf courses, cemeteries, etc.

RURAL AREA

Refers to all territory lying outside of "Urban Areas".

(above quoted from: *Census of Canada 1986* 'Population and Dwelling Counts: Provinces and Territories', Ottawa 1987)

APPENDIX 2: CANADIAN CITIES (CENSUS AGGLOMERATIONS AND CENSUS METROPOLITAN AREAS) 10,000 POPULATION AND OVER†

SIZE CLASS	NEWFOUNDLAND	P.E.I.	NOVA SCOTIA	NEW BRUNSWICK	QUEBEC	ONTARIO	MANITOBA	SASKATCHEWAN	ALBERTA	B.C.	YUKON	CANADA TOTAL
10,000–19,999	CARBONEAR, CA GANDER, CA LABRADOR CITY, CA	SUMMERSIDE, CA		CAMPBELLTON, CA	COWANSVILLE, CA DOLBEAU, CA LACHUTE, CA LA TUQUE, CA MAGOG, CA MATANE, CA MONTMAGNY, CA	COBOURG, CA COLLINGWOOD, CA ELLIOT LAKE, CA HAILEYBURY, CA HAWKESBURY, CA KAPUSKASING, CA KENORA, CA KIRKLAND LAKE, CA LEAMINGTON, CA LINDSAY, CA SIMCOE, CA TILLSONBURG, CA WALLACEBURG, CA	PORTAGE LA PRAIRIE, CA SELKIRK, CA THOMPSON, CA	NORTH BATTLEFORD, CA SWIFT CURRENT, CA YORKTON, CA	CAMROSE, CA LLOYDMINSTER, CA	CRANBROOK, CA DAWSON CREEK, CA FORT ST. JOHN, CA KITIMAT, CA POWELL RIVER, CA PRINCE RUPERT, CA TERRACE, CA	WHITEHORSE, CA	41
20,000–29,999	GRAND FALLS, CA			EDMUNDSTON, CA	ALMA, CA RIVIÈRE-DU-LOUP, CA SAINT-GEORGES, CA SEPT-ÎLES, CA VAL-D'OR, CA	OWEN SOUND, CA PEMBROKE, CA STRATFORD, CA WOODSTOCK, CA			GRAND PRAIRIE, CA			17
30,000–49,999			NEW GLASGOW, CA TRURO, CA	BATHURST, CA	BAIE-COMEAU, CA JOLIETTE, CA RIMOUSKI, CA ROUYN, CA SAINT-HYACINTHE, CA SAINT-JÉRÔME, CA	BROCKVILLE, CA CHATHAM, CA MIDLAND, CA ORILLIA, CA TIMMINS, CA	BRANDON, CA	MOOSE JAW, CA PRINCE ALBERT, CA	FORT MCMURRAY, CA	COURTENAY, CA PENTICTON, CA VERNON, CA WILLIAMS LAKE, CA		26

SIZE CLASS	NEWFOUND-LAND	P.E.I.	NOVA SCOTIA	NEW BRUNSWICK	QUEBEC	ONTARIO	MANITOBA	SASKATCHE-WAN	ALBERTA	B.C.	YUKON	CANADA TOTAL
50,000–99,999		CHARLOTTE-TOWN, CA		FREDERICTON, CA	SALABERRY-DE-VALLEYFIELD, CA SOREL, CA THETFORD MINES, CA VICTORIAVILLE, CA DRUMMOND-VILLE, CA GRANBY, CA SAINT-JEAN-SUR-RICHELIEU, CA SHAWINIGAN, CA	BARRIE, CA BELLEVILLE, CA BRANTFORD, CA CORNWALL, CA GUELPH, CA NORTH BAY, CA PETERBOROUGH, CA SARNIA, CA SAULT STE. MARIE, CA			LETHBRIDGE, CA MEDICINE HAT, CA RED DEER, CA	CHILLIWACK, CA KAMLOOPS, CA KELOWNA, CA MATSQUI, CA NANAIMO, CA PRINCE GEORGE, CA		24
100,000–249,999	ST. JOHN'S, CA		SYDNEY, CA	MONCTON, CA SAINT JOHN, CMA	CHICOUTIMI-JONQUIÈRE, CMA SHERBROOKE, CMA TROIS-RIVIÈRES, CMA	KINGSTON, CA OSHAWA, CMA SUDBURY, CMA THUNDER BAY, CMA		REGINA, CMA SASKATOON, CMA				13
250,000–999,999			HALIFAX, CMA		QUEBEC, CMA	HAMILTON, CMA KITCHENER, CMA LONDON, CMA OTTAWA-HULL (Partly in Province of Quebec), CMA ST. CATHARINES, CMA WINDSOR, CMA	WINNIPEG, CMA		CALGARY, CMA EDMONTON, CMA	VICTORIA, CMA		12
1,000,000 +					MONTREAL, CMA	TORONTO, CMA				VANCOUVER, CMA		3

†See Appendix 1 for definitions   Source: Statistics Canada, *Census Canada 1986, Census Metropolitan Areas and Census Agglomerations—Population*. Ottawa: Ministry of Supply and Services, 1987. Catalogue 93-104.

APPENDIX 3: SELECTED DATA ON CANADA'S CENSUS METROPOLITAN AREAS, 1986

Rank. CMA	1 Population 1986 (000)	2 Population change 1981–1986[a] (%)	3 Recent immigrants, 1981–86 (% of population 5 years and over)	4 Foreign born (% of population)	5 Less than grade 9 (% of population 15 years and more)	6 University degree (% of population 15 years and more)	7 Labour force participation (%)	8 Unemployment rate (%)	9 Labour force engaged in manufacturing occupations (%)	10 Labour force engaged in finance, insurance, real estate and government service (%)	11 Per capita income ($)	12 Index of low Income[b] (%)
1. Toronto	3,427	9.5	4.6	36.0	13.8	13.8	72.5	5.5	22.5	9.6	15,600	11.4
2. Montreal	2,921	2.1	2.2	15.7	21.2	11.0	64.8	11.3	20.4	11.6	12,600	16.3
3. Vancouver	1,381	8.9	4.0	23.4	10.1	12.0	68.3	11.4	12.0	12.3	13,900	11.0
4. Ottawa-Hull	819	10.1	2.5	13.4	10.9	17.6	71.2	7.7	6.9	30.0	15,100	12.5
5. Edmonton	786	6.0	3.1	18.2	9.7	11.9	73.3	10.4	9.0	15.1	13,400	10.7
6. Calgary	671	7.2	3.8	20.6	7.1	14.9	75.3	10.0	8.7	12.2	15,100	10.4
7. Winnipeg	625	5.6	2.6	17.9	13.4	11.3	68.5	7.8	14.5	14.9	12,700	14.1
8. Quebec City	603	3.3	0.7	2.3	18.4	12.0	64.5	11.9	8.7	23.0	11,900	15.0
9. Hamilton	557	2.8	1.8	24.1	14.7	9.1	66.8	7.0	27.4	9.6	13,300	12.3
10. St. Catharines	343	0.2	1.4	20.4	16.7	6.7	63.9	9.0	25.6	8.2	12,200	12.8
11. London	342	4.7	1.8	18.2	11.0	11.7	69.9	7.0	19.4	11.0	12,900	11.7
12. Kitchener	311	8.1	2.2	20.7	15.3	9.9	71.8	6.0	33.4	9.3	12,700	10.7
13. Halifax	296	6.6	1.7	5.9	10.6	14.3	70.1	9.2	6.7	23.4	12,800	12.8
14. Victoria	256	5.8	2.1	20.7	7.7	12.2	62.1	11.3	5.5	22.2	13,100	9.4
15. Windsor	254	1.2	1.9	23.0	15.1	8.5	65.0	9.5	32.3	7.8	13,100	14.9
16. Oshawa	204	9.2	0.3	17.2	12.1	6.6	70.4	6.3	31.3	10.0	13,500	13.8
17. Saskatoon	201	14.6	0.7	9.4	12.3	12.5	70.3	9.7	9.2	11.8	11,300	9.2
18. Regina	187	7.7	0.6	9.4	11.5	14.6	71.6	8.0	6.8	18.8	13,300	11.4
19. St. John's	162	4.6	0.6	3.2	15.0	10.4	65.0	15.3	6.8	14.1	10,600	15.9
20. Chicoutimi-Jonquière	159	0.2	0.3	0.8	19.5	7.2	59.2	17.2	18.3	12.3	10,400	18.5
21. Sudbury	149	−4.6	0.6	10.0	18.9	7.4	62.4	12.3	9.3	13.7	11,400	13.7
22. Sherbrooke	130	3.8	0.8	3.4	20.8	10.7	64.8	11.3	18.3	9.7	10,800	16.5
23. Trois-Rivières	128	2.8	0.2	1.5	22.4	8.0	59.5	15.7	19.7	10.0	10,600	21.5
24. Thunder Bay	122	0.2	0.7	15.2	16.3	7.9	66.8	9.9	14.2	11.1	13,000	9.2
25. Saint John	121	0.2	0.7	4.7	15.6	7.8	61.9	13.5	13.8	11.5	12,600	14.6

NOTES: [a] Population growth is partly due to changes in the size of census metropolitan areas (See Appendix 1 for a description of the method used to delineate CMAs)
[b] Based on Statistics Canada Low-Income Cut Off (LIC), the minimum income necessary to sustain an average size household in each locality.

SOURCE: Statistics Canada, Census Canada 1981, 1986 Profile Series A and B.

APPENDIX 4: SOURCES OF DATA ON HOUSING*

The following list includes the main sources that are likely to be available, and of greatest use, in your community.

A. SOURCES THAT ARE NATIONAL IN SCOPE

1.   Census (decennial; smaller quinquennial census since 1956)

Advantages: Accurate; comprehensive; data available for small areas (census tracts; enumeration areas) since 1941 (maps but no data), 1946 (Prairie cities), 1951 (selected cities), 1961 (all urban areas). In recent years, samples of household data are available on computer tape (Public Use Sample).

Disadvantages: Out-of-date when published; available only every 5 or 10 years.

2.   Household Incomes, Facilities and Equipment Survey (HIFE)

Advantages: Up-to-date; good data on household facilities (and, by inference, use); household data on computer tape.

Disadvantages: Published data do not relate to specific cities.

3.   CMHC Housing Statistics (Annual)

Advantages: Up-to-date; good data on prices and construction.
Disadvantages: Limited variables; no intra-urban data.

4.   Royal LePage Market Surveys (Biannual)

Advantages: Up-to-date; some intra-urban data.
Disadvantages: Price data only.

B. LOCAL SOURCES AVAILABLE IN MOST COMMUNITIES

1.   Property Assessments and Integrated Property Files

Advantages: Data on individual units/households; reliable; *Before 1960s*: wide range of variables, including occupation, housing tenure, and income (sometimes). Some cities (e.g. Toronto) have property files from which up-to-date summary data are available.

Disadvantages: *Since 1960s*: data limited to characteristics of property (esp. address, assessed value and tenure). Difficult to access.

2.   City Directories

Advantages: Up-to-date; data on individual households; easy to use and sample by street and last name.

Disadvantages: Data usually limited to name, address, tenure, head's occupation; may be unreliable, especially in recent years in larger centres.

3.   Multiple Listing Service Reports/TEELA surveys (Monthly, Annual)

Advantages: Up-to-date; easy to use; aggregate data available for sub-areas within larger cities; data on character of individual properties.

Disadvantages: No data on character of occupants.

4.   Special surveys (Irregular)

Municipal and social planning agencies conduct their own surveys, the usefulness of which varies greatly. See local archives for historical material. See municipal and university libraries, and municipal planning departments, for current material.

*Compiled by Richard Harris

APPENDIX 5: OTTAWA: HOUSING PROVISION BY SECTOR FOR SELECTED GROUPS*

			SECTOR PROVIDING HOUSING[1]		
Population Group	State	Household	Voluntary	Voluntary/State	Market
Economically Marginal					
1. Long-term unemployed singles	* city-owned rooming houses for singles (46 units)	* housing provided by relatives or friends (nos. unknown)	* privately funded and run shelters for single men: 3 shelters; avge. no. of clients = 371 × 17 days; for single women: 2 shelters; avge. monthly no. of clients 75 × 13 days duration	* private non-profit and co-operative housing, some with full subsidy for families and singles (2,476), e.g. Centretown Citizens (Ottawa) Corporation (400 + units)	* rooming house units (~1300) * hotel rooms
2. Impoverished elderly	* seniors public housing (5,080) * rent supplements * municipal non-profit	* housing provided by relatives or friends * house-sharing with a family		* private non-profit and co-operative housing directed to seniors (407)	* rooming houses * rental apartments (but 0.3% vacancy rate in rentals i.e. 3 units in 1000)
3. Single parents (>18,000; 83% mother-led) and low-income 2-parent families	* Ontario public housing (100% of units rent-geared-to-income) (3,488) * Rent supplements (1,129) * hotel/motel and other temporary accommodation for emergencies (avge. 78 cases/mo) * municipal non-profit (2,374)	* housing provided by relatives or friends	* refuges for battered women and children in emergencies (2 houses)	* private non-profit and co-operative family housing (2,052)	* Apartments, townhouses
4. Ethnic minorities/ refugees	* as above for singles, elderly, or families, as appropriate	* as above		* as above	* as above

APPENDIX 5—CONTINUED

Population Group	State	Household	Voluntary	Voluntary/State	Market
Economically Marginal					
5. Handicapped[2]					
* psychiatrically (1,978)	* rooming houses * domicillary or boarding hostels (400) * institutions	* provided by family: estimate = 50%		* group homes (~70 places)	* rooming houses * for profit care
* mentally (>1,900)	* institutions	* provided by family: estimate = 50%		* group homes (~112 places)	
* physically (1,541)	* special units within municipal non-profit housing	* provided by family: estimate = 50%		* special units in private non-profits and co-operatives (150) * 48 units with 24-hour care * group homes (35 places)	
6. Street people	* emergency housing for families (36)	* provided by family and friends	* shelters and refuges for shorter (300 places) and longer term visits (144 places)		
7. Participants in drug culture 15,490 alcoholics; 99 other drugs	* detox centres	* provided by family and friends	* detox centres * rehabilitation centres	* group homes for voluntary rehabilitation	
8. Parolees/probationers	* half-way houses (5 for men; 2 for women)			* some contracted spaces in residences serving mixed purposes	

*Compiled by Beth Moore Milroy

[1] Neighbourhood exchange or barter is not included in this description of housing because I am not aware of any studies showing the amount of housing provided in this way. Had day care been selected instead of housing, the modes of provision would have included neighbourhood exchange.

[2] Source of figures: Ottawa-Carleton Regional District Health Council (1985). *Respite Care in Ottawa-Carleton*, pages 3–10. Cited in *Trends 1985*, p. 435.

INDEX